Formalism and Historicity

OCTOBER BOOKS

George Baker, Yve-Alain Bois, Benjamin H. D. Buchloh, Leah Dickerman, Devin Fore, Hal Foster, Daniel Heller-Roazen, Denis Hollier, David Joselit, Rosalind Krauss, Carrrie Lambert-Beattie, Annette Michelson, Mignon Nixon, and Malcolm Turvey, editors

Broodthaers, edited by Benjamin H. D. Buchloh

AIDS: Cultural Analysis/Cultural Activism, edited by Douglas Crimp

Aberrations: An Essay on the Legend of Forms, by Jurgis Baltrušaitis

Against Architecture: The Writings of Georges Bataille, by Denis Hollier

Painting as Model, by Yve-Alain Bois

The Destruction of Tilted Arc: Documents, edited by Clara Weyergraf-Serra and Martha Buskirk

The Woman in Question, edited by Parveen Adams and Elizabeth Cowie

Techniques of the Observer: On Vision and Modernity in the Nineteenth Century, by Jonathan Crary

The Subjectivity Effect in Western Literary Tradition: Essays toward the Release of Shakespeare's Will, by Joel Fineman

Looking Awry: An Introduction to Jacques Lacan through Popular Culture, by Slavoj Žižek

Cinema, Censorship, and the State: The Writings of Nagisa Oshima, by Nagisa Oshima

The Optical Unconscious, by Rosalind E. Krauss

Gesture and Speech, by André Leroi-Gourhan

Compulsive Beauty, by Hal Foster

Continuous Project Altered Daily: The Writings of Robert Morris, by Robert Morris

Read My Desire: Lacan against the Historicists, by Joan Copjec

Fast Cars, Clean Bodies: Decolonization and the Reordering of French Culture, by Kristin Ross

Kant after Duchamp, by Thierry de Duve

The Duchamp Effect, edited by Martha Buskirk and Mignon Nixon

The Return of the Real: The Avant-Garde at the End of the Century, by Hal Foster

October: The Second Decade, 1986–1996, edited by Rosalind Krauss, Annette Michelson, Yve-Alain Bois, Benjamin H. D. Buchloh, Hal Foster, Denis Hollier, and Silvia Kolbowski

Infinite Regress: Marcel Duchamp 1910–1941, by David Joselit

Caravaggio's Secrets, by Leo Bersani and Ulysse Dutoit

Scenes in a Library: Reading the Photograph in the Book, 1843–1875, by Carol Armstrong

Bachelors, by Rosalind Krauss

Neo-Avantgarde and Culture Industry: Essays on European and American Art from 1955 to 1975, by Benjamin H. D. Buchloh

Suspensions of Perception: Attention, Spectacle, and Modern Culture, by Jonathan Crary

Leave Any Information at the Signal: Writings, Interviews, Bits, Pages, by Ed Ruscha

Guy Debord and the Situationist International: Texts and Documents, edited by Tom McDonough

Random Order: Robert Rauschenberg and the Neo-Avant-Garde, by Branden W. Joseph

Decoys and Disruptions: Selected Writings, 1975–2001, by Martha Rosler

Prosthetic Gods, by Hal Foster

Fantastic Reality: Louise Bourgeois and a Story of Modern Art, by Mignon Nixon

Women Artists at the Millennium, edited by Carol Armstrong and Catherine de Zegher

"The Beautiful Language of My Century": Reinventing the Language of Contestation in Postwar France, 1945–1968, by Tom McDonough

The Artwork Caught by the Tail: Francis Picabia and Dada in Paris, by George Baker

Being Watched: Yvonne Rainer and the 1960s, by Carrie Lambert-Beatty

Robert Ryman: Used Paint, by Suzanne P. Hudson

Hall of Mirrors: Roy Lichtenstein and the Face of Painting in the 1960s, by Graham Bader

Perpetual Inventory, by Rosalind Krauss

The Absence of Work: Marcel Broodthaers 1964–1976, by Rachel Haidu

The Filming of Modern Life: European Avant-Garde Film of the 1920s, by Malcolm Turvey

Lucio Fontana: Between Avant-Garde and Kitsch, by Anthony White

Looking for Bruce Conner, by Kevin Hatch

Realism after Modernism: The Rehumanization of Art and Literature, by Devin Fore

Critical Laboratory: The Writings of Thomas Hirschhorn, by Thomas Hirschhorn

Formalism and Historicity: Models and Methods in Twentieth-Century Art, by Benjamin H. D. Buchloh

Formalism and Historicity

Models and Methods in Twentieth-Century Art

Benjamin H. D. Buchloh

An OCTOBER Book

The MIT Press
Cambridge, Massachusetts
London, England

MIT Press books may be purchased at special quantity discounts for business or sales promotional use. For information, please email special_sales@mitpress.mit.edu.

This book was set in Bembo by the MIT Press. Printed and bound in the United States of America.

Library of Congress Cataloging-in-Publication Data

Buchloh, B. H. D.

[Essays. Selections.]

Formalism and historicity : models and methods in twentieth-century art / Benjamin H.D. Buchloh.

pages cm.—(October books)

Includes bibliographical references and index.

ISBN 978-0-262-02852-3 (hardcover : alk. paper)

1. Avant-garde (Aesthetics)—Europe—History—20th century. 2. Art, European—20th century. 3. Avant-garde (Aesthetics)—United States—History—20th century. 4. Art, American—20th century. I. Title.

N6758.B833 2015

709.4—dc23

2014022595

10 9 8 7 6 5 4 3 2 1

With belated gratitude, to the memory of my parents,
Heinrich Gustav Benjamin Buchloh
and
Elisabeth Pawlikowsky

Contents

Acknowledgments

As a procrastinating author, I guess I have hesitated in two directions, dreading the shortcomings of my past writings and fearing the insufficiencies of future ones; thus I was disinclined to either revisit the former or to write the latter, ending up with very little indeed. This condition might begin to explain why the release of the present volume has taken such an inordinately long time. I could quite simply not figure out how to justify the republication of these essays (some of which—including the text that gives the volume its title—had been written at the very beginning of my activities as a critic and historian over thirty-five years ago): it was not compellingly clear to me what they had to contribute to the debates and concerns of the present. Second, my efforts at producing new texts, revisiting the scene of writing again and again in order to increase its precision and to improve its presumed actuality by maintaining a dialogue with new works and with the seemingly ever-more-pressing questions of the present, deferred the periods of patience required for looking calmly at older efforts, which had of course themselves seemed in their time to be similarly actual.

Thus, much time went by before I was able to act on Roger Conover's generous offer to publish a companion volume to my first tome of collected essays, *Neo-Avantgarde and Culture Industry*, published by MIT Press in 2000. That volume collected monographic essays I had written up to that time on individual American and European artists of the post–World War II period; this one groups essays addressing more general historical, and perhaps at times theoretical, issues, with subject matter ranging through various artistic formations in the twentieth century, from the moment of the *retour à l'ordre* in 1915 to developments in the Soviet Union in the late 1920s, from the reception of Constructivism in post–World War II American art to the formation of Conceptual art in the late 1960s, ending its peregrinations with the so-called appropriation artists of the 1980s.

Because of the multiple delays and new beginnings involved in putting this book together, I have accumulated a great number of friends and colleagues to whom I feel grateful for their role in resuscitating the texts before they were completely doomed.

My first thanks goes to Roger Conover for not calling it curtains on the project and tolerating its slow progress. Roger's generosity and patience mark him as the kind of classic editor who seems to be disappearing from the world of publishing, to all of our detriment.

Further, in the distant past, Cathérine de Zegher and Judith Aminoff helped with the increasingly difficult and costly tasks of finding and assembling the illustrations. In more recent years, my most fabulous friend and now important colleague Julia Robinson once again salvaged the project from perdition and brought it back on track, but alas, even with her dynamic support the author was not up to facing a renewed encounter with the old essays, with their antiquated hopes and by now obsolete aspirations.

In this regard, I should acknowledge the many—even if sometimes casual—comments on the old essays made by the extraordinary students with whom I have worked over the past twenty years at Barnard College and Columbia University during the 1990s and at Harvard University since 2005: they have both encouraged and convinced me that rereading some of these essays might be worthwhile—even if only as historical documents from a different moment of writing criticism and history.

I hope that my most esteemed colleagues in the Department of The History of Art and Architecture at Harvard, a group of exceptionally accomplished yet generous and welcoming scholars who have offered me a true academic home if ever I had one, will consider these collected documents worthy of the department's standards.

Similarly, I hope that my other main circle of friends, at *October*, where several of these essays were first published, will decide that reprinting these essays has been justified. At *October*, my colleagues in general have been excellent, but over the years Rosalind Krauss and Yve-Alain Bois, Hal Foster, and, more recently, Leah Dickerman and Devin Fore in particular have given me a stable sense of friendship, the feeling that—in spite of the manifest evidence that utterly different methods and theories now reign in critical and art-historical writing—even the most esoteric of my pursuits and engagements in elusive artistic practices and the antiquated political and social dimensions of artistic production have retained a residual challenge worthy of engagement.

Yet finally it was one individual at *October* who broke the spell of authorial refusal, bringing the manuscript to completion with extraordinary tact and generosity: my dear friend Adam Lehner, Managing Editor of *October*, without whom this book would not have happened.

To follow the strange but common pattern in structuring acknowledgments, the most important thanks come last: to Felix, my beloved son, who grew faster than this book, and to Michelle Harewood, my generous and patient companion, who made it all worthwhile once more by teaching me how to visit the museum.

Introduction

Introducing an Introduction

The following text, "Farewell to an Identity," was written as the introduction to this, the second volume of my collected essays. Before it could appear in that capacity, however, *Artforum* asked me to contribute a text to its end-of-2012 issue, and to conclude that year with a public lament seemed so appropriate a response to the preceding year that I decided to air the introduction ahead of schedule. Still being slightly deluded as to the public's interest and acuity in reading a critic's commentary, I intended to share my increasingly alienated perception that the art world had changed over the past decade in ways that even the most cynical pessimist or most orthodox Marxist critic might not have foreseen.

The essay's title carried a not-so-subtle homage to T. J. Clark's *Farewell to an Idea*. His work, along with that of his great counterfigure, Rosalind Krauss, offered me the most encouragement and inspiration over the decades when the essays in this volume were written. But my title made a more modest claim than Clark's. I was not pronouncing a farewell to the great ideas of Modernism, merely describing what I perceived to be the demise of the historically formed identity and social functions of the critic.

Very much to my surprise, the essay received an unusual number of comments, many of them rather acerbic in their mockery of what was widely (mis-)read as the haughty authorial, if not authoritarian, dismissal of younger artists working in the new contexts of ever-expanding economic and cultural globalization and digitally transmitted forms of communication. The misreading resulted from the text's mournful tone, which, while pointing to a presumably different situation in the recent past, was certainly not intended as an overall dismissal of current practices by active and activist artists. I was not vainly trying to diagnose an apocalyptic endgame but voicing a critical reflection on the structural, discursive, and institutional changes that the social sphere known as the "art world" has undergone in the thirty-some years that I have been participating in it as a critic and historian.

If anything could be misread as "prohibitive" in my essay, it could only be drawn from my argument that a certain type of artistic project with which I had been engaged over a period of time had clearly come to an end. Still, it is true that perhaps because of the distortions of increasing generational distance, I had failed to recognize the extent to which new forms of critical production have already emerged from fundamentally different reflections on how cultural signification and intervention are now placed and practiced. This became most obvious to me in numerous exhibitions in 2013 of new films and media work produced by artists as diverse and different as Dara Birnbaum, Harun Farocki, Pierre Huyghe, Isaac Julien, Steve McQueen, and the late Allan Sekula, as well as the more recent modifications of our concept of the sculptural by artists such as Tino Sehgal, Sarah Sze, and Danh Vo, to name but a few.

As for the collection of essays that the text now introduces, a few preliminary remarks are in order. If any methodological model unifies this group of twelve rather heterogeneous pieces of writing, addressing various topics in the twentieth century from the 1920s to the 1980s, it would be my desire to trace and describe as precisely as possible certain crucial artistic transitions, iterations, and paradigmatic changes, together with their corresponding structural forms, within the extremely specific historical moments in which they occurred.

For example, I discuss conflicts resulting from historical repetitions (such as the monochrome and the collage/montage aesthetic in their various phases in the 1910s, 1950s, and 1980s) and the emergence of crucial neo-avantgarde typologies and practices in their relation to the historical avant-gardes. Equally, I attempt to address the recitation of obsolete genres, such as the portrait and the landscape, that were widely resuscitated in 1980s photography long after their original pictorial dismantlement.

In other texts, I try to grasp the qualitative and quantitative changes brought about by newly emerging epistemes of collective and public experience that generated utterly different material forms of artistic production in tandem with radically altered distribution forms (as in the factographic practices in the 1920s and Conceptualism's linguistic supremacy in the late 1960s).

My approach aimed not only to identify historical and paradigmatic changes as they occurred within the condensed confrontation between different phases and generations, but also to trace those changes as they occurred within a singular oeuvre, either as slow slippages or as suddenly occurring ruptures in the transit from an activist artistic intervention to a cultural sedimentation in a singular artistic trajectory. These shifts move from the sphere of the aesthetic to the ideological sphere and back again, though this is a distinction that proves increasingly difficult to sustain as one enters the present period, with most contemporary practitioners seeming to yield eventually—willingly or not—to the very forces that the once-imagined radicality constitutive of any artistic departure worth its name had most ardently opposed, if not actually attempted to dismantle.

Even in these schematic examples, the potential shortcomings of such a method are evident, the result of a deliberate reluctance to finalize a clear distinction between the artistic/formal sphere and the historical/ideological one. Not surprisingly, some of my attempts to track the structural similarities and historical delays operative in these paradigmatic repetitions have brought immediate rejoinders from my high-modernist colleagues that I am pursuing pseudomorphisms; but I trust that an increasingly acute analysis of history (or structure) will eventually make specific motivations, actual differences, and latent continuity or compulsive repetitions sufficiently transparent to justify such comparisons.

In other words, for better or worse, I have neither applied a universally valid formal, structural, or theoretical model nor attempted to design and write up a grand cohesive historical narrative to haul in more or less speculative sociopolitical determinations. To remain suspended between these two methodological traditions and theoretical perspectives has been my principle, just as I have always perceived myself as suspended between the avant-garde and neo-avantgarde formations, between two continents and their different yet deeply intertwined geopolitical artistic and cultural productions. Facing as many facets of these suspensions in contradiction has always appeared to me to be the most attractive and plausible position, given the limitations of my historical scope (the long twentieth century), the contradictions of my conflicted multifarious generational and artistic interests and identifications, and the inevitable outcome of having spent my professional life since 1976 on two continents.

Undoubtedly, a more consistent and homogeneous method such as the formalist analysis so brilliantly practiced by some of my most venerable friends and colleagues would have yielded more precise results in discussing the artistic objects addressed in this volume. And a rigorously applied analysis of socioeconomical determination and ideological intertwinement between cultural production and actual historical forces would have undoubtedly generated more precise historical accounts. But it is precisely the discrepancies and contradictions between not only these spheres but within individual artistic trajectories and careers as well that have preoccupied me most. An adequate method therefore appeared to me to be one that situated itself between these various force fields. I have always hoped that a fragmentary method, anticipating the contradictions within its own fractured approach, might generate the most accurate historical accounts.

Many such contradictions and transitions are addressed in this volume, and quite often they are microstructures where an aesthetic operation that had been illuminating and subversive in one instance would return in the next season to perform dutifully as political propaganda, or, in the post–World War II period, to deliver the goods according to the rules of capital and consumption.

Very few of the artists whose work has been central to the formulation of my critical models of radical avant-garde and neo-avantgarde practices could ultimately refuse the processes of assimilation to markets and institutions, forfeiting the principles of their initially critical analysis of the interrelationships between discursive, institutional, and critical-political positions (more often than not it has been the interrelation between the three that has preoccupied me most). Daniel Buren, for example, was one of the truly important theoreticians and artists of the late 1960s, analyzing these complex interrelationships between the presumably autonomous sphere of the pictorial and the discursive power of the institution of the museum. Now, after about forty-five years of producing works derived from these principles, a process that has resulted in an extraordinarily complex oeuvre, he seems to have decided that it does not matter anymore if he produces espresso cups for Illy, fashion displays for Marc Jacobs, and silk scarves for Hermès. Even if we recognize that these crossovers into advertisement have become by now a new paradigm for many contemporary artists (from

Jeff Koons and Takashi Murakami to Richard Prince et al.), this intentional mapping of artistic production onto the utterly banal demands of consumption, spectacle culture, and the forms of fashion as pure ideology raises the question of whether the critical strategies that had initially confronted the spheres of institutional and economic power with artistic means were destined to failure from the start, or whether they only caved and dissolved under the pressures of a fundamentally altered system of artistic production and reception.

At the same time, one might pose the opposite question: can works in the present maintain any claim for political opposition and subversive radicality when they deploy the same enlightenment strategies of critical oppositionality that they had formulated at a fundamentally different historical moment (as, for example, in the most recent works by Hans Haacke, or in Martha Rosler's spectacularized restaging of her *Garage Sale* at MoMA in 2012)?

Or is it rather the case that once they themselves have been incorporated into market-distribution networks and institutionalized in museums, these works of art serve only as reminders of their former political aspirations?

A third inquiry motivated some of the essays in this volume, particularly those in which I attempted to clarify the communicative strategies manifest in the work of Marcel Broodthaers. Rather than activist and critical, his artistic propositions might have initially appeared as melancholic. According to all appearances, they seem to have anticipated within their very conception all the forms of acculturation to which they would inevitably be subjected. Therefore, the discussion of Broodthaers' oeuvre as a model remains central to my theoretical concerns in the present, in particular the question of whether an emphasis on the mnemonic can still perform an oppositional function in the production of contemporary art. Broodthaers' almost uncanny capacity to recognize the dialectics of memory and critique, or of obsolescence and avant-gardist innovation—of refusal and withdrawal on the one hand

and the inevitable processes of acculturation on the other—make his allegorical projects highly resonant even forty years after his premature departure. The essay republished here, my first devoted to the artist, was also the first—to the best of my knowledge—to engage the theoretical concept of the allegory, as developed initially in Walter Benjamin's *Origins of German Tragic Drama*, in a discussion of contemporary art in general and of a major figure deploying a post-Duchampian aesthetic in the 1960s and 1970s in particular.

Broodthaers can also teach us how the mnemonic, when conceived naively or cunningly in the practices of the present (as in the work of Christian Boltanski and Anselm Kiefer, for example) as a counterforce to the inevitable processes of spectacularization, remains extremely elusive, if not ultimately even inaccessible. At least we should recognize that he proved the mobilization of historical memory to be a rather dubious strategy when it relied on an imaginary oppositional dimension of a work's innate mnemonic potential alone.

This skepticism had already been formulated by the artist in the late 1960s, demarcating his increasingly complex departure from the legacies of Surrealism. These had been somewhat naively reclaimed at that time by the radical New Left, guided by philosophers such as Herbert Marcuse, who invoked the "remembrance" of different forms of desire and existence, and of alternate forms of social organization, as a Surrealist strategy to oppose the subject's integration within the ruling and repressive regimes of capitalist consumption in the present.

I have otherwise not incorporated any monographic essays in this volume, since these were the subject of my first collection, *Neo-Avantgarde and Culture Industry*, published by MIT Press in 2000, and I hope to bring forth a large group of more recent monographic essays on post–World War II and more recent artists in a third volume, *Refuge and Refuse*.

The last set of questions I would like to pose, finalizing this introduction to the introduction, come in the form of a reflection once again on the current status of the discipline of art criticism. Its decline, if not its final disappearance, is too obvious to lament any further, yet it might be worthwhile to see this decline as a symptomatic forerunner of other disappearances to come. After all, phrasing the situation positively, one could argue that the demise of criticism results at least partially from the critic's and historian's dubious abrogation of the exceptional competence to speak for others (producer, receiver, and the oeuvre itself). Seen in this light, the disciplinary demise might in fact signal a progressive, emancipatory tendency among cultural consumers to increasingly determine their own competences of reading and seeing, that is, the "birth of the reader"—that adage from the early 1960s of the great utopian aspirations for deskilling.

But with the ever-increasing instrumentalization of experience even in its most microscopic structures of everyday life, and the extensive and rapid deskilling of all previously existing differentiations of knowledge in the arts and humanities, methodologically (to say nothing of scientifically) weaker disciplines such as literary and art criticism, which once served as subservient pedagogical supports and historical or discursive introductions to what had previously been considered among the foundational elements of bourgeois subject formation (such as philosophy, literature, and art), will logically disappear first.

But the disappearance of literary, art, and philosophical criticism might also signal the imminent diminution of the former centrality of philosophy, art, and literature themselves, at least in the forms known to us until recently. Perhaps a comparable example might be the deskilling of journalistic expertise that results from the ever-expanding patterns of digital pseudocommunication and their abrogations of universal competence. These indicate a heretofore-unimaginable self-deception that one is actually performing socially valid and productive speech acts and enforcing the myths of a newly founded collective participation. At the same time, they induce an equally unimagined disciplinary disintegration of competences and skills concerning the acquisition of actually productive forms of knowledge, critical analysis, and sociopolitical interaction.

Thus, one of the central questions of the beginning of the twenty-first century concerning artistic and critical cultures might as well be formulated as follows: will the dialectics of deskilling and reskilling in fact generate new dimensions of reader emancipation and bring about a heretofore unimagined participation of universally competent speakers and enabled spectators, or will these tendencies simply amount to a continuously expanding erasure of most of the forms of noninstrumentalized knowledge and experience in visual and literary culture?

After all, every act of painterly deskilling from Cézanne and Seurat onward began as a subversive step to dismantle the problematic epistemological premises of cultural representations under the aegis of bourgeois patriarchy in the nation-state. Until the rise of Modernism, at least, these had claimed an intricate causal connection between the acquired mastery of skills, cultural legitimation, and economic and national authorization. Deskilling in its initial impulses in the late-nineteenth century also opposed those bourgeois claims—simultaneously universal and essentially exclusive—that only extreme forms of bourgeois sublimation provided the preconditions for the formation of any subjectivity. Once that project of contestation had been advanced even further through Cubism, it culminated in the ultimately triumphant declaration of artistic deskilling in Marcel Duchamp's readymade in 1913. At that moment, the emerging egalitarian impulses of these new forms still carried more weight than another force, a rising but not yet recognizable phenomenon, the ultimately devastating social and subjective effects within the rapid emergence of the mass-cultural apparatus of deskilling's practice of total desublimation.

The collective forces of industrial production at the beginning of the twentieth century continued to expand and unleash an unimaginable wealth of means and objects promising to respond to universalized forms of needs and desires. Therefore, the models embodied in Soviet

Productivism, the German Bauhaus, and even in Duchamp's Franco-American readymades had to acknowledge that any further attempts to shore up the representation of certain types of experiences or desires—unconscious or utopian aspirations in particular—would no longer be credible or legitimate.

This was as true for the producer as for the spectator–reader so long as the images were derived from the exclusionary logic of highly skilled artisanal and artistic refinement, imaginary continuities of nation-state traditions, gendered identitarian myths, individuated virtuosity, or fictions of profound and immutable authenticity. Those were some of the answers Duchamp had delivered to Picasso for about a decade before the *retour à l'ordre* mounted its fallacious counterattacks.

Following these paradigmatic changes, the extremely differentiated histories of anti-aesthetic impulses, from Dada and Duchamp to Cage and Fluxus, attempted at all times to articulate this newly emerging historical horizon of the now universally available articulations of emancipated subjectivity and collectively established competences in all fields of experience and their representations. (Lucy Lippard's prognosis formulated at the inception of Conceptual art still offers one of the best examples for these aspirations, touting the liberating impacts of Conceptual art practices as the response to a moment when a supposedly universal leisure culture would newly qualify reading subjects to share and convey a full transformation of their traditional assumptions about cultural representations.)

But, against all expectations of the optimism of the 1960s, the plenitude of newly available leisure time and the supposedly universally available goods and services that actually permeate the Western world have only made the socially calamitous consequences of deskilling all the more evident. Therefore, they now challenge all of our radical aspirations placed in a universal aesthetics of deskilling. Neither the new freedom supposedly gained from the reduction of the demands of labor nor the plenitude of object consumption have generated any new forms of a liberated, self-determining subjectivity and emancipated social relations. Least of all do they sustain a progressive transformation of the collective conditions of subject formation, everyday life, and social hierarchical structures. What then could possibly be the historical functions of an ever-widening programmatic expansion of an aesthetic of universal deskilling?

Quite the opposite. The very objects, goods, and strategies that had promised the utopian transformation of bourgeois society and subjectivity into a socially and subjectively self-determining collectivist reorganization of the means and the conditions of production now return to its recipients as an immense arsenal of heretofore unimaginable forms of domination in the construction of a society of total control, consumption, and spectacularization. Every act of a once supposedly emancipatory and liberating reduction of skills, every gesture of easy gratification seemingly liberated from the necessities of labor, drives the subject into states of ever-deeper dependence and domination.

A consciousness of this conflict first emerged, unbeknownst to all but a few artists of the late 1950s and early 1960s, in the form of the insight that the very processes and strategies that had until recently served the project of emancipation from the myths of skills now had been dialectically turned around, and the anti-aesthetic itself, inadvertently, had become an unknowing ally to the very principles of universal desublimation (Andy Warhol clearly becoming a fateful bringer of this message, the agent and eventually the manifest victim of the news himself). Faced with those newly emerging historical realities in the post–World War II period, and in manifest opposition to such early postwar masters of the new fusion of deskilling and spectacle as Lucio Fontana and Yves Klein, artists such as Jasper Johns and Richard Serra in the United States and Richard Hamilton, Gerhard Richter, and Marcel Broodthaers in Europe repositioned themselves in regard to these questions of skill, deskilling, and reskilling. These artists of the 1960s seem to have wondered whether the dismantling of techniques and genres of disciplinary boundaries of media and spectatorial forms of experience was ultimately still a valid, let alone a mandatory, strategy.

Furthermore, they seemed to ask whether deskilling alone could still guarantee aesthetic practice critical reflection and spectatorial agency. Their reflections addressed these conflicts for the first time since the *retour à l'ordre* in the 1920s, when these questions had been asked. Unlike their originary peers in this realm of the painterly dilemma, they did not deliver the most reactionary responses, artistic self-deceptions of what retrogressive strategies could actually achieve in the moment of crisis; instead, each developed an extremely complex model of a synthesis of the dialectics of deskilling and reskilling, between utter erasure and faint mnemonic fractures of aesthetic resuscitation.

Nowadays, however, it is dubious whether one of the most provocative claims made in Theodor Adorno's aesthetic theory fifty years ago will still hold: that the work of art can generate its opposition only if it assimilates itself mimetically to the most hardened forms of reification, defined by the traditional criteria of an alienated subjectivity and totally reified object relations. Rather, the following question would have to be posed: how can aesthetic practices sustain themselves at all in an era of a total dissolution of the concepts of subjectivity, and its corresponding aesthetic criteria, conventions, and locations? These criteria now seem to emerge from a never-ending fluidity of utter indifference and anomic flexibility, since the symbolic order is no longer addressed as a dialectical structure of emancipatory representation on the one hand and as one of reality's principles of resistance against change and control on the other. If the symbolic now seems to operate as an utterly contingent and aleatory force field of disqualified and dedifferentiated signs, perpetually slipping and shifting, whose sole grounding seems to be the production of instant even if minimal surplus value, and of fleeting seconds of imaginary self-constitution, what then would we recognize as the corresponding aesthetic structures of the future?

Farewell to an Identity

From the perspective of the hegemonic reality principle that has defined modernity—that is, the subject position we have traditionally identified as bourgeois—all forms and practices of artistic and political contestation, transgression, and critique appeared at least initially as suspicious, if not deviant or outright antagonistic to that model of subjectivity.

This dialectic of a fully internalized reality principle and a seemingly compulsive desire for a different order, even disorder, was in fact one of the constitutive conditions of modernity and avant-garde culture from the 1860s until the mid-1960s: Artists had throughout that period created imaginary subjects, models of alternative social relations, languages and spaces of difference, concepts of critique and countermemory and of oppositional transgression. These practices pointed toward profoundly different, and often actually possible alternative models for the cognitive, perceptual, and linguistic structuring of social, sensual, and psychosexual experience. As countermodels, such propositions and strategies were often defined either by taking recourse to subjective or collective negations of existing orders—in primitivizing discourses, for example (from those that privileged the alterity of different geopolitical spaces to those that championed the alterity of unconscious desires)—or by mobilizing techno-scientistic counterdiscourses, emphatically insisting on the fulfillment of the promises of enlightenment culture, which in the actualities of everyday life were being withheld in an order of instrumentalized proto-totalitarian rationality. Or, in a third model, under the conditions of extreme political duress in the late 1920s, for example, artists claimed direct political agency. They explicitly associated themselves with politically transgressive utopian propositions of nonhierarchically ordered social relations or else engaged in outright oppositional struggles against ideological domination and state control.

In keeping with this dialectic, all of the strategies that had been initiated by different avant-garde cultures in various geopolitical contexts were met throughout the history of modernity with a whole arsenal of means by which either to ignore them or defy them, to control them or defer them, to dismiss if not to liquidate them altogether: indifference, quarantine, exclusion, marginalization, pathologization, and, finally, cooptation were the most successful operations in response to the political and social challenges of the historical avant-garde. And, under certain extreme political conditions of authoritarian state power, if none of these strategies could complete the project of containment, stringent state control and brutal oppression would inevitably ensure the continuity of a fully uncontested hegemony and proto-totalitarian social order.

The longer we have studied the history of avant-garde culture, the more compelling the insight has become that the horizons and spaces of utopian thought, and practices of political and artistic transgression, were tolerated within the bourgeois capitalist order only so long as they did not cross these boundaries of discursive and institutional containment (i.e., so long as they ultimately complied with the artistic culture and the conventions of the museum). And what the artists of the late 1960s and early 1970s finally formulated more clearly than anybody before was the fact that the museum had to be recognized as the site where, and the social institution wherein, these forms of acceptance through affirmation, of control through cultural canonization, of tolerance through quarantine, of inversion of meaning through the process of acculturation, had been most successfully implemented.

It was shortly after the emergence of the institutional critiques articulated by artists such as Michael Asher, Marcel Broodthaers, Daniel Buren, and Hans Haacke—and nearly contemporaneous with the bourgeoning critiques of ideological hegemonies in the artistic practices of Louise Lawler, Martha Rosler, Jenny Holzer, and Allan Sekula—that we also encountered Andy Warhol's entry "Art Business vs. Business Art" in his *Philosophy of Andy Warhol (From A to B and Back Again)*, in 1975. Armed with an enlightenment belief in the seemingly unstoppable progress of institutional critique and artistic critiques of the discourse of power, I, for one, at that time considered Warhol's notion of Business Art to be a brilliantly conceived parody of the side effects of an ever-expanding art world—a travesty in the manner of Jonathan Swift's "Modest Proposal." Little did I imagine that, twenty-five years later, it would have become impossible for Warhol's prognostic vision to be mistaken for travesty anymore. Rather, we had to recognize—with belated hindsight—that Warhol had in fact prophesied what we finally came to experience: the total permeation of the cultural sphere by the economic operations of finance capital and its ethos (or rather total lack thereof) and social structures. Only a Cassandra whose ethics and aesthetics were as exceptionally evacuated as Warhol's (unlike other artists at the time who still associated their practices with moral, critical, and political aspirations) could have enunciated this vision. A comparable diagnosis of the explicitly and inevitably affirmative character of modern culture had been formulated by Herbert Marcuse in the early 1960s. Marcuse's tendency to accept if not to exaggerate the inextricably affirmative dimensions of cultural production and to recode them as potentially transgressive operations had appeared to us as a symptom of the philosopher's increasing Americanization. In other words, it was not until the early 1980s, if not even later, that it dawned on some of us that the cultural apparatus had in fact already undergone precisely those transformations whose full spectrum only Warhol had predicted, and that his prognostics were about to attain the status of all-encompassing and seemingly insurmountable new realities.

What were the symptoms of these new conditions of the "common culture" that had emerged perhaps most vehemently in the United States but also abroad during the so-called the Reagan–Thatcher era? And what structural transformations had taken hold in the sphere of artistic production and reception, which we had until that moment naively associated with those other institutions of the public sphere where the production of knowledge and the memory of experience had been socially sustained and collected: the library, the university, and the museum? A number of multifaceted transformations, initially developing slowly yet steadily, soon picked up a precipitous pace and expanded globally. I will enumerate some of these perceived changes, in the manner of a paranoiac whose list of enemies and threats has only increased continuously ever since the first diagnosis of the condition.

The first—and perhaps most startling—symptom was the emergence of a hitherto totally unknown social species, the blindly producing purveyors and the blindly ingesting consumers of culture (blindness, for the time being, simply defined here as the absolute diffidence and total indifference with respect to any remotely rigorous criteria of evaluation). Under the conditions of affluence reigning among the newly emerging subclass of Wall Street financiers, real estate speculators, and state-sponsored plutocrats in Western societies, a new generation of artists—Jeff Koons, Damien Hirst, Takashi Murakami, and Richard Prince, to name only a few—and their respective collectors, speculators, and spectators positioned themselves as the chosen representatives of the culture of these social strata. Their perceptions and consciousness had been partially formed by the politically administered cynicism toward, if not the outright defamation of, the legacies of utopian and critical political thought of the twentieth century—a cynicism all the more triumphant after the fall of the Communist regimes. As the new spectatorial subjects voluntarily embraced the annulment of social and political utopian thinking, artistic production sutured itself to the universal reign of spectacularized consumption. Embracing the new technologies and market formations, the new audiences seemed to seriously believe that an expansion of artistic practices into the registers of the culture industry would compensate for the destruction of the emancipatory promises of the avant-garde cultures of the twentieth century.

Those artists whom one could best identify by their parasitical pose of simulating the grotesques of totalitarian commodity culture are reminiscent of the eponymous protagonist of Bertolt Brecht's 1941 play

The Resistible Rise of Arturo Ui, who gesticulates melodramatically in supposed outrage at the calamitous destruction of the greengrocer's market that he and his gang, the cauliflower merchants, have just brought about. For Koons, Hirst, Murakami, Prince, and their ilk cannot in truth be said to "address" the total fetishization of object relations and the collective cult of marketing and branding; rather, they perform, if anything, parasitic assimilations to the very codes that enforce universal fetishization. They enact an homage to precisely those subjects and corporations that sustain their regimes by enforcing the dictates of a collectively operative pathology, the narcissistic systems of compulsive distinction.

We cannot really call this new social stratum of cultural producers a class, yet its members (if much better dressed and perhaps more polished in their simulated manners) bear astonishing similarities to what Marx had long before identified as the *Lumpenproletariat*. In his essay "The Eighteenth Brumaire of Louis Napoleon" (1852), Marx refers to the lumpens as the "refuse of all classes," including "swindlers, confidence tricksters, brothel keepers, rag and bone merchants, beggars and other flotsam of society," a class fraction that constituted the political power base for Louis Bonaparte of France in 1848. Marx had argued that Bonaparte succeeded to position himself above the two main classes, the proletariat and the bourgeoisie, only by seemingly aligning himself with the lumpens as an apparently independent base of power. In truth, Louis was deeply committed to advancing the material interests of the "finance aristocracy," which, exactly like the *Lumpenproletariat*, had no direct interest in any actual, productive enterprises. The similarities to the people presently populating the various spheres of contemporary cultural production and distribution, the so-called *art world*, are striking, in spite of the semblances of distinction and optical differentiation provided by the apparatus of the fashion industries.

Yet few, if any, of these new spectators could position themselves in the privileged places of the collectors and producers who succeeded in entering the new celebrity culture. At best, the rapidly expanding class of gallery- and museumgoers would define themselves as competent consumers of contemporary art, as the spectatorial strata disseminating the new culture of total affirmation, operating in the institutional and commercial intersections where advertising and the circulation of the commodities of art take place (frenetically active at the openings of gallery and museum exhibitions, the traveling circuits of biennials, auctions, art fairs, and so on). In short, what had emerged in the 1980s was a new public and a new apparatus of cultural industrial production heretofore unknown, and unthinkable, at any earlier moment in the history of modernity. Museum directors like Glenn Lowry at the Museum of Modern Art in New York and Nicholas Serota at Tate Modern in London had the genius to identify the desires and demands of these new publics early on, and they would cater to this new class of cultural consumer and spectacle tourist, whose perceptual sensorium cohered almost magnetically around those artists who created economic surplus value at near mythical rates and with a velocity unheard of in any previous era of cultural production, including even that which underwrote Warhol's own meteoric ascent.

This was the moment when artists such as Marina Abramovic recognized that the time had come when they had to fully and finally identify with the seemingly inescapable order of spectacularization as the foundational modus of their practice. Thus, not only could they triumphantly efface the last residual differences between spectacle and the sphere of cultural production that the neo-avantgarde in its more complex postwar figures and moments had still desperately attempted to maintain; they could also extend the legitimation of spectacle's regime deeper into the registers of subject formation, making their audiences masochistically celebrate their proper subjection to spectacle as the universally valid and incontestable condition of experience.

In this way, contemporary artistic practices have become totally dependent on a neoliberal subjectivity for whom the entire spectrum of once radical avant-garde legacies is now available as gratuitously exchangeable devices, if not gadgets. Under the current cultural dispensation, affirmation of corporate culture can be fused with remnants of a critical subversion of discursive and institutional formations in any imaginable manner. Even formal regressions that had initially been deployed to induce the labor of historical memory can now be turned into more or less instantaneous spectacularization (as evident in the recent work of Christian Boltanski and Anselm Kiefer, to cite only the most prominent exemplars). Just as architects, from the beginning of the twentieth century, have inevitably succumbed (with rare exceptions) to conflating and eventually integrating into their projects both the ideological and economic structures they were bidden to serve, artists have been increasingly integrated into an ever expanding structure of cultural control by mirroring in their work the apparatus of industrialized culture itself. And their production is incorporated immediately within those systems of representation such as advertising and commodity design that stand in constant need of expanding the audiences and consumers of what are now the professionalized and standardized domains of premeditated excess, regress, and transgress—the very parameters that once defined the aesthetic sphere.

Once the radical, utopian sociopolitical horizons that had previously licensed avant-garde practices as agencies of actual transformation of cognition and perception had been foreclosed, all criteria of the judgment of artistic objects were inevitably erased as well. After all, according to what criterion should artistic production be judged, if not by its dialectical capacities of critical negativity and utopian anticipation? What had previously been the rarest of conditions—namely, the exceptional credibility of artistic propositions, wherein a partial and temporary relapse into quasi-mythical forms of experience, called aesthetic, could be reluctantly accepted—had now been turned into the pseudodemocratic claims for universally accessible artistic competence in the sphere of production, buttressed by the matching myths of a universally available competence in the sphere of artistic reception. What had been singularized in the avant-gardes' acts of artistic production precisely by the radicality of their critiques, or by the plenitudes of their anticipatory visions, or by their perpetual redefinitions of what might still qualify credibly as aesthetic experience under the conditions of late capitalist totalitarian consumption, was now effaced in the universal deception of artistically disguised sham operations. A new generation of artists claimed the legacies of Duchamp and Warhol without as much as an atom of the transgressive and subversive intelligence that these two putative forebears had historically initiated. From Olafur Eliasson's apparatus of technocratic deception to the remedial and conciliatory pseudocritiques of Allora & Calzadilla and Francis Alÿs, from the parasitical practices of Francesco Vezzoli, to the spectacularized social sadism of Santiago Sierra (now extending even to the recent work of Thomas Hirschhorn), contemporary artists embrace spectacle in its totality, making it the very basis of their projects, without a shred of evidence that they have so much as attempted the necessary and increasingly difficult steps of devising projects of countermemory and counterspectacle, of the sort manifestly articulated in the work of artists such as Allan Sekula and Harun Farocki.

This state of affairs was at least to some degree the immediate result of a much larger process of deskilling and aesthetic desublimation, the two strategies that had, paradoxically, been defined as integral to the avant-gardes since the first decade of the twentieth century, if not already in the nineteenth-century modernist subversions of the academy and the beaux-arts traditions. Thus, in one of the great paradoxes of the inversion of utopian radicality into its opposite, a condition of universal aesthetic entropy, we have seen how two of the most important artistic epistemes of the twentieth century—the principle of a total deskilling, as embodied in Duchamp's work, and the principle of a universally accessible artistic authorial identity, as embodied in the Romantic lineage from Lautréamont to Joseph Beuys' proclamation that "everyone is an artist"—have in fact resulted in the most catastrophic assimilation of artistic production to the principles of advanced capitalist consumer culture.

Concomitant with this process of deskilling and the consequent effacement of criteria of evaluation and distinction came the deprofessionalization of the critic: deprofessionalization both in terms of the delegitimation of the critical functions within a system of divided powers (i.e., the division between the discursive orders of the museum, the market, the media, the collectors, and, formerly, the historian and the critic) and the dissolution of actual criteria according to which the antinomic hierarchy of artistic production could be evaluated. (By "antinomic hierarchy" I mean the violence of aesthetic differentiation and exclusion as being constitutive of the very definition of aesthetic experience. It is the condition that Adorno once famously described as the fact that every work of art is the fatal and deadly enemy of every other.)

Precisely to sustain this extraordinary paradox of the aesthetic experience—namely, that art offers one last instantiation of mythical experience in order to sublate myth once and for all, and thereby to emancipate art's spectators from myth's reign—was the very ambition of the anti-aesthetic from the beginning. And this defining objective of polarized opposition necessitates the most rigorous distinction and finally the disqualification of hierarchical order. Yet such a challenge to hierarchy is the exact opposite of a seemingly liberal-democratic reign of a laissez-faire aesthetic pluralism serving as the handmaiden of a laissez-faire neoliberal capitalism.

It is not implausible at all, then, that under these historical conditions the industrially produced self and the artistically and politically constituted subject of spectacularized alterity have been increasingly assimilated and eventually collapsed into each other. Or rather, they have been programmatically effaced in order to resemble each other and find a forced reconciliation between artistic principles and the experiential patterns of the fashion and the culture industries. When boundaries are increasingly eliminated, by historical and economic erosion as much as by ideological planning, it is hardly surprising that the attraction is mutual: the rapidly changing cycles of the fashion and culture industries increasingly depend for their mythical reproductions on some allegedly foundational referent, serving to simulate the status of a value-retaining and value-increasing fetish object, which is, of course, the actual function of the visual artistic object today, given its complete and final removal from precisely that sphere which once opened onto a realm of political possibility and the probability of social agency.

One of the questions to be asked, then, is whether any criteria of judgment whatsoever might be reinstituted. And, if so, to which registers of social and subjective experience and construction they could possibly refer. Yet simply by invoking the term "criterion," it becomes instantly evident that the very concept is charged with a profoundly reactionary structuring of experience. After all, the criteria of distinction, of qualitative differentiation, have always been dictated from above, from the judgment seat of power. We have only to remember that it was always bourgeois white men such as T. S. Eliot and Gottfried Benn in the first half of the twentieth century who insisted on the laws of aesthetic quality when confronted for the first time with the possibility of emerging proletarian practices of cultural production. And, later, in the 1960s and '70s, when feminist artistic practices emerged, it was once again the patriarchal authorities who attacked feminist and politicized practices most vociferously. More recently, as artistic practices have emerged increasingly from outside the European and North American orders, the call for criteria of quality has risen anew from the voice of white male patriarchal power, as always in the name of defending tradition. Under these historical circumstances, could it be worthwhile, or even possible, to reconsider the question of the criteria of judgment and evaluation—and, if so, what function could a renewed definition of criteria possibly serve?

The desublimation of criteria entailed by the anti-aesthetic impulses of the twentieth century aimed at a broad spectrum of social effects, of which we can sketch out only the most obvious and important ones: the collectivization of access to cultural representation, the dismantling of the classist exclusivity of bourgeois culture, the disfigurement and eventual elimination of the residual yet powerful mythical implications of visual representations and their innate bond with the desire for prelinguistic and mythical forms of experience. Not even Warhol had succeeded in obliterating all traces of the anti-aesthetic's emancipatory project of cultural desublimation, but he had pointed in the direction of things to come.

Indeed, the artistic practices that have evolved since the late '80s, often by artists claiming Warhol's mantle (yet again, Koons, Hirst, Murakami, and Prince, promulgate precisely the opposite of an emancipatory desublimation). Such practices have instead effected an *actual* desublimation in which the ruling conditions of totalitarian consumer culture have been affirmatively celebrated as utterly inexorable and as intrinsically connected to any and all forms of cultural representation. In other words, we have been confronted with a dual desublimation: the first one dismantles the practices of artistic production themselves, as it programmatically denies that artistic practices might be anything but cynical affirmations of the established order; the second one declares outright that defiance of and distancing from the totalitarian regime of consumption are by now positions altogether unavailable to the contemporary spectatorial subject. These artists, mere barnacles on the Duchamp–Warhol legacies, accept—and their work, wittingly or not, urges us to accept—this framework of a spectacularized culture of consumption that brooks neither contestation nor conflict, transgression nor opposition, and stands impervious to critical negativity and semiological deconstruction.

The seemingly irresistible magnetism of the extreme forms of spectacularized exchange value generated by objects of modernist and postmodernist artistic production has even left its impact on the more industrially advanced spheres of the culture industry. Thus we are witness to an increasingly frantic attraction among the hordes of Hollywood to whatever ruins of artistic practices and institutions they are able to invade and subject to their semiotic and economic takeover. Here the paradox functions as follows: precisely because the artist's role in opening utopian political and semiological perspectives to actual change has been utterly vacated, the former position of the artist and the new position of the full-time employee of the culture industry become not only more similar but also more mutually attractive. Eventually they can easily be collapsed into each other, as witnessed in the emergence of such comically grotesque hybrid and hubristic media creatures such as the first real Hollywood Museum Man, Jeffrey Deitch, or James Franco, who, under the applause of the art world's minions can claim both the movie industry and painting as his prime domains.

With these examples firmly in mind, we have finally to recognize that the spaces and practices of cultural production no longer provide any respite or refuge, no rescue nor redemption from the universal laws of production that have by now permeated every domain of social experience and every fiber of the constitution of the subject, in manners unimaginable only three decades ago when artistic practices still could define themselves as originating in a sphere of oppositionality and critique. Therefore, one of the tasks with which critics and historians might still be entrusted is to define those criteria that are not intrinsically bound to the reconstitution of privileged forms of experience. I will delineate here, by way of multiple lines of inquiry, only the crudest outline of the discursive forms within which these criteria might be established.

First we must query artistic practices specifically with respect to their implicit or explicit reflection on the actually existing conditions of social representation and ideological affirmation. And we would demand of any artistic production that it specifically consider, in each of its instantiations, to whom it is addressed and with whom, if at all, it intends to communicate. Inevitably, under such critical pressures, these practices would come to discover that under current conditions they have assumed as one of their primary tasks the effacement of any reflection on social class. And then we must further pressure artistic practices to reflect on this disavowal, one of the guarantors of an artist's economic success in the present. After all, the enduring and comprehensive amnesia of class is a foundational condition for the culture of the neoliberalist petite bourgeoisie.

This leads us to our next question: what would it mean to sustain, let alone return to, any particular aesthetic value of the past? For example, could we effect a return to the specificity of an autonomous aesthetic experience, such as painting, and reclaim its unique and peculiar temporality? Could we salvage the particularity of any of the great painterly idioms of the past in the discussions of visual representations in the present, under the purview of the digital empires that rule our existence in forms hardly understood, without advocating an aesthetically—and, by implication, a sociopolitically—conservative position?

And if we were indeed to advocate such a return to the slowness of painterly perception, to attempt to redeem or at least preserve any residually accessible forms of the differentiation of subjectivity and to sustain historical memory, how would such ambitions fare within the broader perspective of a collectively structured project of emancipatory cultural politics? Furthermore, how could such a project be enacted, even if only in its most elementary forms of an aesthetic pedagogy—since that is the one domain of praxis to which academics and critics generally have access—rather than within an actual politics, from which they are explicitly barred or from which they are pressured to refrain?

Finally, what is left available to us that we could call criteria of distinction and judgment that would not immediately appear as resignation, melancholia, and a restoration of some lost aesthetic, toppled authority, or relinquished cultural privilege of the bourgeoisie of the past?

One possible strategy is to intensify the annihilating forces of the anti-aesthetic, undoubtedly one of the most precarious and the most difficult courses to sustain, as Andrea Fraser, John Knight, and Tino Sehgal can surely attest. To sustain the anti-aesthetic without fusing it with its own spectacularization is one of the greatest challenges that artists currently face, or so it seems to me—since the spectacularization of negation and the spectacularization of the anti-aesthetic themselves have by now become integral elements in the arsenal of spectacle itself.

Inevitably, one then asks, why not return to the more solid ground of artistic skills, mobilizing what seems to provide a warranty against these forces? After all, a resurrection of skills, a reskilling, has worked very well for reinstituting mythical forms of painterly identity. But the problem, of course, is that what is at stake in the desire for returns of any kind, be they artistic or art historical, is an implicit and explicit restoration of privileged forms of experience, a quest whose reactionary implications are instantly plausible. Shoring up what is being threatened with disappearance might be a perfectly fine *private* motivation, but I doubt that it could qualify as a strategy of cultural and critical politics.

However, another force becomes apparent in the desire for returns, and it appears to be the most important counterdiscourse to collective spectacularization—to wit, the mnemonic functions of culture, both individually and collectively practiced. But with the exception of the extraordinary work of James Coleman and Gerhard Richter, hardly any artistic practice is known to me that has radically committed itself to making the enactment of historical reflection one of its fundamental strategies yet didn't fall prey, as did Kiefer and Boltanski, to the aesthetic instrumentalization and spectacularization of memory, against which memory had initially risen to retrieve alternate histories, different forms of existence, incommensurable models of constructing subjectivity and social relations. And this may well have been the lesson of Marcel Broodthaers, who perpetually posed the question as to whether memory could ever be enacted aesthetically without contributing to an acceleration of the fetishization of culture and an expansion of spectacle itself. Thus the project of imparting visibility to the very classes and peoples, the very spaces and sites, where history has remained nameless and without image and for whom cultural representation would in fact lead to an initiating constitution of historical identity, could be one of the remaining functions of radical cultural practices, rather than an affirmation of past values and privileges now resurrected to reassert the vanishing basis of cultural legitimation defining Western societies.

1

Formalism and Historicity

The idea of an isolated American painting, so popular in this country during the thirties, seems absurd to me, just as the idea of creating a purely American mathematics or physics would seem absurd. … And in another sense, the problem doesn't exist at all; or if it did, it would solve itself. An American is an American and his painting would naturally be qualified by that fact, whether he wills it or not. But the basic problems of contemporary painting are independent of any one country.

—*Jackson Pollock*

I am totally uninterested in European art and I think it's over with.

—*Donald Judd*

The artifacts of recent history rush backwards in time, perpetually receding from our apperception and apprehension; their actuality (their qualities as "acts" performed in a context of historical reality) and their effectiveness (the effects on which those works depended as well as those they created in their particular moment of production) are diminishing in impact, dissolving up to the point of vanishing altogether. It is at precisely this point that the historian steps in. After having neither participated in the decisive acts nor caused any effects, having taken neither risk nor responsibility, the historian elevates works of art to the status of cultural objects, saving them from oblivion by transforming their historical function into an aesthetic one. In the perspective of the historian, the works become magnified idolatries. Bereft of all contextual implications, they now appear as autonomous objects, speaking (and being spoken about) in their own discourse, following their own rules of grammar and having a history of their own, an independent meta-language and a meta-history. This language, being of a secondary mythical, reality (in the definition of Roland Barthes), should be read with the adequate tool of ideological criticism.[1]

Yet since works of art can never be restored to an original level of a primary functional language, the historical method of ideological criticism is capable of revealing their original impact only in an indirect manner. Yet, while their transformation into cultural myth is analyzed, their original intention becomes perhaps more apparent. The formalist approach to artistic practices of the recent past would allow us to talk about a urinal manufactured around 1917 in terms of the wholeness of its Gestalt, the specificity of its material, its sculptural presence. As a result of such an approach, this presumed identity of form and support, which supposedly defines itself and which commands its own space, will now serve as an integral criterion of a judgment of aesthetic quality in Minimalist work (for example when looking at Frank Stella's work or the holistic object quality of Donald Judd's painterly sculpture). Thus one could argue in a first defense of the formalist method that it allows us to deal with a work in an apparently objective manner, perhaps even to recognize the original intentions that motivated the production of such a work, since we are only considering the formal facts at hand.

This formalism of critical description, however, seems to have become the basis for the production of some of the most important American art of the Sixties. The terms that had been once used to describe the phenomena now have become the terms to produce the phenomena. It is a condition that seems to have found its post-Minimal climax in an aphorism pronounced by Joseph Kosuth in 1969:

> Works of art that try to tell us something about the world are bound to fail. … The absence of reality in art is exactly art's reality.[2]

Philosophically speaking, such a position simply introduces a basic concept of logical positivism into aesthetical discussion. And from the purview of art history, it would appear as yet another attempt in a long tradition of artistic propositions in Modernism that had attempted to conjure away the historical and physical materiality of the work of art by acting out narcissistic fantasies about the self-generating artist and the self-referential and autonomous work of art. From symbolism to Yves Klein's concept of immateriality, it has found its most recent version in Kosuth's well-designed tautological corpus.[3]

Daniel Buren's text *Limites Critiques*, written in the very same year as Kosuth's (1969), articulated the dialectical opposite of this formalist position by defining an explicit concept of historicity:

> Art, whatever it may be, is exclusively political. What is called for is the analysis of the formal and cultural limits (and not one or the other) within which art exists and struggles. These limits are many and of different intensities. Although the prevailing ideology and the associated artists try in every way to camouflage them, and although it is too early—the conditions are not met—to blow them up, the time has come to unveil them.[4]

If any specific difference were to be sketched out between recent American and European art, one might find it first by comparing the different attitudes toward the historicity of art. Therefore the following essay—by no means pretending to show the only valid aspect of such a differentiation—focuses on how these attitudes have changed in the work of European and American artists since 1945. Discussing the interrelations between the two geo-political and cultural formations, this essay attempts to trace the transformations that the concept of historicity within artistic practice has undergone both in Europe and the United States in the postwar period.

Postwar Lacunae

> Art publications from France, and *Cahiers d'Art* above all, were another matter; these kept you posted on the latest developments in Paris, which was the only place that really mattered. For a while Parisian painting exerted perhaps a more decisive influence on New York art through black-and-white reproductions than through firsthand examples, which may have been a blessing in disguise, for it permitted some Americans to develop a more independent sense of color, if only thanks to misunderstanding and ignorance.
>
> —*Clement Greenberg*[5]

Indeed, immediate postwar art history, namely that of the Paris and New York Schools of painting, seems to have been formed as much by misunderstandings, omissions and by ignorance of history as by the artistic information which was available at the time, and which has since been handed down to us. For example, Piet Mondrian, during the last four years of his life that he spent in New York, was more recognized by the artists formulating the project of Abstract Expressionism than he had ever been during the twenty-five years that he had spent in Paris where he was practically unknown after the war. Another example of how postwar "art history" was made by omissions and misreadings would be the almost total failure (or refusal) of a reception of the work of the Russian and Soviet avant-gardes.

The reception of the work of Wassily Kandinsky is a particular case in point. His limited concepts of abstract painting and his politically opportunist, not to say reactionary positions had been convincingly criticized already in the Twenties by El Lissitzky (and later by Arnold Schoenberg). Nevertheless, Kandinsky rose to a position of primary importance and became very influential for painterly production in New York as well as in Europe in the postwar period. By contrast, the incomparable reductivist radicality of the Suprematist Kazimir Malevich, the visual and plastic complexity of the paintings of El Lissitzky, and of the sculptural and architectural concepts of Alexandr Rodchenko passed by almost unnoticed until 1962, when Camilla Gray's extraordinary study of the Russian and Soviet avant-garde was published and reintroduced these artists to a broader historical and critical reception.[6]

The same can be said with regard to the artistic and art historical reception of Surrealism, assimilated as it was only in its more traditional painterly positions articulated in the works of figures like Joan Mirò and André Masson, Max Ernst and Yves Tanguy. This is all the more astounding since a profound knowledge and appreciation of these legacies had existed in New York, exceeding by far that of Europe in the late Thirties. One only has to think of the famous exhibitions and catalogs by Alfred Barr, Jr., such as *Cubism and Abstract Art* or *Fantastic Art, Dada, Surrealism*, which offered all the relevant information on the major recent international art in 1936. Thus the question arises again: What kind of information is received by which group of recipients at which particular moment? For what reasons does a particular group choose one set of artistic information, omitting and/or suppressing the other?

Thus one could ask an admittedly rhetorical question: rather than contemplating Mirò and Kandinsky, why did Mark Rothko and Barnett Newman, Clyfford Still and Jackson Pollock, Arshile Gorky and Willem de Kooning not discover the infinitely more radical epistemological changes suggested by artists such as Marcel Duchamp and Francis Picabia, Man Ray and Tristan Tzara, Jean Arp and Kurt Schwitters as the primary sources of artistic information at that time?

One preliminary explanation is clearly to be found in the Americans' awe for the tradition of Parisian painting as it is expressed in Greenberg's essay "The School of Paris" in 1946:

> Paris remains the fountainhead of modern art, and every move made there is decisive for advanced art elsewhere—which is advanced precisely because it can respond to and extend the vibrations of that nerve-center and nerve-end of modernity which is Paris.[7]

From our present-day perspective this statement seems all the more astonishing since artists in Paris by then had themselves become aware of the growing academicism of late Surrealist and late abstract painting of the Ecole de Paris. Jean Dubuffet, for example, tried to posit his art brut figurations against the Surrealists' myths of the individual creator's prolific unconscious. Therefore he attempted to relate artistic practice once again—as the Surrealists had done originally themselves—to the collective potential for artistic production by substituting raw and repugnant materials like foils, sponges and sand for the precious surfaces of late Surrealist painting. As Dubuffet stated in 1947:

> What I am interested in is not the cakes but the bread. If one would be inclined in general to prefer bread to cake, one would end up being very unjust to pastry chefs, and not only to pastry chefs, but also to the institutions, like museums and

> art dealers and critics, which are also a Parisian specialty, nourishing quite a lot of people. ... I would like my paintings to be on the verge of disappearing as paintings. It is at the moment of vanishing that the swan starts singing.[8]

Of course we know that it is pointless to speculate whether artifacts might have changed if more or different information would have been absorbed at specific points in history. Nevertheless it seems valid to acknowledge—in particular in the context of postwar art—the extent to which "reception history" (and its peculiar randomness) has become "production history," and to reveal the degree to which seemingly autonomous aesthetic entities inform themselves art historically, and thereby, historically. From today's European perspective, one begins to question the historicist aspects of some recent American art and to wonder whether a retrospective view will not reveal a cyclical pattern in which each generation from the Abstract Expressionists to the Minimalists will appear as having assimilated, worked through, and enlarged a different set of historical presuppositions of the artistic practices of the twentieth century.

For example, one could voice doubts about the presumed epistemological radicality of Andy Warhol's *Campbell's Soup Cans* (1962) in relation to Duchamp's *Fountain* (1917). Or what about Flavin's *Diagonal of Personal Ecstasy (the Diagonal of May 25, 1963)* (1963), dedicated to Constantin Brancusi, which has certainly to be considered as a key work in international American art of the Sixties? Yet, from a contemporary perspective, is it not a somewhat belabored—at best a very learned—assimilation of different sculptural concepts of the twentieth century, if compared to the still undecipherable complexity of Kurt Schwitters' architectural vision, his *Cathedral of Erotic Misery* (whose title Flavin seems to unconsciously paraphrase)?

Post-Surrealist Dilemma

> The surrealists reacted against the historical conditions "in the service of revolution," trying to accelerate and to intensify the process of the autodestruction of bourgeois consciousness by means of the subconscious. By using the more or less misunderstood and limited methods of psychoanalysis, those artists totally withdrew from society, back into themselves, i.e., the subconscious became the last unit of the dissolving ego; they hoped that from there they could protest more convincingly by throwing their "ego" against the dissociated conditions. That this particular form of protest was infantile did not prevent them from experiencing it as a real protest; on the contrary, it was precisely this infantilism which allowed them to extend their protest to include everything and nothing, believing it to be unlimited.
>
> —*Max Raphael, Reading the New Art, 1938*[9]

When looking at the history of post-Surrealist art in Europe, especially the painting of the School of Paris, it becomes all the more important to recognize the peculiar continuity of local traditions. Although Greenberg's lucid observation from 1946 might sound truthful at first, it coincides neither with the actual Parisian reality at the time, nor with subsequent developments:

> After 1920 the positivism of the School of Paris, which depended in part on the assumption that infinite prospects of technical advance lay ahead of both society and arts, lost faith in itself. It began to be suspected that the physical in art was as historically limited as capitalism itself had turned out to be. Mondrian looked like the handwriting on the wall.[10]

Greenberg's astounding clairvoyance seems to anticipate the ultimate dematerialization of the art object in Conceptual and post-Minimal art, a development which might be called the most original and authentic contribution of American art to the present.[11] One wonders, however, whether he had to relinquish the uncompromising radicality of his original insight into the historical truth of capitalist culture in decline when he made his observations concerning the redevelopment of a local painterly culture ten years later in New York:

> It could be said that, by 1940, Eighth Street had caught up with Paris as Paris had not yet caught up with herself, and that a handful of then obscure New York painters possessed the ripest painting culture of the day.[12]

Indeed, it is only against the background of such a situation "which had not caught up with itself" (once again a reference to either a deliberate or imposed historical ignorance), that one can comprehend certain European developments as well as the high esteem (if not the overestimations) in which certain socially and historically defined artistic identities are held in postwar Europe. Thus the key figures of postwar European art, Georges Mathieu and Yves Klein in Paris, Lucio Fontana and Piero Manzoni in Italy, and finally Joseph Beuys in West Germany are justifying Max Raphael's remark on the Surrealists' infantilism even more in their context. This condition finds its clearest manifestation in the fact that—perhaps with the sole exception of Manzoni—the work of these artists is inextricably bound up with a claim for charisma, an inevitably fraudulent claim as it is.

This idea of the artist as a medium of transcendental experiences stands in distinct opposition to the more traditional image of the artist as a fusion of craftsman, scientist and philosopher, a figure who delivers the work and research results to bourgeois society on the market. By contrast, the historical function of these newly figured hypertrophic identities of European postwar artists, seems to have been to act out not just the urge for a new type of artistic subjectivity but equally, if not more so, the collective needs for a newly formed social hierarchy with the artist as its symbolic center or fountainhead.

Thus these artists had to assume attitudes that oscillate on a broad scale of irrational and archaic behavior: from shaman and high priest to victim and from fool to clown and entertainer.[13] All of these reflect—in very different ways of course—the particular social needs for a new mythical subjectivity. In the case of Mathieu, Klein and Beuys, the subject is spectacularized, in compliance with the reactionary requests of postwar society. In the case of Manzoni, the artist makes a dialectical gesture toward the potential reality of a new collective and recognizes the necessity of the formation of a post-traditional subjectivity.

Mathieu and Pollock

> Were Pollock a Frenchman, there would be, I feel, no need by now to call attention to my objectivity in praising him; he would already be called maître and there would already be speculation in his pictures.
>
> —*Clement Greenberg, 1952*[14]

Certainly one of Mathieu's lasting achievements will be his initiatives to have organized the first exhibitions of the paintings of Wols and Pollock in Paris. And it is characteristic that in Mathieu's eagerness to situate himself among them, and to install his own paintings among theirs, he was not able to discern the fundamental differences between the two artists, and least of all between their work and his own.

If Wols' work completed the last phase of *écriture automatique* and radical subjectivity in painting, Pollock's was an entirely new beginning of the objectification of the process of painting itself. This is most clearly revealed in a comparison between the structural organization of painterly mass in canvases by Pollock and those of Wols. Thus, one of the basic differences between European and American art of that period—and its lasting effects on contemporary practices—becomes evident in Pollock's dominant concern for the decentering of the matter and process of painting, endowing his paintings with the innate radicality of a decentered field of self-referential pictorial processes and traces. Pollock's painting proved that not even the slightest residue of "subjective" imagery should interfere with those forces, and that "artistic" imagination need no longer be superimposed on the viewers' perception. Thus, Pollock shifted abstraction away from Surrealist painting and negated automatist conventions, ultimately suggesting new models of a post-Freudian subjectivity. Pollock reflected on the prevailing conditions of painting and experience under advanced monopoly capitalism—with its potential for increased individual freedom and its actually governing conditions of rapidly diminishing options for the subjective differentiation of experience.

By contrast, Mathieu's work represents a final phase of Surrealist automatism, and the supposedly liberating forces of the subjective unconscious to dissolve objective reification. Although claiming to be the trace of pure velocity and temporality, his "action painting" generates a manifestly frozen gesture. Like an involuntary caricature of Pollock, Mathieu's paintings generate dead hierarchic figures in centralized grounds. At a relatively early moment then, Mathieu's compulsion to restore traditional (artistic) subjectivity in hypertrophic forms, articulates, even if unknowingly, the inescapable condition to have to confront, if not to comply with, the intensifying demands for the spectacularization of (artistic) subjectivity in contemporary culture.

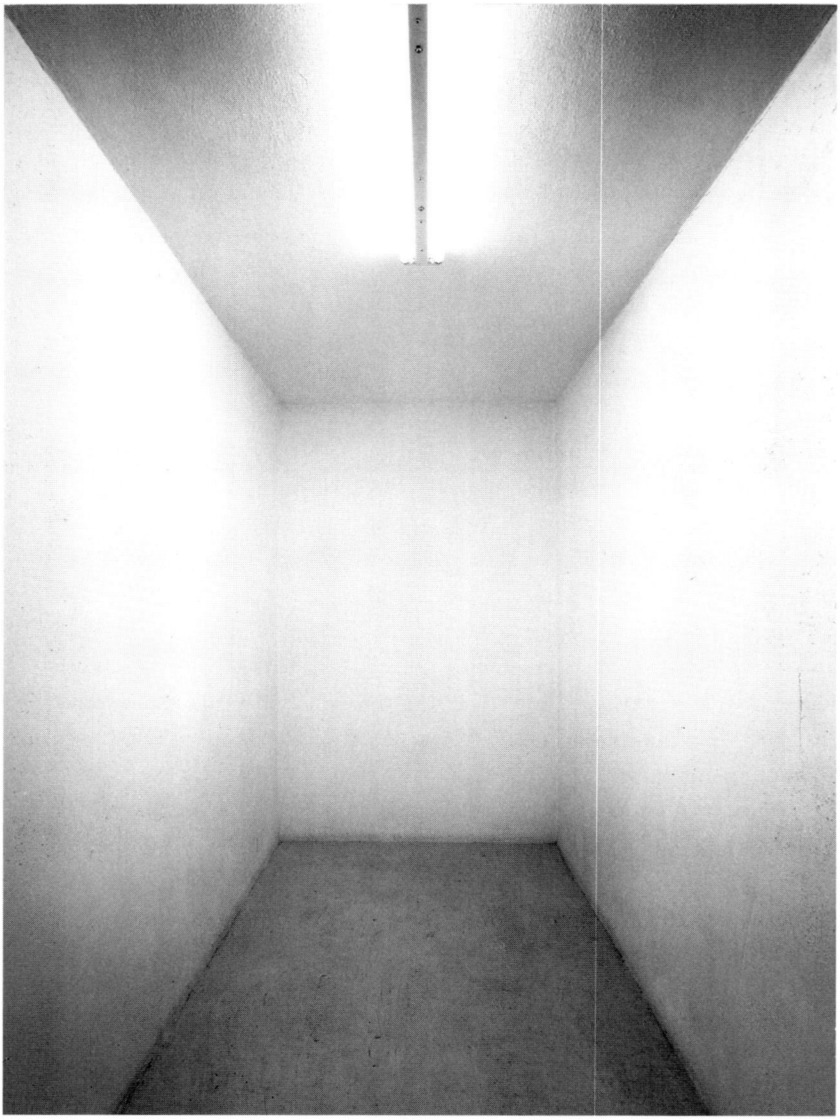

Yves Klein, *Immaterial Room*, 1961. Museum Haus Lange, Krefeld. Photo: V. Dohne. © 2015 Artists Rights Society (ARS), New York/ADAGP, Paris.

KLEIN AND KAPROW

Kaprow and Klein, born in 1927 and 1928 respectively, might well be chosen as another pair of opposites illustrating the history of European and American differences. In fact, they are both members of the first generation of artists that had learned substantially from both their immediate predecessors (i.e., Pollock) and their antecedents in the historical avant-gardes. Kaprow, who had completed his master's thesis on Mondrian with Meyer Schapiro at Columbia University and had studied the work of Pollock extensively, considered his own work as a necessary extension of the projects of these painters:

> Not satisfied with the suggestion through paint of our senses, we shall utilize the specific substances of sight, sound, movement, people, odors, touch. Objects of every sort are the materials of the new art: paint, chairs, food, electric and neon lights, smoke, water, old socks, a dog, movies, a thousand other things which will be discovered by the present generation of artists. Not only will these bold creators show us, as if for the first time, the world which we have always had about us, but ignored, but they will disclose entirely unheard of happenings.[15]

By joining a radical reading of the Surrealist origins of Pollock's painting with the heritage of theatrical activities as they had been performed in revolutionary Russian Futurist theater and Dada activities alike, Kaprow formed the basis for his own work as a new dialectical exchange between the aesthetic and the real. The composer John Cage (with whom Kaprow had studied at the New School in 1957–1958) had set the tone for this new approach:

> I think daily life is excellent and that art introduces us to it and its excellence the more it begins to be like it.[16]

This attitude, which was held by a whole generation of American artists, from Cage and Merce Cunningham to Kaprow and the Fluxus group, from the early work of Robert Rauschenberg to that of Yvonne Rainer, could be summed up as the quest for a new correspondence between life and art on the politicized, historical materialist grounds that the Surrealists had originally aimed for. Typically, this crucial chapter of recent American art continues to be underrated and misrepresented in many ways because it did not produce marketable or museologically classifiable objects. In contrast to Kaprow, the simultaneously developing European position of Klein reveals a state of historical delusion that originates in an artistic narcissism that insists on the false opposition between bourgeois and artistic subject positions. This is what it sounds like:

> Materialism—this quantitative spirit has been recognized as the enemy of liberty. … I love in myself everything that does not belong to me, that is my life, and I detest everything that belongs to me: my education, my psychological and optical inheritance, which is received and traditional, my views, my defects, my qualities, my manias: in one word, everything that leads me irredeemably towards physical, sentimental and emotional death.[17]

Obviously Klein had learned his art historical lessons as well, but unlike Kaprow he tried to conceal his sources—one or two allusions to Malevich not withstanding—with a hypertrophic affirmation of his absolute originality that is symptomatic of his fraudulence and historical disavowal:

> The glaring obviousness of my paternity of monochromy in the twentieth century is such that even if I myself were to fight hard against that fact I should probably never manage to rid myself of it.[18]

Apart from his knowledge of Malevich, Klein seems to have been equally aware of Mondrian's legacy. His first exhibition at Colette Allendy's Paris gallery in 1956 comprised differently colored Unicolor paintings that looked as if they had been executed under the influence of a first encounter with Mondrian's monochrome color rectangles. In a photograph that had been published for the first time in Michel Seuphor's monograph on Mondrian earlier in the very same year, Mondrian's monochrome panels could be seen scattered over the walls of the artist's last studio in New York. One has to admit though that—regardless of whether he was aware of Mondrian nor not—Klein articulates a major formal problem that would soon become one of the crucial arguments made by American artists like Stella and Judd against the European tradition, namely the problem of chromatic and spatial relations and compositionality:

> I was trying to show color, but I realized at the private view that the public were prisoners of a preconceived point of view and that, confronted with all these surfaces of different colors they responded far more to the interrelationship of the different propositions, they reconstituted the elements of a decorative polychromy.[19]

Monochrome paintings had been shown in Paris by Ellsworth Kelly (who had lived and worked in Paris from 1948 to 1954) during his first personal exhibition at the Galerie Arnaud in 1951. And one should of course remember that the monochrome canvases of Lucio Fontana might have been easily known to Klein as well, since he was a frequent traveler to Italy in the early Fifties. And thirdly—if not most importantly—when confronting Klein's claims to an original paternity to monochromy and flatness, wholeness and "object-like" painting, we would have to remember Robert Rauschenberg's monochrome paintings from 1951, unlikely as it is that Klein could have encountered them in reproduction. Finally, the seemingly hermetic mystery of Klein's "genius" had also been subjected to more local, not to say vernacular, influences. Dubuffet' s works such as the Texturologies from 1954, and the monochrome sponge sculptures of the same year, must have been of prime importance for the development of Yves le Monochrome, his discovery of the monochrome in general and his sculptural inventions, the éponges, in particular. It seems that he simply switched from Dubuffet's chthonic monochrome colors to the bright synthetic hues of industrial production, a shift that could either be celebrated as a major change, or that could be discarded as a minor academic problem in the final phases of post-Surrealist painting.

Furthermore, when it comes to Klein's claims to have invented the concept of immateriality, a similar genealogy can be traced once again, since every single one of these immaterial works by Klein has an almost explicit Duchampian predecessor. From Klein's purely indexical paintings which result from the climatic effects on a blank canvas mounted on the roof of his car for the journey Paris–Nice (see by comparison, Duchamp's *Unhappy Readymade*, 1919 and his *Elevage de Poussière*,1920) to Klein's *Portraits-Reliefs* from 1962 (see Duchamp's *With my Tongue in my Cheek*, 1959) to the culminating moment in the certificates for the exchange of pure gold for parts of the *Immaterial Pictorial Sensitivity Zone* (see Duchamp's *Monte Carlo Bonds*, 1924).[20]

Thus Klein—quite in opposition to Kaprow's Happenings—reactivates the artist as a petit bourgeois agent provocateur, a reactionary position which had been lingering around late Parisian Surrealism. It found its most symptomatic figures such as Salvador Dalí, whose techniques of self-scandalizing mythology Klein seems to have studied most thoroughly, attempting to maintain an idea of the artist as a narcissistic elitist, as "a sort of superman," as Marcel Duchamp had once put it.

Klein and Judd

It is all the more astonishing then that Klein's work should have found such an unusual degree of appreciation in the United States. Klein was the first, and for a long time, the only European postwar artist to appear on the cover of *Artforum* (January 1967), on the occasion of his major retrospective at the Jewish Museum in New York. It comes as even more of a surprise that Klein seems to have been the only figure recognized by the younger generation of American artists of the early Sixties, as revealed in Bruce Glaser's interview with Frank Stella and Donald Judd. Finally, Judd in his own writings frequently refers to Klein as the only European painter who dealt with formal issues of prime importance to his own concerns: flatness, abolition of relationality, and the wholeness of the painting as an object. Eventually Judd (born as Klein was in 1928) went as far as including Klein among "the world's best artists" in his essay on Barnett Newman from 1970:

> At the moment, despite the difficulties of comparisons and the excellence of the work of Rothko, Noland and Stella, it's not rash to say that Newman is the best painter in the country. Also the work of these four artists and that by Reinhardt and Lichtenstein, is considerably better than the European painting evident in the magazines and that is shown in New York, except for Yves Klein's blue paintings.[21]

Judd evaluates Klein's work in patently formalist terms, disregarding any implications of the materiality (e.g., the monogolds), or the processes of production (e.g., his *Anthropométries*). From a contemporary European vantage point, it has become even less comprehensible how one could evaluate any artistic production without considering at the same time its manifest political and ideological investments. Klein's became evident in his crypto-fascist statements delivered on the occasion of the "Inauguration of the Pneumatic Epoch":

> Our government pure and scandalous will eliminate the puppets, the Françoise Sagans, the Genets, the George Duhamels, the Einsteins, the Roosevelts, the Pandit Nehrus, the rats and garbage cans.[22]

Judd's formalism seems to have originated in the attitudes of a generation that learned its art history lessons better than its history lessons, and that seems to have been mainly concerned with the problem of inserting its production into the mainstream of modernist formalist traditions. How inaccurate and imprecise such a reading must be, if it is incapable of even identifying the most elementary latent (or manifest) ideological and historical implications of a work?

Fortunately we know of at least one lucid analysis of Klein, published relatively early by the critic Dore Ashton, which proves that American- type formalism was only one possible historical approach to be taken at the time. As Ashton put it in her essay on Klein:

> He was a reactionary in the sense that many of the young intelligentsia were reactionaries in the post-war decade: theirs was a reaction against the great wartime currents of commitment, summarized by existentialism ... when many older French intellectuals were frantic with horror, the fevered prose accompanying the "revolution" in the visual arts was coyly transmundane, limiting itself to exalted discussions of new cosmologies, new psychism, new infinite beyonds, and new brotherhoods in some distant future in the infinite beyonds where "other" art would conquer. ... Under cover of cascades of hyperbolic prose promotion, a host of younger artists stepped out into the world of show business, bringing "reality" to their hungry bourgeois patrons. ... The fossils of one of these lives, dessicated and boring, are on view at the Jewish Museum. No one better

> exemplifies the shift in values, the switch from art as a private affair to art as a public event, than the late Yves Klein. The souvenirs of his life of spectacle are poor dead things. Bereft of the confectioner, the life of his art has vanished.[23]

The opposition of formalism and historicity can perhaps now be more clearly defined. Both concepts should be regarded as the opposite ends of an axis along which artistic production as well as criticism, and the writing of recent art history, seem to be shifting perpetually according to their immanent and historical dynamics. Of course neither one could be called specific to European or American art of the recent decades, but it seems that at precisely the point where the major European artists of the present (Marcel Broodthaers and Daniel Buren, Gerhard Richter and Bernd and Hilla Becher) developed radically altered notions of their relation to history—namely around 1965—a strong formalist identification seems to have defined the American situation. Once again, Judd's apodictic statements, such as those in his essay "Imperialism, Nationalism, and Regionalism" (1975), demonstrate that position:

> Art, dance, music and literature have to be considered as autonomous activities and not as decoration upon political and social purposes.[24]

In spite of Judd's authoritarian prohibition, aesthetic activities do not have to be considered as autonomous activities, and neither must this imply that they can only be considered as "decoration upon political and social purposes."

When the interdependence of aesthetic and historical structures cannot be imagined in any other way than to consider art merely a mimetic appendix to reality (or as its decoration as Judd calls it), this formalist attitude shows either blatant disdain, or naïveté toward the dialectical potential of art. It is precisely the loss of naïveté with regard to history that might be called specific to European art since the late 1950s. An awareness reemerged that—by analyzing their own epistemological presuppositions—artistic practices could not restrict their inquiry to their own discourse alone (nor to the history of that discourse). Rather, they would have to reflect their positions dialectically within a given historical reality, both as dependent and determined forms, and as modes of ideological productivity transforming this reality.

This critical attitude is precisely what prevented the next generation of European artists from following in the footsteps of Yves Klein, who exemplified in the postwar moment the artistic type whose activities Max Raphael had already defined as early as 1938 as being the "caterer of chic":

> Chic is another feeling of contrast. It develops out of two altogether different sources: either the masquerade of outer elegance under which the individual pretends to continue his fight against society, or an abstract idealization and embellishment which develops exactly to the degree to which the real human being becomes a caricature. In the first case dandyism is a conscious irony deriving from the tragic and comical separation of the singular individual from society and the feeling of superiority of the "paradoxical unique" over the bon sens of the philistines; in the second case "embellishment" is the desire of the disproportioned and dehumanized for aesthetical illusion, for false harmony and pretended proportionality, for the fata morgana of all contradictions being resolved. In both cases chic has become an integral element of high art.[25]

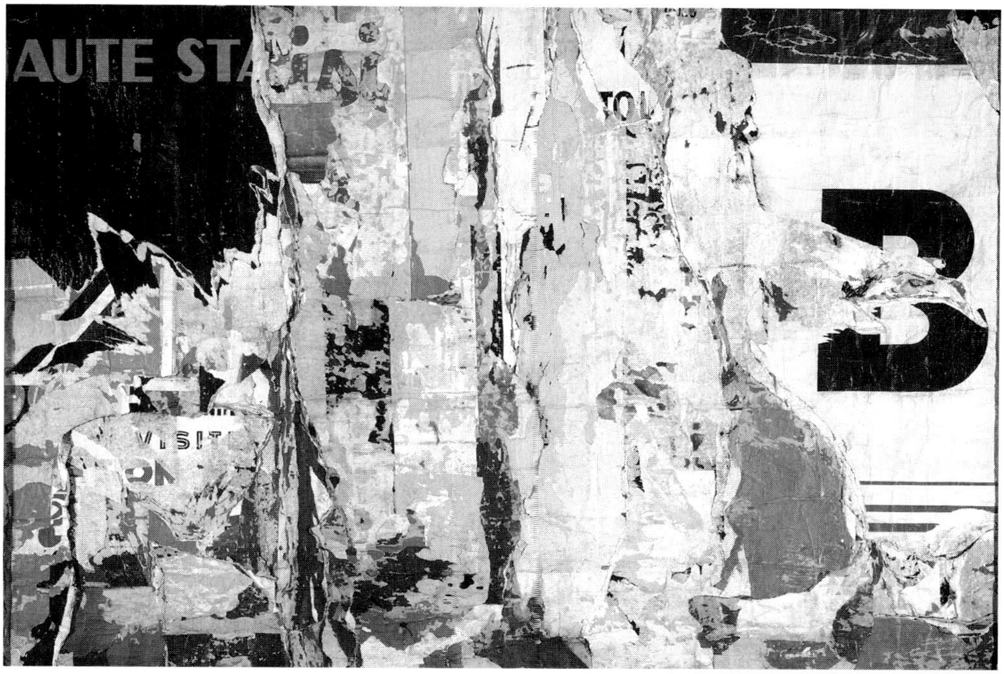

Jacques de la Villeglé, *Avenue de la Liberté (Charenton)*, 1961. Torn posters pasted on canvas, 62½ × 90 in. (159 × 229 cm). Museum Ludwig, Cologne. © 2015 Artists Rights Society (ARS), New York/ADAGP, Paris. Photo: © Rheinisches Bildarchiv: rba_c004464.

VILLEGLÉ'S ANONYMOUS LACERATIONS

> It is within the real, by the real and with the real that the affiche lacérée gains its consistency and imposes its presence. But it's just because he doesn't resign to reality that the anonymous lacerator, who feels the restraint of reification pending on him, acts by protesting in particular against the psychic violation of the masses by the public propaganda. By this he introduces the domain of the potentiality of childhood right into the reality of adults.[26]

It seems useful to emphasize that none of the artists of the subsequent generation, whose work essentially changed the notion of contemporary European art, has been influenced by the Klein legacy. The work of Stanley Brouwn and Hanne Darboven, of Daniel Buren, Palermo and Niele Toroni, of Gerhard Richter and the Bechers, nevertheless articulates transformations of ideas and practices that had already been initiated by European artists of the Fifties and early Sixties, work that had received much less recognition in European, let alone in American art criticism.

This is true, most of all, of Klein's counterfigure, the Italian Piero Manzoni, as well as for the lesser known group of the French décollagistes, Francois Dufrêne, Raymond Hains and Jacques de la Villeglé (and their Italian colleague Mimmo Rotella). "Lacéré Anonyme"—the anonymous lacerations of billboards—is the term used by Villeglé to describe the result of an artistic contract between the artist as "collector" and the anonymous pedestrian committing acts of vandalism against advertisements on urban billboards. The work of the décollagistes could be called the most underestimated and misunderstood artistic position in postwar European art while it might well represent the first legitimate European contribution to the development of a new artistic language after Dada and Surrealism.[27]

Being fully aware of given (art) historical conditions, ranging from the concept of the readymade to Schwitters' collage- and assemblage-aesthetics to the radicality of Pollock's all-over pictorial field which completed the idea of gestural automatism, the décollagistes deliberately transferred painterly actions from the studio and the canvas into the street as early as 1949. Yet their work has been discarded all too easily as simply having transformed Duchamp's readymade into a different materiality, or as having transposed the collage language of Schwitters onto a different scale. In actuality, however, the project of the décollagistes aimed at a far more comprehensive transformation of the Dada legacies, as Villeglé himself pointed out:

> To plunder, to collect, to sign the lacerated affiches, to live with them and to exhibit them in galleries, salons and museums, this is not a questioning of the artwork in the sense of Duchamp's readymade but more a questioning of the professional and traditional artist.[28]

And, in a different text, slightly later:

> After all, I cannot consider the laceration of the anonymous participant or my selection of it as a transcription or objectivization of a singular, lived experience of a gifted and predestined individual, the artist. …
>
> The gestural savagery of a multitude is individualized to become the most remarkable manifestation of "art made by all and not by one" of this period.[29]

The work of the décollagistes departs both from Duchamp's anonymously manufactured objects, aestheticized by declaration, and from Schwitters' found materials, aestheticized by arrangement. The anonymous gesture and the very activity of the collective unconscious (*l'inconscient collectif*) to which Villeglé frequently refers, enter into the realm of artistic reflection, but at a remove from the Surrealists' traditional idealization of the liberating powers of the collective unconscious.

This position had found its most recent articulation in Dubuffet's art brut collection/production, an idiosyncratic fiction (historical, geographical as well as socio-psychological) that attempted to mobilize a seemingly lost innocent productivity to oppose the division of labor and the status of the artist as a specialist in bourgeois society.

With lacéré anonyme, the artist as a flâneur restricts his productive activity to the mere act of choosing an anonymous vandalizing gesture—making it even less of an artistic intervention than Duchamp's "declarative act of pictorial nominalism." In a conscious refusal, the décollagistes cede their position to the collective gestures of vandalism, a counter-productivity which in Villeglé's historical situation appeared to be the sole gesture of opposition against what the artist would identify as "psychic violation by public propaganda."

As a collector who links himself to an anonymous producer of oppositional gestures, the artist acknowledges the potential for collective participation. How such a contract between the artist as collector and anonymous producers would evolve subsequently in the work of Stanley Brouwn and in the systematic documentation of *Anonymous Sculptures* by Bernd and Hilla Becher will be discussed in the following.

The procedural and perceptual specificity in the work of the décollagistes would be certainly legible in "formalist" terms: the abolition of illusionistic space corresponds to the abolition of projective subjectivism in the spectatorial act; the presence of the self-referential opacity of the object demands the presence of a conscious, self-determining spectatorial subject. Nevertheless, Villeglé identified the motivations for his practice by situating the formal and perceptual changes that his work engenders within an explicitly historical frame:

> Lacéré Anonyme opens up with four cuts of the razor blade a window into the flatness of the affiche-objet. A beam of daylight thus cuts through the obscurity of the ways in which the financial and political powers arrive at the ends they impose on mankind. The unknown poetry reveals and destroys the schematizations of propaganda and publicity.[30]

Manzoni's Concepts

> Manzoni is dead, physically dead. He was young. Is there a connection between his untimely death and the attitude that he took on in the context of art? It is most certain that insisting on his kind of humour was not a very comfortable position to have taken. And if this should be the reason, then our inquiry into artistic events, into all kinds of events, will have to be profound and thorough. In any case, Manzoni will be in the history books of the terrible twentieth century.[31]
>
> —*Marcel Broodthaers*

When Broodthaers wrote this eulogy after Manzoni's death in 1963 he considered himself—and was in fact—still a poet and critic whose own visual production would begin only shortly thereafter. Thus those lines could be read in two ways: first, as a profound comprehension of the investigative and analytical nature of Manzoni's work. And second, as a promise to continue Manzoni's legacy, a project which Broodthaers would actually accomplish in his own artistic production. Whereas Klein can be rightfully considered a terminal figure—as of course was true of Mathieu—who left almost no traces in contemporary art, the opposite could be said of Manzoni. Or as stated by the Italian critic Sarenco:

> The work of Klein is conservative, the work of Manzoni is revolutionary. In Klein there is metaphysics, childish obsessions. In Manzoni there is violent irony, desire to change things, a materialist conception of the world. Klein is a man of despair, a romantic, a decadent; his work closes a cycle of the avant-garde. Manzoni is a man of the concrete, a provocateur, his work opens the way of the contemporary avant-garde.[32]

Manzoni should be considered as a key figure for contemporary European art. If Duchamp played games with the epistemological consequences of his work, Manzoni reintroduced those Duchampian attitudes to the postwar period and made them operative. Each step in that progression, from Duchamp to Manzoni and to the next generation, consisted in an increasing differentiation and singularization of the perceptual, cognitive and spatial elements of the contemporary aesthetic structure; and the successive qualitative distillation of these elements and their quantitative extension endowed the work with a new public dimension. And in a dialectical reversal, the progressive dissolution of the work's aesthetic appearance and the abolition of artistic conventions in favor of actual material processes induced a new conceptualization of production.

Lines from Duchamp, Manzoni, and Brouwn

One could suggest that Duchamp's *Three Standard Stoppages* (1913) represented an almost unimaginable step of isolating one particular aspect of spatial plasticity, and as such of course constituted an abstraction, or a conceptualization of a dramatically different kind from those being conceived in Post-Cubist painting at that moment. Duchamp's work was certainly not recognized in Europe until Manzoni's *linea* works (conceived from 1959 onwards), in which the artist defined drawing as a purely spatio-temporal extension (each work is defined by different dimensions ranging from a few meters up to 7200 m, and one—a black

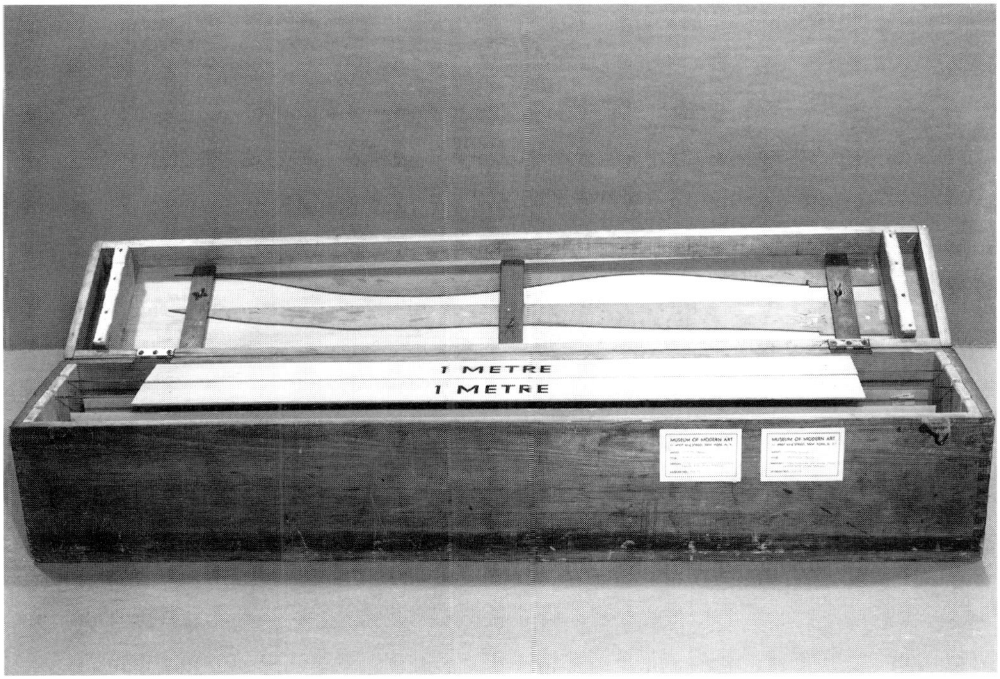

Marcel Duchamp, *Three Standard Stoppages*, 1913–14. Wood box, 11⅛ × 50⅞ × 9 in. (28.2 × 129.2 × 22.7 cm), with three threads, 39⅜ in. (100 cm), glued to three painted canvas strips, 5¼ × 47¼ in. (13.3 × 120 cm), each mounted on a glass panel, 7¼ × 49⅜ × ¼ in. (18.4 × 125.4 × 0.6 cm), three wood slats, 2½ × 43 × ⅛ in. (6.2 × 109.2 × 0.2 cm), shaped along one edge to match the curves of the threads. Katherine S. Dreier Bequest © Succession Marcel Duchamp/ADAGP, Paris/Artists Rights Society (ARS), New York 2015.

wooden tubular body—is identified as a line of infinite length). Manzoni's *linea* works obviously were an immediate influence on Stanley Brouwn's early spatial-conceptual approach to sculpture, evident in works such as his *Piece no. 34* from 1962:

> a walk from a to b; b to a; a to b etc. … 100 times[33]

Brouwn programmatically introduced the concept of a space-time continuum into a sculptural work, or as he defined it in his own formula: distance = length, length = distance.

The materials of *Three Standard Stoppages* range from wooden rulers to gold lettering, from glass panes to metered string pieces, from canvas bases to leather labels, and all of these elements are finally encased in the presentational device of a croquet box which serves as both a fetishistic frame (containing the sculpture in its post-performative state, the sculpture at rest) and as a ludic allusion (promising the sculpture's partial reactivation in the performative display). Equivalent to this range of materials is the perceptual-conceptual complexity of Duchamp's work, shifting from the programmatic examination of the relations of chance operations and sculptural form to the question of a work's conceptual identity and perceptual dissimilarity. All of these aspects culminate in a heretofore unthinkable distinction between the performative state of the sculpture's physical execution and its static mode of display as integral but oppositional elements.[34]

Manzoni's line works (most prominently his *Line 1000 Meters Long*, 1961), while reduced in their presentational devices are by no means less complex in their conception than Duchamp's. The singularization of one constituent feature of the work, in this instance the drawing process as a spatio-temporal extension, is magnified to such a degree that it gains an altogether different, almost monumental public openness and accessibility. By comparison, Duchamp's ludic box appears almost subjectivist, featuring, as it does, a peculiar intimacy.

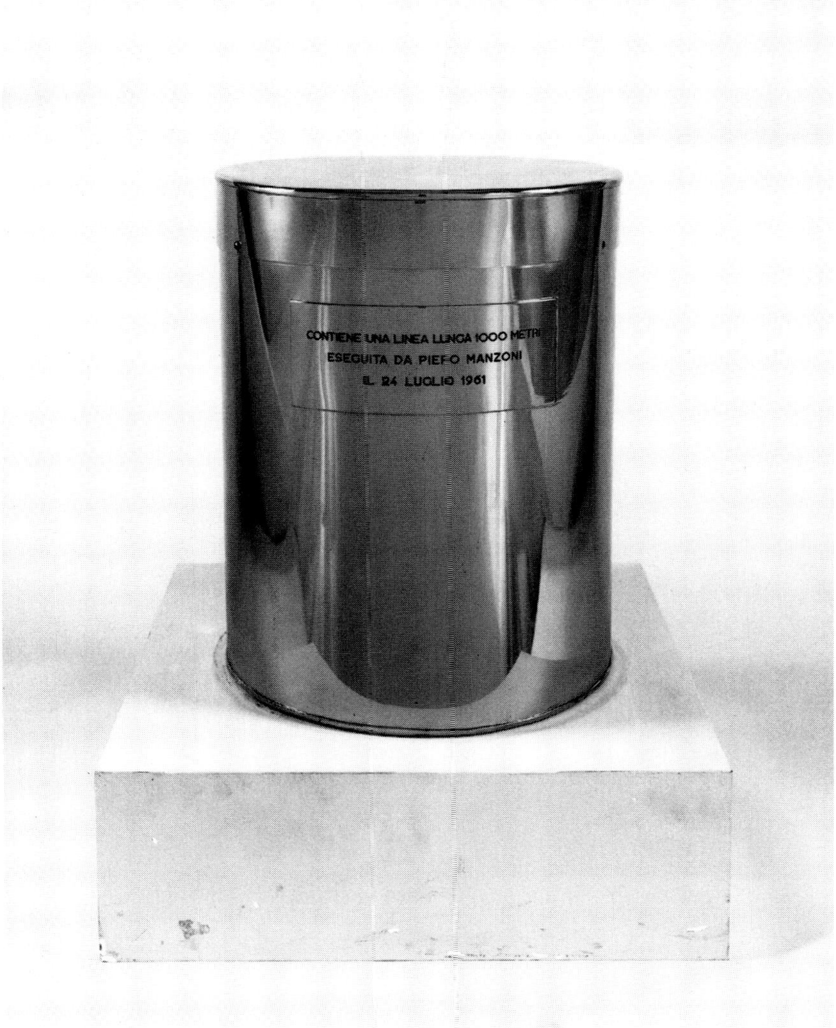

Piero Manzoni, *Line 1000 Meters Long*, July 24, 1961. Chrome-plated metal drum containing a roll of paper with an ink line drawn along its 1,000-meter length; 20¼ × 15⅜ in. diameter (51.2 cm × 38.8 cm). Museum of Modern Art, New York. © 2015 Artists Rights Society (ARS), New York/SIAE, Rome.

Yet while the phenomenon of spatio-temporal extension has been magnified to the level of public monumentality, it has been radically negated in the dialectical withholding of the object's material and visual appearance. Thus it can no longer be perceived in any other way than in the spectator's imaginary conceptualization. By contrast, the device of framing and presentation is now the only material object that is perceptually accessible, as it literally contains the artistic concept and conceals its hidden aesthetic materialization.

Manzoni defines a strategy of perceptual withdrawal that would become increasingly crucial for the formulation of Conceptual art after 1965, replacing perceptual definitions of the work of art by conceptualization. Both the idea of the pure spatial dimension and its material concretion are present. Yet the work as material object negates itself totally in favor of its invisible conceptual dimension. As object, it exists only insofar as it functions to negate the work's appearance—as a containing concealment. The shiny mirroring surface of the chrome container literally reflects and returns the spectator's perceptual expectations from the aesthetic object back onto the viewers themselves.

Thus it becomes evident with hindsight that Manzoni was one of the originators of Conceptual practices who introduced a new attitude of materialist conceptualization and of conceptualized material, or, as Robert Pincus-Witten (one of the first and rare American critics to write about Manzoni) suggested, that "by isolating constituent features of art, Manzoni paraded what he thought the essential futility of art as sensibility."[35] Manzoni's analytical approach initiated a whole spectrum of different attitudes in the subsequent decade. These ranged from the painterly activities of Niele Toroni who would expand Manzoni's systematically ordered, achrome paintings, and who would zero in on the serial order of molecular brushstrokes, or they would generate a new conceptual approach to the process of drawing itself, as in Brouwn's reduction of drawing to a definition of the space-time continuum, or the drawing systems of Hanne Darboven that would increasingly reduce the scope of drawing to the graphic quantification of time.

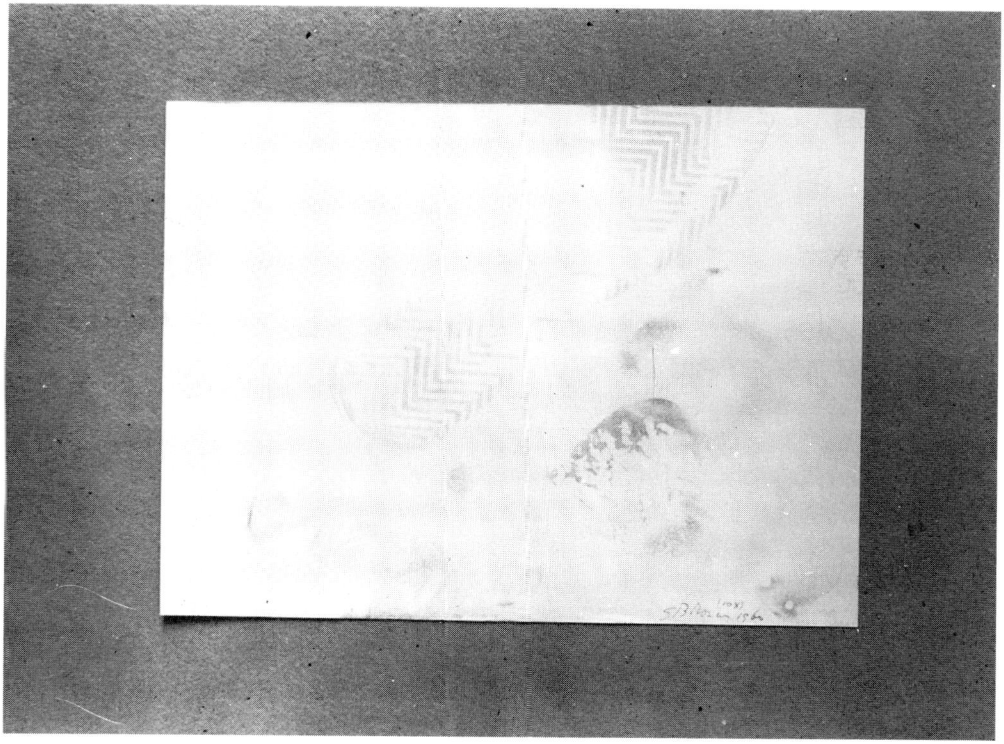

Stanley Brouwn, *Works No. 1–8*, 1962. Footprint on paper. Photo: D. Fischer.

Stanley Brouwn

> A "This way Brouwn" is a portrait of a tiny bit of earth. Fixed by the memory of the city: the pedestrian.
>
> —*Stanley Brouwn*

When Brouwn announced in 1960 that all the shoe shops in Amsterdam should be considered as his first public exhibition, a major step in contemporary European art had been taken. This work not only acknowledged the lasting relevance of Duchamp's readymade concept but at the same time differentiated its meaning and enlarged its functions in various dimensions. The element of quantitative multiplication and serial equivalence had already been introduced by the Nouveaux Réalistes—especially by Arman whom Brouwn had visited in Nice—but in the final analysis, they had left both the concept and the artwork formally and historically in a rather reified state. By contrast, Brouwn's idea of seriality obviously led away from the collectible (and collected) found objects toward the context of a given system and a functioning reality, and into a public, architectural space of simultaneous collective experience.

What is more, Brouwn's shoe shop work announced his future concerns for artistic structures that would be collective, anonymous and participatory, since the physical actions of a pedestrian are among the most common spatio-temporal experiences. In the same year, Brouwn would have anonymous unsuspecting pedestrians produce his first actual works as they walked over large sheets of white paper laid down in the streets of Amsterdam (*Works No. 1–8*, 1960).

Obviously, the collaboration between John Cage and Rauschenberg that had resulted in the *Tire Print* in 1953, had signaled a shift toward a purely indexical approach to drawing (and painting), leading up to the bodily inscriptions of Klein's *Anthropométries* and Manzoni's

Finger Prints in 1960, and eventually to Brouwn's attempts to situate the bodily imprint in public social space. Not surprisingly, Brouwn would shift from merely collecting the traces left by pedestrians on his papers, to actively instigating a dialogue with a participating anonymous subject when he solicits spatial directions from randomly chosen pedestrians:

> The duration of the creation of a "this way Brouwn" is precisely limited, in contrast to what was previously generally done in art. There is no adjusting, no measuring, no rounding-off or embellishment of the result. The time Brouwn really needs to walk from A to B is compressed in the explanation-time of the passer-by in the street. … At the moment of explanation, the situation is still in the future. He (the passer-by) makes a jump in time and space.[36]

It is worthwhile comparing the subject-object and the subject-subject relationships in artistic production that the indexical drawing process has undergone from Klein's *Anthropométries* and Villeglé's lacéré anonyme to Brouwn's randomly chosen pedestrians as active participants. While "objective anonymity" was still a necessary condition in Villeglé's work, his artistic control was still considerable, defined by the act of choosing the vandalized segment according to aesthetic criteria as much as by the act of mounting, framing and signing the chosen fragment.

With Brouwn's work, by contrast, both sides of this new equation of artist and anonymous participant have been inverted. Now, the artist's aesthetic choice is limited to the act of asking an anonymous pedestrian for directions, thus generating the projective spatial production (the anticipatory spatial and temporal operation) in a purely indexical drawing. The result of this cooperation constitutes the totality of Brouwn's work, whose signature is in the form of a stamp. *This Way Brouwn* authenticates a process of production entirely dependent on the cooperation of two individuals. Thus the participation of the anonymous subject in the process of artistic production becomes real, for an instant, since the artist actually eliminates his authorial identity, while his insistence on a dialogical "work" anticipates a self-conscious subject which projects its own self-determined future. As Brouwn has put it:

> It is not the past but the future which has the greatest influence on our ideas and actions.[37]

In the next phase of the development of Stanley Brouwn's work, proposals such as *No. 34* seem to abolish sculptural or painterly materiality altogether and acquire the status of a "mere" verbal definition of a material process:

> a walk from a to b; b to a; a to b etc. … 100 times[38]

This seeming disappearance of all materiality, however, does not lead to a tautological self-referentiality or analytic proposition, symptomatic of certain positions in subsequent Conceptual art. Quite to the contrary, the potential of the work and the necessary execution can be accomplished by anybody in a simple performative practice of (sculptural) activities in everyday life. Thus the highest degree of abstraction—articulated in the commonly developed sense of formalization, the signs of language—corresponds in Brouwn's work to the highest degree of material concretion: the collective potential experience of spatial-temporal change in the activity of taking steps.

The recipient to whom Brouwn addresses his work is a historically conscious subject who no longer supports the more or less complex aesthetic models of an author's heteronomous experience. The artist has accordingly restricted his activities to the most neutral position (and proposition), a written instruction for a performative action which can generate the work's shape and function within any given spatio-temporal reality.

As with Manzoni's proto-conceptual practices, one can trace the impact that Brouwn's work has had on contemporary European and American art, even if that impact at times seems hardly discernible in the well-disguised variations. Manzoni's and Brouwn's materialist radicality and formal abstraction have found followers, imitators, and mere aestheticizations. One example would be a work such as Walter de Maria's *Mile Long Drawing* (Mohave Desert, 1968) which clearly deploys Manzoni's and Brouwn's concepts, in the same way that de Maria's more recent and even more spectacular *Vertical Earth Kilometer* (Kassel, 1977) does. What de Maria adds to the works of Manzoni and Brouwn are precisely those qualities that these artists had deliberately done away with: spectacular size and oppressive symbolism. Another example would be the work of Richard Long, who adds geographical exoticism and a romanticist attitude toward "nature" by re-designing Brouwn's mere spatio-temporal delineations in the structures of mythical archetypes like spirals and concentric circles (photographically documented). All that these artists have achieved, is to have converted Brouwn's radicality back into traditional sculpture. This is evident when one compares any of Long's works of the later Sixties with one of Brouwn's works from 1962: A walk through a grassfield exactly on the same line a–b, every day during a full year.

Once again, it is significant to recognize that Donald Judd, in his essay "Imperialism, Nationalism and Regionalism" (1975), totally ignores the best of the European works of that period, those of Manzoni and Brouwn in particular. Thus he can not only make preposterous statements about the definitive failure of European art, but he also misjudges practices in the present. Typically, Judd expresses his high appreciation for the derivative work of Richard Long, and, worse yet, opposes it in an aggressive non-sensical polemic with an artist like Daniel Buren:

> It becomes a real mess when no one knows the difference between a good artist and a bad one, as they didn't, say, in 1959 between Rauschenberg and Michael Goldberg or Grace Hartigan. Or say now between Richard Long and Daniel Buren or Jan Dibbets.[39]

There are, on the other hand, examples of authentic assimilations and transformations of Manzoni's and Brouwn's concepts, as in the work of the Japanese-American artist, On Kawara, and the German-American artist, Hans Haacke, even though they developed their work eventually in totally different directions. And it should be noted that a younger group of post-Minimalist American artists, like Michael Asher, Dan Graham and Lawrence Weiner, have been fully aware of the functional immediacy of Brouwn's work and hold it in the highest esteem, even though it may not have left obvious traces in their own projects.

Marcel Broodthaers

> I have fabricated instruments which were destined for my usage to understand the aspect of fashion in art, to follow it, and finally to find a definition of that fashion. I am neither painter nor violinist. What really interests me is Ingres. I am not interested in Cézanne and his apples.[40]
>
> —*Marcel Broodthaers*

It was during his sojourn in Brussels in 1962 that Manzoni had declared in his *Carte d'authenticité No. 71* (23/2/1962) that Marcel Broodthaers should be considered a work of art in his entirety and for the future (identified by a red certificate). It seems that for Broodthaers, who was still a poet at the time (as well as a photographer and critic), the encounter with Manzoni may have contributed to his decision to

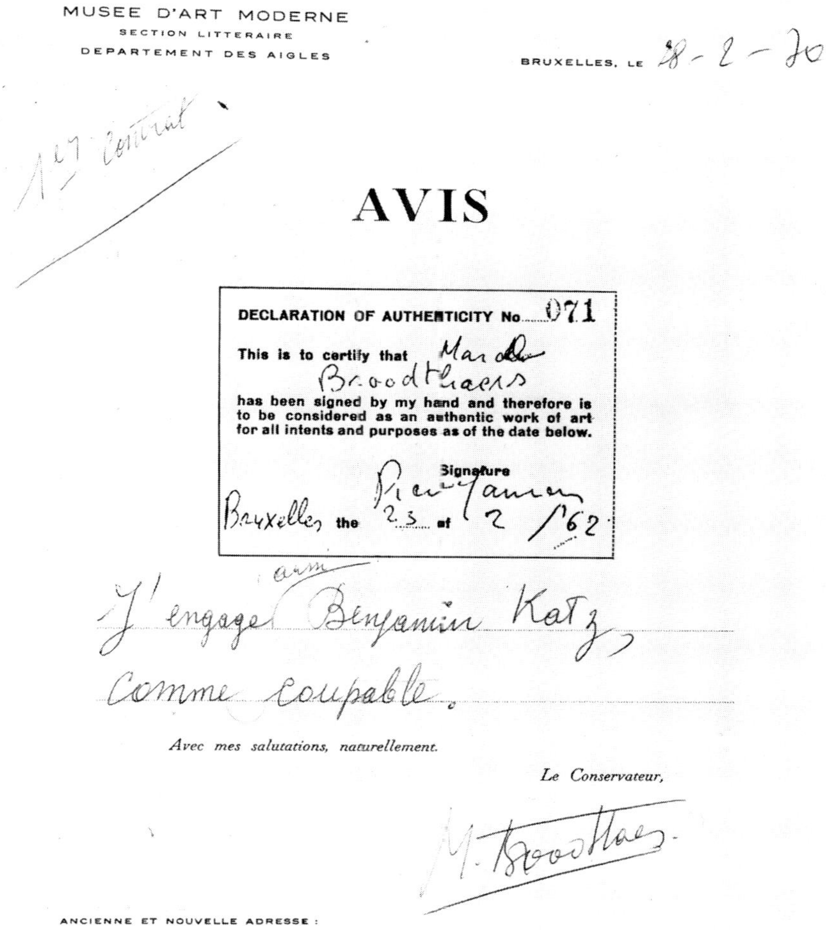

MUSEE D'ART MODERNE
SECTION LITTERAIRE
DEPARTEMENT DES AIGLES

BRUXELLES, LE 28-2-70

1er Contrat

AVIS

DECLARATION OF AUTHENTICITY No. 071

This is to certify that Marcel Broodthaers
has been signed by my hand and therefore is to be considered as an authentic work of art for all intents and purposes as of the date below.

Signature Piero Manzoni

Bruxelles the 23 of 2 /62

J'engage Benjamin Katz
Comme coupable.

Avec mes salutations, naturellement.

Le Conservateur,

M. Broodthaers.

ANCIENNE ET NOUVELLE ADRESSE :
30, RUE DE LA PEPINIERE, BRUXELLES 1 (BELGIUM) TELEPHONE (02) 12 09 54

Marcel Broodthaers, *Musée d'Art Moderne, Département des Aigles, Section Littéraire*, 1968. Installation, Brussels. The work includes Piero Manzoni's Declaration of Authenticity No. 71. 1962. © 2015 The Estate of Marcel Broodthaers/Artists Rights Society (ARS), New York/SABAM, Brussels.

become an artist. Other factors might have been the discovery of the work of George Segal, and Broodthaers' increasingly ambivalent feelings about the preponderance of American pop-art. His very first works, which he showed in 1964 in Brussels under the title *Moi aussi je me suis demandé si je ne pouvais pas vendre quelque chose et réussir dans la vie* (I too have asked myself whether I could sell anything and succeed in life), reveal the strong impression that Manzoni seems to have left on him.

In his very first work, Broodthaers cast the almost complete edition of his recent (and final) volume of poems, *Pense-Bête*, in plaster, thereby literally objectifying the book and reifying poetry in favor of the exhibition value of the contemporary work of art. Conceptually, both artists contemplate the institution of art with a sagacious humor originating in both a deep skepticism and an almost childlike trust in the inevitability of a different future. Broodthaers appears simultaneously in the roles of the acerbic melancholic and the grotesque jester, or rather, he adopts Antonio Gramsci's position of conjoining a pessimism of the intellect with an optimism of the will. Perceptually, Broodthaers' indebtedness to Manzoni surfaces in the juxtapositions of industrial and natural objects, and in the manner that both artists fuse materials and colors, as is evident in his "achromatic" qualities of Broodthaers' plaster assemblages, as much as in his egg, mussel and coal accumulations.

One other contemporary dialogue that marks Broodthaers' early work is his relationship with *Nouveau réalisme*. On the occasion of Arman's first exhibition in Brussels in the early Sixties, Broodthaers inscribed the guest book of the gallery with an accumulation of the syllables dadadada, signaling his doubts about the validity of artistic concepts from different historical contexts when applied to the present without reflection or change.

Later, when asked whether he could identify the origins of his work in *Nouveau réalisme*, he answered:

> My first objects and images, 1964–1965, could not cause such confusion. The literalness shown in the appropriation of the real was intolerable to me because it meant an acceptance pure and simple of the ideas of progress in art … and elsewhere.[41]

While Broodthaers' work tries to distance itself as much as possible from an aesthetic of Neo-Dada, its actual references to Dada and Surrealist ancestors are so frequent that they have been misleading.[42] Broodthaers' first film *La clef de l'horloge (Poème cinématographique en l'honneur de Kurt Schwitters)*—which he produced while still a poet, and the first in a long sequence of films to be made by the artist—arose out of his enthusiasm when seeing his first exhibition of the work of Kurt Schwitters in Brussels in 1957. Aside from several other references to Dada, in particular to works by Duchamp and Man Ray, a perpetual dialogue with the work of René Magritte has misled many of Broodthaers' interpreters, causing them to see him as merely continuing the Dada and Surrealist legacies. Broodthaers had in fact met Magritte shortly after the war and Magritte had introduced the young poet to the work of Mallarmé and Poe, and they remained in contact for a number of years. But it seems that Broodthaers' work—once he had shifted from poet to artist—did not meet at all with the master's approval. As Broodthaers put it:

> This is what Magritte has often reproached me for. He thought of me as more sociologist than artist.[43]

His own appreciation of Magritte, however, appears not to have been without reservations either, as is evident from Broodthaers' statement:

> Magritte with his *Ceci n'est pas une pipe* is less easy. But even so, he was still too much Magritte. This means that he was

> not enough *Ceci n'est pas une pipe*. From this pipe I started on my own adventure.[44]

And having been asked on one occasion whether he would situate himself in a Surrealist perspective, Broodthaers recited the famous line on the abolition of all contradictions from André Breton's Surrealist Manifesto and answered:

> I do hope that I have nothing in common with this state of mind.[45]

The historical positions implicit in Dada and Surrealism that actually seem to have been most crucial to Broodthaers' emerging practice were of course Duchamp's readymade concept from 1913 and the theoretical implications of Magritte's "linguistic" paintings (particularly, *Ceci n'est pas une pipe*, 1928) a painterly response to Ferdinand de Saussure's discovery of the structure of linguistic signs in 1915.

If one aspect of Duchamp's readymade concept had explored the transformation from primary object reality into secondary sign reality (and vice versa), Magritte's inquiry had focused on the secondary nature of the (painted) sign and on the deconstruction of the material significant and the immaterial signifié and their seemingly arbitrary relationship. Broodthaers' work subsequently explored the sign potential of objective reality and the potential objectivity of signs. Since Broodthaers had attended Lucien Goldmann's seminars in Brussels (a disciple of Georg Lukács) and had by that time also read French structuralist theory and semiology extensively, he recognized that neither the production nor the reflection of aesthetic sign-systems could any longer claim the status of a self-contained and self-determined system for the aesthetic object, and thus could not focus on the formal problems of the modernist tradition alone.[46]

With the publication of his *Théorèmes* in 1966, Broodthaers announced the direction that his future investigations would take. Thus he states for example in his Théorème No. 3:

> Every object is the victim of its nature, even in a transparent painting the color still hides the canvas and the moulding hides the frame.[47]

Broodthaers was one of the first artists who reflected the condition of artistic practice as being increasingly overdetermined by elements alien to its proper concerns. For one, it had become the object of commercial speculation to a degree unheard of before and—inasmuch as it was entirely dependent on its museological acculturation—it had also become an object of cultural administration, serving as one of the many representations of the ideological state apparatus. Thus artistic practice could regain its critical role only to the extent that it would recognize its alienated state and reflect on its actual functions of furthering alienation by making its own condition of reification its proper subject matter. In keeping with these intentions, Marcel Broodthaers founded the Musée d'art moderne (Section XIXè siècle) Département des Aigles in 1968 in Brussels.

Naming himself the director of the newly founded museum, the artist invited Dr. Johannes Cladders—the director of a "real" institution, the Museum Abteiberg in Mönchengladbach—to inaugurate the newly founded museum in the presence of a number of guests and friends, among them Daniel Buren. Starting at the point where artistic practice normally comes to an end—in the museum, the place of its official acculturation—this was in fact the first really major and far reaching work by Marcel Broodthaers.

The installation of Broodthaers' first museum fiction consisted of a number of empty wooden crates which normally serve as transportation vehicles for valuable original paintings, and a series of picture-postcards

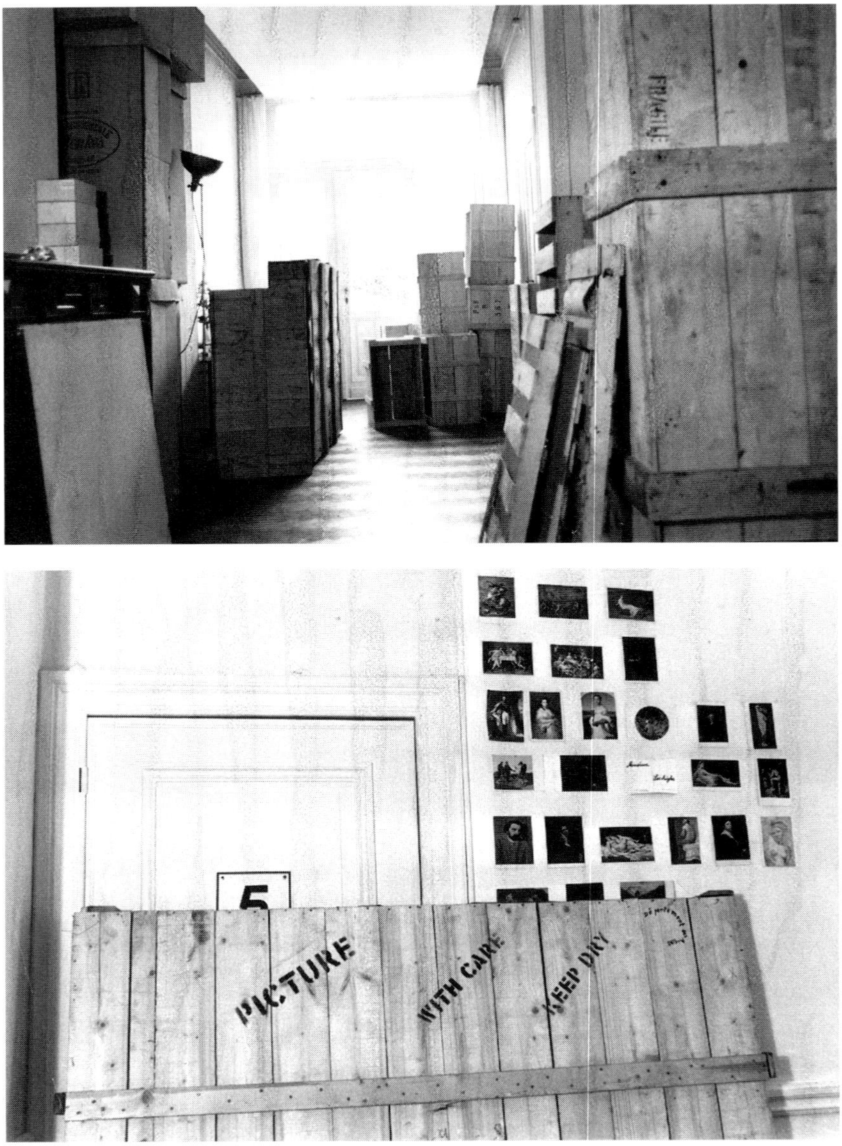

Marcel Broodthaers, *Musée d'Art Moderne, Département des Aigles, Section 19eme Siècle*, 1968. Installation, 30 rue de la Pépinière, Brussels, September 27, 1968. Photo: Maria Gilissen. © 2015 The Estate of Marcel Broodthaers/Artists Rights Society (ARS), New York/SABAM, Brussels.

of more or less famous nineteenth-century paintings on the walls of his apartment declared to be a museum. Broodthaers' Museum of Modern Art thus inverted the traditional hierarchies of cultural organization by substituting the lowest elements of the museum's functional basis (the transport, shipping, distribution and reproduction of images) for the unique hieratic artwork and thus publicly questioned the origins of the power of the hieratic image. In a text on the museum published slightly later, Broodthaers asked:

> Is a picture post-card of a painting by Ingres worth a couple of million?[48]

Thus, not only had the inferior supplemental objects been put into the place and position of the artwork itself but now the artist had reversed his role as well, and assumed that of the director of the museum, becoming in fact "merely" a cultural administrator. Performing yet another reversal of institutional hierarchies and a brilliantly ironic negative cultural revolution, the artist situated these maneuvers within a specific political and historical context when he made the comment that

> l'idée de ce Musée est née de Mai '68 [The idea of this museum was born in May '68].[49]

Broodthaers' museological fictions passed through different states and were enacted in various sections in the following years: the Section XVllè Siècle in Antwerp, Section XXè Siècle bis and Section du Cinéma in Düsseldorf. The project found its conclusion in 1972 with the exhibition *The Eagle from Oligocene to Today—Musée d'art moderne, Section des figures*,[50] which brought together more than 260 items from over 80 public museums and private collections in a structuralist reading of cultural signs and emblems of power (all of the exhibited objects represented the eagle in one form or another, and ranged from relics of natural history to religious and mythological representations, from major works of art to contemporary cartoons, advertising trivialities and the signs of commodity culture.

Each object was accompanied by a black plastic label bearing the catalog number and stating in three languages, "This is not a work of art." Broodthaers had in fact combined the opposing concepts of Duchamp and Magritte—in the first instance the transformation of an object of everyday reality into an (aesthetic) sign by declaration, and in the second the transformation of the sign (the representations of painting) into its real constitutive elements, painterly signifier and painted signified. Or, more humorously, as Broodthaers put it:

> "This is not a work of art" is a formula which I obtained from the contraction of a concept of Duchamp and an antithetical concept of Magritte. This helped me to decorate Duchamp's *Urinoir* with the sign of the eagle smoking the pipe. I believe to have emphasized the principle of authority which makes out of the eagle the colonel of art.[51]

What is more important for Broodthaers' method is the introduction of a third concept bringing de Saussure's linguistic sign-model into the present: Roland Barthes' concept of myth. As a secondary sign system it is superimposed on primary languages to serve ideological interests. When Broodthaers assumes the fictitious role of the museum director and simultaneously negates the aesthetic status of the museum's objects, he designated the museum as the place where artistic production is endowed with the status of a secondary language. Thus the artist engages in an act of artificial or secondary myth construction—the process that Barthes had identified as one of the possible antidotes against mythical speech and ideology at large.

Thus Broodthaers' work opens up two critical perspectives simultaneously, emphasizing the inevitable antagonism between artistic production and its institutional acculturation as primary and secondary languages. Pointing to the transhistorical valorizations given to artistic practices ex post facto by institutions, Broodthaers' fictitious taxonomy points back to the objects' historical status. Situated within a variety of highly differentiated contexts, these objects now appear in a mad taxonomy, each bound to the unique situation on which it depended materially and historically for its original formation. Secondly, Broodthaers' visual language adopts a strategy which might easily be misunderstood. Undoubtedly, he deployed it as a ruse to induce such misunderstandings. In their seemingly nostalgic qualities of typographical and stylistic refinement, his films and books generate an intense experience of obsolescence. The "design" of his work does not appear at all concerned with contemporaneity, least of all does it claim to derive from any aspect of the modernist tradition. Rather, the work seems to be preoccupied with nineteenth-century literary culture.

Broodthaers' profound skepticism against an artistic milieu and its perpetual claims to innovation are derided in the motto "Nouveaux trucs, nouvelles combines" (New tricks, new cheats), which Broodthaers cited from an early French comic-strip *Les Pieds Nickelés* (The Nickel Feet) and which he inserted as a vignette on the covers of two of his major catalogs in Brussels and Paris. While the viewers might be seduced by the works' retrogressive appearance, the artist actually defined his attitude toward the romantic souvenir to be that of the critical historian inside contemporary art itself. When asked at which point the artist would reach the essential state of an "indifferent art" (as opposed to an "engaged art" like poetry which cannot become a commodity), he responded:

> At that moment precisely when one becomes less of an artist, when the necessity of production lowers its roots only into memory itself. I believe that my exhibitions have always and still depend on souvenirs of the epoque in which, I presume,

> the creative situation was one of heroic and solitary form. In other words one of: Read and See. Whereas today it is: May I present to You.[52]

Broodthaers' apparently retrospective fantasy of a more heroic and solitary artistic situation in a somewhat unfathomable past, insists of course dialectically on the necessity of a new spectator/reader of art who has become a fully conscious and self-constituting historical subject.

Along with Robert Barry, Dan Graham and Lawrence Weiner, whose work he held in high esteem, Broodthaers will have to be considered as one of the few artists who used language in a dialectical-materialist manner (as opposed to a theoretical, philosophical or merely poetical one). This positions the work of Marcel Broodthaers historically in the context of so called Conceptual art, even though he explicitly inverted Kosuth's famous formula of Conceptual art, Art as Idea as Idea polemically by countering it with the statement: "As Said Before: Art as Production as Production." When it became obvious, however, that not only the written sentence but even the spoken word could be easily turned into a newly reified commodity, Broodthaers immediately changed positions. His seemingly childish "alphabet paintings" from the early seventies (appearing almost like travesties of Manzoni's letter charts from the late 1950s) and his magnificent major final work *L'éloge du sujet* (The Eulogy of the Subject) radically negate the validity of the heroic gesture of Conceptual art which in his eyes had prematurely claimed to have overcome the burden of the material, the economic and the ideological dimensions of the work of art and its institutional frames. Language as an artistic strategy in Conceptual art had lost its intended status as a primary object and had entered the state of a secondary myth.

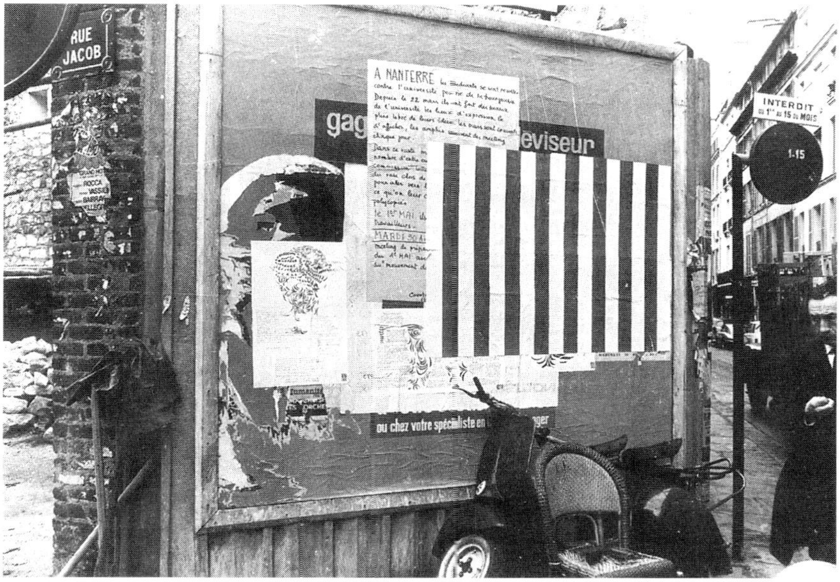

Daniel Buren, *Affichage sauvage*, Paris, April 1968. Imprinted paper with white and green stripes. © DB-ADAGP, Paris/Artists Rights Society (ARS), New York 2015.

DANIEL BUREN

> The difference between art and the world, between art and being, is that the world and being are perceived by real facts (physical, emotional, intellectual) and art visualizes this reality. If the artist's vision of the world were concerned this could be a veritable consciousness of reality. But it deals with a product, art, that is the thing seen by the consumer; thus a fixed and arbitrary reality is proposed, a reality deformed by the individual who, wanting to express his own vision of the world, no longer expresses the real but makes an illusion of reality.[53]
>
> —*Daniel Buren*

Broodthaers' grotesque masquerade of an artist disguised as a museum director pointed to the frameworks within which art is determined and legitimated by the institution of the "Museum." This project of a critical museology—as it evolved in Broodthaers' work after 1968—would soon become a key concern of several other European and American artists who would systematically investigate the historical conditions determining the production and reception of art, its modes of fabrication and distribution, and its principles of installation and display.

With the works of Daniel Buren—who approached these questions latently since 1965 and manifestly since 1969—we are confronted with an entirely different approach. Rather than constructing enigmatic allegorical tableaux, Buren's interventions within both, the legacies of Modernist painting and its institutional and discursive frameworks, are from their inception both more explicit, systematic and theoretically argued.

Broodthaers and Buren became friends in 1968, and Buren's visit to the opening of Broodthaers' first Musée d'art moderne in Brussels would have to be considered as one source for the development of his own project. Yet the parallelism of their critiques of the museum institution originated first of all in their shared interests in French post-structuralist theories and semiology, in particular the work of Roland Barthes and Michel Foucault. Not only were both artists engaged with Barthes' critical model of "myth" but they equally deployed Barthes' concept of the degré zéro of the sign, aiming at a primary language to achieve the dimension of a communicative functional immediacy and transformational efficiency in its relationship to a given historical context. If Broodthaers once said that he made "use of the object as a word at the degré zéro," then Buren suggested that he was engaged with a "zero degree of painting."[54]

Buren has mentioned on several occasions that if there were any postwar European (more specifically, Parisian) influences on his own work, it would in fact have been the work of the painter Simon Hantaï and that of Villeglé and the décollagistes. Not surprisingly then, Buren's early works around 1962 consisted of papiers déchirés that one could situate halfway between Matisse and the décollagistes. In contradiction to the "found paper objects" of the affiche lacérée, however, Buren's décollages consisted of mounted layers of differently colored papers that had been covered with a final layer of white, eventually to be torn off in a random manner to present the final pictorial result. This not only indicates the impact Villeglé's work must have had but also reminds us of the radical inversion of the décollage principle which would occur in Buren's first works after 1965. This is most evident in a project in 1968 during which he actually pasted more than two hundred white and colored striped affiches anonymously onto public billboards in Paris. Simultaneously Buren distributed a similar amount of posters by postal delivery in the context of a museum installation, commenting on the project as follows:

> All these works, executed within a very brief time period in the same city, used the interior and the exterior, static and mobile supports, anonymity (outside of the institution of the museum) and the author's name inside the museum's system.[55]

Here, the activities of the French décollagistes have been literally inverted: the artist is no longer the collector of anonymous acts of vandalism, but has become a conscious agent, positioning himself in public anonymity and in an institutionalized artistic identity. Buren has frequently referred to the instrumental aspect of his work, identifying it as a functional tool of practical investigation, and insisting on the interdependence of his theory and painterly practice. Thus he states for example that the work's appearance "is an instrument of questioning and not a moving and superficial found object."[56]

His interventions give evidence of a potential synthesis of collective and individual practices that are constituted within discursive and institutional limitations. Buren develops this project further than the project of constructivist and neo-plasticist abstraction which had also invested the painterly idiom with a quasi-utilitarian potential, assuming that the non-hierarchical commonality of the painterly sign language would eventually induce actual transformations within the hierarchies of social reality itself. Not surprisingly, Buren has reflected on the problems of painting as one of the most elementary forms of visual signification. As a consequence, he has repeatedly pointed out that his work should be understood first of all as painting (arguing that it should not be considered primarily as an investigation, illustrating his theories or as a purely dematerialized Conceptualist practice).

This self-referential structure of the painterly sign, as opposed to a formalist's notion of self-reference, however, is a dialectical one. But inasmuch as it understands itself to be a materialist practice, it also pays tribute to a painterly tradition that found its most advanced forms within the so-called formalist tradition. Thus Buren has carefully considered the historical trajectory of modernist painting since Cézanne, a development which he once described in a schematic abbreviation:

> Thus contemporary art history would oscillate constantly between two poles symbolized by Cézanne and Duchamp.

> The first represents the positive, open pole, and the second the negative regressive pole. [. .] The history of art thus finds itself really fissured by the impetus given by Cézanne, a fissure enlarged here and there (cf. Mondrian, Pollock, Matisse, Newman, Stella).[57]

One of Stella's central problems had been to present painting as a strictly positivist empirical entity by eliminating every reference to external phenomena and by abolishing every spatial and figurative illusion: painterly facture, compositional order and relations of scale. Precisely through the rigidity of his analysis, Stella had liberated painting from all the hidden conditions that had heretofore determined its operations, while simultaneously achieving at the same time the purest model of contemporary painterly reductivism.

Therefore it seemed hard to imagine that anybody would soon transcend this self-reflexive radicality of Stella's work—at least within the area of painting. Apart from Robert Ryman whose work Buren admired and collected at an early moment—very few artists had in fact singularized the elements of painting to the degree that Stella had in the late Fifties and early Sixties.[58]

It was precisely the phenomenological clarity and the rigorous autonomy of Stella's work that enabled an artist like Buren to take his own investigation in an entirely new direction, discovering a whole range of undetected determinations—inherent, yet external, to traditional painterly production and reception. These merited as precise an analysis as the formal questions that Stella had posed before. This "peripety" of painting, a paradigmatic change induced by Stella whose ramifications would soon be recognized by a large number of Minimalists and Conceptual artists in America and Europe, led in Buren's case to a new dimension of inquiry. His work would now initiate a critical reflection of historical (i.e., political, social, ideological) factors, and would consider them as equal to visual-formal material factors in defining painterly practice. One could argue that even the seemingly formalist concerns of the Minimal artists had initially focused on questions of "form" in the way that Barthes had defined signification—as a process which produces the sense and not as the sense itself. The American critic Roberta Smith therefore understood at best only half of what she saw when she stated, after her first encounter with Buren's work that

> these aspects of Buren's work as well as its formal nature—the broad regular stripes (that is the lack of composition and imagery, and the scale)—involve a logical extension of various ideas in the work of Judd, Flavin, Andre and most overtly, Stella.[59]

First of all this critic failed to grasp any of the theoretical and critical implications of Buren's reductivist approach to painting. And second, the critic erroneously assumes that to acknowledge the impact of Stella's work (which Buren obviously did) would be tantamount to accepting the influence of an entire generation of American Minimal artists who themselves had in fact been equally influenced by Stella.[60] Buren's "objectification" of the painterly support, the decision to use wall surfaces directly, the deconstruction of painting's institutional and discursive frames—all of these strategies led to a project of institutional critique with painterly means that could not be more different from the resuscitation of sculpture under the aegis of Minimalism.

The experience of discomfort many American (and European) artists, curators and critics had in their initial confrontation with Buren's work seems to have resulted first of all from the radicality of this paradigm change. Worse still, Buren introduced this change precisely at a moment when artistic practices in the United States had reached the climax of a heretofore unknown cultural and national autonomy and self-containment, an attitude evident for example when Flavin would call Judd "the first all American sculptor." Paradoxically this climax would occur at the very moment when American artists had reached a peak of historical learnedness: after all it was the Minimalist generation which had for the first time in postwar American art history fully absorbed all the painterly or sculptural lessons, from Cubism to Mondrian and Malevich, from Brancusi to Duchamp and Tatlin.

Precisely at this moment, Buren opened up an entirely new perspective that revealed art to be a highly overdetermined practice and the artist to be an unconscious practitioner, subjected to these determinations like "the bear in the zoo," as Buren once called it. With Buren's work, it seemed, artists were suddenly confronted with a different kind of self-reflexivity if they wanted their work to be taken seriously in the future. The sheer making of art and the delivery of the product no longer appeared sufficient for the newly established standards of mutual recognition between producer and receiver.

Buren stated it thus in one of his typically polemical (and successfully provocative) statements:

> I'll push it further. I believe we are the only ones to be able to claim the right of being "looked at," in the sense that we are the only ones to present a thing which has no didactic intention, which does not provide "dreams," which is not a "stimulant." Each individual can dream himself and without doubt much better than by the trickery of an artist, however great he may be. The artist appeals to laziness, his function is emollient. He is "beautiful" for others, "talented" for others, "ingenious" for others, which is a scornful or superior way of considering "others." The artist brings beauty, dreams, suffering to their domiciles, while "the others," whom I myself consider a priori as talented as artists, must find their own beauty, their own dream. In a word, become adults.

> Perhaps the only thing that one can do after having seen a canvas like ours is total revolution.[61]

This declaration, given in February 1968, not only testifies to the radicality of aesthetic thought in Paris around May '68 but also reads as Buren's definition of artistic practice as one form of ideology critique, operative within the superstructure of the system of art itself. Thus Buren negated simultaneously both the positivist conception of art as an entirely separate and self-reflexive productivity which had governed American modernist painting and sculpture until the mid-Sixties, as he challenged the traditional Marxist position which had ignored the material reality and relative independence of the inherent ideological component of artistic production itself.

Given the magnitude of this paradigmatic change, it is less surprising that the work of Daniel Buren would meet tremendous resistance in the first years of its reception, in particular on the level of public institutions. When, for example, Harald Szeemann's famous exhibition *When Attitudes Become Form* opened at the Kunsthalle Bern in 1969, Buren installed his striped paper works outside the exhibition in various locations. Since he had not been invited to participate in this exhibition of recent post-Minimal and Conceptual art, his work was destroyed and Buren was prosecuted by the local police. Several years later, in 1974, another work was destroyed in the context of an exhibition of contemporary art called Projekt (at the Wallraf-Richartz-Museum in Cologne). While Buren had actually been officially invited to participate on this occasion, his work now lent literal support to an already censored contribution to the exhibition. Confronted with a renewed display of Hans Haacke's suppressed work, copied and pasted to a series of Buren's striped wallpapers, the museum officials destroyed Buren's installation instantly during the opening night.

And yet, the fundamental generational and geo-political contradictions within contemporary art production and reception became evident in a conflict generated when Buren installed a 20 × 10 meter vertically striped cloth hanging from the center ceiling of the museum as his contribution to the Guggenheim International Exhibition in 1971. When five out of twenty-one artists invited to this exhibition raised serious objections to Buren's work, the piece was removed by the museum officials (who had initially approved the artist's project).

This conflict between Buren's "painting" and the Minimalists Flavin and Judd, who had initiated the censorial intervention and who by then were already reaching the zenith of their artistic development, could be considered one of the more illuminating confrontations between the two opposing principles of formalist and historicist aesthetic thought at that time, if we assume that it was in fact more of an aesthetic and theoretical confrontation than a mere conflict of territoriality between American and European artists. One might have to give some credence to Flavin's and Judd's claim that their insistence on the removal of Buren's large-scale work was solely motivated by the fact that their own work would have been visually inaccessible—if only for brief moments—at certain points during the visitors' ambulations on the spiraling ramps of the museum.

Yet it is hard not to suspect at the same time that their primary motivation for the censorious intervention must have been the insight—even if repressed—of having been conceptually and visually upstaged by Buren's coup. After all, their own work appeared obsolete in its naive or affirmative acceptance of the Guggenheim's embracing architectural framework. In manifest opposition to Minimalist sculpture, Buren's piece induced a complex dialectics of perceptual and discursive reflections. Without actually ever becoming a three-dimensional object, the piece shifted continuously from the flat surface of a painting to a voluminous structure circumnavigated by the spectators on the spiraling ramps, culminating in the perception of the fully extended planarity of the front and/or back side of the cloth piece as a quasi-architectural element.

At the same time viewers—descending the ramps—would have experienced the work in a temporal and kinetic dimension, shifting perpetually from the visual crescendo of its fully expanded striated planarity to an extreme diminuendo when the work reduced itself practically to the point of spatial disappearance by becoming a thin, twenty meter vertical line bisecting the vacant circular core of the museum's architecture. Whereas most other works had given themselves over—more or less naïvely—to the dominance of Wright's architecture, those by Flavin and Judd had gone one step further confidently adapting themselves to the architectural structure, as though they wanted to confirm and underline—on a visual and formal level—Buren's theoretical axiom of the museum as an institution of discursive domination and control. Buren, by contrast, was not only fully aware of the institutional implications of the architecture, but quite consciously posited his work in manifest and antagonistic relation to the encircling museum. The huge vertically striped painting in the central void of the spiraling galleries functioned almost like a spine opposing the vertigo of the centrifugal forces of the architecture. Thus, the protective shell of the museum in which the other work had situated itself in a mixture of historical naiveté and economical calculation, was suddenly pierced by Buren's work. Yet, paradoxically, the architectural beauty of the giant cloth piece originated in the underlying theoretical analysis of the historical functions of the museum.

Whenever a new artistic definition seriously questions the fundamental convictions of the preceding period, the former generation's reaction to that provocation will be one of defensive repression. Buren's work in the Guggenheim clearly questioned the foundations of the Minimalists' positivist pragmatism and confronted them with a new dimension of dialectical historical thought. In those general terms, however, the shift should not be understood as a specifically European condition; rather it was an indication of generally changing concepts in the visual arts around 1968 in both Europe and the United States.[62]

With the work of Broodthaers and Buren, artistic practice in Europe became operative and it intervened in the very historical and institutional contexts within which it defined itself and through which its production and reception were determined. This definition of historicity is therefore exactly the opposite of historicism, which one could define as the degree of (art) historical learnedness and knowledge that has entered and modeled a work of art (such as Flavin's and Judd's studious acquisition of the Modernist lineage). The difference between the two attitudes could therefore be seen as a difference of approaches to aesthetic signification. While the first associates the structure of artistic signification with a result, a product, the second most probably would define it as a critical and deconstructive process.

In 1972, on the occasion of Buren's participation in Documenta V, the artist installed a work accompanied by a text, entitled "Exhibition of an Exhibition" (B 51). Placing and dispersing his white-on-white striped wallpapers two weeks before the actual hanging of the exhibition, it happened apparently by accident that Jasper Johns' *Flag* (1954–55) was superimposed onto one of Buren's wall elements, once again forcing the two opposing attitudes toward an ironical showdown of the histories of American and European art. The work of Johns, whom Buren once called irreverently "the Braque of American painting," constituted a crucial step in the reception and painterly reformulation of Duchampian strategies—in particular that of the readymade—a step which would eventually culminate in the self-referential epistemological consciousness of painting as it had been articulated by Stella. Buren's project by contrast—indebted as it was to Stella's, and therefore, ironically enough, in an indirect way to Johns' as well—attempted to negate precisely this process of aestheticization, and to endow his own work with a functional dimension that would intervene within the historical process itself. Buren's project suggested that artistic production should recognize institutional reality and the discursive modes of perceiving, in order to prevent art from becoming a mythical

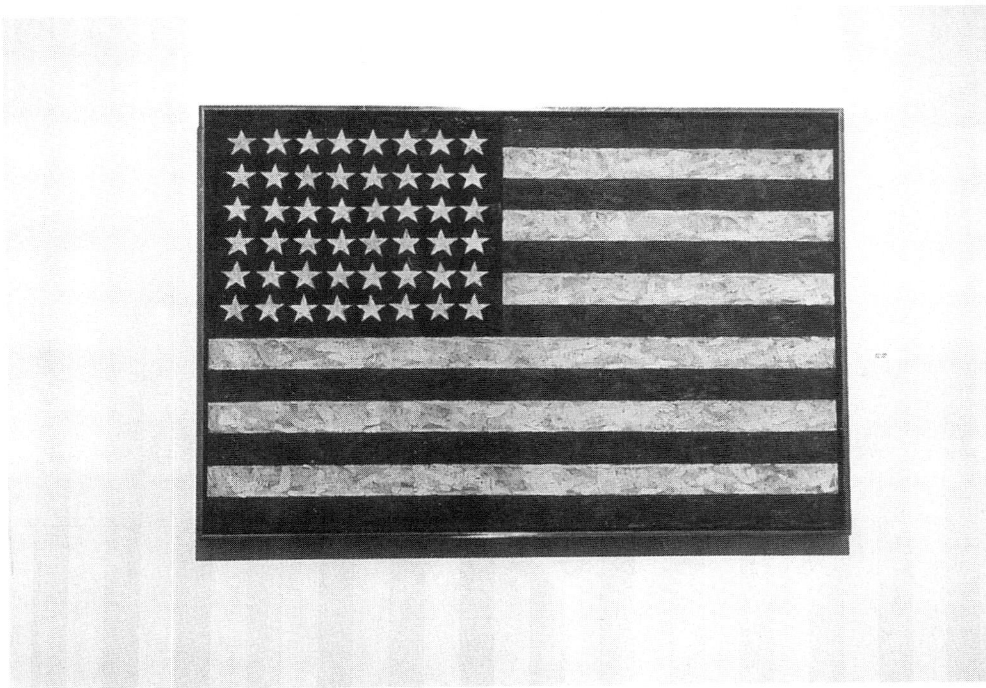

Daniel Buren, *Exposition d'une exposition*, 1972. Photosouvenir of installation at Documenta V, incorporating Jasper Johns' painting *Flag* (1954–55) on white silkscreen paper. Photo: Paolo Mussat Sartor. © DB-ADAGP, Paris/Artists Rights Society (ARS), New York 2015.

substratum of social and political relations and institutional and ideological interests.

It is perhaps also for this reason that Buren in his writings had to attack Duchamp so severely—the artist to whom he owed so much, if nothing else then certainly the principle of his critical investigations.

Niele Toroni

> For me it is not a question of making my work a mythical one, a work which might be the ideal work by repeating its presentation; it is not the question to repeat mechanically for the sake of repetition. It is about a method of critical work being actually valid and necessary: the visible work here and now poses certain questions (it raises questions and it is questioning itself).
>
> —*Niele Toroni*[63]

Along with Daniel Buren, Niele Toroni was the only member of the original "BMPT Group" who continued to develop his artistic work throughout the late Sixties into the Seventies.[64] In 1966, when the "group" first presented its work to the public, it had claimed to be based "on the principle of each artist making one painting over and over again for whatever situation comes up." This attitude had been enacted as late as 1967 in Paris and in Lugano when Buren and Toroni painted each other's paintings and exhibited them in public under the title *Buren, Toroni or anybody*, inviting visitors and reviewers to make their own paintings or to claim those made by the artists as their own.

While Buren would instigate a broad range of systematic investigations into the contemporary determinations of art, ranging from theoretical texts and polemical pamphlets to a highly differentiated system of analytic visual tools that converted his theoretical investigations into artistic practice, Toroni remained more of a traditional painter. Since

1965 he has restricted himself to minute differentiations of his original activity of leaving imprints of color by means of a standard No. 50 brush at an equal distance of 30 cm on various supports (stretched and unstretched canvas, waxcloth, paper, walls, and more recently, on the floor and in outdoor locations).

Undoubtedly it is implied in Toroni's self-imposed restriction that under certain historical circumstances traditionalism in the realm of painting can become one way to pursue a progressive artistic project. We had already encountered this attitude in Buren's initial esteem for the epistemic precision ensuing from a restriction to the visuality of painting alone, an attitude with which the artist had not only opposed the anarchist all-or-nothing voluntarism of Duchamp but which served him equally to criticize Duchamp's followers in American art (from Jasper Johns to Andy Warhol). Yet, as a painter, Toroni is as much of a dialectician as he is a traditionalist, negating painterly practice as seriously as he pursues it.

Toroni, a Parisian of Italian-Swiss descent, would have found himself as attracted to the Italian modernist tradition as to that of Paris. It is not surprising then to find that his central formal strategy, the *empreinte* seems to have had several immediate Italian predecessors. In the early- to mid-Fifties for example, Lucio Fontana had signed a number of his paintings with a thumbprint instead of a signature. This strange gesture had undoubtedly inspired Manzoni in the late 1950s to demarcate his eggs with his individual thumb prints, or, more importantly, to imprint regular rows of serially ordered fingerprints on paper that anticipate the regular spacing of Toroni's empreintes.

For Fontana the imprint would probably have to be read as a sign of ostentatious negation (as was his entire painterly production) of the falsely expressionist and subjectivist attitudes of the gestural painting of neo-Surrealist automatism, which had deluged European postwar painting under the names of *art autre, informel, tachisme*. The gesture of Manzoni is an even more explicit and demonstrative act of replacing the painting in its entirety with the imprint of the thumb, objectivizing, if not reifying, the process of painting altogether. Manzoni literally took the fingerprints, as though he was "booking" that "great culprit," the subjectivist hand of the artist, as André Breton had called it:

> The problem is the glorification of the hand, and nothing else. My hand is the great culprit, how can I accept any longer being the slave of my hand? It is impossible that drawing and painting are still at the point where writing had been before Gutenberg.[65]

This excessive radicality of denying any subjective gestural autonomy, however, seems to lead inevitably to the opposite dilemma of pure painterly determinism. Polemically negating any claims for the continuing validity of automatist writing/painting and its seemingly infinite field of articulations of the unconscious, Manzoni's fingerprints represent the highest degree of invariability. The lines of the skin's imprint—being totally determined in individual biological and genetic nature—are paradoxically more inimitably unique than the most subjective gesture of the unconscious.

As usual, at the extreme end of this spectrum, and far beyond any dialectical attitude, we find Yves Klein. In 1961, Klein produces his own contribution to an emerging aesthetic of the indexical imprint by subjecting this most specific process of mark making to the inexorable logic of spectacularization. Using nude female models, or, as Klein would call them female human brushes, for his *Anthropométries*, his variation of the imprint articulates an autocratic and sexist despotism, producing a public encounter with the total reification of the subject.

Toroni, quite to the contrary, has also remained a traditionalist in his technical means. He would neither touch the paint with the tip of his finger, nor would he possibly think of using anything (or even less, any body) but a standard No. 50 brush as a tool for painterly practice. A

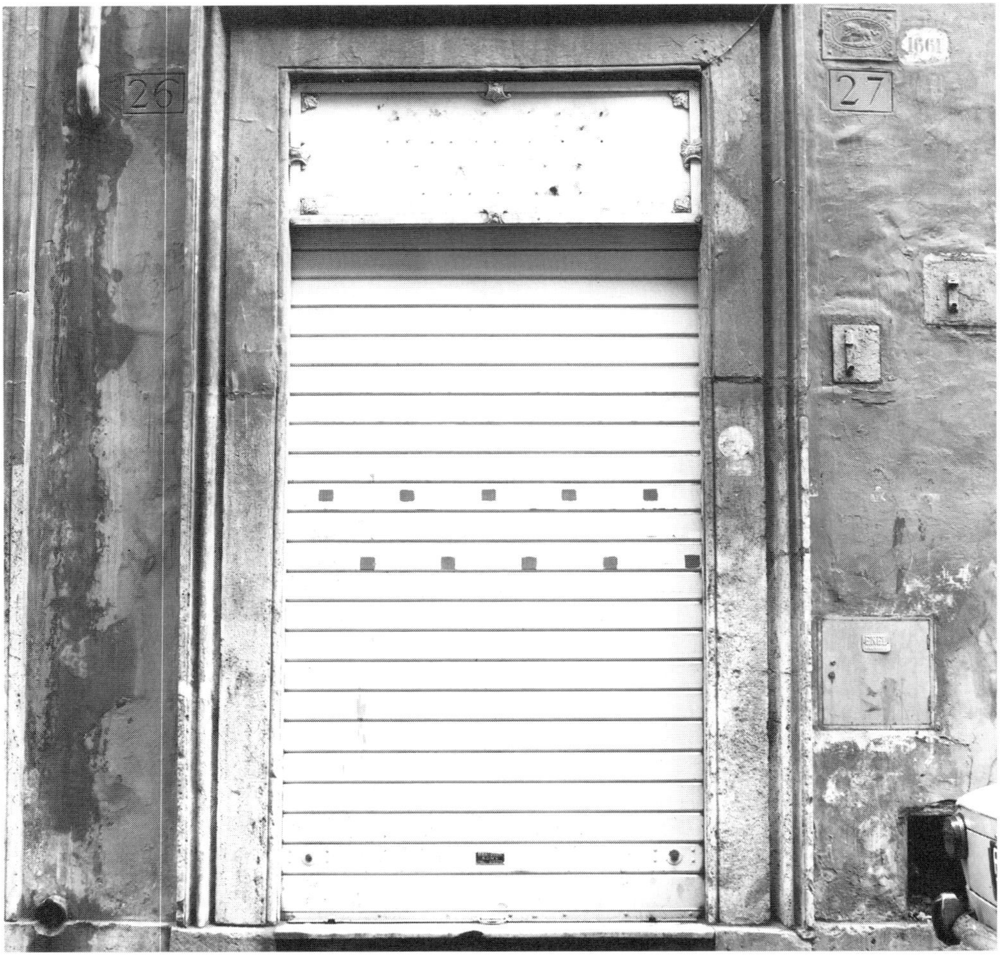

Niele Toroni, *Imprints No. 50*, 1975. © Niele Toroni. Courtesy the artist and Galleria d'Alessandro-Ferranti, Rome.

comparative reading of two quotations from Klein and Toroni might clarify the difference between an artist devoted to spectacle and another devoted to a materialist critique of the myths of culture. Klein defines his project in the following terms:

> My monochrome pictures are not my definite works, but the preparation for my works. They are the left-overs from the creative processes, the ashes. My pictures after all, are only the title-deeds to my property which I have to produce when I am asked to prove that I am a proprietor.[66]

And Toroni on the subject of his empreintes:

> The imprint is neither the image, nor the idea, nor the illusion of an imprint, but in fact the real imprint of a brush No. 50. […] This work is the factum by Toroni, but this work might as well be the factum by everybody else who would systematically apply a brush No. 50 (intervals 30 cm) on a white support (plastic, paper, wall, canvas).[67]

One could hardly imagine a more revealing statement than Klein's claim for creativity and his works as the title deeds of private property: a personal manifesto of petit bourgeois subjectivity (in the tradition of Max Stirner's infamous manifesto *Der Einzige und sein Eigentum* (The Unique and His Private Property). It is of course also the dark, or rather the dull underside of Klein's claims to have reached a radiant transcendence with his painterly immateriality and pure pictorial sensitivity zones. By contrast, Toroni's statement articulates the materialist consciousness of a practitioner fully aware of the discursive limitations of the painterly procedure. To the degree that his practice is transparent in all of its aspects, it serves as a model for subjective and collective acts of cultural self-articulation and self-constitution.

The second key strategy of Toroni's work is the serial repetition of similar or identical visual elements. As was the case with the pure painterly imprint, this strategy was by no means a formal innovation in 1965 when Toroni first showed his work. Apart from Manzoni there had been Arman's accumulations, serial grids of multiplied readymades of the late Fifties, and Warhol's gridded image accumulations of the early Sixties which had "objectified" the painterly process through the means of photography and the silkscreen imprint.

Yet the invention of Toroni's *empreinte* introduced a new dialectic between subjective gesture and objective sign in European art around 1965. The *empreinte* served simultaneously as a particular manual trace of the subject's conscious activity and as the most generalized painterly mark, reduced and objectified in an almost anonymous procedure of applying paint. Thus Toroni continued a tradition which reflected the very process and substance of painting itself in the manner of a readymade object. This tradition ranged from the color chips in Duchamp's *Tu m'* (1919) to Pollock's process of pouring directly from the can and was continued in Rauschenberg's readymade approach to paint when he decided to use color sequences based on the cheapest offers available at the hardware store. It is a painterly paradigm that was articulated once again at the time of Toroni's beginnings most lucidly by Frank Stella: "I wanted to get the paint out of the can and onto the canvas. … I tried to keep the paint as good as it was in the can."[68] Toroni's reflection of the matter and process of painting inserts itself into this tradition all the more when he singularizes the brushstroke and differentiates the act of applying the paint onto the surface from the act of distributing the paint on the surface. By separating these two aspects of the painterly process, by showing that paint as material is not necessarily identical with paint as a spatio-temporal extension, Toroni achieves one of his most original contributions to a critical reflection of contemporary painting. Form as spatio-temporal extension is given in Toroni's work as an abstract definition: the interval of 30 cm, and is thereby not bound to color at all.

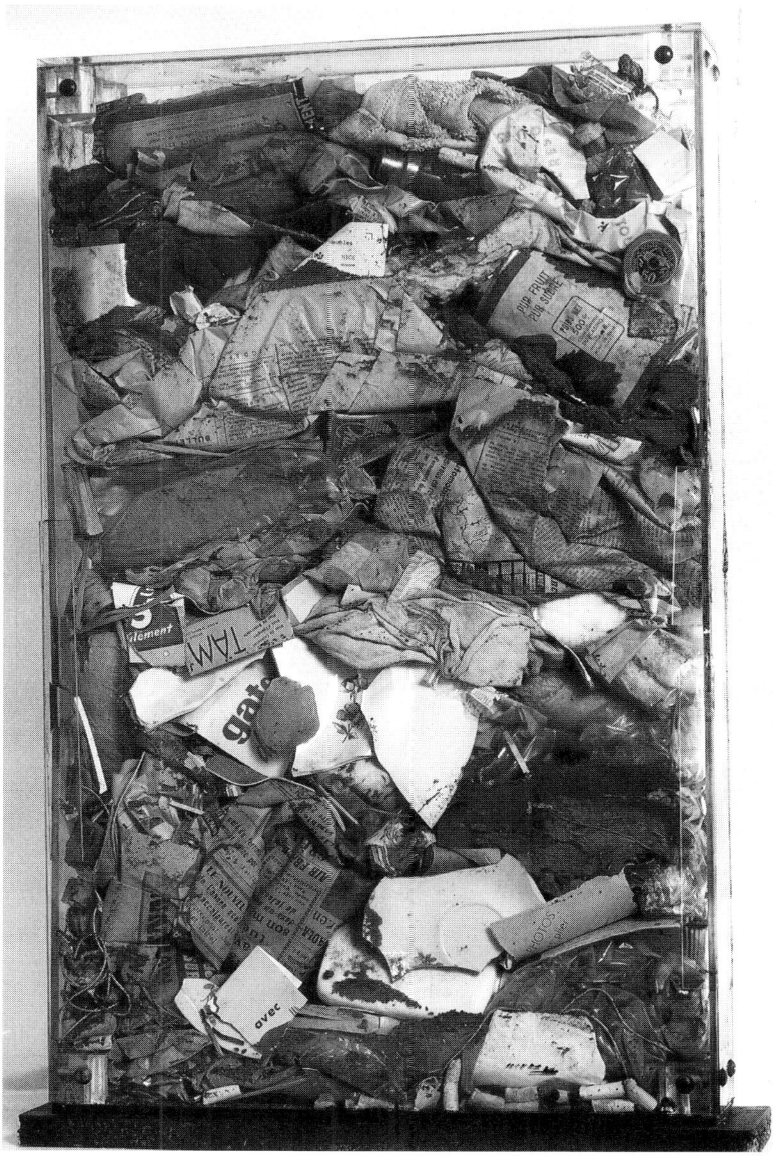

Arman, *Grands déchets bourgeois* (*Large Bourgeois Trash*), 1960. Household garbage in glass box, 26½ × 17⅓ × 3⅞ in. (67.5 × 44 × 9.8 cm). Private collection. © 2015 Artists Rights Society (ARS), New York/ADAGP, Paris.

Color in turn, as paint applied to a surface, is not bound to spatial extension; it exists as a separate, repetitive and objectified imprint.

It is precisely this systematic differentiation of the constituent elements of painting that makes Toroni's work central to the elaboration of a painterly aesthetic after Ryman and Stella in Europe: singularization of the brushstroke, separation of imprint from distribution, hinging the indexical mark in the gridded space of the surface, are all strategies of a radical painterly deconstruction that remind us also once again of comparable attitudes developed by Manzoni and Brouwn. The problem of (non-)composition—having been among the prime concerns of American painting since Ellsworth Kelly and Stella—is equally addressed by Toroni in yet another way that is similar to the solutions worked out by the Minimalists. Abolishing the problem of composition by replacing perceptual principles of spatial order with conceptual principles of distribution, is precisely what Judd had decided when he used mathematical series to structure and position the spatial and material quantities of his work.

What distinguishes Toroni's work from Minimalism primarily is the simplicity of its technical execution. A serial repetition of a spatial distance of 30 cm (probably derived from the gestural experience of a standard body/arm movement in the act of painting without expression or strain) becomes one of the basic definitions of Toroni's work. It is as clearly limited as it is infinite in variety, remaining equally valid on the pages of a book of actual imprints as it is consistent on a scroll of a dozen meters. While the figure remains constant, the surrounding spatial quantities are organized differently within each work.[69]

This highly differentiated separation between the perceptual concreteness of the figure and the conceptual definition of the ground (the processual unit of both constituting Toroni's "form") has also eliminated the last gestural residue of painterly facture. Yet simultaneously it avoids its opposite: the flatly painted color areas within or without geometrical shapes which, according to Stella, should be executed in the manner of the house painter. It opposes even more the Minimalist

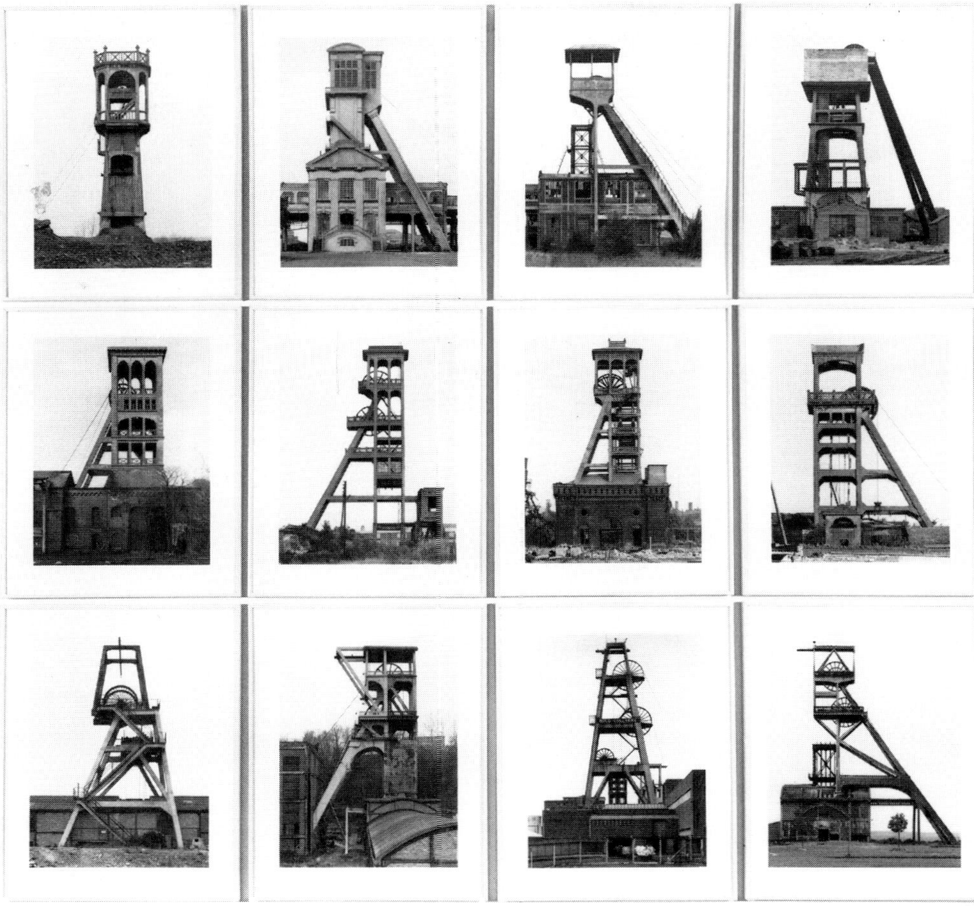

Hilla and Bernd Becher, *Winding Towers (6)*, 1982–83. Courtesy Sonnabend Gallery, New York. Photo: Zindman/Fremont. © Hilla and Bernd Becher.

conviction that purely mechanical techniques like spray-painting or more technologically refined processes like baking enamel paint on metal could achieve a compelling synthesis of subjective and objective processes of painting. If Judd once said that an ideal form would be neither organic nor geometric, it might be said that Toroni has found the ideal form and the ideal process of painterly production.

Accusations of Toroni's simplicity as stereotypical or boring perpetuate false expectations for narrative wealth and powerful variations in artistic practice. Such arguments remind us of Adorno's critique of bourgeois demands on high culture that art should remain powerful and exhilarating whereas the life of the masses should go on to be poor and pitiable. Toroni's art seems in fact to claim the contrary, a feature that might explain the experience of artless serenity emanating from his *empreintes*.

BERND AND HILLA BECHER

> What we decide to photograph is affected by certain necessities. Many of these structures are disappearing. All the time they are being dismantled or rusting or crumbling away. Our main problem is a fight against time.
>
> —*Bernd and Hilla Becher*[70]

With Toroni we saw the traditionalist painter reducing his practice to the painting of minimal gestures that oscillate between the beginning of a subject's conscious activity and the seemingly never ending process of anonymous reification. Bernd Becher could be seen as the dialectical opposite: an artist who has given up painting altogether in favor of another role and other media: sculpture, architecture, photography. Bernd and Hilla Becher started their project of becoming the photographic historians of anonymous industrial architecture in 1957, and when they finally had an opportunity to publish their first volume of photographs in 1970 they identified it as a documentation of *Anonymous Sculptures*.

The work of the Bechers situates itself first of all within the photographic lineage of German Neue Sachlichkeit (i.e., New Objectivity), especially with photographers like Albert Renger-Patzsch and Werner Mantz, who had chosen industrial architecture or serial objects as their subject matter in the Twenties and Thirties. A title like *Anonymous Sculptures*, by contrast, hints at a dialogue with a traditional genre of high art. Yet the work's systematic approach, the consistency with which it deploys sequences (what the Bechers call an *Abwicklung*, or the rotation around a single structure) or series (what they call a typology of images of different structures fulfilling the same function, e.g., twelve different cooling towers) link it to post-Minimal and Conceptual art of the mid- to late Sixties. It can hardly surprise us then that we owe one of the earliest appreciations of the Bechers to Carl Andre who developed seriality and sequential order with utter consequence in sculpture and who placed their artistic project within a rigorously modernist perspective:

> The photographs of the Bechers record the transient existence of purely functional structures, and reveal the degree to which form is determined by the invariant requirements of function.[71]

Bernd Becher's own statement regarding the relationship of their work to contemporary art actually situates it within a more complex set of paradigms:

> The question whether this is a work of art or not is not very interesting for us. Probably it is situated in between the established categories. Anyway the audience which is

> interested in art appears to be the most open-minded and to be willing to think about it.[72]

This statement—in all its ambiguity—defines the artistic object as the result of a declarative act, situating the work of the Bechers also within a Duchampian lineage—one that we have already traced in a variety of European practices of the Sixties. In the case of the Bechers this link is not necessarily caused by a direct confrontation with Duchamp but rather by their encounters with the mediations of Duchamp in the work of the French *Nouveaux réalistes* who exhibited in the late Fifties and early Sixties in the Düsseldorf region, connecting the work of the Bechers in particular with Jean Tinguely's machinic travesties, Arman's object accumulations and Villeglé's notions of "anonymity."

What distinguishes their work first of all from the Duchampian tradition and from *Nouveau réalisme* in particular, is the change from an aesthetic of accumulation and (de)fetishization to one of public structures and productive functions. This is enacted iconographically and formally by the shift to architectural space and to serially ordered photographic documents. This correlation of public space and photography not only pays tribute to the collective subject of the past but also positions the viewer as a self-determining subject in the present. As Bernd Becher noted:

> It is not the selection that is important but what the structures teach us about themselves. [...] We wanted to provide a viewpoint or rather a grammar for people to understand and compare different structures. This is often impossible in their natural setting. [...] We are interested in how people see, we do not want them to look with our eyes but for themselves.[73]

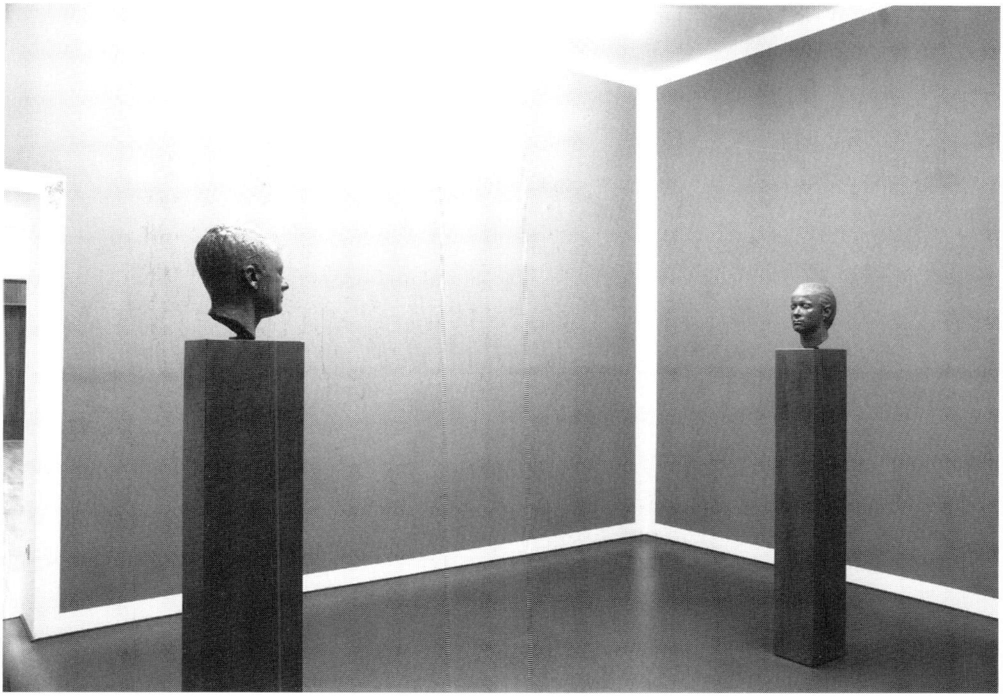

Blinky Palermo and Gerhard Richter, *Wall Painting and Two Sculptures*, 1971. Heiner Friedrich Gallery, Cologne. Photo: Timm Rautert. © 2015 Artists Rights Society (ARS), New York/VG Bild-Kunst, Bonn. © 2015 Gerhard Richter.

The elimination of the author's subjective presence, the definition of an artistic producer who does not want to interfere with the viewers' perception any longer (almost a literal parallel to Buren's quoted statement on this question), finds its correspondence in the anonymous qualities consistently foregrounded in the architectural typologies of the Bechers. Anonymity as a critique of the "author function" has undergone considerable changes from Duchamp's anonymously produced readymades onwards. It re-emerged, as we have seen, in the work of Villeglé and his *Lacéré anonyme* and in Brouwn's *This Way Brouwn* in the active dialogic participations of anonymous producers. Yet the Bechers as historians of anonymous architecture point incessantly backwards toward the collective basis of production and the loss of that collective subjectivity. As artists, by contrast, they have to negate inevitably the validity of any traditional role for the artist as an exceptional subject in the present. It is this very dialectic that Adorno addressed in the final phrases of his *Aesthetic Theory*:

> It is now not the time to imagine the art of the future within a transformed society. Most probably it would be neither like that of the past nor like that of the present, but it would be more desirable that art would disappear altogether once that reality might have changed to a better state, instead of art forgetting the suffering of which it is the expression and which endowed its form with substance. … What else would art have become but the mere writing of history if it would have gotten rid of the memory of accumulated suffering?[74]

Gerhard Richter

> One has to believe in what one is doing, one has to engage oneself wholeheartedly with painting. Once obsessed by this, one goes finally as far as believing that one could change

> humanity by painting. But once you have given up this passion, there is nothing left to do. Then it is highly recommendable to keep one's hands off. Because basically painting is complete idiocy.
>
> —*Gerhard Richter*[75]

From the perspective of this essay we could argue that ever since his arrival in West Germany in 1961, Richter's painting has been engaged in a programmatic dialectics of formalism and historicity. On the one hand we see the artist act as a modernist, consciously eliminating subjective presence, referentiality and expressivity from his work, by reducing his painterly activities to the most elementary analysis of the painterly process. On the other hand we see the artist act as a traditionalist working his way through all the painterly genres and conventions, becoming almost a historian of the various forms of painterly meaning production.

This schism at the center of Richter's painterly production has been described by Roland Barthes in a different context as the "difficulty of the epoch," as a problem of choice between two equally excessive methods, poetry and ideology. According to Barthes, the poetical principle implies "positing a finally impenetrable reality which cannot be reduced any further," while the ideological principle entails "positing a reality which is entirely transparent for history."[76] Such a complex semiological reflection is without precursor in the visual arts in postwar West Germany. It is perhaps for this reason that Richter should be considered the most complex figure among German contemporary artists of the post-Beuys era. Unlike many of the other artists (e.g., Uecker, Piene, Mack) whom he first met when he came to Düsseldorf in 1961, Richter never came under the spell of what was then the rather dominant presence of Arman, Klein, and Tinguely. Neither did he follow the artistic projects outlined by Joseph Beuys that seem to have mesmerized an entire generation of artists (e.g., Immendorff, Kiefer, Palermo, Polke) having started their studies—as did Richter—in the early to mid-Sixties at the Academy in Düsseldorf where Beuys had been teaching since 1961. By contrast, the legacies of Dada, as they were transformed by the artists of the Fluxus movement, certainly had some impact on Richter's attempts to come to terms with the artist's precarious tasks in confronting the recently entered Western capitalist society.

Richter's first public exhibition in 1963 showed his preoccupation with the concept of the readymade and its possible reactivation within present practices. During the *Demonstration for Capitalist Realism* which he performed with Konrad Fischer-Lueg in a furniture department store for one evening, the artists were seated on couches on white pedestals and presented themselves as living sculptures in a rather odd environment of cheap contemporary furniture. In this performance that was as reminiscent of Duchamp as it was explicit in its citation of Manzoni's propositions, the artists declared the store and its contents in their entirety to be considered as a work of art, attempting to find a new relationship between art and reality, or—as Robert Rauschenberg had recently defined his project in the following manner: "Painting relates to both art and life. Neither can be made. (I try to act in that gap between the two.)"[77]

Thus Richter's performance/installation work not only corroborates that the rediscovery of the readymade paradigm was central among most European and American artists of that period, but it tells us more about the importance of Manzoni as a mediator of Duchampian ideas in the early Sixties. In this particular case it is Manzoni's concept of the *Living Sculptures/Sculture Vivante* (1961) and his *Magic Base* (1961) which—by changing everything placed on it into a work of art—finally fulfills Duchamp's prophecy that the whole galaxy of objects would one day be turned into readymades. But Manzoni's spirit of an antimodernist painterly reductivism permeates Richter's work in yet another and totally different way. All of his paintings from the first period (1962 to 1966) were painted in a rather narrow scale of slightly differentiated hues of gray, and as such they operate as quasi-monochrome paintings. Richter called gray the sum of all colors and therefore a "non-color"; deploying in fact the same term that Manzoni had used for his own paintings when he called them achrome or non-color paintings. Richter justified his exclusive deployment of gray in the following manner: "Gray more than any other color, is qualified not to represent anything at all."[78] This statement not only adds a dimension of radical negation to Richter's monochromatic reductivism but to his painterly activities at large, situating them historically in the anti-cultural and anti-aesthetic tradition descending from Duchamp. Rather than perceiving his painting in a lineage of modernist reductivism driven by the project of self-reflexivity, one should situate Richter's chromatic reductivism in his choice of "found photography"—his primary subject matter from 1962 to 1966—in the perspective of a paradigm of the "photographic readymade." As the artist argues, in one of his most enigmatic and provocative statements:

> I wanted to do something which had nothing in common with art whatsoever, at least not as I knew it, nothing to do with painting, composition, color, formal invention, creativity. … Therefore I felt so surprised and attracted by the kind of photography that we all see and use daily in large quantities. All of a sudden I could see this in a different way as an image which gave me a different perception, a mode without all those traditional criteria that I had related to art beforehand. The photograph did not have any style, no concept, no judgment, it rescued me from personal emotion, it had nothing at all, it was pure image. Therefore I wanted to use it not as a medium for painting, but the painting as a medium for the photograph.[79]

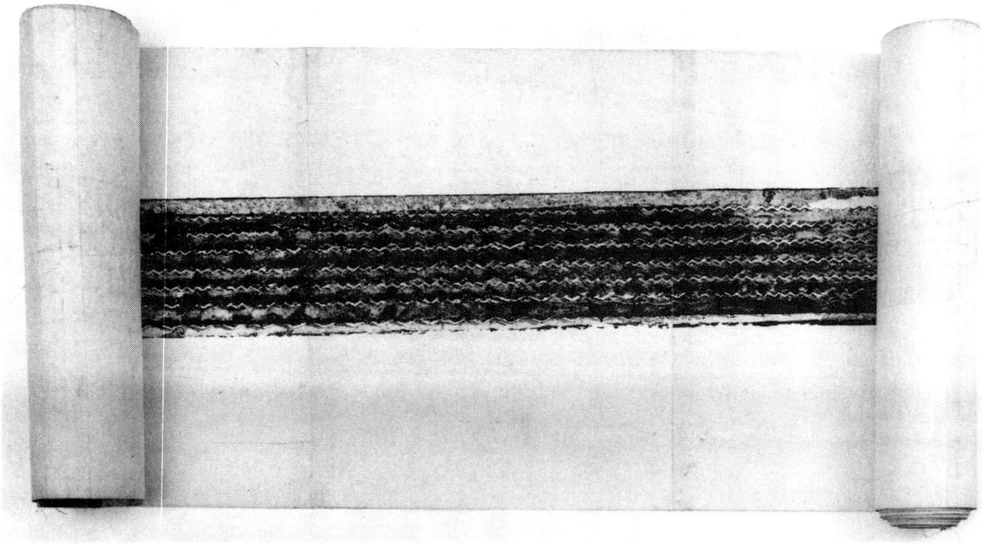

Robert Rauschenberg, *Automobile Tire Print* (detail), 1953. Monoprint: ink on twenty sheets of paper, mounted on fabric, 16½ × 264½ in. (41.91 cm × 671.83 cm) (fully extended). San Francisco Museum of Modern Art. © Robert Rauschenberg Foundation/Licensed by VAGA, New York.

In 1962, at the climax of *Nouveau réalisme* in Europe, most artistic practices were essentially still concerned with the legacies of the readymade as object. At that very moment Richter transferred the focus from the found object to the photographic readymade, an objectified image, addressing reification and fetishization on the level of perception rather than on the level of fetishized object experience. It is a shift that had of course occurred before in Rauschenberg's photo-montage paintings and it had been discerned—without however questioning the paradigm's motivations—as early as 1964 by Max Kozloff:

> The fact that Rauschenberg by now uses all kinds of journalist photography which he transfers by silk-screening it into his paintings as though it were concrete objects, changes in a subtle manner the meaning and the impact of photography on our lives.[80]

We presume that the interaction between historical and artistic processes would actually occur in reverse order, namely that photography's increased impact and presence in social life would motivate artists like Rauschenberg to adopt the paradigm of "found photography" in analogy (and in substitution) to the "found object." Even though Richter's technique differs dramatically from Rauschenberg's, its influence permeates Richter's painterly work, as is evident in Bernice Rose's precise description of the main characteristics of Rauschenberg's dye-transfer technique:

> But perhaps the most consistent expressive device in the work is the scrubbed line created by the transfer tool; the line which conjures the representation but is totally independent of it, weaves its pattern through the work … asserting always the drawn quality as opposed to the printed quality of that image.[81]

While Richter systematically erases gesture from his paintings by anchoring the image in the iconic matrix of the found photograph, he simultaneously erases contour from the reproduction of the photograph, inducing thereby an incessant ambivalence between the painterly signifier and the photographic signified. Again, the specific differences with Rauschenberg's approach become apparent if one recognizes that Rauschenberg maintains at least a partially iconic "narrative" within his found photographic imagery (this is especially obvious in his *Thirty Four Drawings for Dante's Inferno*, 1959–1960).

With Richter, in manifest opposition, "found photography" is absolutely "meaningless." It stands for itself as a category of historically determined visual material, as a collective mode of experience and self-expression, and as such it cannot have any traditionally defined "literary" meaning or illustrative functions. The necessity for painting is derived in Richter's work then from the attempt to maintain a dialectical relationship with photography as a given mass cultural segment of historically formed conventions of perception. Inasmuch as photography enacts the collectively ruling standards of visuality, it is juxtaposed here with the need to critically oppose these conditions by the individual formal gesture of painting. Inasmuch as Richter critically reflects on photography's impact on painting as a historical reality, he analyzes painting's proper historical reality. Not surprisingly then, series of paintings based on photographs have alternated with series of autonomous painterly works, and the same conflict is acted out within each painting itself. This ambiguous wandering between painting as a *discours plein*, which is oriented toward reality, and its opposite approach of a *discours vide*, which is only concerned with its own status as practice, has marked Richter's production ever since his first works in the West.

It is this feeling for historicity, even within the painter's proper activity, the capacity to question the relevance of one's practice while one is practicing it, that position Richter's paintings among the most serious efforts operative as an artist in contemporary culture. Thus

Richter's formal attitudes result from the historicity of his own painterly practice, and as such constitute a highly fragile equilibrium between subjective gesture and objective fact.

This fragility seems to be a feature common to most of the crucial European practices of the Sixties and Seventies. In comparison to the best American art of that period, European art appears almost self-negating, as though it would rather give up its material existence before it would have to give up its historical consciousness. Perhaps this is due to the fact that European artists were—at least for the moment of the Sixties—more concerned with the actually governing conditions of social reality than with an abstract ideal of cultural production. Perhaps it is also due to the fact that their ideas about artistic practices in the present are not primarily engaged with the mere innovation of traditions but rather with a political project that Clement Greenberg had already defined in a prophetic statement in 1939:

> Capitalism in decline finds that whatever of quality it is still capable of producing becomes almost invariably a threat to its own existence. Advances in culture, no less than advances in science and industry, corrode the very society under whose aegis they are made possible. Here, as in every other question today, it becomes necessary to quote Marx word for word. Today we no longer look toward socialism for a new culture—as inevitably as one will appear, once we do have socialism. Today we look to socialism simply for the preservation of whatever living culture we have right now.[82]

NOTES

First published in *Europe in the Seventies: Aspects of Recent Art*, trans. from the German by Barbara C. Flynn (Chicago: Art Institute of Chicago, 1977), pp. 83–111; Excerpts were reprinted in English and Spanish in *New Realisms: 1957–1962: Object Strategies between Readymade and Spectacle*, exh. cat., ed. Julia Robinson (Madrid: Museo Nacional Centro de Arte Reina Sofia, 2010), pp. 77–92. Minor corrections have been made for consistency.

1. The term "ideology" is understood here in the most general way possible, while still remaining relevant, as defined by Karl Mannheim in his *Ideologie und Utopie* (Frankfurt: Suhrkamp, 1952):

> The term "ideology" actually means to say that certain challenged opinions, statements, objectivizations (ideas in the broadest sense of the word) cannot be comprehended alone for themselves, but have to be understood in terms of existential conditions of the subject by being interpreted as functions of these conditions of being. What is more, this means that we somehow reason that the concrete foundation of a subject's existential being is responsible in a constitutional manner for the subject's opinions, statements and recognitions.

2. Joseph Kosuth, *The Sixth Investigation, Proposition 14*, ed. Gerd de Vries (Cologne: Gerd de Vries/Paul Maenz, 1971), n.p.

3. Jean-Paul Sartre—as early as 1947—compared certain aesthetic phenomena of that period to the ideological implications of symbolism's aestheticist attitude:

> But art has never been on the side of the purists. [...] One knows very well that pure art and empty art are one and the same thing, and that aestheticist purism was simply a brilliant defensive manoeuver of the past century's bourgeoisie who preferred being denounced as philistines to being discovered as exploiters.

See "Qu'est-ce que la Littérature?"(I) in *Les Temps Modernes*, February 1947, p. 782.

This quotation is particularly revealing in regard to the development of the visual arts in France (and Europe) where only a few years later the ideas of purity and immaterial emptiness in art became the key concepts of Yves le Monochrome. No wonder then that he became the champion of the newly reinstated bourgeoisie and postwar parvenus of post-fascist West Germany.

4. Daniel Buren, *Limites Critiques*, ed. Yvon Lambert (Paris, 1970); English translation as "Critical Limits," in Daniel Buren, *Five Texts* (New York: John Weber Gallery/ London: Jack Wendler Gallery, 1973), pp. 43–52.

5. Clement Greenberg, "The Late Thirties in New York" (1957), in *Art and Culture* (Boston: Beacon Press, 1961), p. 231.

6. Camilla Gray, *The Great Experiment: Russian Art 1863–1922* (New York: Harry N. Abrams, 1962).

7. Clement Greenberg, "The School of Paris: 1946," in *Art and Culture*, p. 120.

8. Jean Dubuffet, "Causette," invitation-pamphlet for his Portraits exhibition at Galerie René Drouin in 1947, n.p.

9. Max Raphael, "Beschäftigung mit neuer Kunst" (1938), in *Arbeiter, Kunst und Künstler* (Frankfurt: S. Fischer Verlag, 1975), p. 21.

10. Greenberg, "The School of Paris: 1946," p. 120.

11. We do in fact consider all post-Minimalist and Conceptual work to be a manifest exception to the American postwar tradition of historical assimilation. The works of Bruce Nauman and Richard Serra, of Robert Barry and Lawrence Weiner, of Sol LeWitt, Dan Graham and Michael Asher (to name but the most crucial examples) are certainly further removed from any historicism oriented at Europe than any works of the preceding generation. Perhaps Leo Castelli was quite rightfully both punning and paraphSrasing Greenberg's reference to Mondrian, when he commented on the first show of Lawrence Weiner's in his gallery: "This is the writing on the wall."

12. Greenberg, "The Late Thirties in New York," p. 233.

13. It is bewildering—and sometimes amusing—to read the most implausible statements on such irrational attitudes and atavisms again and again in art criticism, and in art history writing, as though the visual arts were a zone protected from reason and the understanding of human behavior. This is especially true of the French and West German Klein exegeses (e.g., Pierre Restany and Paul Wember), or even more so for the recent West German exegesis of the work of Joseph Beuys. But even American criticism seems to fall into this trap as soon as it comes to Beuys. See for example Bernice Rose's matter-of-course reference to Beuys as a shaman in her introductory essay to the catalog, *Drawing Now* (New York: Museum of Modern Art, 1976), p. 16:

> Beuys, while allied to the tradition of automatic drawing, stands alone in his choice of sources and techniques. Instead of resorting to the inchoate individual unconscious, he assumes the role of one to whom the unconscious drive of numerous civilizations has assigned the function of primary executor of fantasies, he assumes the role of shaman.

It would be interesting to find out from the inventors of such notions, how they actually relate those artists' roles and functions to the reality and society within which they supposedly practice their obsolete crafts as shamans. After all, surrounded by a world governed by standards of advanced science, and economics, the artist functions—as archaic as he might be—very well in a highly differentiated and complicated economic and ideological subsystem, called the artworld. At the same time the artist functions supposedly as a shaman for whose sake, healing whom and how, exactly? Most symptomatic, however, seems to be the fact that Beuys' existence as a shaman (and our objection against interpreting him as a shaman raises no questions about his abilities as an artist) has become an integral element to maintain his almost everlasting position of domination in West German postwar art. While Klein and Manzoni disappeared and left the stage to the following generations, Beuys, who began—like them—to make his work in the early Fifties, is still not only the dominating figure in West Germany, but he is perceived as the sole and singular artist to produce the seemingly most authentic work of the present in West Germany.

The question arises, however, as to whether this dominance does not in fact depend more on the everlasting suppression of subjectivity and political memory in Germany, whether his obsolete presence as the artistic father figure does not finally reflect the seemingly never-ending reign of German collective infantilism and the resulting need for archaic mystification.

14. Greenberg, "Partisan Review Art Chronicle, 1952," in *Art and Culture*, p. 153.

15. This is in fact the first time that Kaprow would deploy and define the term "happening," soon to become the central project of his work. See Allan Kaprow, "The Legacy of Jackson Pollock," *Art News* (October 1958), p.27.

16. John Cage, quoted in Richard Kostelanetz, *Conversing with Cage*, 2nd ed. (New York: Routledge, 2003), p. 75.

17. Yves Klein, quoted in Germano Celant's essay on Piero Manzoni in *Piero Manzoni* (London: Tate Gallery, 1974), n.p.

18. Yves Klein's statement from 1957 is reproduced in Yves Klein, *Selected Writings* (London: Tate Gallery, 1974), n.p.

19. Ibid.

20. That Klein was not only familiar with, but deeply fascinated with Duchamp's work is proven by the fact that as early as 1948 he offered the catalog of the famous Surrealist exhibition in the Galerie Maeght to his close friend Arman. This was of course the catalog that carried Duchamp's by now notorious cover with *Prière de toucher*, a life-size foam rubber cast of a breast. See Daniel Abadie, "Conversation avec Arman," in *Arman*, exh. cat., ed. Daniel Abadie (Paris: Galerie nationale du Jeu de Paume, 1998), p. 44. This note was added later to the above quoted reprint of excerpts of this essay in Robinson, *New Realisms*.

21. Donald Judd, "Barnett Newman," *Studio International* (February 1970), reprinted in Donald Judd, *Complete Writings 1959–1975* (Halifax: The Press of the Nova Scotia College of Art and Design/New York: New York University Press, 1975), p. 200.

22. As quoted by Dore Ashton in her essay "Art as Spectacle," *Arts Magazine* (March 1967), p. 44.

23. Ibid.

24. Judd, *Complete Writings*, p. 222.

25. Raphael, "Beschäftigung mit neuer Kunst," p. 133.

26. Jacques de la Villeglé, "Les boulevards de la création," n.d, in Villeglé, *Le lacéré anonyme* (Paris: Centre Georges Pompidou, 1977), p. 57 (my translation).

27. The works of these artists, the "affiches lacérées" and "décollages" were shown in William Seitz's famous exhibition *The Art of Assemblage* at the Museum of Modern Art in New York in 1961, and then later at the New Realists show at the Sidney Janis Gallery in 1962, as well as in a special group show called *L'Affiche lacérée* at the Gres Gallery in Chicago in 1964.

This exhibition included works by all the authentic décollage artists, Dufrêne, Hains, Rotella, and Villeglé. Their work has hardly been dealt with in American and European criticism. As is usually the case with art historical reception (especially that of the recent past), it seems that the radicality of their assault on the traditional (painterly) values equally frightened the collector and the museum curator/historian: they must have questioned the idea of investing money and time into a type of work whose production—by its very definition—was apparently unlimited, resulting from its inherent principles of anonymity and infinite repetition, and aimed at the (symbolic) annihilation of the individual producer.

I have not found a single example to illuminate the ways in which the affichistes were received in the criticism of other artists. Needless to say, Judd does not mention their work at all, and it seems that in this case he once again dismissed and ignored the few really innovative and important contributions to European art of the Fifties. Even for artistic eyes, the implications of this work seem to have been too advanced, or too similar to their own concerns, to be discovered. For once, Pierre Restany does not seem to be altogether wrong in saying:

> Rauschenberg remains a contributor to post-cubist aesthetics, and finally positions himself on this side of Schwitters. He is still bound to a traditional language, a lyrical or expressionist synthesis of cubism, which shows itself clearly in his concerns for composition and painterly presence. The same analysis is valid for Jasper Johns. ... In fact, quite to the contrary of the *Nouveaux réalistes,* these Neo-Dadaists have not realized the extreme consequences of the readymade concept. They (i.e. the American Neo-Dadaists) have not transcended the Dada facts, but instead integrated the found object into aesthetic compositions, into formal structures, which were relevant long ago in expressionist and cubist vocabulary. (Pierre Restany, *Le Nouveau Réalisme* [Paris: Galerie Mathias Fels, 1970], n.p.)

Because of spatial limitations alone, we will deal in the following pages mainly with Villeglé's work and writings, even though the work of all the authentic affichistes would merit equal interest and reading.

28. Villeglé, "Les boulevards de la création," n.d, in Villeglé, *Le lacéré anonyme* (Paris: Centre Georges Pompidou, 1977), p. 55 (my translation).

29. Ibid., p. 59.

30. Ibid., p. 55 (my translation).

31. Marcel Broodthaers, "Gare au défi! Le Pop Art, Jim Dine et l'influence de René Magritte," *Journal du Palais des Beaux-Arts* 1029 (Brussels: Palais des Beaux Arts, 1963), p. 9.

32. Sarenco, *Piero Manzoni: Opere et giorni* (Milan, 1973), n.p. More recently Germano Celant has pointed out the opposition between Klein and Manzoni even more distinctly. Among the many differences that he identifies, the following one seems to be particularly relevant:

> There is therefore a clear contrast between the concept of the spiritual and messianic art that is Klein's and the dialectic and materialistic art of Manzoni. Seen from a psychoanalytic angle there emerges in the former (according to the theories of Norman Brown) a protagonist of sublimation, and therefore of death, while the latter is a champion of the "resurrection" of the flesh, and therefore of life.

See Germano Celant, *Piero Manzoni* (London: Tate Gallery, 1974).

33. Stanley Brouwn, *Catalogue of Works from 1960 to 1975* (Eindhoven: Stedelijk van Abbemuseum, 1976), n.p.

34. Only one other sculptor would make such a distinction a central aspect of his work: Alexandr Rodchenko would explicitly differentiate a display mode and a storage mode in his collapsible folding sculptures of 1918/1919. See the discussion of these terms and Rodchenko's sculptures in my essay "From Faktura to Factography," in this volume.

35. Robert Pincus-Witten, "Ryman-Marden-Manzoni," *Artforum* (June 1972): 50.

36. Stanley Brouwn in Antje von Graevenitz, "The Artist as a Pedestrian: Stanley Brouwn," *Dutch Art and Architecture Today* 1 (June 1977): 2.

37. Ibid.

38. Stanley Brouwn, *Catalogue of Works from 1960 to 1975* (Eindhoven: Stedelijk van Abbemuseum, 1976), n.p.

39. Judd, *Collected Writings*, p. 223.

40. This and the following quotations, unless otherwise indicated, are from Irmeline Lebeer, "Dix mille francs de récompense" (Ten thousand francs reward), an interview with Marcel Broodthaers, published in *Marcel Broodthaers: Palais des Beaux-Arts* (Brussels, 1974), here, p. 64. All quotations from this interview in English translation are taken from *Marcel Broodthaers*, ed. Benjamin Buchloh, Special issue of *October Magazine* 42 (fall

1987): 39–48. The central importance of this interview results from the fact that both parts, questions and answers, were in fact written by Marcel Broodthaers himself, with the critic Irmeline Lebeer only posing as the interviewer.

41. Marcel Broodthaers, *Moules, Oeufs, Frites, Pots, Charbon, Perroquets*, exh. cat. (Antwerp: Wide White Space Gallery, 1966), n.p.

42. One such example would be Nicolas Calas' strictly neo-Surrealist reading (*Artforum*, May 1976), which ultimately does not really aid in understanding Broodthaers' enigmatic work.

43. Irmeline Lebeer, "Dix mille francs de récompense," p. 64.

44. Ibid., p. 65.

45. Ibid., p.66.

46. By 1964 Broodthaers had of course read Roland Barthes' *Le Degré zéro de l'écriture* (1953) and *Mythologies* (1957), both of which had expanded upon de Saussure's linguistic model of the sign and had applied it as a tool for the critical reading of secondary ideological sign systems.

47. Lebeer, "Dix mille francs de récompense," p. 67.

48. Ibid., p. 68.

49. Ibid., p. 65.

50. Broodthaers, *Museum—Museum: Der Adler vom Oligozän bis Heute* (The Eagle from Oligocene to Today), vols. 1 and 2 (Düsseldorf: Kunsthalle Düsseldorf, 1972).

51. Lebeer, "Dix mille francs de récompense," p. 68.

52. Ibid., p. 69.

53. Daniel Buren, "Is Teaching Art Necessary?" *Galerie des Arts* (September 1968); English translation in Lucy R. Lippard, *Six Years: The Dematerialization of the Art Object from 1966 to 1972* (New York: Praeger, 1973), p. 52.

54. Lebeer, "Dix mille francs de récompense."

55. Buren, *Discordance/Cohérence*, ed. R. H. Fuchs (Eindhoven: Stedelijk van Abbe Museum, 1976), p. 4.

56. Ibid., p. 12.

57. Buren, "Standpoints," in *Five Texts*, p. 40.

58. In European painting a comparably radical deconstruction of painting would be initiated only in the mid- to late 1960s, for example in the monochrome wall paintings by the German artist Palermo, and in the *empreintes* paintings by a close colleague and friend of Buren's, the Swiss painter Niele Toroni.

59. Roberta Smith, "On Daniel Buren," *Artforum* (September 1973): 66.

60. Another example of such a misreading, similar to Smith's, would be Barbara Rose's statement from the same moment: "Buren's nondescript and deliberately ephemeral, non-qualifiable pieces vaguely resemble travesties of Stella's stripe paintings.") See Douglas Crimp, "Daniel Buren's New York Work," in *Discordance/Cohérence*, p. 75. Crimp quotes Barbara Rose on p. 77.

Buren has explicitly admitted the relevance of his encounter with Stella's early work—which he had seen for the first time in New York in 1962—for his subsequent investigation of the contemporary problems of painting. But to fully understand the impact of that encounter would require following at least to some extent also the transformations in Buren's response to Stella, a step that the so called formalist critics who discerned this influence only in visual/formal terms seem to have been either unwilling or unable to take. Ultimately—as Douglas Crimp has pointed out—to see stripes in Buren's work and to think only of Stella is therefore typical of the historical limitations of a certain type of American formalist criticism.

61. Buren, in a discussion with André Parinaud in *Galerie des Arts* (February 1968); English translation in Lippard, *Six Years: The Dematerialization of Art*, p. 41.

62. American artists of that moment were equally involved in developing a functional—as opposed to formal—motivation of the aesthetic procedure, though in entirely different directions. Bruce Nauman, for example, inverted the aestheticism of Flavin's fluorescent light works and reinstalled the very same elements (fluorescent light tubes) functionally in his corridor-pieces, generating an immediate and authentic material experience of the work's given and actually operative elements: architectural space, light, color, and the viewer's phenomenological interactions.

63. Niele Toroni, *Quelques évidences a répéter* (Milan, 1973), n.p.

64. Buren in particular has opposed and even violently polemicized against the notion of a "group" and its "name." What he claimed to be at stake was in fact the radical interchangeability of the artists' idioms and actions, and their shared critique of traditional forms of artistic identity and individual production. The group's "acronym" BMPT (Buren, Mosset, Parmentier, Toroni) was typically neither invented nor adopted by the four artists, but was imposed on their activities by a critic, Otto Hahn. Since then, however, it has become somewhat of an established convention—as is often the case in art history—to refer to this formation of artists and their shared activities with the group name they rejected, and we will follow this convention here. The other two members, Parmentier and Mosset, abandoned the group after two years—the first by actively participating in radical politics, the second by joining the world of fashion and interior design. Both ways seem to be once again typical Parisian attempts to escape the problems of artistic production and its contradictions.

65. André Breton as quoted in Jacques de la Villeglé, "Des réalités collectives," in *Dufrêne, Hains, Rotella, Villeglé, Vostell: Sammlung Cremer* (Staatsgalerie Stuttgart, 1971), n.p.

66. Yves Klein, *Selected Writings* (London: Tate Gallery, 1974), p. 35.

67. Niele Toroni, untitled exhibition pamphlet (Brussels: Palais des Beaux Arts, 1973), n.p.

68. Frank Stella in Bruce Glaser, "Questions to Stella and Judd," *Art News*, (September 1966), repr. in *Minimal Art: A Critical Anthology*, ed. G. Battcock, (New York: Dutton, 1968; repr. Berkeley: University of California Press, 1995), p. 157.

69. See for example Niele Toroni, *Cinq Empreintes de Pinceau No. 50* (Paris: Yvon Lambert, 1973).

70. *Bernd and Hilla Becher*, exh. cat. (London: The Arts Council of Great Britain, 1974), p. 58.

71. Carl Andre, "A Note on Bernhard and Hilla Becher," *Artforum* (December 1972), pp. 59–61.

72. Bernd Becher, *Bernd and Hilla Becher*, p. 59.

73. Ibid., p. 60.

74. Theodor W. Adorno, *Aesthetische Theorie* (Frankfurt am Main: Suhrkamp, 1973), 387. English translation as *Aesthetic Theory*, trans. Robert Hullot-Kantor (Minneapolis: University of Minnesota Press, 1998).

75. Irmeline Lebeer, "Gerhard Richter ou la réalité de l'image" (A conversation with Irmeline Lebeer), in *Chroniques de l'art vivant* 36 (February 1973): 13–16.

76. Roland Barthes, *The Death of the Author*, first published in English translation in Brian O'Doherty, *Aspen Magazine* 5–6 (1967), n.p.

77. Dorothy C. Miller, ed., *Sixteen Americans*, exh. cat. (New York: Museum of Modern Art, 1959), 58.

78. Gerhard Richter, letter to Edy de Wilde, February 23, 1975, in *Gerhard Richter: Text 1961–2007*, ed. Dietmar Elger and Hans-Ulrich Obrist (Verlag Buchhandlung König, Cologne, 2008), p. 91.

79. Gerhard Richter, Interview with Rolf Schön, 1972, in *Gerhard Richter: Text 1961–2007*, p. 59.

80. Max Kozloff, "Critical and Historical Problems of Photography" (1964), in *Renderings: Critical Essays on a Century of Modern Art* (New York: Simon & Schuster, 1968), p. 289.

81. Rose, *Drawing Now*, p. 30.

82. Clement Greenberg, "Avant-Garde and Kitsch," in *Art and Culture*, p. 21.

2

Marcel Broodthaers: Allegories of the Avant-Garde

Allegories are to the realm of thoughts what ruins are to the realm of things.

—*Walter Benjamin*

One part of what delights us today was the cause of his death.

—*Charles Baudelaire on Edgar Allan Poe*

To the melancholic eye the world's gear and active machinations disintegrate into hieroglyphs: enigmatic characters that decipher what is normally concealed from the individual involved in the acts of production. Contemplative stasis lays bare to the bone. Pictures and dramas of industrious cultural enterprise tend to become scriptural once the artist addresses his own discourse. Self-referentiality, in the true sense of the word, as an analysis of one's proper material and historical condition of discourse and production, results, as we witnessed with Duchamp, in the epistemological model and the libidinal allegory; or, as in the case of Magritte, in the pictograph and in the rebus. The allegorical mode is dependent on yet another condition: that the objects of its analysis and representation, even though seemingly alive and vital, are in fact historically obsolete. If it seems that allegory saves things of the past from oblivion, it in fact also reveals the degree to which things of the present are encumbered by the past and obsolescence dominates present experience. As much as allegory makes reification its historical subject (of analysis, of memory) it makes ideology its historicized material. In describing one of his procedures for the demarcation and installation of objects, Marcel Broodthaers lists three essentials of allegory—the scriptural, the theatrical, and the ruinous:

> If one trusts the meaning of the inscription, the object itself assumes the character of an illustration referring to a kind of sociological novel. These objects, the mirror and the pipe, submitted to the same number system (or the cardboard box, the clock, and the chair) become interchangeable on the stage of a theatre. Their destiny is ruined.[1]

This could be called the allegorical mode in the work of Marcel Broodthaers: a dialectician by virtue of his abandoned poetical past and his early artistic confrontation and friendship with René Magritte, as well as by his philosophical and political position (he studied with Lucien Goldmann, the disciple of Georg Lukács), he perceived the functions of (his) art under the contemporary conditions to be those of a perpetually renewed reflective criticism of ideology, or, more precisely, of the ideology of art. He recognized the last and only political validity of a nineteenth-century social role model, precisely within the boundaries of that paradox: that of the artist who operates within a highly determined institutionalized space, which claims as its crucial difference from all other social activities its social and political autonomy: the avant-garde.

Born in Brussels in 1924 (the year of the publication of André Breton's first "Manifesto of Surrealism"), Marcel Broodthaers, in contradiction to frequent misperception, was not a second-generation Surrealist in the line of Breton.

In fact, as early as 1947, he joined a group called "Le Surréalisme Revolutionnaire" founded by members of the International European CoBrA Movement: Pierre Alechinsky, Philippe Dotremont, and Joseph Noiret. This group violently attacks the dominance of Breton's esthetic, social, and political positions, which they consider reactionary. One of the first manifestos of this group, published in Brussels on June 7, 1947, "Pas de quartier dans la revolution," carries the signatures of René Magritte, Marcel Mariën, Paul Nougé, Louis Scutenaire, members of the first Surrealist group in Brussels, as well as that of Marcel Broodthaers and other newcomers. The manifesto states the incompatibility between Surrealism and the revolutionary principles of the Communist Party, which was declared the only valid revolutionary force.[2] Only in the early 1950s does Broodthaers cancel his membership in the Belgian Communist Party, but as late as 1974 his criticism against Breton's Surrealism is still virulent.

A close look at the work eventually makes his distance from any attempt at a premature solution of the contradictions between art and politics more apparent, but a programmatic statement of his, replying to the question as to whether he could be situated in a Surrealist perspective, should clarify the problem from the beginning. By denouncing a quote from Breton's second "Manifesto of Surrealism" of 1930, Broodthaers proclaims:

> I know this by heart: "Everything makes us believe that there exists a position of the mind from which life and death, the real and the imaginary, the past and the future, that which can be communicated and that which cannot, the high and the low, cease to be perceived as contradictions." I do hope that I have nothing in common with this state of mind.[3]

If anything, it would be his persistent sense of the contradictions that could be called the most prominent feature in Broodthaers' thoughts and statements and, of course, in his work. The sheer variety of operational modes and material categories of his art offers a spectacle of contradictions and inconsistencies in itself: objects, paintings, and drawings, so-called environmental installations and at least two happenings, books and prints, photos and films, and writings and typography.

Two of the most significant contradictions and oppositional paradigmatic shifts of Modernism from the first decade of this century are at the center of Broodthaers' allegorical methodologies, and both have determined his biography of the poet-turned-painter in an almost exemplary fashion. These are, on the one hand, Magritte's paintings of the late 1920s, and, on the other hand, the dual transformations of both the visual object assuming the status of an epistemological model (i.e., Duchamp's readymade concept) and the linguistic sign becoming the object of semiological and poetical decomposition (i.e., Ferdinand de Saussure and Dada). When Tristan Tzara in his Dada Manifesto (published in *Dada* no. 3, Zurich, December 1918) announces that "we will like a furious wind tear apart the laundry of clouds and prayers and we will prepare the grand spectacle of disaster, the big fire, *decomposition*," it should be apparent from his metaphors of clouds and prayers that this decomposition will be addressing first and foremost the realm of the superstructure and esthetic ideology in particular.

Departing from his earlier poetical works, which included a film called *La clef de l'horloge (Un poème cinématographique en l'honneur de Kurt Schwitters)* (The Key to the Clock [A cinematographic poem in honor of Kurt Schwitters]), 1957, Broodthaers' first work as an artist in 1964 consisted of covering in plaster the bottom half of the almost complete edition of his last volume of poetry, a "found volume of poetry" as he called it, entitled *Pense-Bête* (Think Stupid/Animal). From this point, the perspective of his artistic investigation was clear. Broodthaers was not just analyzing transitional problems arising from making poetry into objects, or from the quasi-magical act of having an object/image, a model of analytical thought, essentially question its own discourse and production; more precisely, he was focusing on the historical and political scandal that is concealed in the seemingly neutral esthetic struggle between these opposing categories. His gallery announcement, accompanying his first exhibition in 1964, makes this point clear:

> I have asked myself as well whether I could not sell anything and become successful in life. I've been good for nothing for quite a while already. I am forty years old now … the idea to finally invent something that would be insincere crossed my mind and I went to work immediately. What was it? Actually, it was objects.[4]

And, from a different angle of irony:

> With the transition towards the visual arts I wanted to turn my back on poetry. Symbolically I wanted to free poetry from its ivory tower and therefore I threw it into the wet plaster to make a kind of sculpture out of it.[5]

The choice of plaster and the process of having casts made or immersing found objects in that white material that takes the life out of the object as much as it objectifies life, is, in the art activities of the early 1960s, neither original nor accidental. The plaster cast, as a highly mechanized mode of production, seems to solve the conflict between the apparently insurmountable presence and dominance of the mechanically reproduced object (in everyday reality and therefore, since Duchamp, logically in the esthetic discourse) and the equally strong human urge to dissolve that domination by the object and liquidate its presence through individual gestures of painting and sculptural invention. The conflict, essentially that between replication and primary process, is

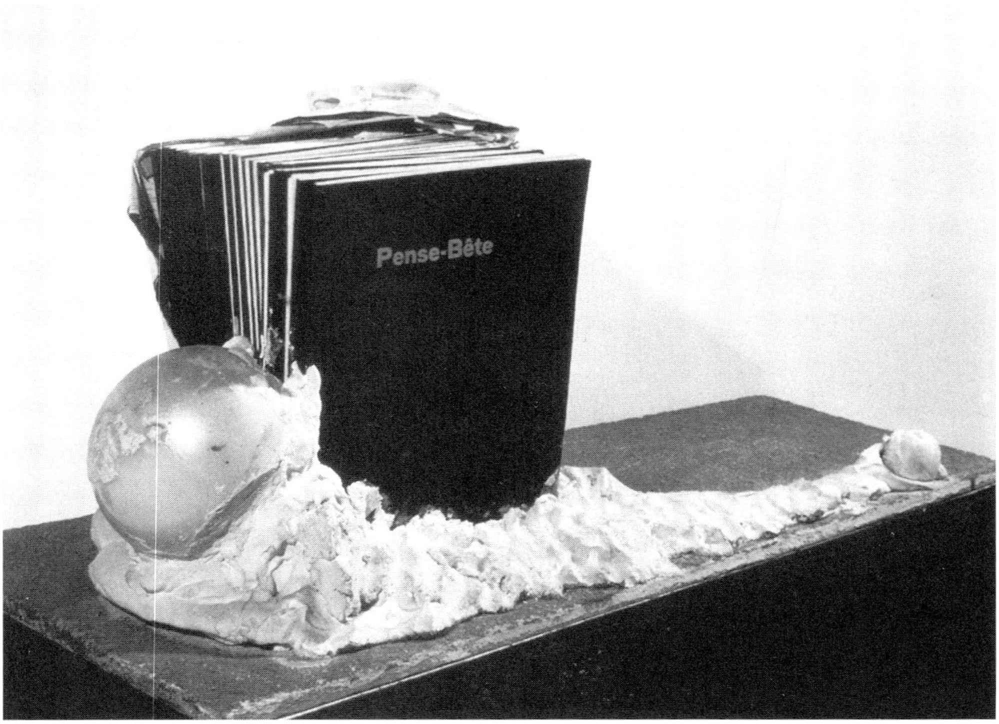

Marcel Broodthaers, *Pense-Bête*, 1964. Books, plaster, paper, plastic spheres, wood, 38½ × 33 × 17 in. (98 × 84 × 43 cm). Collection Anne-Marie and Stéphane Rona. © 2015 The Estate of Marcel Broodthaers/Artists Rights Society (ARS), New York/ SABAM, Brussels.

concretized and incorporated in various cast works, such as Duchamp's *Prière de toucher* (Please Touch), 1947, and his nude-cast in the final work *Étant donnés* (Given), 1946–66; Piero Manzoni's achromatic objects and paintings of 1959 which feature objects like bread-rolls that have been dipped in kaolin; Yves Klein's plaster-cast portraits, 1962; and, of course, in American art, Jasper Johns' paintings such as *Target with Plaster Casts*, 1955, and, most obviously, the work of George Segal from the early 1960s. Broodthaers was living in Paris and working as a freelance writer for a news agency. His first encounters with American Pop Art date from 1963 when he saw exhibitions at the Sonnabend Gallery. His accounts of that experience reflect the ambiguity of his response to an art of recently discovered objects, which would inform his subsequent work:

> In Paris in 1963. The first show that I saw was by George Segal. I was shocked. Therefore I decided to write about the Segal exhibition. I took a flaming critical position against this kind of art—one should not forget that our generation had an artistic background that was essentially surrealist and somewhat *mystique*.[6]

And later:

> How did I become successful? Quite simple. I only followed the footsteps in the artistic sands, which were left by René Magritte and Marcel Duchamp and the very fresh ones by George Segal, Roy Lichtenstein, and Claes Oldenburg.[7]

And even more obviously polemical in his essay "Like Butter in a Sandwich":

> It is evident that if the intellectual muscle fails to function the whole place is overwhelmed by the violence of the attitude. Pop Art is an attitude of the spirit of our times, or rather, this tragicomical actuality.[8]

But simultaneously, we can find statements by Marcel Broodthaers in regard to Pop Art that seem to contradict his critical skepticism. He acknowledges Pop Art as a major influence on his own work:

> Eighteen months ago I saw an exhibition poster of plaster casts by George Segal in Paris: that was my starting point. … Later it was also Lichtenstein, Jim Dine, and Oldenburg.[9]

Or:

> I have been strongly impressed by the image that the American Pop Artists had to offer … I think particularly of Rosenquist, Jim Dine, Oldenburg, and especially Segal.[10]

Broodthaers' relationship to European artists, especially Nouveau Réalisme in France and Italy, which in many ways could be considered the counterpart to American Pop Art, is equally ambiguous. On the one hand, there is no doubt that his early object works from 1964 to '66 bear the marks of a strong awareness of what had been done by artists like Arman, Christo, and Klein (age-wise his peers) during the late 1950s and early 1960s. Formal and material principles of selection and structure, serial accumulation of "found" elements from industrialized urban reality, a renewed reception and understanding of the full range of implications of the historic positions of Dada, all these features that constitute the Nouveaux Réalistes' work are present in Broodthaers' early object work as well.[11] Yet, on first glance, it is obvious that his works take on a radically different perspective on these issues. It comes almost as a surprise to find out that in fact one of Broodthaers' first shows took place in Paris in 1966 at the Galerie J, directed by Janine Restany, a gallery then at the center of Nouveau Réalisme activities. This is especially remarkable given Broodthaers' own comments on that movement:

> My objects and images, 1964–1965, could not cause such confusion [with Nouveau Réalisme]. The literalness shown in the appropriation of the real was intolerable to me because it meant an acceptance pure and simple of the ideas of progress in art … and elsewhere.[12]

There are only two ways to explain these blatant contradictions: either they are examples of an almost mindless opportunism which, after all, is not such a rare feature in the symptomatology of the artist as a social character; or they are phrased in that mode of speaking which the English language identifies as "having one's tongue in one's cheek," a psycho-physiological gesture of refusal to substantiate physically, to commit oneself with the tool of speaking, to what one says. This pattern of empty speech, which we have known as an esthetic tradition in French Dada and Surrealism as *blague*, describes that narcissistic equilibrium of perpetual double negation that reflects and reveals the contradictions in mythical everyday thought and language—the deposit of ideology.

It is this mode of speech that has separated itself from life in order to contradict life that has already separated itself from speech. In a poem called "Ma Rhétorique," published in 1966 (and later used as a tape-recorded text repeated *ad infinitum* by Broodthaers, accompanied by the chatter of a live parrot in its cage), Broodthaers confesses to that mode of speaking:

> Moi Je dis Je Moi Je dis Je
> Le Roi des Moules Moi Tu dis tu
> Je tautologue. Je conserve. Je sociologue.

> Je manifeste manifestement. Au niveau de
> Mer des moules, j'ai perdu le temps perdu.
> Je dis je, le Roi des Moules, la parole des moules.[13]

Mussels, egg shells, plaster casts, suitcases (the husk, the cast, the empty shell), are therefore, from 1964 up to 1967, the most attractive objects and materials for Broodthaers' accumulations, assemblages, and constructs. They seem to embody literally his prime concern: to distinguish the limits between outside husk and inside kernel, frame and body, the interaction between object and subject, or in more precise terms, the gradual transgressions from living dialectics to cultural reification, which determine artistic production. The epithet "King of Mussels" is the grotesque but perfectly accurate description of that artistic role, and its empty mode of narcissistic speech mirrors its surrounding reification, yet it is condemned to continue these passive, pointless, and powerless gestures. Again, Broodthaers' own statements are as ambivalent as they are precise:

> Mussels, eggs, graceless objects without any content other than the air. Only their shells, which obviously express their emptiness. We have to look at the base of things. With my words I deliver reality to you.[14]

In the very same volume of poetry that Broodthaers cast in plaster to transform it into his first object/sculpture, *Pense-Bête,* we find poems that deal with the very phenomenon:

> "The Mussel"
>
> This trickster has avoided the mold of society
> by casting itself into its own proper mold.
> Therefore it is perfect.

Or, in "The Medusa," another animal poem in the same volume, he writes, "the jelly fish is perfect, no shell, nothing but body."

Material and primary process are analogous phenomena, and similarly, functional language on a primary level of discourse is analogous to the esthetic practice of poetry (as opposed to a secondary, mythical level of ideological appropriation).

Broodthaers perceives the various processes that lead into plastic material concretion as processes of reification, commodification, and ideological appropriation. These are the criteria that determine the object-nature of the work of art under capitalism—its shell, its mold, its framework, its form of institutional circulation and commercial distribution is understood as a hidden mode of alienation and domination. This paradoxical nature of the visual arts and their present-day reality (as opposed to Broodthaers' fiction of an artistic past where production and reception were primarily determined by the historical process of political engagement and the formation of individual consciousness)[15] is concretized in the dialectical status of his very first work, the sculpture *Pense-Bête*. With this work he enters that discourse and from 1964 onwards, he develops it with ever increasing acumen and poignancy. He later commented on this work, which terminated his failure as a poet and began his career as an artist:

> For me, this book is an object of interdiction. … Here you cannot read the book without destroying its plastic qualities. I believed that this concrete gesture would have confronted the viewer with this interdiction. But very much to my surprise the viewer reacted in a totally different manner than I had expected. … Nobody was curious to read the text, not knowing whether they were looking at interred prose or poetry, sad or pleasant. Nobody was affected by the interdiction.[16]

The transition from language to object, the object-language of art, and art's capitulation to the status of language are the critical points of Broodthaers' investigation. If material concretion, objectivation within the discourse of art, has become impossible without being simultaneously appropriated by the ideology of the culture industry, and thereby made to support and affirm the very same socio-political conditions that it originally set out to negate, then that discourse itself has to be critically negated. The paradox and dilemma, however, is that this critical negation itself has to assume the status of the object-discourse within which it inscribes itself, unless that critical position wants to accept the idealist fallacy that Broodthaers perceived in most of so-called Conceptual art; that is, the final reification of language under the pretense of liberating art discourse from its object status. Thus, the very same negativity of the objects in Broodthaers' work then entails and ensures their essentially allegorical character as they radically deny any material and formal anticipatory solutions that the visual-plastic discourse traditionally seems to suggest. As allegorical objects they negate the contemporary ideological life of objects and, at the same time, are reminiscent of their past material potential. Broodthaers' position seems to take into account Adorno's criticism of avant-garde art practice:

> Even within radical art there is still so much falsehood, because by anticipating a construction of genuine historical potentiality, in fact art neglects to construct it.[17]

Broodthaers aligns himself within that iconoclastic tradition that denies not only the validity of art's anticipatory vision but, more precisely, insists on revealing the political dependence and ideological determination of an avant-garde practice that perceives itself as acting in a realm of neutral autonomy. One of the key concepts of Modernism has been the idea that the painter operates within strictly self-referential and esthetic parameters, and that means, since the turn of the century, non-representational perceptual and spatial parameters. This tradition of the neutral perceptual, psychological, and/or phenomenological approach to three-dimensional visual phenomena has one of its modernist origins in Cézanne, and this concept is at the center of Broodthaers' criticism. His often seemingly absurd and obscure statements (that may appear redundant, like an eccentric confusion of art history) start to make sense if one looks at them as a critical reading against the grain of art history's self-practiced historical neutrality. For example:

> I am neither painter nor violinist. What really interests me is Ingres. I am not interested in Cézanne and his apples.[18]

Or, when taking about his films:

> In the publicity for this program [films at Brussels, December, 1972] there have appeared the words "essential complement to his visual art" and elsewhere "experimental films." These do not seem to me appropriate to describe the films which I wish to show. It is not cinematographic art ... it is no more and no less than something to talk about like a picture by Meissonier or Mondrian. ... These are just films.[19]

In Broodthaers' terminology, which appears to be as eccentric and idiosyncratic as it is radically negating and criticizing the *idées reçues* of esthetic ideology, this concept of pure plastic art and the neutrality of its spatial operations and containers is polemically demolished in the term "the conquest of space." Accomplished shortly before his death in 1976, one of his very last works is a tiny book (25 × 38 mm) featuring the black silhouettes of the geographical/political shapes and outlines of nations from America to South Africa in alphabetical order. It bears this title: *La conquête de l'espace: Atlas à l'usage des artistes et des militaires* (The Conquest of Space: Atlas for the Use of Artists and the Military).[20]

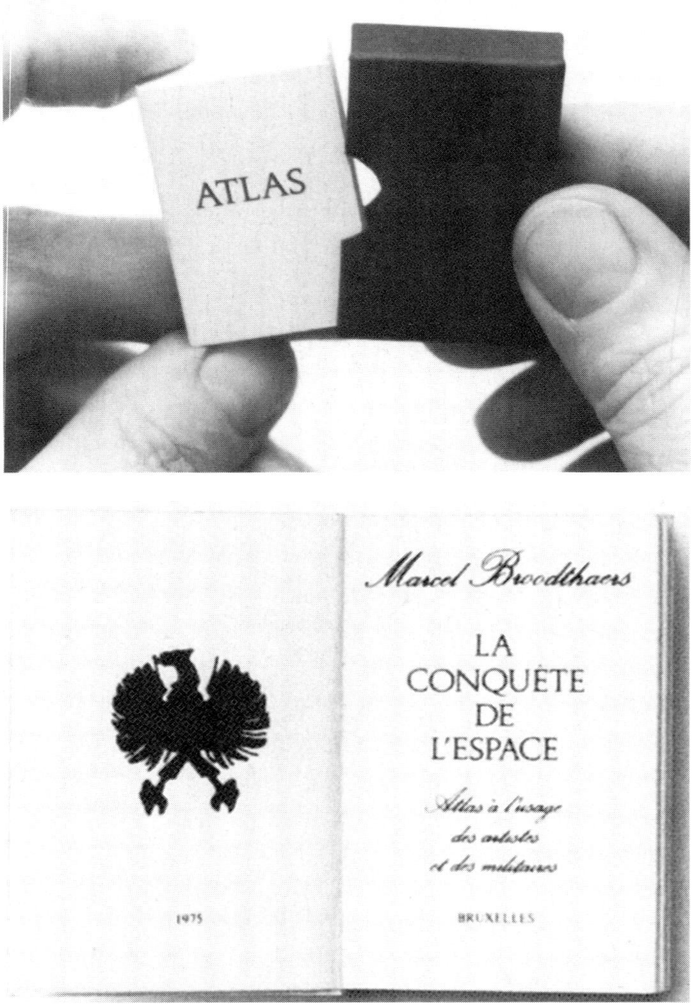

Marcel Broodthaers, *La conquête de l'espace: Atlas à l'usage des artistes et des militaires (The Conquest of Space: Atlas for the Use of Artists and the Military)*, 1975. 38 pp. Edition of 55. Offset print on paper, boxed, 4.4 × 2.9 cm (38 × 25 mm). Published by Lebeer Hossmann (Brussels). © 2015 The Estate of Marcel Broodthaers/Artists Rights Society (ARS), New York/ SABAM, Brussels.

This mock stratagem demarcates precisely the degree to which avant-garde practice, adhering to the delusion that its operations are executed in a historically neutral space, becomes all the more the object of ideological mythification; or more accurately, generates and constitutes that very myth that covers the conditions whose existence and impact the avant-garde denies in its claim for esthetic autonomy. *The Conquest of Space*, with its massivity and concreteness of latent ideology (i.e., socioeconomical and political interests behind the apparatus of the cultural industry), proportionally generates the formal abstraction and neutrality of accredited *autonomous space*. This is the base or underlying apparatus that Broodthaers had in mind when, contemplating the mussels, he requested "that we look at the base of things." Moreover, the seam between this base and its permanent transitions into the secondary language of myth concealing that base is the slim line of Broodthaers' dialectical esthetic critique. His concept of *space* is historically concrete and determined by the political and ideological functions that the work of art assumes in its cultural extrapolation; his concept of *form* is that of *form-determination* in Marx's sense of *circulation-form* (which implies that objects are determined by their commodity-form). In regard to esthetic production, this means that the work is defined by both the institutional framework that guarantees the work's semblance of autonomy as well as by its distributional principles, its circulation-form of *cultural* commodity. Broodthaers' critique is therefore directed dialectically at both the institutionalized autonomy of the avant-garde practice and its historical inefficiency, as well as the commodity status of avant-garde products and the distributional and institutional frameworks governing it. Numerous statements made by Broodthaers made clear that he was systematically addressing these issues in his work:

> Essentially the subject is denied by its use as an operational means for the conquest of space, even if one claims to be engaged only in semantic research or a quest for the Holy Grail. The subject is a type of fraud if it is only considered on the level of thinking.[21]

Or, a few years later:

> If space is really the fundamental elements of artistic construction (either in the form of language or in the form of materials), I would have to oppose it with the philosophy of what has been written with a certain common sense. … The constant search for the definition of space serves only to cover up the essential structure of art as a process of reification. Every individual, perceiving a function of space, and even more so if it is a convincing one, appropriates it either mentally or economically. … Space can only lead to paradise.[22]

Broodthaers' versatility in imbuing visual signs with historical material concretions and including the full range of their inherent dialectics (the contradictions of the reality from which they arise as ideological meaning, as well as their own contradictory nature in shaping and determining that reality and our reading of it) is puzzling. No sign seems to have the same meaning twice, no semiological element or function is secured. No wonder then that the rebus, the riddle that challenges the reader's vision and dictates reading to the eyes with the pleasantry of children's games, has been one of Broodthaers' favorite strategies to decipher the interdependency and interaction of fragmented language and reified imagery, which both constitute the discourse of art as ideology. In one of these works, which he conceived as a cover design for the English art magazine *Studio International*, children's alphabet blocks are assembled on the front page to form the line fin(e) (a)rts, with the letter *e* having been substituted by the image of the eagle and the letter *a* by an ass, thus making the sentence into another pun on the perpetual renewed proclamation of the end of the arts.[23] That this work is again a polemical statement on certain forms of Conceptual art prevailing in the early 1970s becomes even more apparent when we look at the back of the same magazine where a paid advertisement, designed by

Broodthaers for a commercial gallery, appears disguised as art (or vice versa). The advertisement employs again the same alphabet blocks in no apparent order. Images (of a horse, zebra, watch, dog, umbrella) alternate with alphabetical letters and numbers. Each cube carries a handwritten caption that constructs the following sentence: "éléments du discours ne peuvent servir l'art, une faute d'ortographe cachée vaut un fromage" (elements of discourse cannot serve art, a hidden orthographer's mistake is worth a cheese).[24] The same attitude had been voiced by Broodthaers in a theoretically more explicit aphorism which again was part of a cover design for an art magazine. The text read "View: according to which any artistic theory functions as an advertisement for the artistic product, whereas the artistic product functions as an advertisement for the powers under which it was born. There is no other space, but this view according to which … etc., etc., …"[25]

A series of works, begun in 1968, concomitant with the foundation of the Musée d'Art Moderne, Département des Aigles, Section XIXe Siècle and concluded around 1971, when Broodthaers began a new type of serially arranged typographical "paintings," screened on traditional canvas, is entirely based on the rebus principle. These plaques, printed and embossed plastic sheets (85 cm ×120 cm) look like the predecessors—or afterimages—of advertisements and commercial signs from the period of transition from private manufacture to organized enterprise. Their outdated "factory-style" (in material, production, and typography) situates them with that of the Duchampian readymades and they share with them the secret attraction and delusion of dysfunctionalized objects that seem to bespeak a more humane past stage in the development of the means of production. Broodthaers called them *poèmes industriels*. As they shift between vision and reading they balance object and sign. Hybrids of ideogram and pictograph, their function is to simultaneously perform and deconstruct the ideological and the esthetic sign. The epistemological relevance on the level of the integration of language into art is comparable to that of Duchamp's in regard to readymade objects. In Broodthaers' *poèmes industriels* it becomes apparent that language, under the extreme pressure of its collective abuse as a means for oppression and exploitation, can only function as poetry if it disintegrates into its own allegory: the plaques are more monuments to the individual word than are the serialized, objectified language of concrete poetry that marked Broodthaers' original former position and practice as a poet.

In Broodthaers' *poèmes industriels* the syntactic structure, consistent with the development of poetry since Dada (and since Tzara and Schwitters in particular), has been fragmented and stripped to the discrete semantic unit, the enigmatically purposeless word. The lowest, most subservient and functional elements of syntax and grammar—the punctuation marks—suddenly appear to be liberated from their roles and assume a gregarious visual importance in their own right; the disproportionately enlarged commas or acute accents, as for example in the plaques *Cinéma I* and *Cinéma II*, appear to be floating in the typographical field like mechanically produced clouds from a factory chimney, whereas the blown-up periods as marks of punctuation and order in *Cinéma I* take on the faces of clocks with their hands at noon in the identically cast, but differently screened relief-plaque *Cinéma II*. The word "*modèle*," in both plaques identical as a quote from an industrial commodity, underlines the "patented" nature of objectified language. The same act of typographical liberation occurs in the enlarged exclamation mark in the plaque *La signature, serie I, tirage illimité*, 1969, where the rhetorical sign is juxtaposed with an unidentifiable flag (whose missing center stripe suggests that the exclamation mark was cut out of its body) and embossed words (an alphabetical enumeration of the centers of political student revolts at that time: Amsterdam, Berlin, Nanterre, Paris, Milan, Brussels). These words remain blind-stamped letters, whereas the periods separating them are printed in color. The most complex of the plaques is the first, bearing the title *Museum—enfants non admis* (Museum—children not admitted). Again, as in the *Cinéma* signs, the

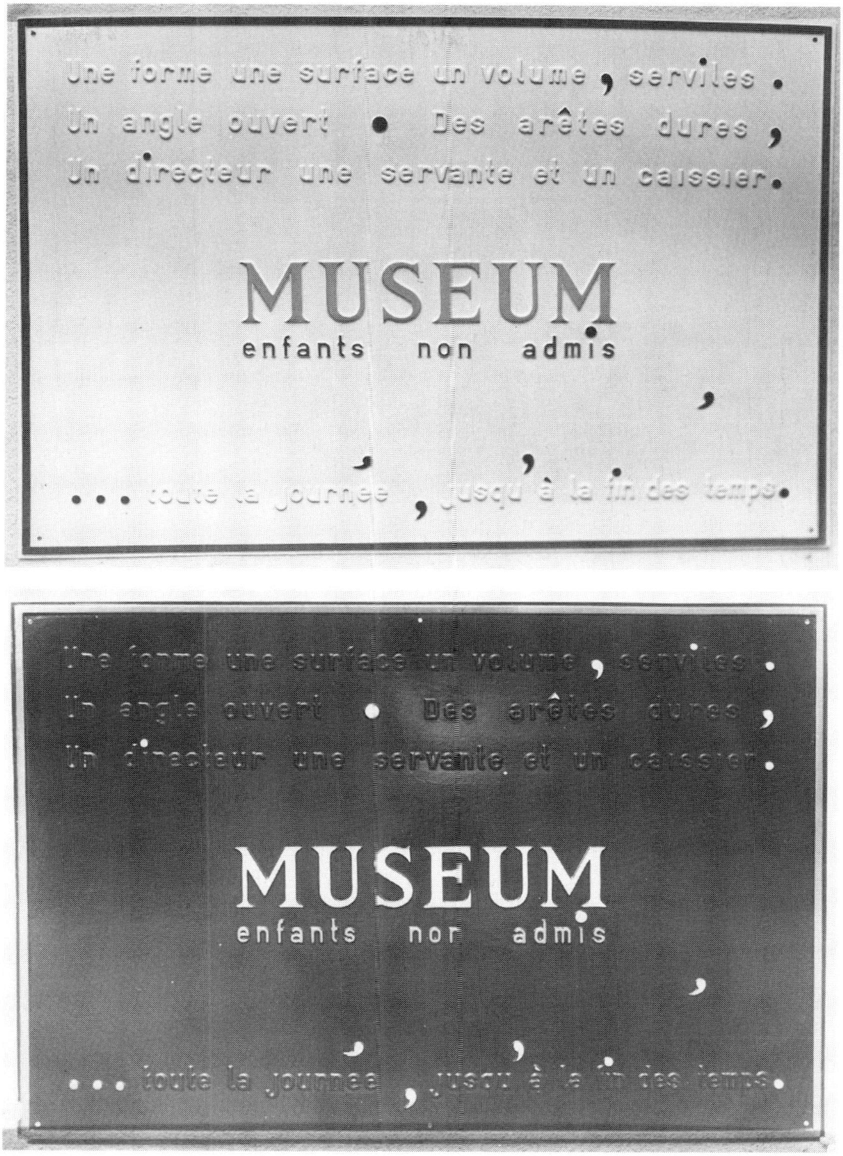

Marcel Broodthaers, *Museum—Enfants non admis*, 1968–1969. Edition of 7. Blind stamp and print on plastic board, 32⅔ × 47½ in. (83 × 120 cm). Private collection. © 2015 The Estate of Marcel Broodthaers/Artists Rights Society (ARS), New York/SABAM, Brussels.

name of the primary institution of the cultural industry is centered in a white rectangular field. The four lines of text, blind-stamped, with the exception of the conspicuously black periods, commas, and acute and circumflex accents that seem to float randomly like amoebas (or perhaps tadpoles) over the field, read as follows: "A form, a surface, a volume, subservient, an open angle, hard fishbones, a director, a female servant and a cashier. All day long, until the end of times."

This is a listing of the essentials of the institutionalized and rigidly ordered hierarchical space of avant-garde culture from which life has been banned and has vanished. The haunting melancholy of this still life of hardly visible white words is a surreal juxtaposition of metonymy and metaphor. Metonymy is employed insofar as historically isolated and disconnected elements of a purely formal discourse of plasticity in art—form, surface, volume, and open angle—are disqualified as subservient and pointless in comparison to the power of the political structure that dominates them, a structure here represented by "director and employee" and the economic order. Similarly, metaphor describes the work's evocation of a blank and hard skeleton of a dead fish, a true still-life element from the iconographical tradition of *vanitas* representations, which seems to be materially concretized and reflected in the blank white surface of the industrially produced plaque and colorless letter-relief.

It remains to be seen whether the fishbone metaphor relates to the obsolete elements of a formalist artistic discourse, or whether it refers to the abstractness of the governing power structure, or whether it quite simply stands for a vanished life, with its humorous dialectical complement in the phrase prohibiting children access into the realm of reification. The bottom line of the relief adds the equivalent notion of temporal experience to the object experience of the still life: the *semper idem* of the perpetually identically *toute la journée* and *jusqu'à la fin des temps* coalesces presence and future into an abstraction of spatialized time, where there is no room for development and growth, change and dialectical flux, continuum and memory.

However, to the same degree that Broodthaers reveals the historical nature of esthetic reality in its contemporary practices of cultural institutionalization and commercial reification to be a seemingly hermetically closed system that does not allow for any movement or dialectical change, nor any interaction with the essentially political nature of historical reality, he nonetheless insists on a dimension within human experience that subverts and rejects the stasis and passivity of reification.

The very act of reading itself achieves emancipatory potential inasmuch as it destroys the domination of the object over the subject, and liberates language and the individual's conscience from the limitations and bonds of interest and function. It is at this point that the frequent image of children's alphabet cubes and awkwardly drawn or painted, scattered, discrete letters become transparent hieroglyphs for new reading lessons—Broodthaers once summarized a whole group of these works in an exhibition under the title: *Apprendre à lire* (Learn to read); such operations suggest a new alphabet for a history lesson that would still have to be learned by mankind.

The formal and material transformation of the alphabet as the basic condition of radically (in the true sense of starting from the root of the word) changing our material apprehension of the world, is at the origin of the typographical revolution that accompanies the major movements of twentieth-century art. El Lissitzky, for example, in his comments on the design for his children's book, *Of Two Squares*, stated:

> By reading, our children are already acquiring a new plastic language, they are growing up with a different relationship to the world and to space, to shape and to color; they will surely also create another book.[26]

In Marcel Broodthaers' vision, one that has been broken by the unaltered conditions of bourgeois capitalist life, this new alphabetical order is perceived dialectically as both more emphatic in its anticipation and more pathetic in its avowed skepticism:

> This would be an a.b.c.d.e.f. ... of diversion, an art of diversion ... g.h.i.j.k.l.m.n.o.p.q.r.s.t.u.v.w.x.y.z. ... To forget. To sleep, serenely, well thinking. New horizons shape themselves. I see new horizons approaching me and the hope of another alphabet (see catalogue).[27]

The deadpan statement "(see catalogue)" that crudely terminates the visionary and divinatory promises becomes even more grotesque as a negation of such Utopian euphoria when one actually discovers that the catalog pages that Broodthaers refers to are simple reproductions of typesetters' font-schemes and font-sample-sheets that exemplify various typefaces by spelling "The Fine Art of Printing" in various sizes.

When one realizes that these readymade typographical schemes are a contribution to a catalog of so-called Conceptual art, the work's dialectic comes full circle. It insists on the collective historical necessity for the "new alphabet," even as it denies the validity of the individual artist's premature solutions by denouncing them as susceptible to cultural and ideological appropriation (since they are esthetic decisions, as opposed to material, political ones) and by negating them in the deadpan confrontation with the font-schemes of basic typography. It is on those grounds that one has to understand why Broodthaers' extremely developed sense of the meaning of typography leads him to a typographical design in his numerous books and prints as well as in his paintings and films, a design that assumes the mask of a conservative classicism. Obviously, for the reasons indicated above, he could not align his usage of written language with the revolutionary typography of Dada and Constructivism. By negating their validity for his own

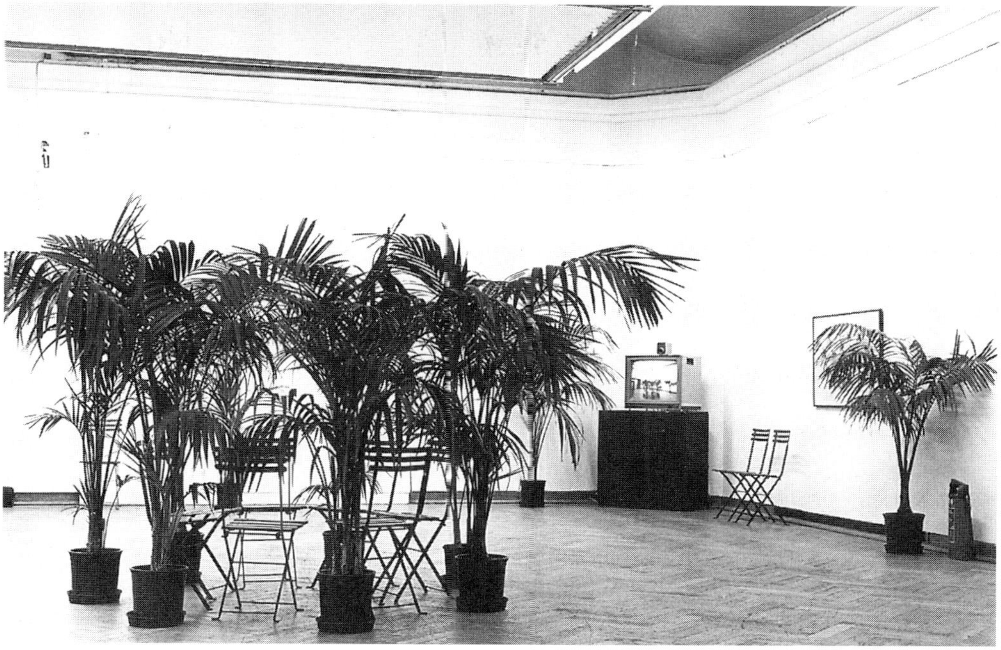

Marcel Broodthaers, *Un Jardin d'Hiver*, first version, in *Carl Andre, Marcel Broodthaers, Daniel Buren, Victor Burgin, Gilbert & George, On Kawara, Richard Long, Gerhard Richter*, Palais des Beaux-Arts, Brussels, January 9–February 3, 1974. 36 palm trees in pots (1.75 m × 2.20 m); 6 nineteenth-century photographic prints, from a book, framed, 31⅘ × 49 in. (81 × 124.5 cm); 16 folding garden chairs painted, iron and wood; 2 vitrines containing 16 nineteenth-century original gravures; 4 exhibition catalogs; and video monitor with camera on a column wrapped with red cloth.

work and its historical context, however, he continued all the more to insist on the original subversion and poetical potential of the new alphabets and their typographical concretion.

NOTES

First published in *Artforum* 18, no. 9 (May 1980): 52–59. All translations by Benjamin H. D. Buchloh unless otherwise noted. Minor corrections have been made for consistency.

1. Marcel Broodthaers, interview with Irmeline Lebeer, "Dix-mille francs de récompense," in *Marcel Broodthaers*, exh. cat. (Brussels: Palais des Beaux Arts, 1974), p. 66.

2. See Marie-Pascale Gildemyn, in *Marcel Broodthaers*, pp. 10, 26.

3. Broodthaers, interview with Irmeline Lebeer, "Dix-mille francs de récompense," p. 64.

4. Marcel Broodthaers, invitation card for exhibition for Galerie St. Lambert, Brussels, 1964, n.p.

5. Marcel Broodthaers, in Ludo Beekers, "Interview with Marcel Broodthaers," *Museums Journal* 15, no. 4 (Amsterdam, 1970): 66.

6. Ibid., p. 70.

7. Marcel Broodthaers, invitation card for exhibition at Galeries d'aujourd'hui, Brussels, 1965, n.p.

8. Marcel Broodthaers, "Comme du beurre dans un sandwich," *Phantomas* 51/61 vol. 12 (Brussels, 1965): 295.

9. Broodthaers, "Marcel Broodthaers par Marcel Broodthaers," *Journal des Beaux Arts* 1068 (Brussels, 1965): 5.

10. Marcel Broodthaers, in Ludo Beekers, "Interview with Marcel Broodthaers," p. 66.

11. A much closer connection can be traced between Broodthaers and the Italian artist Piero Manzoni, who, even though not a Nouveau Réaliste in the strict sense of their manifesto, shared a whole range of their programmatic concerns about the interrelationships between art and reality.

His sense for organic materials and processes in art, as opposed to those of the classical categories of the modernist tradition, his awareness of the radically changed notion of the readymade concept, connect his work much more directly with that of Broodthaers' than that of the Nouveaux Réalistes.

He declared Marcel Broodthaers in his certificate no. 71 on February 23, 1962, as "an authentic work of art for all intents and purposes" for lifetime. And Broodthaers' necrologue on Manzoni, written in 1963 when he was still a poet, clearly reveals the deep respect and friendship he felt for this extraordinary artist:

> Manzoni is dead, physically dead. He was young. Is there a connection between his untimely death and the attitude that he took on in the context of art? It is most certain that insisting on this kind of humor was not a very comfortable position to have taken. And if this should be the reason, then our inquiry into artistic events, into all kinds of events, will have to be profound and thorough. In any case, Manzoni will be in the history books of the terrible twentieth century.

See Marcel Broodthaers, "Gare au Défi," *Journal du Palais des Beaux Arts* 1029 (Brussels, 1963).

12. Broodthaers, interview with Irmeline Lebeer, "Dix-mille francs de récompense," p. 66.

13. See the exhibition catalog *Moules, Oeufs, Frites, Pots, Charbon, Perroquets* (Antwerp: Wide White Space Gallery, 1966), n.p.

14. Broodthaers, "Marcel Broodthaers par Marcel Broodthaers," p. 5.

15. "I believe that my exhibitions have always and still depend on souvenirs of the epoch in which, I presume, the creative situation was one of heroic and solitary form. In other words one of: Read and See. Whereas today it is: May I present to you." Broodthaers, interview with Irmeline Lebeer, "Dix-mille francs de récompense," p. 66.

16. Ibid.

17. T. W. Adorno, *Aesthetische Theorie: Gesammelte Schriften*, vol. 8 (Frankfurt: Suhrkamp, 1970), p. 129.

18. Broodthaers, interview with Irmeline Lebeer, "Dix-mille francs de récompense," p. 64.

19. See Michael Compton, *A Program of Film by Marcel Broodthaers* (London: Tate Gallery, 1977).

20. Published by Editions Lebeer Hossmann (Brussels, 1976).

21. Broodthaers, "Complément indispensable à la suite de neuf tableaux … ," *Actualité d'un Bilan* (Paris: Yvon Lambert, 1972) p. 37.

22. Broodthaers, interview with Irmeline Lebeer, "Dix-mille francs de récompense," p. 66.

23. *Studio International* 188, no. 970 (London, 1974).

24. Cheese as metaphor for money is derived from La Fontaine's fable "Le Corbeau et le Renard," which a few months before had served already as a model to unmask the hidden tricks of the trade when Broodthaers replied to an "Hommage" exhibition that was installed by two young artists in his honor with the question, "Mais qui mangera le fromage?" (But who will eat the cheese?).

25. See *Interfunktionen* 11 (Cologne, 1974).

26. El Lissitzky, quoted in Sophie Lissitzky-Kueppers, *El Lissitzky* (New York, 1968), p. 359.

27. Flyer by Marcel Broodthaers, distributed on the occasion of the first installation of *Un Jardin d'Hiver*, Brussels, January 1974.

3

Figures of Authority, Ciphers of Regression: Notes on the Return of Representation in European Painting

> The crisis consists precisely in the fact that the old is dying and the new cannot be born; in this interregnum a great variety of morbid symptoms appears.
>
> —*Antonio Gramsci, Prison Notebooks*

How is it that we are nearly forced to believe that the return to traditional modes of representation in painting around 1915, two years after the Readymade and the Black Square was a shift of great historical or aesthetic import? And how did this shift come to be understood as an autonomous achievement of the masters, who were in fact the servants of an audience craving for the restoration of the visual codes of recognizability, for the reinstatement of figuration? If the perceptual conventions of mimetic representation—the visual and spatial ordering systems that had defined pictorial production since the Renaissance and had in turn been systematically broken down since the middle of the nineteenth century—were reestablished, if the credibility of iconic referentiality was reaffirmed, and if the hierarchy of figure-ground relationships on the picture plane was again presented as an "ontological" condition, what other ordering systems outside of aesthetic discourse had to have already been put in place in order to imbue the new visual configurations with historical authenticity? In what order do these chains of restorative phenomena really occur and how are they linked? Is there a simple causal connection, a mechanical reaction, by which growing political oppression necessarily and irreversibly generates traditional representation? Does the brutal increase of restrictions in socioeconomic and political life unavoidably result in the bleak anonymity and passivity of the compulsively mimetic modes that we witness, for example, in European painting of the mid-1920s and early 1930s?

It would certainly appear that the attitudes of Neue Sachlichkeit and Pittura Metafisica cleared the way for a final takeover by such outright authoritarian styles of representation as Fascist painting in Germany and Italy and Socialist Realism in Stalinist Russia. When Georg Lukács discussed the rise and fall of expressionism in his "Problems of Realism," he seemed to be aware of the relationship of these phenomena, without, however, clarifying the actual system of interaction between proto-Fascism and reactionary art practices: "The realism of Neue Sachlichkeit is so obviously apologetic and leads so clearly away from any poetic reproduction of reality that it can easily merge with the Fascist legacy."[1] Paradoxically, however, both traditional Marxism and standard liberalism exempt artists from their responsibilities as sociopolitical individuals: Marxism through its reflection model, with its historical determinism; liberalism through its notion of the artist's unlimited and uninhibited freedom to produce and express. Thus both political views extend to artists the privilege of assuming their determinate necessity to produce unconscious representations of the ideological world.

But would it not be more appropriate to conceive of these radical shifts of the period between the wars, with such decisive selections of production procedures, iconographic references, and perceptual conventions, as calculated? Should we not assume that every artist making these decisions would be aware of their ramifications and consequences, of the sides they would be taking in the process of aesthetic identification and ideological representation?

The question for us now is to what extent the rediscovery and recapitulation of these modes of figurative representation in present-day European painting reflect and dismantle the ideological impact of growing authoritarianism; or to what extent they simply indulge and reap the benefits of this increasingly apparent political practice; or, worse yet, to what extent they cynically generate a cultural climate of authoritarianism in order to familiarize us with the political realities to come.

In order to analyze the contemporary phenomenon, it may be useful to realize that the collapse of the modernist idiom is not without precedent. The bankruptcy of capitalist economics and politics in the twentieth century has been consistently anticipated and accompanied by a certain rhythm of aesthetic manifestations. First there is the construction of artistic movements with great potential for the critical dismantling of the dominant ideology. This is then negated by those movements' own artists, who act to internalize oppression, at first in haunting visions of incapacitating and infantilizing melancholy and then, at a later stage, in the outright aculation of manifestations of reactionary power. In the present excitement over "postmodernism" and the "end of the avant-garde," it should not be forgotten that the collapse of the modernist paradigm is as much a cyclical phenomenon in the history of twentieth-century art as is the crisis of capitalist economics in twentieth-century political history: overproduction, managed unemployment, the need for expanding markets and profits, and the resultant war-mongering as the secret promise of a final solution for late capitalism's problems. It seems necessary to insist upon seeing present developments in the larger context of these historical repetitions, in their nature as response and reaction to particular conditions that exist outside the confines of aesthetic discourse.

If the current debate does not place these phenomena in historical context, if it does not see through the eagerness with which we are assured from all sides that the avant-garde has completed its mission and has been accorded a position of comfort within a pluralism of meanings and aesthetic masquerades, then it will become complicit in the creation of a climate of desperation and passivity. The ideology of postmodernism seems to forget the subtle and manifest political oppression which is necessary to save the existing power structure. Only in such a climate are the symbolic modes of concrete anticipation transformed into allegorical modes of internalized retrospection. If one realizes that melancholy is at the origin of the allegorical mode, one should also realize that this melancholy is enforced by prohibition and repression. What is taken as one of the key works for postmodernist aesthetics and the central reference for any contemporary theory of the return to allegory in aesthetic production and reception, Walter Benjamin's *The Origin of German Tragic Drama*, was written during the dawn of rising Fascism in Germany. Its author was well aware of the work's allusion to contemporary artistic and political events, as is confirmed by Benjamin's friend Asja Lacis:

> He said that he did not consider this thesis simply as an academic investigation but that it had very direct interrelationships with acute problems of contemporary literature. He insisted explicitly on the fact that in his thesis he defined the dramaturgy of the baroque as an analogy to expressionism in its quest for a formal language. Therefore I have, so he said, dealt so extensively with the artistic problems of allegory, emblems, and rituals.[2]

Or, as George Steiner describes it in his introduction to the English edition of Benjamin's study:

> As during the crises of the Thirty Years' War and its aftermath, so in Weimar Germany the extremities of political

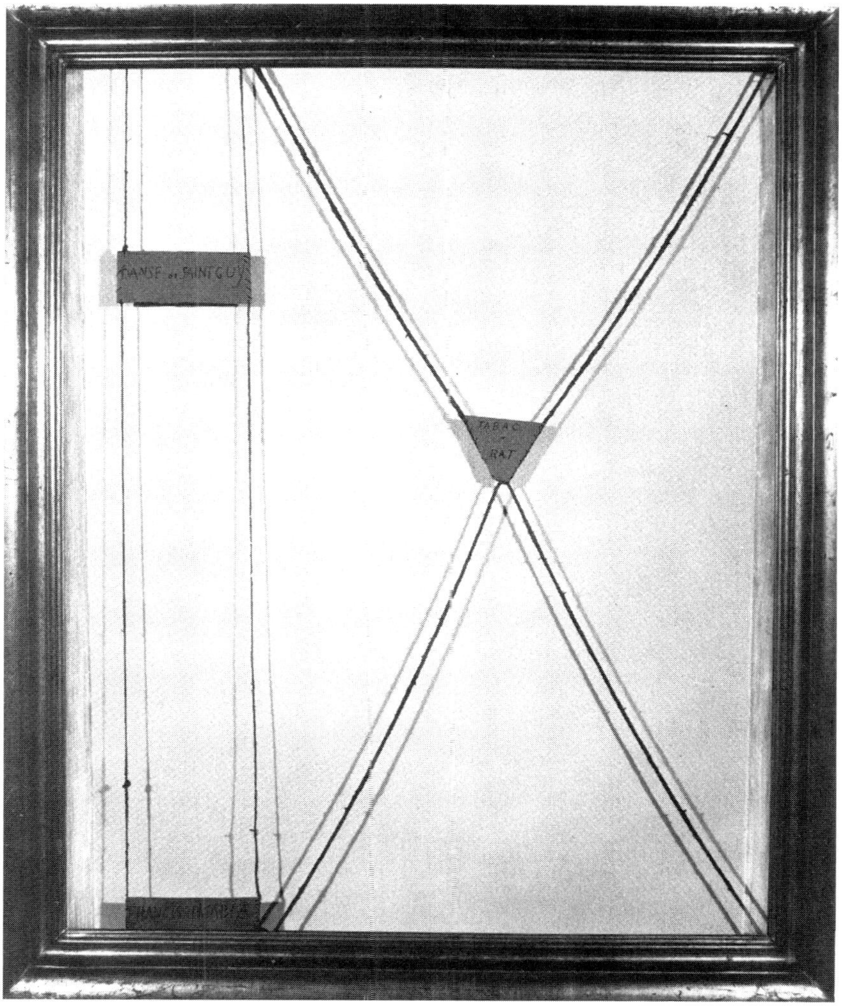

Francis Picabia, *Tabac-Rat*, 1919–1921 and ca. 1948–1949. Ink, cord, and cardboard in an open frame, 35⅞ × 27½ in. (91 × 70 cm) Succession Picabia, Paris.

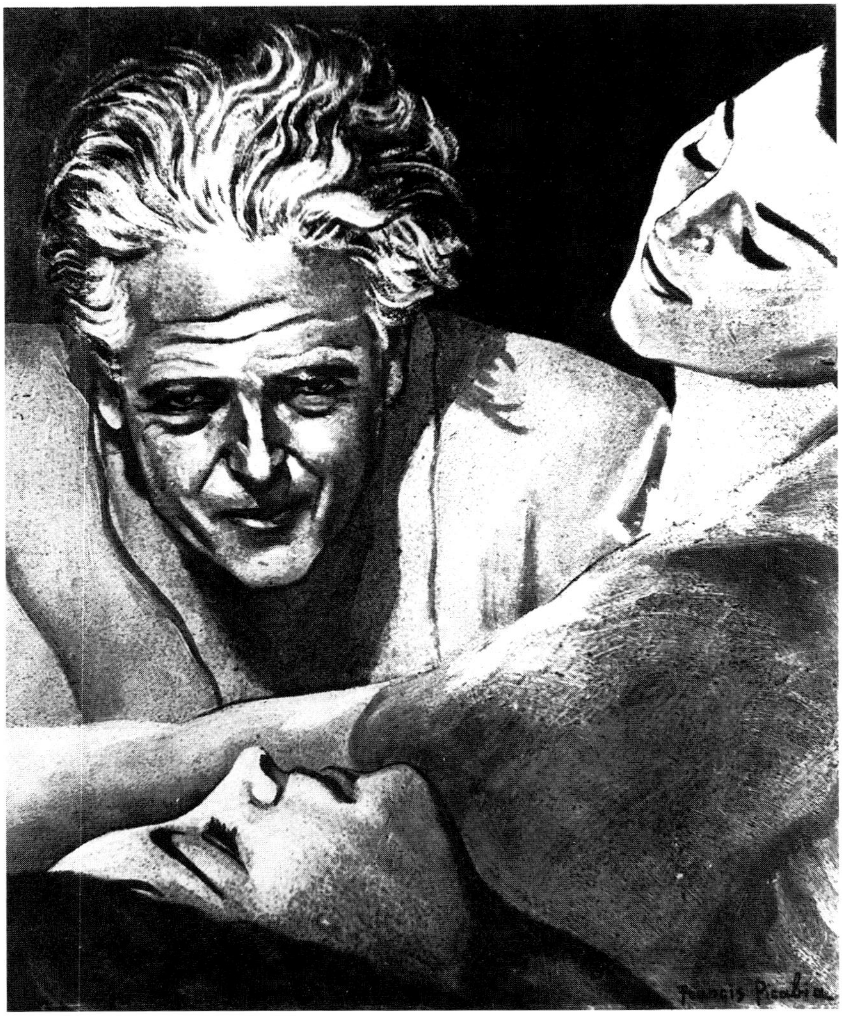

Francis Picabia, *Self-Portrait*, 1942. Oil on canvas, 32¾ × 28¼ in. (83 × 72 cm). Private collection. © 2015 Artists Rights Society (ARS), New York/ADAGP, Paris.

> tension and economic misery are reflected in art and critical discussion. Having drawn the analogy, Benjamin closes with hints towards a recursive theory of culture: eras of decline resemble each other not only in their vices but also in their strange climate of rhetorical and aesthetic vehemence. ... Thus a study of the baroque is no mere antiquarian archival hobby: it mirrors, it anticipates and it helps grasp the dark present.[3]

Repression and Representation

It is generally agreed that the first major breakdown of the modernist idiom in twentieth-century painting occurs at the beginning of the First World War, signaled by the end of Cubism and Futurism and the abandonment of critical ideals by the very artists who had initiated those movements. Facing the deadlock of their own academicization and the actual exhaustion of the historical significance of their work, Picasso, Derain, Carrà, and Severini—to name but a few of the most prominent figures—were among the first to call for a return to the traditional values of high art. Creating the myth of a new classicism to disguise their condition, they insisted upon the continuation of easel painting, a mode of production that they had shortly before pushed to its very limits, but which now proved to be a valuable commodity which was therefore to be revalidated. From this situation originated their incapacity or stubborn refusal to face the epistemological consequences of their own work. Already by 1913 their ideas had been developed further by younger artists working in cultural contexts that offered broader historical, social, and political options to dismantle the cultural tenets of the European bourgeoisie. This is particularly the case with Duchamp in Paris and New York, and Malevich and the Constructivists in Russia. But, even in Paris, such artists as Francis Picabia recognized the imminent demise of Cubism. Upon his return from his first journey to New

York in 1913, he wrote, "But, as you know, I have surpassed this stage of development and I do not define myself at all as a Cubist anymore. I have come to realize that one cannot always make cubes express the thoughts of the brain and the feelings of the psyche."[4] And in his "Manifeste de l'Ecole Amorphiste," published in a special issue of *Camera Work* in 1913, he was even more explicit: "One has said of Picasso that he studies objects in the way a surgeon dissects a cadaver. We do not want these bothersome cadavers anymore which are called objects."[5]

Even in 1923 these polemics continued among various factions of the Parisian avant-garde. On the occasion of the first performance of Tristan Tzara's play *Le Coeur à Gaz* at the Soirée du Coeur à Barbe, a fistfight broke out in the audience when one of the artists present jumped onto the stage and shouted, "Picasso is dead on the field of battle."[6] But even artists who had been allied with the Cubist movement realized by the end of the second decade that it was exhausted without, however, necessarily advocating a return to the past. Blaise Cendrars, for example, in his text "Pourquoi le cube s'effrite?" published in *La Rose rouge* (May 1919), announced the end of the relevance of the Cubist language of form. On the other hand, in the very same year a number of ideological justifications appeared for the regression that had begun around 1914–15. Among the many documents of the new attitude of authoritarian classicism is a pamphlet by the Cubist dealer Léonce Rosenberg, *Cubisme et Tradition*, published in 1920, and Maurice Raynal's "Quelques intentions du cubisme," written in 1919 and published in 1924, which stated, "I continue to believe that knowledge of the Masters, right understanding of their works, and respect for tradition might provide strong support."[7] If properly read, this statement, in its attempt to legitimize the academicization of an aging and ailing Cubist culture, already reveals the inherent authoritarian tendency of the myth of a new classicism. Then as now, the key terms of this ideological backlash are the idealization of the perennial monuments of art history and its masters, the attempt to establish a new aesthetic orthodoxy, and the demand for respect for the cultural tradition. It is endemic to the syndrome of authoritarianism that it appeal to and affirm the "eternal" or ancient systems of order (the law of the tribe, the authority of history, the paternal principle of the master, etc.). This unfathomable past history then serves as a screen upon which the configurations of a failed historical presence can be projected. In 1915, when Picasso signals his return to a representational language by portraying the Cubist poet Max Jacob, recently converted to Catholicism, in the guise of a Breton peasant, drawn in the manner of Ingres, we get a first impression of the degree of eclecticism that is necessary to create the stylistic and historical pose of classical simplicity and equilibrium, with its claim to provide access to the origins and essentials of universal human experience. Subsequently this historicist eclecticism becomes an artistic principle, and then, as in Jean Cocteau's "Rappel à l'Ordre" of 1926, it is declared the new avant-garde program.

In Picasso's work the number and heterogeneity of stylistic modes quoted and appropriated from the fund of art history increase in 1917: not only Ingres' classical portraits but, as a result of Picasso's journey to Italy in the company of Cocteau, the iconography of the Italian *commedia dell'arte* and the frescoes of Herculaneum (not to mention the sculpture of the Parthenon frieze and the white-figure vases at the Louvre, the peasant drawings of Millet, the late nudes of Renoir, and the pointillism of Seurat, as Anthony Blunt, Christopher Green, and other Picasso scholars have pointed out). And, of course, there is the self-quotation of synthetic Cubist elements, which lend themselves so easily to the high sensuousness of Picasso's decorative style of the early twenties.

Again it is Maurice Raynal who naively provides the clue to an analysis of these works when he describes Picasso's 1921 *Three Musicians* as "rather like magnificent shop windows of Cubist inventions and discoveries."[8] The free-floating availability of these Cubist elements and their interchangeability indicate how the new language of painting—now wrenched from its original symbolic function—has become reified as "style" and thus no longer fulfills any purpose but to refer to itself as an aesthetic commodity within a dysfunctional discourse. It therefore enters those categories of artistic production that by their very nature either work against the impulse to dissolve reification or are oblivious to that impulse: the categories of decoration, fashion, and *objets d'art.*

This transformation of art from the practice of the material and dialectical transgression of ideology to the static affirmation of the conditions of reification and their psychosexual origins in repression has been described as the source of a shift toward the allegorical mode by Leo Bersani:

> It is the extension of the concrete into memory and fantasy. But with the negation of desire, we have an immobile and immobilizing type of abstraction. Instead of imitating a process of endless substitutions (desire's ceaseless "traveling" among different images), abstraction is now a transcendence of the desiring process itself. And we move toward an art of allegory.[9]

This becomes even more evident in the iconography of *Pittura Metafisica,* which de Chirico and the former Futurist Carrà initiated around 1913. The conversion of the Futurists, parallel to that of the Cubists, involved not only a renewed veneration of the cultural tradition of the past—as opposed to their original fervent antipathy to the past—but also a new iconography of haunting, pointlessly assembled quotidian objects painted with meticulous devotion to representational conventions. De Chirico describes his paintings as stages decorated for imminent but unknown and threatening acts, and insists on the demons that are inherent in the objects of representation: "The metaphysical work of art seems to be joyous. Yet one has the impression that

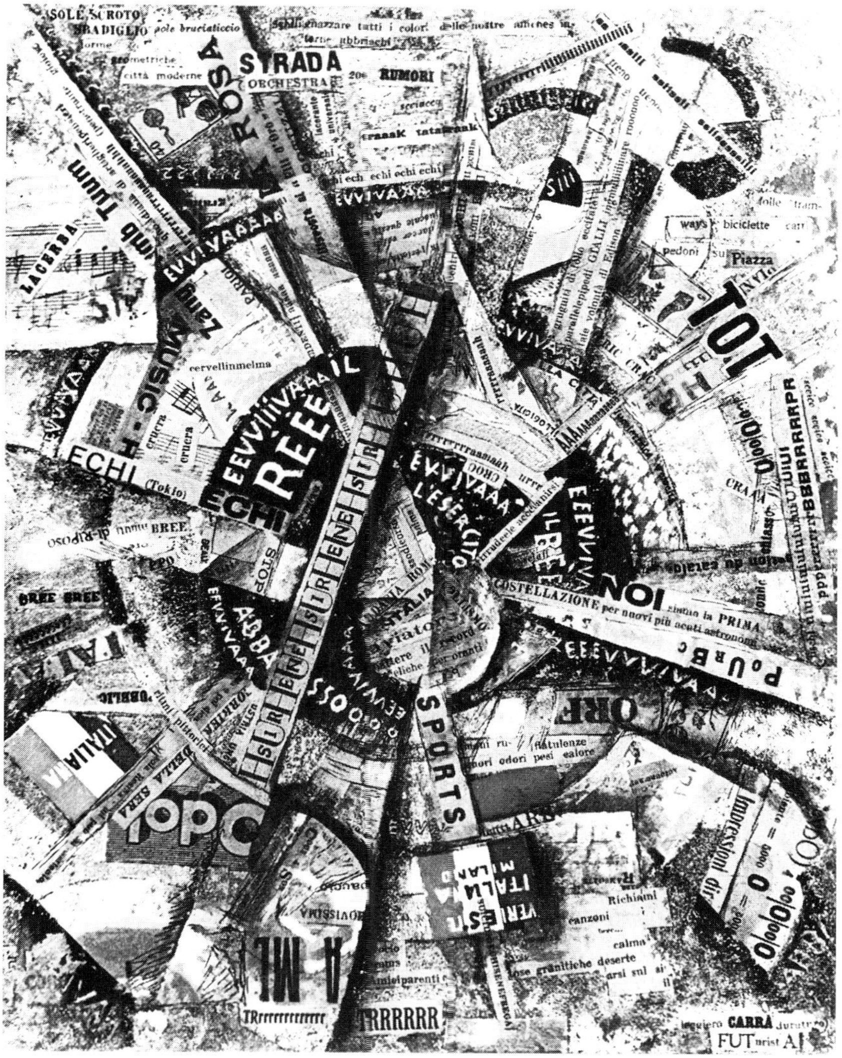

Carlo Carrà, *Patriotic Celebration*, 1914. Pasted paper and newsprint on cloth, mounted on board, 15¼ × 12 in. (38.5 × 30 cm). Private collection. © 2015 Artists Rights Society (ARS), New York/SIAE, Rome.

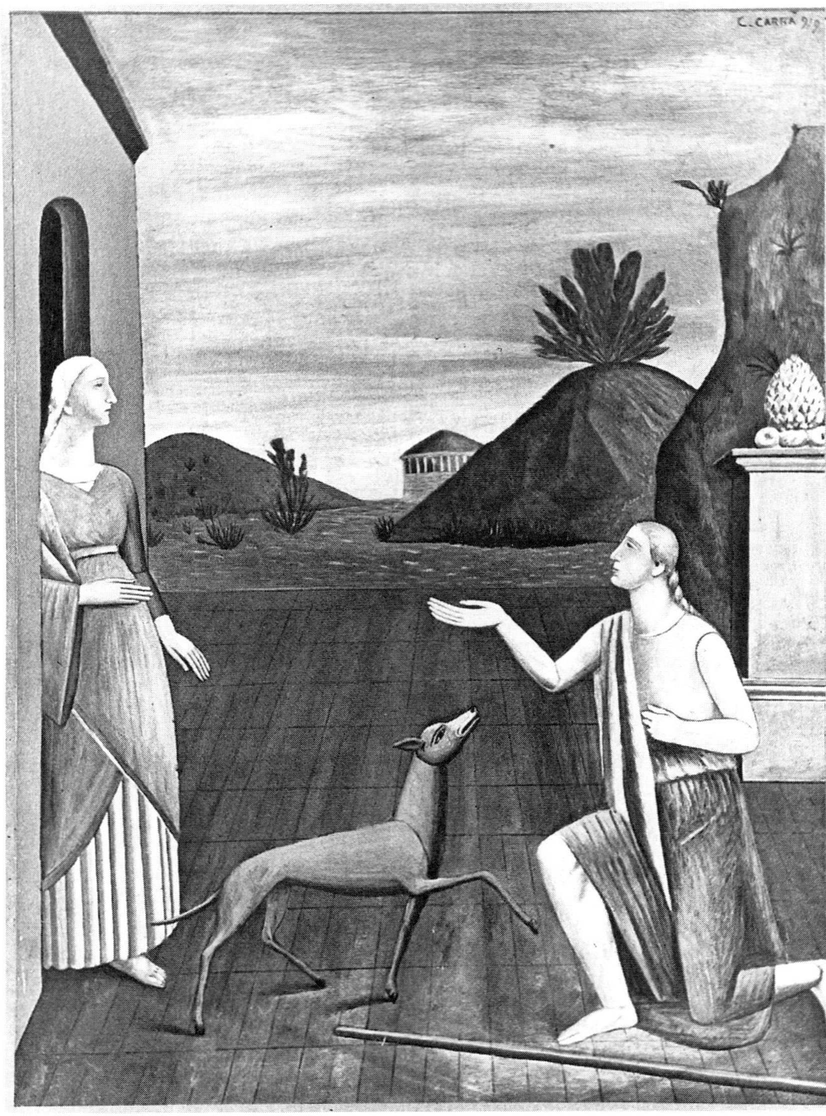

Carlo Carrà, *The Daughters of Loth*, 1919. Oil on canvas, 43¼ × 31½ in. (110 × 80 cm). Private collection. © 2015 Artists Rights Society (ARS), New York/SIAE, Rome.

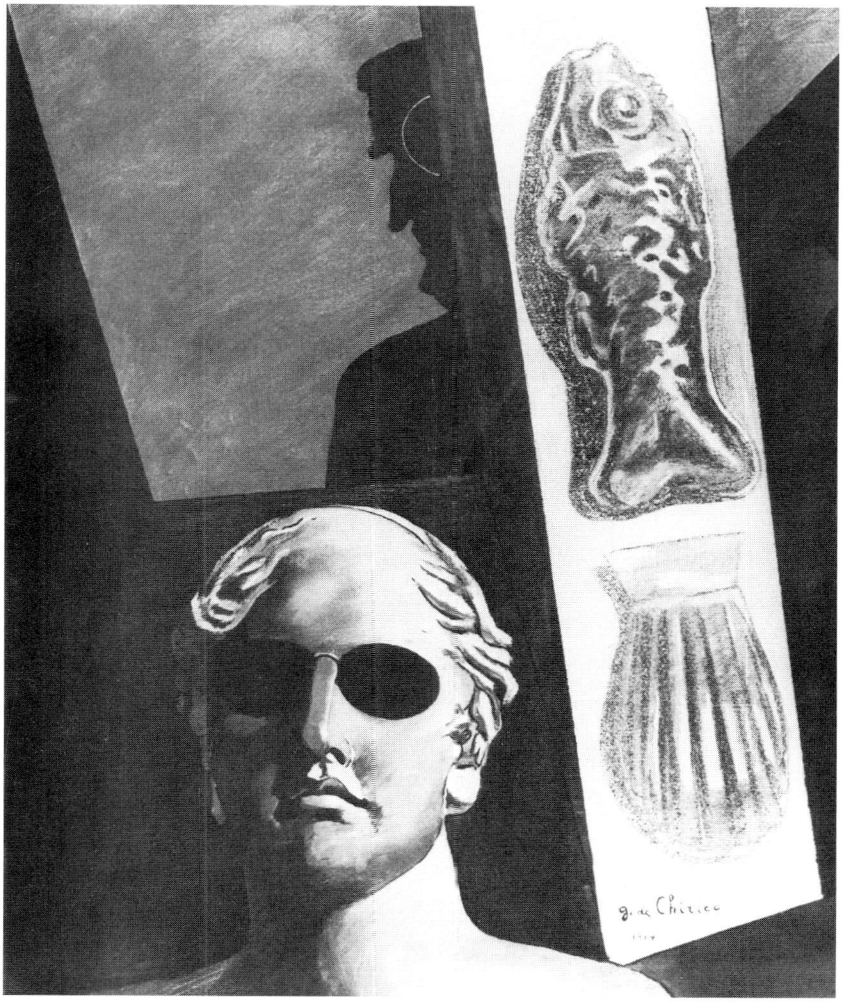

Giorgio de Chirico, *Premonitory Portrait of Guillaume Apollinaire*, 1914. Oil on canvas, $32\frac{1}{8} \times 25\frac{1}{2}$ in. (81.5×65 cm). Musée National d'Art Moderne, Centre National d'Art et de Culture Georges Pompidou, Paris. © 2015 Artists Rights Society (ARS), New York/SIAE, Rome.

something is going to happen in this joyous world."[10] De Chirico speaks of the tragedy of joy, which is nothing other than the calm before the storm, and the canvas now becomes the stage upon which the future disaster can be enacted. As the Italian historian Umberto Silva pointed out, "De Chirico is the personification of Croce's Italian disease: not quite fascism yet, but the fear of its dawn."[11]

As was the case in Picasso's conversion, the Futurists now fully repudiated their earlier nonrepresentational modes and procedures of fragmentation and pictorial molecularization. They further rejected the collage techniques by which they had forced the simultaneous presence of heterogeneous materials and procedures within the painted surface, and through which they had underlined the interaction of aesthetic phenomena with their social and political context. It is surely no accident that one of Severini's first paintings to manifest his return to history is a work called *Maternity*, which represents a mother suckling an infant in the traditional pose of the Madonna. Even more conspicuous perhaps is the case of Carrà, who had been one of the most important Futurists due to his development of non-mimetic pictorial signs, his systematic transgression of verbal and visual codes through the insertion of verbal fragments within painting, and his mechanization of pictorial production processes and their juxtaposition with pictorialized remnants of mechanical production processes. Carrà turned at that time to representational depictions of biblical scenes in the manner of Tuscan painting.

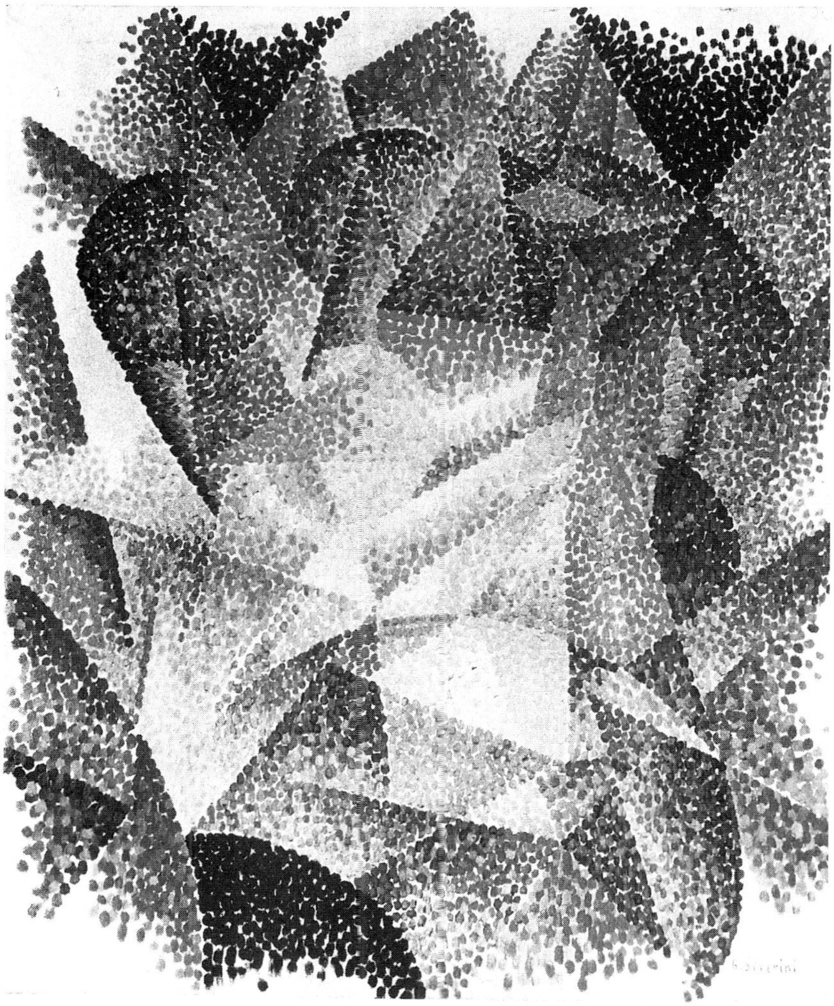

Gino Severini, *Spherical Expansion of Light (Centrifugal)*, 1914. Oil on canvas, 24⅜ × 19¾ in. (62 × 50 cm). Private collection. © 2015 Artists Rights Society (ARS), New York/ ADAGP, Paris.

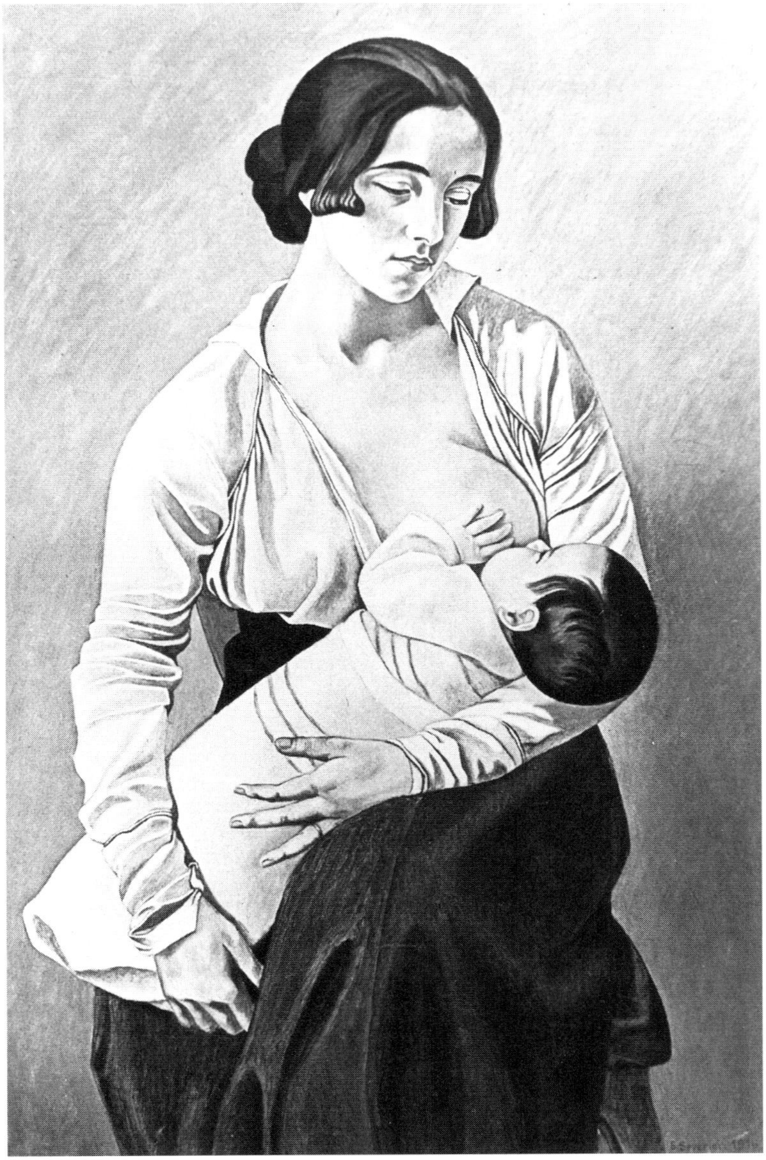

Gino Severini, *Maternity*, 1916. Oil on canvas, 36¼ × 25½ in. (92 × 65 cm). Museo dell'Academia Etrusca, Cortone. © 2015 Artists Rights Society (ARS), New York/ADAGP, Paris.

Art, Past and Master

To the very same extent that the rediscovery of history serves the authoritarian purpose of justifying the failure of modernism, the atavistic notion of the master artist is reintroduced to continue a culture oriented to an esoteric elite, thus guaranteeing that elite's right to continued cultural and political leadership. The language of the artists themselves (or rather these particular artists, for there is an opposite definition of artistic production and culture simultaneously developing in the Soviet Union) blatantly reveals the intricate connection between aesthetic mastery and authoritarian domination. Three examples from three different decades may serve to illustrate this aesthetic stance:

> Hysteria and dilettantism are damned to the burial urns. I believe that everybody is fed up now with dilettantism: whether it be in politics, literature, or painting.
>
> —Giorgio de Chirico, 1919[12]

> Socialism has only been invented for the mediocre and the weak. Can you imagine socialism or communism in Love or in Art? One would burst into laughter—if one were not threatened by the consequences.
>
> —Francis Picabia, 1927[13]

And finally, Picasso's notorious statement from 1935:

> There ought to be an absolute dictatorship … a dictatorship of painters … a dictatorship of one painter … to suppress all those who have betrayed us, to suppress the cheaters, to suppress the tricks, to suppress mannerisms, to suppress charms, to suppress history, to suppress a heap of other things.[14]

Like senile old rulers who refuse to step down, the stubbornness and spite of the old painters increase in direct proportion to the innate sense of the invalidity of their claims to save a cultural practice that had lost its viability. When, in the early 1920s, the former German Dadaist Christian Schad attempts a definition of the Neue Sachlichkeit by portraying members of the Weimar hautemonde and demimonde in the manner of Renaissance portraits; when, in 1933, Kazimir Malevich portrays himself and his wife in Renaissance costumes; then obviously the same mechanism of authoritarian alienation is at work. In a text from 1926 Schad delivers a complete account of the syndrome's most conspicuous features:

> Oh, it is so easy to turn one's back on Raphael. Because it is so difficult to be a good painter. And only a good painter is able to paint well. Nobody will ever be a good painter if he is only capable of painting well. One has to be born a good painter. ... Italy opened my eyes about my artistic volition and capacity. ... In Italy the art is ancient and ancient art is often newer than the new art.[15]

The idealization of the painter's craft, the hypostasis of a past culture that serves as a fictitious realm of successful solutions and achievements that have become unattainable in the present, the glorification of the Other culture (in this case Italy), all of these features—currently discussed and put into practice once again—recur through the first three decades of twentieth-century modernism. They seek to halt that modernism and to deny its historical necessity as well as to deny the dynamic flux of social life and history through an extreme form of authoritarian alienation from these processes. It is important to see how these symptoms are rationalized by the artists at the time of their appearance, how they are later legitimized by art historians, and how they are finally integrated into an ideology of culture.

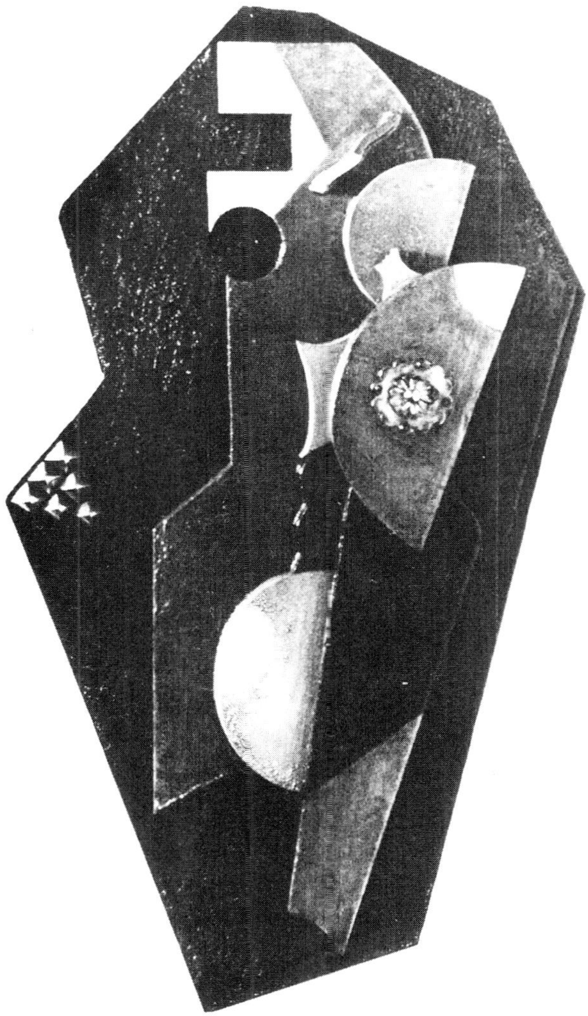

Christian Schad, *Portrait of a Woman (Relief)*, 1920. Painted wood relief with collage, 23⅝ × 11¾ × 4 in. (60 × 30 × 10 cm). Private collection.

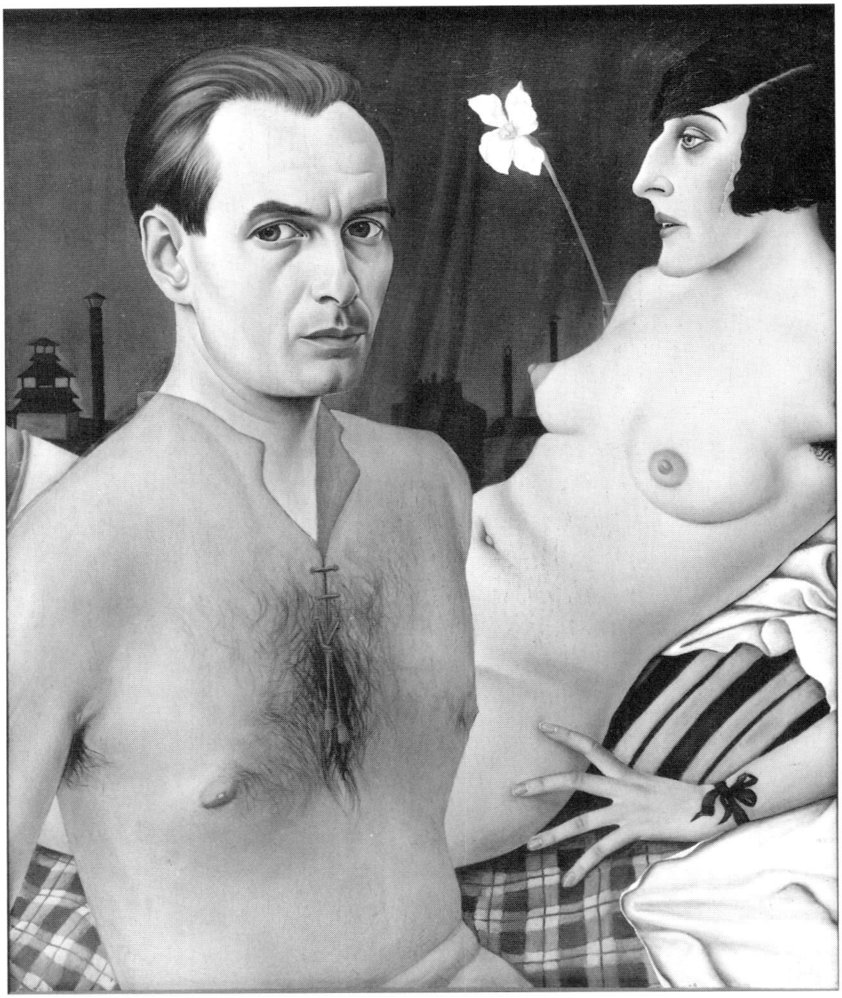

Christian Schad, *Self-Portrait with Model*, 1927. Oil on canvas, 29⅞ × 24½ in. (76 × 62 cm). Private collection. © 2015 Christian Schad Stiftung Aschaffenburg/ARS, New York/VG Bild-Kunst, Bonn.

Kazimir Malevich, *Black Cross*, 1915. Oil on canvas, 31½ × 31½ in. (80 × 80 cm). Musée National d'Art Moderne, Centre National d'Art et de Culture Georges Pompidou, Paris.

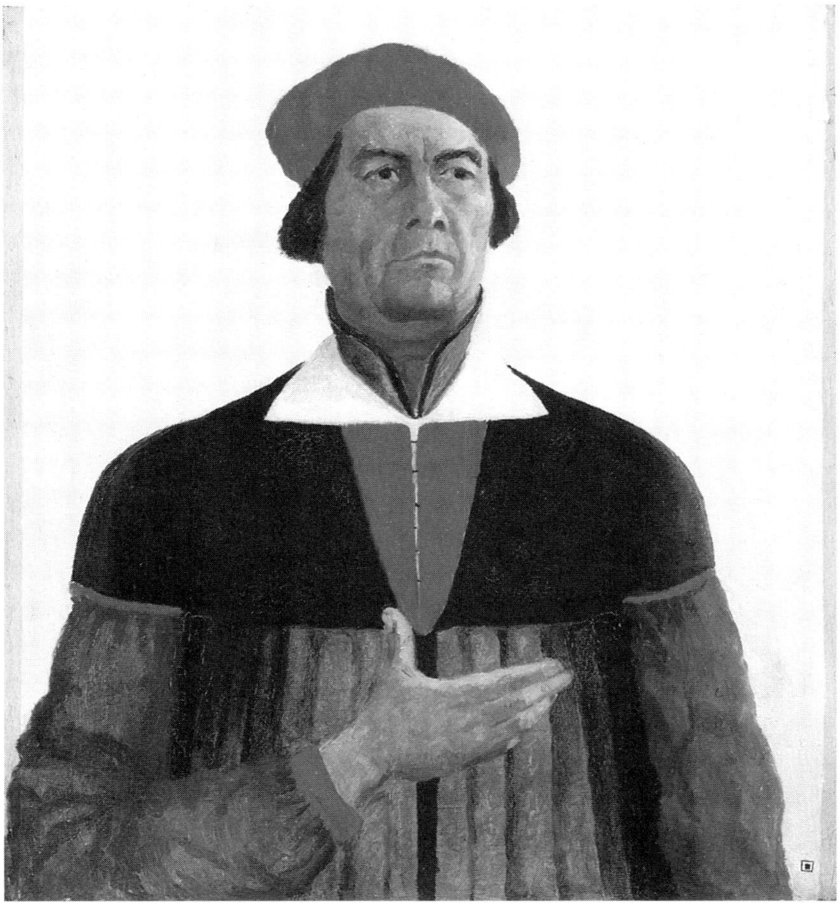

Kazimir Malevich, *Self-Portrait*, 1933. Oil on canvas, 28¾ × 26 in. (73 × 66 cm). State Russian Museum, Leningrad.

The concepts of "aesthetic paradox" and "novelty," essential features of avant-garde practice, serve as explanations for these contradictions. Here, for example, is Christopher Green's justification for Cocteau's and Picasso's neoclassicism:

> For Cocteau a return to narrative clarity and to form in the novel did not mean a denial of paradox, and in the same way neither did a return to representation in painting. Indeed it seems possible that it was at least partially out of a sense of paradox that Picasso turned against the anti-representational dogma associated with Cubism to revive Ingres in 1915. ... Cocteau suggests that where audacity had become convention—as in the Parisian avant-garde—the resurrection of the old modes could create a special kind of novelty: that looking backwards the artist could even more dramatically look forward. There is no direct evidence that Picasso consciously aimed to create such a paradox, but the fact remains ... that by turning back he did achieve novelty and that his perverse development of Synthetic Cubism and representational styles alongside one another between 1917 and 1921 was calculated to throw the paradox implicit in his progressive move backwards into the highest possible relief.[16]

The degree of congruity between Cocteau's antimodernist stance (or should we say cliché of ahistorical thought?) and the arguments against avant-garde practice in the art press's current discussion of postmodernism is striking. The stereotype of the avant-garde's audacity having become convention is, of course, used primarily by those who want to disguise their new conservatism as its own kind of audacity (Cocteau at the time of "Rappel à l'Ordre" had just turned to Catholicism). They deny the fact that conventionalization itself is a maneuver to silence any form of critical negation, and they wish to share in the benefits that bourgeois culture bestows on those who support false consciousness as it is embodied in cultural conventions. With regard to historical eclecticism, the congruity between the neoclassicists of the 1920s and the contemporary figuration is even more astounding. Intellectual acrobatics are needed to make the ideological stance look like an organic historical necessity, as opposed to a construct determined by extreme social and political factors. Whatever we are to understand by a "progressive move backwards" or "paradox as novelty," and however Green's observation of Picasso's "perverse development" indicates his limited awareness of the contradictions resulting from the art historian's need to accommodate a cultural notion of the master who necessarily moves from achievement to achievement, it becomes even more evident that the art historian's maneuvers cannot explain the contradictions when we read:

> His [Picasso's] work between 1917 and 1921, ranging as it did from a gay Synthetic Cubism to a sober Classicism repeatedly confirmed the irrelevance for him of having a style and the relevance for him of Cocteau's idea of "style." The bright color planes of Cubism are right for the carnival brilliance of the 1918 *Arlequin*, the sheer figurative weight of Roman fresco painting and of Ingres' *Madame Moitessier* were right for the monumental stability of *La Femme assise lisant*; the implication was that any style, old or new, could be adapted to Picasso's needs, could be made subject to his will.[17]

Style, the very gem of reified art-historical thinking, the fiction that there could be a pictorial mode or a discursive practice that might function autonomously—traditionally rejected by artists—is now applied by the artists to imbue these exhausted modes with historical meaning. "All the wasms have become isms," is a vulgar contemporary variation on the theme of historicism put forward by the self-styled spokesman of postmodernist architecture, Charles Jencks.

Style then becomes the ideological equivalent of the commodity: its universal exchangeability, its free-floating availability indicating a historical moment of closure and stasis. When the only option left to aesthetic discourse is the maintenance of its own distribution system and the circulation of its commodity forms, it is not surprising that all "audacities have become convention" and that paintings start looking like shop windows decorated with fragments and quotations of history.

None of the manifold features of this eclecticism should be seen as random; they confirm one another in an intricate network of historical meaning, which may, however, be read differently from the intentions of the authors or the interests of their audience and the art historians who constitute their cultural reception. This transformation of the subversive function of aesthetic production to plain affirmation necessarily manifests itself in every detail of production. The discovery of "history" as a treasure trove into which one might dip for the appropriation of abandoned elements of style is but one obvious step. The secret attraction of the iconography of Italian theater for Picasso and others at that time becomes more comprehensible in such a perspective. The Harlequins, Pierrots, Bajazzos, and Pulcinelles invading the work of Picasso, Beckmann, Severini, Derain, and others in the early 1920s (and, in the mid-1930s, even the work of the former Constructivist/Productivist Rodchenko in Russia) can be identified as ciphers of an enforced regression. They serve as emblems for the melancholic infantilism of the avant-garde artist who has come to realize his historical failure. The clown functions as a social archetype of the artist as an essentially powerless, docile, and entertaining figure performing his acts of subversion and mockery from an undialectical fixation on utopian thought.[18]

This carnival of eclecticism, this theatrical spectacle, this window dressing of self-quotation becomes transparent as a masquerade of alienation from history, a return of the repressed in cultural costume. It is essential to the functioning of historicism and its static view of history that it assemble the various fragments of historical recollection and

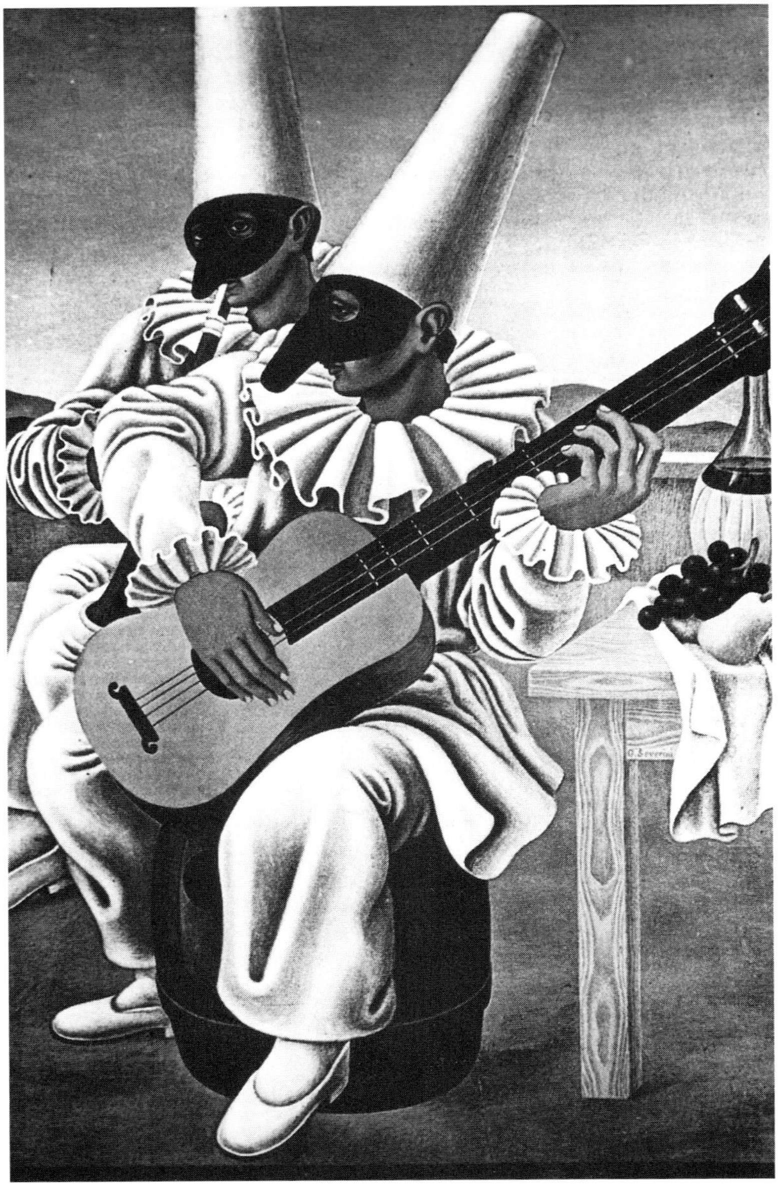

Gino Severini, *The Two Clowns*, 1922. Oil on canvas, 36¼ × 24 in. (92 × 61 cm). Gemeentemuseum, The Hague. © 2015 Artists Rights Society (ARS), New York/ADAGP, Paris.

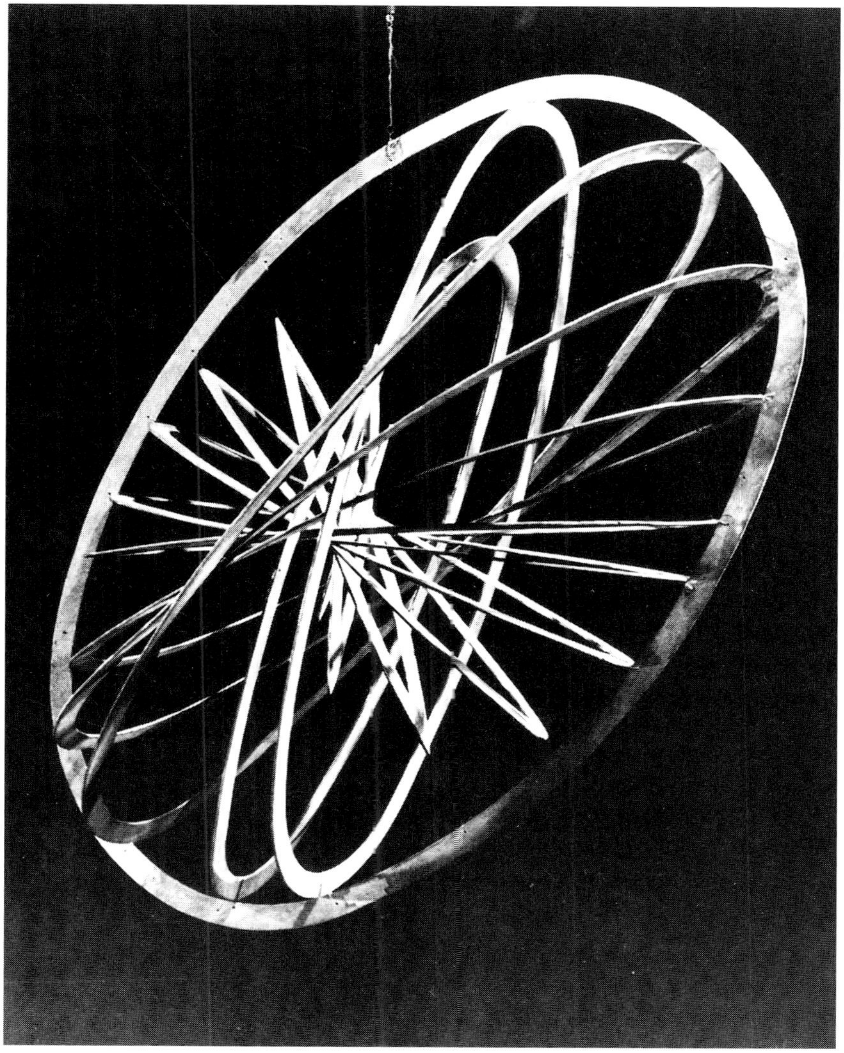

Alexander Rodchenko, *Oval Hanging Construction No. 12 (Mobil)*, ca. 1920. Painted plywood and wire, 33 × 23 × 21 in. (83.5 × 58 5 × 53.3 cm). Private collection. © Estate of Alexander Rodchenko/RAO, Moscow/VAGA, New York.

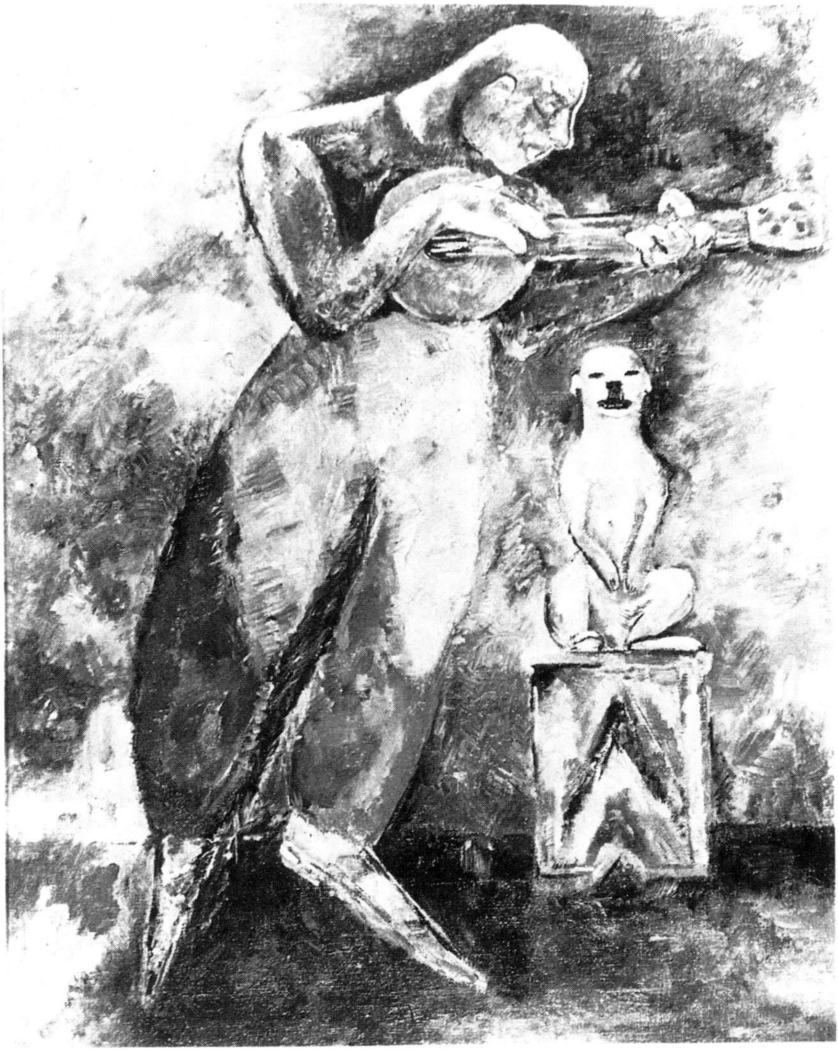

Alexander Rodchenko, *Romance (Circus Scene)*, 1935. Oil on canvas, 35½ × 27¼ in. (90.5 × 69 cm). Tretayakov Museum, Moscow. © Estate of Alexander Rodchenko/RAO, Moscow/VAGA, New York.

incantation according to the degree of projection and identification that these images of the past will provide for the needs of the present. Quite unlike the modernist collage, in which various fragments and materials of experience are laid bare, revealed as fissures, voids, irresolvable contradictions, irreconcilable particularizations, pure heterogeneity, the historicist image pursues the opposite aim: that of synthesis, of the illusory creation of a unity and totality which *conceals* its historical determination and conditioned particularity.[19] This appearance of a unified pictorial representation, homogeneous in mode, material, and style, is treacherous, supplying as it does aesthetic pleasure as false consciousness, or vice versa. If the modernist work provides the viewer with perceptual clues to all its material, procedural, formal, and ideological qualities as part of its modernist program, which therefore gives the viewer an experience of increased *presence* and autonomy of the self, then the historicist work pretends to a successful resolution of the modernist dilemma of aesthetic self-negation, particularization, and restriction to detail, through *absence*, leading to the seductive domination of the viewer by the Other, as Julia Kristeva has described the experience of alienation and perversion that ideology imposes on the subject.

The Returns of the New

> The meaning structure of art seems to have been undergoing reorganization while the market merely faltered briefly and then regained its stride. The 1970s may turn out to have been a revanchist period in which controlling influences within audience and market elites regrouped to reestablish the stratification of the audience and its objects, thereby reasserting, for example, the preeminence of painting as artifactual meaning bearer and as tangible investment.
>
> —*Martha Rosler, "Lookers, Buyers, Dealers, Makers: Thoughts on Audience"*

Perceptual and cognitive models and their modes of artistic production function in a manner similar to the libidinal apparatus that generates, employs, and receives such models. Historically, they lead a life independent of their original contexts and develop specific dynamics: they can be easily reinvested with different meanings and adapted to ideological purposes. Once exhausted and made obsolete by subsequent models, these production modes can generate the same nostalgia as does iconic representation for an obsolete code. Emptied of their historical function and meaning, they do not disappear but rather drift in history as empty vessels waiting to be filled with reactionary interests in need of cultural legitimation. Like other objects of cultural history, aesthetic production modes can be wrenched from their contexts and functions, to be used to display the wealth and power of the social group that has appropriated them.

To invest these obsolete modes with meaning and historical impact requires, however, that they be presented as *radical* and *new*. The secret awareness of their obsolescence is belied by the obsession with which these regressive phenomena are announced as innovation. "The New Spirit of Painting," "The New Fauves," "Naive Nouveau," "Il Nuove Nuove," "The Italian New Wave" are some of the labels attached to recent exhibitions of retrograde contemporary art (as though the prefix *neo* did not indicate the restoration of preexisting forms). It is significant in this regard that the German Neoexpressionists who have recently received such wide recognition in Europe (presumably to be followed by a similar acclaim in North America) have been operating on the fringes of the German art world for almost twenty years. Their "newness" consists precisely in their current historical availability, not in any actual innovation of artistic practice.

The historical specificity of iconographic codes is generally more apparent than that of production procedures and materials. It had seemed until recently, for example, that the representation of saints and clowns, of female nudes and landscapes, was entirely proscribed as an authentic expression of individual or collective experience. This proscription did not extend, though, to less conspicuous aspects of pictorial and sculptural production. Excited brushwork and heavy impasto paint application, high-contrast colors and dark contours are still perceived as "painterly" and "expressive" twenty years after works by Frank Stella, Robert Ryman, and Gerhard Richter demonstrated that the painted sign is not transparent, but is a coded structure which cannot be an unmediated "expression." Through its repetition the physiognomy of this painterly gesture so "full of spontaneity" becomes, in any case, an empty mechanics. There is only pure desperation in the recently reiterated claim of "energism," which betrays a secret foreboding of the instant reification that awaits such a naive notion of the liberating potential of apolitical and undialectical aesthetic practices.

But the intentions of the artists and their apologists remain to be understood, because contrary to their claim of psychic universality they in fact "express" only the needs of a very circumscribed social group. If "expressivity" and "sensuousness" have again become criteria of aesthetic evaluation, if we are once again confronted with depictions of the sublime and the grotesque—complementary experiential states of modernism's high-culture products—then that notion of sublimation which defines the individual's work as determined by alienation, deprivation, and loss is reaffirmed. Lillian Robinson and Lise Vogel describe this process:

> Suffering is portrayed as a personal struggle, experienced by the individual in isolation. Alienation becomes a heroic disease, for which there is no social remedy. Irony masks resignation to a situation one cannot alter or control. The human situation is seen as static, with certain external forms varying but the eternal anguish remaining. Every political system is perceived to set some small group into power, so that changing the group will not affect our "real" (that is, private) lives.

> ... Thus simply expressed, the elements of bourgeois ideology have a clear role in maintaining the status quo. Arising out of a system that functions through corporate competition for profits, the ideas of the bourgeoisie imply the ultimate powerlessness of the individual, the futility of public action, and the necessity of despair.[20]

Modernist high culture canonized aesthetic constructs with the appellation "sublime" when the artists in question had proven their capacity to maintain utopian thought in spite of the conditions of reification, and when, instead of actively attempting to change those conditions, they simply shifted subversive intentions into the aesthetic domain. The attitude of individual powerlessness and despair is already reaffirmed in the resignation implicit in a return to the traditional tools of the craft of painting and in the cynical acceptance of its historical limitations and its materially, perceptually, and cognitively primitivist forms of signification.

Such paintings, experienced by a certain audience as sensuous, expressive, and energetic, perform and glorify the ritual of instant excitation and perpetually postponed gratification that is the bourgeois mode of experience. This bourgeois model of sublimation—which has, of course, been countered by an avant-garde tradition of negation, a radical denial of that model's perpetrations of the extreme division of labor and specialization of sexual role behavior—finds its appropriate manifestation in the repeated revitalization of obsolete representational and expressive pictorial practices. It is not accidental that Balthus—champion of the bourgeois taste for high titillation with his scopophilic pictures of sleeping or otherwise unaware adolescent female nudes—has recently received renewed acclaim and is regarded as one of the patriarchal figures of the "new" figuration. Nor is it accidental that not *one* of the German Neoexpressionists or the Italian Arte Ciphra painters is female. At a time when cultural production in every field is becoming increasingly aware of, if not actively countering, the oppression of traditional role distinctions based on the construction of sexual difference, contemporary art (or at least that segment of it that is currently receiving prominent museum and market exposure) returns to concepts of psychosexual organization that date from the origins of bourgeois character formation. The bourgeois concept of the avant-garde as the domain of heroic male sublimation functions as the ideological complement and cultural legitimation of social repression. Laura Mulvey has analyzed this phenomenon in the context of the "visual pleasure" of cinematic experience:

> Woman then stands in patriarchal culture as signifier for the male other, bound by a symbolic order in which man can live out his phantasies and obsessions through linguistic command by imposing them on the silent image of woman still tied to her place as bearer of meaning, not maker of meaning.[21]

And Max Kozloff puts it explicitly in the context of the visual arts:

> Further scouting might produce more evidence that virility is often equated with the probing of space or the masterful brushing of a surface. The metaphor of sculptural extension or battling with the canvas is easily sexualized because it conflates two desirable goals associated with the energy of creation. With Expressionist theory, German and American, we are never far removed from its special aura. … The imagery of modern art, of course, is rich with overtones of masculine aggression and depersonalization of woman.[22]

The abandonment of painting as sexual metaphor, which occurred around 1915, implied not only formal and aesthetic changes but also a critique of traditional models of sublimation. This is most evident in Duchamp's interest in androgyny and in the Constructivists' wish to abolish the production mode of the individual master in favor of one oriented toward collective and utilitarian practice. In contradistinction, those painting practices which operate under the naive assumption that gestural delineation, high-contrast color, and heavy impasto are immediate (unmediated, noncoded) representations of the artist's desire propagate the traditional role model; and they do so far more effectively than those painting practices that systematically investigate their own procedures. The former's attraction and success, its role and impact with regard to notions of high culture, and the hierarchy of the visual arts, are governed by its complicity with these models of psychosexual organization. Carol Duncan has described how psychosexual and ideological concepts interrelate, how they are concealed and mediated in early twentieth-century expressionist painting:

> According to their paintings, the liberation of the artist means the domination of others; his freedom requires their unfreedom. Far from contesting the established social order, the male-female relationship that these paintings imply—the drastic reduction of women to objects of specialized male interests—embodies on a sexual level the basic class relationship of capitalist society. In fact such images are splendid metaphors for what the wealthy collectors who eventually acquired them did to those beneath them in the social as well as the sexual hierarchy. However, if the artist is willing to regard women as merely a means to his own ends, if he exploits them to achieve his boast of virility, he, in his turn, must merchandise and sell himself—an illusion of himself and his intimate life—on the open, competitive avant-garde

> market. He must promote (or get dealers and critic friends to promote) the value of his special credo, the authenticity of his special vision, and—most importantly—the genuineness of his anti-bourgeois antagonism. Ultimately, he must be dependent on and serve the pleasure of this very bourgeois world or the enlightened segments of it that his art and life seem to contest.[23]

Inasmuch as this sexual and artistic role is itself reified, *peinture*—the fetishized mode of artistic production—can assume the function of an aesthetic equivalent and provide a corresponding cultural identification for the viewer. Not surprisingly, then, both German Neoexpressionists and Italian Arte Ciphra painters draw heavily upon the stock of painterly styles that predate the two major shifts in twentieth-century art history: Fauvism, Expressionism, and Pittura Metafisica before Duchamp and Constructivism; Surrealist automatism and Abstract Expressionism before Robert Rauschenberg and Piero Manzoni—the two essential instances in modern art when the production process of painting was radically questioned for its claim on organic unity, aura, and presence, and replaced by heterogeneity, mechanical procedures, and seriality.

The contemporary regressions of "postmodernist" painting and architecture are similar in their iconic eclecticism to the neoclassicism of Picasso, Carrà, and others. A variety of production procedures and aesthetic categories, as well as the perceptual conventions that generated them, are now wrested from their original historical contexts and reassembled into a spectacle of availability. They postulate an experience of history as private property; their function is that of *decorum*. The gaudy frivolity with which these works underscore their awareness of the ephemeral function they perform cannot conceal the material and ideological interests they serve; nor can their aggressivity and bravura disguise the exhaustion of the cultural practices they try to maintain.

The works of the contemporary Italians explicitly revive, through quotation, historical production processes, iconographic references, and aesthetic categories. Their techniques range from fresco painting (Clemente) to casting sculpture in bronze (Chia), from highly stylized primitivist drawing to gestural abstraction. Iconographic references range from representations of saints (Salvo) to modish quotations from Russian Constructivism (Chia). With equal versatility they orchestrate a program of dysfunctional plastic categories, often integrated into a scenario of aesthetic surplus: freestanding figurative sculpture combined with an installation of aquatint etchings, architectural murals with small-scale easel paintings, and relief constructions with iconic objects.

The German Neoexpressionists are equally protean in their unearthing of atavistic production modes, including even primitivist hewn wood polychrome sculpture, paraphrasing the expressionist paraphrase of "primitive" art (e.g., Jörg Immendorff). The rediscovery of ancient teutonic graphic techniques such as woodcuts and linocuts flourishes (e.g., Baselitz, Kiefer), as does their iconography: the nude, the still life, the landscape, and what these artists conceive of as allegory.

Concomitant with the fetishization of painting in the cult of *peinture* is a fetishization of the perceptual experience of the work as *auratic*. The contrivance of aura is crucial for these works in order that they fulfill their function as the luxury products of a fictitious high culture. In the tangibility of the auratic, figured through crafted surface textures, aura, and commodity coalesce. Only such synthetic uniqueness can satisfy the contempt that bourgeois character holds for the "vulgarities" of social existence; and only this "aura" can generate "aesthetic pleasure" in the narcissistic character disorder that results from this contempt. Meyer Schapiro saw this symbiotic relationship between certain artists and their patrons in 1935: "The artist's frequently asserted antagonism to organized society does not bring him into conflict with his patrons, since they share his contempt for the public and are indifferent to practical social life."[24]

The aesthetic attraction of these eclectic painting practices originates in a nostalgia for that moment in the past when the painting modes to which they refer had historical authenticity. But the specter of derivativeness hovers over every contemporary attempt to resurrect figuration, representation, and traditional modes of production. This is not so much because they actually derive from particular precedents, but because their attempt to reestablish forlorn aesthetic positions immediately situates them in historical secondariness. That is the price of instant acclaim achieved by affirming the status quo under the guise of innovation. The primary function of such cultural re-presentations is the confirmation of the hieratics of ideological domination.

National Identity and Product Protection

> But the European has been unhoused for a long time, he is a *déraciné*, and as he could in no way face up to it and did not have the courage to admit it, he became a *parvenu*. To be a *parvenu* means to maintain the pretense of being at home in the world. …
>
> —*Otto Freundlich, Bulletin D, 1919*

If the raison d'être of historicist work is that of private property, and if fashion is the discourse in which it manifests and maintains itself, then it is only natural that the work itself has the characteristics of the cliché: compulsively repeated gestures emptied of meaning and congealed into grotesques. Beyond the obsolete and stereotyped conception of the artist's role and character; beyond the fetishized conventions, procedures, and materials that we have analyzed; these clichés are most easily recognized in the artists' call for a return to national culture with its "roots and laws."

Carrà's demand for *italianità* in the 1920s now recurs in both Italian and German painting as the claim of national cultural identity. But such a claim cannot hide its economic function as product protection in the increasingly competitive international art market. Its ideological function has been defined by Fredric Jameson in another context:

> National allegory should be understood as a formal attempt to bridge the increasing gap between the existential data of everyday life within a given nation-state and the structural tendency of monopoly capital to develop on a worldwide, essentially transnational scale.[25]

Just as history has been rediscovered as an inexhaustible source for fictions of identity and subjectivity in commercial culture (fashion, advertising, etc.), so the regressive practices of "high" cultural production provide luxury goods directed at the identity and subjectivity of the managerial class. When Lenin said, "Nationality and Fatherland are essential forms of the bourgeois system," he could hardly have anticipated that "history" would subsequently assume the same function. The nostalgia of artistic production for its own past conventions corresponds to this class's nostalgia for its past processes of individuation at the time of its historical ascendancy.

The very same call for a return to the fictions of national and cultural identity as we observed in the regressive art of the 1920s is now taking place in Arte Ciphra and Neoexpressionism. Frequent references to the late de Chirico and the painterly manner of Mario Sironi's work of the 1920s occur in contemporary Italian painting, while the current German painters refer to the pictorial characteristics and production techniques of German Expressionism.

The reference to Expressionism in contemporary West German art is the natural move to make at a time when the myth of cultural identity is to be established specifically against the dominance of American art during the entire period of reconstruction. Since the Second World War, Expressionism, the "German intuition" of early twentieth-century modern painting, has received increasing esteem. It had of course lacked just this esteem in the post–World War I period, prior to its eventual suppression under Fascism. But during the early 1960s skyrocketing prices indicated that Expressionism had achieved the status of a national treasure, the best of the pre-Fascist heritage of German culture. As opposed to the political radicalism of Berlin Dada, Expressionism presented an avant-garde position acceptable to the newly reconstituted upper middle class, and it thus became the key object for historical study, collection, and speculation. The apolitical humanitarian stance of the expressionist artists, their devotion to spiritual regeneration, their critique of technology, and their romanticization of exotic and primal experience perfectly accorded with the desire for an art that would provide spiritual salvation from the daily experience of alienation resulting from the dynamic reconstruction of postwar capitalism.

The generation of contemporary Neoexpressionists—now in their forties—received their education during this period from artists who had themselves only recently learned the lessons of post-Surrealist automatism as represented by *art informel* and Abstract Expressionism. The first "scandals" of individual achievement of the present generation occurred in the early 1960s, when they "dared" to reintroduce figurative subject matter and highly expressive gestural and chromatic qualities into their art. Their "courage" consisted, then, precisely in committing themselves to the emerging myth of Germany's cultural heritage and national identity through the adoption of the artist s traditional role and the willful ignorance or rejection of all the aesthetic, epistemological, and philosophical developments of the first two decades of the century.

Originally—that is, in the early to mid-sixties—some of these artists had produced work of considerable interest. (The early activities of Jörg Immendorff at the Düsseldorf Academy and his subsequent LIDL happening, and the early work of the East German "primitivist" painter

A. R. Penck are cases in point.) But subsequent to their discovery by the market and museums, these painters underwent a stylistic streamlining that resulted in the "movement" of Neoexpressionism. The first step was the return to large-scale easel painting. For that purpose individual eccentricities of aesthetic activity had to be sacrificed, as did all references to twentieth-century developments contesting the practice of painting. The second step was the conversion of the various idiosyncratic activities of the artists into a homogeneous Neoexpressionist style.

The Neoexpressionists and their apologists understandably reject an exclusive alignment with the German Expressionist patrimony, since their painterly erudition and ambition extends to an assimilation of the pictorial standards of the New York School and the economic value set by it. Any art that wants to supplant the dominance of American art through the programmatic return to a national idiom can only be successful on the market if it acknowledges the dominant "foreign" style. After all it had been the major problem of postwar European painting that it never achieved the "qualitative" level of the New York School (just as, according to Greenberg, the major problem facing American painting before the war was attaining the level of "quality" of the School of Paris). This is particularly evident in the work of the Neoexpressionist Georg Baselitz, whose canvases' size and scale, drawing, and painterly gesture owe as much to Abstract Expressionism as to German Expressionism.

The successful institutionalization of Neoexpressionism has required a complex and subtle set of maneuvers by the market and museums. For example, historical continuity had to be established in order to legitimize the Neoexpressionists as heirs to the German cultural heritage. A recent example of how this authentication may be achieved is a spectacular case of *Geschichtsklitterung* (eclectic historicist construct): the *First Study for a Sculpture* by Baselitz. The large-scale seated figure, hewn out of a wood block, raising its right arm in such a way that hostile critics have called it a Fascist gesture, was recently shown at the Whitechapel Gallery in London. For this exhibition, it was surrounded by the late

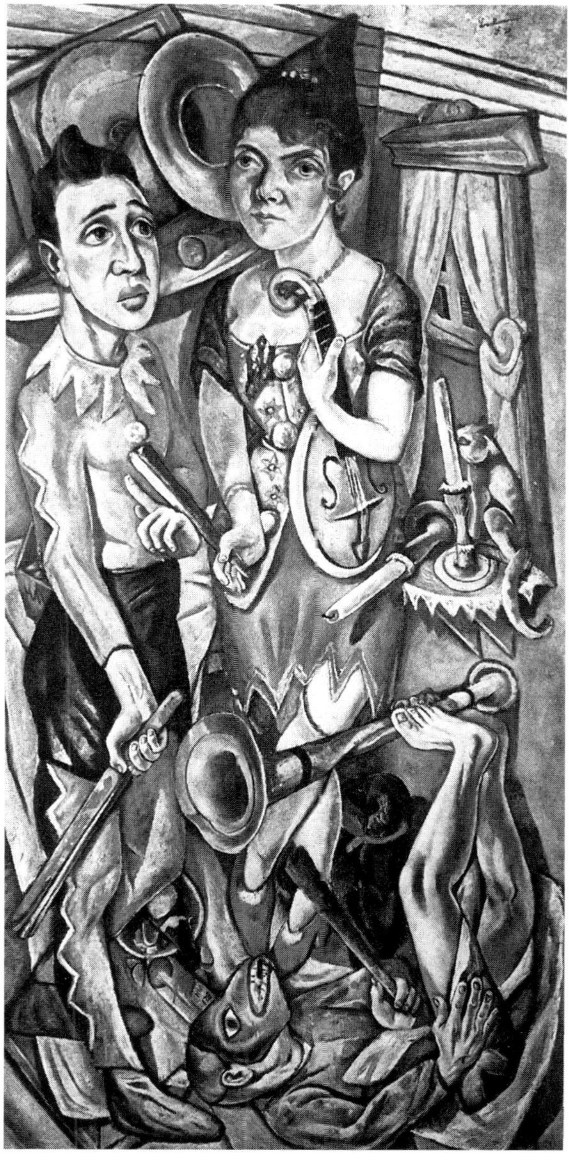

Max Beckmann, *Carnival*, 1920. Oil on canvas, 73⅜ × 36 in. (186.6 × 91.5 cm). Private collection. © 2015 Artists Rights Society (ARS), New York/VG Bild-Kunst, Bonn.

triptychs of Max Beckmann, thus establishing the historical pedigree, the continuity of specifically German art. Thus accredited with authenticity, local products can succeed on the international market.

A second strategy, complementing this contrived national continuity, is that of carefully placing the work in the context of the contemporary international avant-garde. For example, a reproduction of a painting by the Neoprimitivist Penck appears on the frontispiece of a catalog for a recent exhibition of the Italian artists Fabro, Kounellis, Merz, and Paolini at the Kunsthalle Bern—one of the strongholds of German Neoexpressionism. And more overtly, the catalog introduction states the museum director's proposal to combine work by this group of truly significant Italian artists with that of the Neoexpressionists who are described as their "nordic" counterparts. Thus the intellectual subtlety and analytic clarity of these Italian artists is conferred upon the reactionary German artists, when the proper German peers of these Italians are, of course, Darboven, Palermo, and Richter.

Critical Clichés, Manufactured Visions

> Social reasons for this impotence [of historicism]: the fantasy of the bourgeois class ceases to focus on the future of the forces of productivity which it released. The specific *Gemütlichkeit* of the middle of the century results from this conditioned fading away of social fantasy. The desire to have children is only a weaker stimulation of potency in comparison to the images of the future that this social fantasy once engendered.
>
> —*Walter Benjamin, "Zentralpark"*

When art emphasizing national identity attempts to enter the international distribution system, the most worn-out historical and geopolitical clichés have to be employed. And thus we now see the resurrection of such notions as the nordic versus the Mediterranean, the teutonic versus the Latin. A typical formulation of the clichéd idea of German character appears in an art historian's comment on a Neoexpressionist painter's work: "The tendency of German art to literature, to profound allegories, and ideological symbolism, [and] to the mysticism and ecstasy of an exuberant imagination has found expression here."[26]

Just as the art itself resorts to cliché as the reliable strategy for operating within an obsolete context, so the critics and curators who have become the spokesmen of the "new art" resurrect a critical language of false naiveté and bloated trivialities which forms the terminology of the new subjectivity. The lack of historical specificity and reflection upon methodology, the willful ignorance of radical changes in other fields of research bearing upon aesthetic practice (semiology, psychoanalysis, criticism of ideology) are particularly revealing. Take for example the British art historian and curator Nicholas Serota discussing the manner in which one of the Neoexpressionist painters

> has adopted the seemingly more traditional ground of the painter of still life. He has created for himself a kind of theatre in which the absurd object, emblems, allegory and metaphor are used to reinterpret universals such as the creation and awakening of life, the interaction of natural forces, human emotions and ideologies and the experience of death. For a comparison one has to look back to the triptychs of Beckmann, though Beckmann's use of narrative structure is quite different.[27]

Or, more hyperbolically, Rudi Fuchs, Dutch art historian and director of one of Europe's most active museums in exhibiting contemporary art, claims that

> painting is salvation. It presents freedom of thought of which it is the triumphant expression. … The painter is a guardian angel carrying the palette in blessing over the world. Maybe the painter is the darling of the Gods.[28]

And the German art historian Siegfried Gohr, in a text published by London's Whitechapel Gallery, writes:

> The relationship between beauty and terror, eros and death, those time-honored themes of art, are presented again by the painting. Negativity, death is introduced as a theme.[29]

The lack of formal and historical complexity in the painters' works and the attendant avoidance of genuine critical analysis of their contrived "visions" results inevitably in a stereotypical critical language. Here, for example, are two virtually identical statements by two critics writing about different painters:

The motifs which Georg Baselitz time and again employs in his paintings are insignificant as content. They are only meaningful within his pictorial method: as formal points of departure.[30]

The value of the motif in these paintings of Lüpertz's lay only in the way in which he used it as a starting point for the development of a meaningful activity.[31]

As was the case in the call to order by regressive artists of the 1920s, a growing aggressivity is now becoming apparent in the manner that these clichés of vision and language are propagated. With the demise of liberalism, its underside—authoritarianism—no longer feels inhibited. And it thus comes to the fore in the guise of irrationality and the ideology of individual expression. In reaction against social consciousness and political awareness, proto-Fascist libertarianism prepares the way for the seizure of state power. Without questioning the reasons for the failure of enlightenment, the end of modernism and the enforced silencing of its critical potential are taken as excuses for indulging in defeat.

The following programmatic statements, couched in a pastiche of Deleuze and Guattari, Stirner, and Spengler, fervently advocate the received ideas of petit-bourgeois anarchism in relation to Arte Ciphra:

> Arte Ciphra exposes itself as an art of the most extreme subjectivism. … The disillusionment is the strongest with those who even at the beginning of the seventies still believed in an immediately imminent collapse of capitalism-generated by criticism and revelation. … Now it is much more important to develop new forms which relate to pure intensity, to the indivisibility of desire and to the unconscious fixations of desire. Desire therefore assumes a revolutionary position. But as desire itself is always a part of infinitely complicated and ambivalent interdependences, its particular fixations must come to bear in their totality, even if they are partially "regressive," "bourgeois," or "nonrevolutionary." … The failure of bourgeois enlightenment—well understood long ago in political and ideological thought—was not acknowledged by this art of the seventies … Arte Ciphra attempts a formation of the "here and now."… Its aim is the opposite of utopia—it is *atopia,* the discovery of the other in the immediacy of the present.[32]

And here, in the explicitly proto-Fascist language of an Italian critic:

> The new force of art is born from this very tension, turning a relationship of quantity into a relationship of intensity. The work is taken from a socially underprivileged position back to an individual centrality, reestablishing the creative need by means of an image in opposition to the shapeless fogginess of social needs.[33]

Rather than face up to its own bankruptcy and the necessity of political change, this frankly elitist notion of subjectivity ultimately opts for the destruction of the very historical and cultural reality that it claims to possess. The secret longing for destruction as a solution to contradictions that can only be met in political, not cultural, terms, manifests itself in fantasies of catastrophe. This climate of finality—when the end of a class is mistaken for the end of the world—generates apocalyptic and necrophilic visions, first in high art, then spread throughout the culture. Eventually self-destruction can be seen as an act of heroism. These tendencies are again to be found in the painting of Neoexpressionism and its accompanying criticism:

> It represents one of the great tyrannical gestures in aesthetics: an emperor burning down a city to make way for a new and grander one. As a theme it belongs of course to a larger topological framework which dates back to the beginning of time: renewal and purification through fire. ... Fire destroys but it also cleanses.[34]

And:

> Last year ... I accompanied Lüpertz to the Ruhleben crematorium on the outskirts of the city. As we walked slowly down a wide path to the modern crematorium ... a pale of black smoke began to rise slowly from the chimneys. Suddenly the silence was broken by the sharp report of rifles firing on the British artillery range hidden behind the crematorium. The conjunction was typical of Berlin. Inside the building was the pair of paintings by Lüpertz. ... They have a quality of universal truth.[35]

The historical "authenticity" of these works is contained, then, in the very retardation and regression that they enact: the continuing domination of the obsolete. In the pathetic farce of their repetition-compulsion, we can still recognize the tragic failure of the original forms of the protest of Expressionism. In the mockery and mimicry of contemporary Neoexpressionism we see the afterimage of that anarchic and subversive but ultimately apolitical radicalism that was doomed to failure, to be appropriated by the very forces that it had set out to oppose. It is Lukács, once again, who has described this mechanism:

> Mythologizing the problems allows one to avoid looking at the phenomena which are criticized as being part of capitalism, or to render capitalism in such a spurious, distorted, and mystified form that the critique does not generate a confrontation of the problems but a parasitic complacency with the system; by inversion, even an affirmation coming from the "soul" can be derived from this critique. … Without doubt, expressionism is only one of the many bourgeois ideological currents eventually leading to fascism, and its role as ideological preparation is not any more or less important than currents of the imperialist epoch, inasmuch as they express decadent parasitic features, including all the fake revolutionary and oppositional forces. … This schism is deeply inherent in the character of anti-bourgeois expressionism and this abstracting impoverishment of content not only indicates the tendency of expressionism; it is from the very beginning its central, insurmountable stylistic problem, because its extraordinary poverty of content marks a blatant contradiction of the pretense of its performance, of the hybrid subjective pathos of its representation.[36]

The mock avant-garde of contemporary European painters now benefits from the ignorance and arrogance of a racket of cultural *parvenus* who perceive it as their mission to reaffirm the politics of a rigid conservatism through cultural legitimation.

Postscript

This essay was written in the fall of 1980. Since then the fictions and realities of the art world—in terms of the amount of attention devoted in museums and in the art marketplace to the work discussed here—have fulfilled my own worst fears. What in 1980 still seemed the eccentricities of a particular group of aficionados, collectors, and dealers, have in the meantime been heralded as the new art historical norms: late Picabia, late de Chirico, Raoul Dufy, and of course Balthus. With these guideposts in mind, historians of twentieth-century art are now encouraged to rewrite history from the perspective of the Reagan era.

Not since the 1920s has cultural production (or at least that segment of it controlled by the market) made such aggressive claims in asserting its reactionary political affiliations and in its defense of a notion of culture that is right-wing, sexist, and elitist, but also willfully ignorant of the implications of cultural production in different circumstances and contexts. In this respect, I hope that in spite of its sketchiness this essay's depiction of a broader historical panorama may still be of some help in understanding particular cultural formation in the present. (For a recent, thorough discussion of the political and cultural milieu of Europe between the wars—unfortunately unavailable at the time I wrote this essay—see Kenneth Silver, "Esprit de Corps: The Great War and French Art, 1914–1925," Ph.D. diss., Yale University, 1981.)

In another respect, however, reality has proven the severe limitations of an art historical attempt to clarify present-day conditions in terms of a reception-compulsion of unresolved problems of the past, or in terms of a recycling of artistic strategies which may serve the stereotypical interests of a class that resists, with equal fervor, change in both political and cultural practice. The present situation, then, may perhaps be less profitably compared with the twenties than I originally suspected, presenting instead conditions that are altogether quite unique and specific.

While certain American critics now celebrate the "Germanness" of German *angst* in painting, the authenticity of its reflection upon the Fascist past, and its reconstruction of national self-consciousness, seldom do they (or, of course, the paintings in question) reflect upon the real *fears* (and practices of protest) brought on by the aggressive policies of the Reagan administration and by the deployment of missiles on the territory likely to be the first "war theater." In a recent interview—in true Picabia manner, at the wheel of his luxurious sports car—the most bombastic of the German painters claimed, "My generation doesn't worry much about survival." Here one recognizes, once again, what motivates this generation of artists: profound cynicism and contempt for the social and political reality that surrounds them. They share this contempt with their clients, who are grateful that these artists have put art back where *they* always thought it belonged: on their walls and in their vaults and in the museum (to receive its institutional blessings).

These paintings, then, function as the perfect mirage (and herein lies the secret of their attraction and success): they assure us that, in a period of conservatism and defunding, the arts are flourishing, and that those who rule are generous in their support of the arts (if it abides by their standards). They tell us that even in the realm of culture, the old means of production are still the most viable since they (after all) produce affluence and excellence. But this notion of a culture of excellence is no longer acceptable on historical grounds; indeed, by virtue of its exclusivity and its contempt for the social reality within which it exists, the proposition itself advocates cultural barbarism.

These paintings function as a perfect mirage in another sense as well: they project a mirage-image of individuality and personal freedom.

In their mode of production and their iconography, as well as their object-status as auratic works of art, they pretend to be the last bastion against the destruction of individuality and the totalitarian conditions of mass culture.

When it comes to the production of handcrafted luxury objects, American myth (and the commercial reality to which it contributes) holds that Europeans do it better. This is due in part to the typical American cliché of the European individual as bound to an identity afforded by his or her ancient nation-state, that is, possessing an identity more ingrained with history, more solid, more profound. The new European paintings bring just these clichés to bear, providing the warranty for a satisfaction of precisely those desires for the deeply rooted, the deeply felt, and the solidly produced: in other words, for the true individuality that only the few can have. At the same time, current European painting (German painting in particular) offers an additional attraction that European art of the sixties and seventies—which passed by largely unnoticed in the United States—refused to offer. This new European painting is the first international avant-garde in which reverberates the profound influence of American Abstract Expressionism. What makes Anselm Kiefer, A. R. Penck, and Georg Baselitz so attractive to Americans (in particular) is that they teach a new art history lesson, one that begins with Picasso and Matisse, passes through German Expressionists and the Surrealists (especially Fautrier and the later postwar painting), and then decisively registers the extraordinary impact of Still, de Kooning, Kline, and Pollock. Who would not be seduced by the reflection of one's own national culture in the art of a succeeding generation, especially in a different geopolitical context? So, when we look at a painting by Kiefer, for example, we see first of all a German national asserting through his art a national authenticity and identity, but also tackling or toying with the distant monstrosity of German Fascism, simultaneously exorcising its power in today's society and performing for us the labor of mourning occasioned by a barbarism that has quickly receded into the past. But, at the same time, we see an obedient disciple, who now for the first time has encapsulated the lessons of the "School of New York," in exactly the way that generation after generation of American avant-garde artists learned their lessons from the European schools.

Thus the aesthetic mirage fulfills (almost miraculously) all our needs at the same time. It keeps at bay our worst fears about the present—the here-and-now of the Age of Reagan—by projecting them onto the distant historical reality of authoritarian politics in other countries. It vigorously asserts the perpetuation of a hierarchical organization of society and the rule of the individual, emphasizing the cultural legitimation of nationalism as an essential feature of that individualism. And, as with all colonialized representations, it provides an image of obedience and assent: the various foreign cultures validate the hegemony of the dominant culture. (The recent Museum of Modern Art "survey," for instance, showed examples of German, French, Italian, and English, as well as Canadian and Australian Neoexpressionism.)

While one might imagine that flooding the market with manufactured originality would have to be carefully avoided, it seems that, for the time being at least, that familiar ideologeme—the private, individual, nationalistic, male artist—remains powerful and (paradoxically) can easily withstand and inflationary accumulation and sheer endless repetition of the same originality.

One other shortcoming of this essay—a major one in retrospect—is that it does not make any attempt to analyze the current situation in terms of its economy. Now, more clearly than ever before, drastic structural shifts have taken place in the art world. The number of corporate and private collectors has increased tremendously, and, if nothing else, it has become apparent that investment in art, if well managed, can generate interest and revenue exceeding most other small-time investment gambles of the affluent. (We are, after all, not talking about real business, but only about the destruction of surplus capital, which traditionally has been invested in luxury goods.) As in the case of all luxury

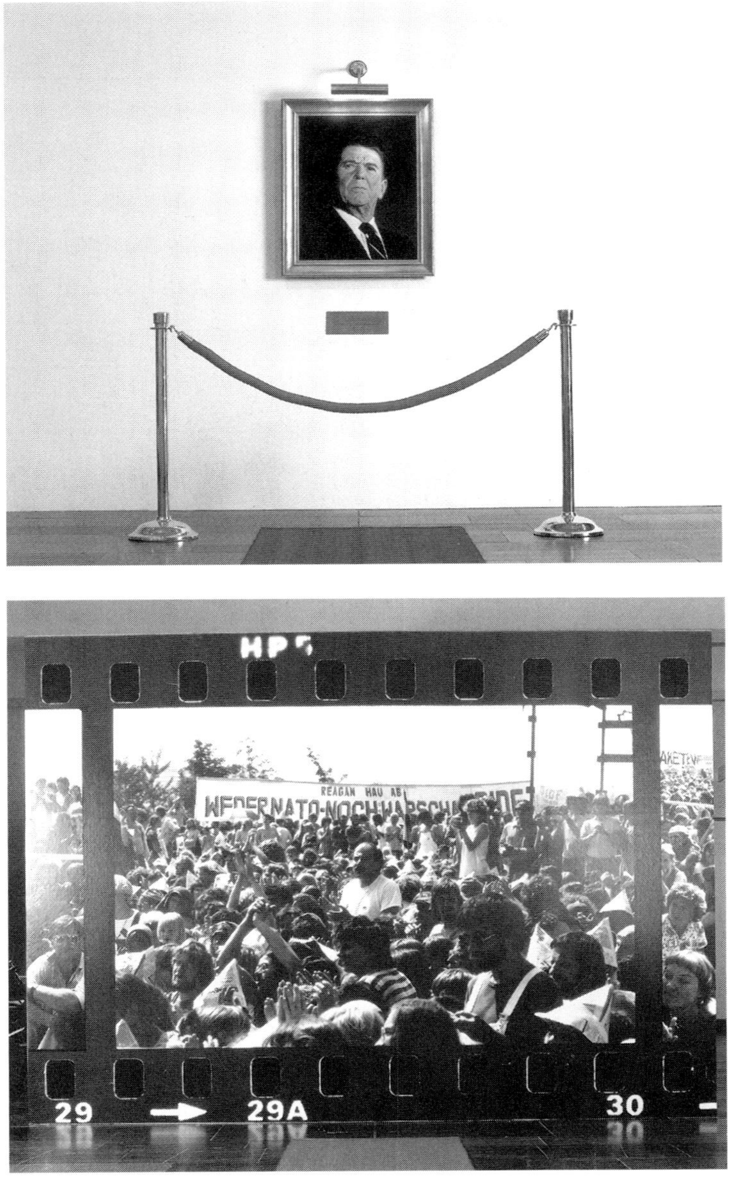

Hans Haacke, *Oil Painting, Homage to Marcel Broodthaers*, 1982. Installation; overall dimensions determined by exhibition space. Oil painting in gold frame, 35½ × 29 in. (90 × 73.5 cm); brass picture lamp; brass plaque with title, 4½ × 12 in. (11.4 × 30.4 cm); brass stanchions with velvet rope; red carpet runner, 35 in. wide (89 cm), length variable; photomural. Photomural represents anti-Reagan/anti–nuclear weapons demonstration, Bonn, June 10, 1982, during Reagan's state visit. First exhibited at Documenta 7, Kassel, Germany, June 19–September 28, 1982. Photo: Udo Reusching. Collection Eli Broad Family Foundation, Los Angeles. © 2015 Hans Haacke/Artists Rights Society (ARS), New York/VG Bild-Kunst, Bonn.

goods (e.g., designer clothes), the desire to possess artworks and the need to use them for the constitution of individuality and social identity not only grows constantly, but can be massively propagated as well. With the rising number of speculators in this gamble, the number of certified artists and products participating in the race has to be dramatically increased. Not only can the original artists not produce quickly enough, but also the products they do produce move very quickly out of the price range of the many newcomers to this (new) stock exchange. We then see the emergence (as in the East Village) of substitute designer ware (often more interesting than the stepped-up manufacturing of the original masters). Now even the most liberal critics have to recognize as historical reality the fact that High Culture has indeed merged its enterprise with the conditions of the cultural industry.

These, then, are the issues that this essay failed to address in 1980. Their thorough discussion and analysis in terms of the present, and not in the guise of an art historical exemplum, remains to be carried out.[37]

NOTES

First published in *October* 16, Art World Follies (spring 1981): 39–68; reprinted with postscript in *Art After Modernism: Rethinking Representation*, ed. Brian Wallis (New York: New Museum of Contemporary Art, 1984), pp. 106–135. All translations by Benjamin H. D. Buchloh unless otherwise noted. Minor corrections have been made for consistency.

1. Lukács, "Grösse und Verfall des Expressionismus," p. 147.

2. Asja Lacis, *Revolutionär im Beruf: Berichte über proletarisches Theater, über Meyerhold, Brecht, Benjamin und Piscator*, ed. Hildegard Brenner (Munich: Rogner & Bernhard, 1971), p. 44.

3. George Steiner, "Introduction," in Walter Benjamin, *The Origin of German Tragic Drama*, trans. John Osborne (London: New Left Books, 1977), p. 24.

4. Francis Picabia, "Comment je vois New York," in *Francis Picabia* (Paris: Musée National d'Art Moderne, 1976), p. 66.

5. Francis Picabia, "Manifeste de l'Ecole Amorphiste," in *Francis Picabia*, p. 68.

6. See William Rubin, *Picasso* (New York: Museum of Modern Art, 1980), p. 224. The awareness of Picasso's decline eventually developed even among art historians who had been previously committed to his work: "Picasso belongs to the past. ... His downfall is one of the most upsetting problems of our era" (Germain Bazin, quoted in Rubin, *Picasso*, p. 277).

7. Maurice Raynal, "Quelques intentions du cubisme," *Bulletin de l'effort moderne*, no. 4 (1924): 4.

8. Ibid.

9. Leo Bersani, *Baudelaire and Freud* (Berkeley: University of California Press, 1978), p. 98.

10. Giorgio de Chirico, "Ueber die metaphysische Kunst," in *Wir Metaphysiker* (Berlin, n.d.), p. 45.

11. Umberto Silva, *Kunst und Ideologie des Faschismus* (Frankfurt, 1975), p. 18.

12. Giorgio de Chirico, *Valori Plastici* 3–4 (Rome, 1919). This phenomenon finds its earliest explicit manifestation in de Chirico's declaration "Pictor sum classicus," with which he concludes emphatically his call for a return to the law of history and classic order, a manifesto called "The Return to the Craft" published in *Valori Plastici* in 1919. Like Carlo Carrà in his "Pittura Metafisica," also published in 1919, de Chirico not only requests the return to the "classic" tradition and the "masters" of that tradition (Uccello, Giotto, Piero della Francesca), but to the specific *nationality* of that tradition. This is the most obvious of the three historical fictions in that authoritarian construct of a return to the past, since the nation-state as a socioeconomic and political ordering system did not exist at the time of these masters' production.

It is only logical to find Carrà's name subsequently among the artists who signed the "Manifesto of Fascist Painting" in 1933 which reads as follows: "Fascist Art rejects research and experiments. ... The style of Fascist art has to orient itself towards antiquity."

It seems that with increasing authoritarianism in the present the projection into the past has to be removed further and further away—from Renaissance to antiquity in this case. More explicitly we find this substitution of present history by mnemosynic fictions of past history in an essay by Alberto Savinio, published in *Valori Plastici* in 1921: "Memory generates our thoughts and our hopes ... we are forever the devoted and faithful sons of Memory. Memory is our past; it is also the past of all other men, of all men who have preceded us. And since memory is the ordered recollection of our thoughts and those of the others, memory is our religion: *religio*."

When the French art historian Jean Clair tries to understand these phenomena outside of their historical and political context, his terminology, which is supposed to explain these contradictions and save them for a new reactionary anti-modernist art history writing, has to employ the same clichés of authoritarianism, the fatherland, and the paternal heritage: "[These painters] come to collect their paternal heritage, they do not even dream of rejecting it. ... Neoclassicism is lived as a meditation on the exile, far from the lost fatherland which is also that of painting, the lost fatherland of paintings." See Jean Clair, "Metafisica et Unheimlichkeit," in *Les Réalismes* 1919–1939 (Paris: Musée National d'Art Moderne, 1981), p. 32

13. "Francis Picabia contre Dada ou le Retour à la Raison," in *Comoedia* (March 14, 1927): 1. "The Return to Reason" and "The Return to Order" not only espoused almost identical programs of authoritarian neoclassicism, but also shared the same supposed enemies and targets of attack. Dada was, of course, one of them, so it seems useful in this context to recall the attitudes of the literary neoclassicist T. S. Eliot toward Dada: "Mr. Aldington treated Mr. Joyce as a prophet of chaos and wailed at the Rood of Dadaism which his prescient eye saw bursting forth at the tap of the magician's rod. ... A very great book may have a very bad influence indeed. ... A man of genius is responsible to his peers, not to a studio full of uneducated and undisciplined coxcombs." See T. S. Eliot, "Ulysses, Order and Myth," *The Dial* 75 (1923): 480–483.

14. Pablo Picasso, in conversation with Christian Zervos, in *Cahiers d'Art* 10, no. 1 (1935): 173.

15. Christian Schad, in *Christian Schad*, exh. cat. (Vienna: Galerie Würthle, 1927), n.p. See also a nearly identical statement by the former Expressionist Otto Dix: "The new element of painting for me resides in the intensification of forms of expression which *in nuce* exist already as givens in the work of *old masters*" (in *Das Objekt ist das Primäre*, Berlin, 1927). Compare this with the statement by George Grosz, a peer of Schad and Dix: "The return to French classicist painting, to Poussin, Ingres, and Corot, is an insidious fashion of *Biedermeier*. It seems that the political reaction is therefore followed by an intellectual reaction" (in *Das Kunstblatt*, 1922, as a reply to Paul Westheim's inquiry "Towards a New Naturalism?").

16. Christopher Green, *Léger and the Avantgarde* (New Haven: Yale University Press, 1976), p. 218.

17. Ibid.

18. When Max Beckmann in the 1920s referred to himself as the "alienated clown and the mysterious king" he expressed precisely the unconscious dilemma of the artist's fluctuation between authoritarian rule and melancholy, as George Steiner puts it in his introduction to *The Origin of German Tragic Drama*: "Prince and Puppet are impelled by the same frozen violence" (p. 18). Renato Poggioli described this dilemma without coming to an adequate understanding: "Aware that bourgeois society looks at him only as a charlatan the artist deliberately and ostentatiously assumes the role of the comic actor. From this stems the myth of the artist as *pagliaccio* and mountebank. Between the

alternating extremes of self-criticism and self-pity, the artist comes to see himself as a comic victim and sometimes as a tragic victim, although the latter seems to be predominant." See Renato Poggioli, "The Artist in the Modern World," in *The Spirit of the Letter* (Cambridge, Mass.: Havard University Press, 1965), p. 327.

This new icon of the clown is only matched in frequency in the paintings of that period by the representation of the *manichino*, the wooden puppet, the reified body, originating from both shop window decoration and from the props of the classical artist's studio. If the first icon appears in the context of the carnival and the circus as the masquerades of alienation from present history, the second appears on the stage set of reification. With due historical transformation we can observe parallel phenomena in the iconography of the "New Painting." As described in the following example: "The comic and the self-effacing aspects ... loom very large (and very small in the work of many recent artists). Miniaturization, stick figures, dimpled dollies, micro freaks and the humanoid progeny of Krazy Kat are all part of an ever increasing Lilliputian population; the doll house syndrome is very much with us." See Klaus Kertess, "Figuring It Out," *Artforum* (November 1980): 30. Or, a more adequate critical understanding of these phenomena: "In another of a long string of ironic (?) refusals of virtuosity and 'sensitivity,' painters have recently adopted a reduced brutish figuration (seemingly chosen from a lexicon of the drastically damaged mentally) whose nihilism strikes not at any society in particular but at 'civilization'—a familiar desperate move" (Martha Rosler, unpublished notes on quotation).

19. These "concealed collages" in painting represent a false unification. Fredric Jameson describes this analogous attempt at unification in literature: "the mirage of the continuity of personal identity, the organizing unity of the psyche or the personality, the concept of society itself, and not least, the notion of the organic unity of the work of art." See *Fables of Aggression* (Berkeley: University of California Press, 1980), p. 8. The term "painted collages" was used by Max Ernst in his "Au-delà de la Peinture" in 1936 to describe the painting of Magritte and Dalí. Of course Ernst was not able to provide a historical differentiation between the original collage techniques and their implications and the attempt of renewed painterly unification of fragmentation, fissures, and discontinuity of the plastic language. Since then several authors have described the phenomenon of the "painted collage" in the neoclassicist paintings and their peculiar unreal spatiality, a surface and pictorial space that seem to be made of glass or ice. See, for example, Wieland Schmied, "Pittura Metafisica et Nouvelle Objectivité," in *Les Réalismes* 1919–1939, exh. cat. (Paris: Centre Georges Pompidou, 1980), p. 22. This is of course the spatial configuration of the static melancholic experience which is fixated on the authoritarian images of the alien and the ancient and that recognizes itself in the shimmering surface of classicist painting that seems to contain life in a shrine. The most haunting image of this idealized classical beauty is given in Baudelaire's poem "La Beauté":

Je suis belle, ô mortels! comme un rêve de pierre,
Et mon sein, où chacun s'est meurtri tour à tour,
Est fait pour inspirer au poète un amour
Eternel et muet ainsi que la matiere.

Je trône dans l'azur comme un sphinx incompris;
J'unis un coeur de neige à la blancheur des cygnes;
Je hais le mouvement qui déplace les lignes,
Et jamais je ne pleure et jamais je ne ris.

20. Lillian Robinson and Lise Vogel, "Modernism and History," *New Literary History* 3, no. 1 (1971): 196.

21. Laura Mulvey, "Visual Pleasure and Narrative Cinema," *Screen* 16, no. 3 (1975): 7.

22. Max Kozloff, "The Authoritarian Personality in Modern Art," *Artforum* 12, no. 8 (May 1974): 40.

23. Carol Duncan, "Virility and Domination in Early Twentieth Century Painting," *Artforum* 12, no. 9 (December 1973): 38.

24. Meyer Schapiro, quoted in Kozloff, "The Authoritarian Personality in Modern Art," p. 40.

25. Jameson, *Fables of Aggression*, p. 94.

26. Siegfried Gohr, "Remarks on the Paintings of Markus Lüpertz," in *Markus Lüpertz: "Stil" Paintings*, ed. Nicholas Serota (London: Whitechapel Gallery, 1979), n.p.

27. Nicholas Serota, *Markus Lüpertz*, n.p.

28. R. H. Fuchs, *Anselm Kiefer*, exh. cat. (Venice: Venice Biennale, 1980), p. 62.

29. Gohr, "Remarks," in *Markus Lüpertz*, n.p.

30. R. H. Fuchs, *Georg Baselitz-Bilder 1977–1978* (Eindhoven: Van Abbemuseum, 1979), n.p.

31. Gohr, "Remarks," n.p.

32. Wolfgang Max Faust, *Arte Ciphra*, exh. cat. (Cologne, 1979), p. 14.

33. Achille Bonito Oliva, "The Bewildered Image," *Flash Art* 96–97 (April 1980): 35.

34. Fuchs, *Anselm Kiefer*, p. 57.

35. Serota, *Markus Lüpertz*, n.p.

36. Lukács, "Grösse und Verfall des Expressionismus," p. 116.

37. I have limited my investigations here to European phenomena, even though I am aware that a comparable movement is presently emerging in North America. The reasons for such a limitation are best described by Georg Lukács:

We will restrict our observations to Germany, even though we know that expressionism was an international phenomenon. As much as we understand that its roots are to be found everywhere in imperialism, we know as well that the uneven development in the various countries had to generate various manifestations. Only after a concrete study of the development of expressionism has been made can we come to an overview without remaining in the abstract. (Georg Lukács, "Grösse und Verfall des Expressionismus" [1934], in *Probleme des Realismus*, vol. 1, *Gesammelte Werke*, vol. 4 [Neuwied: Luchterhand Verlag, 1971], p. 111)

4

Allegorical Procedures: Appropriation and Montage in Contemporary Art

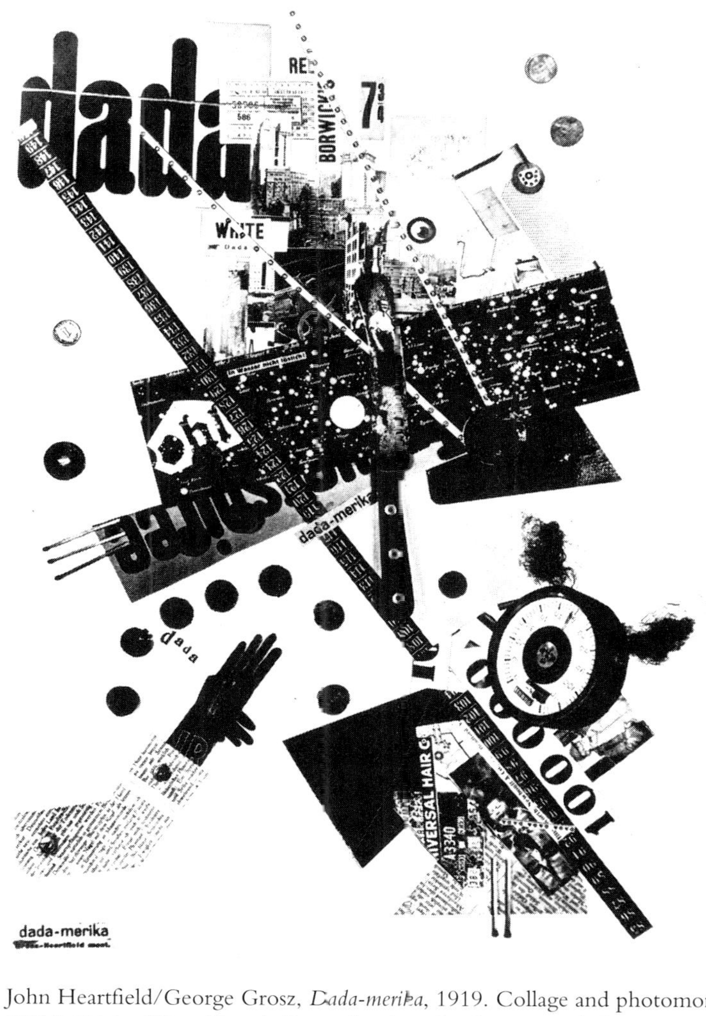

John Heartfield/George Grosz, *Dada-merika*, 1919. Collage and photomontage, 10¼ × 7½ in. (26 × 19 cm). Reproduction after lost original.

From the very moment of its inception, it seems that the inventors of the strategy of montage were aware of its inherently allegorical nature: to speak in public with hidden meaning, in response to the prohibition of public speech.[1] George Grosz for one reminisces as follows:

> In 1916, when Johnny Heartfield and I invented photomontage … we had no idea of the immense possibilities or of the thorny but successful career that awaited the new invention. On a piece of cardboard, we pasted a mishmash of advertisements for hernia belts, student songbooks, and dog food, labels from Schnapps and wine bottles and photographs from picture papers, cut up at will, in such a way as to say in pictures, what would have been banned by the censors if we had said it in words.[2]

In a highly condensed form, Grosz charts the terrain of montage as well as its allegorical methods of confiscation, superimposition, and fragmentation. He outlines its materials as much as he points to the dialectic of montage esthetics: to range from a meditative contemplation of reification to a powerful propaganda tool for mass agitation. Historically, this dialectic is embodied most eminently in the oppositional practices of two German Dada artists, the opposition between the collage work of Kurt Schwitters and the montage work of John Heartfield.

The inventors of the collage/montage techniques understood just as clearly that they performed operations on the pictorial or poetical signifying practice, which ranged from the most subtle and minute interference in linguistic and representational functions to the most explicitly and powerfully programmatic propaganda activities. This becomes apparent in Raoul Hausmann's recollections of 1931, when he ponders the development from phonetic Dada poems to the political polemics of the Berlin Dada group:

> In the conflict of opinions, people often argue that photomontage is only possible in two ways: one being the political, the other being the commercial. … The Dadaists, after having "invented" the static, the simultaneous and the purely phonetic poem, now applied the same principles with consequence to pictorial representation. In the medium of photography, they were the first to create out of structural elements from often very heterogeneous materials or locales a new unity that tore a visually and cognitively new mirror image from the period of chaos in war and revolution; and they knew that their method had an inherent propagandistic power which contemporary life was not courageous enough to absorb and to develop.[3]

The dialectical potential of the montage technique to which Hausmann refers found its historical fulfillment in the fundamental contradiction of the consequences spawned by the collage/montage model. On the one hand we witness its increasing psychological interiorization and estheticization in the work of Max Ernst and of Surrealism at large (and its subsequent, still continuing exploitation in advertising and product propaganda). On the other hand, we encounter the historically simultaneous development of politically revolutionary montage and agitprop practices in the work of El Lissitzky, Alexandr Rodchenko, and Heartfield (and the logical conclusion of an almost complete disappearance of montage's public social function from history, except for some isolated pursuits in contemporary individual practices that we will focus on in the following).

Parallel with the emergence of montage practices in literature, film, and the visual arts, we witness the development of a theory of montage in the writings of numerous authors since the late 1920s: Sergei Eisenstein, Lev Kuleshov, and Sergei Tretyakov in the Soviet Union; Bertolt Brecht, Heartfield, and Walter Benjamin in Weimar

Germany; and Louis Aragon in France. It is in particular the theory of montage as it was developed in the later writings of Walter Benjamin, in close association with his theories on allegorical procedures in Modernist art, that is of significance if one wants to develop a more adequate reading of certain aspects of montage models in the present, their historical predecessors, and the meaning of the transformations of these models in contemporary art.

In his analysis of the historical conditions that generated allegorical practices in European Baroque literature, Benjamin suggests that the rigid immanence of the Baroque—its worldly orientation—leads to the loss of an anticipatory, utopian sense of historical time, and thereby generates a static, almost spatially conceivable experience of time. The desire to act and produce, and the idea of a public political practice, recedes behind a generally dominant attitude of melancholic contemplation. Similar to the general perception of the world's perishable nature during the Baroque, the world of material objects is perceived as becoming invalid in the emerging transformation of objects into commodities, a transformation that occurred with the general introduction of the capitalist mode of production. This devaluation of objects, their split into use value and exchange value and the fact that they would ultimately function exclusively as producers of exchange value, would—still according to Benjamin—profoundly affect the collective experience of objects under the conditions of modernity.

But it is in particular in his later writings, especially in the "fragments" on Baudelaire, that Benjamin developed a theory of allegory and montage based on the structure of the commodity fetish as it had been defined by Karl Marx. Planning to write a chapter entitled "The Commodity as Poetical Object," in his Baudelaire study, Benjamin wrote a preparatory fragment that contains *in nuce* an almost programmatic description of collage/montage esthetics: "The devaluation of objects in allegory is surpassed in the world of objects itself by the commodity. The emblems return as commodities."[4] Language and image, taken into the service of the commodity by advertising, were allegorized by the montage techniques of juxtaposing and fragmenting depleted signifiers.[5] The allegorical mind sides with the object and protests against its devaluation to the status of a commodity by devaluating it for the second time in allegorical practice. By splintering signifier and signified, the allegorist subjects the sign to the same division of functions that the object has undergone in its transformation into a commodity. It is this repetition of the original act of depletion and the new attribution of meaning that redeems the object.

The allegorist perceives the essential site of the procedure in the scriptural element of writing, where language is incorporated into a spatial configuration. Thus Dadaist poets deplete words, syllables, and sounds of all traditional semantic functions and references until they become purely visual, opaque and concrete shells and skeletons. The purely phonetic dimension of language signals their dialectical complement in the Dada and Cubo-Futurist sound poems, where psychosomatic expression is freed from the spatial shells and skeletons of language and the usages of imposed and instrumentalized forms of communicative meaning.

The procedure of montage is therefore one in which all allegorical principles are executed simultaneously: appropriation and depletion of meaning, fragmentation and dialectical juxtaposition of fragments, and the systematic separation of signifier and signified. In fact, in yet another aphorism from Benjamin's fragments on Baudelaire we find an exact description of these procedures:

> The allegorical mind arbitrarily selects from the vast and disordered material that his knowledge has to offer. It tries to match one piece with another to figure out whether they can be combined. This meaning with that image, or that image with this meaning The result is never predictable since there is no organic mediation between the two.[6]

Benjamin's theory of montage ultimately outlines a historical critique of perception. The beginning of the Modernist avant-garde emerged at a historical turning point where, under the impact of the rising participation of the masses in collective production, all traditional models of perception that had served in the character formation of the bourgeois subject now had to be rejected in favor of models that acknowledged explicitly those social facts of a newly emerging historical situation where, as Benjamin would phrase it in his central essay, "The Work of Art in the Age of Mechanical Reproduction" (1934), "the sense of equality had increased to such a degree that equality was gained even from the unique, by means of reproduction."[7]

These perceptual changes denied any qualification of subject or object as singular and unique, dismantling by implication the hierarchical social order as much as the system of the bourgeois character structure. Techniques and strategies of montage, dismantling hierarchies and emphasizing tactility, established a new physiology of perception, anticipating and initiating transformations of the individual psyche as well as those of the larger social organization.

The transformation of the commodity into an emblem—a phenomenon that Benjamin had observed primarily in the poetry of Baudelaire—had come full circle in the readymades of Duchamp. Here the willful declaration of the unaltered object as meaningful, and the act of its appropriation, had allegorized the very act of creation by bracketing it with the anonymous procedures of mass-production. It seems that the traditional separation of the pictorial or sculptural construct into procedures and materials of construction, as much as the division between a pictorial/sculptural signifier and a signified, no longer occur in Duchamp's readymades. Rather, all three coalesce in the allegorical gesture of appropriating a preexisting object, thus negating any individual conception and production of the pictorial/sculptural sign altogether.

Duchamp's proposal for an inverted readymade, his infamous *Rembrandt as Ironing Board*, 1919, suggested the transformation of an actual cultural icon into an object of use value. It would find less of a following since it went beyond the culturally accepted limits of iconoclasm. Yet, the desire for communicative use value has not resurfaced in art since the 1930s—most likely because it has been generally submerged by the emphasis on pictorial exchange value in the period after World War II.

At the same time, this emphasis on the manufactured signifier and its mute existence made those hidden factors apparent that determine the work and the conditions under which it is perceived. These latent structures of a discursive system range from presentational devices and the institutional framework to the conventions of meaning-assignment within art itself. It seems that what Yve-Alain Bois observed in regard to Robert Ryman's paintings is only half the truth in Duchamp's work: "The narrative of process establishes a primary meaning, an ultimate originating referent that cuts off the interpretive chain."[8] The mechanically reproduced image of the once unique auratic work functions as the ideological complement to the manufactured commodity that the readymade frames in its allegorical schema. Duchamp's *L.H.O.O.Q.*, 1919, could be recalled as one of the first instantiations of a Dadaist allegorical montage, driven by the principle of appropriation. In his citation of a mass-reproduced icon of cultural history, Leonardo's *Mona Lisa*, Duchamp subjected the printed image first of all to the essentially allegorical procedure of confiscation. Subsequently, he inscribed the image with a textual insertion that could only come alive in its phonetic performance.

As is well known, beginning in the late 1950s and throughout the development of Pop art, commodity images/objects were juxtaposed with mechanically reproduced high-cultural icons in the work of Robert Rauschenberg, Andy Warhol, and Roy Lichtenstein. More importantly, as an example of an allegorical operation in the tradition of Duchamp's *L.H.O.O.Q.*, however, one would have to recognize the amazing complexity of an early work within that emerging reception of Dada practices in the early 1950s.

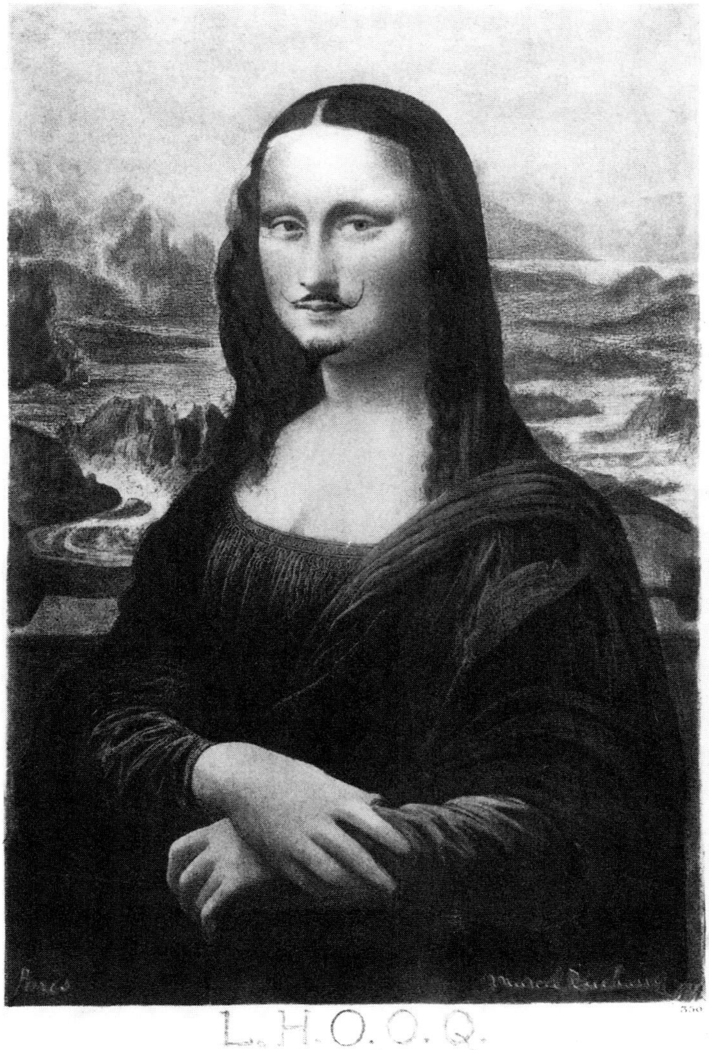

Marcel Duchamp, Replica of *L.H.O.O.Q.*, 1919, from *Box in a Valise* (*Boîte-en-Valise*), 1941–42. Collotype hand-colored with watercolor, 7¾ × 4⅞ in. (19.6 × 12.4 cm). Philadelphia Museum of Art, The Louise and Walter Arensberg Collection, Philadelphia. Photo: Lynn Rosenthal, 1992. © Succession Marcel Duchamp/ADAGP, Paris/Artists Rights Society (ARS), New York, 2015.

In 1953 Rauschenberg obtained a drawing from Willem de Kooning after having informed him of his intention to erase the drawing, and to make it the subject of a work of his own. Once Rauschenberg had executed the erasure as carefully as possible, a process which left vestiges of pencil and the imprint of the drawn lines visible as clues of an earlier drawing that had been based on similitude, the erasure was framed in a gold frame and an engraved metal label attached to the frame identified it as a work by Robert Rauschenberg entitled *Erased de Kooning Drawing*, dating it 1953.[9]

At the climax of the Abstract Expressionist idiom, this work may have been perceived as a sublimated patricidal assault by the new generation's seemingly most advanced artist. By now it appears to us, however, rather to have been one of the first examples of allegorization in postwar New York School art. Its procedures of appropriation, its depletion of the confiscated image, the superimposition or doubling of a visual text by a second text, and the shift away from purely perceptual attention to an act of reading, from the central substantive structure of the "work" to the device of the frame, all make it correspond eminently with the demands of the allegory in the definition that we have suggested. Where perceptual data are withheld or removed from the traditional surface of display, the gesture of erasure shifts the focus of attention to the appropriated historical construct on the one hand, and to the devices of framing and presentation on the other.

Furthermore, Rauschenberg's appropriation confronts two opposite paradigms of drawing almost programmatically: that of de Kooning's traditional denotative lines, and that of the purely indexical functions of the erasure. And yet, all the dispersed elements of this work seem to have become materially and semiotically congruent: the traditional drawing procedure as denotative gesture is displaced by *drawing* as erasure. And the proposition that a constructed sign now might have to critique the traditional substantive or organic models of figurative

Robert Rauschenberg, *Erased de Kooning Drawing*, 1953. 19 × 14½ in. (48.3 × 36.8 cm). San Francisco Museum of Modern Art (SFMOMA), San Francisco, CA. Courtesy Leo Castelli Gallery, New York. Photo: Walter Russell. © 2015 Robert Rauschenberg Foundation/Licensed by VAGA, New York.

representation, sublates and sublimates the pronunciation of a merely parricidal motivation.

A second, equally conspicuous example of an emerging allegorical aesthetic within that moment would be Jasper Johns' *Flag*, 1954–55. This painting not only indicated the beginning of the Duchamp reception in American art, and thus the beginning of Pop art, but more precisely, it introduced a pictorial method to New York School painting that had been previously unknown: the appropriation of an object/image whose structural, compositional, and chromatic aspects determined the painter's decision-making process in advance of the execution of the painting.

Thus, the rigid iconic/symbolic structure of the flag functions like a template or a matrix, bracketing first of all the two apparently exclusive discourses of high art and mass culture. Yet this semblance of a fusion of the oppositional spheres paradoxically reveals the irreconcilable gap between them all the more. One could argue that to the very degree that the work emerging from the reception of the readymade aesthetic in American Pop art addresses mass culture and mechanically reproduced imagery as abstract universal conditions, this work fails to clarify its historically specific framing conditions: those of its proper reification as art within the institutional framework of the museum, those of the ideology of Modernism, and those of the distribution form of painting as a commodity.

Therefore we are encountering only well-balanced and well-tempered modes of appropriation at that moment in American painting. And the successful synthesis of relative radicality and relative conventionality, would demarcate the positions of American Pop art from the mid-1950s onwards in general. Its program would always remain one of liberal reconciliation, aiming at the mastery of the conflict between individual artistic practice and collective mass cultural production, between the mass-produced imagery of low culture and the icon of individuation that each painting within the sphere of high culture mythically embodies.

Here lies one of the explanations of the social success of Pop art, and the secret behind its present rediscovery and glamorous institutionalization. If read against the historical moment which was dominated by Abstract Expressionist aesthetics and ideology, Rauschenberg's *Erased de Kooning Drawing* and Johns' first *Flag* might have appeared at first to be scandalous representations that denied the validity of traditional concepts of individual expression and authorship. Compared to the radical epistemology and seemingly inexhaustible shock of Duchamp's three-dimensional, unaltered readymade, however, they are delicate constructs of compromise, refining gestural definition and juxtaposing individualized painterly craftsmanship with seemingly anonymous mechanicity.

It could easily turn out to be one of the great ironies of history that an element of truth was contained in Clement Greenberg's conservative formalism after all. He refrained from acknowledging the impact of Duchamp's work—and of the work of the Pop artists, for that matter—because it lacked, as he perceived it, the specific self-referentiality that could empirically and critically verify itself with regard to all the perceptual and material conditions determining the perception of the painterly object. For all of its obvious failures, Greenberg's empirico-critical position at least did not succumb to the delusion of a premature reconciliation between high art and mass culture, as it was implicit in the work of Duchamp's followers.

It would take the work of two more generations for other practices to emerge in the mid-1960s that would reflect simultaneously on both legacies in their recent emanation as Pop and Minimalist strategies. Conceptualism would finally integrate Greenberg's self-referential formalist analysis of the pictorial/sculptural construction with the historical ramifications of Duchamp's readymade and its consequences.

In the work of artists such as Michael Asher, Marcel Broodthaers, Daniel Buren, Dan Graham, Hans Haacke, and Lawrence Weiner, we encounter both an examination of the framework that determines the

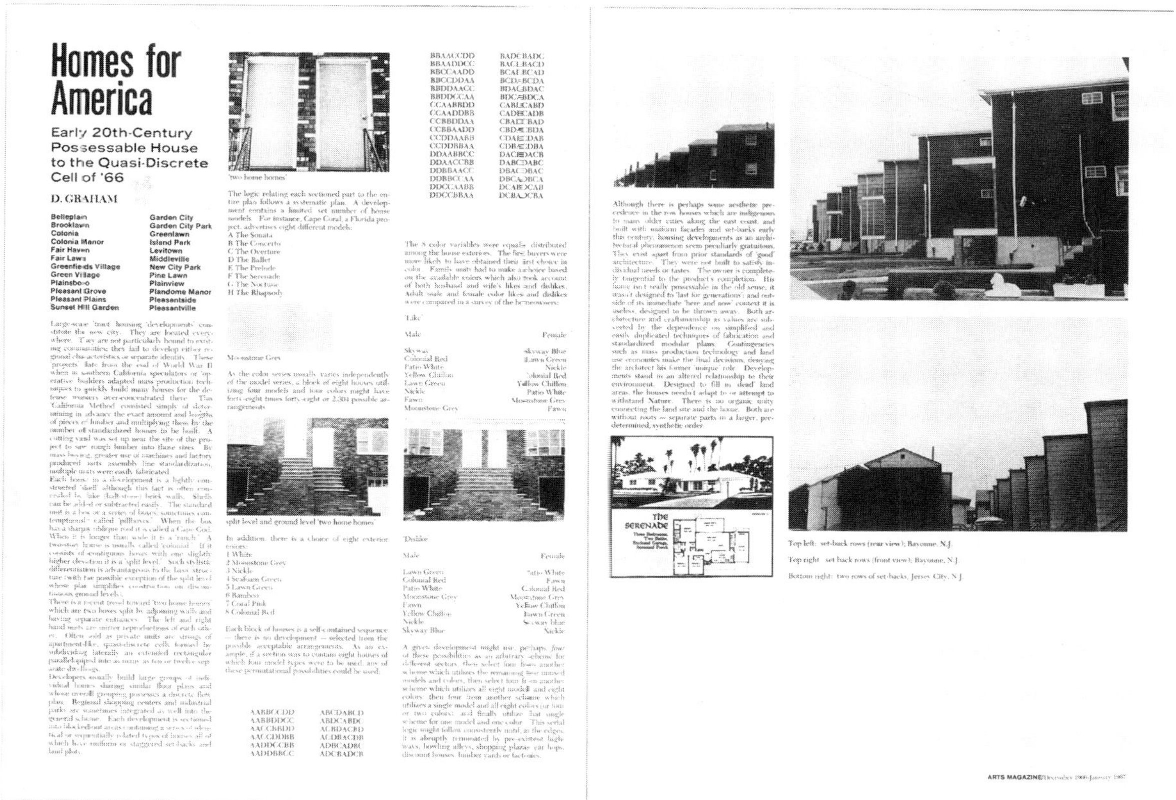

Homes for America

Early 20th-Century Possessable House to the Quasi-Discrete Cell of '66

D. GRAHAM

Belleplain	Garden City
Brooklawn	Garden City Park
Colonia	Greenlawn
Colonia Manor	Island Park
Fair Haven	Levitown
Fair Lawn	Middleville
Greenfields Village	New City Park
Green Village	Pine Lawn
Plainsboro	Plainview
Pleasant Grove	Plandome Manor
Pleasant Plains	Pleasantside
Sunset Hill Garden	Pleasantville

Dan Graham, *Homes for America*. Layout for *Arts Magazine*, December 1965–January 1966. © Dan Graham. Courtesy the artist and Marian Goodman Gallery, New York.

reading conventions of artistic signs, as well as an analysis of the structuring principles of the sign itself. A work such as Graham's 1966 *Homes for America*[10] was conceived as an art-magazine article, and it becomes now fully readable as an early example of allegorical deconstruction in Conceptual art. In this work, the institutional framework, as much as the distribution form, the economic materiality of the support system, as much as the physical site of the work's ultimate existence, are foregrounded as the very parameters that determine the function and reading of the work from its very inception.

Since his *Homes for America* focused on what was then the primary distribution form of esthetic information, the printed magazine page and the photo reproduction, Graham would refer to that form—not surprisingly—as a sort of "disposable readymade." On the one hand, the work inscribed itself within the historical context of Minimal sculpture's self-reflexivity. Yet simultaneously it denied the validity of such self-reflexivity by introducing a public and popular "subject matter" (in this case, serialized, standardized, suburban prefabricated architecture).

The linguistic and semiotic interests of these early Conceptual artists led to a renewed reading and rediscovery of Stéphane Mallarmé. In particular, his investigations of the spatialization of the linear, temporal dimension of reading and writing. Independently of each other, both Graham and Broodthaers, for example, had become aware of the historical consequences of Mallarmé's work. In his essay "Information," written and partially published in 1967, Graham discussed Mallarmé's 1866 project for "The Book."[11] The symbolist poet had conceived a book whose multidimensional geometry implied a complete restructuring of reading and writing, one that was fundamentally different from the reading conventions as they had been known since the invention of the printed letter.

Two years later, in 1969, Broodthaers published his version of an "hommage" to Mallarmé, citing his *Un coup de dés jamais n'abolira le hasard* which exercised literally all the principles of allegorical

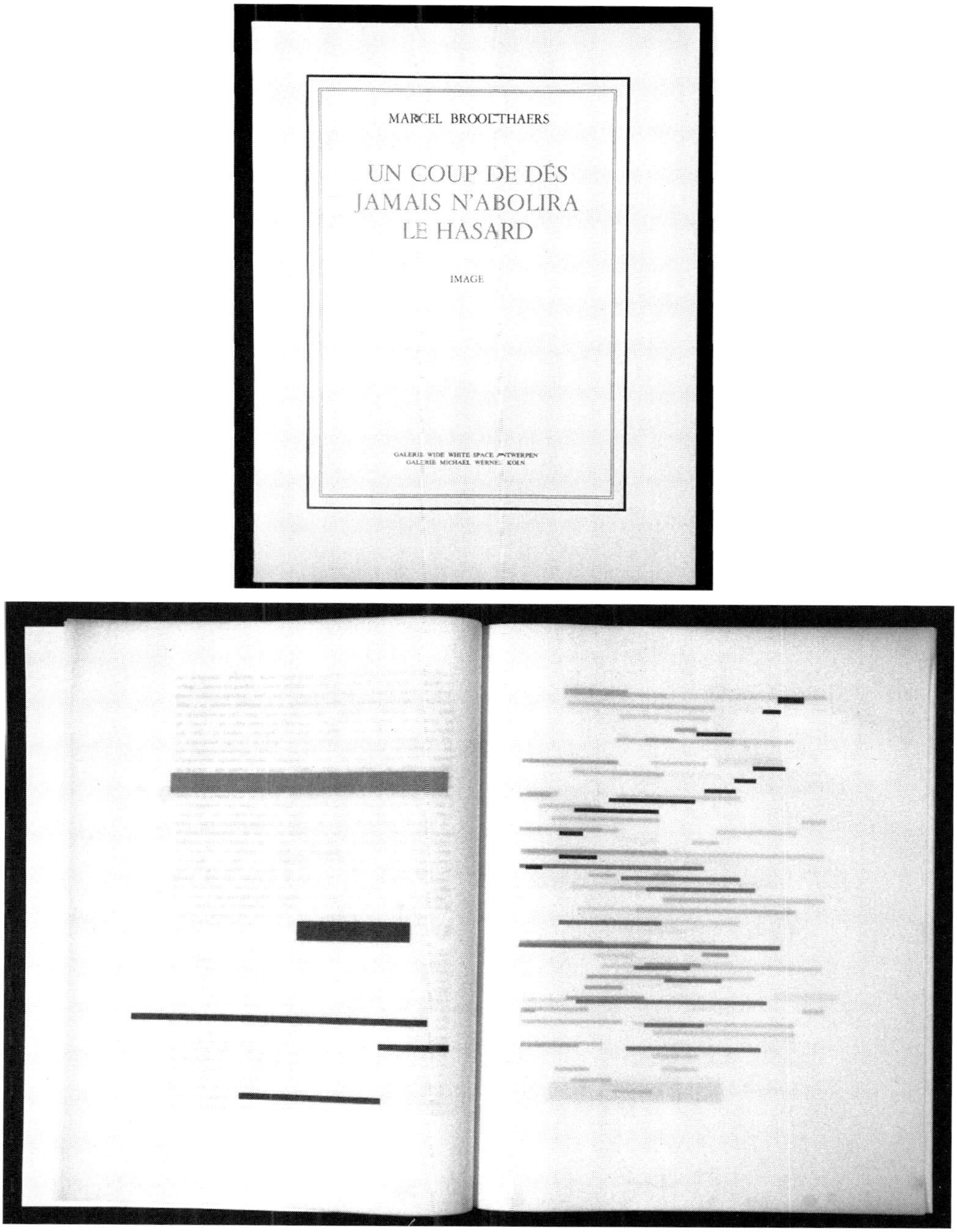

Marcel Broodthaers, *Un coup de dés jamais n'abolira le hasard*, 1969. Edition of ninety on transparent mecanographic paper, 32.5 × 25 cm. Wide White Space, Antwerp/Galerie Michael Werner, Cologne. © 2015 The Estate of Marcel Broodthaers/Artists Rights Society (ARS), New York/SABAM, Brussels.

appropriation and montage as Benjamin had developed them.[12] Broodthaers' own *Un coup de dés jamais n'abolira le hasard* confiscated the presentational details, format, design, and typography of the cover of Mallarmé's *Un coup de dés* as it had been published posthumously by Editions Gallimard in Paris in 1914. Mallarmé's name on the cover, however, was now replaced in a semblance of bold parricidal displacement by that of Marcel Broodthaers' own.

In a manner reminiscent of Rauschenberg's erasure of de Kooning's drawing, Broodthaers operated on the scriptural configurations of Mallarmé's poem: the actual text of the poem was reduced from its spatial and graphic extensions, and was newly condensed and conventionalized as a continuous text. Its textual and graphic avant-gardism seemingly downgraded and disarticulated, Broodthaers' *Un coup de dés* relocated the poem to the site of the original's preface, a text which was now dropped from the book altogether.

While the text's semantic and lexical information were depleted, the visual and spatial dimensions of the poem's original configuration were maintained on the page, as it were, in the shadowy opaque black bars (*sous rature*) that followed the former textual display down to the most minute detail. Mallarmé's typographical modifications of his lexical structures (the position, placement, size, weight, and direction of the poem's spatialized scripture) disappeared, or rather, were sublated, within the pure graphic/linear demarcations of the erasures.

Since Broodthaers' book was printed on semi-transparent tracing paper, the pages could be "read" not only in the traditional linear, horizontal left-to-right reading pattern that is ordered on a vertical plane. But the translucency of the pages also invited reading along an axis of lateral, superimposed planes as well as an inversion of the recto/verso reading order. Thus Broodthaers' allegorical procedures deconstructed the positivist prison-house of Modernism, alternating between a focus on the institutions of artistic practice and on the discursive structure determining modernism's objects.[13]

In a rather different manner, yet central to our study of the phenomenon of allegorical appropriation, one should see how Daniel Buren employed this strategy in 1972 in order to transfer the viewer's attention from exhibited objects to the underlying frameworks that determine the conditions of their presentation and their perception. In a work entitled *Exhibition of an Exhibition*, his installation for *Documenta 5* in Kassel in 1972, Buren inserted his work into each of the previously determined sections of the exhibition (painting, sculpture, advertising, propaganda posters, *art brut*, etc.).[14]

His interventions consisted of the attachment of identical wall elements (white stripes 8.7 cm wide printed on white paper) that served to demarcate the framing and display devices of the seemingly neutral institution of the gallery space and its architectural conventions. Covered in each exhibition segment by another type of work or object (paintings, posters, or sculpture when the paper elements covered a base), it was only in one exhibition segment (the section on post-Minimal and Conceptual art, curated by Konrad Fischer and entitled *Light and Idea*) that Buren's element was actually presented as an autonomous, self-sufficient structure in the manner of an abstract painting.

The most spectacular collision occurred when by apparent coincidence Johns' *Flag*, 1954–55, was placed on one of the demarcated wall areas. This "chance encounter" not only revealed the historical distance between the two works, and more importantly, the specificity with which Buren had overcome the randomness of Johns' attempt to fuse high art and mass culture, but it also pointed further backward to the problematic implications of Duchamp's aesthetic of the readymade, as we discussed them briefly above. Buren's critique of Duchamp was directed first of all at the anarchist willfulness of Duchamp's decision to ignore the institutional and discursive framing devices that made the conception of the readymade possible at all. Second, his critique was directed against the purely iconic mediation between avant-garde and mass culture that Duchamp, and after him Johns and the American Pop artists, had engaged with.

By contrast, Buren's analytic approach to the governing institutional and discursive conditions of presentation, mediation and reception of a work of art in the present historical situation was infinitely more specific. It recognized the actually existing frames within which spectatorial desire and reading competence are currently contained, and that make a merely iconic and populist mediation between mass culture, commodity object, and avant-garde art ultimately pointless and abstract.

One of the first works of that post-Minimal generation to actually incorporate the commodity structure directly into the conception of the work and into the elements of its presentation was Hans Haacke's contribution to the summer festival "L'art vivant américain" at the Maeght Foundation, St. Paul de Vence, France, in 1970. Haacke complied with the organizer's request to contribute to a "non-profit avant-garde festival" by linking his contribution to the concealed promotion of saleable objects at the foundation. Haacke's "performance" consisted of a tape-recorded litany of prices and descriptions of prints for sale in the bookstore of the Maeght Gallery foundation. The recording was interrupted only by news agency teletype reports, read over the phone from the office of the newspaper *Nice-Matin*, and it seems that only the fear of audience protest deterred the organizers from banning Haacke's work.

The historical record of attempts by museum authorities and exhibition organizers to censor Haacke's strategies to reintroduce the repressed elements of culture into the official face and functions of cultural institutions, attests to the truly allegorical qualities of Haacke's work. In a number of projects Haacke has chosen to write *art history* as *commodity history*. This is most prominent, for example, in the chronology and genealogy of the succession of owners of the *Asparagus Still Life* by Edouard Manet (a work by Haacke banned from an exhibition in Cologne in 1974), and in a similar work delineating the provenance of Seurat's *Les Poseuses*.[15] More recently, Haacke has investigated the economic practices and manoeuvers of Peter Ludwig, the major cultural "benefactor" and collector, uncovering the actual benefits and privileges that the apparently selfless generosity of the patron implies, as for example in his work *Der Pralinenmeister* (*The Master Chocolate Maker*, 1981).[16]

In an American context, two works from the late 1970s must also be mentioned as prefiguring contemporary allegorical strategies of appropriation: Louise Lawler's untitled 1978 installation at Artists Space in New York,[17] which—among several other elements—incorporated a painting from 1883 by Henry Stullmann representing a racehorse (loaned by the New York Racing Association), and Michael Asher's contribution to the 73rd American Exhibition at the Art Institute of Chicago in 1979, which appropriated a bronze replica of Jean-Antoine Houdon's life-size marble sculpture of George Washington. Due to their enigmatic procedures these works have received little or no critical attention, yet they both anticipated and prefigured the newly developing strategies of the crucial practices of the 1980s under consideration in this essay.[18]

Lawler's installation made those supplemental elements, generally considered marginal, yet necessary for the production of a work and its exhibition, the central subject of her installation. Thus the actual objects of Lawler's contribution to the exhibition consisted first of all of the appropriated painting of a racehorse, appearing displaced and decontextualized. It functioned as the mere allegorical shell of painting at the moment of painting's reactionary reemergence in the culture at large. Furthermore, two stage lights illuminated the arrangement and spectacularized the innocuous racehorse painting. One of the lights confronted the viewer's eyes directly from above the painting (interfering thus with perception of the painting itself, almost inhibiting it), and the other was directed outward, through the exhibition space, projecting its light out of the window and casting a large shadow of the window frame onto the street. Thereby it connected the isolated exhibition space with its urban setting and brought the presence of the institution and exhibition to the attention of the immediate neighborhood. Lawler's catalog

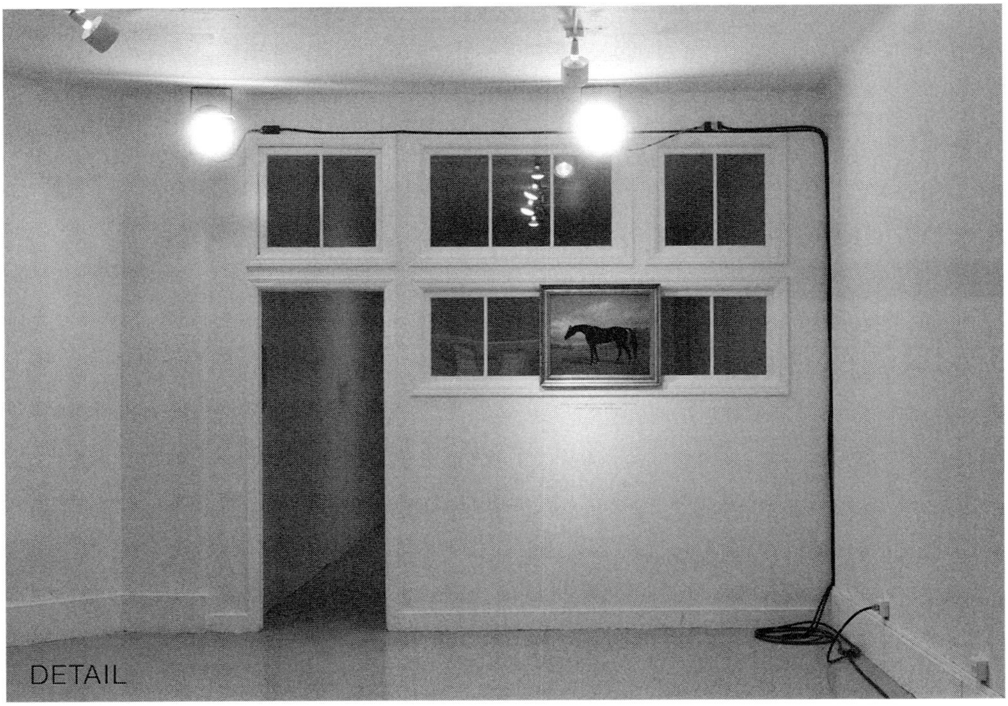

Louise Lawler, *Untitled Installation at Artists Space, New York*, 1978. One oil painting borrowed from the New York Racing Association, Aqueduct Racetrack, painted by Henri Stulman in 1883. 2 VNSP par 64 1,000-watt lights hung over the painting, one directed at the viewer, the other through the space. At night this projects the shape of the windows onto the ground floor of the building across the street. © Louise Lawler. Courtesy the artist and Metro Pictures, New York.

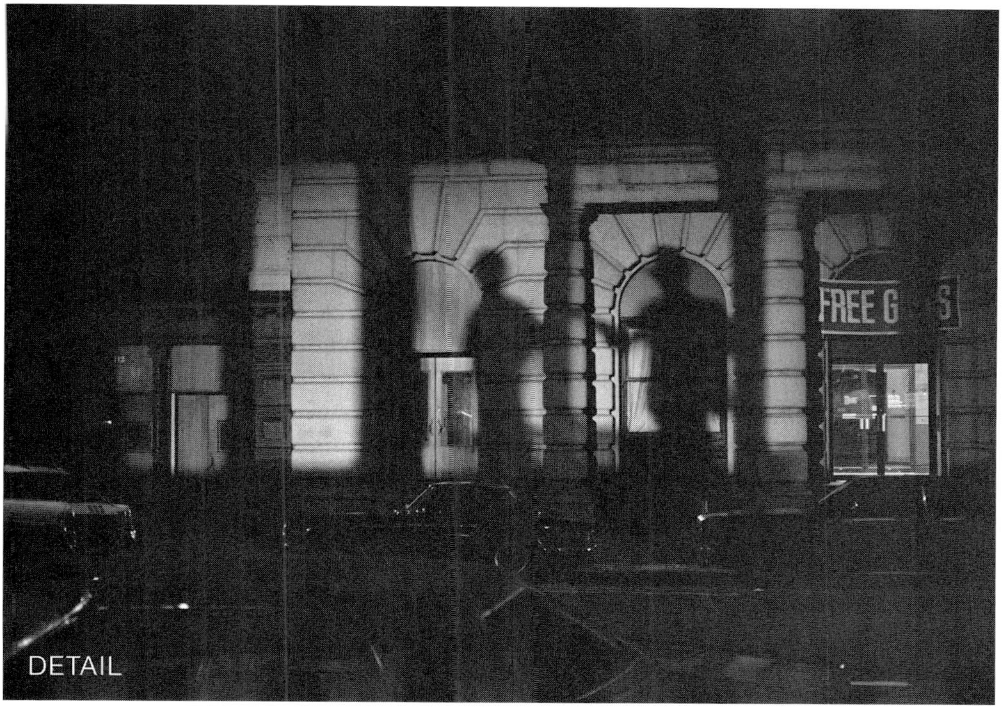

Louise Lawler, *Untitled Installation at Artists Space, New York*, 1978. Exterior view of the installation: spotlights projecting window frame onto the street. © Louise Lawler. Courtesy the artist and Metro Pictures, New York.

contribution for the exhibition, by contrast, consisted solely in the graphic design for a new logo for the institution Artists Space in New York that exhibited her work. Lastly, a poster with that logo as its sole information was distributed outside of the exhibition to disseminate knowledge about Artists Space and increase its visibility in the manner of a newly emerging product or corporation.

It was with the work of this group of artists that questions of site specificity were programmatically expanded to include the analysis of the discursive framing devices and a critique of the institutional conventions of exhibition and display (their material and economic support systems, as much as the physical, socio-political and the linguistic components of those elements that previous reflections on site specificity had considered exclusively in spatial, or at best, in architectural terms). Ultimately, as a result of this expanded concept of site specificity, new questions, specifically concerning the mode of address, and the actually existing audience expectations toward contemporary culture, became integral for the production of these artists.

Anyone taking seriously the implications of this project of a *situational esthetics* as it was developed in the late 1960s would have to recognize its ramifications for the cognitive and perceptual conditions of future art production. Furthermore, one would have to realize from now on—so it seemed at least—that any return to an unconditional autonomy of art would be extremely problematical if not outright impossible.

Of course this did not imply a doxa either. Lawrence Weiner's reduction of esthetic practice to its linguistic definition, Buren's and Asher's analysis of the historical place and function of esthetic constructs within institutions, or Haacke's and Broodthaers' operations revealing the material conditions of those institutions as ideological frameworks, would articulate positions that could be logically continued and that would have to be developed further.

Yet it is important to understand that the dialectical response to these positions would not be, as some seem to have thought, a return to some obscure historical conventions of figurative and neo-expressionist painting and sculpture, or, more importantly, to the commodity camouflage that they provide. Rather, what the new generation of artists emerging in the mid- to late Seventies confronted, was not only the precision with which the Conceptual generation of the Sixties and early Seventies had analyzed the place and function of esthetic practice within the discourses and institutions of Modernism. But the new generation would now re-orient its attention and address the ideological discourses *outside* of the Modernist framework, focusing on those mass cultural discourses that condition and control the experience of everyday life. And it was this constellation of Conceptualist precision and critical mass cultural analysis that brought about the paradigmatic shift in the work of artists as Dara Birnbaum, Jenny Holzer, Barbara Kruger, Louise Lawler, Sherrie Levine, Martha Rosler and Cindy Sherman.

In their projects, the languages of television, advertising, and photography, and the ideology of everyday life, were subjected to a formal and linguistic analysis that essentially followed Roland Barthes' model of a secondary mythification in his classic essays *Mythologies* (1957), which according to Barthes, attempt to deconstruct the mythical constructions of ideology. Barthes' strategy of secondary mythification publicly repeats the semiotic and linguistic devaluation of primary language by myth. Therefore it could be considered as both a historical sequel and a structural analogue to Benjamin's theorization of allegorical procedures that were defined—as we argued above—by the reiterated devaluation of the object once it had become the commodified object.

It seems justifiable therefore to transfer the notion of montage and allegory from the context of the avant-garde practices of the first half of the century, into a reading of recent and contemporary work, and to extend the ramifications of an esthetics of allegorical montage into the present, modified and mediated through a method of critical mythology.

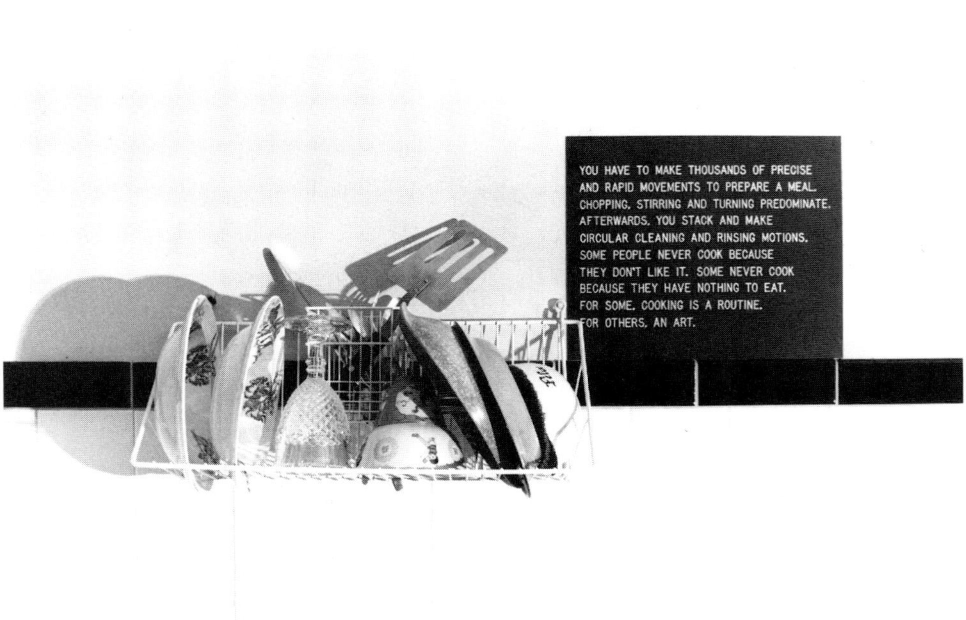

Jenny Holzer, *Untitled ("Essay" Series)*, 1981. Engraving on metal plate, 12 × 10 in. (30.5 × 24.5 cm). Private collection, New York. Photo: Louise Lawler. © 2015 Jenny Holzer, member Artists Rights Society (ARS), New York.

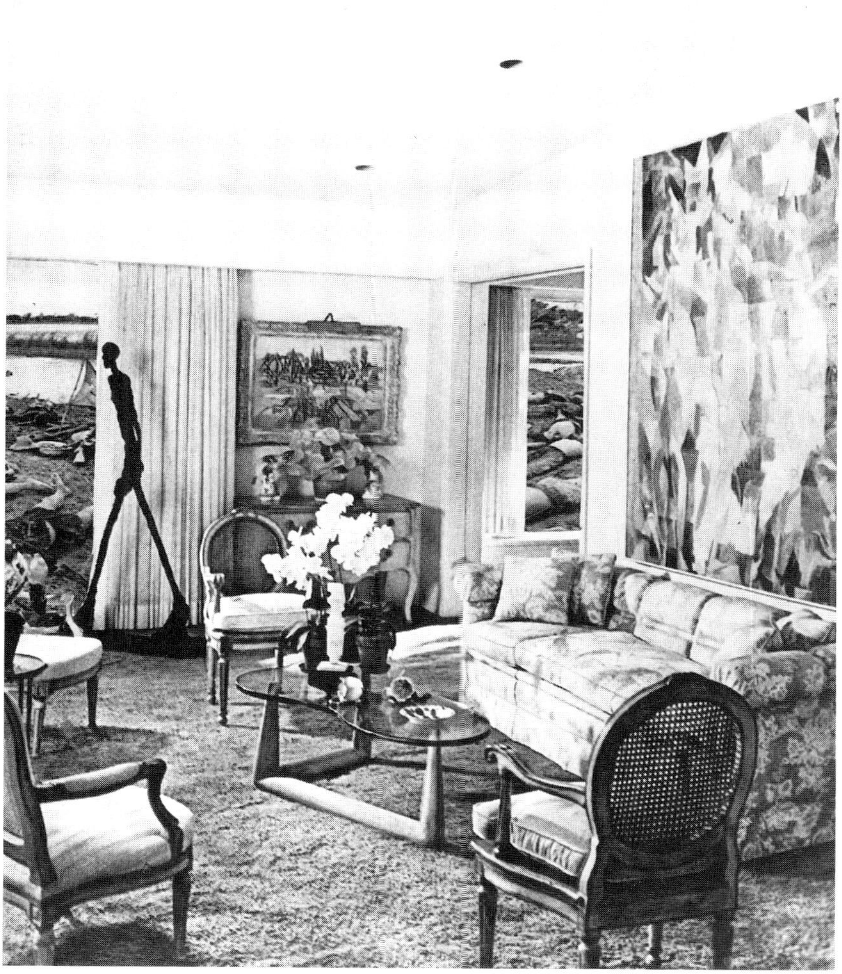

Martha Rosler, *House Beautiful: Giacometti*, from the series *Bringing the War Home*, 1968. Photomontage printed as color photograph, 8 × 10 in. (20.3 × 25.4 cm). © Martha Rosler.

The political spectrum within which these artists operate—inasmuch as it can be read in the work itself and inasmuch as it can be isolated at all from the current climate of cynical pessimism—encompasses a variety of positions. They range from the apparently outright denial of production and dialectical construction in the work of Levine to the position of cultural activism in Rosler's work. By contrast, Holzer's anarcho-situationist position trusts the strategy of an unmediated street activity in which anonymous posters confront language and its daily ideological performances with acts of a seemingly self-generated linguistic *détournement*. Birnbaum's videotapes and video installations deploy a similar set of situationist strategies of *détournement* with regard to the language conventions operative within the spectacularized framework of corporate media production.

The risk of Levine's position of a programmatic aesthetic passivity is that it might function ultimately in secret alliance with the static conditions of social life in general. These had been previously reflected in Warhol's passive affirmative practices that were ultimately only concerned with the work's finite commodity structure, considering the innovation of artistic product design as the solely accessible space of social variance.

By contrast, Rosler's activist position runs the risk of ignoring the structural specificities of the work's circulation form and of the determining factors of its distribution system within contemporary art institutions (the gallery, the museum, the fashion circuit). In isolating itself from this system completely, Rosler's work risks a failure of communication already on the first level of a mere reception of current art practices. This is all the more problematical when the work's larger claims are in fact to engage the spectators in types of communicative action that would lead toward radical political awareness and change. The dilemma underlying Holzer's work is that it ignores the mediating framework of the institutions within which language as ideology is historically placed, for the sake of her direct actions upon this particular condition of language. As a consequence the work has to claim an apparent independence from these institutions (i.e., the museum and the gallery space) and it can pretend to a false immediacy and radicality (i.e., direct action on language in the street) which inevitably leads toward an increasing number of compromises with the very framework that the work's false radicality claims to have dismissed. Finally, the risk for Birnbaum's work is that it could be integrated so successfully into the advanced technologies and linguistic perfection of governing television ideology that its original impulse of critical deconstruction could disappear in a perfect blending of a technocratic estheticization of art practices, and the media's perpetual need to rejuvenate its looks and products by grafting itself onto the esthetics of the avant-garde.

The inability of current art history and criticism to recognize the necessity and relevance of this new generation of artists working within the parameters of allegorical appropriation results partially from art history's almost total failure to develop an adequate reading of Dada and Productivist theory and practices, particularly of the activities of "factography" and documentary work and the range of agitprop production that emerged from it—for example, in the work of Ossip Brik, Vladimir Mayakovsky, Lyubov Popova, and Sergei Tretyakov, as much as the still essentially ignored key figure of montage practice, John Heartfield. Once these activities are admitted to the framework of legitimization that art history provides, their consequences for contemporary practice will become more readable.

At the very moment when even the analysis of the institutional framework could be safely absorbed and integrated into the codex of exhibition topics since the supremacy of the museum had been widely reaffirmed by a general return to traditional production procedures—Michael Asher abandoned the liberally delegated option to adorn the institution's repressive tolerance, by expanding the focus of the field of critical deconstruction. An untitled installation, consisting of a number of spatially dispersed elements, was his contribution to the exhibition

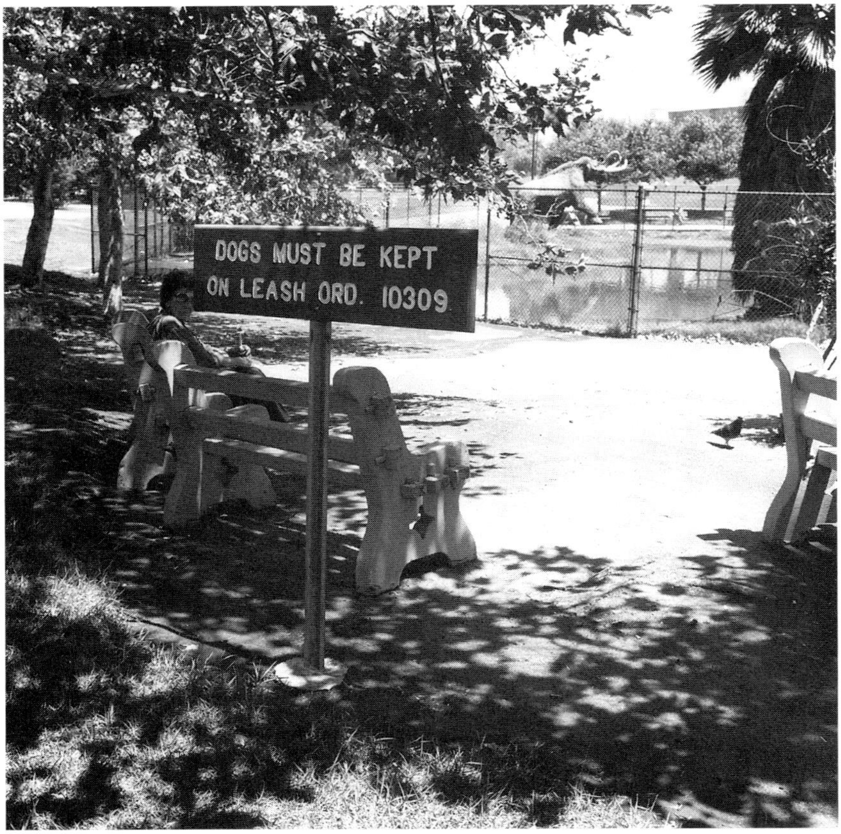

Michael Asher, Los Angeles County Museum of Art, California, USA, "Art in Los Angeles—*The Museum as Site: Sixteen Projects*," July 16–October 4, 1981. Photo: Michael Asher. © Michael Asher Foundation.

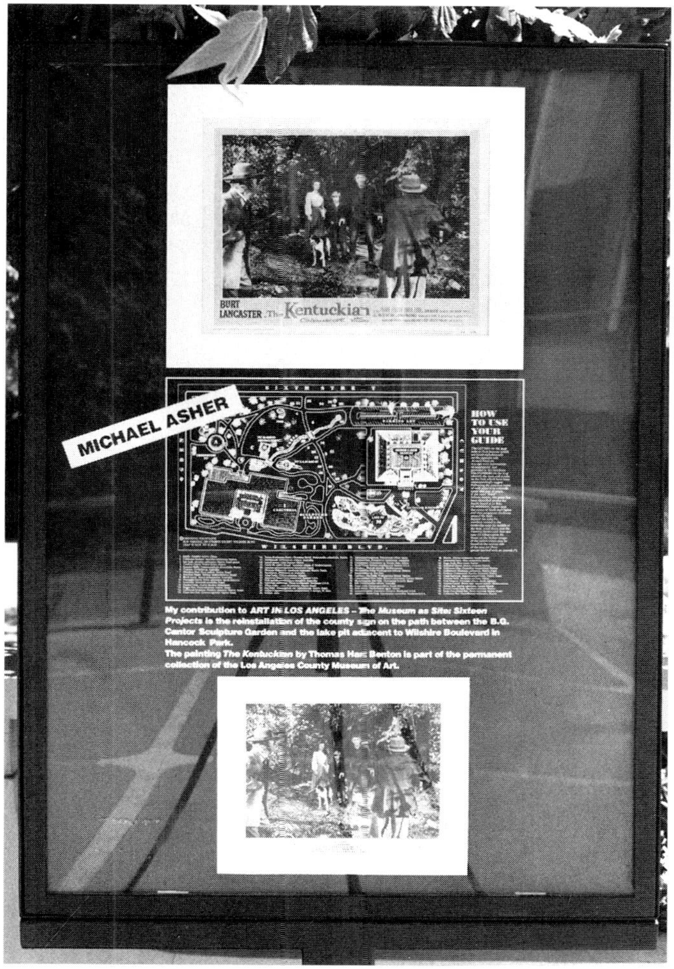
BURT LANCASTER
The Kentuckian
MICHAEL ASHER
HOW TO USE YOUR GUIDE
SIXTH STREET
WILSHIRE BLVD.
My contribution to ART IN LOS ANGELES – The Museum as Site: Sixteen Projects is the reinstallation of the county sign on the path between the B.G. Cantor Sculpture Garden and the lake pit adjacent to Wilshire Boulevard in Hancock Park.
The painting The Kentuckian by Thomas Hart Benton is part of the permanent collection of the Los Angeles County Museum of Art.

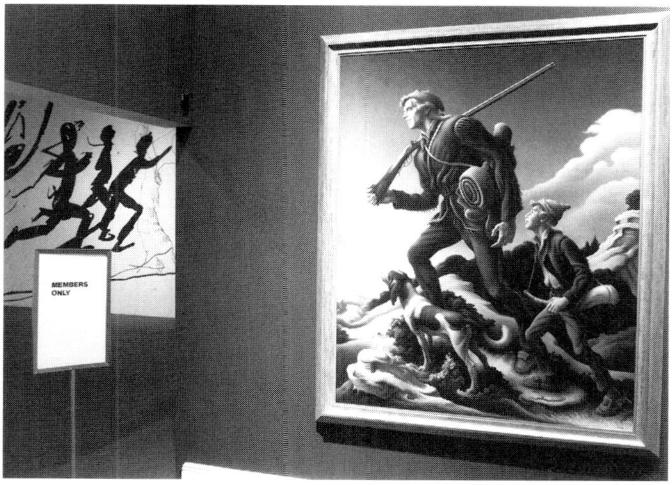
MEMBERS ONLY

The Museum as Site: Sixteen Projects in 1981 at the Los Angeles County Museum of Art. Asher's work integrated three fragments from heterogeneous discourses: the first element was a wooden sign with the inscription "dogs must be kept on leash ord. 10309."

Asher replaced the sign that had been previously lifted by vandals from the park surrounding the museum, and he had the sign produced by the park authorities themselves to match the rustic, handcrafted look of the original. The second element was a poster, displaying a color reproduction and a black-and-white still photograph showing the same scene from the movie *The Kentuckian* (1955).

This poster was placed on a brass placard in the main entrance court where the museum normally announces its special events and lectures. Along with those two images (which showed Burt Lancaster as "The Kentuckian" stepping out of a forest with a child, a woman, and a dog, facing two men with rifles), a map of the museum's park indicated the location of the replaced wooden sign, and identified it as one element of Asher's contribution to the exhibition. In a third element the viewer was furthermore informed that the museum's permanent collection housed a painting by Thomas Hart Benton entitled *The Kentuckian*, 1955, which had been commissioned on the occasion of the film's original release. The painting, depicting Lancaster and a little boy, a dog, and a blossoming plant on the top of a mountain, was originally in Lancaster's collection, and had been later donated by the actor to the museum.

Inside the museum, the visitor could in fact find Benton's painting in its usual place in the permanent collection, without any additional information referring to Asher's temporary appropriation. Asher provided fewer clues or instructions here than in his previous works, enticing the viewers to assemble and synthesize the various elements of his installation. The work's utterly ephemeral existence and the dispersion of its elements made it likely that parts (or all) of the installation remained unrecognized by those viewers who had recently become once again readjusted to traditional works of painting and sculpture with highly condensed and centralized visual regulations.

Placed with the context of Asher's project, Benton's stridently anti-Modernist painting signaled all the more the artist's overtly sexist, racist, and chauvinist positions dating from the McCarthy era. But Asher's project also contemplated the absurd historical situation of an easel painting that had been commissioned by a movie corporation from a reactionary master of representational painting, that had served as a promotional gadget for the release of a film, and that had been donated subsequently by the movie star to the collection of the museum.

The constellation of elements in Asher's allegorical construction also provided a discomforting historical example of the political implications of a breakdown of Modernist thinking, and a concomitant return to traditional models of representation. Asher's work seemed to perceive itself as operating from within a historically comparable situation. It responded to the cultural symptoms of a newly asserted cultural and political authoritarianism by confronting its viewers with a work that demanded an allegorical analysis of a disseminated and decentered structure.

The reinstallation of the dog sign in the park of the museum—as an act bordering on travesty in response to the exhibition's topic *The Museum as Site*—evidently denied the historical interest of an academicized notion of site specificity. It allegorizes simultaneously—as a textual and iconic reference—the hidden dimension of authoritarianism in representational painting. Furthermore, the reference to the movie and its star (who—as the donor of the painting—functions as a new type of patron of the museum) confronts the museum's ever increasing entanglement with the entertainment industry. Asher's brilliant diagnostics specifically pointed to the then imminent and henceforth rapid transformation of the institutions of high culture into mere appendices of the culture industry (which since then has become an uncontested rule). And while the work's analytical specificity focused first of all on the local cultural contradictions in Los Angeles, the installation transcended the limits of that context, developing a model that critically reflected the universal conditions of artistic production.

Ultimately it is in the materiality and status of objects in Asher's installation, their placement as much as their interrelationship, that the work's complex references become fully evident. Each element continues to exist within its own context to the same degree that it enters the superimposition of discourses that now constitute Asher's "work." By repositioning Benton's painting within its historical context (i.e., its place and function, its patron and original purpose), it acquired also a sudden, exemplary significance for contemporary painting and its conceits.

Whereas the technically reproduced images, the poster and still photograph that were placed in the museum's showcase doubled their representational status by assuming temporarily and peripherally the status of art objects, clarifying the unique, auratic object's dependence on technical reproduction. The only element manufactured specifically for the purposes of this installation was paradoxically the most quotidian, the most functional of all objects, the wooden sign in the park.

In Asher's appropriations, the discursive fragments are, however, never transformed into a finite status as art objects. Their given historical status and functions (e.g., as ideological discursive elements, for example) are always maintained. The ephemerality of these elements (e.g., lobby card, park sign), as much as their dispersed presentation, operates in tandem with an apparent lack of productive artistic presence and authorial identity And to the extent that the reading and viewing of this work suggest the absence of a unified, authorial subject, the work opposes the condition of becoming merely an aesthetic fetish and resists the commodification of cultural practice.

Thus, while the refusal of production in Asher's work primarily decenters reading, it also attempts to generate an awareness of the various layers of ideological overdetermination within the production and reception of cultural practice in the present. Unlike Levine's negation of production, however, which suggests a position of self-effacing complacency or melancholic contemplation, Asher's allegories manifest the hidden network of relations and discourses, the institutionally mediated interests and powers that constitute the framing devices of contemporary culture. Nevertheless, it has to be said, that within the distributional system of the gallery framework itself, Levine's work functions—for the time being, at least—as one of the strongest negations of the mythical singularity of the work of art and its indisputable status as a commodity. Her work's melancholic strategies threaten not only the current reaffirmation of an expressive creativity, but also that myth's implicit affirmation of private property and corporate enterprise as the economic parameters of culture.

At the very historical moment when a reactionary middle class struggles to expand its privileges, buttressing an oligarchic hegemony searching for cultural legitimation, and when hundreds of minor talents in painting obediently provide gestures of free expression, Levine's work subverts this spectacle of a mythical individuality. While continuing practices defined by Duchamp and updated by Warhol, her allegorical appropriations prove that Baudelaire's sexist diagnosis was wrong when he argued that the poetical was necessarily alien to female nature since melancholy was outside the female emotional experience. With Levine and Lawler enter the female dandy, whose disdain has been sharpened by the experience of phallocratic oppression in the so-called art world, and whose sense of resistance to domination is therefore more alert than that of their male colleagues practicing painting in the present.

In the current historical situation, male artists inevitably adopt the psychosexual standards of obsolete role models and provide products for the market, but they fail to change esthetic practice as much as they fail to challenge the conventions of subject construction. By contrast, artists like Asher, Lawler and Levine radically redefine artistic practice by transcending traditional character formation and social role play. And to the very extent that they criticize the commodity form of culture and the current practices of instant institutionalization, they fail to enter cultural reception altogether since they do not fulfill the public's expectations, and do not abide by the rules of culturally acceptable deviation. As one author stated lucidly,

> to exemplify an attitude within which the bourgeois world can first and foremost find its identity, that of the enchanted consumer. ... By doing so, the ideological condition of the *posthistoire* which late capitalism claims for itself, would equally be reaffirmed by art practice.[19]

The contemporary allegories use methods of appropriation and montage without estheticizing them in a newly auratic disguise of the commodity.

We might even find strategies and procedures of quotation and appropriation in contemporary painting (for example in the work of David Salle or Julian Schnabel), but painting inevitably proposes a reconciliation with the very social contradictions that contemporary culture should precisely articulate. With few exceptions, the ultimate subject of painting is always a newly centralized author, whereas in contemporary montage procedures the ultimate subject is—following Barthes' brilliant prognosis—always the reader/viewer.

After all, it is in the critical analysis of the actual procedures and materials of production and reception that a work's historical legitimacy will become evident. In expanding the spacing of its elements, in isolating the discursive fragments of its appropriation, and by redirecting the viewing/reading to the frame, the new montage work decenters authorial subjectivity as much as it confronts the viewing/reading subject with acts of its proper dispersal.[20] Yet the viewing/reading subject remains always within a dialectical relation to the text, since it is simultaneously constituted and negated in these acts of quotation. Precisely to the degree that the various sources and authors of quoted "texts" are left intact and fully identifiable in a truly contemporary montage, the viewers/readers encounter a decentered text that completes itself in the acts of their reading/viewing and through the comparison of the original and subsequent layers of meaning that the appropriated text/image has acquired.

It is important to recognize in what way and to what extent the notion of fragmentation in allegorical procedures differs from the phallocratic tendency in painting which associates fragmentation with broken saucers, burnt wood, and crumpled straw. Levine confiscates historical objects, canceling their innate authenticity, their historical function, and their meaning—in true allegorical fashion. In her seemingly random selection of imagery from the history of Modernism, representations are literally torn from the hermetic totality of the ideological discourses within which they now operate. Just as Benjamin had identified devalorization as one of the fundamental principles of allegory, Levine devalues the objects of appropriation by negating the aestheticized commodity status of photographs (for example those by Walker Evans, Edward Weston, Eliot Porter) in her willful, seemingly random acts of re-photographing and re-presentation, emphatically restating their actual status as multiplied, technically reproduced imagery.

Levine's apparently radical denial of authorship—like Warhol's before her—might fail to recognize the socially acceptable, if not ideologically desirable, features it implies: to publically affirm the final dismantling of the subject, and to sustain a detached and passive complacency in the face of the static conditions of a totally reified existence. And these faint historical spaces, opened between original and reproduction, easily seduce the viewer into a fatalistic acceptance, since they do not enact a dimension of critical negativity that would imply an activist model of practice, but merely an affirmative and melancholic contemplation.

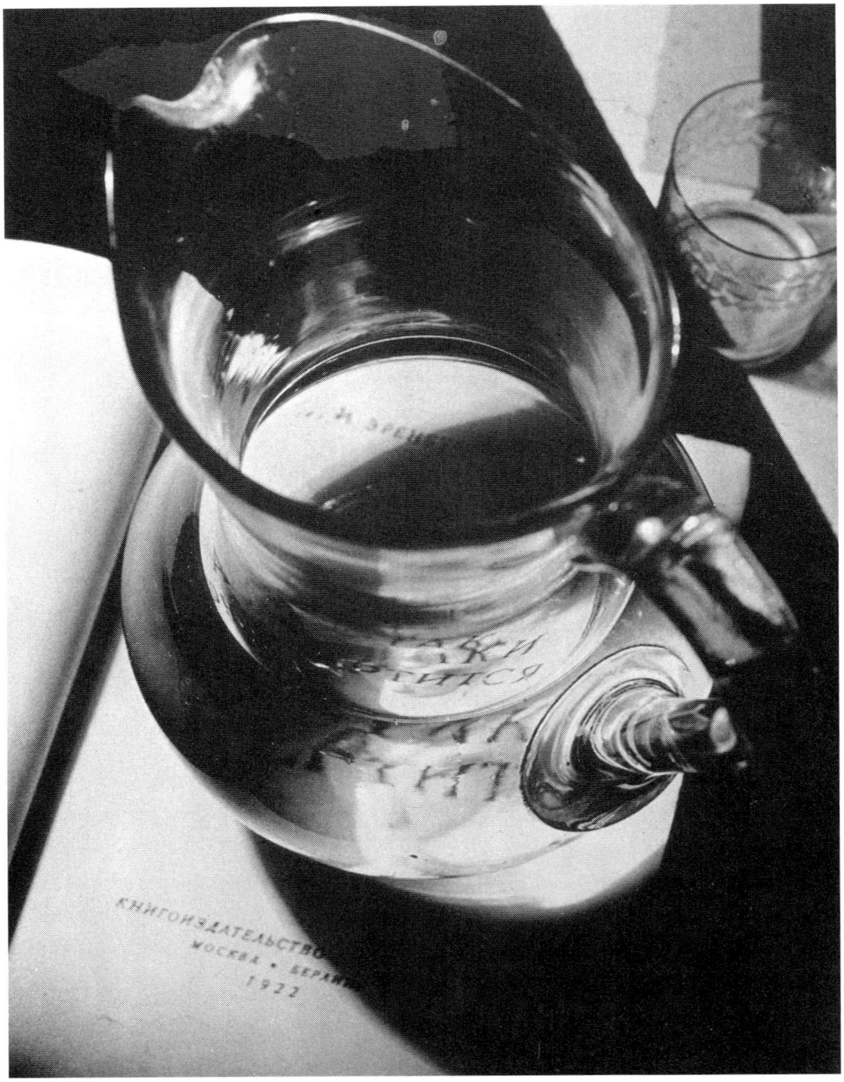

Sherrie Levine, *After Rodchenko: 2*, 1987–1998. Silver gelatin prints, 12 photos, 8 × 6 in. (20.3 × 15.2 cm). © Sherrie Levine. Courtesy the artist and Paula Cooper Gallery, New York.

Levine's position and that of Martha Rosler differ precisely in their attitudes regarding social context and the historic authenticity of their objects of appropriation. Levine's work embodies the ambivalence of the artist (and intellectual) who lacks or disavows class identity and political perspective, inevitably exerting a certain fascination over those contemporary critics who are equally ambivalent toward their affiliations with the powers and privileges that the middle class provides. This attitude is evidenced in the following statement by Levine:

> Instead of taking photographs of trees or nudes, I take photographs of photographs. I choose pictures that manifest the desire that nature and culture provide us with a sense of order and meaning. I appropriate these images to express my own simultaneous longing for the passion of engagement and the sublimity of aloofness. I hope that in my photographs of photographs an uneasy peace will be made between my attraction to the ideals these pictures exemplify and my desire to have no ideals or fetters whatsoever. It is my aspiration that my photographs, which contain their own contradiction, would represent the best of both worlds.[21]

In spite of his devotion to allegorical theory and its concrete implementation as he discerned it in the work of Baudelaire and the Surrealist montage work of the 1920s, Benjamin was aware of the inherent danger of melancholic complacency and of the violence of passive denial that the allegorical subject imposes upon itself as well as upon the objects of its choice. The contemplative stance of the melancholic subject, the "comfortable view of the past," as he argued, must be exchanged for the political view of the present.[22] This theoretical position was developed further in "The Author as Producer," a text in which all reflection upon allegorical procedures has been abandoned and in which Benjamin comes closest to the development of a factographic, Productivist position, as it had already been outlined for example in the late 1920s in the writings of Ossip Brik and Sergei Tretyakov.[23]

Now, according to Benjamin, the new author must first of all address the Modernist framework of isolated producers and try to change the artist's position from that of a caterer of esthetic goods to that of an active force in the transformation of the existing cultural apparatus itself. This differentiation in Benjamin's positions could help us to elucidate in the present a comparison between Levine's allegorical work and Rosler's activist communicative work, specifically her approach toward photographic conventions and the histories that they embody. Such a comparative reading is specifically suggested by Rosler's *The Bowery in Two Inadequate Descriptive Systems* (1974–75), and her critical essay "In, around, and afterthoughts (on documentary photography)."[24]

Both works address photographic conventions as language practices, analyze their historical and ideological functions and consider the varying affiliations with the social and political conditions at large, rather than assuming a stance of aesthetic neutrality that the program of photographic Modernism had prescribed. *The Bowery in Two Inadequate Descriptive Systems* is a photo-text work whose photographic component consists of black-and-white images of Bowery store fronts, reciting and restaging the conventions of street photography and social documentary, paraphrasing photographs from Berenice Abbott to Walker Evans. The complementary language component of the work consists of typewritten word lists, in a design that mockingly embraces the highly serious administrative sobriety of the looks of Conceptual art. Language, however, returns here with the vengeance of its repressed somatic and social dimension, since it lists a vast array of linguistic variations on the subject of drunkenness. At the same time, Rosler's seemingly crude attempts to mimic the style of the great urban "documentarians" is of course as thoroughly disappointing to the eye cultivated in photographic modernity as Levine's photographs are to the collector's hand. It is not

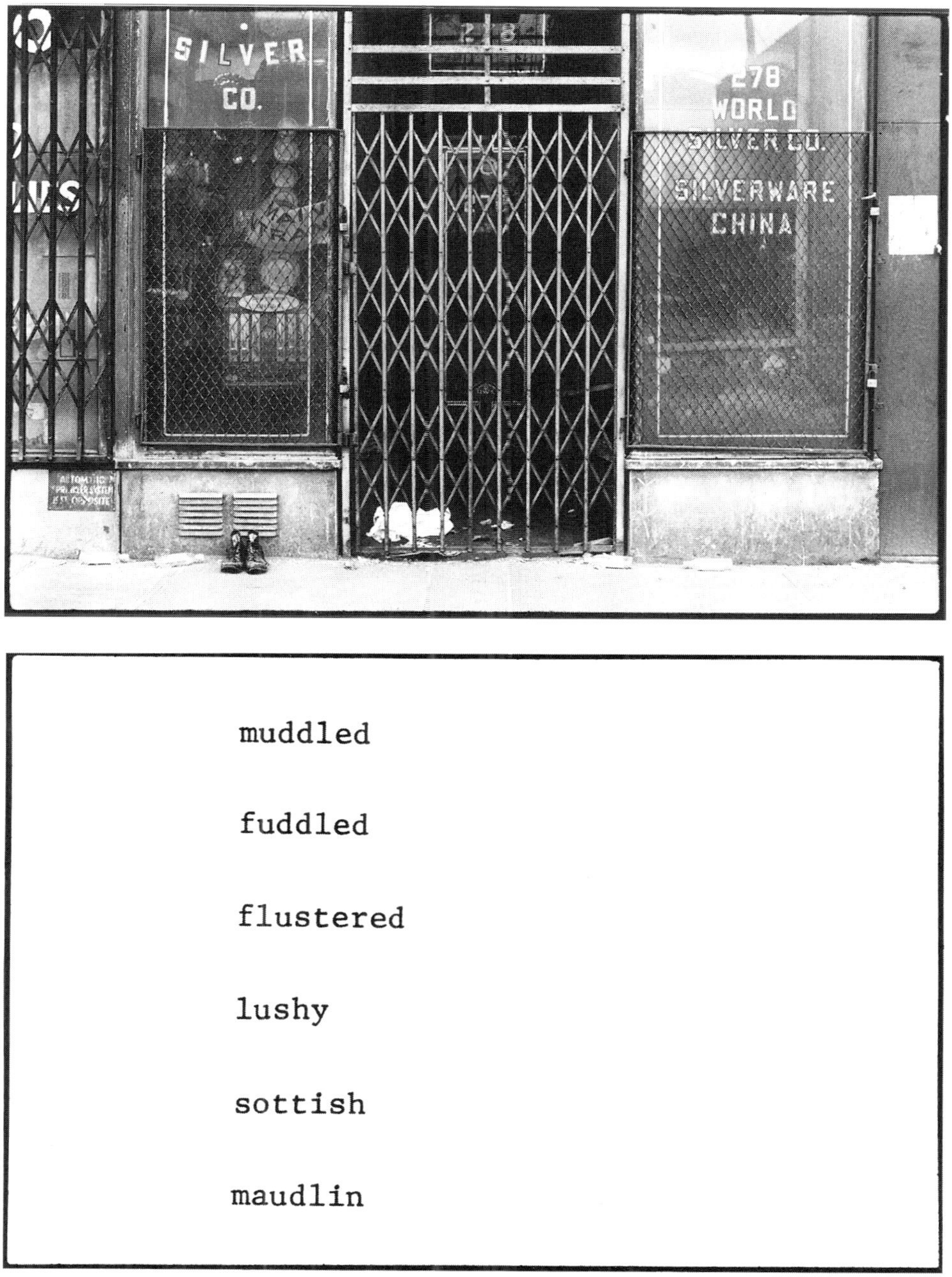

Martha Rosler, *The Bowery in Two Inadequate Descriptive Systems*, 1975–76. Silver gelatin prints, 8 × 10 in. (20.3 × 25.4 cm). © Martha Rosler.

surprising then that in an interview on the work Rosler describes *The Bowery* in an explicitly allegorical terminology:

> In *The Bowery* the photographs are empty and the words are full of imagery and incident. … A lot of photographers made pictures of Bowery bums. That upset me because I thought it was a false endeavor, that it involved a pretense that such photos were about the people when they were really about the sensibility of the photographers and the viewers. It's an illicit exchange between the photographer and the viewer. They provide the raw materials for a confirmation of class and privilege. … I wanted to make a point about the inadequacy of that kind of documentary by contrasting it with verbal images. … I didn't want to use words to underline the truth value of the photographs, but rather words that undermined it. I felt that just as the images are expected to be poetic but aren't even "original"—they follow a tradition of street-photography and have more to do with commerce than with anything else, since they're shopfronts—the words would be a kind of unexpected poetry. Their ironic humor would cut against and be cut against by the deadpan photographs.[25]

In the same interview, not surprisingly, Rosler introduces the question of a contemporary collage practice and its historical functions into the discussion of her work. Her definitions coincide with an outline of contemporary montage as I have tried to develop it in the course of this essay:

> I think it's even more valid to talk about contradiction than about collage, because much of the collaging consists of contradiction, putting things together that don't go together, but that are connected in some way. … Many of the

> contradictions I want to talk about in my work are not simple riddles of existence but things that arise from the system we live under which makes impossible and conflicting demands on us. I like to point to situations in which we can see the myths of ideology contradicted by our actual experience.[26]

Rosler insists on a model of artistic practice as critical intervention, clarifying in acts of allegorical repetition the historical meaning and the inadequacy of contemporary documentary production when reiterating photographic conventions. Thus her essay "In, around, and afterthoughts (on documentary photography)" analyzes the historical and political implications of contemporary (documentary) photography. Confronting the material reality of the "subjects," i.e., the present-day living conditions of the famous "victims" of photography, Rosler transforms the current interest of certain photographers who have turned back to the history of their own discipline by re-photographing "in the manner of the masters."

If Levine's abstract and radical denial of production and authorship would place her cultural model ultimately on the side of the existing power structure, Rosler's strategy by contrast constructs a photographic and artistic practice outside of Modernism's claims for neutrality and autonomy. It positions her, paradoxically, within cultural traditions of political commitment that could fail to communicate in the present precisely because of its lack of power within the governing discursive conventions and institutions.

The work of Dara Birnbaum inhabits a third position that is equally distant from Levine's and from Rosler's work. While it embodies all the concerns that had originated in Pop art, and had been subsequently developed in Minimal and post-Minimal art of the late 1960s and early 1970s, it does not merely employ rediscovered Pop art strategies, as is fashionable in the context of 1980s painting. Thus Birnbaum states for example that she wants "to define the language of video-art in relation to the institution of television in the way that Buren and Asher had defined the language of painting and sculpture in relation to the institution of the museum."[27]

Birnbaum's work operates programmatically within both frames: looking at the conditions of high culture—its isolation and privileged position, its commodity status and fetish existence—while simultaneously adopting the perspective of mass culture in its most advanced form: the television industry. This strategy, to integrate both perspectives in a dialectical exchange, has the potential to affect the languages of both art and television, though the work has not assumed a comfortable position in either institution.

In a traditional gallery situation, the work's references (both implicit and explicit) to the past decade of sculptural thinking become instantly readable. Birnbaum's video work emerges out of that historical moment in sculpture when artists such as Bruce Nauman and Dan Graham began to use video to radicalize a phenomenological understanding of viewer-object relationships as they had been introduced in the context of Minimal sculpture. The analytical video installations and performances of the post-Minimalist artists not only focused increasingly on the phenomenology of the viewing process, but involved either author and audience, audience and object, or audience and architecture in an explicit and active interchange.

With the growing theatricalization of video and performance art in the mid-1970s and its increasing tendency toward narcissistic estheticization, video activities of politically conscious artists would increasingly address television. At that time, video tapes such as Richard Serra's *Television Delivers People* (1973) emerged. Rather than addressing the language of television itself, previously produced videotapes had simply channeled artistic performance material on videotape through television.

Nam June Paik's pioneering video/television work of the mid- to late 1960s had argued in the context of Fluxus that the visual culture of the future would be contained within television as the primary social practice of visual meaning production, just as visual culture in the 19th century had been profoundly affected by the invention of photography. Birnbaum logically refers to Paik as one of her prime influences. Equally important for the development of her work was her collaboration with Dan Graham on a major project entitled "Local Television News Program Analysis for Public Access Cable TV."[28]

It is crucial to understand to what extent Birnbaum's work is anchored in the structures that determine collective perceptual experience considering that it appropriates segments from broadcast television and focuses first and foremost on the meaning of the techniques and the specific language conventions and genres of television. The ideological functions and effects of the genres become transparent in the formal analysis of the conventions and the allegorical juxtapositions of the genre quotations. Due to its revelatory deconstructive procedures, the work does not participate in the proliferation of artist-produced, innovative media strategies which only bring television ideology esthetically up to date. Birnbaum's videotapes appropriate television footage ranging from sitcoms and soap operas such as *Laverne and Shirley* and *General Hospital* to live broadcast material such as *Olympic Speed Skating* and commercials for the Wang Corporation. The artist's works are ideally destined for television broadcast, where they could most effectively clarify their functions in situ and operate in the manner of a typical *détournement*. But the work's contradictory status of being situated primarily within art-world production and distribution position it—for the time being—solely within the framework of an avant-garde discourse within the sphere of high art. Were her works to be actually shown at some point on commercial television, their essentially esthetic strategies might become all the more apparent, and their critical potential might decrease. The striving for a process of acceptance by the media—necessary as it is for Birnbaum—is therefore also her work's most vulnerable aspect. This becomes most evident in a work such as Birnbaum's *Remy/*

Grand Central: Trains and Boats and Planes, 1980, where a corporation's "support" for young artists results in a commissioned simulacrum of an advertisement that at best could be perceived as a parody and at worst could be misperceived as merely a more sophisticated form of advertisement. It is not surprising then that the work's potential for affirming a final, totalitarian synthesis of the culture industry and of esthetic production would occur *in nuce* in Birnbaum's own production of new footage that mimics advertising conventions rather than addressing itself with her typical critical acuity to found footage and its genres, which is the rule in almost all of Birnbaum's other tapes.

Technology/Transformation: Wonder Woman, 1978–79, unveils *Wonder Woman*, a favorite emblem of American puberty fantasies, that has grown historically from a comic-book figure to a nationally broadcast television series. This advance to a status of national cult provides an image of crisis which, like the resurrection of Superman in film, feeds on a collective desire for icons that represent monolithic powers: heroes, parents, and the nation-state. The seemingly inexhaustible special effects that corporate television and film producers draw upon when state power most urgently needs to be mystified appear to be the prime focus of this tape. Birnbaum's video work on the iconography of *Wonder Woman* runs parallel to the manner in which Lichtenstein's paintings had placed themselves within and against the graphic techniques of comic-book reproduction in the 1960s.

At the same time, Birnbaum's deployment of filmic loops recalls Bruce Conner's strategy of repeating found film segments as much as it reminds us of Warhol's strategies of serializing commodity imagery. The quotational loops in Birnbaum's work break the temporal continuity of the television narrative and split it into self-reflexive elements. As a result of the precision with which Birnbaum employs these allegorical procedures, we discover with unprecedented clarity to what degree the theater of professional facial expressions, performed by television actors in close-ups on the screen, has become the site of domination itself.

This becomes particularly evident in the ingenious juxtaposition of segments from a live broadcast of women speed skating at the Olympics and a segment from the "real-life" soap opera *General Hospital* in her tape *POP-POP-VIDEO: General Hospital/Olympic Women Speed Skating*, 1980. Here the artist juxtaposes a series of reverse-angle shots in which a female doctor confesses to her paternal male colleague her failure in handling a communication breakdown with a tightly counterpointed spectacle of Olympic vigor and velocity. The splendor of this neo-futuristic imagery that celebrates the subjection of the female body to athletic instrumentalization only fails to become a new Leni Riefenstahl series on color TV because of the constant intercutting with the spectacle of neurotic collapse in the features of the female doctor.

The tape, which extracts segments from the game show *Hollywood Squares*, confirms Walter Benjamin's enigmatic observation that neurosis has become the psychological equivalent of the commodity. Birnbaum's selection of details and the formal procedures to which she submits her quotations reveal the extent to which even the facial expressions of hyperactive television performers implement ideology. The serial repetition allows for a sudden insight into the extent to which the actors' faces themselves have become the site of the total instrumentalization of the individual, down to the very last feature of a spectacle of the physiognomic. Thus the patterns of behavior on the screen already exemplify what television ultimately aims to achieve within the viewer: pure exercises in mimetic submission.

In contrast to other video artists of her generation, Birnbaum does not use her competence in the analysis of television techniques to develop a new video gadgetry, employed for the sake of "pure pleasure" or "formal play," whose purpose it is always to estheticize ideology. In all instances we find that the "visual pleasure" of Birnbaum's tapes is balanced by cognitive shock. For example, in her work *Wonder Woman*, the citation of special effects manifestly serves to reveal their patriarchal violence, offering sexualized images of power and technological mirages

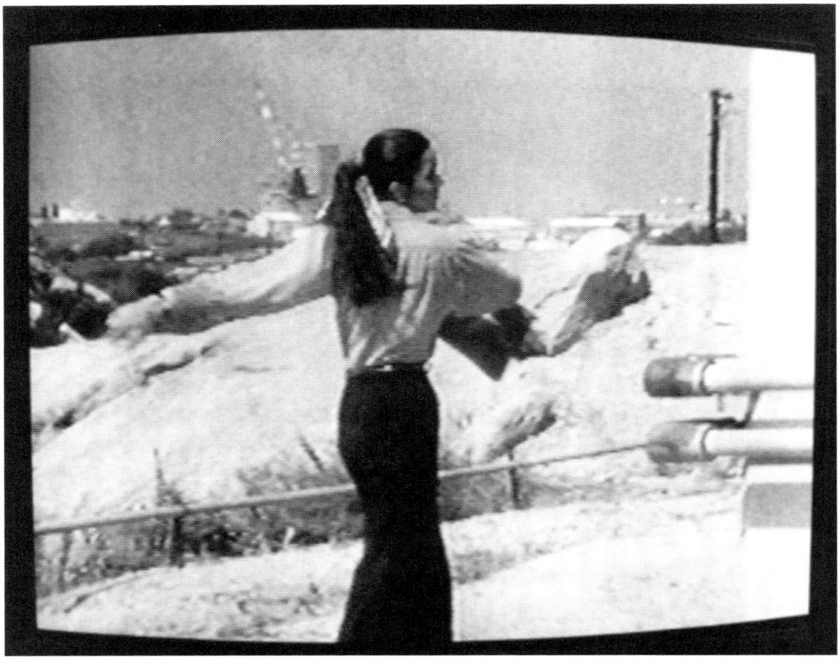

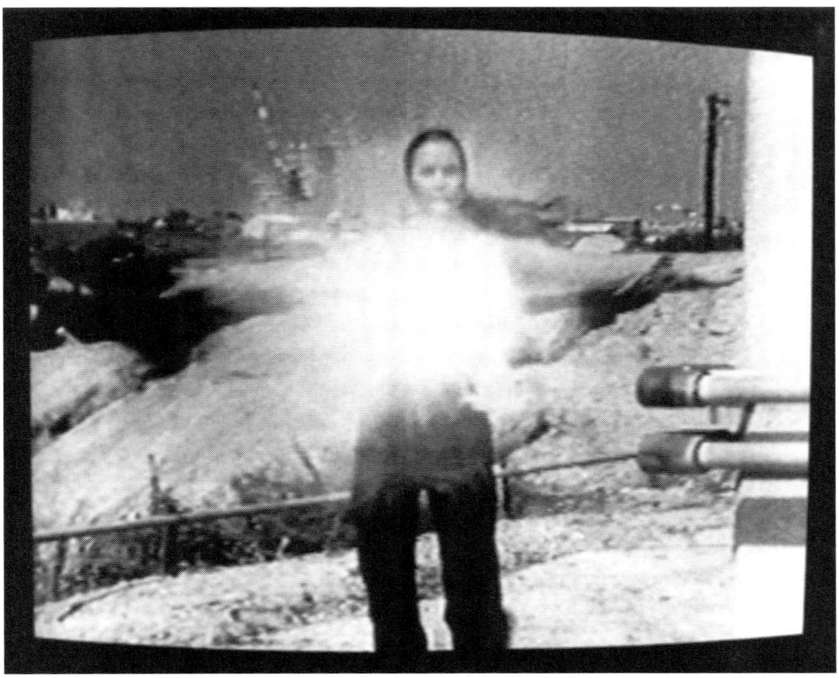

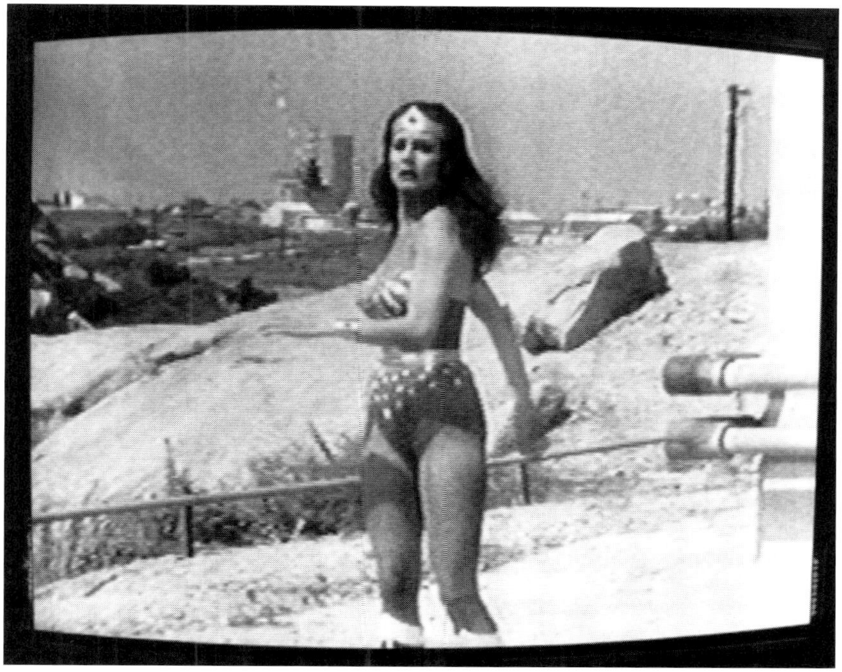

Dara Birnbaum, *Technology/Transformation: Wonder Woman*, 1978–79. Single-channel video, color, sound, 5 minutes, 50 seconds. © Dara Birnbaum. Courtesy Dara Birnbaum, Electronic Arts Intermix, New York, and Marian Goodman Gallery, New York/Paris.

as a diversion from the reality of social and political life; here the cognitive shock originates partially in the recognition that these sexist representations of a female figure correspond to an actual historical situation in which radical political practice seems to have been restricted to feminist practice alone.

This dialectical approach becomes all the more transparent in the juxtaposition of sound and imagery that occurs in the second part of the tape. While in the first part, staccato serializations and freeze-frame images of a spinning, running, fighting Wonder Woman are accompanied by an original soundtrack that is subjected to the same formal procedures as the images, the second part of the tape consists merely of the lyrics (in white letters on a blue background) of a disco song, accidentally also called "Wonder Woman."[29]

These graphic, scriptural representations of pure phonetics, of female sighs and of lyrics that we are normally supposed to hear, but not to read, invert the split of the phonetic and graphic elements of language which we saw earlier in Duchamp's pun. Here, in the scriptural allegorization of the disco song, we become aware that even the most minute and discrete phonetic elements of such popular music (sighs, moans, etc.) are as soaked in sexist and reactionary political ideology as the larger syntactic and semantic structures of the lyrics, or even the physiognomic performances of the actors. The dimension of sound plays a very important role in Birnbaum's tapes in general—it does not merely serve as a phonetic illustration to which sound in film and television have been usually reduced. Thus the restoration of sound as a separate discursive element, running as an equivalent parallel to the visual text, makes the viewer aware of the hidden functions that sound fulfills in industrially produced television.

In one of Birnbaum's recent works, *PM Magazine*, 1982, a four-channel video and sound installation, the function of sound is extrapolated even further.[30]

At the same time, the presentational devices of the video work are deliberately positioned in a dialogue with painting and sculpture, which make the work emphatically self-conscious of the museum framework within which it is constituted.[31] In this complex installation, the framework of the museum is bracketed on the one hand with the design language of commercial display and advanced media technology, and the historic dimension of avant-garde agitprop montage, on the other. In the video element of the installation, the *PM Magazine* trailer, state-of-the-art animation techniques are juxtaposed with recycled icons of the 1950s American dream of leisure time and consumption. In the same way that the visual material is processed in four three-minute loops, the soundtrack of the trailer—or the key motifs of it—are run through four channels. Once again it is the auditory dimension that generates the work's effects of decentralization. The elements of the installation could only become congruent as "text" within the individual experience of an active viewer. As a result of Birnbaum's self-reflexive structuring of the material, the television conventions and their technological implementation become transparent as the ultimate representational system in which ideology constitutes its subjects.

While it is essential for the work of Birnbaum and Rosler to operate simultaneously inside and outside the framework of institutionalized art distribution, Levine's work functions exclusively within this framework. Only as a commodity can the work fulfill all its functions, and yet, paradoxically, for the time being it cannot be sold. Its ultimate triumph is to repeat and anticipate in a single gesture the abstraction and alienation from historical context to which work is subjected in the process of commodification and acculturation. In this respect Levine's and Birnbaum's works reveal an historical affinity with the position of Warhol, the first American dandy to systematically deny individual creation and productivity in favor of a blatant reaffirmation of the conditions of cultural reification. Warhol's once subversive trajectory ended in the institutions of fame and fashion, as surely as de Sade had ended in the Bastille. The fate of his work, which had once subverted painting by precisely the same allegorical techniques of confiscating imagery, bracketing high-art and mass-cultural discourses, individual production and mechanical reproduction, was to produce the most singularized and rarefied icons of Pop art.

As we have seen, all the artists discussed here appropriate and quote the images and materials that they use for their allegorical investigations, in the very manner that the radical Conceptual artists of the late 1960s had questioned why artistic practice should be relegated to the status of a spectacularized commodity of individuation. If they have been successful in their critiques, it will be only a temporary success—until acculturation will find new ways to accommodate their production. For ultimately it is the visual representation rather than the textual articulation of a construct that imbues it with material reality, the basis of the commodity form and of institutional acculturation alike. Unlike the artists we considered here, Roland Barthes, when deconstructing the reigning contemporary myths of design, of objects of consumption and of advertising in his *Mythologies* (1957), he did not have to consider the problems of ownership and copyright. In certain respects his approach can still be considered as the originary model for the critique of ideology as it has been developed in the work of the artists analyzed here. But the visual object/image transformed into artistic practice has become—and remains—the essential ideological correlate of private property.

Notes

First published in *Artforum* 21, no. 1 (September 1982): 43–56. All translations by Benjamin H. D. Buchloh unless otherwise noted. Minor corrections have been made for consistency.

1. The introduction of this essay largely follows an argument that has been developed in Ansgar Hillach's attempt to define a notion of montage in the avant-garde of the 1920s and its relationship to Walter Benjamin's concept of allegory. See Ansgar Hillach,

"Allegorie, Bildraum, Montage," in *Theorie der Avantgarde* (Frankfurt: Edition Suhrkamp, 1976), pp. 105–142. For a more specific analysis of the complexities and historical changes of Benjamin's allegory-model, I refer the reader to Harald Steinhagen, "Zu Walter Benjamin's Begriff der Allegorie," in *Form und Funktionen der Allegorie* (Stuttgart: Metzler, 1979), pp. 666ff., and Jürgen Naeher, *Walter Benjamin's Allegorie-Begriff als Model* (Frankfurt: Klett-Cotta, 1975).

For a more recent English account of Benjamin's theory of allegory, see Bainard Cowan, "Walter Benjamin's Theory of Allegory," *New German Critique* 26 (1982): 109–122. Cowan's claim that Benjamin's theory of allegory "has gone virtually without thorough explication," however, indicates, as does his text, that he is not at all familiar with the German literature on the subject.

2. George Grosz, quoted in Hans Richter *Dada: Kunst und Antikunst* (Cologne: Dumont, 1963). English translation in Dawn Ades, *Photomontage* (London, Phaidon, 1976), p. 10.

3. Raoul Hausmann, "Fotomontage," *A–Z* 16 (May 1931). Reprinted in *Raoul Hausmann*, exh. cat. (Hannover: Kestnergesellschaft, 1981), pp. 51ff.

4. Walter Benjamin, "Zentralpark," in *Gesammelte Schriften*, vol. 1, part 2 (Frankfurt: Suhrkamp, 1974), pp. 657–690.

5. The spatialization of time and the adoption of a contemplative stance toward the world that Benjamin discussed in 1935 as the experiential conditions of allegory in the European Baroque were discussed in 1928 by Georg Lukács as the essential features of the collective condition of reification:

> Neither objectively nor in his relation to his work does man appear as the authentic master of the process; on the contrary, he is a mechanical part incorporated into a mechanical system. He finds it already pre-existing and self-sufficient, it functions independently of him and he has to conform to its laws whether he likes it or not. As labor is progressively rationalized and mechanized, his lack of will is reinforced by the way in which his activity becomes less and less active and more and more contemplative. The contemplative stance adopted towards a process mechanically conforming to fixed laws and enacted independently of man's consciousness and impervious to human intervention, i.e., a perfectly closed system, must likewise transform the basic categories of man's immediate attitude to the world: it reduces space and time to a common denominator and degrades time to a dimension of space.

See Georg Lukács, "Reification and the Consciousness of the Proletariat," in *History and Class Consciousness* (Cambridge, Mass.: MIT Press, 1971), p. 89.

6. Benjamin, "Zentralpark," p. 681. The famous anecdote in which Kurt Schwitters described the origin of the term "Merz" as a result of his encounter with an advertising for the "Kommerzbank" contains equally *in nuce* all the essential features of the allegorical procedure: fragmentation and depletion of conventional meaning are followed by acts of willful meaning-assignment which generate the poetical experience of primary linguistic processes.

7. Walter Benjamin, "The Work of Art in the Age of Mechanical Reproduction," in *Illuminations* (New York: Schocken, 1978), p. 223.

8. Yve-Alain Bois, "Ryman's Tact," *October* 19 (winter 1981): 94.

9. More recently, Calvin Tomkins has argued that the label, identifying the work as a project by Robert Rauschenberg, was actually designed and produced by Jasper Johns. See Calvin Tomkins, "Everything in Sight: Robert Rauschenberg's New Life," *New Yorker* (May 23, 2005): 75.

10. Dan Graham, *Homes for America*, in *Arts Magazine* (December/January, 1966–67).

11. Dan Graham, "The Book as Object," *Arts Magazine* (May 1967); repr. first in an extended version in Dan Graham, *End Moments*, self-published, New York, 1969; later repr. in Dan Graham, *Rock My Religion*, ed. Brian Wallis (Cambridge, Mass.: MIT Press, 1993), pp. 26–30.

12. Marcel Broodthaers, *Un coup de dés jamais n'abolira le hasard* (Antwerp: Wide White Space Gallery/Cologne: Michael Werner Gallery, 1969).

13. Beginning with his foundation of a fictitious museum in Brussels in 1968 where the icons of Modernism were presented as postcard images, the project culminated with his large-scale installation *The Eagle from the Oligocene until Today (The Museum of Eagles)*, presented in Düsseldorf in 1972, where 266 artifacts representing the image of the eagle were once again submitted to the process of abstraction from history in the construction of a secondary mythical fiction. See Marcel Broodthaers, *Der Adler vom Oligozän bis Heute* (The Eagle from the Oligocene until Today), exh. cat., vols. 1 and 2 (Düsseldorf: Kunsthalle Düsseldorf, 1972).

14. Daniel Buren, "Exposition d'une exposition," in *Documenta 5*, exh. cat. (Munich: Bertelsmann, 1972). See also Daniel Buren, *Rebondissements/Reboundings* (Brussels: Daled-Gevaert, 1977).

15. The work traced the transfer of Manet's *Asparagus Still Life* from its original French owners, through various German Jewish families and its enforced sale under the Nazi regime, to its eventual "donation" by Hermann Josef Abs, the former chief financial officer of the Nazi regime, to the Wallraf-Richartz Museum on the occasion of its 150th anniversary in 1972.

16. The works referred to are documented in the following publications: Edward Fry, *Hans Haacke* (Cologne: Dumont, 1972); Hans Haacke, *Framing and Being Framed* (Halifax: Nova Scotia College of Art and Design, 1975); Hans Haacke, *Der Pralinenmeister* (Cologne: Paul Maenz Gallery, 1981); English edition, *The Master Chocolate Maker* (Toronto: Art Metropole, 1982).

17. See the exhibition catalog ———, *Louise Lawler, Adrian Piper, Cindy Sherman* (New York: Artists Space, 1978). The blank space in the catalog's title signaled the intentionally anonymous participation of the artist Christopher d'Arcangelo.

18. For a notable exception of a discussion of Michael Asher's installation, see Anne Rorimer, "Michael Asher: Recent Work," *Artforum* (April 1980), and my own essay "Michael Asher and the Conclusion of Modernist Sculpture (1979), in *The Centennial Lectures at the Art Institute of Chicago*, ed. Susan Rossen (Chicago: Art Institute of Chicago, 1983); republished in revised and expanded form in Buchloh, *Neo-Avantgarde and Culture Industry* (Cambridge, Mass.: MIT Press, 2000).

19. Annegret Jürgens-Kirchhoff, *Technik und Tendenz der Montage* (Giessen: Anabas Verlag, 1978), p. 191.

20. Rosalind Krauss introduced the linguistic concept of "spacing" into the discussion of collage/montage aesthetics in the period from 1910 through the 1920s. See for example her essay "The Photographic Conditions of Surrealism," *October* 19 (winter 1981).

21. Sherrie Levine, unpublished, undated statement, ca. 1980.

22. Walter Benjamin, *Angelus Novus* (Frankfurt: Suhrkamp, 1966), p. 204.

23. Walter Benjamin, "The Author as Producer," in *The Essential Frankfurt School Reader*, ed. Andrew Arato and Eike Gebhardt (New York: Urizen Books, 1978), pp. 254–269.

24. Martha Rosler, *Three Works*, ed. Benjamin Buchloh (Halifax: Nova Scotia College of Art and Design, 1981).

25. Martha Rosler, interview by Martha Gever, *Afterimage* (October 1981): 15.

26. Ibid.

27. Dara Birnbaum, interview with the author, unpublished.

28. Dan Graham, *Video—Architecture—Television*, ed. Benjamin Buchloh (Halifax: Nova Scotia College of Art and Design, 1979).

29. Birnbaum happened to come across this relatively obscure disco song while she was editing the television footage.

30. Variations of the work have been installed at the Hudson River Museum, at the Art Institute of Chicago's *74th American Exhibition*, and at *Documenta 7* in Kassel.

31. Two panels on opposing walls—one framing one monitor, and one framing three monitors—featured large black-and-white photostat images that had been extracted from the television footage screened in the installation's videotape. A wall surface was painted bright blue for the three-monitor panel and bright red for the one-monitor panel. The panels possessed the qualities of the kind of enlarged photographic imagery that might be encountered in trade-show displays, yet at the same time they were slightly reminiscent of the grand-scale exhibition panels in the later Productivist work of El Lissitzky, such as his installation for the Soviet Pavilion of the International Pressa Exhibition in Cologne in 1928 with Sergei Senkin, or the International Hygiene Exhibition in Dresden in 1930, in which photomontage techniques were expanded to the level of agitprop architecture. Birnbaum's panels have lost their "agit" dimension for the sake of the museum "prop." As such they enter a dialectical relationship with the current return to large-scale figurative multi-panel painting, which uses quotation merely as an end to legitimize historicism.

5

The Museum Fictions of Marcel Broodthaers

> Here, again, a new form of expression was involved. Instead of painting something new, my aim was to reproduce the paintings and the objects that I liked and collect them in a space as small as possible. I did not know how to go about it. I first thought of a book, but I did not like the idea. Then it occurred to me that it could be a box in which all my works would be collected and mounted like in a small museum, a portable museum so to speak.
>
> —*Marcel Duchamp*[1]

As usual, the reflection upon the origins of the artist's concern to integrate within the conception of a work, the final forms of distribution and the conditions of reception and acculturation, the modes of reading that ensue from them and that are contained within the practices of institutionalization, has to take its point of departure in a reference to the work of Marcel Duchamp. Undoubtedly, his description of the origins of the portable museum *La Boîte-en-Valise,* on which he started to work in 1936 and which was announced for publication in 1941, reveals his anticipation of the final destination that his *oeuvre* would reach in the immanent process of acculturation: the museum.

It is the dialectic of institutionalization and the transformation of artistic practice into the object of the aesthetic cult on the one hand, and the conditions of technical reproduction as he had introduced them into the high art discourse with the definition of his readymades on the other, that demarcate the dimensions within which the conception of the *Boîte-en-Valise* is situated.

If Duchamp's concern for the destruction of the aura and the abolition of the hieratic individual object had been the focal point of his invention of the readymade strategy in 1914, in 1941 he had to focus on an entirely different question: how to encounter the immanent acculturation of the readymade? Even though Robert Lebel argues that "characteristically one year before the war Duchamp foresaw that he must pack his bags in as small a space as possible,"[2] it seems rather obvious that Duchamp's motivation behind the project *From or by Marcel Duchamp or Rrose Sélavy (The Box in a Valise)* was not the result of pragmatic concerns. Rather, as it was more obviously the case with Duchamp's installation work in 1938 for the "Exposition Internationale du Surréalisme" entitled *Twelve Hundred Coal Bags Suspended from the Ceiling over* a *Stove* as well as in 1942 for his installation work for the exhibition "First Papers of Surrealism" in New York, Duchamp was at this time dealing with the problems of cultural institutionalization and reception. As he perceived Surrealism to be on the verge of becoming an officially accepted cultural practice, gradually re-converting its original radical position into that of a comfortable position of easel painting production, he responded in both instances with contributions to the problems of the retrospective exhibition that openly denounce its validity and criticize the quasi-religious veneration of the acculturation.

In both installations the actual visibility of the paintings was extremely reduced and the material elements of the work (coal sacks and dust and an electrically illuminated coal brazier in the one, and

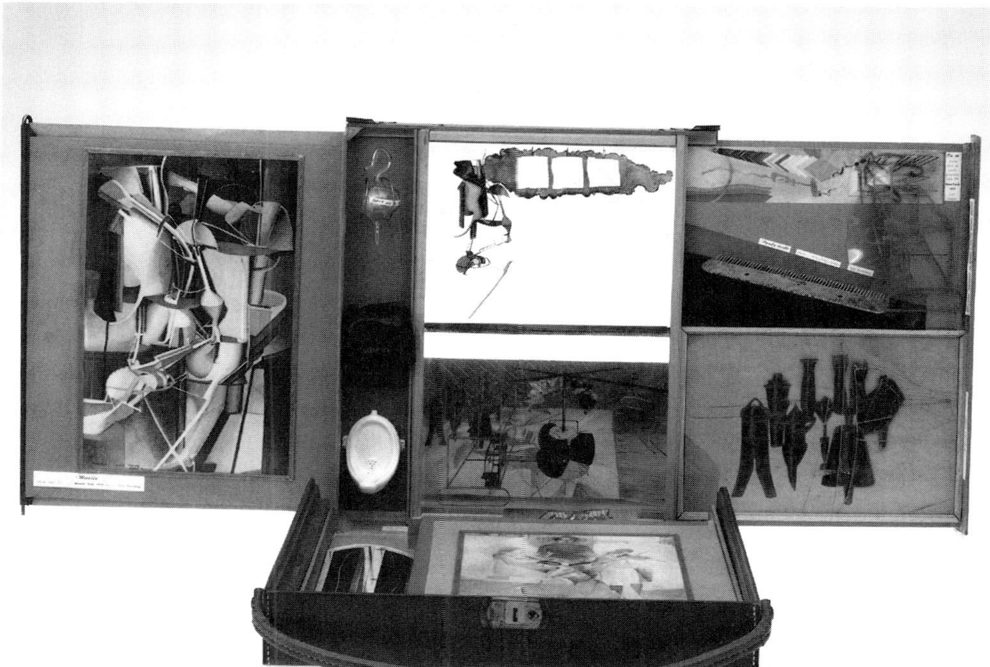

Marcel Duchamp, *Box in a Valise (La Boîte-en-Valise)*, 1935–41. Brown leather valise with handle containing sixty-nine miniature replicas and printed reproductions and one original, *Virgin (No. 2)*, 1938, hand-colored collotype. Valise (closed): 16 × 14¾ × 4¼ in. (40.6 × 37.5 × 10.8 cm). Philadelphia Museum of Art, The Louise and Walter Arensberg Collection, 1950. © Succession Marcel Duchamp/ADAGP, Paris/Artists Rights Society (ARS), New York, 2015.

twine strung like cobweb throughout the painting exhibition in the other) certainly emphasized the obsolescence that Duchamp revealed as the quintessential feature of these exhibitions of Surrealist paintings and sculpture—obsolescence of both the mode of pictorial production that had gradually taken over the Surrealist program and the obsolescence of the format of the retrospective exhibition itself which, in anticipation of the final status of the acculturated work within the museum institution, converts the inherent dynamic rupture of the aesthetic construct into an object of contemplation. As Duchamp is reported to have said in 1945 in regard to the conception of his cover proposal for the magazine *View*: "Vintage cobweb? Indeed not!" He was clearly aware of the transformation to which the work of his friends and peers within the Surrealist movement already had been subjected and that the same destiny was waiting in the reception process of his own, more radical work of the Dada period. We can therefore speculate that it is this challenge that Duchamp tries to meet in 1936 when he begins his work on the design and production of the *Valise* that is offered to the public in 1941.

The false neutrality of a traditional documentation of his work in a book format is explicitly rejected by Duchamp in an interview with J. J. Sweeney as an "idea he did not like." Therefore the creation of a portable miniature museum in the format of a traveling salesman's sample case, containing reduced color reproductions of a large number of Duchamp's paintings from the pre-readymade period and three miniature reproductions of actual three-dimensional readymades seemed to be a more attractive solution. We might wonder whether Duchamp's exhilarating description of his activities of smuggling the various elements of the edition of the valise "with the fake passport of a cheese merchant" from occupied Paris to Marseille is not a partially ironic commentary on his ideas about the transformation that an artist's work undergoes in retrospective exhibitions, institutional collecting and display.

The most conspicuous features of Duchamp's portable museum are the miniaturization and the spatial and temporal versatility of the container or the framework of his museum. Like in the writing of Lewis Carroll, the objects with which we seemed to be acquainted—e.g., the readymades *Fountain*, *Traveler's Folding Item* and *Air de Paris*—return in their museum presentation in a shrunken format that induces a vision of spatio-temporal distance, the reminiscence of objects affecting their scale. Or, what is more likely, the loss of immanence and rigor of the readymade, as it once ruptured the discourse of high art and its unique auratic objects, by doubling it with the discourse of technically reproduced objects is now literally embodied in their reduced existence as they have undergone the cultural process of reception and institutionalization.

Since Roland Barthes' *Mythologies* (1957), we have come to understand that processes of cultural reception are essentially defined as the subjection of primary language to the interests of a secondary mythological language, the language of ideology. Clearly, as Barthes argues, the language of art is more susceptible to the interested appropriations by the demands of bourgeois ideology than the language of poetry and mathematics, which are complete in themselves and therefore resist interpretation and secondary superimposition of meaning. However, Barthes outlines an aesthetic strategy that he calls the process of secondary mythification, the creation of a fictitious myth that anticipates within the aesthetic construct, itself mimetically its ultimate destiny of mythification. And it is due to that strategy that certain practices of primary language can resist partially or temporarily the process of mythification that is defined by the extraction of human practice from the condition of history, by the isolation and specialization of subversion (e.g., the autonomous practice of art) in order to prevent a systematic and general criticism of bourgeois conditions, by the leveling of oppositional terms, the quantification of quality, the sum total of these particular functions allowing the general tendency of myth to transform the historical into the natural or the essential. As Barthes puts it in his classical definition of the functions of the myth:

> But myth is a peculiar system, in that it is constructed from a semiological chain which existed before it: it is a second order semiological system. That which is a sign (namely the associative total of a concept and image) in the first system becomes a mere signifier in the second. We must here recall that the materials of mythical speech (the language itself, photography, painting, posters, rituals, objects. etc.), however different at the start, are reduced to a pure signifying function as soon as they are caught by myth. Myth sees in them only the same raw material; their unity is that they all come down to the status of a mere language. Whether it deals with alphabetical or pictorial writing, myth wants to see in them only a sum of signs, a global sign, the final term of a first semiological chain. And it is precisely this final term that will become the term of the greater system which it builds and of which it is only a part.[3]

Undoubtedly Marcel Duchamp's *Boîte-en-Valise*, the portable museum from 1941, in its miniaturization and emphasis on technical reproduction of both the unique hand-crafted original painting and the technically produced object, the readymade, in its assimilation of the art object to the sample box of the traveling salesman, constitutes an early example of that mimetic practice in which a fictitious secondary construction of mythical language is inscribed within the very conception of the work itself in order to anticipate and "vanquish myth from inside" in the process of acculturation. All the functions of the museum, the social institution that transforms the primary language of art into the secondary language of culture, are minutely contained in Duchamp's case: the valorization of the object, the extraction from context and function, the preservation from decay and the dissemination of its abstracted meaning. Particularly in the form that the *Boîte-en-Valise* imposes on the objects, the displacement and extraction from context, the ultimate fate of the primary language is anticipated: it becomes literally enshrined in a container that allows arbitrary movements in time and space, multiple ownership and privacy of possession and meaning assignment.

By literally anticipating the ultimate destination of the object in the structural definition of the work, Duchamp also changes the role of the artist as creator into that of the collector and conservator, who is concerned with the placement and transport, the evaluation and the institutionalization, the display and the maintenance of the work of art. This change of the artist's role into that of the collector is consistent with Duchamp's original definition of the artist as a *flâneur* who—as it seems—randomly selects with a gesture of divine disinterest, objects from the totality of technical reproduction and singles them out as the readymade. Hannah Arendt has pointed out in the context of Walter Benjamin's attitude toward the material reality of history how intricately connected the *flâneur* and the collector were as social characters of the late nineteenth century and how they determined artists' and writers' role behavior still in the first two decades of the twentieth century as well:

> The figure of the collector, as old fashioned as that of the *flâneur*, could assume such eminently modern features in Benjamin because history itself—that is, the break in tradition which took place at the beginning of this century—had already relieved him of this task of destruction and he only needed to bend down, as it were, to select his precious fragments from the pile of debris. In other words, the things themselves offered, particularly to a man who firmly faced the present, an aspect which had previously been discoverable only from the collector's whimsical perspective. … I do not mean to assert that Benjamin shifted his emphasis from the collection of books to the collecting of quotations (exclusive with him) overnight or even within one year,

> although there is some evidence in the letters of a conscious shifting of emphasis.[4]

The constitution of identity within an assemblage of (self) quotations—it had been one of Benjamin's imaginary projects, as Arendt mentions, to write a book that consisted entirely of quotations—is the historical reality of Duchamp's *Boîte-en-Valise.*

The strategy of assembling a work from quotations seems to sign over the individual producer's acts of decision and choice, self-determination and material transformation in social interaction to a totality of inescapable predicaments: those of the discourse, those of the conditions of reception, those of the social institution within which the production and reception are historically contained. In the work's attempt to dissolve reification within the very medium and the site where they are produced, in the necessity to mimetically anticipate its subjection to ideology by inscribing itself as precisely as possible into those very systems that determine its historical status, it seems to fail to maintain any claim for autonomy and rupture in favor of a complacent, melancholic, and passive contingency upon the conditions of rule that it set out to disrupt. It is no mere coincidence or irony of history that Joseph Cornell, the master of that quietism, who spent a life on the perpetual repetition of that ritual of entombment of quotations from a vanishing world, whose claim for historical legitimacy and demand for interacting presence were literally reduced to the box-sized space self-determination at its ultimate level of interiority, was actively involved in the assembling and production of the first edition of Marcel Duchamp's *Boîte-en-Valise.* Yet in Duchamp's case, the box is more mundane, a traveler's item rather than a shrine of contemplation, and the quotations that it contains are strictly referring to the artist's own past and historical production, thus keeping the fetishization at bay and retaining some of its original duplicity in regard to the demand of the mythification process of culture.

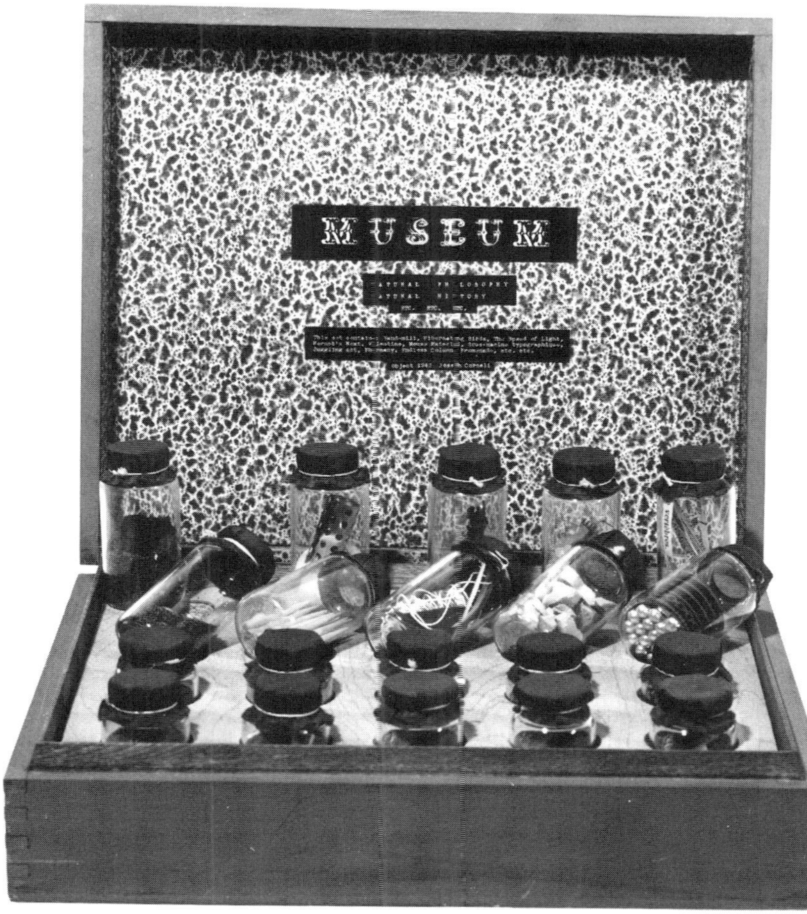

Joseph Cornell, *The Museum*, 1942. Musée National d'Art Moderne, Centre National d'Art et de Culture Georges Pompidou, Paris. © The Joseph and Robert Cornell Memorial Foundation/Licensed by VAGA, New York.

Once again, as usual, any attempt to establish an historical background for the reflection upon the origins of the contemporary artist's concern for the conditions of reception would have to take as its other point of departure those instances of aesthetic practice that did not—as was the case with Duchamp—focus primarily on the linguistic conditions of object production, but that approached the spatial and architectural conditions of framing and containing the language of art and that analyzed the conventions of institutional conservation, containment and display as an historical language of its own in order to transform it: El Lissitzky's first demonstration room, commissioned by the "International Art Exhibition" in Dresden in 1926 for the display of the "new constructive art" (Lissitzky) and his second demonstration room commissioned by Alexander Dorner, the director of the Hannover Museum in 1926 for the installation of the museum's twentieth-century collection, installed in 1928 at the Niedersaechsische Landesgalerie, Hannover. In both projects, Lissitzky changes programmatically the conventions of viewing by changing the conventions of institutional display, in a manner that he perceives to be consequential and consistent with the demands and new definition of spatial, pictorial and architectural codes as they were inherently given with post-Cubist art production itself. In his description of the functions of the museum display installation, Lissitzky argues:

> In the large scale international picture exhibitions the visitor feels like being in a zoo where he is simultaneously attacked by a thousand different beasts. In my exhibition room the objects should not assault the viewer all at the same time. If the viewers were traditionally lulled into passivity while they were passing the pictures, our design should make the individual active. This should be the function of the room.

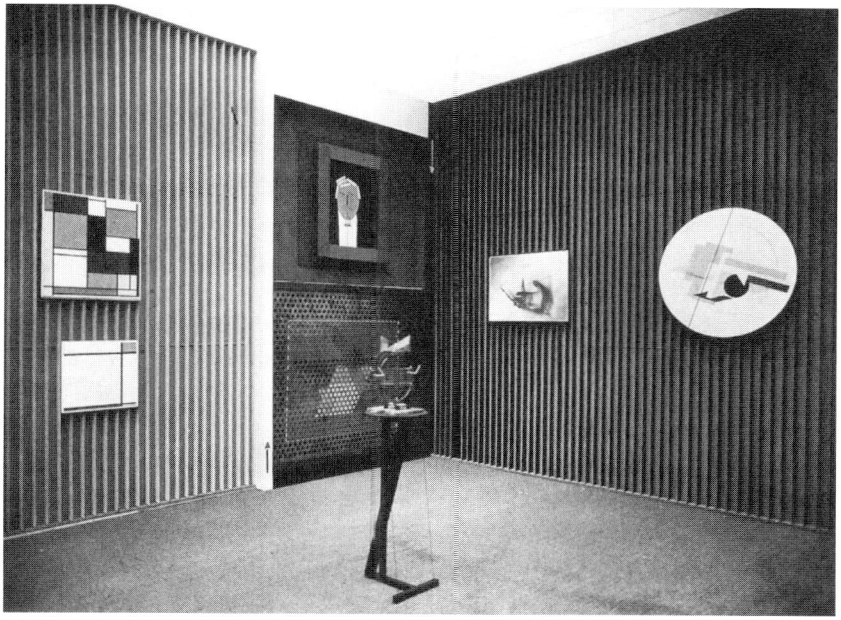

El Lissitzky, view toward northeast corner of *Raum für konstructive Kunst*, Internationale Kunstausstellung Dresden, 1926. Photo: Alexander Paul Walther. © 2015 Artists Rights Society (ARS), New York.

And later, in the same text, he concludes:

> The viewer will be physically forced to interact with the objects in the exhibition.[5]

This program of the transformation of the optical mode of perception toward a tactile mode, from the bourgeois mode of antisocial contemplation of aesthetic constructs to the revolutionary mode of active participation and distraction, is shortly thereafter elaborated theoretically in Walter Benjamin's famous essay "The Work of Art in the Age of Mechanical Reproduction," as well as in the later notes on Surrealism. In the work of Lissitzky it is the immediate result of a systematic analysis of the perceptual conventions (and the forms of meaning production that they entail), the modes that are embedded in easel painting as a mode of pictorial production and consequently in the convention of display and institutional, i.e., architectural, presentation that they require. Lissitzky's design for exhibition spaces and museum cabinets therefore addresses directly the core of that institutional architectural language—the false neutrality of the wall space with its seemingly universal white or monochrome surface and the false timelessness and immobility of the picture's place.

Contingency and particularity are therefore the prime features of Lissitzky's design element in the first demonstration room and in the second demonstration room. The paintings and sculptures on display in these exhibition/museum spaces are no longer presented as epiphanic moments of supreme aesthetic truth and universal validity, but as particular objects of historical study, with which the viewer has to actively engage in order to generate an exchange of "reading" and "meaning." The contingency of this act upon institutional mediation and the viewers' particularized interest is constantly emphasized in Lissitzky's design details: the moveable wall panels that reveal or obscure individual paintings according to the choice of the viewer, the display walls with highly structured relief surfaces that change color, according to the viewer's position, from white through gray to black, thus underlining in a very concrete manner the constant shifting of viewing conditions and their dependence on external circumstances that interfere with any false assumption about the universal and autonomous readability of aesthetic constructs outside of their specific conditions of presentation and reception. Architectural scale and utilitarian function of Lissitzky's productivist design for exhibition/museum interiors which situate the work historically, along with Alexandr Rodchenko's design for a Worker's Club as he presented it at the "Exposition Internationale des Arts Décoratifs" in Paris in 1925, make the actual paintings that are displayed in it look strangely distant and remote. They become specimens of a different moment in the history of production of visual meaning, dating from a situation that has been determined by different conditions of perception. It is in this distancing effect of instant historicization that Lissitzky's museum architecture and Duchamp's display case coincide. They differ in that the first enters the framing conditions, the discourse and the social institution that contain them on every possible level and, while transforming them radically, achieves a new dimension of aesthetic use value. The second simulated the subjection of aesthetic practice to the conditions of cultural reception, mimicking its ultimate destiny as commodity and reproduction, and ends up close to the passivity and fetishization that all parodic quotations of ideology seem to imply. But those are observations in retrospect and neither solution could be sustained in the contemporary practice of the neo-avantgarde of the Forties since the work of the first—or rather, the misunderstanding of it—ended up in the dilemma of design and the work of the second in the industry of gimmicks. Different tactics and practices were to be developed in the work of the artists of the 1960s. Once they had worked their way through the delusions that post–World War II neo-avantgarde license seems to have provided and they realized that the walls of the museum were not only those of the "prisonhouse of language," but also those of the domestication and social control of aesthetic practice.

Marcel Broodthaers' first work as an artist in 1964—as opposed to his preceding poetic works, which included a film called *La clef de l'horloge (Un poème cinématographique en l'honneur de Kurt Schwitters)* (The Key to the Clock [A cinématographic poem in honor of Kurt Schwitters]), 1957—was to sink in plaster the bottom half of his last volume of poetry, entitled *Pense-Bête*. This transformation from poet to artist, exemplified in an allegorical model, revealed that it is necessary to eliminate the reading in order to conserve the material status of the sign as an object. Broodthaers later commented on this work.

> For me this book is an object of interdiction. ... Here you cannot read the book without destroying its plastic qualities. I believed that this concrete gesture would have confronted the viewer with this interdiction. But very much to my surprise the viewer reacted in a totally different manner than I had expected. ... Nobody was curious to read the text, not knowing whether they were looking at interred prose *or* poetry, sad or pleasant. Nobody was affected by the interdiction.[6]

Within Broodthaers' very first work the future strategy of inscribing the work into the institutional frame is already apparent as a dialectical approach toward the conditions of contemporary object production. If primary language and material objectification within the discourse of art cannot exist outside of the secondary language of mythification, and they support and reaffirm the socio-political conditions that they set out to negate, then the discourse of object production itself has to be negated, the paradox being that the critical negation has to assume the structure and status of the discourse into which it inscribes itself. As Broodthaers put it in the catalog of his first one-man exhibition in 1966: "Every object is the victim of its nature, even in a transparent painting the color hides the canvas and the molding hides the frame."[7]

The essential structure of art "as a process of reification" determines Broodthaers' first work where the gesture of material definition functions like an institutional frame that contains and conserves, obscuring the object of reading in order to materialize it in the virtual space of the aesthetic object. This institutional space and its various framing devices, its techniques of containment, the factual site where the transformation from primary into secondary language takes place, will henceforth become the field of Broodthaers' investigations, in particular the series of museum and exhibition fictions that he produced after 1968.

The artist as founder of museums is not foreign to the history of Modernism. Charles Baudelaire for one in 1861–1863 was working on a project on "lost museums and museums to be founded." And obviously Broodthaers was familiar with the actual museum foundations by nineteenth-century artists, such as the Musée Gustave Moreau that had been rediscovered by the Surrealists and that had become a secret place of veneration in Paris. In 1974 we see Broodthaers initiate a campaign to save a nineteenth-century museum by the eccentric Brussels painter Antoine Wiertz, arguing that "from a current artistic point of view, this strange museum should be regarded as a place where theoretical inflation is embodied, certainly worth conserving and still able to function as a critical model."[8]

But we can equally assume that Broodthaers in 1968 was familiar with the museum foundations of the avant-garde: with Duchamp's *Boîte-en-Valise* certainly, if not with the "Museum" boxes by Joseph Cornell from the mid- to late Forties, and most likely also with the fictions that Claes Oldenburg constructed around his *Store* in 1961 and the collection that was later to become the *Mouse Museum*, the self-appointment as director and the publication of an official letterhead of the Ray Gun Manufacturing Company Inc., whose purpose it was to "protect art through reversals and disguises, from the bourgeois, from commercialism, from rivalry, from all the forces that might destroy art."[9]

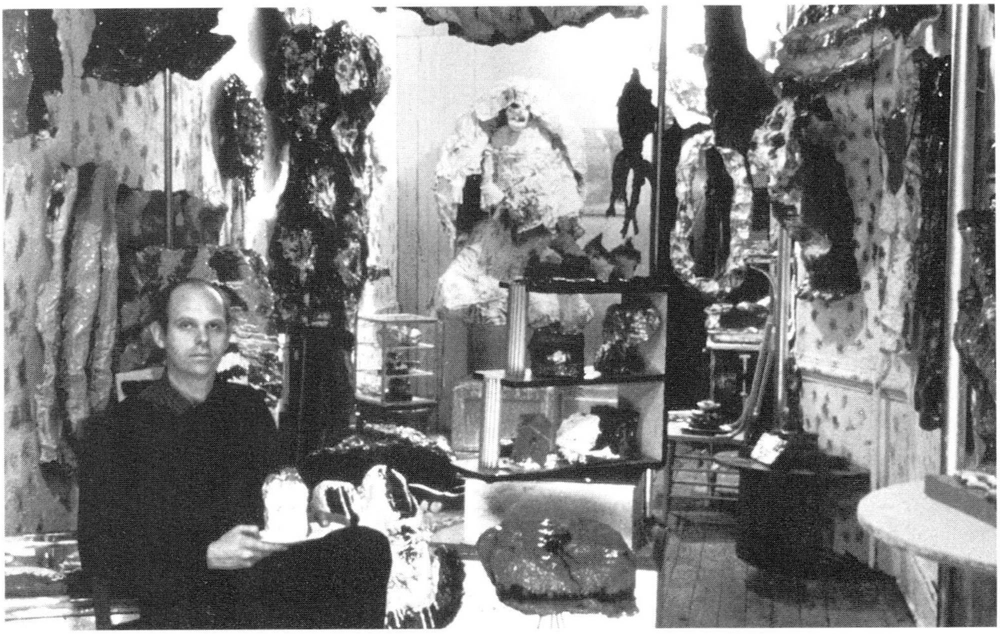

Claes Oldenburg in *The Store*, 107 East 2nd Street, New York, December 1961–January 1962. © Claes Oldenburg. Courtesy Paula Cooper Gallery, New York.

Clearly those references are only of secondary importance in the formation of Broodthaers' first museum fiction that he staged on September 27, 1968, in his former studio at Rue de la Pépinière in Brussels. This installation initiated a series of museum fictions and exhibition constructs—the series that was announced under the auspices of the *Musée d'Art Moderne, Département des Aigles*, ending in 1972 with the installation of the *Section des Figures (The Eagle From Oligocene to today, Düsseldorf)*—and the ultimate installation was staged at the Palais Rothschild in Paris under the title *L'Angélus de Daumier* in 1975.

All the framing elements of aesthetic production and reception, that determine and contain it invisibly, yet powerfully, were made explicit constitutive elements in Broodthaers' secondary mythogical construction.

The *Musée d'Art Moderne, Département des Aigles, Section 19eme Siècle*, as it was officially called on the letterhead that Broodthaers had designed and printed on the occasion of the opening and for the purposes of future correspondence, was directed by the artist as "conservateur." When Broodthaers said in retrospect that his museum was "born of the spirit of May '68," this reference should not be mistaken as a nostalgic note that passes on the aura of distant political radicality to the muteness and immobility of the art-object. The role reversal that is performed in the artist as museum director for a day (the first museum installation actually lasted for exactly one year at the Rue de la Pépinière) had a material background in the events of 1968. When, during the cultural revolution of May 1968 in Paris, the students occupied the Théâtre de l'Odeon, and its director, Jean-Louis Barrault, eventually stood in solidarity with their aims to form new Soviet-type structure of self-government and administration of the theater, a group of artists, students and political activists, Broodthaers among them, occupied for a short time the Palais des Beaux-Arts in Brussels in order to force its director to resign and to take over the artistic, political and administrative directorship of this institution. Broodthaers' subsequent coup in the studio can therefore certainly be seen as an allegorical commemoration of the events of May 1968 at a moment in time when the futility of these events and their eventual suppression might have already become apparent.

The museum was officially opened on the evening of September 27, 1968, and the inauguration speech was delivered by Johannes Cladders, a "real" museum director (of the Museum Mönchengladbach, then one of Germany's most active museums committed to the support of contemporary avant-garde art), whom Broodthaers had invited for this occasion.

The attending guests, a crowd consisting of friends of Broodthaers, artists and collectors, critics and curators, found themselves in an environment consisting of a number of variously sized empty picture crates, carrying the usual stenciled inscriptions "Picture, with care, keep dry" and "Tableau-fragile," that Broodthaers had borrowed from the Palais des Beaux-Arts. This display was augmented by spotlights and ladders, equipment used for the installation of exhibitions and the only reference that the bewildered audience could find in regard to the museum's devotion to the nineteenth century was a group of thirty color picture postcards reproducing well-known nineteenth-century French paintings by Ingres, David, Courbet and Corot, Meissonnier, Puvis de Chavannes and Horace Vernet. A truck from the Palais des Beaux-Arts in Brussels was parked in front of the artist's studio and inscriptions on the windowpanes reading "Musée/Museum," from the inside as well as from the outside were indicating to the visitors the transformation of the site of production into the fictitious institution of reception.

Broodthaers' installation assembled, as it seemed, all the elements of contingency and containment that institutionalized the work of art and constituted framing conditions: the containers of transportation and dissemination as well as the authoritative rituals of meaning assigned them. Like Duchamp's *Boîte-en-Valise*, Broodthaers' *Musée d'Art Moderne* takes the means of transportation as literally and seriously into

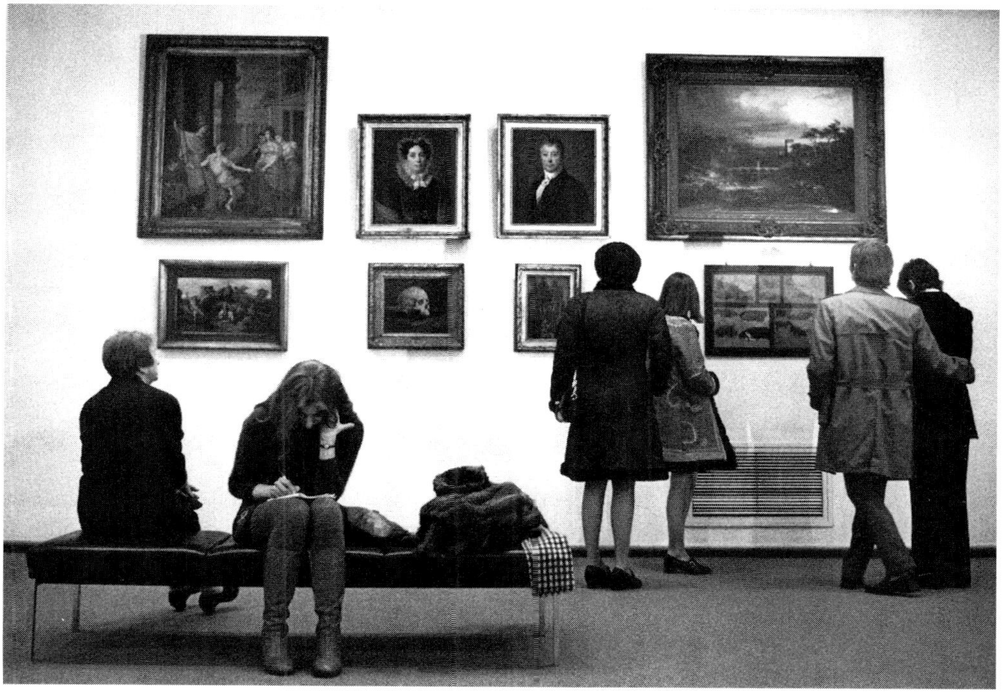

Marcel Broodthaers, *Musée d'Art Moderne, Département des Aigles, Section 19ème Siècle*, 1969. Installation, Kunsthalle Düsseldorf. Photo: Maria Gilissen. © 2015 The Estate of Marcel Broodthaers/Artists Rights Society (ARS), New York/SABAM, Brussels.

account as it takes the technology of dissemination and its forms for the outward status of the once auratic existence of the unique work of art. Broodthaers' selection of postcards from the beginning of Modernism encompasses that historical moment that initiates the gradual disintegration of the auratic work. As contemporary technical reproductions of original works of art they equally speak of the conclusion of that historical period in allegorical disguise. The dialectic definition of allegorical practice, as given by Walter Benjamin, describes Broodthaers' activity exactly: the redemption of the object of the past from oblivion as the ritualized repetitions of the devaluation of objects in the present, in anticipation of their fate on the market and their subjection to ideology—the very process that Barthes defines as mythification. What is, however, only implicit in Duchamp's work in general and in the *Boîte-en-Valise* in particular, the reference to the social institution that contains the practice of art as a discourse, is now at the center of Broodthaers' work. The place of production, the artist's studio (in this context, see Daniel Buren's essay "The Function of the Studio"), is exchanged for the institutionalized space of reception, the museum. The place of origin of the work of art and place of final destination are reversed and integrated.

It was only logical that in the final museum fiction that Marcel Broodthaers conceived for his exhibition, *L'Angélus de Daumier*, 1975, this reversal was reversed. At the climax of his life, when the work was finally about to enter official culture, the studio that had once been transformed into the museum was now reconstructed inside the museum itself. *Salle Blanche*, as the life-size plywood reconstruction of Broodthaers' two-room studio in the Rue de la Pépinière was called, replicated the architectural detail of the studio in all exactitude. From the architectural molding to the trompe-l'oeil radiators, the artist's studio, the site of production, which had once been converted into fiction, was now reconstructed inside the museum space itself, roped off from access, distant in material, space and time. The architectural

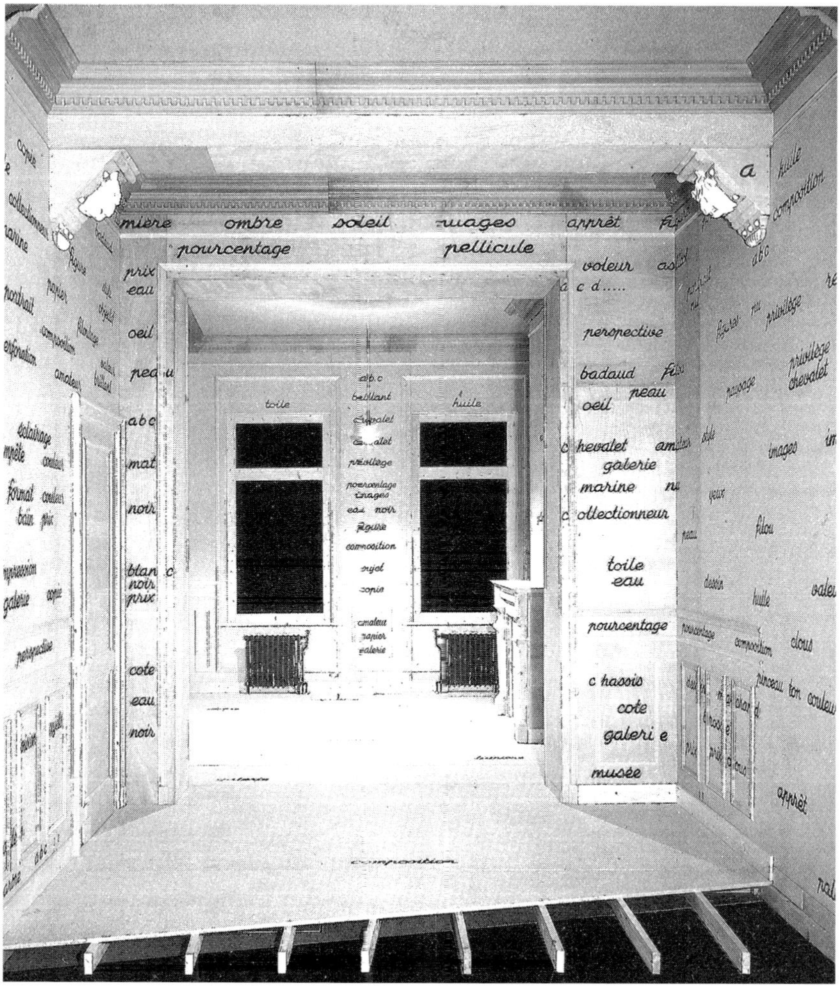

Marcel Broodthaers, *Salle Blanche*, in *L'Angélus de Daumier*, 1975. Centre national d'art contemporain, Hôtel Rothschild, Paris, October 2–November 10, 1975. © 2015 The Estate of Marcel Broodthaers/Artists Rights Society (ARS), New York/SABAM, Brussels.

container in its entirety seemed to have assumed the qualities of the wooden shipping crate, and their stenciled inscriptions had now been turned into calligraphic inscriptions covering the walls and placed sporadically on the floor. The vocabulary was that of the nineteenth-century academy painters and the inscriptions seemed to have taken on the function of the iconographic references of the picture postcards in the original foundation of the *Musée d'Art Moderne*. Juxtaposed with *Salle Blanche*, that had been roped off from the public, was the former salon of Madame de Rothschild, once the owner of the Palais in which the museum was now located. This salon, normally not accessible to the public, containing the original eighteenth- and nineteenth-century furniture and decoration, as well as part of the private collection of the Rothschild family, was now open to the public for the duration of Broodthaers' exhibition.

Broodthaers' museum fictions seem to address both the language and the architecture of the social institution within which the discourse of art is framed and contained. Further yet, they reach to the origins of the historical institution and the discourse within which they are fabricated as secondary myths and anticipate the penultimate status of the aesthetic construct in the present moment. It is within that scale that Broodthaers' work "vanquishes myth from inside," that it avoids the parodic fetishization that we discovered in Duchamp's *Boîte-en-Valise*. It equally succeeds in overcoming the architectural neutrality of design, that which he called "decor," that he anticipated for any practice that restricted itself only to the visual and architectural elements of the ideological discourse of Modernism and the museum institution.

New York, March 1983

Notes

First published in French and English in *Museums by Artists*, ed. A. A. Bronson and Peggy Gale (Toronto: Art Metropole, 1983), pp. 45–56. All translations by Benjamin H. D. Buchloh unless otherwise noted. Minor corrections have been made for consistency.

1. Marcel Duchamp, interview with J. J. Sweeney, in *The Complete Works of Marcel Duchamp*, ed. Arturo Schwarz (London: Thames & Hudson, 1969), p. 513.

2. Ibid.

3. Roland Barthes, *Mythologies* (New York: Farrar, Straus & Giroux, 1972), p. 114.

4. Hannah Arendt, "Introduction," in Walter Benjamin, *Illuminations* (New York: Schocken, 1969), p. 45.

5. El Lissitzky, "Demonstrationsräume," in *El Lissitzky*, ed. Sophie Lissitzky-Kueppers (Dresden: VEB Verlag der Kunst, 1967), pp. 2–3.

6. Irmeline Lebeer, "Dix-mille francs de récompense," interview with Marcel Broodthaers, in *Marcel Broodthaers*, exh. cat. (Brussels: Palais des Beaux-Arts, 1974), p. 66.

7. Marcel Broodthaers, *Moules, Oeufs, Frites, Charbon, Perroquets*, exh. cat. (Antwerp: Wide White Space Gallery, 1966), n.p.

8. Marcel Broodthaers, "Wiertz-Museum," *Studio International* 186, no. 970 (October, 1974): 114.

9. Claes Oldenburg, "Notebooks" (1960), quoted in *Claes Oldenburg*, ed. Barbara Rose (New York: Museum of Modern Art: 1970), pp. 62ff.

6

From Faktura to Factography

As the first director of the Museum of Modern Art, Alfred Barr largely determined the goals and policy of the institution that was to define the framework of production and reception for the American neo-avant-garde. In 1927, just prior to the founding of the museum, Barr traveled to the Soviet Union. This was to have been a survey journey, like the one he had just completed in Weimar Germany, to explore current avant-garde production by artists working in the new revolutionary society. What he found there, however, was a situation of seemingly unmanageable conflict.

On the one hand, he witnessed the extraordinary productivity of the original modernist avant-garde (extraordinary in terms of the number of its participants, both men *and* women, and in terms of the variety of modes of production: ranging from Kazimir Malevich's late suprematist work through the Laboratory Period of the constructivists, to the Lef Group and the emerging productivist program, as well as agitprop theater and avant-garde films screened for mass audiences). On the other hand, there was the general awareness among artists and cultural theoreticians that they were participating in a final transformation of the modernist vanguard aesthetic, as they irrevocably changed those conditions of art production and reception inherited from bourgeois society and its institutions. Then, too, there was the growing fear that the process of that successful transformation might be aborted by the emergence of totalitarian repression from within the very system that had generated the foundation for a new socialist collective culture. And last of all, there was Barr's own professional disposition to search for the most advanced, modernist avant-garde at precisely the moment when that social group was about to dismantle itself and its specialized activities in order to assume a different role in the newly defined process of the social production of culture. These conflicting elements are clearly reflected in the diary that Barr kept during his visit to the Soviet Union:

> … went to see Rodchenko and his talented wife. … Rodchenko showed us an appalling variety of things—suprematist paintings (preceded by the earliest geometrical things I have seen, 1915, done with compass)—woodcuts, linoleum cuts, posters, book designs, photographs, kino set, etc. etc. He has done no painting since 1922, devoting himself to the photographic arts of which he is a master. … We left after 11 p.m.—an excellent evening, but I must find some painters if possible.[1]

But Barr was no more fortunate in his search for painting during his visit with El Lissitzky: "He showed also books and photographs, many of them quite ingenious. … I asked whether he painted. He replied that he painted only when he had nothing else to do, and as that was never, never."[2]

And, finally, in his encounter with Sergei Tretyakov, it became clear that there was a historical reason for the frustration of Barr's expectations. For Tretyakov enunciated the position these artists had adopted in the course of transforming their aesthetic thinking in relation to the emerging industrialization of the Soviet Union: the program of productivism and the new method of literary representation/production that accompanied it, *factography*. Barr's diary tells us that Tretyakov "seemed to have lost all interest in everything that did not conform to his objective, descriptive, self-styled journalistic ideal of art. He had no interest in painting since it had become abstract. He no longer writes poetry but confines himself to reporting."[3]

This paradigm change within modernism, which Barr witnessed from the very first hour, did not make a strong enough impression on him to affect his future project. He continued in his plan to lay the foundations of an avant-garde art in the United States according to the model that had been developed in the first two decades of this century in western Europe (primarily in Paris). And it was this perseverance, as much as anything else, that prevented—at least until the late 1960s—the program of productivism and the methods of factographic production from entering the general consciousness of American and European audiences.

In 1936, when Barr's experiences in the Soviet Union were incorporated in the extraordinary exhibition *Cubism and Abstract Art*, his encounter with productivism was all but undocumented. This is particularly astonishing since Barr seems to have undergone a conversion toward the end of his journey, one which is not recorded in his diary, but which he publicly expressed upon his return in "The Lef and Soviet Art," his essay for *Transition* published in the fall of 1928. Surprisingly, we read in this article, illustrated with two photographs of Lissitzky's exhibition design for the 1928 *Pressa* exhibition in Cologne, the following, rather perspicacious appraisal of the ideas and goals of the Lef Group:

> The *Lef* is more than a symptom, more than an expression of a fresh culture or of post-revolutionary man; it is a courageous attempt to give to art an important social function in a world where from one point of view it has been prostituted

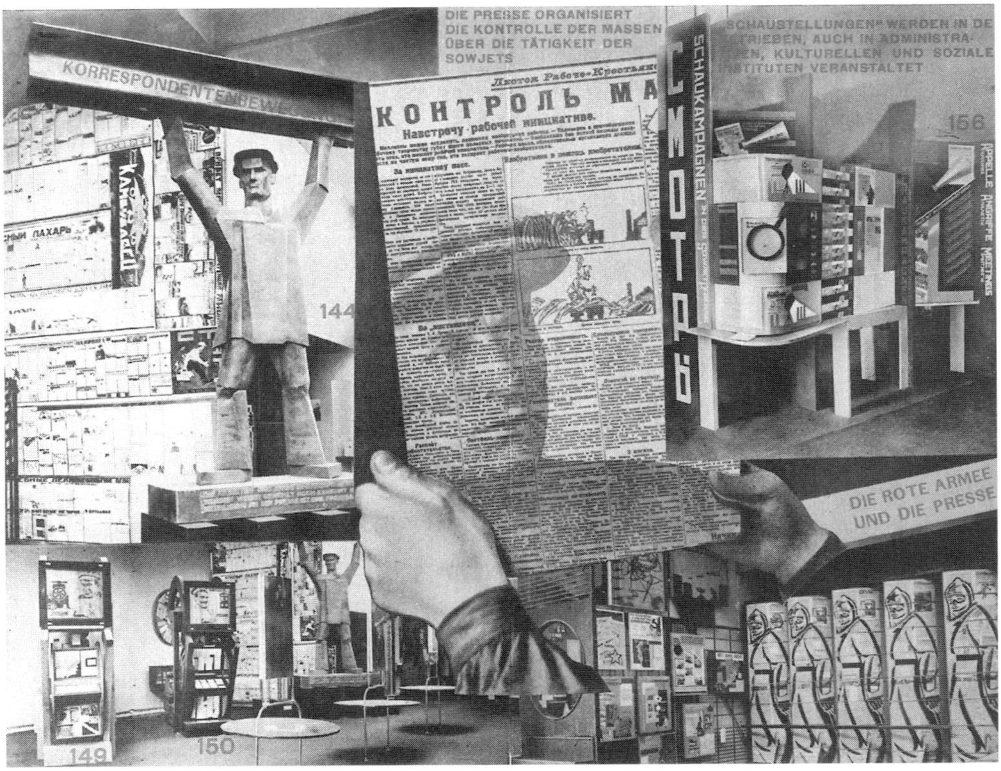

El Lissitzky, photomontage for catalog accompanying the Soviet Pavilion at the *International Pressa Exhibition*, Cologne, 1928. © 2015 Artists Rights Society (ARS), New York/VG Bild-Kunst, Bonn.

> for five centuries. The *Lef* is formed by men who are idealists of Materialism; who have a certain advantage over the Alexandrian cults of the West—the *surréaliste* wizards, the esoteric word jugglers and those nostalgics who practice necromancy over the bones variously of Montezuma, Louis Philippe or St. Thomas Aquinas. The *Lef* is strong in the illusion that man can live by bread alone.[4]

But European and American interests in the modernist avant-garde refused to confront the implications seen so clearly by Barr. Instead, what happened at that moment, in the process of reception, was what had been described in 1926 by Boris Arvatov, who along with Alexei Gan, Sergei Tretyakov, and Nikolai Tarabukin made up the group of productivist theoreticians. Arvatov wrote about the painters who refused to join the productivists:

> Those on the Right gave up their positions without resistance. … Either they stopped painting altogether or they emigrated to the Western countries, in order to astonish Europe with home-made Russian Cézannes or with patriotic-folkloristic paintings of little roosters.[5]

It is against this background that I want to pursue the following questions: Why did the Soviet avant-garde, after having developed a modernist practice to its most radical stages in the post-synthetic cubist work of the suprematists, constructivists, and Laboratory Period artists, apparently abandon the paradigm of modernism upon which its practice had been based? What paradigmatic changes occurred at that time, and which paradigm formation replaced the previous one?

For the sake of detail and specificity I will limit myself in what follows to a discussion of only some aspects of the respective paradigms that generated the crucial concern for *faktura* in the first period, and that made *factography* the primary method in the second period of Russian avant-garde practice.

Faktura was first defined in the Russian context in David Burliuk's futurist manifesto, "A Slap in the Face of Public Taste," of 1912, and in Mikhail Larionov's "Rayonnist Manifesto" of the same year. In the works of Malevich from 1913 to 1919 *faktura* was a major pictorial concern, as it was at that time for painters such as El Lissitzky, Lyubov Popova, and Olga Rozanova, who had their origins in synthetic cubism and who had been profoundly influenced by Malevich's suprematism. Further, it remained the central concept in the nonutilitarian objects produced by Alexandr Rodchenko, Vladimir Tatlin, and the Stenberg brothers, sometimes referred to as the Laboratory constructivists. During an extremely hectic period of approximately seven years (from 1913 to 1920) the essential qualities of *faktura* were acquired step by step and developed further by the individual members of that avant-garde.

By 1920 it seemed to them that they had brought to their logical conclusion all the major issues that had been developed during the preceding fifty years of modernist painting. Therefore the central concern for a self-reflexive pictorial and sculptural production was abandoned after 1920—gradually at first, then abruptly—to be replaced by the new concern for factographic and productivist practices that are indicative of a more profound paradigmatic change.

Faktura

Attempts are being made in the recent literature to construct a genealogy for the Russian vanguard's concern for *faktura*, claiming that it originates in Russian icon painting. Vladimir Markov's 1914 text "Icon Painting"—after Burliuk and Larionov the third to address *faktura* explicitly—had established this specifically Russian source, arguing that

> through the resonance of the colors, the sound of the materials, the assemblage of textures (*faktura*) we call the people to beauty, to religion, to God. … The real world is introduced into the icon's creation only through the assemblage and incrustation of real tangible objects and this seems to produce a combat between two worlds, the inner and the outer.[6]

But the specifically Russian qualities of *faktura* are nonetheless challenged by other details of this production. For the religio-transcendental function assigned by Markov to the term *faktura* is just too close to the essential pursuit of the beginning of a collage aesthetics as defined in 1912 by, for example, Georges Braque who argued that color and shape operated simultaneously but completely independent of each other. Similarly, Tatlin's request in 1913 that "the eye should be put under the control of touch" is very similar to Marcel Duchamp's contemporaneous statement that he wanted to abolish the supremacy of the retinal principle in art. And, in the simultaneous discussions of the term, any references to specifically Russian or religious functions are too rapidly jettisoned to maintain the credibility of Markov's argument. Already in 1916 Tarabukin wrote a definition of *faktura* that would essentially remain valid for the entire period of Laboratory constructivism to follow:

> The form of a work of art derives from two fundamental premises: the material or medium (colors, sounds, words) and the construction, through which the material is organized in a coherent whole, acquiring its artistic logic and its profound meaning.[7]

What qualifies this concern for *faktura* as a paradigmatic feature (differentiating it at the same time from previous concerns for *facture* in the works of the cubists and futurists in western Europe) is the quasi-scientific, systematic manner in which the constructivists now pursued their investigation of pictorial and sculptural constructs, as well as their systematic interrogation of the perceptual interaction that these constructs generate. The equation between colors, sounds, and words established by Tarabukin no longer followed the neo-romantic call for *synaesthesia* that one could still hear at this time from Wassily Kandinsky and Frantisek Kupka. Running parallel with the formation of structural linguistics in the Moscow Linguistic Circle and the Opoyaz Group in Petersburg in 1915 and 1916 respectively, the constructivists developed the first systematic phenomenological/semiological grammar of painting and sculpture. With the same analytic accuracy used to analyze the *interrelationships* of their various functions—what Saussure would call the syntagmatic axis—they would now define the separate material and procedural qualities equally relevant for the constitution of a perceptual phenomenon. Furthermore, they addressed the apparatus of visual sign production, that is, production procedures as well as the tools of these procedures. It was precisely the systematic nature of this investigation that led Barr in 1927 to see "an appalling variety of things" in Rodchenko's work.

When in 1920–21 Rodchenko arrived more or less simultaneously at his sculptural series *Hanging Constructions* (a series subtitled *Surfaces Reflecting Light*) and at the triptych *Pure Colors: Red, Yellow, Blue*, he had developed that separation of color and line and that integration of shape and plane to its logical conclusion that the cubists had initiated with such excitement. With some justification he declared, "This is the end of painting. These are the primary colors. Every plane is a plane and there will be no more representation."[8]

Even at this point in Rodchenko's development *faktura* already meant more than a rigorous and programmatic separation of line and drawing from painting and color, more than the congruence of planes with their actual support surface, more than emphasizing the necessary self-referentiality of pictorial signifiers and their contiguity with all other syntagmatic functions. It already meant, as well, more than just the object's shift from virtual pictorial/sculptural space into actual space. We should not take the reference to *Surfaces Reflecting Light* as anything less than an indication of the potential involvement of these artists with materials and objects in actual spaces and the social processes that occur within these spaces.

Faktura also meant at this point, and not for Rodchenko alone, to incorporate the technical means of construction into the work itself, and to link them with existing standards of the development of the means of production in society at large. At first this happened on the seemingly banal level of the tools and materials that the painter employs—shifts that still caused considerable shock thirty years later with regard to Pollock's work. In 1917 Rodchenko explained his reasons for abandoning the traditional tools of painting and his sense of the need to mechanize its craft:

> Thenceforth the picture ceased being a picture and became a painting or an object. The brush gave way to new instruments with which it was convenient and easy and more expedient to work the surface. The brush which had been so indispensable in painting which transmitted the object and its subtleties became an inadequate and imprecise instrument in the new non-objective painting, and the press, the roller, the drawing pen, the compass replaced it.[9]

The very same conviction about laboratory technology is concretized in Rodchenko's systematic experimentation with pictorial surfaces as traces or immediate results of specific procedures and materials: metallic and reflective paint are juxtaposed with matte gouaches; varnished oil colors are combined with highly textured surfaces. It is this technologic of Rodchenko's experimental approach that seems to have prevented aesthetic comprehension for even longer than did Duchamp's most advanced work of 1913, such as his *Three Standard Stoppages* or his readymades. With its emphasis on the material congruence of the sign with its signifying practice, on the causal relationship between the sign and its referent, and its focus on the indexical status of the sign, Rodchenko's work has defied for the longest time a secondary level of meaning/reading.[10]

Further, this emphasis on the processual qualities of painting was linked to a serially organized configuration, a structure that resulted as much from the commitment to systematic investigation as from the aspiration toward science with which artists wanted to associate their production. It is this nexus of relationships that tied the essential features of the modernist paradigm eventually to the socially dominant modes of control and management of time and perceptual experience in the Soviet Union's rapidly accelerating process of industrialization.

Faktura is therefore the historically logical aesthetic correlative to the introduction of industrialization and social engineering that was imminent in the Soviet Union after the revolution of 1917. For that reason *faktura* also became the necessary intermediary step within the transformation of the modernist paradigm as we witness it around 1920. When in 1921 A. V. Babichev, the leader of the Working Group for Objective Analysis (of which Rodchenko and Stepanova were members), gives a definition of art production, his statement is strikingly close to ideas of Taylorism, social engineering, and organized consumption, as they became operative at that time in both western European and American society. Thus Babichev states:

> Art is an informed analysis of the concrete tasks which social life poses. ... If art becomes public property it will organize the consciousness and psyche of the masses by organizing objects and ideas.[11]

Finally, the notion of *faktura* already implied a reference to the placement of the constructivist object and its interaction with the spectator. To emphasize spatial and perceptual contiguity by mirror reflection—as hinted in Rodchenko's project for constructions whose reflective surfaces would mirror their surroundings—means, once again, to reduce the process of representation to purely *indexical* signs.[12] Matter seemingly generates its own representation without mediation (the old positivist's dream, as it was, of course, that of the early photographers). Contiguity is also incorporated in the kinetic potential of Rodchenko's *Hanging Constructions*, since the sculptures' movements by air currents or contact literally involve the viewers in an endless phenomenological and potentially tactile loop established by their own movements in the time/space continuum.

In the discussions of the Group for Objective Analysis from 1921, *construction* was defined as the organization of the kinetic life of objects and materials which would create new movement. As such it had been juxtaposed with the traditional notion of composition, as Varvara Stepanova had defined it:

> Composition is the contemplative approach of the artist in his work. Technique and industry have confronted art with the problem of construction as an active process, and not a contemplative reflection. The "sanctity" of a work as a single entity is destroyed. The museum which was a treasury of this entity is now transformed into an archive.[13]

If these lines sound familiar today it is not only because Stepanova's text had considerable impact on the thinking and practice of her peers, but rather because, more than ten years later, precisely the same historical phenomenon is described and analyzed in a text that is by now rightfully considered one of the most important contributions to twentieth-century aesthetic theory. I am speaking, of course, of Walter Benjamin's

1935 essay "The Work of Art in the Age of Mechanical Reproduction," and the following excerpt might be compared with Stepanova's 1921 statement:

> What they [the Dadaists] intended and achieved was a relentless destruction of the aura of their creations, which they branded as reproductions with the very means of production. ... In the decline of middle-class society, contemplation became a school for asocial behavior; it was countered by distraction as a variant of social conduct. ... [Dada] hit the spectator like a bullet, it happened to him, thus acquiring a tactile quality. ... (Thus the dada work restores the quality of tactility to the art of the present day, a quality which is important to the art of all periods in their stages of transformation.)[14]

The historical observations by Stepanova and their subsequent theorization by Benjamin have another correlative in the work of El Lissitzky from the period 1925–27. Already in 1923 in his *Prounenraum* for the Grosse Berliner Kunstausstellung, Lissitzky had transformed tactility and perceptual movement—still latent it Rodchenko's *Hanging Construction*—into a full-scale architectural relief construction. For the first time, Lissitzky's earlier claim for his *Proun-Paintings*, to operate as transfer stations from art to architecture, had been fulfilled.

It was, however, not until 1926, when he designed and installed in Dresden and Hannover what he called his *Demonstration Rooms*—room-sized cabinets for the display and installation of the non-representational art of his time—that one finds Stepanova's theoretical analysis fully confirmed in Lissitzky's practice. The vertical lattice relief-construction that covers the display surfaces of the cabinet, and that changes hue and value from white, through gray, to black according to the viewer's position clearly engages the viewer in a phenomenological

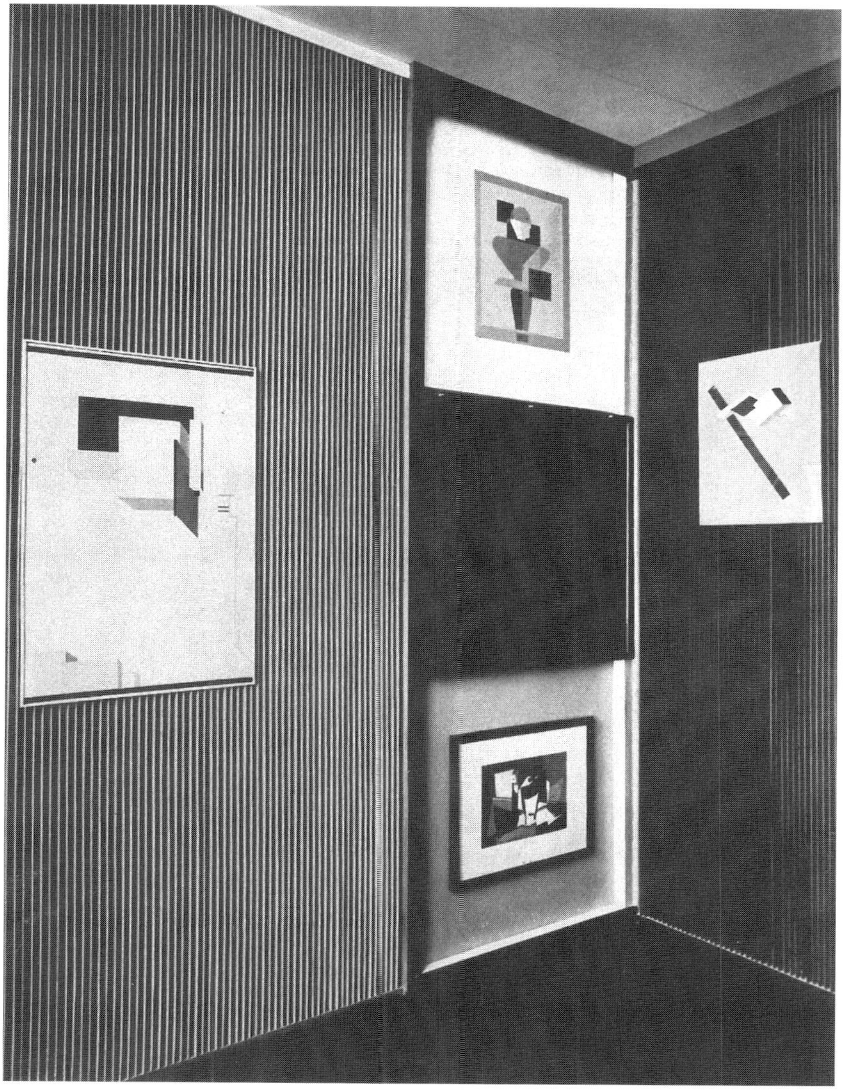

El Lissitzky, views toward walls 1 and 2 of *Kabinett der Abstrakten*, 1928. Provinzialmuseum, Hannover. Installation view shows aluminum relief walls and corner cabinet with movable panel.

exercise that defies traditional contemplative behavior in front of the work of art. And the moveable wall panels, carrying or covering easel panels on display, to be shifted by the viewers themselves according to their momentary needs and interests, already incorporate into the display system of the museum the very functions of the archive that Stepanova predicted as the museum's social and historical destiny. In the late 1920s, Lissitzky wrote a retrospective analysis of his *Demonstration Rooms*, and once again it is crucial to compare his ideas with those of both Stepanova and Benjamin in order to realize how developed and current these concerns actually were in the various contexts:

> Traditionally the viewer was lulled into passivity by the paintings on the walls. Our construction/design shall make the man active. This is the function of our room. … With each movement of the viewer in space the perception of the wall changes; what was white becomes black, and vice versa. Thus, as a result of human bodily motion, a perceptual dynamic is achieved. This play makes the viewer active. … The viewer is physically engaged in an interaction with the object on display.[15]

The paradox and historical irony of Lissitzky's work was, of course, that it had introduced a revolution of the perceptual apparatus into an otherwise totally unchanged social institution, one that constantly reaffirms both the contemplative behavior and the supposed sanctity of historically determined works of art. This paradox complemented the contradiction that had become apparent several years earlier when Lissitzky had placed a suprematist painting, enlarged to the size of an agitational billboard, in front of a factory entrance in Vitebsk. This utopian radicalism in the formal sphere—what the conservative Soviet critics later would pejoratively allude to as formalism—in its failure to communicate with, and to properly address the new audiences of

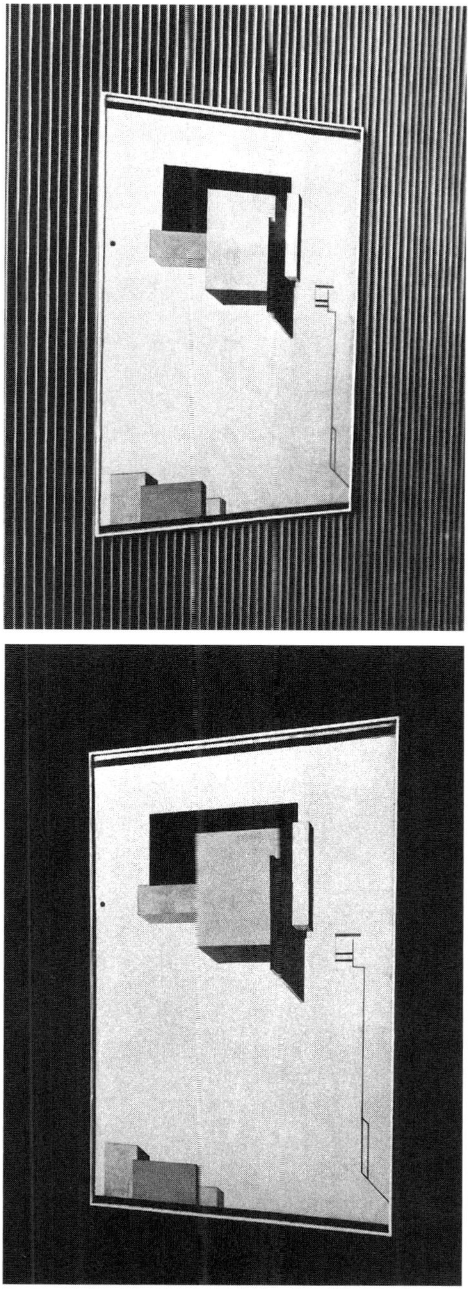

El Lissitzky, *Floating Volume*, 1919. Installed in El Lissitzky's *Kabinett der Abstrakten*. The two views indicate change from white to black depending on the viewer's position. © 2015 Artists Rights Society (ARS), New York/ VG Bild-Kunst, Bonn.

industrialized urban society in the Soviet Union, became increasingly problematic in the eyes of the very groups that had developed constructivist strategies to expand the framework of modernism.

It had become clear that the new society following the socialist revolution (in many respects a social organization that was comparable to the advanced industrial nations of western Europe and the United States at that time) required systems of representation/production/distribution which would recognize the collective participation in the actual processes of production of social wealth, systems which, like architecture in the past or cinema in the present had established conditions of *simultaneous collective reception*. In order to make art once again "an informed analysis of the concrete tasks which social life poses," as Babichev had requested, and in order to "fill the gulf between art and the masses that the bourgeois traditions had established," as Meyerhold had called for, entirely new forms of audience address and distribution had to be considered. But around 1920 even the most advanced works among the non-utilitarian object constructions—by Rodchenko, the Stenberg brothers, Tatlin, and Konstantin Medunetsky—did not depart much further from the modernist framework of bourgeois aesthetics than to establish models of epistemological and semiotic critique. No matter how radical, these were at best merely a negation of the perceptual conventions by which art had previously been produced and received.

With sufficient historical distance it becomes clearer that this fundamental crisis within the modernist paradigm was not only a crisis of representation (one that had reached its penultimate status of self-reflexive verification and epistemological critique). It was also, more importantly, a crisis of audience relationships, a moment in which the historical institutionalization of the avant-garde had reached its peak of credibility. Any new legitimation was only to be obtained by a redefinition of its relationship with the new urban masses and their cultural demands, a conflict, after all, that the Western European avant-garde since Dadaism experienced with the same intensity. One of the Western responses had been an entrenchment in traditional models—the "*rappel à l'ordre*"—and the subsequent alignment of many of its artists with the aesthetic needs of the Fascists in Italy and Germany. Other factions of the Paris avant-garde responded to the same crisis with an increased affirmation of the unique status of high art, trying to resolve the contradictions of their practices by newly endorsing the blatantly obsolete conventions of pictorial representation.

In the early 1920s, the Soviet avant-garde (as well as some members of the de Stijl group, the Bauhaus, and of Berlin Dada) developed different strategies to transcend the historical limitations of modernism. They recognized that the crisis of representation could not be resolved without at the same time addressing questions of distribution and audience. Architecture, utilitarian product design, and photographic factography were some of the practices that the Soviet avant-garde considered capable of establishing these new modes of simultaneous collective reception.[16] Arvatov gives a vivid account of the gradual transition from the modernist position in the Russian avant-garde to the factographic and utilitarian aesthetic:

> The first to retire were the expressionists, headed by Kandinsky, who could not endure extremist pressure. Then the suprematists, headed by Malevich, protested against the murder of the sanctity of art, since they were convinced of the complete self-sufficiency of art. They could not comprehend any other form of art production but that of the easel. … In 1921 the Institute for Artistic Culture, which had once united all the Left artists, broke up. Shortly thereafter the Institute started to work under the banner of productivism. After a long process of selection, after an obstinate fight, the group of nonrepresentational constructivists crystallized within the group of the Left (Tatlin, Rodchenko, and the

> Obmochu-Group), who based their practice on the investigation and treatment of real materials as a transition to the constructive activity of the engineer. During one of the most important meetings of the Inchuk a resolution was passed unanimously to finish off with the self-sufficient constructions and to take all measures necessary in order to engage immediately with the industrial revolution.[17]

PHOTOMONTAGE: BETWEEN *FAKTURA* AND FACTOGRAPHY

The relatively late discovery of photocollage and montage techniques seems to have functioned as a transitional phase, operating between the fully developed modernist critique of the conventions of representation, which one sees in constructivism, and an emerging awareness of the new needs to construct iconic representations for a new mass audience. Neither Lissitzky nor Rodchenko produced any photocollage work before 1922, and only as late as 1919—when these artists had already pushed other aspects of post-cubist pictorial and sculptural problems further than anyone else in Europe (except, of course, for Duchamp)—did the collage technique proper enter their work at all. It seems credible that in fact Gustav Klucis, a disciple of Malevich and a collaborator with Lissitzky, was the first artist to transcend the purity of suprematist painting by introducing iconic photographic fragments into his suprematist work in 1919, the very date that John Heartfield and George Grosz, Raoul Hausmann and Hannah Hoech have claimed as the moment of their invention of photomontage.

In any case, by 1919 photomontage was widespread and commonly used in advertising and commercial photography, and the question of who actually introduced the technique into the transformation of the modernist paradigms of painting is ultimately of minor importance.[18] What is far more crucial is to find out in what way these artists (who might very well have "discovered" the technique for their own purposes quite independently of one another) related to the inherent potential and consequences of the reintroduction of (photographic) iconic imagery at precisely the moment when mimetic representation had seemingly been dismantled or was claimed to have been definitively abandoned.

Yet, when announcing his claims to have priority for the invention of the technique, Klucis also underlines the essential difference between the Soviet type of photomontage and that of the Berlin Dadaists when he writes in 1931:

> There are two general tendencies in the development of photomontage: one comes from American publicity and is exploited by the Dadaists and Expressionists—the so called photomontage of form; the second tendency, that of militant and political photomontage, was created on the soil of the Soviet Union. Photomontage appeared in the USSR under the banner of LEF when non-objective art was already finished. … Photomontage as a new method of art dates from 1919 to 1920.[19]

The hybrids that Klucis, Lissitzky, and Rodchenko created with their first attempts at collage and photomontage reveal the difficulty of the paradigmatic transformation inherent in that procedure, and the concomitant quests for a solution to the crisis of representation in the period from 1919 to '23. But these hybrid forms also suggest an answer to these questions, and they define the qualities and functions which the new procedures legitimizing iconic representation would have to offer. The conflict appeared roughly as follows:

On the one hand, these artists did not want to sacrifice any of the supreme modernist virtues they had achieved in their pictorial and sculptural work, primarily the transparency of construction procedures; the self-referentiality of the pictorial signifying devices; the reflexive

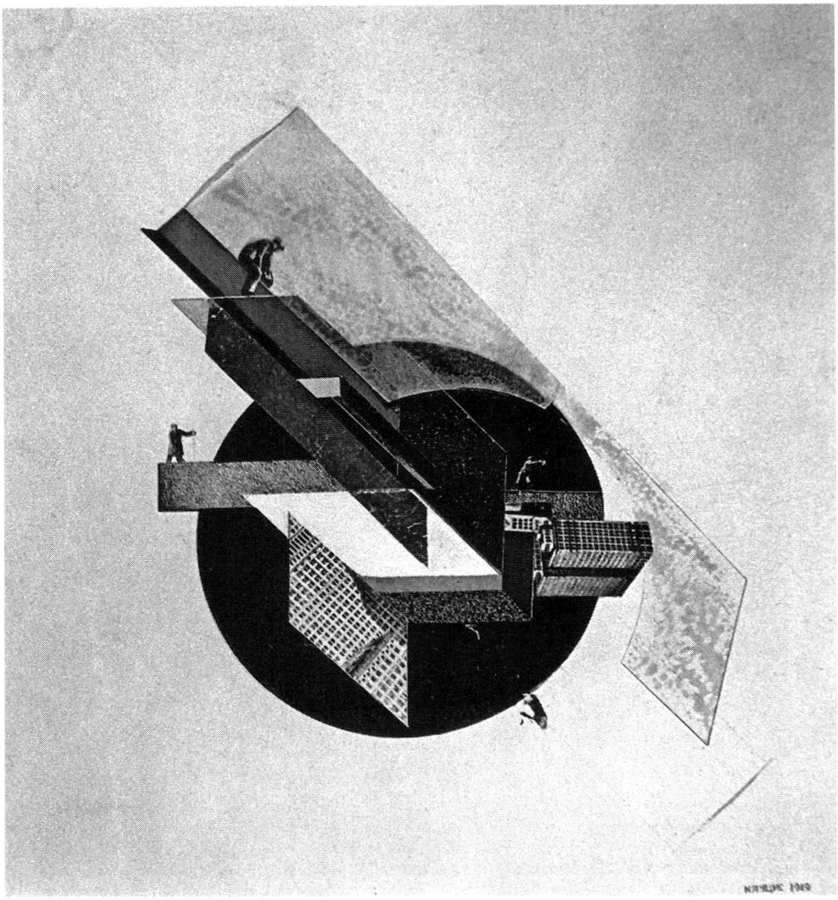

Gustav Klucis, *The Dynamic City*, 1919. Gouache, foil, and photomontage on paper. Private collection.

spatial organization; the general emphasis on tactility; and the constructed nature of their representations. On the other hand, photocollage and photomontage reintroduced into the aesthetic construct—at a moment when its modernist self-reflexivity and purification had semiotically reduced all formal and material operations to purely indexical signs—unlimited sources for a new iconicity of representation.

It was, however, a new type of iconicity, one that was mechanically produced and reproduced, and therefore—to a generation of media utopians—the most reliable and desirable one. Looking at the photomontage work of 1923 such as Hausmann's *Tatlin at Home*, or such as Rodchenko's series *Pro Eto*, one might well wonder whether the exuberance, willfulness, and quantity of the photographic quotations and their juxtapositions were not in part motivated by their authors' relief at having finally broken the modernist ban on iconic representation. This stood of course in extreme contrast to the Parisian cubists' earlier collage work, in which iconic representation had of course ultimately reappeared as well (even though only in the most minute references), but which had never made use of photographic iconic images.

But obviously, the rediscovery of a need to construct iconic representations did not result primarily from the need to overcome the strictures of modernism. Rather it was a necessary strategy to implement the transformation of audiences that the artists of the Soviet avant-garde wanted to achieve at that time. "Photomontage," an anonymous text (attributed by some scholars to Rodchenko) published in *Lef* in 1924, not only traces the historic affiliation of photomontage's conglomerate image with the strategies of advertising, juxtaposing photomontage's techniques and its iconic dimensions with the traditional techniques of modernist representation, but also introduces the necessity of *documentary* representation, explicitly in order to reach the new mass audiences:

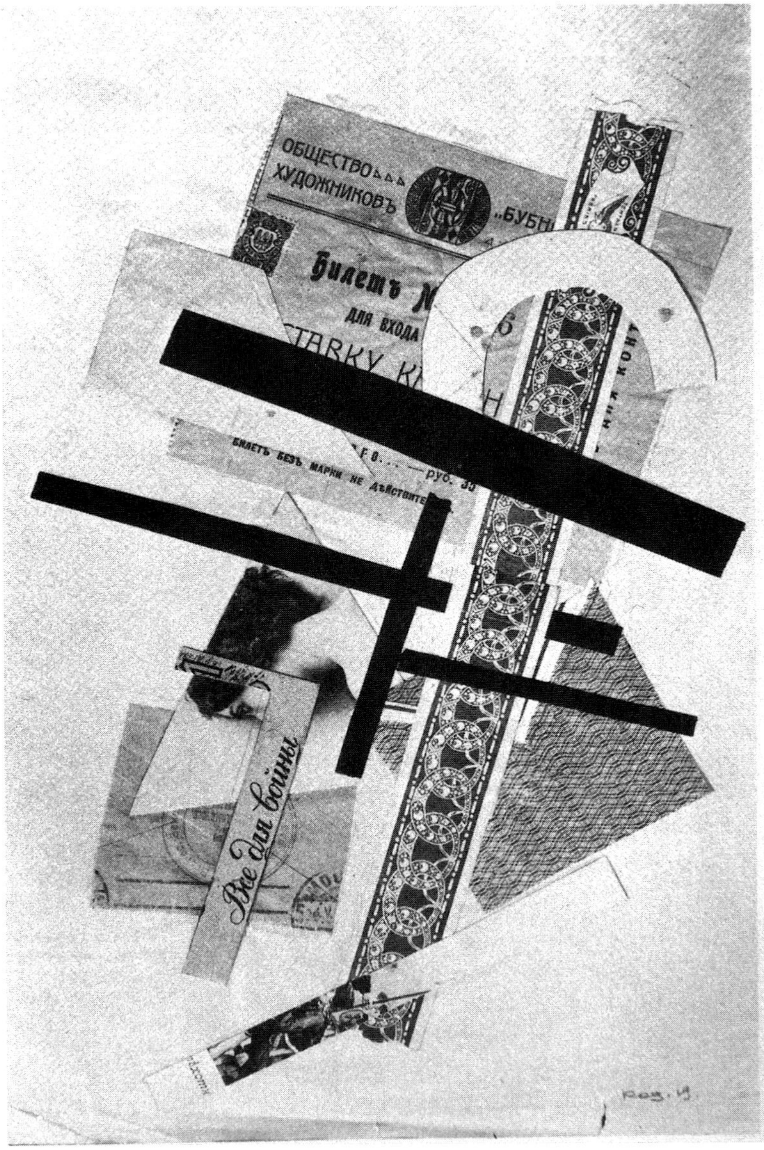

Alexander Rodchenko, *Ticket No. 1*, 1919. © Estate of Alexander Rodchenko/RAO, Moscow/VAGA, New York.

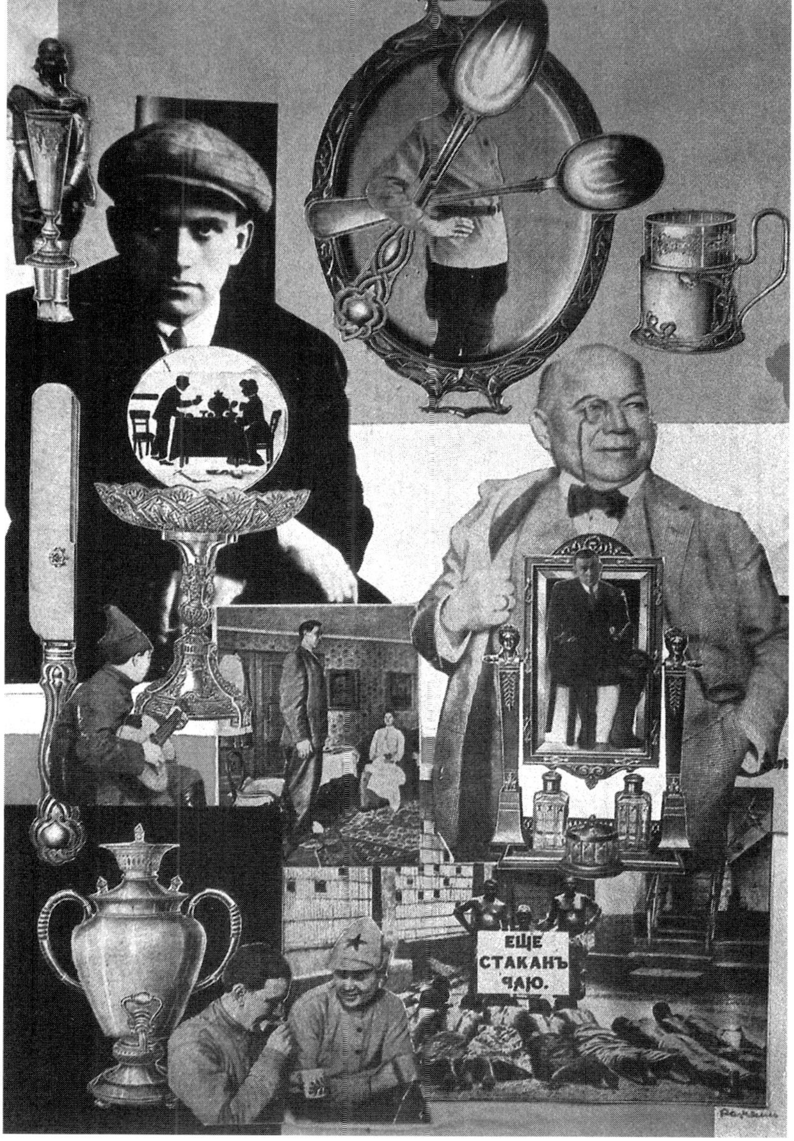

Alexander Rodchenko, photomontage for *Pro Eto*, 1923, c. 1950. Gelatin silver photomontage, $6\frac{11}{16} \times 4\frac{3}{8}$ in. (15 × 10 cm). © Estate of Alexander Rodchenko/RAO, Moscow/VAGA, New York.

> By photomontage we understand the usage of the photographic prints as tools of representation. The combination of photographs replaces the composition of graphic representations. The reason for this substitution resides in the fact that the photographic print is not the sketch of a visual fact, but its precise fixation. The precision and the documentary character give photography an impact on the spectator that the graphic representation can never claim to achieve. ... An advertisement with a photograph of the object that is being advertised is more efficient than a drawing of the same subject.[20]

Unlike the Berlin Dadaists who claimed to have invented photomontage, the author of this *Lef* text does not disavow the technique's intrinsic affiliation (and competitive engagement) with the dominant practices of advertising. Quite the contrary, the author seems to invite that competition by defining photomontage from the start as an agitational tool that addresses the Soviet Union's urban masses. It is with this aspect in mind that the practitioners of photomontage could not accept the confinement of the medium to the forms of distribution they had inherited from collage: forms limited by the single, rectangular sheet of paper, its format, scale, and size of edition entirely determined by the most traditional studio notions of unique, auratic works of art.

While (with the exception of the work of John Heartfield) most western European photomontage remained indeed on the level of the unique, fabricated image—paradoxically folding into the singularity of this montage object a multitude of fragmented and technically reproduced photographic images from mass-cultural sources—the strategies of the Soviet avant-garde seem to have shifted away rather rapidly from a mere reenactment of that historical paradox. The productivist artists realized that in order to address a new audience not only the techniques of production would have to be changed but the forms of distribution

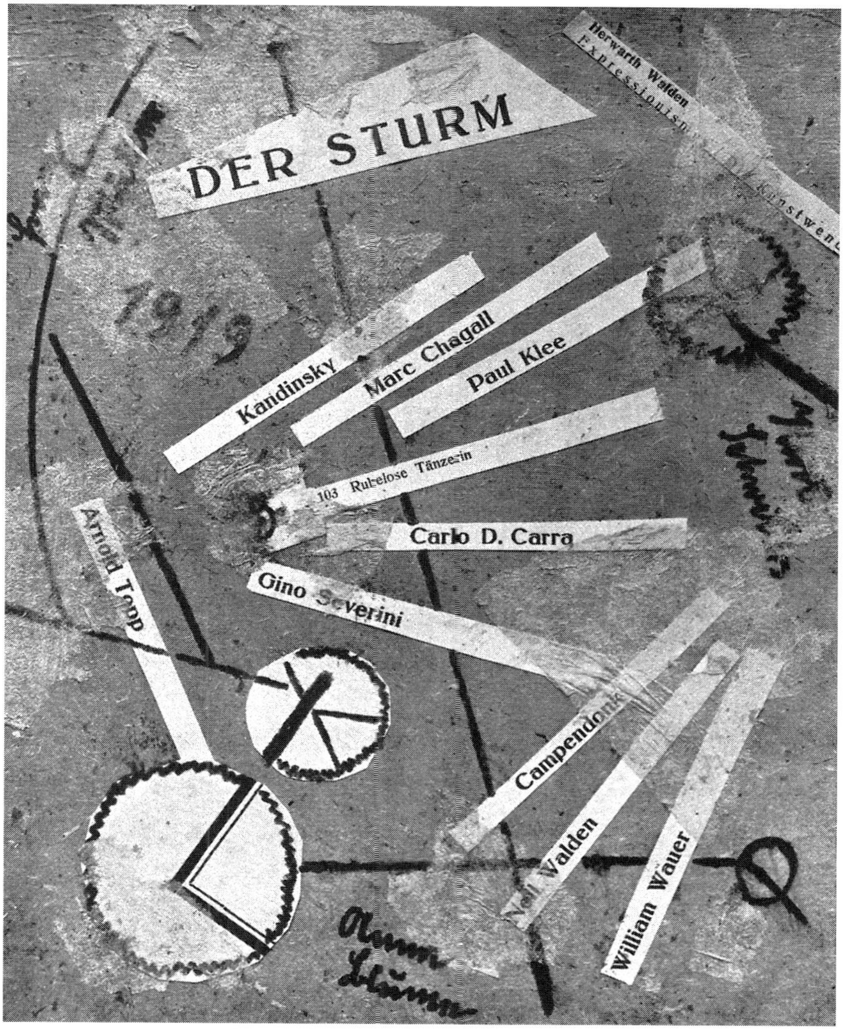

Kurt Schwitters, *Untitled (Der Sturm)*, 1919. © 2015 Artists Rights Society (ARS), New York/VG Bild-Kunst, Bonn.

and institutions of dissemination and reception would have to be transformed as well.

If the Berlin Dadaists seem to have believed that the artistic procedure of photomontage carried transformative potential qua *procedure*, montage would become integrated in the work of Rodchenko and Lissitzky as only one among several techniques—typography, advertising, propaganda—that attempted to redefine the representational systems of the new society.

From Modernism to Mass Culture

In 1926 Lissitzky developed a theory of contemporary art that not only associated aesthetic practice with the needs of its audience and patron class as prime determinants of the forms that production would assume, but it also linked standards of modernist practice to distribution developments occurring in other media of communication: books, graphic design, film. Although his beliefs were buoyed by the same naïve optimism toward the enlightening power of technology and the media that would ten years later limit the ultimate relevance of Walter Benjamin's essay, Lissitzky's is not a mere "machine aesthetic." Rather, it is an attempt to establish an operative aesthetic framework that could focus attention simultaneously on the existing needs of mass audiences and on the available techniques and standards of the means of artistic production. Like Benjamin in his later essay, Lissitzky considers aesthetic forms and their procedures of production in the light of history rather than in terms of universal categories. Yet unlike Benjamin, he perceives the ensuing transformations as a product of social needs and political functions rather than as a result of technological changes. The text is important for the clarification of Lissitzky's motivation in the following years, when he decided to abandon almost all traditional forms of graphic and photographic, let alone painterly or sculptural production, and to concentrate exclusively on those practices that would establish the new "monumentality"—the conditions of simultaneous collective public reception:

> It is shortsighted to suppose that machines, i.e., the displacement of manual by mechanical processes, are basic to the development of the form and the figure of an artifact. In the first place it is the consumers' demand that determines the development, i.e., the demand of the social strata that provide the "commissions." Today this is not a narrow circle anymore, a thin cream, but everybody, the masses. ... What conclusions does this imply in our field? The most important thing here is that the mode of production of words and pictures is included in the same process: photography. ... [In America] they began to modify the relation of word and illustration in exposition in the direct opposite of the European style. The highly developed technique of facsimile electrotype (half-tone blocks) was especially important for this development; thus photomontage was born. ... With our work the Revolution has achieved a colossal labor of propaganda and enlightenment. We ripped up the traditional book into single pages, magnified these a hundred times, ... and stuck them up as posters in the streets. ... The innovation of easel painting made great works of art possible, but it has now lost its power. The cinema and the illustrated weekly have succeeded it. ... The book is the most monumental art form today; no longer is it fondled by the delicate hands of a bibliophile, but seized by a hundred thousand hands. ... We shall be satisfied if we can conceptualize the epic and the lyric developments of our times in our form of the book.[21]

The degree to which Lissitzky focused at that time on the question of audience as a determinant of form, and on the perspective of creating conditions for simultaneous collective reception, becomes even more obvious in the essay's initially surprising equation between the reading space of the printed page and the space of dramatic experience in the theater. According to Lissitzky, the page (and its traditional layout and typography) shares conventions of confinement with the theater—the peep-show as he calls it—where the spectator is separated from the performers, and the spectator's gaze is contained—as in traditional easel painting—in the central perspective of the proscenium stage. The revolutionary transformation of book design in Lissitzky's work ran parallel to the revolution of the theatrical space. This is evident, for example, in Lissitzky's stage design in 1929 for Meyerhold's theater and its central, open-stage construction. Already in his 1922 book *Of Two Squares* (reading lessons for children, as he called it), Lissitzky had stated that " the action unrolls like a film" and that the method of typographical montage would generate the tactility of experiencing the readers' movements through time and space.[22]

The total integration of the dramatic experience of theatrical/cinematographic space and the perceptual experience of static signs of graphic/photographic montage and typography is successfully achieved in 1928 in Lissitzky's first major exhibition design, a project for the International Press Exhibition, Pressa, in Cologne. Not surprisingly, we find on the first page of the catalog that Lissitzky created to accompany the design of the USSR Pavilion the announcement, "Here you see in a typographic kino-show the passage of the contents of the Soviet Pavilion."[23]

Rather than thinking of Lissitzky's involvement with the design of exhibitions merely as a task-oriented activity that remains marginal to the central concerns of his work (as have most authors considering these projects), it seems more adequate to see them, along with Lissitzky's subsequent involvement with the propaganda journal *USSR in*

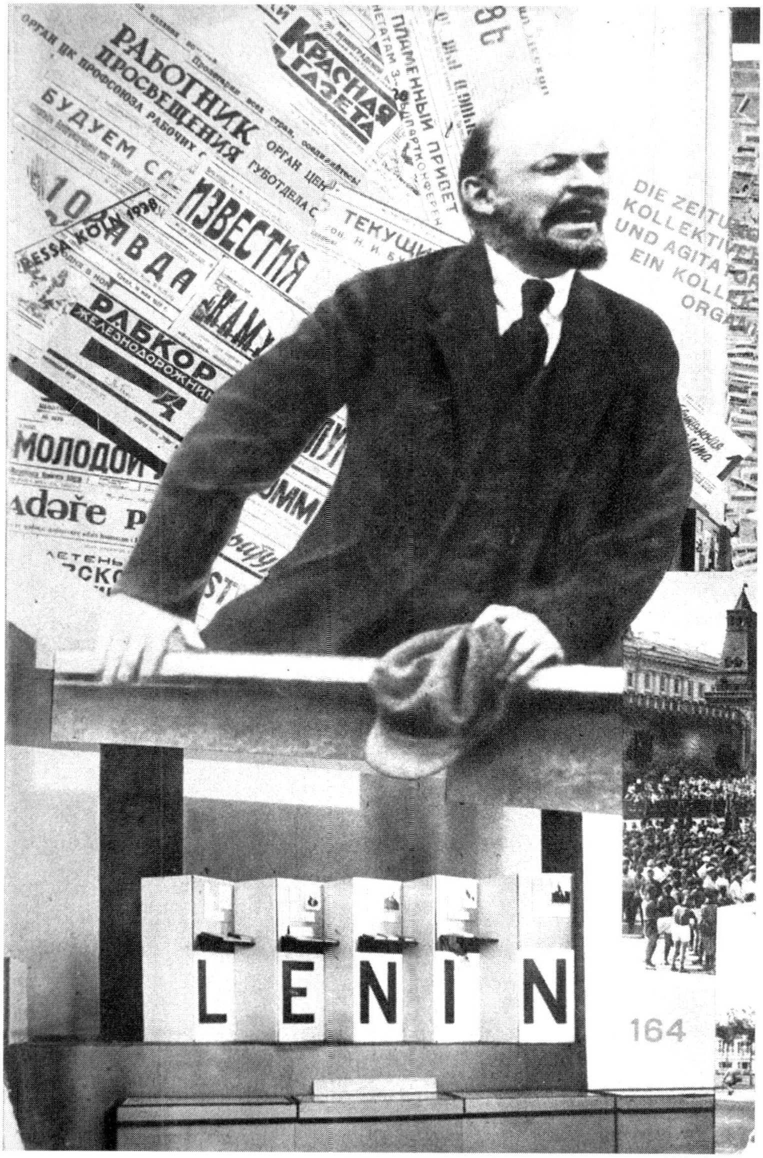

El Lissitzky, photomontage for catalogue accompanying the Soviet Pavilion at the *International Pressa Exhibition*, Cologne, 1928. © 2015 Artists Rights Society (ARS), New York/VG Bild-Kunst, Bonn.

Construction, as a logical next step in the development of his own work, as well as a necessary next phase in the radical transformation of modernist aesthetics and art production as it had been occurring within the Soviet avant-garde since 1921, in particular since the rise of productivism. We have no reason to doubt the sincerity of one of the last texts Lissitzky wrote, shortly before his death in 1941, a table of autobiographical dates and activities, where the entry under the year 1926 reads, "In 1926 my most important work as an artist began: the design of exhibitions."[24]

In 1927 Lissitzky had been commissioned to install his first "commercial" exhibition design in the Soviet Union, the exhibition of the Polygraphic Union, a relatively modest project in Moscow's Gorky Park. Unlike the 1926 design for the *International Contemporary Art Exhibition* in Dresden, or the cabinet design for the Hannover Landesmuseum in 1927, this project was conceived and produced as a set for a trade show rather than an exhibition of contemporary art; furthermore, it was the result of the collaboration of a group of artists.

Klucis, the "inventor" of photomontage, Lissitzky's colleague and disciple from Vitebsk, where both had struggled to come to terms with the legacy of Malevich's suprematism in 1919–20, was one of the collaborators in the project, as was Solomon Telingater, who would later emerge as one of the major figures in the revolution of Soviet typographic design. It is in the catalog of this exhibition—a book design project that was jointly produced by Lissitzky and Telingater—that we find Lissitzky's essay "The Artist in Production."

This text in many ways does not only constitute Lissitzky's own productivist manifesto (Rodchenko and Stepanova's text, officially entitled "Productivist Manifesto," had appeared already in 1921, and Ossip Brik's manifesto "Into Production" had appeared in *Lef* in 1923), but it is also the first text in which Lissitzky develops most succinctly his ideas about the uses of photography in general and the functions of photomontage in particular:

> As a result of the social needs of our epoch, and the fact that artists acquainted themselves with new techniques, *photomontage* emerged in the years following the Revolution and flourished thereafter. Even though this technique had been used in America much earlier for advertising, and the Dadaists in Europe had used it to shake up official bourgeois art, it only served political goals in Germany. But only here, with us, photomontage acquired a clearly socially determined and aesthetic form. Like all other great art, it created its own laws of formation. The power of its expression made the workers and the Komsomol circles enthusiastic for the visual arts and it had great influence on the billboards and newspapers. Photomontage at its present stage of development uses finished, entire photographs as elements from which it constructs a totality.[25]

Lissitzky's 1927 text not only traces an astonishingly clear history of the technique of photomontage and its origins in advertising technology, but it also clearly indicates his awareness that the functions of the technique within the historical context of the Soviet avant-garde were to be entirely different from that of the Berlin Dadaists. More important is the insight that the technique is only valid if it is bound into the particular needs of a social group. That is to say, Lissitzky already at this moment disavows photomontage as a new artistic strategy that supposedly has value *qua* artistic operation and innovational mode of representation/production. The inherent potential of photomontage—the production of iconic, documentary information, already addressed in the anonymous text from *Lef* of 1924—is now fully developed in Lissitzky's definition of the functions of the technique in 1927. Accordingly, the morphology of the products of that technique would change substantially by comparison with its original manifestations in 1919–23.

Those features that the technique of photomontage had inherited from its origins in collage, and the cubist critique of representation, now were gradually abandoned. Also abandoned was the overlap of photomontage with the techniques of modern advertising. In the Dada context, these techniques seemed to have generated the extreme juxtapositions and fragmentations necessary to invert the origins and functions of advertising. After all it had been the first task of the constructed artificiality of montage to subvert, if not to destroy, the totalizing and mythical nature of the commodity.

The shifts toward the documentary invoked by Lissitzky would become increasingly apparent in the gradual return to the primarily *iconic* functions of the photograph, increasingly deleting the *indexical* potential of the photograph altogether (as it had still been visible in Lissitzky's photograms of the 1920s), and, more importantly, the actual indexical structure of the agglomerated fragments of the photomontage itself, where the network of cuts and fissures, of the jutting edges and unmediated transitions from fragment to fragment, had been as important, if not more so, than the actual iconic representations contained within these fragments themselves.

Thus *faktura*, as an essential feature of the modernist paradigm that underlay the production of the Soviet avant-garde until 1923, was also replaced in the sphere of the photographic by a new concern for the *factographic* capacity of the photograph, supposedly rendering aspects of reality visible without interference or mediation. It was at this moment—in 1924—that Rodchenko decided to abandon photomontage altogether and to engage in single-frame still photography, which transforms montage through the explicit choice of camera angle, the framing of vision, the determinants of the filmic apparatus, and the camera's superiority over the conventions of human perception.

In Lissitzky's essay this change is clearly indicated in the phrase which argues that "photomontage in its present stage of development uses finished entire photographs as elements from which it constructs a totality." It appears now that homogeneity in the single print is favored over fragmentation, and that iconic representation of an absent referent is favored over the indexical materiality of the trace of a verifiable process, just as the tactility of the construction of incoherent surfaces and spatial references is exchanged for the monumentality of the camera-angle's awesome visions and the technological media optimism that it conveys.

Yet while it is evident that the premises of the modernist paradigm of photomontage were vacated at this moment, and that a programmatic commitment to new audiences entirely changed the nature of artistic production, it seems no more appropriate to neglect or condemn Lissitzky's or Rodchenko's work from this period (nor their subsequent involvement with Stalin's State Publishing House in the 1930s) as propaganda, than it would be appropriate to condemn certain Surrealist artists (those in particular who developed what Max Ernst was to call the technique of the "painted collage") as being responsible for providing advertising's new visual and textual strategies, to conquer and invade the spaces of the unconscious, operative to this very day.

Pressa: Exhibition Design between Photomontage and Propaganda

Partially as a response to his first successful exhibition design in Moscow in 1927, a committee chaired by Anatoly Lunacharsky, then still the radical minister of cultural affairs, decided to ask Lissitzky (together with Rabinowich, who later withdrew from participation) to design the Soviet Pavilion at the forthcoming International Exhibition of Newspaper and Book Publishing in Cologne, the first exhibition of its kind. Since the decision of the committee was made on December 23, 1927, and the exhibition was to begin in the first week of May 1928, Lissitzky and his collaborators had four months to plan and produce the design of the exhibition. Apparently just two days after the committee had appointed him, Lissitzky submitted a first general outline that foresaw the formation of a "collective of creators" with himself as the general coordinator of the design. Among the approximately thirty-eight members of the collective, only a few, among them the stage designer Naumova, had previously participated in exhibition design and the decoration of revolutionary pageants.[26] The largest group within the collective consisted of agitprop graphic designers, shortly thereafter to become some of the most important graphic designers of the Soviet avant-garde. The majority of the 227 exhibits were produced and assembled in the workshops for stage design in the Lenin Hills in Moscow. The other elements were designed in Moscow as well, but produced and assembled in Cologne under the supervision of Lissitzky and Sergei Senkin, who had traveled to the site of the exhibition to supervise and install the Soviet Pavilion.

The centerpiece of the exhibition was in fact a large-scale photomontage that Lissitzky had designed with Senkin's assistance. This *photofresco*, as Senkin called it, measured approximately seventy-two by eleven feet and depicted, in constant alternation of camera angles, of close-ups and long-shots, the history and importance of the publishing industry in the Soviet Union since the Revolution, and its role in the education of the illiterate masses of the newly industrialized state. Thus the photofresco, *The Task of the Press Is the Education of the Masses* (its official title), functioned as the centerpiece of an exhibition that was devoted to documenting the achievements of the Revolution in the educational field for a skeptical, if not hostile western European public.

The actual structure of the photofresco followed the strategies that Lissitzky had laid out in the essay that accompanied the catalog of his first exhibition design in 1927. Large-scale photographic prints were assembled in an irregular grid formation and the visual dynamic of the montage resulted from the juxtaposition of the various camera angles and positions, but no longer from a jagged linear network of seams and edges, and of heterogeneous photographic fragments that had defined the aesthetics of photomontage.

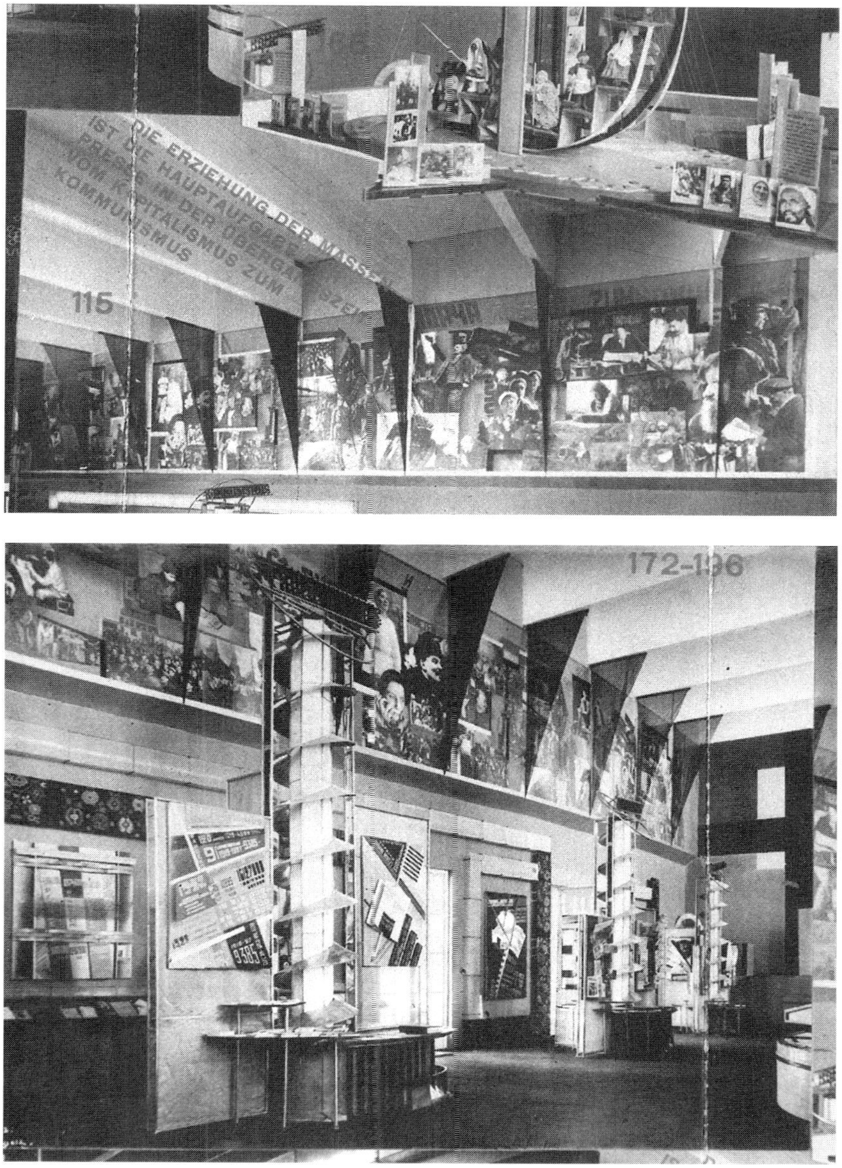

El Lissitzky (in collaboration with Sergei Senkin), photofresco at the *International Pressa Exhibition*, Cologne, 1928. © 2015 Artists Rights Society (ARS), New York/VG Bild-Kunst, Bonn.

While the scale and size of the photofresco—it was installed on the wall at a considerable height—aligned the work with a tradition of architectural decoration and mural painting, the sequencing of the images and their emphatic dependence on camera technology and movement related the work equally, if not more emphatically to experiences of cinematic viewing, such as that of the newsreel. In their mostly enthusiastic reviews, many visitors to the *Pressa* exhibition actually discussed the theatrical and cinematic aspects of the photofresco. One critic reminisces that one went through "a drama that unfolded in time and space. One went through expositions, climaxes, retardations, and finales."[27] Reviewing both the Dresden *Hygiene Exhibition* design by Lissitzky and the Cologne *Pressa* design, even a less well-disposed critic still had to admit the design's affiliation with the most advanced forms of cinematic production:

> The first impression is brilliant. Excellent the technique, the arrangement, the organization, the modern way it has been constructed. Propaganda, propaganda, that is the keynote of Soviet Russian exhibitions, whether they be in Cologne or in Dresden. And how well the Russians know how to achieve the visual effects their films have been showing us for years![28]

Even though Lissitzky did not meet Dziga Vertov until 1929 (inaugurating a friendship that lasted until Lissitzky's death in 1941), it is very likely that in 1927–28 he was drawing not only upon the collage and montage sources of cubism, Dadaism, and constructivism, but equally upon the cinematic montage techniques that Vertov had used in the first *Kino-Pravda* films, and used still more daringly and systematically in his work after 1923.

In his manifesto "We," published in *kinofot* in 1922, and illustrated by a compass and ruler drawing by Rodchenko from 1915, Vertov had called film "an art of movement, its central aim being the organization of the movements of objects in space."[28] Hubertus Gassner speculates that this manifesto had considerable influence on Rodchenko, as well as the constructivists in general, and led him away from drawing and painting into the photographic montage production that Rodchenko published two issues later in the same journal.[29]

It seems, however, that Vertov only voiced a concern that, as we saw above in several instances, was very much at the center of the constructivist debate itself, to make "construction" and "montage" the procedures that would transform the passive, contemplative modes of seeing. Sophie Küppers argues in fact that it was rather Vertov who had learned the montage technique from Lissitzky's earliest experiments with the photogram and the photomontage, and that it was primarily Lissitzky's techniques of transparency and the double exposure as variants of photographic montage that left a particularly strong impression on Vertov's own work in the mid-1920s. According to Küppers, it would be only in the later work produced by Lissitzky for the magazine *USSR in Construction* that we could recognize an actual influence of Vertov's *Kino-Pravda*.

In spite of the obvious parallels between the cinematographic montage and the photomontage, and leaving once again aside the question of historical priority and influence, it seems more important to clarify in this context the specific differences that existed between the mural-sized photomontages and exhibition designs of Lissitzky and the montage of Vertov's *Kino-Pravda*. Clearly the still photograph and the new photomontage, as Lissitzky defined it, offered features that the moving imagery of the film lacked: aspects of the same subject could be compared and contrasted and could be offered for extensive reading and viewing; complicated processes of construction and social transformation could be analyzed in detailed accounts that ran parallel with statistics and other written information; and the same subject could, as Rodchenko argued, be represented simultaneously "at different times and in different circumstances." This practice of a "realistic constructivism," as the critic Gus called Lissitzky's exhibition design, had in fact brought about a substantial change within collage and photomontage aesthetics. One could sum up to argue that what had been the strategy of *contingency* in collage, the strategy by which different textures and materials had been juxtaposed to emphasize the divergence of the fragments, had now become the stringency of a conscious construction of documentary factographic information.

In an excellent recent study of Russian constructivism, Christina Lodder has argued that it was the failure of the constructivists to actually implement their productivist program (due to shortage of materials, lack of access to industrial facilities, disinterest on the part of the engineers and administrators of the State manufacturing companies) that drove these artists into the field of typography, publication and poster design, agitational propaganda and exhibition design.[30] The emergence of a strong antimodernism, backed by the Party as a result of Lenin's New Economic Policy in 1921, required the return to traditional values in art and laid the foundations for the rise of socialist realism. Lodder argues further that it was as a result of these changes, and as an attempt at competition with these reactionary forces, that Lissitzky's and Rodchenko's work at that time employed iconic, photographic representation and abandoned the radical syntax of the montage aesthetic. The problem with this criticism, however—as with all previous rejections of the later work of Rodchenko and Lissitzky—is in particular the fact that precisely those criteria of judgment that were originally developed within the framework of modernism are now applied retroactively to a practice of representation that had deliberately and systematically disassociated itself from precisely that framework in order to lay the foundations of an alternate model of art production that would correspond to the needs of a newly industrialized collective society. As we have seen, these conditions required radically different production procedures and modes of presentation and distribution, and any serious historical critique or evaluation will have to develop its criteria from within the actual intentions and conditions that motivated and determined the origin of these practices.

Lissitzky's exhibition design does overcome the traditional limitations of the avant-garde practice of photomontage, and reconstitutes it within the necessary conditions of simultaneous collective reception that were given in the cinema and in architecture. Further, in his new practice of montage, Lissitzky incorporated the method of "systematic analytical sequence," as Tretyakov was to define it shortly afterward. Tretyakov wrote in 1931 that the photographer/artist should move from the single-image aesthetic to the systematic photographic sequence and the long-term observation:

> If a more or less random snapshot is like an infinitely fine scale that has been scratched from the surface of reality with the tip of the finger, then in comparison the photoseries or the photomontage lets us experience the extended massiveness of reality, its authentic meaning. We build systematically. We must also photograph systematically. Sequence and long-term photographic observation—that is the method.[31]

Modernism's Aftermath

In spite of the fact that even the most conservative international newspapers reported enthusiastically on Lissitzky's *Pressa* design, and that he received a medal from the Soviet government in recognition of the success of this project as well as having been named an honorary member of the Moscow town Soviet, he seems to have been personally dissatisfied with the results. This is evident in a letter that he wrote on December 26, 1928, to his Dutch friend, the de Stijl architect J. J. P. Oud:

> It was a big success for us but aesthetically there is something of a poisoned satisfaction. The extreme hurry and the shortage of time violated my intentions and the necessary completion of the form—so it ended up being basically a theater decoration.[32]

We will, however, find neither in Lissitzky's letters, nor in his diary entries any private or public disavowal or signs of regret about having abandoned the role of the modernist artist for that of the producer of political propaganda in the service of the new Communist state. Quite the opposite: the letters we know Lissitzky to have written during the years of his subsequent involvement with both the design of exhibitions for the government and his employment by Stalin's State Publishing House on the magazine *USSR in Construction* clearly indicate that he was as enthusiastically at work in fashioning the propaganda for Stalin's regime as were Rodchenko and Stepanova, who were at that time involved in similar tasks. Clearly Lissitzky shared the naive utopianism that also characterizes Walter Benjamin's later essay, an optimism that T. W. Adorno criticized immediately in his first response to the text:

> Both the dialectic of the highest and the lowest [modernism and mass-culture] bear the stigmata of capitalism, both contain elements of change. … Both are torn halves of an integral freedom, to which however they do not add up. It would be romantic to sacrifice one to the other, either as the bourgeois romanticism of the conservation of personality and all that stuff, or as the anarchistic romanticism of blind confidence in the spontaneous power of the proletariat in the historical process—a proletariat which is itself a product of bourgeois society.[33]

But it is also clear by now that both Lissitzky's and Benjamin's media optimism prevented them from recognizing that the attempt to create conditions of a simultaneous collective reception for the new audiences of the industrialized state would very soon issue into the preparation of an arsenal of totalitarian, Stalinist propaganda in the Soviet Union. What is worse, it would even deliver the aesthetics and technology of propaganda to the Italian Fascist and German Nazi regimes. And only a little later we see the immediate consequences of Lissitzky's new montage techniques and photofrescoes in their successful adaptation for the ideological needs of American politics and the campaigns for the acceleration of capitalist development through consumption. Thus, what in Lissitzky's hands had been a tool of instruction, political education, and the raising of consciousness of the newly literate proletarian masses of the Soviet Union, was rapidly transformed into an instrument for enforcing the silence of conformity and obedience in the Fascist countries of Western Europe.

The "consequent inrush of barbarism" of which Adorno speaks in the letter to Benjamin as one possible result of the undialectical abandonment of modernism was soon to become a historical reality. As early as 1932 we see the immediate impact of the *Pressa* project in its adaption for the propaganda needs of the Fascist government in Italy. Informed by the members of the Italian League of Rational Architecture, in particular Bardi and Paladini (who was an expert on the art of the Soviet avant-garde), the architect Giuseppe Terragni constructed an enormous mural-sized photomontage for the Exposition of the Fascist Revolution.[34] It would require a detailed formal and structural analysis to identify the transformations that took place within photomontage aesthetics once they were put to the service of Fascist politics. It may suffice here to bring only one detail to the attention of the reader, a detail in which that inversion of meaning under an apparent continuity of a formal principle becomes apparent, proving that it is by no means simply the case of an available formal strategy being refurbished with a new political and ideological content.

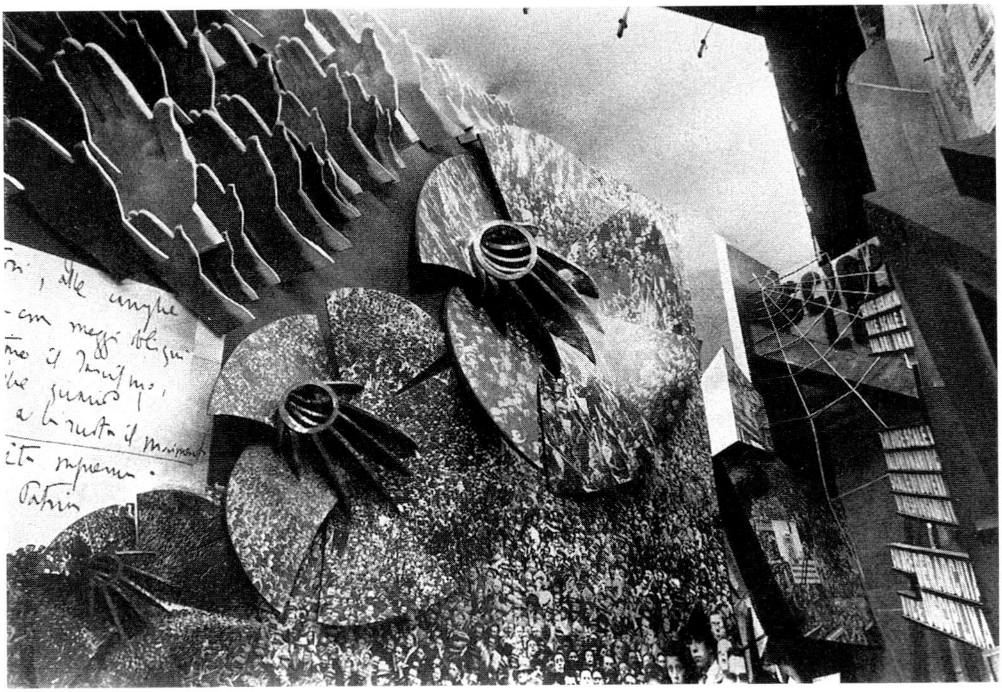

Giuseppe Terragni, photomontage mural for the Exposition of the Fascist Revolution, 1932.

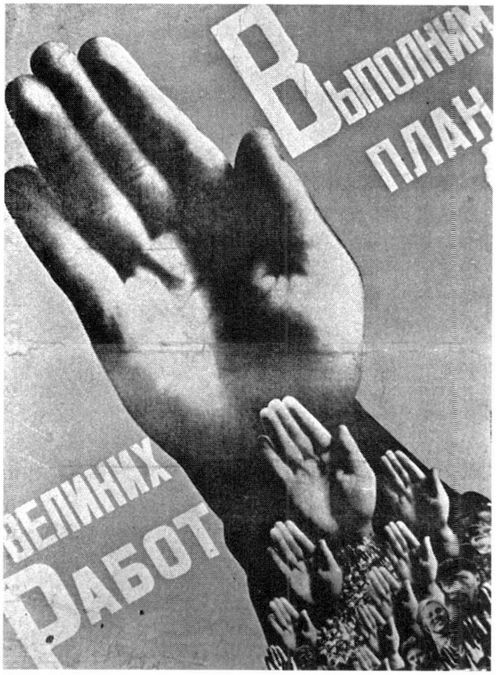

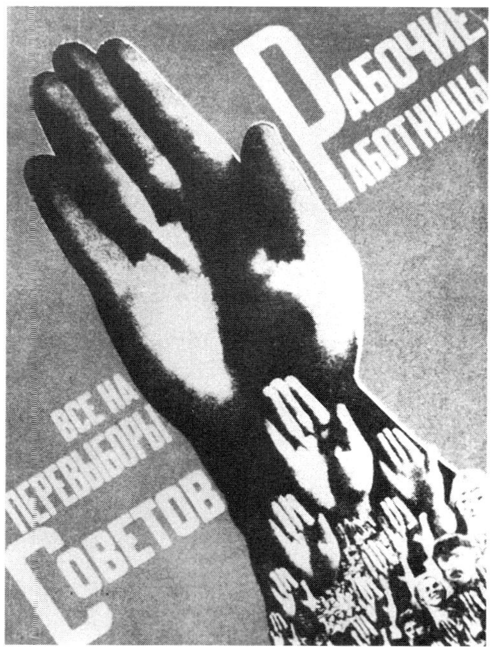

Gustav Klucis, photomontage poster (two versions), 1930.

The detail in question is the representation of the masses in Terragni's photomural, where a crowd of people is contained in the outlines of a relief shaped like the propeller of a turbine or a ship. Clearly it was one of the most difficult tasks, in constructing representations for new mass audiences, not only to establish conditions of simultaneous collective viewing, but further, to actually construct representations of the masses themselves, to *represent* the collectivity. One of the most prominent examples of this necessity is an early photomontage poster by Klucis, which in fact seems to have been so successful that Klucis used the same visual configuration for two different purposes.[35] The subject of the poster in both versions is the representation of political participation in the decision-making processes of the new Soviet state. In Klucis's poster, this participation is encouraged by an outstretched hand within which hundreds of faces are contained: thus the individuation resulting from the participation in political decisions and subordination under the political needs of the collectivity seem to be successfully integrated into one image. In Terragni's photomural the same structure has been deployed; this time, however, the overall form of the outstretched hand of the voting individual is replaced by the outlines of a mythical and monumental image of a machine (the propeller, the turbine) which—inadvertently accurate for the conditions of Fascism—contains and controls the masses of the people.

And it is clear that the Fascist image means what it unknowingly conveys: that the subordination of the masses under the state apparatus in the service of the continuing dominance of the industrial ruling class and its political and economic interests, has to be masked behind the image of technological progress and mastery. Abstracted as it is, however, from the interests of those who are being mastered, it appears as an image of anonymity and subjugation rather than one of individual participation in the construction of a new collective.

Significantly, even the elementary traces of the principles of photomontage are abandoned once the technique of the photomural is

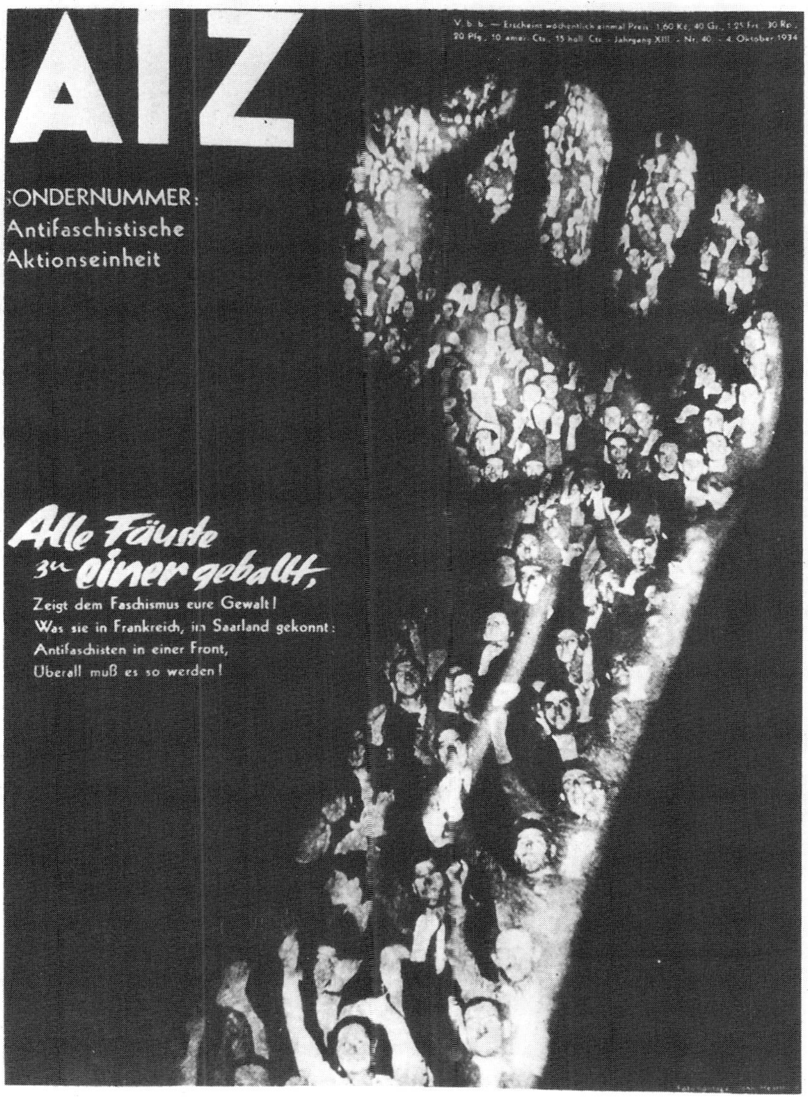

AIZ 40/1934

John Heartfield, *All Fists Have Been Clenched as One*, 1934. Photomontage cover for special issue against fascism of *Arbeiter Illustrierte Zeitung*, vol. 13, no. 40.

employed for the propaganda purposes of the German Fascists. In the same manner that they had discovered Eisenstein's films as a model to be copied for their purposes (Leni Riefenstahl studied his work thoroughly for the preparation of her own propaganda movies), they had also recognized that the achievements of the Russian artists in the field of exhibition design could be employed to serve Fascist needs to manipulate the urban and rural masses of Germany during the crisis of the post-Weimar period. When the German Werkbund, which had just been turned into a Fascist organization, put together a popular photography show in 1933, called *The Camera*, the organizers explicitly compared their exhibition design with that of the Russians (without, of course, mentioning Lissitzky's name):

> If you compare this exhibition with the propaganda rooms of the Russians that received so much attention during the last years, you will instantly become aware of the direct, unproblematic, and truly grandiose nature of the representation of reality in this room. These pictures address the spectator in a much more direct manner than the confusion of typography, photomontage, and drawings. ... This hall of honor is so calm and grand that one is almost embarrassed to talk any longer about propaganda in this context.[36]

To erase even the last remnants of modernist practice in photomontage, the seams and the margins where the constructed nature of reality could become apparent—and therefore its potential for change would become obvious—would now become the standard in totalitarian propaganda. Construction was replaced by the awe-inspiring monumentality of the gigantic, single-image panorama. What had once been the visual and formal incorporation of dialectic principles in the structuring of montage—in its simultaneity of opposing views, its rapidly changing angles, its unmediated transitions from part to whole and back

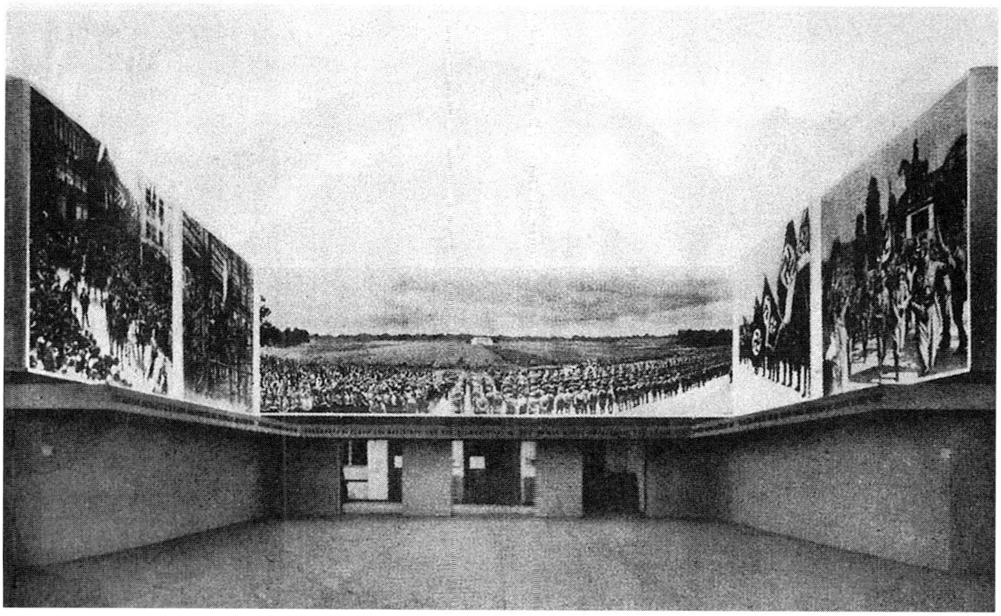

Photomural at the German Werkbund exhibition *Die Kamera*, Berlin, 1933.

to parts—had plausibly embodied the relationship between individual and collectivity as one that is constantly to be redefined. Now that dialectic construction of social relations was displaced by the unified spatial perspective (often the bird's-eye-view) that travels over uninterrupted expanses (land, fields, water, masses). Thus the perspective of governance and control, of the surveillance of the rulers' omnipresent eye, is naturalized, and nature serves as the metaphor of a pacified social collective without history or conflict.

It remains to be determined at what point, historically as well as structurally, this reversal takes place within the practices of photomontage during the 1930s. Unification of the image and its concomitant monumentalization were—as we saw—to some extent even already operative in Lissitzky's work for the *Pressa* exhibition. These tendencies were of considerable importance for the success of his enterprise. And according to Stepanova's own text, Rodchenko had abandoned photomontage principles as early as 1924, replacing them by single-frame images and/or series of single-frame images with highly informative documentary qualities. At what point these factographic dimensions turned into the sheer adulation of totalitarian power, however, is a question that requires future investigation. That this point occurs within Rodchenko's work, if not also in Lissitzky's, for the journal *USSR in Construction*, is a problem that modernist historians have tried to avoid by styling these artists as purist heroes and martyrs who had to sacrifice their commitment to the spiritual realm of abstract art by their enforced involvement with the state.

A revision of this comforting distortion of history is long overdue. It is a distortion that deprives these artists—if nothing else—of their actual political identity (their commitment to the cause of Stalinist politics was enthusiastic and sincere and came unforced, as is evident from the fact that an artist such as Tatlin, who did not work for the state agencies, continued to live his private, if economically miserable existence without harassment). It is a distortion that also deprives us of the understanding of one of the most profound conflicts inherent in modernism itself: that of the historical dialectic between individual autonomy and the representation of collectivity through visual constructs. Clearly the history of photomontage is one of the terrains in which this dialectic was raised to the highest degree of its contradictory forces. In 1928 Stepanova could still trace this terrain's development through an apparently neutral political terminology in characterizing the climax of the productivist factographic position:

> Within its short life, photomontage has passed through many phases of development. Its first stage was characterized by the integration of large numbers of photographs into a single composition, which helped bring into relief individual photo images. Contrasts in photographs of various sizes and, to a lesser extent, the graphic surface itself, formed the connective medium. One might say that this kind of montage had the character of a planar montage superimposed on white paper ground. The subsequent development of photomontage has confirmed the possibility of using photographs as such … the individual snapshots are not fragmented and have all the characteristics of a real document. The artist himself must take up photography. The value of the photograph itself came to assume primary importance; the photograph is no longer raw material for montage or for some kind of illustrated composition but has an independent and complete totality.[37]

Yet it should not really surprise us that we encounter the first signs of a new authoritarian monumental aesthetic resulting from the very rejection of the photomontage legacy in favor of a new unified imagery. Already two years later, from within the Soviet Russian reflection upon the purposes and functions of the technique of photomontage itself, we witness the rise of that concern for the new monumentality and heroic pathos that would become the prime feature of the German fascist attack on the legacy of photomontage quoted above. In 1930, in his text "The Social Meaning of Photomontage," the critic O. L. Kusakov writes,

> The solution to the problem of the proletarian, dynamic photomontage is inherently connected to the simultaneous solution of the question for a monumental style, since the monumentality of the tasks of the construction of socialism requires a heroic pathos for the organization of the consciousness of the spectators. Only in a successful synthesis of dynamics and monumentality—in conjunction with the constitution of a dialectical relationship between the levels of life—can photography fulfill the functions of an art that organizes and leads life.[38]

Thus it seems that Babichev's original, utopian quest and prognosis for the future functions of a postmodernist factographic art to become "an informed analysis of the concrete tasks which social life poses," one that will "organize the consciousness and psyche of the masses by organizing objects and ideas," had become true within ten years' time, although in a manner that was perhaps quite different from what he had actually hoped for. Or we could say that the element of social engineering, latent and inherent in the very notion of social progress as a result of technological development which art was supposed to enact and mediate, had finally caught up with modernism's own originary orientation toward science and technology as its underlying paradigms for a cognitively and perceptually emancipatory practice.

This historical dialectic seems to have come full circle in Rodchenko's career. In 1931 he worked as artist-in-residence on the site of the construction of the White Sea Canal in order to document the

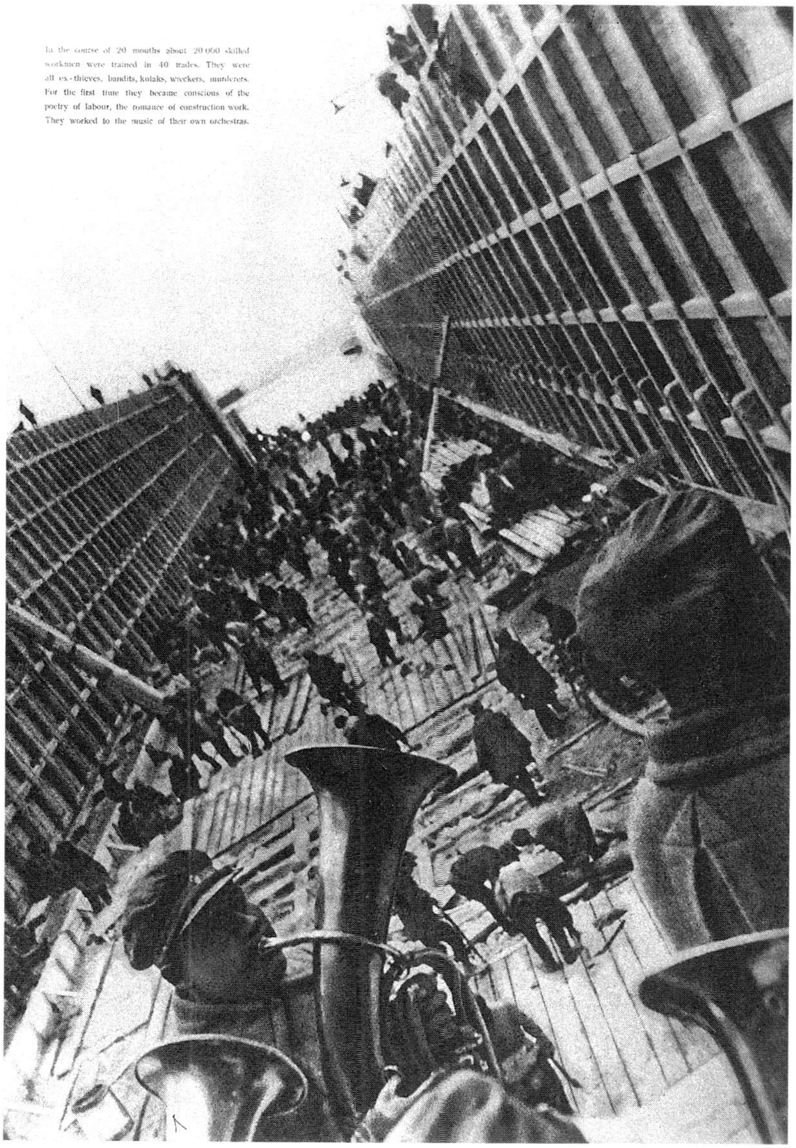

In the course of 20 months about 20 000 skilled workmen were trained in 40 trades. They were all ex-thieves, bandits, kulaks, wreckers, murderers. For the first time they became conscious of the poetry of labour, the romance of construction work. They worked to the music of their own orchestras.

Alexander Rodchenko, page from the magazine *USSR in Construction*, no. 12, December 1933, special issue on the construction of the Stalin Canal. © Estate of Alexander Rodchenko/RAO, Moscow/VAGA, New York.

heroic technological achievements of the Stalin government and to produce a volume of photographic records. Apparently in the first year alone of his stay more than 100,000 workers lost their lives due to inhuman conditions in the forced labor camps. While it is unimaginable that Rodchenko would not have been aware of these conditions at the construction site that he photographed for almost two years, his subsequent publications on the subject only project a grandiose vision of a doubly dominated nature. The one of the rivers and forests harnessed by technology and the one of the criminal and hedonistic impulses of the prerevolutionary and counter-revolutionary subjects mastered through the process of socialist re-education in the forced labor camps of the White Sea Canal.[39] While it is undoubtedly clear that at this time Rodchenko did not have any other choice than to either comply with the interest of the State Publishing House if he wanted to maintain his role as an artist who participated actively in the construction of the new Soviet society (and we have no reason to doubt this to be his primary motive), or to perish, we have to recognize at least that by 1931 the goals of factography had been clearly abandoned.

However, any contempt meted out from a Western perspective at the fate of modernist photomontage and factographic practice in the Soviet Union during the 1930s, or at its eventual transformation into totalitarian propaganda in Fascist Italy and Germany, seems historically inappropriate. For at the very same moment the technique was adapted to the specifically American needs of ideological deployment. Once again, as in Germany, the tradition of photomontage itself had to be attacked first of all in order to clear the ground for the new needs of the monumental propaganda machines. Here is Edward Steichen's American variation on the theme of an antimodernist backlash in favor of his version of a "productivist" integration of art and commerce in 1931:

> The modern European photographer has not liberated himself as definitely [as the American commercial photographer]. He still imitated his friend, the painter, with the so-called photomontage. He has merely chosen the *modern* painter as his prototype. We have gone well past the painful period of combining and tricking the banal commercial photograph. It is logical therefore that we find many modern photographers lined up with architects and designers instead of with painters or photographic art salons.[40]

Ten years later Steichen staged his first project at the Museum of Modern Art, the exhibition *Road to Victory*. Once again its propagandistic success depended almost entirely, as Christopher Phillips has shown, on a debased and falsified version of Lissitzky's exhibition designs.[41] In this case it was Herbert Bayer who provided American industry and ideology with what he thought Lissitzky's ideas and practice had attempted to achieve. Bayer was well suited to this task, having already prepared an elaborate photomontage brochure for the National Socialists' *Deutschland Ausstellung* of 1936, staged to coincide with the Berlin Olympics. When asked by Christopher Phillips about his contribution to this project for the Nazis, Bayer's only comment was, "This is an interesting booklet insofar as it was done exclusively with photography and photomontage, and was printed in a duotone technique."[42] Thus, at the cross-section of politically emancipatory productivist aesthetics and the transformation of modernist montage aesthetics into an instrument of mass education and enlightenment, we find not only its imminent transformation into totalitarian propaganda, but also its successful adaptation for the needs of the ideological apparatus of the culture industry of Western capitalism.

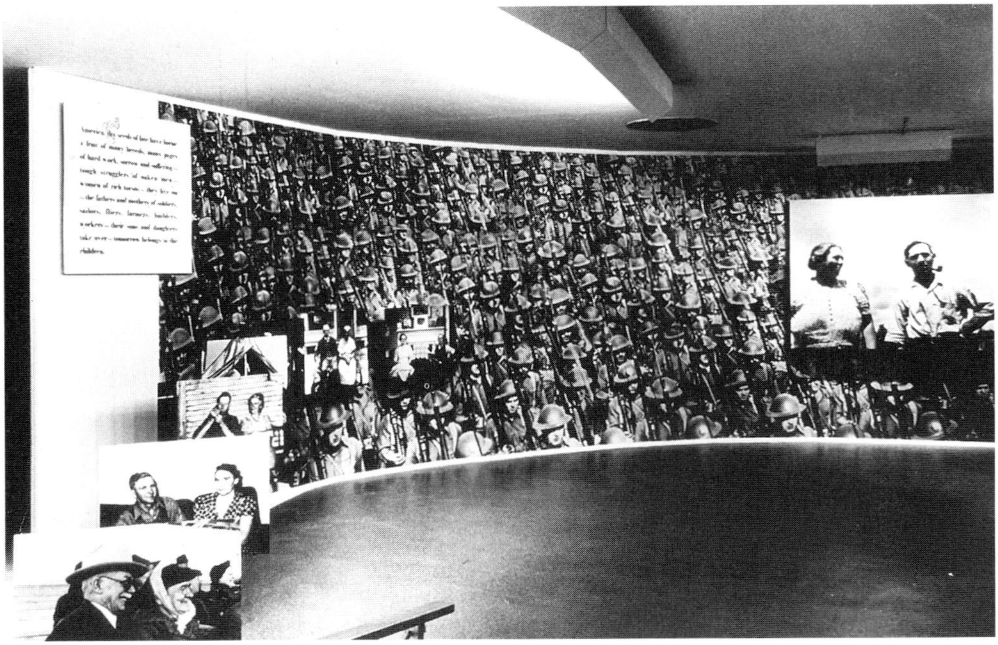

Herbert Bayer, photomural for the exhibition *Road to Victory*, curated by Edward Steichen, at the Museum of Modern Art, New York, 1942. Photograph by Samuel H. Gottscho. Courtesy The Museum of Modern Art Archives, New York. © 2015 Artists Rights Society (ARS), New York/VG Bild-Kunst, Bonn.

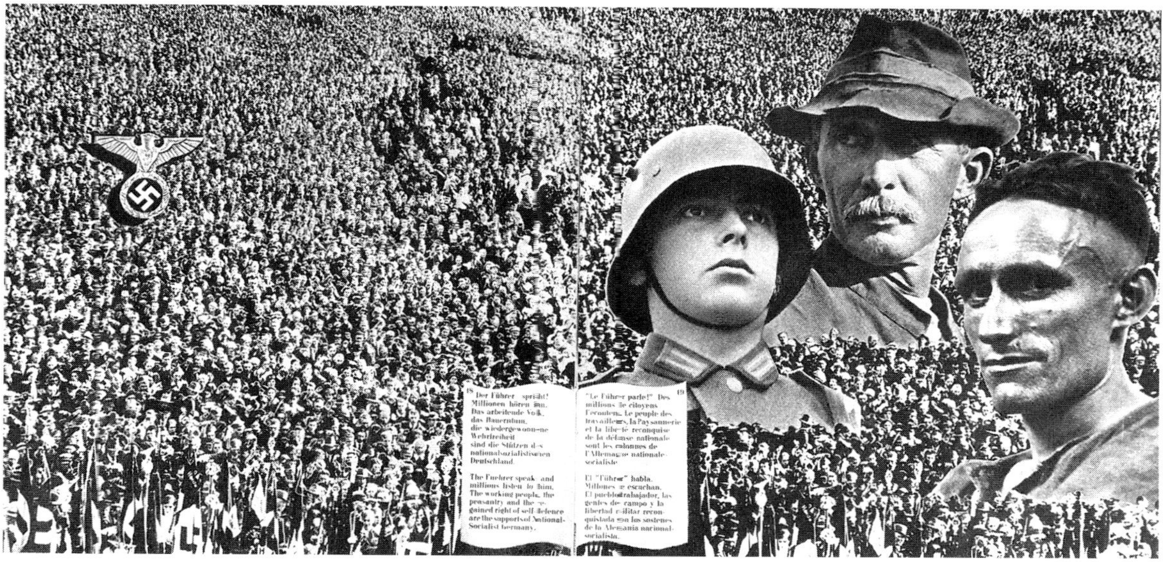

Herbert Bayer, photomontage for brochure accompanying the exhibition *Deutschland Ausstellung*, Berlin, 1936. © 2015 Artists Rights Society (ARS), New York/VG Bild-Kunst, Bonn.

Notes

First published in *October* 30 (autumn 1984): 82–119. All translations by Benjamin H. D. Buchloh unless otherwise noted. Minor corrections have been made for consistency.

1. Alfred Barr, "Russian Diary 1927–1928," *October* 7 (winter 1978): 21.

2. Ibid., 19.

3. Ibid., 14.

4. Alfred Barr, "The Lef and Soviet Art," *Transition* 14 (fall 1928): 267–270.

5. Boris Arvatov, *Kunst und Produktion* (Munich: Hanser Verlag, 1978), p. 43.

6. Yve-Alain Bois, in his essay "Malévich, le carré, le degré zéro" (*Macula*, no. 1 [1976]: 28–49), gives an excellent survey of the original discussion of the question of *faktura* among the various factions of the Russian avant-garde. More recently Margit Rowell has added references such as Markov's text, quoted here, that had not been mentioned by Bois. In any case, as Bois has argued, it is pointless to attempt a chronology since the many references to the phenomenon appear simultaneously and often independently of one another.

As early as 1912 the question of *faktura* is discussed by Mikhail Larionov in his "Rayonnist Manifesto," where he calls it "the essence of painting." Larionov furthermore argues that the "combination of colors, their density, their interaction, their depth, and their *faktura* would interest the truly concerned to the highest degree." A year later, in his manifesto "Luchism," Larionov states that "every painting consists of a colored surface, its *faktura* (that is, the condition of that colored surface, its timbre) and the sensation that you receive from these two aspects." Also in 1912, we find David Burliuk differentiating between "a unified pictorial surface A and a differentiated pictorial surface B. The structure of a pictorial surface can be 1. *Granular*, 2. *Fibrous*, and 3. *Lamellar*. I have carefully scrutinized Monet's *Rouen Cathedral* and I thought 'fibrous vertical structure.' … One can say that Cézanne is typically *lammellar*." Burliuk's text is in fact entitled "Faktura." Bois also quotes numerous references to the phenomenon of *faktura* in the writings of Malevich, for example, where he calls Cézanne the inventor of a "new faktura of the pictorial surface," or when he juxtaposes the *linear* with the *textural* in painting.

The concern for *faktura* seems to have been still central in 1919, as is evident from Popova's statement that "the content of pictorial surfaces is *faktura*."

Even writers who were not predominantly concerned with visual and plastic phenomena were engaged in a discussion of *faktura*. This is the case for example of Roman Jakobson in his essay "Futurism," where he identifies *faktura* as one of the many strategies of the new poets and painters who were concerned with "the unveiling of the procedure: therefore the increased concern for *faktura*; it no longer needs any justification, it becomes autonomous, it requires new methods of formation and new materials."

Quite unlike the traditional idea of *factura* or *facture* in painting, where the masterful "facture" of a painter's skilled hands spiritualizes the mere materiality of the pictorial production, and where the "hand" becomes at the same time the substitute or the totalization of the identifying signature (as the guarantee of authenticity, it justifies the painting's exchange value and maintains its commodity existence), the new concern for *faktura* in the Soviet avant-garde emphasizes precisely the mechanical quality, the materiality, and the anonymity of the painterly procedure from a perspective of empirical-critical positivism.

It demystifies and invalidates not only the claims for the authenticity of the spiritual and the transcendental in the painterly execution but, as well, the authenticity of the exchange value of the work of art that is bestowed on it by the former. For the discussion of the Markov statement and a generally important essay on the phenomenon of *faktura*, see also Margit Rowell, "Vladimir Tatlin: Form/Faktura," *October* 7 (winter 1978): 94ff.

7. Nikolai Tarabukin, *Le dernier tableau* (Paris: Editions Le Champ Libre, 1972), p. 102; cited in Rowell, "Vladimir Tatlin," p. 91.

8. Alexander Rodchenko, "Working with Mayakovsky," manuscript 1939, published in excerpts in *From Painting to Design*, exh. cat. (Cologne: Galerie Gmurzynska, 1981), pp. 190–191.

9. Alexander Rodchenko, exhibition pamphlet at the exhibition of the Leftist Federation in Moscow, 1917, cited in German Karginov, *Rodchenko* (London: Thames & Hudson, 1975), p. 64.

10. The terminological distinction is of course that of C. S. Peirce as Rosalind Krauss has first applied it to Duchamp's work in her essay "Notes on the Index," *October*, nos. 3 and 4 (summer and fall 1977).

11. A. V. Babichev, cited in Hubertus Gassner, "Analytical Sequences," in *Alexander Rodchenko*, ed. David Elliott (Oxford: Museum of Modern Art, 1979), p. 110.

12. See Krauss, "Notes on the Index."

13. Varvara Stepanova, quoted in Camilla Gray, *The Russian Experiment* (New York/London: Thames & Hudson, 1971), pp. 250–251.

14. Walter Benjamin, "The Work of Art in the Age of Mechanical Reproduction," in *Illuminations*, trans. Harry Zohn (New York: Schocken Books, 1969), p. 238. The last sentence of this quotation, set into parenthesis, is taken from the second version of Benjamin's essay (my translation).

15. El Lissitzky, "Demonstrationsräume," in *El Lissitzky*, ed. Sophie Lissitzky-Küppers (Dresden: VEB-Verlag der Kunst, 1967), p. 362.

16. The problem of the creation of conditions of simultaneous collective reception is dealt with in an essay by Wolfgang Kemp, "Quantität und Qualität: Formbestimmtheit und Format der Fotografie," in *Foto-Essays zur Geschichte und Theorie der Fotografie* (Munich: Schirmer/Mosel, 1978), pp. 10ff.

17. Arvatov, *Kunst*, p. 43.

18. The two essays that trace the history of photomontage in the context of the history of photography and the history of emerging advertising technology are Robert Sobieszek, "Composite Imagery and the Origins of Photomontage," parts I and II, *Artforum* (September/October 1978): 58–65, 40–45. Much more specifically addressing the origins of photomontage in advertising techniques is Sally Stein's important essay "The Composite Photographic Image and the Composition of Consumer Ideology," *Art Journal* (spring 1981): 39–45.

19. Gustav Klucis, preface to the exhibition catalog *Fotomontage*, Berlin, 1931, cited in Dawn Ades, *Photomontage* (London/New York: Pantheon, 1976), p. 15.

20. Anonymous, *Lef*, no. 4 (1924), repr. in *Art et Poésie Russes* (Paris: Musée national d'art moderne, 1979), pp. 221ff.

21. El Lissitzky, "Unser Buch," in *El Lissitzky*, pp. 357–360.

22. Yve-Alain Bois, "El Lissitzky: Reading Lessons," *October* 11 (winter 1979): 77–96.

23. Lissitzky, *Katalog des Soviet Pavillons auf der Internationalen Presse-Ausstellung* (Cologne: Dumont Verlag, 1928), p. 16.

24. Lissitzky, *Proun und Wolkenbügel* (Dresden: VEB Verlag der Kunst, 1977), p. 115.

25. Lissitzky, "Der Künstler in der Produktion," *Proun*, pp. 113ff.

26. For a detailed description of the history and the procedures of the work for the *Pressa* exhibition design, see Igor W. Rjasanzew, "El Lissitzky und die *Pressa* in Köln 1928," in *El Lissitzky*, exh. cat. (Halle: Staatliche Galerie Moritzburg, 1982), pp. 72–81.

27. Ibid., p. 78.

28. Ibid., p. 79.

29. Hubertus Gassner, *Rodchenko Fotografien* (Munich: Schirmer/Mosel, 1982), p. 121.

30. Christina Lodder, *Russian Constructivism* (New Haven: Yale University Press, 1983).

31. Sergei Tretyakov, "From the Photoseries to the Long-Term Photographic Observation," in *Proletarskoje Foto*, IV (1931), p. 20; repr. in German translation in *Zwischen Revolutionskunst und Sozialistischem Realismus*, ed. Hubertus Gassner and Eckhart Gillen (Cologne: Dumont Verlag, 1979), pp. 222ff.

32. Lissitzky, *Proun*, p. 135.

33. Theodor W. Adorno, Letter to Walter Benjamin, London, March 18, 1936, repr. in *Aesthetics and Politics* (London: New Left Books, 1977), pp. 120ff.

34. Herta Wescher wrote in 1968 in her history of collage that P. M. Bardi's work *Tavola degli orrori* had been modeled upon Lissitzky's montage work published in Western journals. For Paladini, Wescher argues, the relationship was even more direct since he had been born in Moscow of Italian parents and had developed a strong interest in the Soviet avant-garde. In response to the exhibition of the Soviet Pavilion at the Venice Biennale in 1924, he published a study *Art in the Soviet Union* (1925). See Wescher, *Collage* (Cologne: Dumont Verlag, 1968), pp. 76ff.

35. Gustav Klucis's first version of the photomontage poster in 1930 reads, "Let us fulfill the plan of the great projects," and it was meant as an encouragement to participate in the five-year plan of 1930. The second version of the poster is identical in its image of an outstretched hand, which in itself contains a large number of outstretched hands and an even larger number of photographic portraits, but this time the inscription exhorts the women of the Soviet Union to participate in the election and decision-making process of their local soviets. This poster seems to have also had an influence on John Heartfield, who transformed Klucis's outstretched hand into an outstretched arm with a fist, giving the salute of the Communist International under the slogan, "All fists have been clenched as one," on the cover of the *AIZ*, no. 40 (1934).

Here, as well as in Klucis's and Terragni's work, the image of the masses is contained in a synecdochic representation. In Klucis's and Heartfield's photomontages it is, however, the synecdoche of the human body as a sign of active participation, whereas in the Terragni montage it is the synecdoche of the machine that subjugates the mass of individuals. The inscription in Terragni's photomontage mural reads accordingly, "See how the inflammatory words of Mussolini attract the people of Italy with the violent power of turbines and convert them to Fascism."

36. Kemp, *Foto-Essays*, p. 14.

37. Stepanova, "Photomontage" (1928), English translation in *Alexandr Rodenchenko*, ed. Elliott, pp. 91ff.

38. O. L. Kusakov, "Die soziale Bedeutung der Fotomontage," *Sovetskoe Foto*, no. 5 (Moscow, 1930), p. 130. Quoted from the German translation in *Zwischen Revolutionskunst und Sozialistischem Realismus*, pp. 230ff.

39. Gassner makes a first attempt at assessing these facts with regard to Rodchenko's career at large in his doctoral thesis on the artist, "Rodchenko-Fotografien," especially pp. 104ff, and n. 475. The problem is, however, that he seems to base his information on the working conditions at the White Sea Canal and the number of victims on the "testimony" of Alexander Solzhenitsyn's writings, clearly a source that would have to

be quoted with extreme caution in a historical study. The main work on Lissitzky's, Rodchenko's, and Stepanova's collaboration with Stalin's State Publishing House remains to be done.

40. Edward Steichen, "Commercial Photography," *Annual of American Design* (New York, 1931): 159.

41. Christopher Phillips, "The Judgment Seat of Photography," *October* 22 (fall 1982): 27ff, provides detailed information on Steichen's history and practice of exhibition design at the Museum of Modern Art in New York. Allan Sekula's essay, "The Traffic in Photographs" (repr. in *Modernism and Modernity*, Halifax: Nova Scotia College of Art and Design, 1983), gives us the best discussion of the *Family of Man* exhibition by Steichen and also touches upon the issues of exhibition design in general.

42. I am grateful to Christopher Phillips for providing me with this information and for his permission to quote from his private correspondence with Herbert Bayer, as well as for his lending me the brochure itself. *Deutschland Ausstellung 1936* was also published as an insert in the design magazine *Gebrauchsgraphik* (April 1936).

7

READYMADE, *OBJET TROUVÉ*, *IDÉE REÇUE*

In his famous paper, "The Creative Act," delivered in 1957 at the meeting of the American Federation of the Arts in Houston, Marcel Duchamp concluded with the following remark:

> All in all the creative act is not performed by the artist alone; the spectator brings the work in contact with the external world by deciphering and interpreting its inner qualifications and thus adds his contribution to the creative act.[1]

Thus, more than ten years before Roland Barthes wrote his essay "The Death of the Author" (1968), which was to become one of the cornerstones of the postmodernist debate, and more than ten years before any notion of reception aesthetics was seriously discussed in the context of art history, Duchamp prepared the ground for the final (however delayed) realization that, in visual constructs as well as in writing, a text is made of multiple writings. As Barthes stated, it is

> drawn from many cultures and entering into mutual relations of dialogue, parody, contestation, but there is one place

> where this multiplicity is focused and that place is the reader, not as was hitherto said, the author. The reader is the space on which all the quotations that make up a writing are inscribed without any of them being lost; a text's unity lies not in its origin but in its destiny.[2]

This, of course, had been all along the dislodging message of Duchamp's work ever since the first readymade assemblage with a bicycle wheel in 1913, and the radicality of that message alone explains the extraordinary delay of its reception into the culture.[3] As Barthes traces the origins of this development back to the nineteenth century, particularly to the poetical project of Stéphane Mallarmé, we can now more easily recognize the degree to which the Symbolist poet and the Dada artist shared a concern for "substituting language itself for the person who until then had been supposed to be its owner" (Barthes).

In 1918, Duchamp inserted into his last painting, *Tu m'*, a hand with an outstretched index finger, painted by a professional sign painter, and placed this collaborative sign in the company of the shadows of his readymades.[4] Thus not only the paradigm of the readymade appeared as a *parole*, as an act of linguistic choice and designation, an act of naming, but Duchamp also emphasized the quintessentially collaborative nature of the readymade. The declarative mode of the readymade (and its indexical sign status, as Rosalind Krauss has extensively discussed it)[5] point to the same dimension: the work of art appears as a performative operation, in the sense that Barthes defines it:

> The fact is (or, it follows) that writing can no longer designate an operation of recording, notation, representation, "depiction" (as the Classics would say); rather it designates exactly what linguists, referring to Oxford philosophy, call a performative, a rare verbal form (exclusively given in the first person and in the present tense) in which the enunciation has

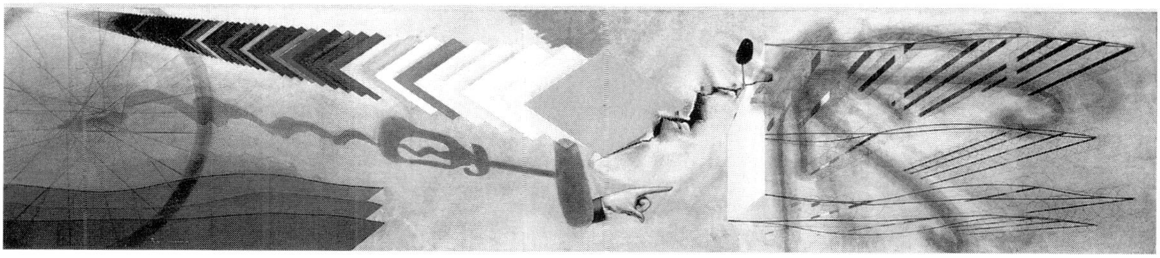

Marcel Duchamp, *Tu m'*, 1918. Oil on canvas, with bottle brush, three safety pins, and one bolt, 27½ × 119⁵⁄₁₆ in. (69.8 × 303 cm). Yale University Art Gallery, New Haven. Gift from the Estate of Katherine S. Dreier. © Succession Marcel Duchamp/ADAGP, Paris/Artists Rights Society (ARS), New York, 2015.

> no other content (contains no other proposition) than the act by which it is uttered—something like the I declare of kings or the I sing of very ancient poets.[6]

But let us return for a moment to our analogy at the beginning of this essay, that between de Saussure's and Barthes's "Death of the Author" on the one hand, and that of Duchamp's "Death of the Creative Artist" on the other. As tempting as this analogy might appear at first and even though it might seem possible to substantiate the argument in a more detailed comparison, the equation suffers from one elementary misconception: the fact that an analysis of the linguistic signifier in writing does not necessarily apply to the material (visual, corporeal, sculptural) signifying practices of Duchamp's work with readymade objects.

De Saussure himself had warned against a simplistic expansion of the field of linguistic analysis into other areas of human experience. He emphasized that the observations of his *Cours* were properly adaptable only to the system of linguistic signs, and—as he cautioned explicitly—any utopian aspiration for a general science of signs had to be considered for the time being with skepticism. And, more importantly for our argument, even in the relatively late essay by Barthes we find a cautioning remark against a simplistic transfer from the linguistic sphere of referentiality, denotation and narrative to that of pure "writing":

> As soon as a fact is narrated no longer with a view to acting directly on reality but intransitively, that is to say, finally outside of any function other than that of the very practice of the symbol itself, this disconnection occurs, the voice loses its origin, the author enters into his own death, writing begins.[7]

While Barthes clearly specifies the conditions under which the linguistic sign is severed from its referent, he implies by no means that this is always the case in each act of enunciation. Furthermore, in reading this passage it becomes even more obvious that it would be difficult to argue that Duchamp's readymade merely functions as an object that—like poetical writing—"no longer acts with a view directly on reality." Yet it would be equally difficult not to admit that the readymade is also the object *par excellence* that acts "on reality, but intransitively … outside of any function other than that of the very practice of the symbol itself." After all, it is precisely this innate structural ambiguity that determines the readymade's significant allegorical nature: it is not only a *nominalistic* act, neither a mere linguistic interference like an analytic proposition, nor is it only a mass-produced anonymous object, a commodity, a fetish that is positioned within the discursive and institutional framework of aesthetic propositions and institutional definitions.

In recent theoretical developments, the linguistic signifier has become the privileged model according to which all other modes of experience are structured (for example in Jacques Lacan's notion of the linguistic structure of the unconscious, Louis Althusser's theorization of ideology as a *langue*, and Jean Baudrillard's concept of the fetish as a mere code). Yet the putative supremacy of the linguistic signifier over all other functions (the economic, the corporeal, the material production and exchange in the labor process), and the exclusion of any notion of the referent, is obviously problematical in a discussion of the paradigm of the readymade and its subsequent transformations in artistic practice. If we reduce the readymade concept to its linguistic dimension, its nominalistic activity alone, we falsify a paradigm that started out as an attempt at dislodging all transcendental modes of thinking and seeing: we would deny the implicit political dimension of this radical decentralization of the subject and the paradigm would lose all its critical potential and original subversive force.

One argument that seems to have been made in the early 1960s was that Duchamp's "invention" of the readymade in 1913 (if we consider in fact the *Bicycle Wheel* a readymade, in spite of its assembled

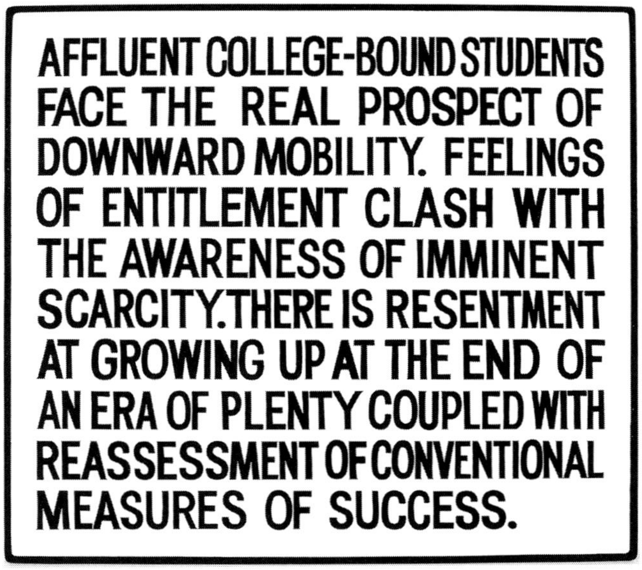

Jenny Holzer, *Living: Affluent College-Bound Students* ..., 1981. Hand-painted enamel on metal sign, 21 × 23 in. (53.3 × 58.4 cm). Text: *Living*, 1980–82. © 2015 Jenny Holzer, member Artists Rights Society (ARS), New York. Courtesy the artist and Cheim & Read, New York.

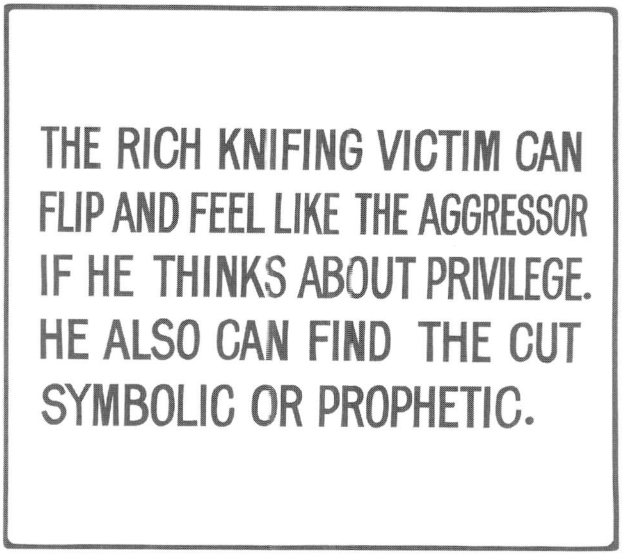

Jenny Holzer, *Living: The Rich Knifing Victim Can Flip* …, 1981. Hand-painted enamel on metal sign, 21 × 23 in. (53.3 × 58.4 cm). Text: *Living*, 1980–82. © 2015 Jenny Holzer, member Artists Rights Society (ARS), New York. Courtesy the artist and Cheim & Read, New York.

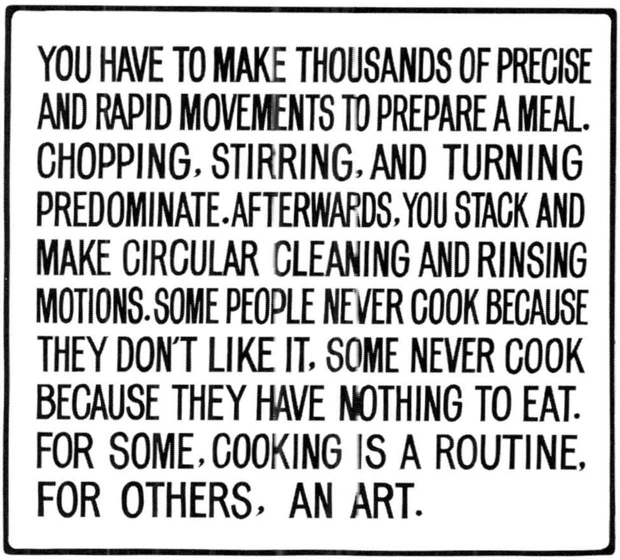

Jenny Holzer, *Living: You Have to Make Thousands of Precise* …, 1981. Hand-painted enamel on metal sign, 21 × 23 in. (53.3 × 58.4 cm). Text: *Living*, 1980–82. © 2015 Jenny Holzer, member Artists Rights Society (ARS), New York. Courtesy the artist and Cheim & Read, New York.

character) was the single most important and consequential aesthetic strategy of the twentieth century. What seemed to place this strategy above its closest historical competitors, collage and geometric abstraction (which were not only vying simultaneously for the position of the supreme artistic strategy of the twentieth century, but with whom the readymade was also formally and epistemologically connected) was the fact that the readymade seemed to embody in a single lapidary gesture the object relations of the twentieth century (those of production, consumption, and possession), and it seemed to be capable of doing this better than any other known form of representation. Like the discovery of the photograph (another strategy of pictorial representation with which the readymade shares essential features), the readymade seemed to make all other pictorial conventions and devices at least partially, temporarily, if not definitely obsolete. Henceforth, any argument for their continuation required complex or reactionary maneuvers of defense, conservative reasoning, and an orientation toward past values and anterior practices.

This is all the more visible now, at the very moment when the strategy of Duchamp's readymade not only seems to have lost its viability in contemporary art, but worse yet, when those strategies that the readymade seemed to have replaced (gestural, expressive-figurative painting, and craft oriented production procedures) have returned to the foreground as promises of individuality and subjectivity, or, more ambitiously, posture as resistance against mass-cultural desublimation.

The history of the readymade can therefore illustrate the degree to which discursive formations are subjected to a multiplicity of forces and interests, latent and manifest, external and internal, during the varying moments of social reception. Furthermore, this history demonstrates also that for extended periods of time, it is precisely the radical paradigmatic changes that remain most often excluded from the general reception process. By contrast, those configurations that follow the patterns of affirmation rather than of rupture, patterns that promise continuity rather than transformation, maintain or cyclically reestablish their grasp on public cultural representations that obscures if not obstructs, the impact that actual radical paradigmatic shifts could have had. Unlike in empirical scientific discourses, the shifts in aesthetic practices of production and reception apparently are not governed by any concept of truth-value, verifiability or revisionary correction and necessary agreement. Presumably, it would be simplistic, however, to conclude prematurely that the discourse of aesthetic formations simply follows the same dynamics of other unverifiable representational systems like fashion or advertising that are simply subjected to the general pressures and interests of larger ideological formations.

But the paradoxical fate of aesthetic formations is far more complex. If a particular paradigm is admitted into the reception process that is controlled by the cultural and ideological apparatus at all, it may enter this reception process for various reasons. Perhaps its inevitability has become scandalously apparent, and finally the culture caves in under the pressure of the historical evidence (consider for example the pressure that was exerted by photography on "high" art in the mid- to late nineteenth century). Or a culture may realize that certain paradigms can finally be admitted because their originally threatening subversion has diminished, or it has come under control, or it has simply evaporated since the conditions under which the radical paradigm was formulated no longer apply to the circumstances of experience in the present (for example, the enthusiastic reception that the art of the Soviet avant-garde has been finally accorded in the last ten years). Finally, a paradigm change may be admitted after a long period of exclusion, neglect, and/or repression, if it turns out that the ruling system of representation, and the institutions that control it are no longer properly serving the needs of ideology. Therefore they have to update their arsenal by admitting different modes of perceptual experience, even if they have to take the risk of inviting a partial breakdown of earlier, and more conventional ordering systems.

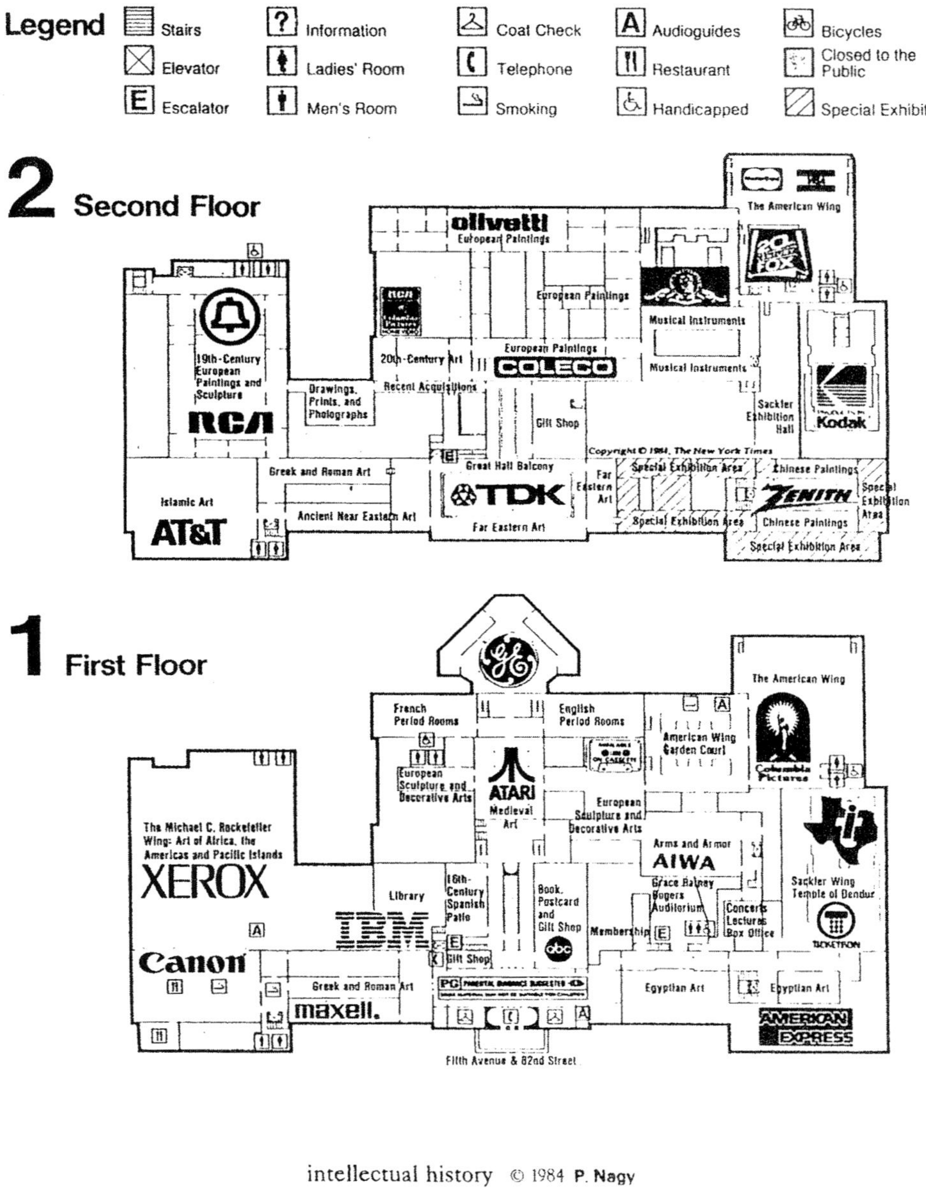

Peter Nagy, *Intellectual History*, 1984. Black-and-white photocopy, 11 × 8½ in. (28 × 21.5 cm). © Peter Nagy. Courtesy the artist.

As is well known, the radicalization of Duchamp's paradigm in the Fluxus and Happening project was for the most part shunned by the institutions that controlled the artistic production of their time. These institutions instantly made sure that Pop art would emerge as the splendid historical compromise between the manifest contradictions ruling a society of consumption and its elite cultural, hangovers. Pop art offered a compromise that was more conciliatory and accommodating to both sides of the ideological divide. On the one hand, one had to update the artistic vision of reality within the advanced capitalist strategies of production and consumption (i.e., one had to acknowledge their specific object relationships). On the other hand, an art was necessary that maintained sufficient distance from the collapse of all cultural standards, that reaffirmed the unmitigated status of an art of the museum.

After all, it seems that precisely to the degree that a work of art sustains these contradictions, to the degree that artistic practice is a practice of manifest disavowal, the work can generate the compelling and irresistible quality of suggestion that imbues it with the power of the fetish object. Only then does it seem worthy to be collected, conserved, and only then is its attraction and success as a commodity guaranteed, and only then can it become an object of discourse and an object of institutionalization. Therefore it seems that what caused the particular failure of Fluxus, as a radical attempt to take Duchamp's paradigm literally and turn it into actual practice, was based on a deeper misconception: a failure to acknowledge that it is not within a linguistic system alone that a "performative" act takes place. Furthermore, Fluxus did not take into account (or did not accept) that there is no unmediated relationship between the producer (author, creator) and the recipient (reader) of a work of art. If the reader is the final destination, as Duchamp and Barthes tried to convince us the reader is positioned, however, at the end of a complex system of institutional and discursive mediations. And it is only on this level of mediation that artistic practice acquires its intricate involvement with ideology, not primarily in the consciousness of its author or the needs of its recipients.

Discursive practices such as Fluxus that (temporarily) failed to signify within the conventions of the coding system, did not fail as texts, but as *objects*. They did not fail because of their lack of legibility (it is not as though they were not perfectly lucid, audible *paroles* in a system of *langue*), but they failed primarily as institutional objects. Their refusal to share the practices and forms of institutional, commercial or discursive (academic) distribution and their resistance against the required conventions of fetishistic meaning structures barred their access to the framework of art historical reception.[8]

If one argues, however, that artistic practice can (temporarily) fail to signify as a result of its disregard for linguistic conventions, discursive status, object conditions, and institutional positioning, then it should also be possible to argue the opposite case: namely that artistic practice can fail to generate meaning, if it does not transcend, but affirms and abides by all of the requirements that rule at a particular historical moment the triangular relationship between language, object, and institution (if we agree that it is in this triangular field that the "reader" is constituted, rather than continue to assume that the reader, or spectator, could be a neutral force that exists as a category of its own).

It is almost impossible to distinguish whether these artists who have programmatically committed themselves to producing a traditional art of the museum simply have produced a completely institutionalized discourse, or whether it is not the institutions themselves who have produced these artists. It seems that for these affirmative individuals cultural production is synonymous with the task of securing the patrimony, asserting its continued rule and increasing its power. These artists accept a notion of culture as a continuous representation of—and for—the dominant visions of social order. Their latent, if not unconscious ideological agenda wants to defy any notion of culture as a process of a constant contestation of power formations, or as an intrusion of suppressed meanings into officially accepted representations, and as a challenge to the ideological concepts of a traditionally confined group of recipients.

Confronted with the reality of a hegemonic cultural industry and with the experience of the instant transformation of all cultural production into spectacle, this type of work continues to pretend to an unchallenged and unthreatened continuity of the artist's social role, place, and production procedures. However, in order for an artist to promote these myths, and to imbue them with credibility, now the same mechanisms and techniques have to be employed which the culture industry, corporate advertising, and product design have long utilized in promoting their own products. As though they had learned their lessons from the managers and designers of advertising campaigns (who, until recently took most of their clues from the works of artists) these artists now have their public appearance managed according to similar principles.

In a variation of Baudrillard's famous concept of the "passion for the code" that rules systems of representation and our relationship to them, one could argue that in the world of "high art" it is the "nostalgia" for the code (for the conditions of production of the code, e.g., the role model and behavior of the male avant-garde studio artist) that governs the self-image of these artists as much as it determines the expectations of their recipients. Thus at the core of the work itself we find not only a fetishized notion of high art in general, but also a fetishization of its particular historical configurations.

The ever more visible affinities between the worlds of fashion, design, and advertising and the world of so-called postmodern high art are not simply explained by mutual economic dependence. Rather it is an elective affinity resulting from their increasingly similar techniques of embodying and conveying ideology and their shared relationships to the powers that organize the culture industry. The growing number of artists' personality profiles in the media, the photo features of the artists' studios (and wives and children) and the use of artists as male fashion models provide us with the double-bind message that is the structural hallmark of all successful advertising. On the one hand artists have to vouch for their traditional authenticity and the originality and exclusivity of their production (in the same manner that mass-produced schlock is advertised through image campaigns reminiscing about aristocratic and high bourgeois lifestyles). On the other hand these artists have to assure us that to invest in them is as secure as buying shares in a designer's label. In fact, the author is only an author at this point if he is potentially functioning like a corporation, while a designer's corporation can be successful only if it presents itself as an *auteur*. Here, then, is an unexpected reconciliation of the traditional dialectic of high culture and mass culture.

Paradoxically the central argument to legitimate these practices has been focused on the precarious balance between the historical concept of the bourgeois subject and the emergence of a universal power of mass-cultural formations that threatens to destroy subjectivity altogether. This dialectic relationship was already recognized by Theodor W. Adorno in 1938 as the inescapable conflict for all high art production:

> But the autonomy of the work of art, and therefore its material form, is not identical with the magical element in it. The reification of a great work of art is not just loss, any more than the reification of the cinema is all loss. It would be bourgeois reaction to negate the reification of the cinema in the name of the ego, and it would border on anarchism to revoke the reification of a great work of art in the spirit of immediate use values. "Les extremes me touchent" (Gide), just as they touch you, but only if the dialectic of the lowest has the same value as the dialectic of the highest, rather than the latter simply decaying. Both bear the stigmata of capitalism, both contain elements of change. … Both are torn halves of an integral freedom, to which however they do not add up. It would be romantic to sacrifice one to the other, either as the bourgeois romanticism of the conservation of personality and all that stuff, or as the anarchist romanticism

> of blind confidence in the spontaneous power of the proletariat in the historical process—a proletariat which is itself a product of bourgeois society.[9]

Embedded in Adorno's argument, or at least in one half of it, is no doubt a case against the aesthetics of the readymade. It almost seems as though he was voicing an explicit attack (certainly a proper description) on Duchamp's "productivist" proposal for the reversal of the readymade—the *Utilizer un Rembrandt comme planche à repasser* (Use a Rembrandt as Ironing Board)—when he argues that it would "border on anarchism to revoke the reification of a great work of art in the spirit of immediate use values."

On the one hand, one could easily extend Adorno's argument to all artistic practices that are motivated by an anti-aesthetic impulse, or at least the impulse to criticize their proper discursive and institutional conditions: for example those artistic practices of critical negation that are engaged in an effort to define different distribution forms and to constitute different audiences. On the other hand—as it might appear in a superficial reading of Adorno—his argument seems to justify the contemporary conservative position which, like the new art of the museum, implicitly claims a position of resistance against the process of mass-cultural desublimation, and against the destruction of historical consciousness.

In a manner analogous to the arguments made for postmodern architecture against the disastrous consequences of the deployment of international style Modernism in the service of corporate capitalism, one could argue that the notion of progress inherent in Modernist thinking had lost all its credibility since the critical negativity of Modernist art (its model of ascetic reduction and the denial of aesthetic gratification) had unknowingly contributed to the decline and the decay of the experience of history and subjectivity through its aesthetic representations. By decreasing—if not, as it seemed, eliminating—from itself all dimensions of subjectivity and experience of historical (individual, regional, national) memory, it has supposedly sacrificed the complexity and sophistication of the legacy of bourgeois cultural practice, and has thus unwillingly assisted in the "onrush of barbarism" as Adorno calls it in the same letter.

Furthermore, one could argue that in Modernism's self-imposed restrictions to absolute reductivist "simplicity," to a critical negativity in the guise of a mimicry of mass-cultural formations (as was the case, most notably of course, with Duchamp's readymade and all art that has followed it conceptually, materially, and formally), artistic production has declined ultimately to the conceptual joke, to an esoteric and elitist specialist's game that has lost its audience, or forced it to accept a seemingly endless self-reflexive repetition of one-liners and one-move gestures. In the same manner that a conservative interpretation of Adorno's argument could somewhat rightfully suggest that all deconstructive involvements with the mass-cultural practices of advertising and television, are futile in the face of their incessant and voracious desire to absorb and transform all criticism instantly into newly updated strategies of ideological cooptation. And finally, Adorno certainly suggested on many occasions that any attempt at an explicitly political art practice under present circumstances would not only be condemned to futility, but also, by its very exclusion of the aesthetic would have already collaborated in the destruction of subjectivity since it has agreed to the subject's final and complete submission to the mechanisms of political control and administrative power.

If these are some of the contradictions within which art production and reception are currently contained, it should be obvious that not any one particular concept or strategy, such as the "readymade," "abstraction," or even "figurative expressivity," could remain historically independent, valid, and unaffected by them. We are, of course, aware that the majority of contemporary artists and almost all constituencies of contemporary reception (museums, institutions, dealers, collectors, and viewers) act as though these conditions not only do *not*

Sherrie Levine, *After Piet Mondrian: 2*, 1983. C-print, 20 × 16 in. (50.8 × 40.6 cm). © Sherrie Levine. Courtesy the artist and Paula Cooper Gallery, New York.

affect art production but have no purchase whatsoever on the actually existing conditions in the art world. It is this massive system of interlocking disavowals that defines the institutionalized art discourse of the present all the more as a continuous process of intensified collective fetishization of culture: the disavowal of its obsolescence (first with regard to its discursive prefigurations in twentieth-century art history, and second regarding the technical means and standards of representation-production by which it is surrounded); the disavowal of its failure to live up to the standards or the ambitions, commitments and achievements that marked the practice of artists throughout the twentieth century (one sometimes wonders what it must feel like for artists in the present to be confronted with the minds and with the integrity of artists of previous generations and to realize that they themselves will at best enter history as the successors to Bernard Buffet).

Thirdly, the disavowal with regard to their audiences: to know that they produce for corporate lobbies, investment collections, and speculating Yuppies while they pretend to be involved in the crafting of a unique aesthetic construct that claims to be universally communicative and accessible.

This system of disavowals, however, has its dialectical correlative in the practices of radical negation: political artists refuse to admit that the continued hegemony of the institutions, their corporate support, and the supremacy of the official cultural practices have created a historical reality with which all contemporary art practices have to come to terms. When a cultural production contents itself to remain in the shadows of a tolerated marginality without constantly assaulting the formations of power and ideology in official culture, it becomes subject to its own processes of disavowal and ideological delusions.

Consequently, it will suffer from a lack of specificity and accuracy, because it abstains from the confrontation with art's proper reality principle (that of the market and of the institutions of official culture). Only in that confrontation can aesthetic practice find its inextricable entanglement with economic reality on the one hand, and ideology on the other, without ever submitting fully to either one.

The works of a younger generation of artists, like Louise Lawler, Sherrie Levine, and Allan McCollum, seem to confront these conditions programmatically and precisely in the present. Obviously, it is indebted in many respects to the generation of the 1960s. Yet it is important to realize that even within the short period of a decade (1968–1978) the determining conditions inside artistic production have changed to such an extent that although these artists are seemingly all involved in a critical approach to "found" and "given" institutional and discursive structures of framing, their concerns are of an entirely different nature.[10]

The artists of the 1980s take the moments and the sites where traditional art production concluded its activities as their point of departure. Their work begins, in almost all instances, at the level where traditional work had already been processed through the various mechanisms of acculturation (strategies of presentation, practices of dissemination and reproduction, institutional positioning, the affirmation of authorship and ownership, and the modes of viewing that these generate as a cultural compound). While all of these contingencies had been always constitutive of artistic production, they had been obliterated as "marginal," if not excluded from the purely "perceptual" experiences of traditional artistic constructs, all the more powerful since they had been traditionally concealed, if not eliminated from the work's "central core."

In critical opposition, these artists in the 1980s now recognize, even foreground, the reality, if not the primacy of all ancillary mechanisms. They conceive and structure the "body" of their work out of the totality of supplements that are crucial in establishing the functions of a cultural representation. Finally, and to a varying degree in each individual work, one can discover a reflection on that precarious zone of transition between the status of the high cultural object, its discursive conventions and institutional claims, and the gradual transition of these

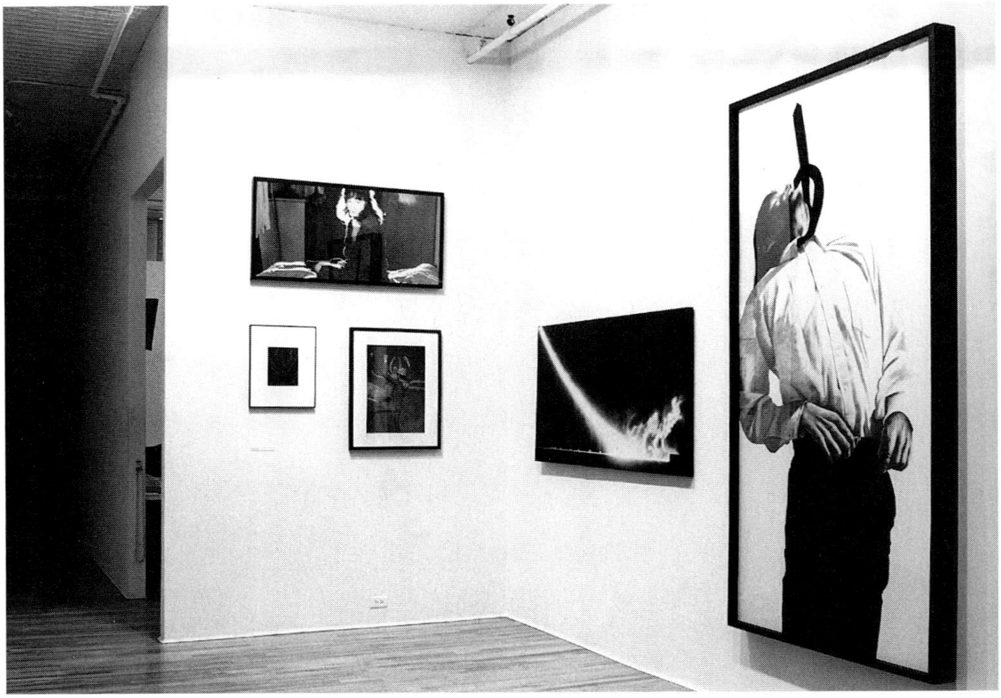

Louise Lawler, *Arranged by Louise Lawler, Metro Pictures, New York City*, 1982. Installation of Metro Pictures artists: Cindy Sherman, James Welling, Laurie Simmons, Jack Goldstein, and Robert Longo. © Louise Lawler. Courtesy the artist and Metro Pictures, New York.

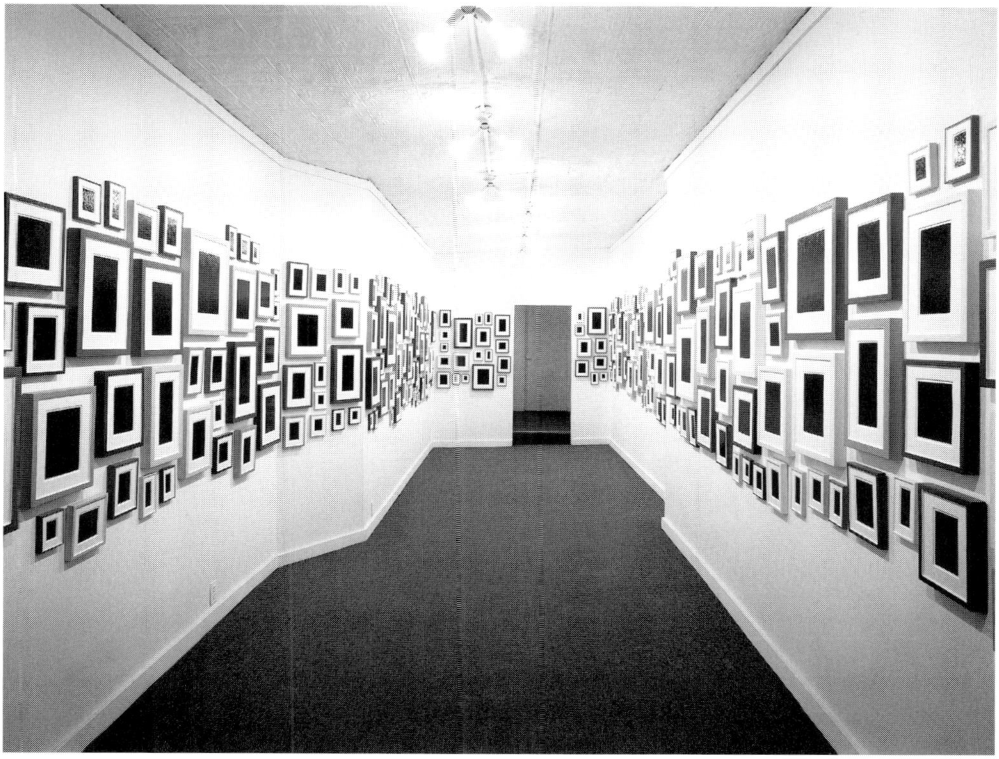

Allan McCollum, *Plaster Surrogates*, 1982–84. Enamel on cast Hydrostone. Size variable, each unique. Installation Cash Newhouse Gallery, New York, 1984. © Allan McCollum. Courtesy the artist.

constructs (or de facto congruence) with mass-cultural figurations or the practices of the culture industry. The revelation of these hybrid transitional zones belies the credibility of a continued pretense to be still securely contained within an uncontaminated system of high art. And it reveals the necessity to recognize the actually governing structural parallelisms in both domains of perception, simultaneously determining contemporary artistic and ideological experiences.

NOTES

First published in *Dissent: The Issue of Modern Art in Boston*, exh. cat. (Boston: I.C.A., 1985), pp. 106–122. Minor corrections have been made for consistency.

1. Marcel Duchamp, "The Creative Act," in *The Essential Writings of Marcel Duchamp*, ed. Michel Sanouillet and Elmer Peterson (London: Oxford University, 1975), p. 138.

2. Roland Barthes, "The Death of the Author," in *Image, Music, Text* (New York: Hill & Wang, 1977), p. 148.

3. It is certainly not incidental that at exactly the same time Ferdinand de Saussure also declared the "death of the author" in his *Cours de linguistique générale*. Saussure had clarified that the speaker of a language entered a preexisting system of signs (*langue*), constituting the speaker in the speech act (*parole*) rather than the speaker constituting himself/herself in an autonomous act of language- and self-definition.

4. This synecdoche of the hand with an outstretched, pointing, designating index finger dates of course, as is well known, from the days of advertising's naive childhood (when it could still admit to its manipulation of perception). Two more examples may suffice to indicate the ubiquity of advertising's index hand in the visual arts of the 1920s: in 1922 we find it on the cover of the proto-surrealist publication *Le Coeur a barbe* which anticipates Fluxus design in almost every other aspect as well. In 1923 we find it on several pages of El Lissitzky's book design for Wladimir Mayakovsky's poems *For the Voice (For Reading Out Loud)*. This sign, universally present in either engraved or lithographic advertising images in the nineteenth century, subsequently appears almost like a Fluxus trademark in a large number of Fluxus publications (primarily those designed by George Maciunas). Whether Maciunas took his reference from Duchamp's *Tu m'* or, what is more likely, from advertising design directly, is less important than to recognize that in each case the emphasis is on the declarative, performative act of indexical pointing and of naming the found object and transferring it from one discursive context to a different one.

5. Rosalind Krauss, "Notes on the Index: Parts 1 and 2," in *The Originality of the Avant-Garde and Other Modernist Myths* (Cambridge, Mass.: MIT Press, 1985), pp. 196–210.

6. Barthes, "Death of the Author," pp. 145ff.

7. Ibid., p. 142.

8. It is not accidental that no other artistic practice since World War II has been ignored almost completely in the way that the activities of the Fluxus and Happening artists were all but erased from history. Only recently has interest emerged very sporadically. The explanations for this will still have to be found and cannot simply be given by the fact that Fluxus and Happening did not produce any merchandise. What is more important, they also refused to produce an art for the museums, and, what is possibly even more self-destructive, an art that does not reproduce well in art history books, magazines and color slides.

A similar situation, less decisive, however applies to some of the most important artists of the post-Minimal and Conceptual generation of the 1968 period (Michael Asher, Robert Barry, Dan Graham, John Knight, Lawrence Weiner). They have been consistently ignored by almost all major American museums both in exhibitions and acquisitions (one cannot find a single work of theirs in either the collection of the Museum of Modern Art or in the Whitney Museum of American Art). However, both institutions have rushed to embrace, exhibit and acquire the work of the generation of artists that came, as it were, to the historical rescue of the credibility of these museums by devoting themselves to a massive production of museum art. It seems that painting galleries, like sculpture gardens, living room couches, and corporate lobbies, produce their own institutional needs and discursive voids that have to be filled. And it seems that one does not have to worry about an absence of aesthetic opportunism that rushes in to fill these voids at all times and costs.

9. Theodor W. Adorno, letter to Walter Benjamin, March 18, 1936, cited in *Aesthetics and Politics*, ed. Fredric Jameson (London: Verso, 1977), p. 123.

10. For an extensive discussion of the relationship between the artists of this generation—most notably Michael Asher, Marcel Broodthaers, Daniel Buren, and Hans Haacke—and their importance for the younger generation of artists, see my essay, "Allegorical Procedures: Appropriation and Montage in Contemporary Art," originally published in *Artforum* 21, no. 1 (September 1982): 43–56; repr. in this vol.

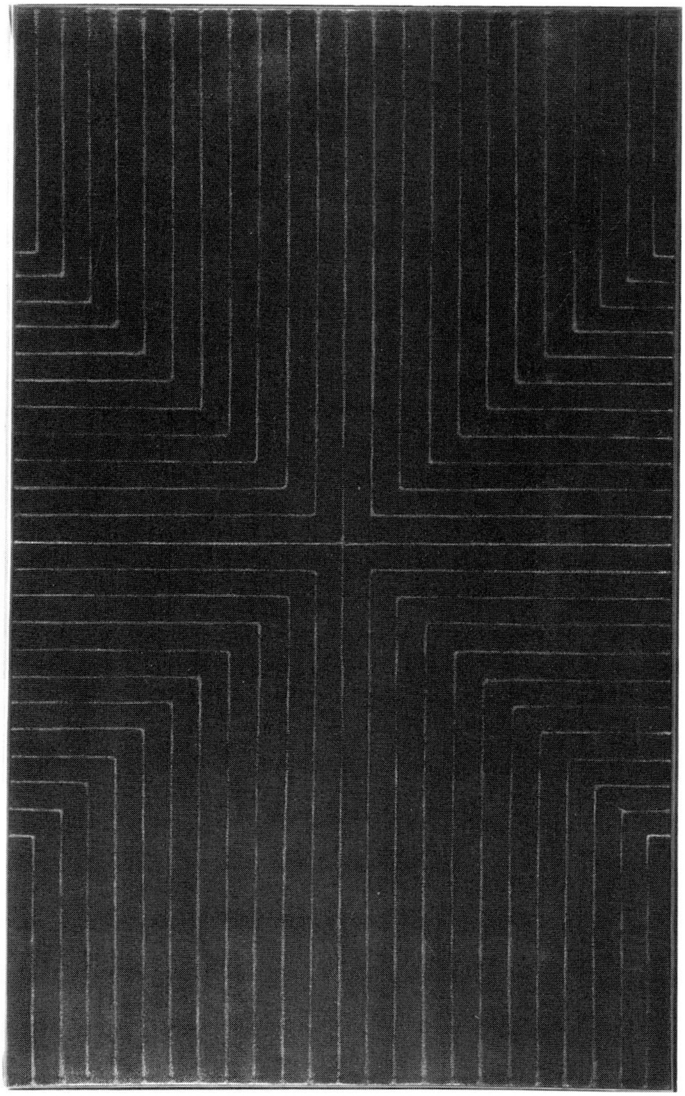

Frank Stella, *Die Fahne Hoch*, 1959. Black enamel on canvas, 121½ × 73 in. (309 × 185 cm). Whitney Museum of American Art. Photo: Geoffrey Clements. © 2015 Frank Stella/Artists Rights Society (ARS), New York.

> There were two problems that had to be faced. One was spatial and the other was methodological. In the first case I had to do something about relational painting, i.e., the balancing of various parts with and against each other. The obvious answer was symmetry—make it the same all over. The question still remained though, of how to do this in depth. A symmetrical image or configuration placed on an open ground is not balanced out in the illusionistic space. The solution I arrived at—and there are probably quite a few, although I know of only one other, color density—forces illusionistic space out of the painting at a constant rate by using a regulated pattern. The remaining problem was simply to find a method of paint application which followed and complemented the design solution. This was done by using the house painter's technique and tools.[8]

Stella's subsequent claim that he "tried to keep the paint as good as it was in the can," as well as his actual usage of metallic powder that was mixed into the emulsion, completed these terms as he outlined them in 1959. Obviously, all of these terms situate painting in a competitive relationship with the readymade and the sculptural relief. Simultaneously, Stella's paintings reflect on the precarious condition of gesture, and its displacement by pure facture (as had been obviously the case in the work of all serious painters after Fontana and Jasper Johns since the mid-1950s).

The historical synthesis of the two fundamental challenges to painting occurs precisely at that moment when the prevailing relevance of both paradigms, photography and readymade, is fully recognized for the first time in the postwar period.[9] The first proves painting's enduring competence in relation to photography and *mechanical reproduction* by reducing it semiotically to the sign of the index. The second proves painting's compatibility with the prevailing processes of *technical production* by reducing it materially to the status of the readymade. As one critic put it succinctly at a relatively early moment:

> Neither Manzoni's paintings, nor Rauschenberg's *White Paintings* for that matter, were statements about abstraction. The Rauschenbergs were screens which registered the shadow of spectators. Hence they functioned as isolated rectangles of environment.[10]

And Klein's paintings have been recognized even more explicitly in their formal, structural, and material parallelism to Duchamp's readymades:

> The phenomenon of Duchamp's Readymades is in certain respects the opposite antecedent of Klein's Milan show. … There is a sense in which the sight of a gallery hung with eleven virtually identical pictures raises more immediately than a Readymade the issue of the irrelevance of the uniqueness of a material object of art.[11]

It is as important to recognize the historical continuity that relates painting in the mid-1960s to the paradigms that had been developed in 1913–1919, as it is important to emphasize the relative continuity between the first and the second generation of neo-avantgarde painters from the early 1950s to the early 1960s against the artificial division that Greenberg and his followers have drawn.[12]

In his exhibition *Three American Painters* (1965) and the catalog essay that accompanied it, Michael Fried included Frank Stella in a group of second-generation New York School painters who were generally called the "color-field" painters. Fried's choice is of particular historical interest in retrospect, since Stella's painting at that moment seemed to offer sufficient continuity with the legacy of Greenberg's theories and yet to extend and update the ideas of the second generation.

At the same time, Stella seems to have appeared to Fried as a guardian against the "neo-Dadaist" tide that Johns and Rauschenberg had initiated and that was now rising further as Pop art. What Fried failed to recognize, however, was not only the fact that Stella was a very close friend of a young group of artists who violently rejected color field painting, but that he was in many respects already the driving force behind this group whose work would soon emerge as "Minimal art." While Fried's description and analysis of the radical innovations of the New York School painters were generally advancing beyond Greenberg's notions, leading up to recognize the peculiar conditions of painting in the confrontation with photography and mechanical reproduction, it is the final hypothesis of an independently existing realm of visual experience—his notion of a bastion of pure opticality—that prevents him from understanding the implications of Stella's work (and ultimately, that of Pollock and Morris Louis, for that matter). This failure prepares the way for Fried's subsequent misperception of the work of the Minimal artists. Not only did Fried inherit Greenberg's resentment of Duchamp, he seems to have also inherited his astonishing capacity of selective art historical memory.

At the conclusion of Abstract Expressionism and *informel* painting in the mid-1950s, the depletion of the painterly gesture from any expressive connotation becomes one of the key concerns of that second generation of postwar artists. Yet, when it comes to mechanical mark-making processes that displaced the conventional forms of drawing, for example, Manzoni's and Ryman's works of the late 1950s are as profoundly implicated in a historical dialogue with the analytical laboratory positions in Russian and Soviet Constructivism (e.g., Rodchenko's compass and ruler drawings in 1919, or even earlier, Duchamp's *Three Standard Stoppages* from 1913) as they depended upon, as Ryman claims, his admiration for the work of Mark Rothko (or Barnett Newman, for that matter). The athletic calligraphy of the New York School (as Robert Rosenblum once called it) was now transformed into the scriptural, the repetitive, the molecular movement of the brush, increasingly scrutinized and objectified. European and American artists who responded to these paradigmatic changes were clearly motivated by similar concerns. Comparable to his more visible peer Stella, Ryman serialized the brush marks in his paintings already in the late 1950s, by stacking them up mechanically, as it were, almost identical in size (width, length, and quantity of pigment applied). Yet their minuscule variations made them still legible as brushstrokes, not as the mere mechanical painterly imprints they would become in the work of Niele Toroni ten years later.

More importantly, however, in one of Ryman's paintings from 1961, a column of horizontal, fairly equalized brush marks suddenly turns into a stack of signatures toward the bottom of the painting. Thus Ryman performs in his work what will become a crucial feature in Toroni's as well: the dialectics of facture, operating in perpetual suspense between a gesture of transcendentality and the functions of a trademark that guarantees authenticity like the signature itself. In his discussion of Malevich's work, Yve-Alain Bois has brilliantly described this dialectic:

> Facture, in terms of painterly touch, is only a substitute for the signature of the artist (this is now no longer a body that acts, but it is a spirit) and it becomes the guarantee of the "authenticity" of the painting: caught in a movement that is both transcendental and commercial, textural facture remains the object of a profound ambiguity.[13]

Facture méchanique

Ryman develops a wide range of factural devices; his brushstrokes are differentiated by length and width, by quantity and pigment charge, and by the directions of arm and hand movement. Thus he opens an entirely new realm of infinite aestheticization of the once goal-oriented "laboratory" investigation of the basic pictorial elements of pictorial language (subjecting it thus inevitably to the fetishization that this process of infinite aesthetic variation implies). By contrast, in Toroni's work, the variety of factures is reduced to a single type of painterly imprint, since he deconstructs painting's modernist self-reflexivity at that very moment when modernism's originally critical force of self-reflexivity has become painting's mythical purpose.

"The liberation of line from the task of figuration," as Michael Fried had identified one of the major achievements of Pollock's paintings and those of his follower Morris Louis, had been—like the monochrome—one of the central concerns of painters after Cubism. The abolition of any and all iconic functions of linear definition (line as contour, binding and describing figures or spatial configurations) had been replaced since 1913 in the work of the most advanced artists by a definition of the linear as a spatiotemporal formation, or as the immediate trace of a process. It was conceived of as a structure that existed on its own terms, independent of the author's creative, expressive, or skillful hand, the *patte* as Félix Fénéon had called it.

This mechanization of drawing—in analogy to the monochrome—was articulated in the development of two complementary strategies: the first one revealed the force of gravity as the prime determining factor in placing structures and materials on planar surfaces (in the way that Duchamp executed the principle in *Trois Stoppages Étalons* in 1913, or as Jean Arp performed it slightly later in his *Squares Arranged According to the Laws of Chance* in 1916–17). The second strategy was developed primarily in the Russian and Soviet context by Olga Rozanova's or Lyubov Popova's exploration of facture and by Rodchenko's usage of mechanical drawing tools that had been banned from artistic drawing for centuries, such as the compass and ruler (let alone the house painter's brush and the paint roller). Popova stated, for example, in 1919:

> Line as color and as the vestige of a transverse plane participates in, and directs, the forces of construction. … Texture is the content of painterly surfaces.[14]

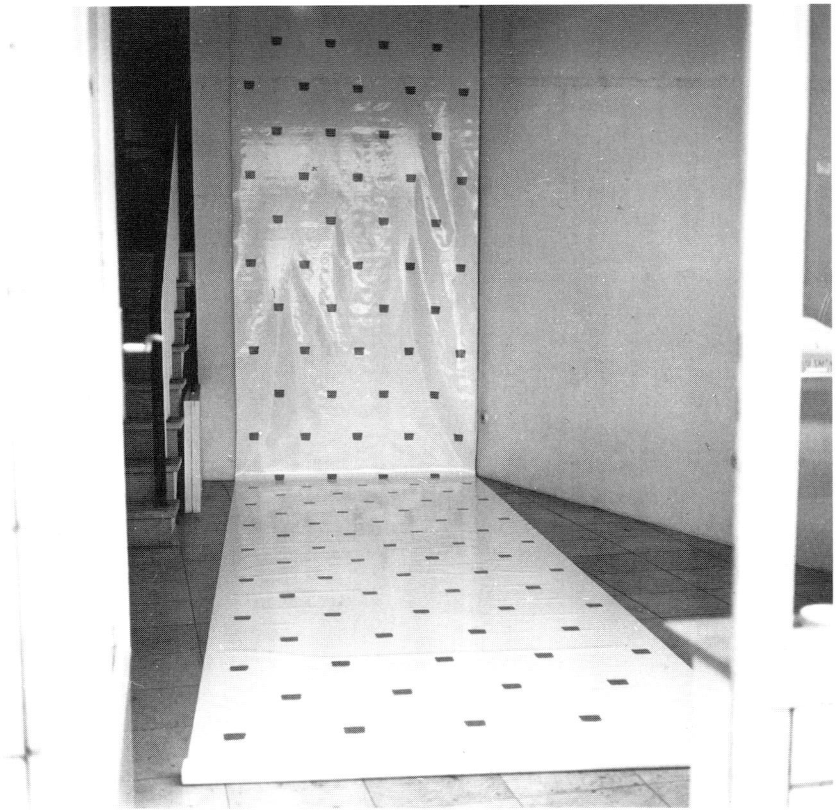

Niele Toroni, *Imprints No. 50* (1972). Acrylic on wax cloth, various dimensions. © Niele Toroni. Courtesy the artist and Galerie Michael Werner, Cologne.

If the recognition of the index as the semiotic foundation of drawing and of pictorial line is one of the essential discoveries of modernist painting, then this recognition is radicalized even further in the decision to present the brushstroke as a singular, isolated unit altogether. This logical step had of course been taken in work which evolved from Suprematism, such as Rozanova's *Green Stripe* (1917), or in some of the paintings by Popova from the same period.

In his essay "Three American Painters," Fried gives an astonishing description of the radical transformation of drawing procedures that had entered Abstract Expressionism through the stain technique, in which he—unknowingly, it seems—recapitulates the Soviet avant-garde's original concerns with mechanizing drawing almost as programmatically as the artists of the 1960s had repeated it themselves:

> Roughly the essence of this synthesis resides in the fact that thinned pigment soaked and stained into unsized canvas can be made to assume configurations which appear not to be bounded by anything like a drawn outline … but it conveys the strong impression of not having been circumscribed by any cursive, draughtsmanlike gesture. It resists being read as drawn. … At the same time the stain technique identifies the painted image with its woven ground, almost as if the image were thrown onto the latter from a slide projector. Finally it has been observed that the stain technique entails relatively depersonalized execution. Because the liquid pigment is for the most part either poured onto the horizontal canvas, rubbed into it with sponges or rolled on with commercial rollers, the technical virtuosity and bravura touch associated with painterliness from the Venetians to de Kooning is renounced from the start.[15]

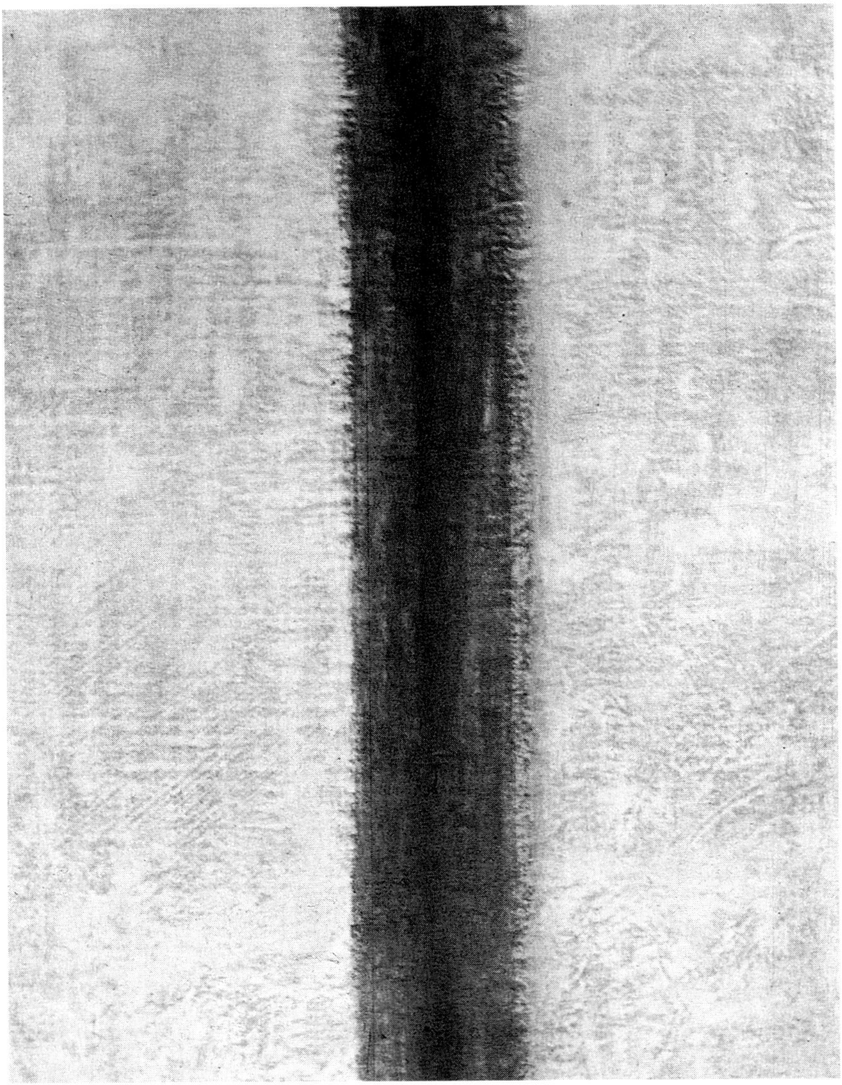

Olga Rozanova, *Green Stripe*, 1917. Oil on canvas, 30 × 20⅞ in. (71 × 53 cm). State Museum–Preserve Rostor, Kremlin.

Six years after Fried's essay, the quasi-photographical qualities of the stained images of the so-called color field painters were once again mentioned (we have to assume in direct reference to Fried's acute observation). This time, however, it is Harold Rosenberg who deplores the loss of gestural originality and authenticity, of the expressive force and auratic presence that he had of course venerated (and projected upon) the "athletes of gesture" in Abstract Expressionism:

> As colored images the canvases of Frankenthaler, Louis and Olitski were arresting. … The weakness of these paintings is in the quality of their absorbed color, which they all share on a didactic basis. While the soaked-in paint produces a uniform transparency, it results in a thinness that diffuses the eye instantaneously across the entire surface of the picture. As a result the image in these paintings is all there is to them. Their quality is akin to that of the photograph or color reproduction; they could be cast on a screen without much loss. Perhaps this is what endears the work of these artists to art-historian curators, who are habituated to thinking of paintings as they appear in slides and reproductions.[16]

Fried's description of the ramifications of the stain procedure is remarkable first of all because of the precision with which he identifies the indexical qualities in Louis' painting, culminating in his comparison of Louis' "images" with photographic light projections. Nothing could in fact reveal more adequately the historical ties between the stain technique and the reconceptualization of line that had occurred in the post-Cubist avant-garde.[17]

Yet Fried's description remains problematic in several ways. First of all, because—in his eagerness to secure the continuing primacy of New York School artists—he ignores or he deliberately obscures—as had Greenberg—the historical predecessors in painting's ineluctable trajectory toward the indexical structure. But Greenberg and Fried not only ignored the strategies of the avant-garde (Fried at one point calls Duchamp "at best an amusing inventor"), they also refused to recognize that an emphasis on tactility had already reappeared within Abstract Expressionism itself, and not just with the second generation of color field painters. This misperception becomes evident when Fried refers to Newman's paintings as "executed by conventional means," when in fact Newman's painterly methods were as unconventional as those of Pollock or Louis: after all, already in Newman's painting *Onement II* in 1948 the process of painting had been foregrounded as a purely indexical procedure. More astonishing even was the fact that Newman presented the brushstroke as a singularized synecdoche of the process of painting itself. In his work from the late 1940s onward, Newman often used masking tape as a drawing template: its edge either rigidified the drawing (when the template was used as a ruler) or the tape doubled up as a linear/planar relief, against whose mechanical rigidity the matter of paint and the manual brushwork had to be activated.

When looking at Newman's work, we cannot fail to recognize the importance of procedure, the fact that painting is physically constituted as process, as trace, as the activation of various materials on diverse surfaces. The very same development would of course occur in other contexts of the postwar period, as for example in the foregrounding of the indexicality of painting in Johns' work and the subsequent mechanical execution and singularization of the brushstroke in Stella's proud (re-)discovery of the house painter's brush. It would reemerge simultaneously in Europe, as for example in Fontana's singularized slashing and piercing gestures, or in Manzoni's mechanization of singular line drawings in the *Linee*.

Yet, in order to relegitimate an untenable aestheticist and antihistorical position that had come under assault since the mid-1950s, Fried deploys Greenberg's concept of opticality, which reclaimed autonomy for the aesthetic construct and defined a purely visual experience that

Barnett Newman, *Onement II*, 1948. Oil on canvas, 60 × 36 in. (152 × 91 cm). Wadsworth Atheneum Museum, Hartford. © 2015 The Barnett Newman Foundation, New York/Artists Rights Society (ARS), New York.

had been dismantled in 1913 precisely by those pictorial strategies that foregrounded painting's tactility. The idealist notion of opticality prevents Fried from recognizing the inherently dialectical quality of tactility embodied in the indexical, singularized structure: that it functions simultaneously as the pure trace of a process and as a sign originating in the materiality of painterly production.

But it is not until Ryman's and Toroni's work that the dialectic of process and pictorial sign will appear most programmatically, as though it was performed in a laboratory experiment. And it is only in their work that the analytical approach to facture's indexicality and singularity now manifestly constitutes painting as the outcome of a complex interaction between multiple factors and forces: between tool, material, and surface, between procedure and gesture, suspended between the trace of matter and the trace of bodily performance—all are displayed now with an exemplary transparency. In the development of this logic from Ryman's to Toroni's work between 1958 and 1968, the indexical brush mark becomes not only increasingly isolated and regularized but also increasingly systematical: size and placement now become the subject of rigorous serial repetition rather than merely aim at an approximate regularity. Furthermore, what distinguishes Toroni's work from the early work of Ryman and Stella is the emphatic limitation to the individual brush mark as the smallest, repeatable, identical module of painterly operation while maintaining at the same time a margin of chromatic variation within a rigorously fixed format of composition, chroma, and facture.

It appears, then, that all of these features—the indexical brushstroke, the monochromatic order, the non-relational composition on a rectangular, more often square support—in short, what we could call painting on the cognitive and semiotic level of the index and the readymade—had been fully rediscovered in the mid-1950s and would subsequently become the key features of painting in the first half of the 1960s. But what concerns us here is obviously not who "invented" what strategy at what point in time, but rather to understand why these strategies appear as historically ineluctable, evident in the simultaneous and parallel occurrence of similar, if not identical, pictorial operations during that period. Such a comparative approach will hopefully not prevent us from perceiving the actual differences that exist between each individual artist's work and the specific, innate authenticity of each artist's operations that are of equal, if not greater, interest to us in this context.

The Grid and Non-Relational Composition

The assertion that the painting's canvas/support competes as a visual entity with the visual units assembled on its surface—as is evident in the compositional grid that functions as a cognitive map of that supporting surface—emerges originally once again as a strategy from within Cubist concerns. It finds one of its earliest, fully resolved examples in Robert Delauney's *First Disk* (1912), and in many paintings emerging shortly thereafter within the context of the Russian and Soviet post-Cubist avant-garde. Malevich's *Black Square* from 1913–15 would obviously be the most prominent example—as we already mentioned—in particular its permutations in the systematic breakdown of the square into quadrangular modules delimiting the canvas's horizontal and vertical expanse and their superimposition, superficially—if not erroneously—often referred to as a figuration of cruciformity, as in Malevich's *Black Cross* (the very structure of the quadrant as a form of modular mapping that Ad Reinhardt would later adopt as the principle of his mature work). It is with these geometrical all-over formations in 1915 that the pictorial plane is divided into more or less regular sections, and with Mondrian's geometric all-over formations in 1918–1919 (as for example in *Lozenge with Gray Lines*, 1918, and *Checkerboard with Light Colors*, 1919, both at Gemeentemuseum, The Hague) that compositional relationalism had been definitely replaced by systematized surface organizations. These chart—just as Johns' *Flags* or *Targets* would forty years later—the pictorial plane in a predictable, calculated manner that excludes all subsequent compositional choices, once the first decision for a parameter or a permutation had been made.[18]

Central holistic imagery and its counterpart, the non-relational grid, invalidate all traditional expectations for composition to function as a complex play of spatial and planar relationships, to generate a perceptual balance of tensions and weights, a vivid interaction of chromatic, linear, and spatial pictorial elements. This serialization of pictorial planar elements is transferred from the plane to the volumetric body by Rodchenko in 1920. Volumetric serialization evolved here directly from a concentric planar structure that had already been implicit in Delauney's concentric circular structure. Yet to the degree that the virtual space of planarity is transformed into the actual space of volume, a new dimension emerges within what had been until now a merely spatial structure: the new kinetic and performative potential of sculpture adds temporal sequentiality to the perception of spatial simultaneity.[19]

The strategy of a serialized or non-relational, holistic composition was available not only in the work of the original avant-garde, but continued or resurfaced in the various paraphrases and elaborations of the postwar artists, whether they were directly connected to the avant-garde of the 1920s like Josef Albers (whose *Homage to the Square* made this one of its foundational epitstemes) or whether they were the rediscoverers of that work, like the already mentioned examples of the neo-avant-garde of the '50s and early '60s.

Modular seriality, central symmetrical imagery, and the literal correspondence between figure, ground, and support (as well as monochromy and molecular brushwork) would become once again—as we have argued before—among the most salient formal operations in the paintings of Johns, Klein, and Manzoni from 1953 to 1955 onward. However, not only would these artists recognize the degree to which these pictorial conditions were overdetermined by the concept of Duchamp's readymade, but that painting in the twentieth century would remain intrinsically suspended between the photograph and the mechanically produced object.

This reflection alone made artists like Johns, Rauschenberg, and Ryman, let alone the Europeans, *persona non grata* with both Greenberg and Fried. A holistic central image defying internal relations, as much as figure-ground relations and illusionistic depth, such as Johns' *Targets* or *Flags* had of course not only been the defining structure of Delauney's *First Disk*, it had also been the striking quality of the *Urinal* or the *Bottle Rack*. It is precisely for those formal qualities—not for their inherent cognitive or philosophical implications—that Judd would eventually admit the Duchampian readymades to be among the possible antecedents for Minimal art, at the very same moment of the 1970s when he finally came around to reluctantly recognize Malevich's historical precedent as well.

But this could occur only at a later point, when Minimal art had been more firmly established. In 1966, in the famous interview between Stella, Judd, and Bruce Glaser, we still had been confronted with an extremely selective knowledge of European art history that considered Vasarely, Kandinsky, Gabo, and Pevsner at the forefront of Constructivist abstraction. This ignorance, or rather, this strategically displayed bad faith—the apogee of post-Greenbergian historical repression—certainly allowed the critics and artists at that time to believe that the introduction of non-relational compositional principles was in fact an achievement all their own.

The pictorial order of Ryman's work and later of Toroni's paintings—the systematic distribution of imprints with a brush no. 50 at a distance of thirty centimeters—follow at first sight the mapping principle of the grid. This principle had signaled—beyond the mere reformulation of pictorial composition—the radically egalitarian qualities within a non-hierarchical organization: here, the universal equivalence of all constituent elements of the collective production process had been ideally articulated. At the same time—and paradoxically not recognized by

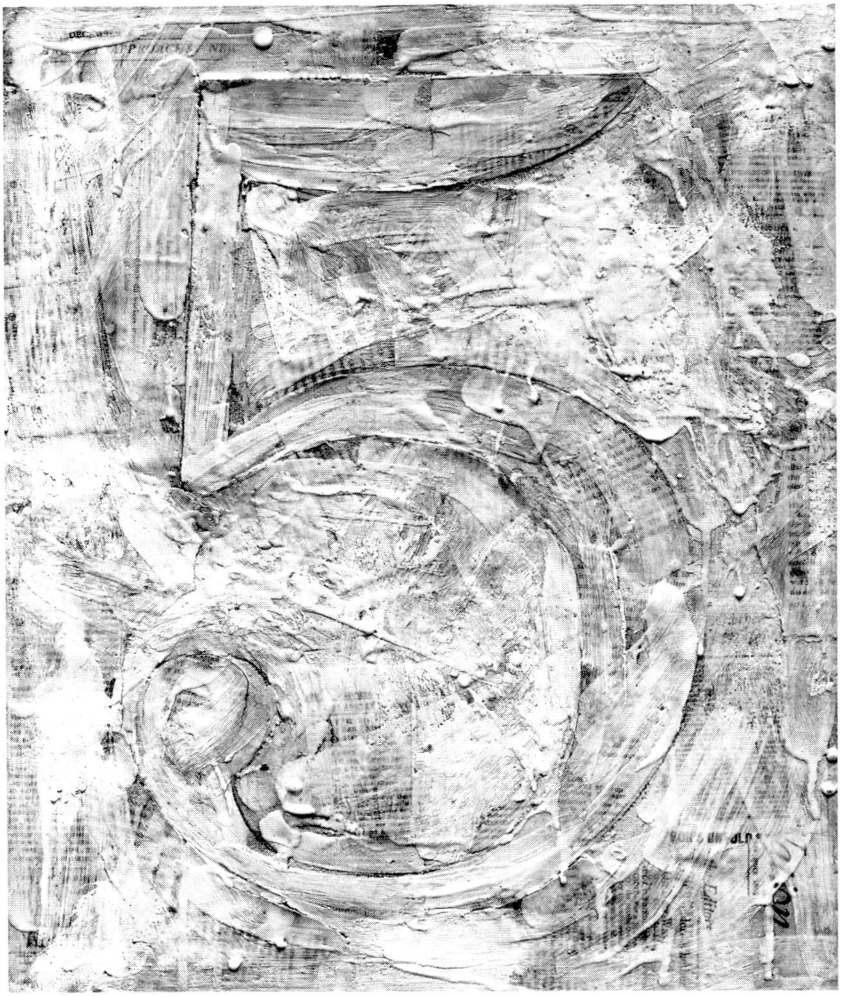

Jasper Johns, *Figure 5*, 1955. Encaustic and collage on canvas, 17½ × 14 in. (44.5 × 35.6 cm). Collection of the artist. © Jasper Johns/Licensed by VAGA, New York.

the heroic aspirations of the original avant-gardists—the distributional system of the grid also imposed a network of rigorous administrative rationality, an order of preestablished determination onto the aesthetic construct that seemed to prohibit—once and for all—intuition and initiative, if not individual decision-making processes within painterly production altogether.

It is first of all this temporal, performative dimension in Ryman's and Toroni's paintings that would distinguish them from the modernist grid distribution of their avant-garde predecessors. As they foreground procedure and production, it becomes impossible to differentiate whether these imprints are to be read as progressions and process, that is, whether one perceives the sequentiality of one imprint after another, or whether one perceives the imprints' simultaneity as a field of equivalent elements. While the processual nature of Toroni's painting emphasizes their sequentiality, the serial grid distribution emphasizes the simultaneity of these pictorial marks.

What Rosalind Krauss had observed for the order of the grid in painting in the twentieth century in general is equally true for Toroni's distribution of the synecdochies of painting in a grid system: they can be read simultaneously as centrifugal and centripetal. The imprints thrive from their originating point on the pictorial surface out into architectural space, where they establish a relationship to the reality of utilitarian and functional objects: this is the object status of the readymade against which they have to measure themselves, if they want to maintain their aesthetic credibility. When read centripetally, however, the imprints seem to adhere and insist on the pictorial surface alone, thereby foregrounding their status as mere painterly synechdoche and processual trace. As the index of painting, they emphasize the absolute difference that separates them from all other objects in real space. As autotelic elements of the language of painting, claiming to be involved exclusively with the conventions of that language, they posit their heteronomy from both the laws of use value and from those of sign exchange value.[20]

To the degree that Ryman's and Toroni's compositional principles regularize and systematize the elements of pictorial perception, forcing them to the threshold of rigor and boredom, they inevitably establish a reference to the generally governing conditions of repetition in object— and time experience outside of artistic production. One could speculate that the organization of time in the mechanical production process of everyday life would here be mimetically repeated in the rigorous repetition of identical pictorial elements. Therefore, Thierry de Duve's remarks about Ryman could be applied equally, if not more so, to Toroni's work, who certainly shares in this respect all the features of the Duchampian legacy that determines the practice of Minimal artists at large:

> And here we are dealing with a fact of our epoch that is not at all new ... but that massively occupies the forefront at the moment when Minimalism emerges: the resolution to replace the age old painterly craft, the archaic artisanal competence of painting, with the terms of industrial mechanization against which painting nevertheless had attempted to defend itself. Now, the oldest procedures of the craft of painting are treated as just that, as mere procedures. This means that the continuity of the painterly practice which corresponded to the rhythms of the labors and the structures of the day will from now on have to be cut into the smallest possible discrete units, into mere elements and parts of sequential and repeatable time fragments. The body of the painter mimics the model of the assembly line, he internalizes the social division and the organization of labor in order to resist it all the more. If the artist wants to survive, he has to industrialize his own body in the work process. This is a fact of the epoch and it is particularly evident in all of the serial and repetitive artistic principles.[21]

These artists enact a gesture of solidarity with those who produce under the conditions of alienated labor by inscribing the very mechanization of collective production within the aesthetic itself—within its processes as well as within its products. The myth of the aesthetic construct as the epitome of non-alienated productivity—and in particular the version of that myth which emerges from the history of pictorial abstraction as an unmediated transcendental and spiritual presence—is negated here in a manifest assimilation of abstraction to the dominant conditions of alienated labor and the collective conditions of a society of administration. The stereotypical repetition of the unit and the unified composition of the grid in Ryman and Toroni no longer appear as the promise of a radical non-hierarchical field of emancipated social relations, but function as the painterly equivalents of the collectively governing conditions within a highly regularized and controlled everyday life.

At the same time, in their apparent assimilation of the painterly process to a rigorously controlled temporal experience, Ryman's and Toroni's paintings dialectically negate those very conditions. To the extent that their paintings disassociate themselves from the hierarchical ordering structures of conventional compositions and subjective execution, their serial equality opposes the hierarchical ordering principles operative outside of pictorial reality. To the degree that their painting, in its semblance of an assimilation to the alienating procedures of mechanized labor, sides with those that are actually subjected to the conditions of alienation, it also refuses to fulfill any claim that artistic production should deliver a compensatory aesthetic plenitude, which would only affirm the division of labor by which culture's intricate link with domination is maintained.

Mythical qualities seem to be an inevitable result of the newly enforced meaning assignment that the reiteration of modernist pictorialist strategies provides for both, the reconstituted bourgeois audiences and neo-avantgarde artists. More than that, it seems that the parasitical nature of these recycled pictorial strategies has to be imbued with renewed credibility in a manifest link to the culture of spectacle. While the paradigmatic investigation of the modernist painters prided itself in its autonomy, transparency, and purposelessness (in its parallelism to pure scientific research or positivist empiricism), the neo-avantgarde increasingly has to employ the mode of the mystifying spectacle-presentation (as we saw in the case of Klein in particular) to legitimate its persistent recapitulation of modernist strategies.

If this mythification of painting under the auspices of spectacle is one of the inevitable conditions of the reiterated paradigms, then fetishization seems to have become its necessary counterpart. Once the postwar reception had resuscitated these painterly paradigms, the neo-avantgarde had to assume a position where the originary critical investigations of the avant-garde would become merely a point of departure for the continuation of production. Neither the subsequent developments nor the inherent consequences of the original paradigms (for example, the transformation of the abstraction of the Soviet avant-garde into Productivist practice) could be taken into account, as they would lead—by necessity—beyond the threshold where the newly acquired positions of the neo-avantgarde artist could be maintained.

This entrenchment, the institutionalization of a rupture that is extracted from an entirely different moment of the history of the discourse, generates an aesthetic surplus value upon which the ultimate success of the neo-avantgarde is based: only as such can it provide models of cultural identity to the reconstructed (or newly instituted) liberal bourgeois audiences of the post–World War II period. Thus in its radical denial, in its refusal to aestheticize the features of the original rupture of the paradigm that have become available through historical reception and repetition (and the wealth of pictorial surplus that comes along with them), Ryman's and Toroni's work has avoided the spectacular conventionalization of their own practice (before the work is inevitably subjected to it by the institutions).

While their painting upholds the radicality of the original modernist negation with an ostentatious simplicity against the extreme refinement that the reductivist pictorial procedures had undergone in the reception of the neo-avantgarde, its radicality has by now become mythical itself. Thus Ryman's and Toroni's work can be read first of all as a critical paraphrase of the reception of the paradigmatic features of modernist painting: monochromy, facture and indexical structure, the compositional grid, and the fallacy of their historical repetition and aestheticization. In its self-imposed limitations to the extreme specificity of modernist reduction, their work encounters, however, a dialectic condition that is different from the problem of its aestheticization: the ineluctable institutionalization of its own practices and paradigms.

To the same degree that it insists on the exclusively painterly means of its practice, Ryman's and Toroni's work (unlike that of Buren) is ultimately subjected to the full impact of an unreflected condition: the discourse of the institutionalization of the neo-avantgarde. Even though it attempts to maintain itself in manifest opposition to that discourse in its emptiness and repetitiveness, its modernist loss of the referent is not resolved—as Bois claims for Ryman—through an "endless sleight of hands, and excess of reflexivity."[22] It attempts in vain to counteract the failure of its signifying practices and to maintain a relationship with a referent by an incessant repetition of that condition that results in the process of a fetishistic substitution.

Modernism's failure to recognize the absence of the referent as its quintessential historical dilemma has thus led to a continuous process of neo-avantgarde substitutions. Each generation increases the necessarily fetishistic nature of that historical disavowal, even when it constitutes itself explicitly—as do Ryman and Toroni—in gestures of a systematic defetishization of the visual. While modernism's original negativity succeeded in abolishing the tendencies of fetishization that were inherently given with the increasing pressure to disavow the loss, and the lack of the referent within its signifying practices, the work of the neo-avantgarde fails to recognize that ultimately the practice of negation has become part of the institutionalized discourse and has therefore become part of the dynamic of fetishization itself.

Notes

An earlier version of this essay was published in *October* 37 (summer 1986): 41–52.

1. Yve-Alain Bois gives us the chronology of the first monochrome paintings in his essay "Malévich, le carré, le degré zéro," *Macula* 1 (Paris, 1978): 28–49.

2. Antoine Pevsner and Naum Gabo, "The Realistic Manifesto," in *The Tradition of Constructivism*, ed. Stephen Bann (New York: Viking Press, 1974), pp. 3–11.

3. Ryman, in Phyllis Tuchman, "An Interview with Robert Ryman," *Artforum* (May, 1971): 46–54. Robert Ryman has argued on several occasions that it is in fact wrong to discuss his work in terms of a history of the monochrome since, as he says, the inherent color values and tones of the changing supports in his work, and the wide range of tonal changes within the color white itself, make him a painter of the color white. While this position is of course correct with regard to his work, it in fact confirms our argument that the achromatic definition of painting's proper constituents (including, if not foregrounding, its supports and framing devices) functions historically as the complementary formation to monochromy itself.

4. Yve-Alain Bois refers to this text from Jean Arp's and El Lissitzky's *Kunstismen* in his essay "Malevich, le carré, le degré zéro," p. 37. The actual text can be found on pp. ix–x of El Lissitzky's and Jean Arp's anthology *Kunstismen* (Munich, 1925; repr. New York: Arno Press, 1968).

5. See Yves Klein, "The Monochrome Adventure," as quoted in Nan Rosenthal's essay "Assisted Levitation: The Art of Yves Klein," in *Yves Klein 1923–1962: A Retrospective* (New York: Guggenheim Museum, 1982), p. 105.

6. Félix Fénéon, as quoted by Paul Signac, *D'Eugène Delacroix au Néo-Impressionisme* (1911) (Paris: Editions Hermann, 1964), p. 148.

7. Clement Greenberg, "Art after Abstract Expressionism," *Art International* 6, no. 8 (1962): 30.

8. Frank Stella, "Lecture at Pratt Institute," in *Frank Stella*, ed. Robert Rosenblum (New York: Penguin Books, 1971), n.p.

9. For an earlier attempt to analyze the condition of contemporary painting as one that operates continuously between photography and the paradigm of the readymade, see my essay "Ready Made, photographie et peinture dans la peinture de Gerhard Richter," in

Gerhard Richter, ed. Daniel Abadie, exh. cat. (Paris: Centre Georges Pompidou, 1977), pp. 11–58. English translation in my *Neo-Aventgarde and Culture Industry* (Cambridge, Mass.: MIT Press, 2000), pp. 365–404. For a later essay on similar questions in the context of the work of Robert Ryman, see Thierry de Duve, "Ryman irréproductible," in *Parachute* (fall 1980): 19ff. Even though I disagree with de Duve in many respects, in particular with his uncritical approach to Greenberg's formalist aesthetics, and his continued commitment to the idea that artistic practice could operate outside of socio-political and ideological interests, de Duve has developed several aspects of the problems that I discuss in this essay, specifically the collision between Greenberg's ideas about painting and those of Johns' or Rauschenberg's which Greenberg had of course ignored or rejected. While de Duve gives a clear observation of the problem—the first that I know of—he nevertheless refrains from drawing any conclusions.

10. Robert Pincus-Witten, "Ryman, Marden, Manzoni," *Artforum* (June 1972): 52.

11. Rosenthal, "Assisted Levitation," p. 107.

12. Evidence for this generational relationship and the importance of the mediating figures Rauschenberg and Johns is ample. See, for example, Frank Stella's comments on the influence of Rauschenberg's monochromatic paintings on his *Black Paintings*, as discussed by Brenda Richardson:

> Further, Stella did not think of these paintings as black and white, but only as black (what he felt to be a neutral non-color). Although he had not seen them at the time, he says he was influenced by descriptions of Rauschenberg's all black paintings more than by the black and white works of his abstract-expressionist predecessors.

See Brenda Richardson, *Frank Stella: The Black Paintings* (Baltimore: Baltimore Museum of Art, 1976), p. 3.

13. Bois, "Malévich," p. 37.

14. Published in *Russian Art of the Avant-Garde: Theory and Criticism, 1902–1934*, ed. John E. Bowlt (New York: Viking Press, 1976), pp. 146ff. For another systematic investigation of the phenomenon of texture or facture in the twentieth century that is actually theorized as well as practiced, see Lyubov Popova's diagram that distinguishes painting from "the depiction of reality" and argues that "texture is the content of painterly surfaces" (ibid.).

15. Michael Fried, *Three American Painters* (Cambridge, Mass.: Fogg Art Museum, 1965), p. 37.

16. Thierry de Duve, apparently unaware of the comparable passage in Fried's essay, quotes Rosenberg's observations from his text "Time in the Museum," reprinted in *Artworks and Passages* (New York, 1971), p. 105. See de Duve, "Ryman irréproductible," p. 27.

17. Rosalind Krauss was of course the first to apply Charles Sanders Peirce's semiotic terminology, which systematically differentiates the visual signs of index, icon, and symbol to the work of Duchamp and others. She developed in particular an analysis of the shift from the iconic qualities of drawing to the indexical qualities of the trace or the material procedure, approaching the equivalent of the photographic image and the condition of the readymade. See Rosalind Krauss, "Notes on the Index: Parts 1 and 2," in *The Originality of the Avant-Garde and Other Modernist Myths* (Cambridge, Mass.: MIT Press, 1985), pp. 196–210.

18. It is ironic that Fried's extremely pertinent observation—that the Cubist pictorial analysis had essentially taken place in the oval center field of the painting's rectangle—did not propel him to look into the immediate consequences of Cubism, where precisely this problem was addressed. Instead of recognizing the changes that Delauney's, Mondrian's, and Malevich's works introduce in 1915, he credits Frank Stella as having been the first to have resolved a problem, that—in his view—Mondrian had only tentatively approached: to integrate the four corners of the painting into the process of analyzing the center of pictorial planarity, and to conceive of an exact reciprocal correlation between support surface and figure. Limitations of space prohibit me from arguing further on behalf of the extraordinary and exemplary proposition inherent in Delauney's *First Disk*. But if further evidence were needed to corroborate my perhaps at first slightly surprising argument, one has only to contemplate Stella's own subsequent development, which leads straight to the tondos of randomly mapped chromatic segments.

19. In a first step, Duchamp's *Trois Stoppages Étalons (Three Standard Stoppages)* had transplanted the segregated and faceted pictorial planes of Cubism into the tactile stability of a literalist three-dimensional relief space. As though this were not radical enough, Duchamp then proceeded to redefine these pictorial segments and invest them with a processual, a temporal, and a kinesthetic dimension, identifying materials and procedures, the existing determining forces of physicality (i.e., gravity) and the work's traditionally hidden presentational devices (e.g., the pictorial frame and the sculptural base) as the key elements that define aesthetic decisions and spectatorial experience in a latent if not repressed manner. Rodchenko's stereometric hanging constructions from 1920–21 introduce these factors (and their transparent segregation) into the domain of post-Cubist relief construction in a similar fashion. If the comparison between the two works might appear odd at first glance, one has only to point to the one aspect in Rodchenko's work that is often overlooked: the fact that the concentric stereometric sculptures were intended to be folded and put into storage after exhibition, and to be reopened or unfolded for subsequent display purposes. Thus sculpture was defined for the first time by a differentiation or alternation of exhibition mode and storage mode. This performative quality of Rodchenko's work is clearly related to the performative quality in Duchamp's elaborate display and storage system in the *Three Standard Stoppages*.

20. See Rosalind Krauss' essay "The Originality of the Avant-Garde," as well as her earlier essay on the subject, "Grids," both in her *The Originality of the Avant-Garde and Other Modernist Myths*, pp. 151–170 and pp. 9–22, respectively. See also John Elderfield's earlier approach to the complex problem of grid-structures in the twentieth century in his essay "Grids," *Artforum* 10 (May 1972).

21. Thierry de Duve, "Ryman," p. 26 (my translation).

22. Yve-Alain Bois, "Ryman's Tact," *October* 19 (winter 1981): 93–104.

9

Cold War Constructivism

> America is the bearer of a new civilization, whose task is simultaneously to cultivate and industrialize a continent. It is the ideal ground on which to work out an educational principle which strives for the closest connection between art, science, and technology.
>
> —*László Moholy-Nagy, The New Vision (1938)*

Between the *Triumph of the Will* in 1936, and the *Triumph of American Painting* in 1958 (the year of the European tour of *The New American Painting*), art history also witnessed a number of relative failures. One such case was the failure of geometric reductivist abstraction—in particular, Russian and Soviet Constructivism—to reenter Western European and American reception in the post–World War II period. In this essay, the exemplary subject is the artist Naum Gabo (a member of the historic avant-garde) and his fate within the discursive, institutional, and economic spaces of the newly established, thriving postwar culture—the neo-avantgarde.[1]

The problematic reception in 1948 of Constructivism and Gabo's transition from avant-garde to neo-avantgarde artist raises two questions: First, what personal, aesthetic adjustments and what historical, political adaptations were required of Gabo? Second, what determined the critical reception of Gabo's work, inside the history of postwar culture, for example, by one of the major critics of the American neo-avantgarde, Clement Greenberg? What maneuvers was Greenberg obliged to perform, initially to accommodate Gabo's work, only to subsequently exclude it from integration into the critical, institutional, and aesthetic framework of the 1950s?

Naum Gabo left Moscow in 1922 for Berlin. In the early 1930s, after a brief stay in Paris, he fled the German Nazis to settle in England, where he remained until his departure, in 1946, for the United States. Why he left England then remains unclear; after all, this was the country he later frequently called his "real home." He had a firmly established circle of friends there, many of whom occupied increasingly powerful positions. Further, Gabo's apparently unproblematic continuation of the prewar tradition of geometric abstraction had found at that time more credibility and critical support in the British Isles than anywhere else in Europe.

Gabo, the artist, emerged from the history of Soviet Constructivism just when the type of reductivist geometric sculpture was about to lose all credibility in the United States. Gabo, the citizen, arrived in New York just when any association with the Soviet Union had become increasingly suspect, and definitely a liability, given the American climate of vindictive anti-Stalinism and aggressive anti-Communism.

In fact, a typical strategy during this period was to decry the threat of Communism by pointing to the cultural aberration in Soviet art and architecture, exemplified by Socialist Realism. Thus in 1948, in his essay "Irrelevance versus Irresponsibility," Clement Greenberg wrote,

> The truly new horror of our times is not, perhaps, totalitarianism as such, but the vulgarity it is able to install in places of power—the official vulgarity, the certified vulgarity.[2]

Similarly, in the first major American art magazine article on Gabo, Serge Chermayeff (then director of the New Bauhaus, Chicago, and later of the Institute for Design) presented Gabo by juxtaposing his work with several pages of Socialist Realist painting.[3]

By contrast, Gabo's own attitude had not at all been that of the fervent anti-Communist he would soon become after his arrival in the United States. Only four years earlier, in a rather obscure journal *World Review*, published in London, and dedicated to contemporary Soviet politics and culture, Gabo had written:

> Many students of Russian art are inclined to wonder whether that art, in its contemporary phase, does really represent the genuine spirit of Russia, and whether it is not annihilated by the imposition of the leading ideology of the government party. … Their main argument can be summarized thus: Russian art is no longer the free expression of a free artistic mind; it is supervised by a very strict and dogmatic tendency; it is no longer interested in that free development of all sorts of experiments which is so necessary to the progress of a creative mind; any possible advance is held back by the attempt to keep art on the level of the masses, whereas it should be just the other way round. Such arguments, plausible as they may sound to the layman, are fundamentally misplaced. … But there was and is another very important side to the Russian attitude towards art: that to the Russian mind, art represents a social phenomenon, first and foremost; it is the expression of a collective event, and the work is valued mostly from the point of view of its social utility. It is, and

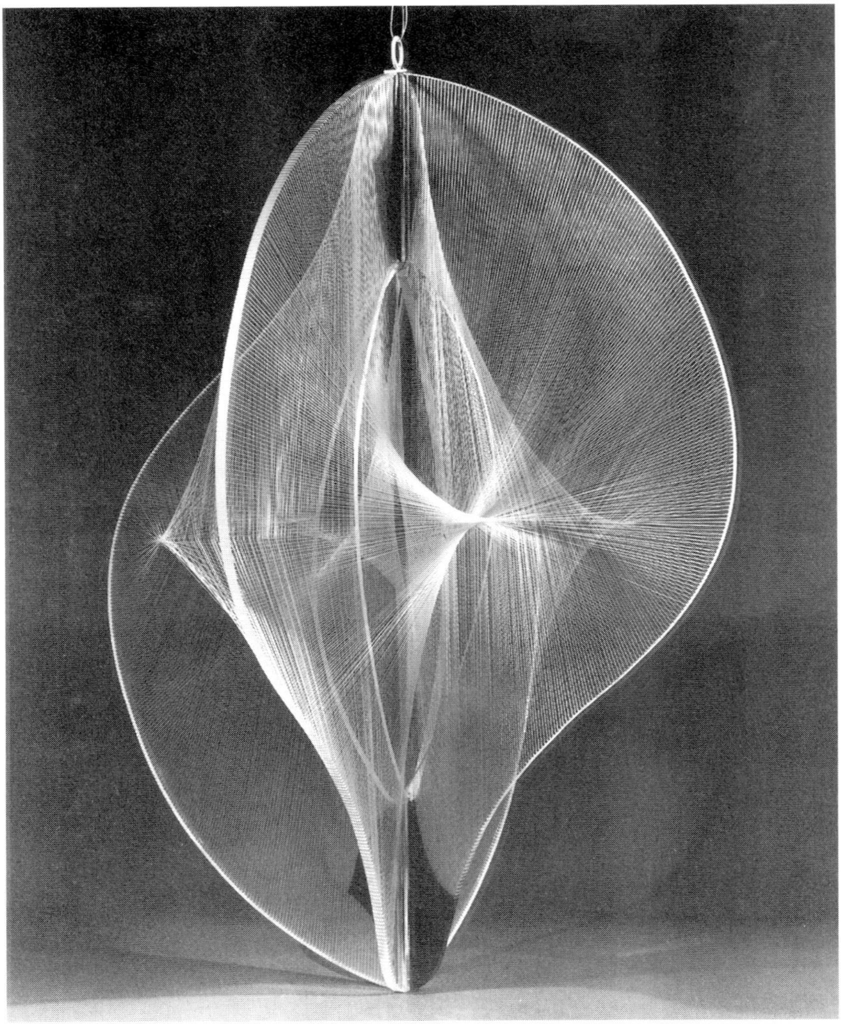

Naum Gabo, *Linear Construction in Space No. 2* (1949/1972–73). Perspex with nylon monofilament, 36¼ in. (92 cm) high. Tate, London. © Nina and Graham Williams/ Tate, London, 2015.

> was, valued almost entirely in so far as it accomplishes an obvious social function for the use of all and not merely a few privileged ones.
>
> This stream of naturalistic art, with an emphatically social theme, is flowing now broad and deep in Russian art, and it is entirely irrelevant whether that art is, at the present stage, of high or low quality, from the point of view of refined Western technique. … It is true that, at the moment, the constructive movement is not encouraged in the Soviet Union, but this may be an inevitable and, to a certain extent, understandable phase of transition, which need not alarm any artistic mind. One has to bear in mind that for more than twenty years, the Soviet Union has been developing itself under potential wartime conditions. The abstract movement is still in the process of growth and has not yet found its full application in the life of the masses. It has, nevertheless, slowly penetrated, and is continuing to do so, in the shaping of the edifice of the New Union. In due course and through these demands, it will also find its way into the emotions and aesthetic demands of the masses.[4]

These sentences are as surprising as they will remain rare. While there is no shortage of ideological justifications for Socialist Realism in the Eastern/Western European debates of the 1930s and 1940s, one would not easily find such a position affirmed among Soviet emigrés. Most astonishingly, Gabo's position recognized the complicated dialectical relationship between progressive modernist geometrical abstraction and reactionary neoclassicist figurative Socialist Realism. Further, it dared to consider the historical reality of Socialist Realism as a necessary transition stage in a long process of cultural consciousness-raising and political education among the masses. Most provocatively, Gabo's attitude courageously argued that this phenomenon might be partially dependent on the precarious conditions inflicted on the new state by external military threats—at first from German Fascism and later from American Cold War anti-Communism.

For Socialist Realism to appear sufficiently horrifying after 1945, Western European and American intellectuals had to argue that after 1922 party politics made it impossible to work in any other mode, unless an artist were willing to face deportation, imprisonment, or death. After his arrival in the United States, Gabo became one of art history's key eyewitnesses to ascertain these accounts. Along with his brother, Antoine Pevsner, he would soon deliver a version of that moment in Constructivist history that would be endlessly repeated, almost *verbatim*, in identical terms, by scholars such as Herbert Read, George Heard Hamilton, Andrew Carnduff Ritchie, Eduard Trier, Robert Goldwater, and many others, from the early 1950s into the late 1970s. The "master statement," issued in 1949 by Gabo himself, read as follows:

> At the end of the Civil War, they (i.e., the Party) took over cultural affairs and were given the job of drawing up our programmes. It only took them a few years to liquidate everything alive in art. They closed the School and brought in new teachers. … The Party's hostility soon became very disturbing. We were attacked from all sides and no longer had the right to reply. To do so would have meant prison. Our only remaining choice was exile.[5]

It is now understood that this particular period of artistic transformation was occasioned by an internal artistic debate, which, among other consequences, led to Gabo's and Pevsner's departure from the Wchutemas (of which Gabo was never an officially appointed faculty member, although he shared a studio and periodically gave seminars). While apparently rabid and unrelenting, this debate certainly did not involve Party officials, but rather included artists like Malevich, who insisted on the departure of Kandinsky and Chagall, and like Rodchenko, who forced out into the open conflicts between the Productivist program and the increasingly aestheticized Constructivist practices of Gabo and Pevsner.[6]

It seems reasonable, for example, to assume that El Lissitzky was addressing, among others, the work of Gabo and Pevsner in his essay on "The New Russian Art" when he wrote:

> *And finally, the materials were imbued with a symbolic meaning: iron stood for the willpower of the proletariat, glass was as clear and pure as its consciousness.* Thus, a new sculptural body had been constructed, but it was not at all a machine; it did not perform any work and did not serve any utilitarian function. But this art still had one merit, in that it ruptured the old conception of art. Thus, the process of transcending the institution of art altogether began. … The position of the artist in the world was changed: the materials of his profession became more varied; new conditions of reception emerged. Nevertheless, the artists still moved on the same old orbit. The merit of Tatlin and his colleagues consisted of the fact of having acquainted artists with actual space and contemporary materials. … *But this group ended up in a kind of fetishism of materials and forgot the necessity of a new plan.*[7]

In contrast to the extremely well-informed scholars and general audiences of the prewar period,[8] it appears that the European and American public of the immediate postwar years was completely ignorant of that aspect of Russian and Soviet avant-garde history and its critical debates, and these readers and spectators would remain so for at least another twenty years. The work of the most important Soviet artists (and the corresponding concepts of writers and theoreticians) would be censored from reception by those who actually witnessed the transformation from Constructivism to Productivism and who had emigrated to the West, like Gabo, Pevsner, and Kandinsky. From then on, that history would be simply disavowed by these witnesses and ignored by historians and critics who were determined to write the history of twentieth-century art according to the biased accounts provided by these witnesses.

In his classic 1967 study *Painting and Sculpture in Europe, 1880–1940*, George Heard Hamilton not only repeats once again Gabo's account, but he also seems to candidly identify its tilted perspective:

> As Malevich's influence declined, the task of opposing the materialistic direction of Tatlin's and Rodchenko's teaching fell to two artists, Naum Gabo (1890–1977) and his elder brother Anton Pevsner (1886–1962). … Long after they had left Russia, where Socialist Realism had become the dominant Soviet aesthetic, Gabo and Pevsner, through their work and activity in Western Europe and America, maintained the tradition of Russian abstract design. It is only an historical accident that their mode of expression … has since been known as "Constructivist" and was eventually so accepted by the artists themselves. The latter term properly should be identified with a social and political point of view which would grant the artist none of the autonomy, and the work of art none of the spiritual primacy, which they have demanded.[9]

The strategies for such a reorganization of the history of Constructivism now seem obvious: first of all, it was necessary to disinherit the actual historical participants, and to deny the development of the movement; then, to erase its commitment to mass audiences and ignore its utilitarian dimensions; and finally, to reorient it toward European and American concepts of artistic autonomy and modernism.

To achieve the first task of successfully disregarding those artists who, in fact, had actually developed Constructivism, it was crucial to establish oneself as the movement's originator and leader: Gabo and Pevsner both dedicated themselves with considerable eagerness to the dissemination of this myth. In a 1947 article in the Waterbury *Sunday Republican* of Gabo's new Connecticut hometown, the artist was already describing himself as the "founder and leader of the Constructivist school."[10] Or, as the *New Yorker* critic Robert Coates phrased his version of the same testimony, presumably freshly received from the witness: "In fact, since the death, a while ago, of their great co-peer Moholy-Nagy, they [Gabo and Pevsner] just about are the Constructivist movement."[11] It should be remembered that at this time Tatlin, Rodchenko, Stepanova, Melnikov, and two of the Vesnin brothers were still alive and working in Moscow (El Lissitzky had died in 1941).

The most astounding reconstruction of Constructivist history, however, was delivered by Pevsner in an interview with Rosamond Bernier for the French journal *L'Oeil*. She introduced her article with the formula that by now had become standard: "The founders of the Constructivist movement, Antoine Pevsner and his brother Naum Gabo, were forced, by the political events, to leave their country." She then proceeded to ask Pevsner about the other Constructivist artists in the group, and he replied:

> There were no others. I repeat it again and again: it was only Gabo and myself who invented Constructivism. Tatlin and Rodchenko picked up our ideas, but they falsified them by applying them to a functional art that was subjected to serve practical purposes. By contrast, we have always declared … that we were partisans of pure art, of *l'art pour l'art*.[12]

For Gabo and Pevsner, this was the very moment in which they could secure for themselves the mythical role as originators of Constructivism,

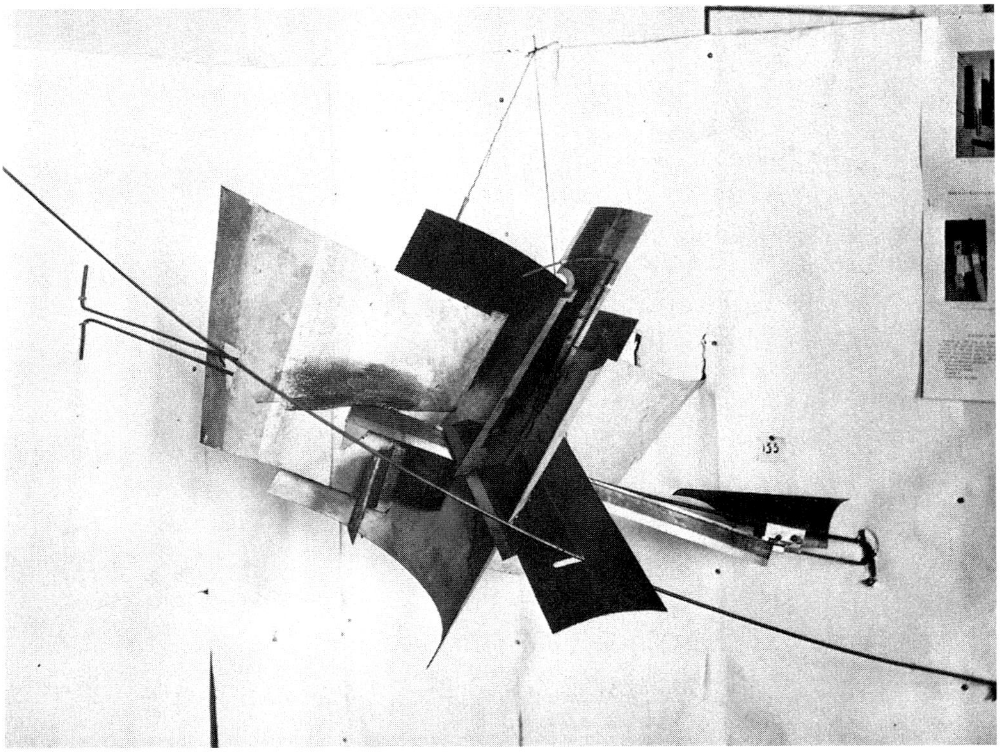

Vladimir Tatlin, *Corner Counter-Relief*, 1915. Iron, aluminum, and primer. Photographed at the 0.10 exhibition, December 1915–January 1916. The original work is lost. Photo: State Film, Photographic and Sound Archive, Leningrad.

and to block the reception of Russian and Soviet Constructivism for postwar audiences. These Western European and American audiences were as eager to reconstruct the institution of modernist high culture as they were anxious to depoliticize the heroic tradition of its opponents—the *historical* avant-garde of the 1915–1925 period. However, that avant-garde tradition had to be reinstituted in such a way that it would supply the radical aesthetic goods without any of the political strings originally attached to the work of the Constructivists, especially to that of their Productivist followers. This unlikely synthesis of contradictory needs could be performed successfully only under the guise of a complete abstraction of the Constructivist avant-garde's artistic practices (here, artistic practices would include their *aesthetic* commitment, as well as their *social* and *political* involvements). Gabo and Pevsner performed these abstractions by fusing irreconcilable contradictions in their work, and they were adequately rewarded: soon they would be considered as the first, the *true*, and the only "Russian Constructivist" artists, and their work would actually dominate all art historical accounts and sculptural histories of the 1950s and 1960s.

In addition they provided the ideological argument to legitimize this blatant falsification of the Constructivist project. Typically, Gabo wrote:

> My art is generally recognized as the art of Constructivism. But the word "constructivism" was also claimed in the 1920s by a group of "constructive" artists that actually wanted to liquidate art. … They requested that the artist should devote his life to the construction of material goods. … My friends and I opposed this conception. … I believe, by contrast, that art is an elementary, real part of human life, the most immediate and effective means of communication among the members of human society.[13]

The final task, then—the conventionalization of the avant-garde and its reorientation toward the autonomy concept of modernism—was accomplished through a renewed commitment to an anti-materialist, anti-utilitarian notion of art, evident here in the abstract universality of art as "a means of human communication."

Thus, the antimodernist assault on the presumably autonomous status of art (mounted, and, in many instances, successfully achieved by the Constructivist and Productivist aesthetic of the Soviet avant-garde) was refuted. This reconstruction necessarily erased those voices which, since the1920s, had clearly criticized the inherent conceptual limitations of the modernist legacy and the type of Constructivist sculpture produced by artists like Gabo and Pevsner. It is to these voices that Gabo refers with a typical Cold War term, calling them the "liquidators" of art.

As early as 1926, the Productivist theoretician Boris Arvatov had attacked that very notion of a self-sufficient purity Gabo now attempted to resuscitate in 1948:

> While the totality of capitalist technology is based on the highest and latest achievements and represents a technique of mass production (industry, radio, transport, newspaper, scientific laboratory), bourgeois art, in principle, has remained on the level of individual crafts, and therefore has been isolated increasingly from the collective social practice of mankind, and has entered the realm of pure aesthetics. ... The lonely master is the only type in capitalist society—the type of specialist of "pure art"—who can work outside of an immediately utilitarian practice, because his work is not based on machine technology. From here originates the total illusion of art's purposelessness and autonomy, from here art's bourgeois fetishistic nature.[14]

While there is no certainty that this statement by Arvatov and similar ones by El Lissitzky were written with specific reference to Gabo and Pevsner, both identify the problem of the *fetishism* of so-called Constructivist materials, and this problem is pivotal for any reconsideration of their work. El Lissitzky had been among the first artists to understand that the concept of autonomy in modernism was particularly problematic: it stood in manifest contradiction to the assertion that the work would simultaneously provide an experience of formal, material, and structural radicality, and, thereby, anticipate and implement social and political "progress."

One of the key concerns of the Constructivists and the Productivists had been precisely the disentanglement of their practice from this mythology. Further, they attempted to develop strategies and production procedures that would concretize their aesthetic and political commitments, according to the original implications of the modernist critique: they sought to activate and expand its audience, to abolish the work's cult and exhibition value, to deny its falsely auratic status, and, most importantly, to actually develop new strategies that would gradually anchor aesthetic practice to the social and political reality of the new mass-audiences.

El Lissitzky's statement reveals his foresight about Constructivism's eventual transgression of modernism's aesthetic limits: he foresaw that it would, at that point, inevitably cling to a mythology which claimed that new materials and production procedures had inherent progressive values. However, such materials and procedures originally had been developed as *functional* strategies, intended to dismantle governing aesthetic preconceptions, rather than to carry perceptual or actual value and meaning, *qua material* or *qua process*.

It must be remembered that the Constructivist commitment to industrial materials in sculpture originated both from an emphatic, Futurist embrace of industrial mass-culture, and from an anti-aesthetic impulse that insisted on the work's contingency and ephemerality.

Opposed to traditional emphasis on sculpture's presumed universal validity and static perpetuity, this new type of sculpture underlined temporal, functional, and dynamic qualities (see, for example, El Lissitzky's 1920 design for a *Tribune for Lenin*). The work of Gabo and Pevsner (and most of Moholy-Nagy's) fulfilled the worst expectations about the fetishization of materials and process that El Lissitzky and Arvatov had anticipated. In fact, this "Perspex School of Constructivism" pretended that the contradictions within the modernist aesthetic could be resolved, at least superficially, through the use of new technological materials (celluloid, perspex, nylon, wire, chrome, steel), in whose inherent aesthetic qualities they firmly believed. However, it is on the level of materials that their sculpture acquired its mythological qualities in the first place: to its postwar audience, these qualities signaled the perfect fusion of their apparent devotion to scientific and technological progress, on the one hand, and, on the other, "spiritual autonomy" and "exquisite abstract beauty," as the English critics put it.

During the reconstruction period, the dominant notion of industrial progress refused to address any of the social, economic, and political questions posited by the Constructivists. Further, such works had appeal because this fetishization process was so ideally suited to disembody the actual Constructivist sculptural practices and to make the new techno sculpture appear truly progressive: it embraced technology and industrial production, providing new high-culture icons, for both the collective adaptation to industrial consumption and the incumbent industrialization of culture itself.

Paradoxically, we learn that as late as 1936—in apparent contradiction to their postwar commitment to pure, autonomous spirituality—Gabo and Pevsner were perceived as potential builders for monumental, utilitarian architecture. Here, for example, is Alfred Barr's (presumably) unintentionally comic statement:

> Pevsner is more powerful, more intellectual in his approach and more inclined to force his materials so that … his constructions take on superficially something of the character of sculpture, while Gabo's are more in the spirit of architecture. Some of Gabo's constructions have, in fact, been projects for semi-architectural monuments, but it is his pupil Lubetkin, and not himself, who has had the privilege of designing the Constructivist Penguin Pond for the London Zoo.[15]

And even after the war, some of these architectural visions materialized, albeit—as was the case with the Penguin Pond—in somewhat different contexts and for unexpectedly different patrons. The promotional text for the publication of Gabo's A. W. Mellon lectures (delivered in 1959, published in 1962), stated:

> Among his most famous works are *Construction Suspended in Space* (Baltimore Museum of Art); a constructed relief in the U.S. Rubber Co. Building, Rockefeller Center, New York; and a free-standing 85-foot construction in Rotterdam, Netherlands (for the department store De Bijenkorf).[16]

To accomplish this complex ideological mission, on the level of formal and structural definition, all of the specific features of Constructivist sculpture had to be mythified. Transparency of construction and transparency of the sculptural body had been among the essential strategies in the works of Kobro, Medunetsky, Ioganson, Rodchenko, and the Stenberg brothers. These strategies had originally increased the spectator's awareness of the sculptural construct as being temporary and transient, and had pointed to the utilitarian potential of the object. This emphasis on its constructed nature, and its continuous transformation resulting from the collective social production process (the *Machbarkeit*, as Bertolt Brecht would call it), equally emphasized its participatory

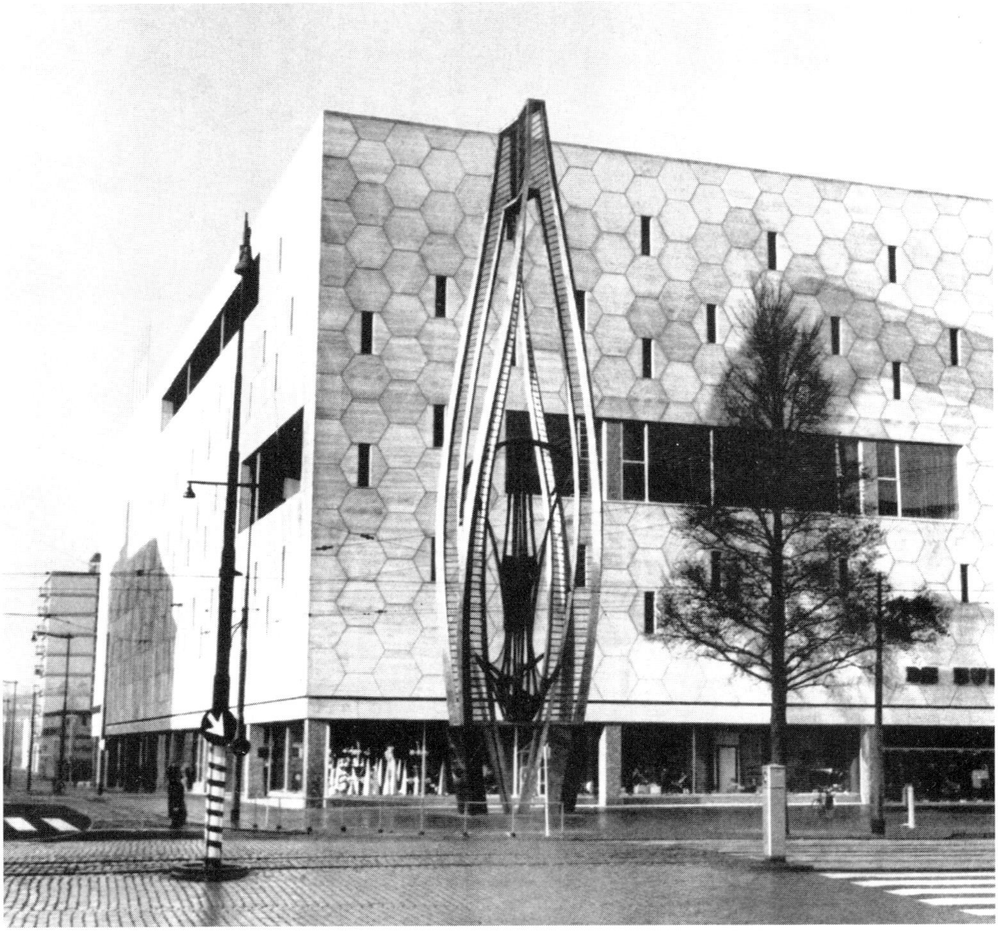

Naum Gabo, *De Bijenkorf Sculpture*, 1958. Rotterdam, De Bijenkorf Department Store. © Nina and Graham Williams.

dimension and contextual contiguity. At the same time, construction and transparency abolished the contemplative mode, in favor of a new tactility, a mode of activating its spectators, as Walter Benjamin would describe it.

By contrast, with Gabo and Pevsner, as well as with Moholy-Nagy, transparency had acquired a "purely visual" value. This is, for example, evident in one of Moholy-Nagy's statements on the subject of materials:

> This composition demonstrates three types: transparent walls, circumscribed by the thick edges of the plastic or wire. One is moderately transparent (rhodoid), the second perfectly transparent (plexiglass), and the third supertransparent (air).[17]

The second, equally important paradigmatic feature of Constructivist sculpture had been the foregrounding of inherent physical forces, which determined the structure and position of the sculptural construct. In Gabo's and Pevsner's postwar work, gravity, weight, and tension were aestheticized as stylistic devices, generating the advanced techno-scientistic appearance of the gadget, while no longer performing any of the functional tasks demonstrated by the wire in Tatlin's work or the collapsible, serial, volumetric elements in Rodchenko's *Hanging Constructions*.

The third and final question concerns materials. In many of Gabo's postwar works (and in almost all of Pevsner's work of that period), there is a partial or complete return to the traditional medium of bronze. This decision categorically rejects all of the artists' earlier claims associated with the new materiality of Constructivist sculpture, as they had initially voiced them in their *Realistic Manifesto*. This programmatic falsification of Constructivist thought is best indicated by the discrepancy between the structural and material elements in Gabo's *Bijenkorf* sculpture (1958): it sits on its black marble base, with its bronze-wire network faking tension and structural function. Clearly, it had to be an impossible historical task to simultaneously *maintain* the Constructivist legacy and *withdraw* from its integral program of a materialist and socialist art production into an emphatic renewal of a completely abstracted art practice, insisting on its pure spirituality and transcendental beauty aimed at buttressing the newly reaffirmed Western consumer cultures. And these contradictions were of course heightened further by attempting to position such work in the public sphere, in the guise of newly conceived monumental sculpture, without having analyzed the conditions of Western economic and political reality and the needs of its audiences. Thus there was no consideration at all of the audiences for whom sculpture would be produced nor for its situation in public space: these issues were totally excluded from the concerns of the artists, and, most certainly, from those of the new patrons of public sculpture—state agencies or corporate enterprises.

Obviously then, Gabo's and Pevsner's art production had detached itself systematically from all questions of concrete specificity, regardless of whether these were questions of production, concerning the discursive and institutional conditions of practice, or of reception, addressing the relationships of a work to both its presumed and actual audiences and to the cultural, political, and economic conditions determining that audience.

Paradoxically, it was precisely this reorientation toward a modernist autonomy that placed Gabo dangerously close to that tradition of abstract art, particularly the European Abstraction-Création and Cercle et Carré and the American Abstract Artists group, which was just about to be displaced by the much-heralded emergence of the New York School aesthetic. As early as 1936, Alfred Barr had concluded his brief (but epochal) study *Cubism and Abstract Art* with these rather astonishing remarks:

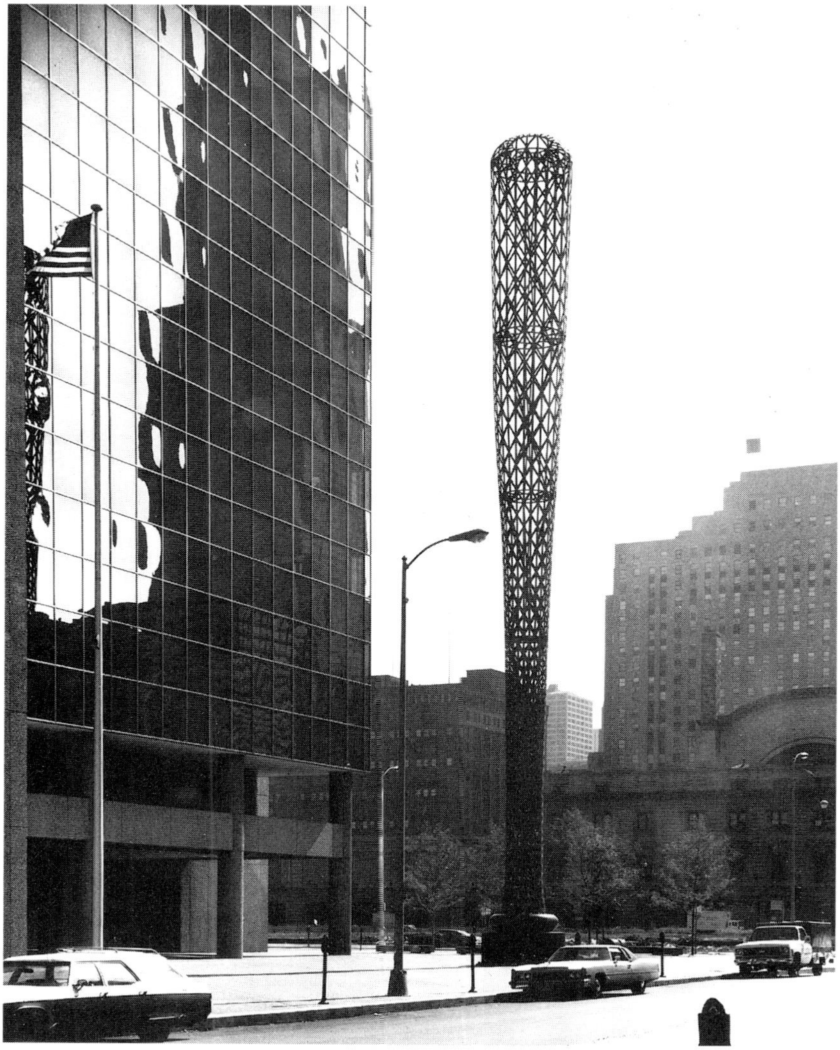

Claes Oldenburg and Coosje van Bruggen, *Batcolumn*, 1977. Steel and aluminum painted with polyurethane enamel, 96 ft., 8 in. (29.5 m) high × 9 ft., 9 in. (3.0 m) diameter, on base 4 ft. (1.2 m) high × 10 ft. (3.1 m) diameter. Collection Harold Washington Social Security Center, 600 West Madison Street, Chicago. Courtesy the artist and Paula Cooper Gallery, New York. © 1977 Claes Oldenburg and Coosje van Bruggen.

> At the risk of generalizing about the very recent past, it seems fairly clear that the geometric tradition in abstract art … is in the decline. … The non-geometric biomorphic forms of Arp and Miro and Moore are definitely in the ascendant. The formal tradition of Gauguin, Fauvism and Expressionism will probably dominate, for some time to come, the tradition of Cézanne and Cubism.[18]

Just when the geometric reductivist and supposedly "European" legacy was about to be displaced by the emergence of Abstract Expressionism, Robert Goldwater, another pivotal figure of this period, described the same attitude in his "Art Chronicle" of July 1947:

> Here, in art, as elsewhere, this country has a more important international burden to carry. … There is a growing inclination to shy away from what is, by now, due to long exposure, our easy acceptance of the compositional and technical virtuosity of pure abstraction, to embrace an art in which emotion has not been subjugated, and uncontrolled feeling breaks through the boundaries of the medium. One tends to say "So what" to the beautifully mastered forms of abstraction. … This is the effect produced by so many members of the American Abstract Artists group.[19]

To complicate matters even further, Gabo had to define his own position from this point on with explicit reference to the actual "threat" (as he surely perceived it) posed by the "deep irrationality and collective politics" of the Surrealist aesthetic, which increasingly dominated the New York sensibility in the late 1940s. Accordingly, Gabo deemed it necessary to voice his critique of the political potential of Surrealism, already withering in its New York School incarnation. In a *New Yorker* piece of 1948, Gabo wrote:

> I don't believe in trusting the subconscious. I don't care for the transitional acceptance of the crowd either. Artists are done for, if they go in for effects that attract the man in the street.[20]

Once again Gabo had to realign himself and stake out his territory, and once again he was forced to redefine his position in manifest contradiction to those positions he had espoused until that very point. Now, it was no longer a question of his past membership in the Soviet avant-garde, when (as *Time Magazine* put it in 1953), he was "still the darling of the Bolsheviks." Rather, it was his more recent involvement with the relatively progressive Socialist circle in London, grouped around Herbert Read in the late 1930s, that created difficulties for him. While the presence of Surrealism had made itself felt in London as well, the conflicting aesthetic positions had appeared more balanced during that period, and Gabo had been able to fend off comfortably any critical accusations that might have been leveled against his work. For example, when questioned in 1936 by the so-called "theorists of art" as to whether his work was too rational, ignoring the power and value of imagination and free-ranging fantasy (as Gabo put it, whether "our works lack the mythical element"),[21] he could still reply with references to the architectonic and social dimension of art. Or, as he wrote one year later, in 1937:

> The constructive idea has given back to sculpture its old forms and faculties, the most powerful of which is its capacity to act architectonically. … By architecture I mean not only the building of houses, but the whole edifice of our everyday existence.[22]

But as we have already seen, shortly after his arrival in New York, this collective dimension had to be obliterated. An interview with the curator of his first retrospective exhibition (a joint exhibition, in 1948, with Pevsner) at the Museum of Modern Art suggests that the social and architectural dimension by that time had already been erased from his memory: "In 1923, in Germany, my work hovered on the verge of architecture. But now, it is more mature, self-sufficient, or pure art."[23]

In 1948, however, the New York situation was by no means as homogeneous and unified as it would soon be portrayed: the various arguments lodged against the legacy of academicized abstract-geometric art, and for the Surrealist liberation were not easily reconciled. These contradictions are most evident in the positions voiced by yet another critic, Clement Greenberg, who at that time was still quite far from being the unequivocal champion and spokesman of Abstract Expressionism he would soon become. His description of the conflicts and paradoxes with which the Americanized Constructivist Gabo was confronted appears to be the most accurate. In "The Situation at the Moment" Greenberg assured us that

> when it comes to the Zeitgeist we Americans are the most advanced people on earth, if only because we are the most industrialized. … After all, the easel painting is on its way out; abstract pictures rarely go with the furniture, and the canvas, even when it measures ten feet by ten, has become a kind of a private journal. … Perhaps the contradiction between the architectural destination of abstract art and the very, very private atmosphere in which it is produced, will kill ambitious painting in the end. As it is, this contradiction, which lies outside of the autonomy of art, defines specifically the crisis in which painting now finds itself.[24]

Surprising as it may be, this article makes one speculate whether, at least for a short period, Greenberg's position was approximating that of the original Constructivists. Thus, for example, when he mentions "the architectural destination of abstract art," the statement seems to echo El Lissitzky's famous comment that he considered his *Proun* paintings as "transit stations between painting and architecture."

In a more explicit essay published later that year, Greenberg drew even more astonishing conclusions, based on his diagnosis of the end of abstract art in the late 1930s. In distinct opposition to his subsequent beliefs, Greenberg all but declared the end of painting in his essay "The New Sculpture":

> I do not mean to suggest that painting will soon decline as an art. … What is to be pointed out is that painting's place as the supreme visual art is now threatened, whether it is in decline or not. And I want also to call attention to sculpture, an art that has been in relative desuetude for several centuries but which has lately undergone a transformation that seems to endow it with a greater range of expression for modern sensibility than painting now has. This transformation, or revolution, is a product of Cubism.[25]

In this statement, Greenberg foresaw a future for post-Cubist art which was in fact totally opposed to Barr's prognosis: he argued that the logical evolution of Cubism would inevitably lead into three-dimensional spatial, sculptural, and (probably) architectural constructs. However, even more astonishing is Greenberg's historical awareness: when he traced the historical lineage of the new sculpture, Greenberg did not hesitate to name Dadaists (like Schwitters or Arp) or Constructivists (like Tatlin, Gabo, or Pevsner), all of whom would soon disappear from his memory. In fact, this amnesia would become so complete that, when asked why the references to Dadaism and Constructivism had all but vanished from his later argument, Greenberg simply replied that he did not think about it because he had not seen enough of it.[26]

In 1948, however, Greenberg could still remember:

> Thence the new sculpture grew through the bas-relief constructions that Picasso and then Arp and Schwitters created by raising the collage above the picture plane; and from there Picasso … along with the Russian Constructivists Tatlin, Pevsner and Gabo … at last delivered it into the positive truth of free space, altogether away from the picture plane.[27]

What could Greenberg possibly have meant when he spoke about "the positive truth of free space altogether away from the picture plane"? This is a conceptual and perceptual condition apparently profoundly at odds with the foundations of Greenberg's later, neo-modernist aesthetic, with its notorious emphasis on flatness and opticality. To clarify this question, we must read further:

> This new, pictorial, draftsman's sculpture has more or less abandoned the traditional materials of stone and bronze in favor of ones more flexible under such modern tools as the oxyacetylene torch: steel, iron, alloys, glass, plastics. It has no regard for the unity of its physical medium and will use any number of different materials in the same work and any variety of applied colors—as befits an art that sees in its products almost as much that is pictorial as is sculptural.[28]

While the first statement addresses the new sculpture's historical lineage, the second speaks to its production aesthetic. But a few paragraphs later, there is a third important statement dealing with the reception aesthetic of the new sculpture, defining the requisite cognitive and perceptual conditions of the audience, which justify the structure and morphology of this new work:

> Sculpture has always been able to create objects that seem to have a denser, more literal reality than those created by

> painting; this, which used to be its handicap, now constitutes its greater appeal to our newfangled, positivist sensibility, and this also gives it its greater license. It is now free to invent an infinity of new objects and disposes of a potential wealth of forms with which our taste cannot quarrel in principle, since they will all have their self-evident physical reality, as palpable and independent and present as the houses we live in and the furniture we use.[29]

But, of course, this is not the Clement Greenberg most of us would encounter, in 1961, in *Art and Culture*, the widely disseminated first collection of his essays. While the essay "The New Sculpture" was included in this collection, it carried two dates (1948 and 1958), indicating that it had been extensively rewritten in the intervening decade.

Obviously, to forge a new aesthetic of reconstruction, Greenberg had to make several elisions, adaptations had to be made within the text, and outside of it in actual history where former participants and criteria would now have to be erased and eliminated. The 1958 revised version of the passages just quoted reads:

> The new construction sculpture points back, almost insistently, to its origins in Cubist painting: by its linearism and linear intricacies, by its openness and transparency and weightlessness, and by its preoccupation with surface and skin alone, which it expresses in blade or sheet-like forms. Space is there to be shaped, divided, enclosed, but not to be filled. The new sculpture tends to abandon stone, bronze and clay for industrial materials like iron, steel, alloy, glass, plastics, celluloid, etc., etc., which are worked with the blacksmith's, the welder's and even the carpenter's tools.[30]

And a few paragraphs later, still in this 1958 version, Greenberg described (apparently affirmatively) the inversion of each and every quality of Constructivist sculpture in the work he was considering, and he made sure to provide the ideological legitimation for these inversions of the Constructivist legacy:

> To render substance entirely optical and form, whether pictorial, sculptural or architectural, as an integral part of ambient space—this brings anti-illusionism full circle. Instead of the illusion of things we are now being offered the illusion of modalities; namely that matter is incorporeal, weightless and exists only optically, like a mirage. This kind of illusionism is stated in pictures whose paint surfaces and enclosing rectangles seem to expand into surrounding space … but better yet in Constructivist and quasi-Constructivist works of sculpture. Feats of "engineering" that aim to provide the greatest possible amount of visibility with the least possible expenditure of tactile surface belong categorically to the free and total medium of sculpture. The constructor-sculptor can, literally, draw in the air with a single strand of wire that supports nothing but itself.[31]

It is immediately apparent that this new perspective on Constructivism implied an almost violent dematerialization and depoliticization of the complex formal and material dialectic of Constructivist sculpture. This literal *disembodiment of sculpture*, as we might call it, also implied a complete disembodiment of the viewer's perceptual experience, as Greenberg (with no hesitation) phrased it, in 1958:

> And even should sculpture be compelled eventually to become as abstract as painting, it would still have a larger realm of formal possibilities at its command. The human

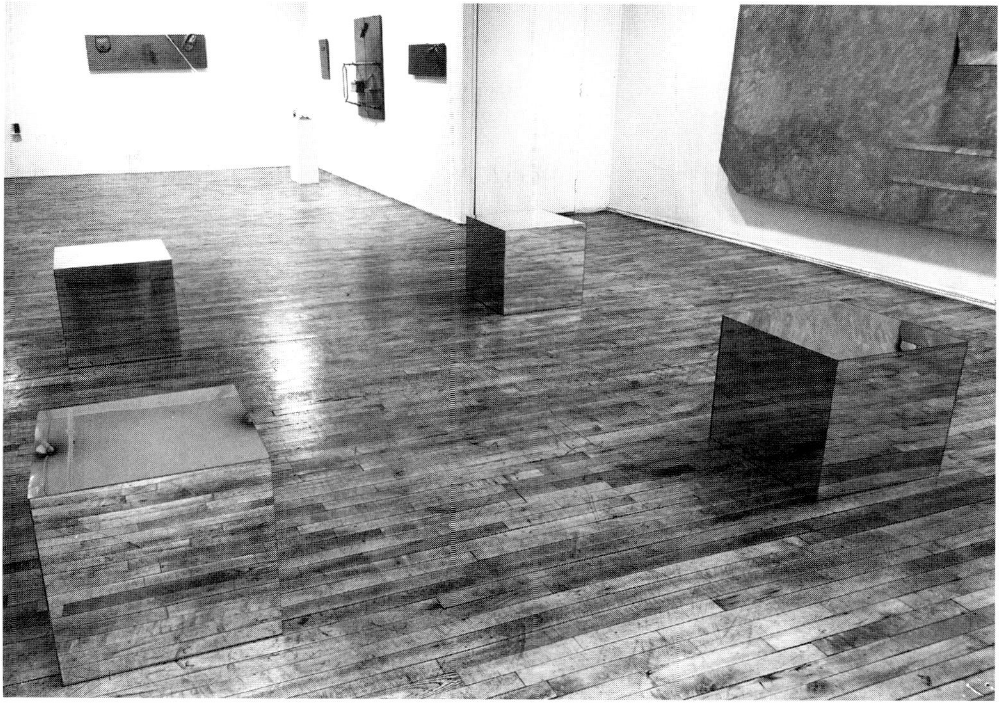

Robert Morris, *Mirrored Cubes (Untitled)*, 1965. Installation Green Gallery, 1965 (destroyed). Courtesy Leo Castelli Gallery, New York. Photo R. Burckhardt. © 2015 Robert Morris/Artists Rights Society (ARS), New York.

> body is no longer postulated as the agent of space in either pictorial or sculptural art; now it is eyesight alone, and eyesight has more freedom of movement and invention within three dimensions than within two.[32]

Thus, Constructivism—in the works of Gabo and Pevsner, and most certainly in the words of Greenberg in 1958—finally had reached the stage of the "mirage." What had once been tactile and contingent had become "optical," what had been rigorously anti-illusionistic in emphasizing weight, physical mass, and process, in foregrounding surface and texture, and in "baring the structural device" had turned into an "illusion of modalities."

If the tension wire in Tatlin's work had originally functioned as an important element in the contextualization of the sculptural construct in architectural space (revealing mass and weight as essential features of sculptural perception), it became now, through a magic trick of dematerialization, an object that "supports nothing but itself" in Greenberg's vision. Here we witness the construction of the neo-modernist aesthetic, with all of its requirements and its amazing conceptual and terminological *volte face*. This text seems to have been the first instance in which Greenberg used the concept of "opticality," a term that would circulate for at least the next twenty years as a key concept in the neo-modernist aesthetic, particularly in the criticism of Michael Fried.

Yet, in this case, despite its efforts to transform Constructivism into an idealist and ahistorical aesthetic, that key term was at least still applied to its complicated relationship with historical avant-garde legacies. But even this residual relationship was eclipsed soon after, and it was ultimately restricted to an almost exclusive reference to Cubism alone.

Apparently yet another type of elision was necessary, and it is equally evident in the text. This adjustment occurred within Greenberg's own attempt to eliminate all contradictions from the new aesthetic. While in the original 1948 version he could still affirm "our positivist sensibility," he had to modify this in 1958 to merely mention a "positivist aspect of the modernist aesthetic." Most importantly, in the original version Greenberg credited sculpture as having "a self-evident physical reality," describing it with this astonishing comparison: "as palpable and independent and present as the houses we live in and the furniture we use."[33] Greenberg's emphasis on the positivist dimension of this aesthetic led him to reveal (perhaps involuntarily) the dull and pragmatic dimension of positivism. Clearly, this furniture analogy would have been extremely discordant with the discourse of the tragic, the sublime, and the transcendental that supported Abstract Expressionism in 1958. Accordingly, this surprising statement—which could have easily been misread as an ingenuous anticipation of Minimal sculpture—was deleted from the revised version.

A few years later, such maneuvers were no longer necessary. Greenberg's reconstruction of the history of modernism (from which some of the most important contributions now had been deleted) were thoroughly and successfully institutionalized. In fact, Greenberg's reconstruction modernism had become the *doxa* which, well into the 1960s, was hardly questioned by American and European critics, curators, and audiences alike.[34]

Notes

First published in Serge Guilbaut, ed., *Reconstructing Modernism: Art in New York, Paris, and Montreal* (Cambridge, Mass.: MIT Press, 1986), pp. 85–110. Minor corrections have been made for consistency.

1. The distinction between the post–World War II neo-avantgarde and the historical avant-garde of the 1915–35 period was first developed in Peter Bürger's *Theorie der Avantgarde* (Frankfurt: Suhrkamp, 1974); translated into English as *Theory of the Avant-garde* (Minneapolis: University of Minnesota Press, 1984).

2. Clement Greenberg, "Irrelevance versus Irresponsibility," *Partisan Review* 15, no. 5 (May 1948): 579.

3. Serge Chermayeff, "Naum Gabo," *Magazine of Art* 41 (February 1948): 56–59. Michel Seuphor adopted this juxtaposition of Russian and Soviet modernist art to Socialist Realism in the conclusion of his important article "Au temps de l'avant garde," in the French journal *L'Oeil* (November 1955): 24–39. This first major sketch in post-war France of the history of Russian Constructivism concluded with an unusually large number of color reproductions of Socialist Realist paintings.

4. Naum Gabo, "The Concepts of Russian Art," *World Review* (June 1942): 48–53.

5. Naum Gabo, quoted by Jean Clay, *Visages de l'art moderne* (Lausanne: Éditions Rencontre, 1969), pp. 70–120.

6. For a discussion of the relationship between Gabo and Pevsner and the Moscow Free State Art Studios (VKhuTEMAS), see Christina Lodder, *Russian Constructivism* (New Haven: Yale University Press, 1983), pp. 34, 109–130.

7. El Lissitzky, "Neue Russische Kunst," in Sophie Lissitzky-Küppers, *El Lissitzky* (Dresden: Verlag der Kunst, 1967), p. 354 (my translation; emphasis added).

8. Most notably, Alfred Barr's seminal exhibition *Cubism and Abstract Art* included and/or reproduced in the catalog a number of central works from the Russian and Soviet avant-garde, including works by Alexandr Rodchenko, Vladimir Tatlin, Lyubov Popova, and Varvara Stepanova. A year later, in spite of its obvious limitations, Carola Giedion-Welcker's study *Modern Plastic Art* (published in English and German in 1937) was even more developed in its comprehension of the new sculptural phenomena. Both Barr's and Giedion-Welcker's vision of Constructivist sculpture was more advanced in the mid-1930s than virtually every other study to be published during the first two decades after the war. Not only does Giedion-Welcker reproduce Tatlin's counter-reliefs, corner-reliefs and, of course, the *Monument to the Third International*, but she also documents those sculptural works which, in spite of their seminal position, will soon vanish mysteriously from the art history of twentieth-century sculpture: Rodchenko's *Oval Hanging Construction*, works by Katarzyna Kobro, and the work of the Laboratory Constructivists Konstantin Medunetsky and the Stenberg Brothers.

The suspicion that the repression of the Russian and Soviet avant-garde from the art-historical reception process during the period of the geopolitical reconstruction after the war (which was also that of the reconstruction of modernism) was at least partially determined by such obvious factors as the rabid anti-Communism of the postwar period is corroborated by the fact that this elimination seems to have taken place at a different pace, and to a different degree, in the various geopolitical contexts. While in the West German and the American contexts the elimination of historical memory seems to have been all but complete for many years to come, the French situation seems less distorted in its political relationship with the Soviet Union, and it seems to have also allowed for a more open and liberal reception of the Constructivist legacy.

As for the actual falsification of (art) history, in the attitudes of postwar scholars toward the Russian and Soviet avant-garde, it is particularly amazing to witness the persistent repetition of these ideological clichés about the prohibition and prosecution of Constructivist art in the Soviet Union after 1921. Not a single study of that period mentions the artistic and political debates among the artists themselves, or the gradual transformation from the Constructivist aesthetic into the Productivist aesthetic, initiated from within the ranks of the artists, critics, and theoreticians of that generation. The typical attitude regarding these phenomena can be found in every single sculpture history of that period, and it seems that once the ideological cliché had been set up, it was repeated for generations to come. One of the first to change that critical legacy was Herbert Read who seemed to have become something like the mouthpiece of Gabo and Pevsner, voicing the ideological cliché with more distinction: "For a few years, the politicians were too busy to interfere in such matters, but five years later they felt compelled to call a halt. The movement was suppressed, its promoters silenced or exiled, but they had already created, not merely a new movement in art, an advance in the evolution of style, but an altogether new kind of art, Constructivist art, and its practice was to spread from Moscow throughout the world." See Read, *Modern Sculpture* (London: Faber & Faber, 1941), p. 93. Or, ten years later in the German context, in 1954, it was Eduard Trier who phrased it, "The so-called revolutionary masses of Russia [*sic*] destroyed these hopes [of the Constructivists] already in 1922, when abstract constructivism was prohibited by the state and when it was interrupted or eliminated as undesirable" (Trier, *Moderne Plastik* [Berlin: Geb. Mann, 1954], p. 74).

Or, in a third example from the seemingly inexhaustible repertory of ideological clichés, as late as 1969 in a study by an eminent American scholar: "But in 1922 the government suppressed the movement (of Constructivism), saying it was of no service to the state." See Robert Goldwater, *What Is Modern Sculpture?* (New York: Museum of Modern Art, 1969).

For an attempt to clarify the actual transformation of aesthetic theory and practice in the Soviet Union after 1920, and a first study to discuss the collaboration between Stalin's propaganda ministry and artists like Alexandr Rodchenko and Varvara Stepanova, see Hubertus Gassner, *Rodchenko Fotografien* (München: Schirmer & Mosel, 1982) and Hubertus Gassner and Eckhart Gillen's anthology of documents, *Zwischen Revolutionskunst and Sozialistischem Realismus* (Cologne: Dumont, 1979). As to Lissitzky's work for the same ministry, and a first discussion of the transformation of his aesthetic theory and practice, see my essay "From Faktura to Factography," *October* 30 (fall 1984): 82–119 (reprinted in this vol.).

9. George Heard Hamilton, *Painting and Sculpture in Europe, 1880–1940* (New York: Penguin, 1967), p. 352.

10. Naum Gabo, quoted in the *Sunday Republican* (Waterbury), June 8, 1947.

11. Robert M. Coates, "Naum Gabo," *New Yorker* (February 21, 1948): 43–44. To give another example from 1953: "We started Constructivism in 1915. … In the past, my work has been prosecuted—thrown out of Russia, attacked in Germany. The narrow-minded sculptors who are so derogatory, who try to destroy it, believe only in materialist art. … When I came to Berlin, as far as I know, there were no Constructivists. Afterwards Constructivism emerged in Berlin, in France, in Holland and in England. They are teaching Constructivism in Yale, Harvard, MIT, N.Y.U. Brooklyn. We have started something which is rolling, something of the human spirit. As yet, Constructivism has not yet reached its full maturity" (Naum Gabo, quoted by A. L. Chanin in "Gabo Makes a Construction," *Art News* 52, no. 7 [November 1953]: 46).

The myth of Gabo as the "founder and leader" of the Constructivist movement will be repeated from 1947 on through the next thirty years. Thus, for example, Hilton Kramer in 1966: "Naum Gabo, the Russian sculptor and theorist who founded the Constructivist movement half a century ago. … As Alexei Pevsner makes clear in his memoir—Constructivism was the creation of Gabo alone. It was Gabo who formulated the theory, devised the sculptural syntax to realize it and produced the first Constructivist masterpieces." In Kramer, "Gabo and Constructivism: History Revised," *New York Times*, no. 3127 (1966). Or, still ten years later in the context of an exhibition at London's Tate Gallery: "The work of Naum Gabo, for over sixty years the leading exponent of Constructivism…" (Corinne Bellow, press release, The Tate Gallery, London, October 18, 1976).

12. Rosamond Bernier, "Propos d'un sculpteur," Antoine Pevsner interviewed by Rosamond Bernier, *L'Oeil* 28 (November 1956): 28–35. Bernier concludes: "'Don't forget, Gabo and I are the only Constructivists,' the artist reminded me when I was about to leave the studio." It is important to know that on the occasion of the publication of this interview, even Gabo explicitly corrected the outrageous claims made by his brother and disassociated himself from these remarks. See Naum Gabo, "Statement," *L'Oeil* 29 (April 1957): 61.

13. Naum Gabo, as quoted by Trier, *Moderne Plastik*, p. 74 (my translation).

14. Boris Arvatov, *Kunst und Produktion: Entwurf einer Proletarisch—Avantgardistischen Aesthetik 1921–1930* (Munich: Hanser, 1972), pp. 11–12 (my translation).

15. Alfred Barr, *Cubism and Abstract Art* (New York: Museum of Modern Art, 1936), p. 138.

16. Naum Gabo, *Of Divers Arts*, The A. W. Mellon Lectures in the Fine Arts, 1959, Bollingen Series 35:8 (Washington, D.C.: National Gallery of Art, 1962).

17. László Moholy-Nagy, in Goldwater, *What Is Modern Sculpture?*, p. 69.

18. The statement is astonishing not only because of its prognostic accuracy, but also because of the fact that Barr's catalog and exhibition were—and would remain for

decades to come—the most comprehensive and exact documentation of the post-Cubist pictorial and sculptural practices of abstraction. This was true, in particular, for its unusually developed documentation of the artists of the Russian and Soviet avant-garde, whose reception in the Western world after 1945 concerns us here primarily. Barr's statement poses an important question, and we will not be able to answer it in this context; neither will we be able to answer why his prognosis would turn out to be so accurate. More precisely, why would the legacies of geometric abstraction—in their various forms and formations (e.g., groups such as Cercle et Carré, Abstraction/Création, and American Abstract Artists)—become increasingly unacceptable toward the end of the 1930s, and remain definitely rejected in American art of the 1940s and 1950s, entailing the almost complete obliteration of an entire generation of American abstract artists from the map of modernism.

19. Robert Goldwater, "A Season of Art," *Partisan Review* 14, no. 4 (July–August 1947): 414ff.

20. Naum Gabo, quoted by Robert Coates, *New Yorker* (March 20, 1948): 25.

21. Naum Gabo, "Constructive Art,' *Listener* (November 4, 1936): 846–848.

22. Naum Gabo, in *Circle: International Survey of Constructive Art* (London: Phaidon, 1937).

23. Quoted in Chanin, "Gabo Makes a Construction," pp. 34–37.

24. Clement Greenberg, "The Situation at the Moment," *Partisan Review* (January 1948): 81–84.

25. Clement Greenberg, "The New Sculpture," *Partisan Review* (June 1949): 641.

26. In a discussion with the author on the occasion of the 1981 Vancouver conference "Modernism and Modernity"; see *Modernism and Modernity* (Halifax: Nova Scotia College of Art and Design, 1983), p. 271.

27. Greenberg, "The New Sculpture " p. 640. Greenberg, in 1948, had obviously not yet quite determined the full canon of Abstract Expressionism, nor had he singled out the masters of the movement. Quite the contrary: the list of artists that he mentions at the end of the essay is, with the exception of David Smith, remarkably atypical (it includes Burgoyne Diller, who at that time was still one of the most outspoken defenders of geometrical abstraction). It is also a list of distinctly secondary figures, including Peter Grippe, Adaline Kent, David Hare, and Richard Lippold. But most of all it is astonishing because the achievements of Abstract Expressionism would precisely not occur in the field of sculpture; quite the opposite, as Greenberg himself would later admit, this would be the domain of its most obvious weaknesses and failures.

28. Ibid.

29. Ibid.

30. Clement Greenberg, "The New Sculpture" (revised version), in *Art and Culture* (Boston: Beacon Press, 1961), p. 142. I would like to thank Yve-Alain Bois for having brought the differences between the two versions of the essay to my attention.

31. Ibid., p. 144.

32. Ibid., p. 193.

33. Greenberg, "The New Sculpture" (1948), p. 641.

34. A further example of the workings of reconstruction modernism: in this text, Greenberg can still mention David Smith's work in the context of his discussion of Constructivist sculpture, but soon he will have to extract him from any such reference, in order to start rewriting modernist sculptural history—not only according to the new terms of a reconstructed modernist aesthetic, but also according to the particular interests and investments of what had become by then his urgent project: the construction of an autonomous and hegemonic local neo-avantgarde. Soon Greenberg would say, by contrast, that in Smith's sculpture "there is no flavor in it of (de) Stijl or of the Bauhaus or even of Constructivism." See Greenberg, "David Smith's New Sculpture," in *David Smith*, ed. Garnett McCoy (New York: Praeger, 1973), p. 222.

10

Conceptual Art 1962–1969: From the Aesthetics of Administration to the Critique of Institutions

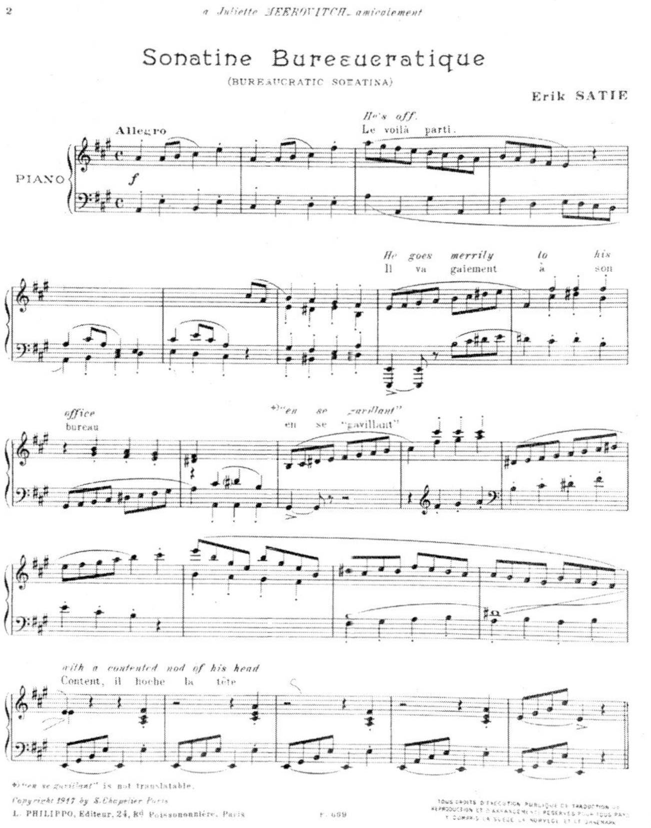

Erik Satie, *Sonatine bureaucratique*, 1917.

> This monster called beauty is not eternal. We know that our breath has no beginning and that it will never end, but we can conceive, before anything else, and think of the world's creation and of its end.
>
> —*Guillaume Apollinaire, Les Peintres cubistes*

> Allergic to any relapse into magic, art is part and parcel of the disenchantment of the world, to use Max Weber's term. It is inextricably intertwined with rationalization. What means and productive methods art has at its disposal are all derived from this nexus.
>
> —*Theodor W. Adorno, Aesthetic Theory*

A twenty-year distance separates us from the historical moment of Conceptual Art. It is a distance that both allows and obliges us to contemplate the movement's history in a broader perspective than that of the convictions held during the decade of its emergence and operation (roughly from 1965 to its temporary disappearance in 1975). Thus, to historicize Conceptual Art requires, first of all, a clarification of the wide range of often conflicting positions, and the mutually exclusive types of investigation that were generated during this period. But beyond that there are broader problems of method and of "interest." For at this juncture, any historicization has to consider what type of questions an art-historical approach—traditionally based on the study of visual objects—can legitimately pose, or hope to answer, in the context of artistic practices that explicitly insisted on operating outside of the parameters of formally ordered perceptual objects, and most of all, outside of those of art history and criticism. Furthermore, any historicization must also address the currency of the historical object, i.e., the motivation to rediscover Conceptual Art from the vantage point of the late 1980s: the dialectic which links Conceptual Art, as the most rigorous elimination of visuality and traditional definitions of representation, to this decade of a rather violent restoration of traditional artistic forms and procedures of production.

It is with Cubism, of course—in what can be seen as Cubism's tribute to the legacy of Stéphane Mallarmé—that elements of language surface programmatically within the visual field for the first time in the history of Modernist painting. It is at that very moment that a parallel is established between the emerging structuralist analysis of language and the formalist examination of representation. But Conceptual practices went beyond such a mapping of the linguistic model onto the perceptual model, passing beyond the spatialization of language and the temporalization of visual structures.

Typically, one of the many proposals inherent in Conceptual Art was to replace the object of spatial and perceptual experience by linguistic definitions alone (defining, for example, the "work" as an analytic proposition). Thus it constituted the hitherto most consequential assault on the artistic object—its visuality, its commodity status, and its distribution form. Confronting—perhaps for the first time in the postwar period—the full range of the implications of Marcel Duchamp's legacies, Conceptual practices reflected furthermore upon the construction—or rather the death—of the author, just as much as they redefined the conditions of receivership and the role of the spectator. Thus they generated that period's most rigorous investigation of the conventions of pictorial and sculptural representation and engaged in a critique of the traditional paradigms of visuality.

The historic phase in which Conceptual Art was developed comprised from the beginning such a complex range of mutually opposing approaches that any attempt at a retrospective survey must be beware of the forceful voices (mostly those of the artists themselves) that demand respect for the purity and orthodoxy of the movement. Precisely because of this range of variations of Conceptual Art, it would seem imperative to resist a construction of its history in terms of a stylistic homogenization. This would falsely limit a rather contradictory and complex history to a select group of individuals and a set of strictly defined practices (such as, for example, an exclusive focus on the activities initiated by Seth Siegelaub in New York in 1968 or the authoritarian quests for orthodoxy by the English *Art & Language* group).

As is usual with stylistic formations in the history of art, the origin and the name of the movement (to use the term as it was coined by Henry Flynt in 1961) are heavily contested by its major participants. Robert Barry, Joseph Kosuth, and Lawrence Weiner, for example, vehemently denied in recent conversations with the author any historical connection to or even knowledge of the Fluxus movement of the early 1960s, the context in which the term was first used. Nevertheless at least with regard to the invention of the term it seems correct when Henry Flynt claims that he is

> the originator of concept art, the most influential contemporary art trend. In 1961 I authored (and copyrighted) the phrase "concept art," the rationale for it and the first compositions labeled "concept art." My document was first printed in *An Anthology*, ed. La Monte Young, New York, 1962.[1]

This moment, then, requires more than a mere reconstruction of that movement's self-declared primary actors, or a scholarly obedience to their proclaimed purity of intentions and operations.[2] Their convictions were voiced with the (by now often hilarious) self-righteousness that continues the tradition of hypertrophic claims made in avant-garde declarations of the twentieth century. For example, one of the campaign statements by Joseph Kosuth from the late 1960s asserts: "Art before the modern period is as much art as Neanderthal man is man. It is for this reason that around the same time I replaced the term work for *art proposition*. Because a conceptual work of art in the traditional sense, is a contradiction in terms."[3]

It seems crucial to remember that the oppositions within the formation of Conceptual Art arose partly from the different readings of Minimal sculpture (and those of its pictorial equivalents in the paintings of Robert Mangold, Robert Ryman, and Frank Stella) and in the consequences the generation of artists emerging in 1965 drew from those readings. Yet, divergences also resulted from the differing impact different Minimalist artists had on each member of the new generation. For example, Dan Graham seems to have been primarily engaged with the work of Sol LeWitt since he not only organized LeWitt's first one-person exhibition in his gallery, called The Daniels Gallery in 1967, but he also wrote one of the first essays on this artist, entitled "Two Structures: Sol LeWitt." In 1969, he concluded the introduction to his self-published volume of writings entitled *End Moments* as follows: "It should be obvious the importance Sol LeWitt's work has had for my work. In the article here included (written first in 1967, re-written in 1969) I hope only that the after the fact appreciation hasn't too much submerged his seminal work into *my* categories."[4]

Mel Bochner, while clearly indebted in his early work to his friendship with Sol LeWitt, wrote one of the first essays on Dan Flavin (it is in fact a text-collage of accumulated quotations, all of which relate in one way or another to Flavin's work).[5] Shortly thereafter, the text-collage as a presentational mode would in fact become integral to Bochner's activities, for in the same year he organized what was probably the first truly conceptual exhibition (both in terms of materials being exhibited and in terms of presentational style). Entitled *Working Drawings and Other Visible Things on Paper Not Necessarily Meant to Be Viewed as Art* (at the School of Visual Arts in 1966), the exhibition included works by most of the Minimal artists along with works by a number of then still rather unknown Post-Minimal and Conceptual artists. Having assembled drawings, sketches, documents, tabulations and other paraphernalia of the production process, the exhibition limited itself to presenting the "originals" in Xeroxes assembled into four loose-leaf binders which were installed on pedestals in the center of the exhibition space.

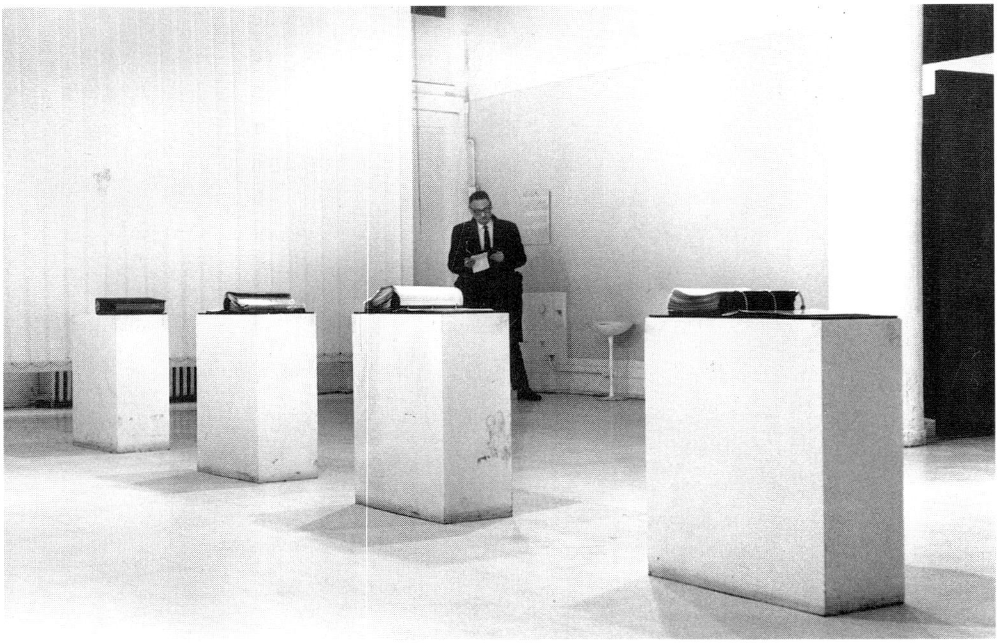

Mel Bochner, *Working Drawings and Other Visible Things on Paper Not Necessarily Meant to Be Viewed as Art.* Four identical ring-binder notebooks, each containing one hundred Xeroxed pages of studio notes, working drawings, and diagrams collected and Xeroxed by the artist; displayed on four sculpture stands. Installation, School of Visual Arts Gallery, New York, December 1966. © Mel Bochner. Courtesy the artist.

While one should not overestimate the importance of such features (nor should one underestimate the pragmatics of such a presentational style), Bochner's intervention clearly transformed both the format and the space of exhibitions. Furthermore, Bochner's implementation of these strategies in 1966 indicates that the transformation of the gallery space, of the devices of exhibition and display, and of the object of art itself had already been a common concern of the generation of Post-Minimal artists before they were to be ostentatiously announced as having undergone a revolutionary breakthrough two years later in Seth Siegelaub's exhibitions and publications (e.g., *The Xerox Book*).

A third example of the proximity between the generation of the Minimalists and that of the Conceptualists is given by Joseph Kosuth who seems to have consciously chosen Donald Judd as his key historical reference: thus at least one of the early tautological neon works from Kosuth's *Proto-Investigations* is dedicated to Donald Judd. Furthermore, throughout the second part of "Art after Philosophy" (published in November 1969) Judd's name, work, and writings are invoked with the same frequency as those of Marcel Duchamp and Ad Reinhardt. At the end of this essay Kosuth explicitly states: "I would hastily add to that, however, that I was certainly much more influenced by Ad Reinhardt, Duchamp via Johns and Morris, and by Donald Judd than I ever was specifically by LeWitt. … Pollock and Judd are, I feel, the beginning and end of American dominance in art."[6]

Sol LeWitt's *Structures*

Apparently, LeWitt's proto-conceptual work of the early 1960s originated in an understanding of the essential dilemma that has haunted artistic production since 1913, when its basic paradigms of opposition were first formulated—a dilemma that could be described as the conflict between structural specificity and random organization. On the one hand, there is an explicit need for a systematic reduction, and an

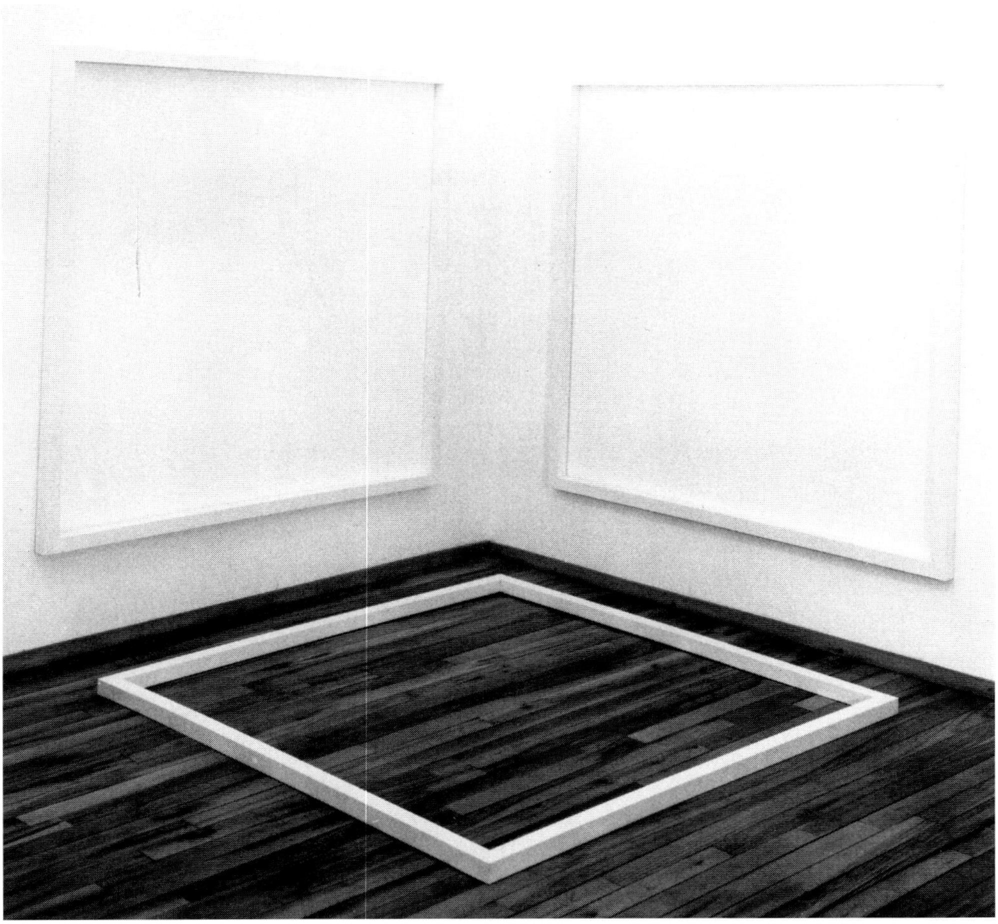

Sol LeWitt, *Wall/Floor Piece ("Three Squares")*, 1966. White lacquered steel in three parts, 29½ × 29½ × 1⅝ in. each (74.9 × 74.9 × 4.1 cm). © 2015 The LeWitt Estate/Artists Rights Society (ARS), New York. Courtesy Paula Cooper Gallery, New York.

empirical verification of the perceptual data of a visual structure. On the other hand there is a desire that wishes to assign a new "idea" or meaning to a randomly chosen object (in the manner of Mallarmé's "transposition") as though the object were a new and empty (linguistic) signifier.

This was the dilemma that Roland Barthes had first described in 1956 as the "difficulty of our times" in the concluding paragraphs of *Mythologies*:

> It seems that this is a difficulty pertaining to our times: there is as yet only one possible choice, and this choice can bear only on two equally extreme methods: either to posit a reality which is entirely permeable to history, and ideologize; or, conversely, to posit a reality which is ultimately impenetrable, irreducible, and, in this case, poeticize. In a word, I do not yet see a synthesis between ideology and poetry (by poetry I understand, in a very general way, the search for the inalienable meaning of things).[7]

Both critiques of the traditional practices of representation in the American postwar context had at first appeared mutually exclusive and had often fiercely attacked each other. For example, Reinhardt's extreme form of self-critical, perceptual positivism had gone too far for most of the New York School artists. It had certainly surpassed the claims of Clement Greenberg and Michael Fried, the apologists of American-type Modernism who had constructed a paradoxical dogma of transcendentalism and self-referential critique. On the other hand, Reinhardt was as vociferous as they were—if not more so—in his contempt for the opposite of his perceptual positivism, namely the Duchampian tradition. This is most evident in Reinhardt's frequently condescending remarks about Duchamp. For example, when confessing, "I've never approved or liked anything about Marcel Duchamp.

You have to choose between Duchamp and Mondrian"; and, even more so in his outright disapproval for the Duchampian legacy that he detected in the theories of John Cage, and the work of Robert Rauschenberg, when stating that "the whole mixture, the number of poets and musicians and writers mixed up with art. Disreputable. Cage, Cunningham, Johns, Rauschenberg. I'm against the mixture of all the arts, against the mixture of art and life you know, everyday life."[8]

What passed by seemingly unnoticed was the fact that both of these critiques of representation had generated highly comparable formal and structural results (e.g., Rauschenberg's monochromes in 1951–1953 and Reinhardt's monochromes such as *Black Quadruptych* in 1955). Furthermore, even while conceived from opposite vantage points, the critical arguments accompanying such works systematically denied the traditional principles and functions of visual representation, and they constructed astonishingly similar litanies of negation. This parallelism is evident, for example, in two texts. The first was prepared by Cage for Rauschenberg's White Paintings in 1953, and the second is Reinhardt's 1962 manifesto "Art as Art." First Cage:

> To whom, No subject, No image, No taste, No object, No beauty, No talent, No technique (no why), No idea, No intention, No art, No feeling, No black, No white no (and). After careful consideration I have come to the conclusion that there is nothing in these paintings that could not be changed, that they can be seen in any light and are not destroyed by the action of shadows. Hallelujah! the blind can see again; the water is fine.[9]

And here is Ad Reinhardt's manifesto for his own principle of "Art as Art":

> No lines or imaginings, no shapes or composings or representings, no visions or sensations or impulses, no symbols or signs or impastos, no decoratings or colorings or picturings, no pleasures or pains, no accidents or ready-mades, no things, no ideas, no relations, no attributes, no qualities—nothing that is not of the essence.[10]

Reinhardt's empiricist American formalism (condensed in his "Art as Art" formula) and Duchamp's critique of visuality[11] reappear *verbatim* in Kosuth's historically rather unlikely fusion of the two positions in the mid-1960s, leading to his own formula, which he propagated since 1966, "Art as Idea as Idea." It should be noted, however, that the strange admixture of the nominalist position of Duchamp (and its consequences) and the positivist position of Reinhardt (and its implications) was not only accomplished in 1965 with the beginnings of Conceptual Art. It had been well prepared in the work of Frank Stella, who in his *Black Paintings* from 1959 claimed the apparently mutually exclusive traditions of Rauschenberg's and Reinhardt's monochrome paintings as simultaneous points of the departure of his work. Finally, it was LeWitt's response to Stella—in particular work such as his *Structures*—that had demarcated precisely that specific transition in which language and visuality had been integrated for the first time in a structural model.

The surfaces of these *Structures* from 1961 to '62 (some of which used single frames from Eadweard Muybridge's serial photographs) carried inscriptions in bland lettering, self-referentially identifying the hue and the shape of those surfaces (e.g., "*red square*") and the conditions of the inscription itself (e.g., "*white letters*"). Since these inscriptions named either the support or the inscription (or, in the middle section of the painting, both support and inscription in a paradoxical inversion), they created a continuous conflict in the viewer/reader. A conflict not just over which of the two functions of reading or viewing should be performed initially in response to the painting. Rather, a conflict concerning

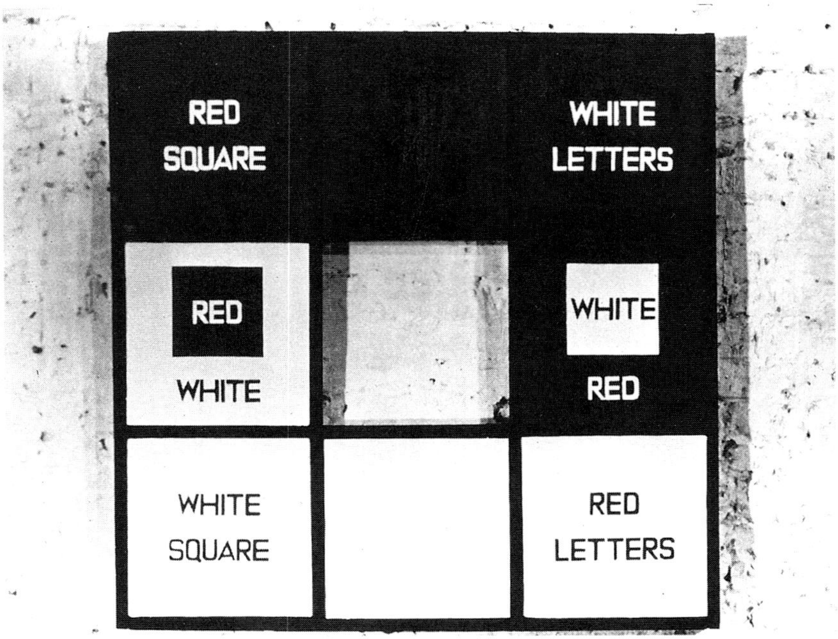

Sol LeWitt, *Untitled (Red Square, White Letters)*, from the series *Structures*, 1962. Oil on canvas, 36 × 36 in. (91 × 91 cm). Private collection. © 2015 The LeWitt Estate/Artists Rights Society (ARS), New York. Courtesy Paula Cooper Gallery, New York.

the reliability of the given information and the sequence of that information: was the inscription to be given primacy over the visual qualities identified by the linguistic sign, or was the perceptual experience of the visual, formal, and chromatic element anterior to its mere denomination by language?

Clearly this "mapping of the linguistic onto the perceptual" was not arguing in favor of "the idea"—or linguistic primacy—or suggesting that the work of art from now on should be merely considered as an analytic proposition. Quite to the contrary, the permutational character of the work suggested that the viewer/reader should systematically perform *all* the visual and textual options the painting's parameters allowed for. This included an acknowledgment of the painting's central, square element: a spatial void that revealed the underlying wall surface as the painting's architectural support in actual space, thereby ultimately even suspending the reading of the painting between architectural structure, pictorial conventions and linguistic definition.

Rather than privileging one over the other, LeWitt's work (in its dialogue with Jasper Johns's legacy of paradox) insisted on forcing the inherent contradictions of the two spheres (that of the perceptual experience and that of the linguistic experience) into the highest possible relief. Unlike Frank Stella's response to Johns, which had forced Modernist self-referentiality one step further into the ultimate *cul de sac* of its positivist convictions (his notorious statement "what you see is what you see" would attest to that just as much as the development of his later work).[12] To what extent the problem of this dilemma haunted the generation of Minimal artists becomes evident when almost ten years later, in an interview with Jack Burnham, Robert Morris would still seem to be responding (if perhaps unconsciously) to Stella's notorious statement:

> Painting ceased to interest me. There were certain things about it that seemed very problematic to me. … There was a big conflict between the fact of doing this thing, and what it looked like later. It just didn't seem to make much sense to me. Primarily because there was an activity I did in time, and there was a certain method to it. And that didn't seem to have any relationship to the thing at all. There is a certain resolution in the theater where there is real time, and *what you do is what you do.*[13]

Sol LeWitt's dialogue (with both Johns and Stella, and ultimately, of course with Greenberg) developed a dialectical position with regard to Modernism's positivist legacy. In contrast to Stella, his work now revealed that the compulsion for painting's empiricist self-reflexivity not only originated in a scientific positivism (which—as the founding logic of capitalism—is foundational to industrial forms of production just as much as to its science and theory). Worse yet, Lewitt recognized that for an artistic practice that internalized this positivism by insisting on a purely empiricist approach to vision, there would be only one ultimate destiny: to aspire to the conditions of tautology. It is therefore not surprising that when LeWitt formulated his second text on Conceptual Art—his "Sentences on Conceptual Art" from the spring of 1969—the first sentence should programmatically state the radical difference between the logic of scientific production and that of artistic production:

1. Conceptual artists are mystics rather than rationalists. They leap to conclusions that logic cannot reach.

2. Rational judgments repeat rational judgments.

3. Irrational judgments lead to new experience.[14]

Robert Morris's Paradoxes

> The problem has been for some time one of ideas—those most admired are the ones with the biggest, most incisive ideas (i.e., Cage and Duchamp). … I think that today art is a form of art history.
>
> —*Robert Morris, letter to Henry Flint, August 13, 1962*

Quite evidently, Morris's approach to Duchamp, in the early 1960s, had already been based on reading the readymade in analogy with a Saussurean model of language: a model where meaning is generated by structural relationships. As Morris recalls, "My fascination with and respect for Duchamp was related to his linguistic fixation, to the idea that all of his operations were ultimately built on a sophisticated understanding of language itself."[15]

Accordingly, Morris's early work (from 1961 to 1963) already pointed toward an understanding of Duchamp that transcended the limited definition of the readymade as the mere displacement of traditional modes of artistic production by a new aesthetic of the performative speech act ("this is a work of art if I say so").

In marked distinction from the Conceptualists' subsequent exclusive focus on the unassisted readymades, Morris, who had discovered Duchamp from the late 1950s onwards, had been particularly engaged with works such as Duchamp's *Three Standard Stoppages* (1913) and the *Notes for the Large Glass (The Green Box)*. Morris's own production from the early 1960s, in particular works like *Card File* (1962), *Metered Light Bulb* (1963), *I-Box* (1963), *Litanies and the Statement of Aesthetic Withdrawal*, also entitled *Document* (1963), indicated a reading of Duchamp that clearly went beyond Johns's, leading toward a structural and semiotic definition of the functions of the readymade. As Morris described it retrospectively in 1970 in his essay "Some Notes on the Phenomenology of Making":

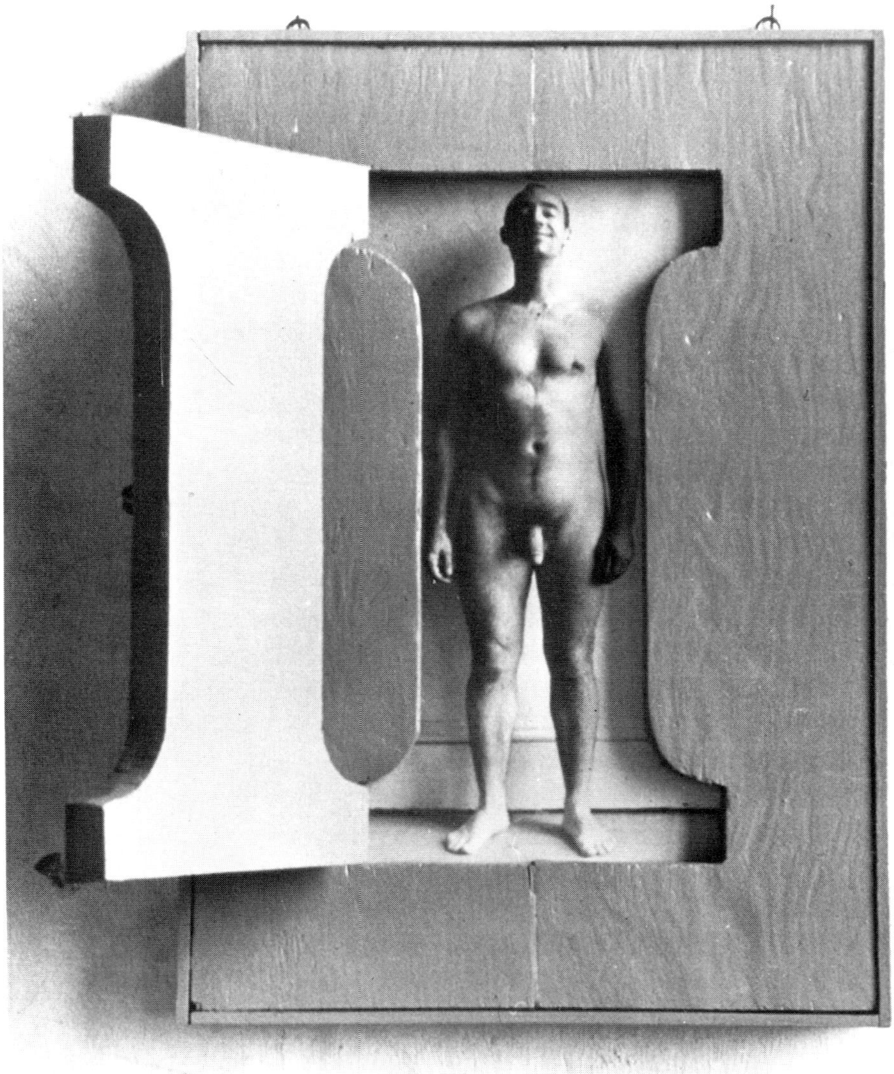

Robert Morris, *I-Box*, 1962. Painted plywood cabinet, Sculptmetal, and gelatin silver print, 19 × 13 × 1½ in. (48.3 × 33 × 3.8 cm). Collection Barbara Bertozzi Castelli. © 2015 Robert Morris/Artists Rights Society (ARS), New York.

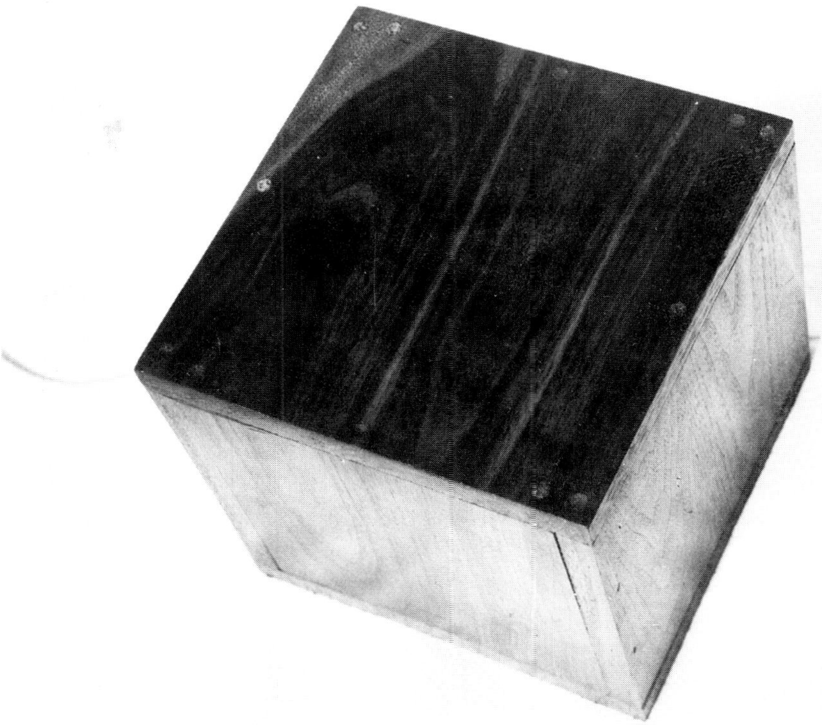

Robert Morris, *Box with the Sound of Its Own Making*, 1961. Walnut and recorded tapes (original) and compact disc (reformatted by artist), 46 × 9¾ × 10 in. (116.8 × 24.8 × 25.4 cm). Seattle Art Museum. Gift of Mr. and Mrs. Bagley Wright. © 2015 Robert Morris/Artists Rights Society (ARS), New York.

> There is a binary swing between the arbitrary and the non-arbitrary or "motivated" which is ... an historical, evolutionary, or diachronic feature of language's development and change. Language is not plastic art but both are forms of human behavior and the structures of one can be compared to the structures of the other.[16]

While it is worth noticing that by 1970 Morris already reaffirmed apodictically the ontological character of the different categories of "plastic art" versus that of "language," in the early 1960s his assaults on the traditional concepts of visuality and plasticity had already begun to lay some of the crucial foundations for the development of Conceptual Art, an art practice that emphasized the parallels, if not the identity of artistic production with the production and systems of linguistic signs. Most importantly, as early as 1961 in his *Box with the Sound of Its Own Making,* Morris had ruptured both the Modernist quest for medium-specific purity as much as its sequel in the positivist conviction of a purely perceptual experience operating in Stella's visual tautologies and the early phases of Minimalism. Furthermore, by counteracting the supremacy of the visual with that of an auditory experience of equal, if not higher importance, he renewed the Duchampian quest for a non-retinal art. In Morris' *Box with the Sound of Its Own Making* as much as in the subsequent works, the critique of the supremacy of the traditional categories of the visual and formal is enacted not only in the acoustic and tactile disturbances of the presumed purity of perceptual experience, but it is performed as well through a literalist act: one which simply withholds from the viewer practically all (at least traditionally defined) visual information.

This strategy of a "perceptual withdrawal" leads in each of the works from the early 1960s to a different analysis of the constituent features of the structured object and the modes of reading that it generates. In *I-Box*, for example, the viewer is confronted with a semiotic pun (on the words "I" and "eye") just as much as with a structural sleight of hand from the tactile (the viewer has to manipulate the box physically to see the *I* of the artist) through the linguistic sign (the letter *I* defines the shape of the framing/display device: the "door" of the box) to the visual representation (the nude photographic portrait of the artist) and back. It is of course this very tripartite division of the aesthetic sign—its separation into material object, linguistic sign, and photographic representation—that we will encounter in infinite variations, didactically simplified (to operate as stunning tautologies) and stylistically designed (to take the place of paintings) in Kosuth's so called *Proto-Investigations* done some time after 1966.

In *Document (Statement of Aesthetic Withdrawal)* Morris takes the literal negation of the visual even further in clarifying that after Duchamp the readymade is not just a neutral proposition (in the manner of an underlying statement such as "this is a work of art if I say so"), but that beyond being a tool to restructure the aesthetic object, the readymade transforms the work of art to become the ultimate subject of a legal definition and the result of institutional validation. In the absence of any specifically visual qualities and due to the manifest lack of any artistic or manual competence as a criterion of distinction, all the traditional criteria of aesthetic judgment—of taste and of connoisseurship—have been programmatically voided. The result of this is that the definition of the aesthetic becomes on the one hand a matter of linguistic convention and on the other the function of both a legal contract and an institutional discourse (a discourse of power rather than taste).

This erosion not only undermines the hegemony of the visual, but equally all claims for any other aspect of the aesthetic experience as being autonomous and self-sufficient. That the introduction of legalistic language and an administrative style of the material presentation of the artistic object could effect such an erosion had of course been prefigured in Duchamp's practice as well. In 1944 he had hired a notary to inscribe a statement of authenticity on the verso of his 1919 *L.H.O.O.Q.*, affirming that "this is to certify that this is the original 'ready-made' *L.H.O.O.Q.* Paris, 1919."

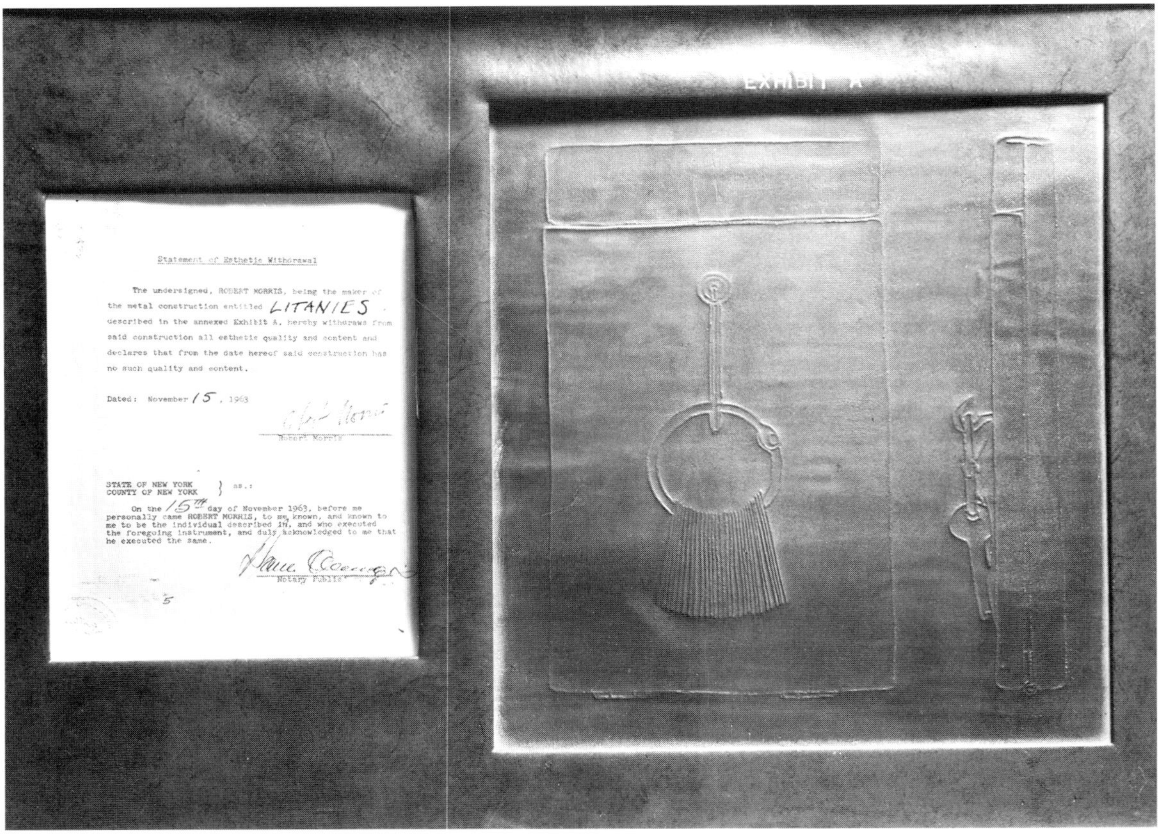

Robert Morris, *Document*, 1963. Typed and notarized statement on paper and sheet of lead mounted in imitation leather mat, 17⅝ × 23¾ in. (44.8 × 60.4 cm). Museum of Modern Art, New York. Gift of Philip Johnson. © 2015 Robert Morris/Artists Rights Society (ARS), New York.

What was possibly still a pragmatic maneuver with Duchamp (although certainly one in line with the pleasure he took in contemplating the vanishing basis for the legitimate definition of the work of art in visual competence and manual skill alone) would soon become one of the constituent features of subsequent developments in Conceptual Art. Most obviously operating in the certificates issued by Piero Manzoni defining persons or partial persons as temporary or lifetime works of art (1960–61), the certificate as a strategy of authentification emerges simultaneously in Yves Klein's decision to assign zones of immaterial pictorial sensibility to the various collectors who acquired them.

But this newly emerging aesthetic of linguistic conventions and legalistic/administrative arrangements not only denies the validity of the traditional studio aesthetic, it also canceled the aesthetic of production and consumption which had still governed Pop Art and Minimalism. Just as the Modernist critique (and ultimate prohibition) of figurative representation had become the increasingly dogmatic law for pictorial production in the first decade of the twentieth century, so Conceptual Art now instated a prohibition of any and all visuality as the inescapable aesthetic rule for the end of the twentieth century. Just as the readymade had negated not only figurative representation, authenticity, and authorship while introducing repetition and the series (i.e., the law of industrial production) to replace the studio aesthetic of the handcrafted original, Conceptual Art came to displace even that image of the mass-produced object and its aestheticized forms in Pop Art, replacing an aesthetic of industrial production and consumption with an aesthetic of administrative and legal organization and institutional validation.

EDWARD RUSCHA'S BOOKS

Another major example of these tendencies—acknowledged both by Dan Graham as a major inspiration for his own *Homes for America*, and by Kosuth, whose "Art after Philosophy" names him as a proto-Conceptual artist—would be the early book work of Edward Ruscha. Among the key strategies of future Conceptual Art that were initiated by Ruscha in 1963 were his decisions to choose the vernacular (e.g., architecture) as referent, to deploy photography systematically as the representational medium and, finally, to develop a new distribution form (e.g., the commercially produced book as opposed to the traditionally crafted *livre d'artiste*).

Typically, reference to architecture in any form whatever would have been unthinkable in the context of American-type formalism and Abstract Expressionism (or within the European postwar aesthetic for that matter) until the early 1960s. The devotion to a private aesthetic of contemplative experience with its concomitant absence of any systematic reflection of the social functions of artistic production and their potential and actual publics had, in fact, precluded any exploration of the interdependence of architectural and artistic culture, be it even in the most superficial and trivial forms of architectural décor.[17]

While it would be fair to argue that a developed artistic reflection on the problematic relationship between visual culture and public space does not reemerge until the early 1960, it was certainly part of the project of Pop and Minimal Art in the early 1960s, in particular in the work of Bernd and Hilla Becher, Claes Oldenburg and Edward Ruscha, to initiate a new reflection on the possibilities of anonymous and monumental sculpture (even in its negation as the anti-monument) and a reflection on its links to vernacular architecture, reflections which insisted simultaneously on a reconsideration of the intersection between public architectural and private domestic spaces.

In January 1963 (the year of Duchamp's first American retrospective, held at the Pasadena Art Museum), Ruscha, at the time a relatively unknown Los Angeles artist, decided to publish a book entitled *Twentysix Gasoline Stations*. The book, modest in format and production, was as removed from the tradition of the artist's book as its iconography opposed every aspect of the official American art of the 1950s and early

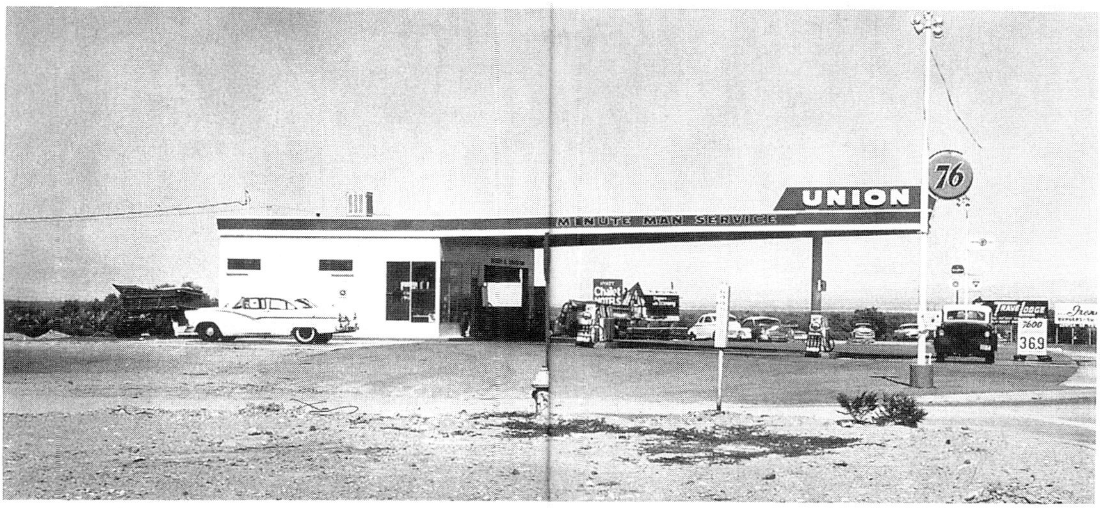

UNION, NEEDLES, CALIFORNIA

Edward Ruscha, *Twentysix Gasoline Stations*, 1962. 48-page book, 26 photographic illustrations; black offset printing on paper, 7$\frac{1}{16}$ × 5$\frac{1}{2}$ × $\frac{3}{8}$ in. (17.9 × 14 × 0.5 cm).

1960s: the legacy of Abstract Expressionism and Color Field painting. The book was, however, not so alien to the artistic thought of the emerging generation, if one remembers that only one year before a slightly better-known artist from New York by the name of Andy Warhol had exhibited a serial arrangement of thirty-two stenciled paintings depicting Campbell Soup cans arranged like objects on shelves in the Ferus Gallery. While both Warhol and Ruscha accepted a notion of public experience that was inescapably contained in the conditions of consumption, both artists altered the mode of production as well as the form of distribution of their work in such a manner that a different public was potentially addressed.

Ruscha's vernacular iconography evolved every bit as much as Warhol's from the Duchamp and Cage legacy of an aesthetic of "indifference," and from the commitment to an anti-hierarchical organization of a universally valid facticity, appearing as mere affirmation. Indeed, the principle of random sampling and aleatory choices from an infinity of possible objects (such as Ruscha's *Twentysix Gasoline Stations*, or later, Warhol's *Thirteen Most Wanted Men*) would soon become one of the essential strategies of the aesthetics of Conceptual Art: one could think of Alighiero Boetti's *The Thousand Longest Rivers*, of Robert Barry's *One Billion Dots*, of On Kawara's *One Million Years*, or, most significantly in this context, of Doug Huebler's life-long project, entitled *Variable Piece: 70.*[18] In all of these works, as well as in similar ones by Stanley Brouwn or Hanne Darboven, an arbitrary, abstract principle of pure quantification replaces in each case the traditional principles of pictorial or sculptural organization and/or of any compositional relational order.

In the manner that Ruscha's books shifted the formal organization of the representation into the register of mass distribution, the modus of the presentation itself became equally transformed: instead of lifting photographic (or print-derived) imagery from mass-cultural sources and aestheticizing these images by transforming them into painting (as Warhol and the Pop Artists had practiced it), Ruscha would now deploy photography directly, and reproduce it in an unmediated manner in an appropriate medium of reproduction, the printed book. And it was a particularly laconic type of photography at that, one that explicitly situated itself as much outside of all conventions of art photography as outside of those of the venerable tradition of the documentary photograph, furthest of all from the traditions of what had been called "concerned" photography. This devotion to a deadpan, anonymous, amateurish approach to photographic form corresponds exactly to Ruscha's iconographic choice of architectural banalities. Thus at all three levels—iconography, representational form, and mode of distribution—the given conventions of the artistic object no longer seemed acceptable in their traditionally specialized and privileged positions. As Victor Burgin would later describe these changes with hindsight: "One of the things Conceptual Art attempted was the dismantling of the hierarchy of media according to which painting (sculpture trailing slightly behind it) is assumed inherently superior to, most notably, photography."[19]

Dan Graham's Magazines

Accordingly, even in 1965–66, at the earliest stage of Conceptual practices, we witness the emergence of diametrically opposed appproaches: Kosuth's *Proto-Investigations* on the one hand (according to their author conceived and produced in 1965) and a work such as Graham's *Homes for America* on the other.[20] Published in *Arts Magazine* in December 1966, the latter is a work which—unknown to most and long unrecognized—programmatically emphasized structural contingency and contextuality, addressing crucial questions of presentation and distribution, of audience and authorship.

At the same time the work linked Minimalism's esoteric and self-reflexive aesthetics of permutation to a new reflection of the architecture of mass culture (thereby redefining the legacy of Pop Art that had exclusively focused on the objects of consumer culture, but had not considered its spatial and architectural conditions). The Minimalists' detachment from any representation of contemporary social experience upon which Pop Art had insisted, however furtively, resulted from their attempt to construct models of visual meaning and experience that juxtaposed formal reductivism with a structural and phenomenological model of perception.

By contrast, Graham's work argued for an analysis of (visual) meaning which defined signs as both structurally constituted within the system of linguistic functions and that was simultaneously grounded in the referent of social and political experience. Further, Graham's dialectical conception of visual representation polemically collapsed the difference between the spaces of production and those of reproduction (what Seth Siegelaub would call in 1969 the difference between primary and secondary information).

> For many years it has been well known that more people are aware of an artist's work through (1) the printed media or (2) conversation than by direct confrontation with the art itself. For painting and sculpture, where the visual presence—color, scale, size, location—is important to the work, the photograph or verbalization of that work is a bastardization of the art. But when art concerns itself with things not germane to physical presence, its intrinsic (communicative) value is not altered by its presentation in printed media.
>
> The use of catalogues and books to communicate (and disseminate) art is the most neutral means to present the new art. The catalogue can now act as the primary information for the exhibition, as opposed to secondary information about art in magazines, catalogues, etc. and in some cases the "exhibition" can be the "catalogue."[21]

Anticipating the work's actual modes of distribution and reception, within its very structure of production, Graham's *Homes for America* was the first work to have eliminated the difference between the artistic construct and its (photographic) reproduction, the difference between an exhibition of art objects and the photographic records of its installation, the difference between the architectural space of the gallery and the space of the catalog and the art magazine.

Joseph Kosuth's Tautologies

In opposition to this, Kosuth was arguing, in 1969, precisely for the continuation and expansion of Modernism's positivist legacy, and doing so with what must have seemed to him at the time the most radical and advanced tools of that tradition: Ludwig Wittgenstein's logical positivism and language philosophy (he emphatically affirmed this continuity when, in the first part of "Art after Philosophy," he states, "Certainly linguistic philosophy can be considered the heir to empiricism"). Thus, even while claiming to displace the formalism of Greenberg and Fried, he in fact updated Modernism's project of self-reflexivity. For Kosuth stabilized the notion of a disinterested and self-sufficient art by subjecting both Wittgenstein's model of the language game as well as the Duchampian model of the readymade to the strictures of a model of meaning that operates in the tradition of a paradox of modernity which Michel Foucault has called "empirico-transcendental" thought. This is to say that in 1968 artistic production is still the result, for Kosuth, of artistic intention as it constitutes itself above all in self-reflexivity (even if it is now discursive rather than perceptual, epistemological rather than essentialist and optical).[22]

At the very moment when the complementary formations of Pop and Minimal Art had, for the first time, succeeded in criticizing the legacy of American-type formalism and its prohibition of referentiality, this project is all the more astounding. The privileging of the literal over the referential axis of (visual) language—as Greenberg's formalist aesthetic had entailed—had been countered in Pop Art by a provocative devotion to the iconographies of mass culture. Then, both Pop and Minimal Art had continuously emphasized the universal presence of the industrial means of reproduction as inescapable framing conditions for artistic means of production, or, to put it differently, they had emphasized that the aesthetic of the studio had been irreversibly replaced by an aesthetic of production and consumption. And finally, Pop and Minimal Art had exhumed the repressed history of Duchamp (and Dadaism at large), phenomena equally unacceptable to the reigning formalist aesthetic thought of the late 1950s and early 1960s. This makes Kosuth's narrow reading of the readymade all the more astonishing since in 1969 he had explicitly claimed that he had encountered the work of Duchamp primarily through the mediation of Johns and Morris, rather than through an actual study of Duchamp's writings and works.

As we have seen before, the first two phases of the reception of Duchamp's *oeuvre* by American artists from the early 1950s (Johns and Rauschenberg) up to Warhol and Morris in the early 1960s had gradually opened up the full range of the implications of Duchamp's readymades. As Rosalind Krauss has suggested, at least Johns's understanding at that point already transcended the earlier reading of the readymade as merely an aesthetic of declaration and intention:

> If we consider that Stella's painting was involved early on, in the work of Johns, then Johns's interpretation of Duchamp and the readymade—an interpretation diametrically opposed to that of the Conceptualist group outlined above—has some relevance in this connection. For Johns clearly saw the readymade as pointing to the fact that there need be no connection between the final art object and the psychological matrix from which it issued, since in the case of the readymade this possibility is precluded from the start. The *Fountain* was not

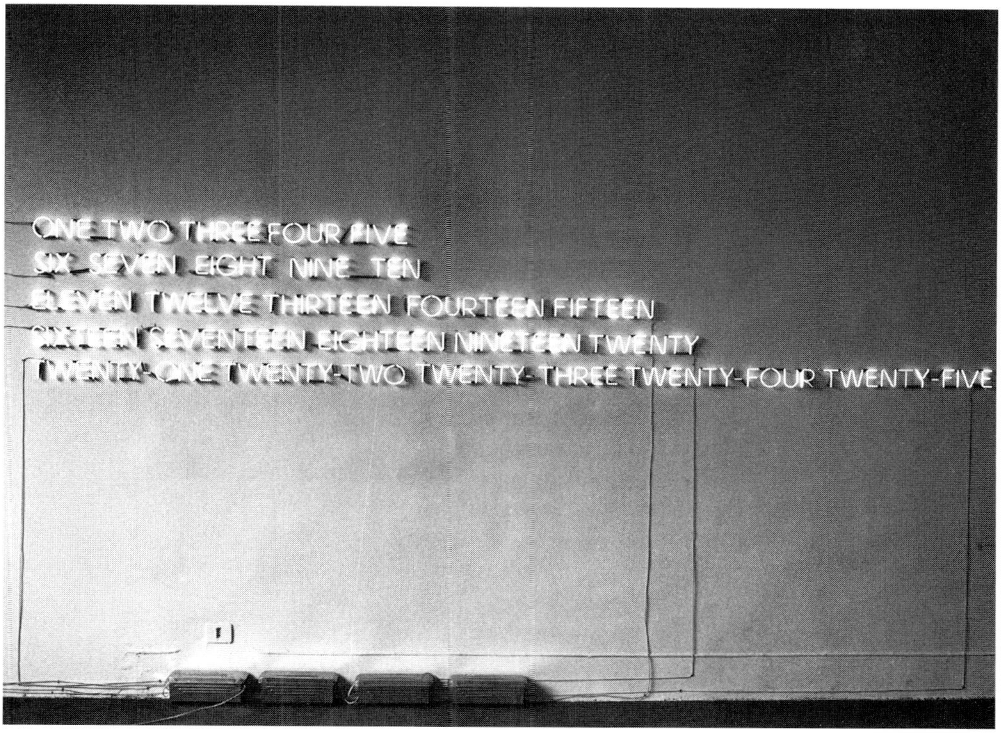

Joseph Kosuth, *Five Fives (to Donald Judd)*, 1965. Blue neon, transformers, 36½ × 218½ in. (92.7 × 555 cm). © Joseph Kosuth/Artists Rights Society (ARS), New York.

> made (fabricated) by Duchamp, only selected by him. Therefore there is no way in which the urinal can "express" the artist. It is like a sentence which is put into the world unsanctioned by the voice of a speaker standing behind it. Because maker and artist are evidently separate, there is no way for the urinal to serve as an externalization of the state or states of mind of the artist as he made it. And by not functioning within the grammar of the aesthetic personality, the *Fountain* can be seen as putting distance between itself and the notion of personality per se. The relationship between Johns's *American Flag* and his reading of the *Fountain* is just this: the arthood of the *Fountain* is not legitimized by its having issued stroke-by-stroke from the private psyche of the artist; indeed it could not. So it is like a man absentmindedly humming and being dumbfounded if asked if he had meant that tune or rather another. That is a case in which it is not clear how the grammar of intention might apply.[23]

It is therefore all the more puzzling to see that after 1968—what one could call the beginning of the third phase of the Duchamp reception—the understanding of this model by Conceptual artists still foregrounds intentional declaration over contextualization. This holds true not only for Kosuth's "Art after Philosophy," but equally for the British *Art & Language* group, as is evident in the introduction to the first issue of the journal in May 1969 when they write:

> To place an object in a context where the attention of any spectator will be conditioned toward the expectancy of recognizing art objects. For example placing what up to then had been an object of alien visual characteristics to those expected within the framework of an art ambience, or by

> virtue of the artist declaring the object to be an art object whether or not it was in an art ambience. Using these techniques what appeared to be entirely new morphologies were held out to qualify for the status of the members of the class "art objects." For example Duchamp's "readymades" and Rauschenberg's "Portrait of Iris Clert."[24]

A few months later Kosuth based his argument for the development of Conceptual Art on just such a restricted reading of Duchamp. For in its limiting view of the history and the typology of Duchamp's *oeuvre*, Kosuth's argument—like that of Art & Language—focuses exclusively on the "unassisted readymades." Thereby early Conceptual theory not only leaves out Duchamp's painterly work but avoids such an eminently crucial work as the *Three Standard Stoppages* (1913), not to mention *The Large Glass* or the *Étants donnés* or the *Boîte en valise* (1943).

What is worse, however, is the fact that even the reading of the unassisted readymades is extremely narrow, reducing the infinite complexity of the readymade model merely to that of an analytical proposition. Typically, both Art & Language and Kosuth's "Art after Philosophy" refer to Robert Rauschenberg's notorious example of an aesthetics of the performative ("This is a portrait of Iris Clert if I say so"), based on the rather limited understanding of the readymade as an act of willful artistic declaration. This understanding, which had been the most advanced and typical of the early 1950s, continues in Judd's famous lapidary norm (and patently nonsensical statement), quoted a little later in Kosuth's text: "if someone calls it art, it's art."

What Art & Language and Kosuth shared in 1969 was precisely this foregrounding of the linguistic performative inherent in each readymade, namely the implicit declaration "this is a work of art," over and above all other aspects implied by the readymade (its structural logic, its features as an industrially produced object of use and consumption, its seriality, and the manifest dependence of its "meaning" on discursive and institutional contexts). And most importantly, according to Kosuth, this implied that artistic propositions constitute themselves in the negation of all referentiality, be it that of the historical context of the (artistic) sign or that of its social function and use:

> Works of art are analytic propositions. That is, if viewed within their context-as-art, they provide no information what-so-ever about any matter of fact. A work of art is a tautology in that it is a presentation of the artist's intention, that is, he is saying that that particular work of art is art, which means, is a definition of art. Thus, that it is art is true a priori (which is what Judd means when he states that "if someone calls it art, it's art").[25]

Or, shortly thereafter, in the same year, Kosuth writes in *The Sixth Investigation 1969 Proposition 14* (a text which has mysteriously vanished from the collection of his writings):

> If one considers that the forms art takes as being art's language one can realize then that a work of art is a kind of proposition presented within the context of art as a comment on art. An analysis of proposition types shows art "works" as analytic propositions. Works of art that try to tell us something about the world are bound to fail. … The absence of reality in art is exactly art's reality.[26]

Kosuth's programmatic efforts to reinstate a law of discursive self-reflexivity in the guise of a critique of Greenberg's and Fried's visual and formal self-reflexivity are all the more dumbfounding since a considerable part of "Art after Philosophy" is dedicated to the elaborate construction of a genealogy for Conceptual Art, in and of itself a historical project (e.g., "All art [after Duchamp] is conceptual [in nature] because art exists only conceptually") This very construction of a lineage already contextualizes and historicizes, and thereby succeeds, of course, in "telling us something about the world"—the world of art, at least; that is, it unwittingly operates like a synthetic proposition (even if only within the conventions of a particular language system) and therefore denies both the purity and the possibility of an autonomous artistic production that would function, within art's own language-system, merely as an analytic proposition.

One could argue that one of the achievements of Kosuth's renewed pursuit of self-referentiality brings the Modernist project full circle to its final (and originary) state of tautology. This renewal of a radical aesthetic of self-critical abstraction completes the project of a Modernist aesthetic that had begun with Symbolism's exclusive concern with the conditions and the theorization of art's own modes of conception and reading. Such an argument, however, would still not allay questions concerning the altered historical framework within which such a cult of self-reflexivity inevitably finds its historical determination. Even within its Symbolist origins, the Modernist theology of art was already gripped by a polarized opposition. The religious veneration of self-referential plastic form as the pure negation of rationalist and empiricist thought can simultaneously be read as nothing other than the inscription and instrumentalization of precisely that rationalist order—even or particularly in its negation—within the realm of the aesthetic itself (the almost immediate and universal application of Symbolism for the cosmos of late nineteenth-century commodity production would attest to this).

This dialectic came to claim its historical rights all the more forcefully in the contemporary, postwar situation. Under the conditions of a rapidly accelerating fusion of the culture industry with the last bastions of an autonomous sphere of high art, self-reflexivity increasingly (and inevitably) shifted away from its roots in logical positivism toward the cunning of the advertisement campaign. And furthermore, a newly established postwar middle class, coming fully into its own in the 1960s, could identify comfortably with the late Modernist model of the tautology and its accompanying aesthetic of administration. This aesthetic of administration is structured exactly in analogy to that class's social identity, since its tasks are to administer labor and to organize and supervise the distribution of commodities, rather than to actually engage in material production. This class, having become firmly established as the most common and powerful social class of postwar society, is the one which, as H. G. Helms wrote in his book on Max Stirner, "deprives itself voluntarily of the rights to intervene within the political decision-making process in order to arrange itself more efficiently with the existing political conditions."[27]

This aesthetic of a newly established power of the order of the administrative found its first fully developed literary voice in a phenomenon like that of the *nouveau roman* of Alain Robbe-Grillet. It was no accident that such a profoundly positivist literary project would then serve, in the American context, as a point of departure for Conceptual Art. But, paradoxically, it was at this very same historical moment that the social functions of the tautological principle would find their most lucid analysis, through a critical examination launched in France. Thus one finds, in the early writing of Roland Barthes, at the very moment of the *nouveau roman*'s beginnings, a discussion of the tautological:

> *Tautology*. Yes, I know, it's an ugly word. But so is the thing. Tautology is the verbal device which consists in defining like by like ("*Drama is drama*"). … One takes refuge in tautology as one does in fear, or anger, or sadness, when one is at a loss for an explanation. … In tautology, there is a double murder: one kills rationality because it resists one; one kills language because it betrays one. … Now any refusal of language is a death. Tautology creates a dead, a motionless world.[28]

Ten years later, at the same moment that Kosuth was discovering tautology as the central aesthetic project of his era, the phenomenon came once again under theoretical scrutiny in France. But now, rather than being discussed as a linguistic and rhetorical form, it was analyzed as a general social effect: as the seemingly inescapable behavioral reflex under the conditions of everyday life in late capitalism, once the requirements of the advanced culture industry (i.e., advertisement and media) had been put in place in the formation of spectacle culture. What still remains open for discussion, of course, is the extent to which Conceptual Art of a certain type shared these conditions, or even enacted and implemented them in the sphere of the aesthetic—accounting, perhaps, for its subsequent proximity and success within a world of advertisement strategists—or, alternatively, the extent to which it merely inscribed itself into the inescapable logic of a totally administered world, as Adorno's notorious term had identified it. This is the description of the conditions of tautology as given by Guy Debord in 1967:

> The spectacle is essentially tautological, for the simple reason that its means and its ends are identical. It is the sun that never sets on the empire of modern passivity. It covers the entire globe, basking in the perpetual warmth of its own glory.[29]

A Tale of Many Squares

The visual forms that correspond most accurately to the linguistic form of the tautology are the square and its stereometric rotation, the cube. Not surprisingly, these two forms proliferated in the painterly and sculptural production of the early-to-mid-1960s. This was the moment when a rigorous self-reflexivity was bent on examining the traditional boundaries of Modernist sculptural objects to the same extent that a phenomenological reflection of viewing space was insistent on re-incorporating architectural parameters into the conception of painting and sculpture.

The square and the cube permeated the morphology of Minimalist sculpture to such an extent that in 1967 Lucy Lippard considered it appropriate to circulate a questionnaire among a fair number of artists, investigating the role of these forms, and to publish the results of the inquiry. In his response to the questionnaire, Donald Judd, in one of his endless attempts to detach the morphology of Minimalism from similar investigations of the historical avant-garde in the earlier part of the twentieth century, displayed the aggressive dimension of tautological thought (disguised as pragmatism, as was usual in his case) by simply denying that any historical meaning could be inherent in geometric or stereometric forms:

> I don't think there is anything special about squares, which I don't use, or cubes. They certainly don't have any intrinsic meaning or superiority. One thing though, cubes are a lot easier to make than spheres. The main virtue of geometric shapes is that they are not organic, as all art otherwise is. A form that's neither geometric nor organic would be a great discovery.[30]

How pervasive the square actually was in the art of the early-to-mid-1960s is all too obvious: the work from the late '50s such as paintings by Reinhardt and Ryman and a large number of sculptures from the early 1960s onwards (Andre, LeWitt for example) deployed the tautological form in endless variations. Paradoxically, even Kosuth's work from the mid-1960s—while emphasizing its departure from painting's traditional object status and visual/formal design—continues to display the definitions of words on large, black, square photostats. By contrast one only has to think of Barnett Newman's or Jasper Johns's work as immediate predecessors of that generation to recognize how infrequent, if not altogether absent the square had been at that moment.

As the central form of visual self-reflexivity, the square abolishes the traditional spatial parameters of verticality and horizontality, thereby canceling the metaphysics of space and its conventions of reading. It is in this way that the square (beginning with Malevich's 1915 [slightly irregular] *Black Square*) incessantly points to itself: as spatial perimeter, as plane, as surface and, functioning simultaneously, as support. But, with the very success of this self-referential gesture, demarcating the form as purely pictorial, the square painting paradoxically but inevitably assumes the character of a relief/object situated in actual space. It thereby invites a viewing/reading of spatial contingency and architectural contextuality, insisting on the imminent and irreversible transition from painting to sculpture.

This transition was performed in the proto-Conceptual Art of the early-to-mid-1960s in a fairly delimited number of specific pictorial operations. It occurred, first of all, through the emphasis on painting's *opacity*. The object-status of the painterly structure could be underscored by unifying and homogenizing its surface through monochromy, serialized texture, and gridded compositional structure; or it could be emphasized by literally sealing a painting's spatial transparency, thereby altering its material support: shifting it from canvas to unstretched fabric or metal. This type of investigation was developed systematically, for example, in the proto-Conceptual paintings of Robert Ryman, who employed all of these options separately or in varying combinations in the early-to-mid-1960s; or, after 1965, in the paintings of Robert Barry, Daniel Buren, and Niele Toroni.

Secondly—and in a direct inversion and counter-movement to the first—the emphasis on painting's object-status could be achieved by foregrounding, in a literalist manner, painting's transparency. This entailed establishing a dialectic between pictorial surface, frame, and architectural support by either literally opening up the painterly support as in Sol LeWitt's early *Structures* or by inserting transparent surfaces into the conventional frame of viewing as in Ryman's fiberglass paintings,

Robert Barry, *4 Red Squares,* 1967. Acrylic on canvas, 60 × 60 in. (152 × 152 cm). © Robert Barry. Courtesy the artist and Yvon Lambert Gallery, New York.

Buren's early nylon paintings, or Michael Asher's and Gerhard Richter's glass panes in metal frames, all being produced between 1965 and 1967. Or as in the early work of Robert Barry (such as his *Painting in Four Parts*, 1967, in the FER-Collection) where the square, monochrome, canvas objects now seemed to assume merely the role of architectural demarcation and the designation of the site and placement of a painting. Functioning as decentered painterly objects, these pictorial substitutes delimit the external architectural space in a manner analogous to the serial or central composition of earlier Minimal work which still defined internal pictorial or sculptural space. In Barry's *Square Canvas* (1967), which is to be placed at the exact center of the architectural support wall, the pictorial work is now conceived as programmatically shifting the reading from a centered, unified, pictorial object to an experience of architectural contingency, and thereby it incorporates the supplementary and overdetermining strategies of curatorial placement and of the conventions of installation (traditionally disavowed in painting and sculpture) into the *conception* of the painterly work itself.

And thirdly—and most often—this transition is performed in the "simple" rotation of the square, as originally evident in Naum Gabo's famous diagram from 1937 where a volumetric and a stereometric cube are juxtaposed in order to clarify the inherent continuity between planar, stereometric, and volumetric forms. This rotation generated cubic structures as diverse as Hans Haacke's *Condensation Cube* (1963–65), Robert Morris's *Mirrored Cubes* (1965), or Larry Bell's simultaneously produced *Mineral Coated Glass Cubes*, and Sol LeWitt's *Wall/Floor Piece ("Three Squares")* (1966). All of these (beyond sharing the obvious morphology of the square/cube) engage in the dialectic of opacity and transparency (or in the synthesis of that dialectic, the condition of mirror-reflection as in Morris's *Mirrored Cubes* or Larry Bell's aestheticized variations of the theme). At the same time that they engage in the dialectic of opacity and transparency, they also initiate a breakdown of the traditional distinction between frame, support and surface. Thereby—while displacing the traditional opposition of figure-ground relationships—they open up yet another dialectic that constitutes sculpture—that between sculptural object and architectural container.

The deployment of any or all of these strategies (or, as in most cases, their varying combinations) in the context of Minimal and Post-Minimal art, i.e., proto-Conceptual painting and sculpture, resulted in a range of hybrid objects. They no longer qualified for either of the traditional studio categories of painting or sculpture, nor could they be identified as relief or architectural decoration—the compromise terms traditionally used to bridge the gap between these categories. These objects demarcated another spectrum of departures toward Conceptual Art. Not only did they destabilize the boundaries of the traditional artistic categories of studio production, by eroding them with modes of industrial production in the manner of Minimalism, but they went further in their critical revision of the discourse of the studio versus the discourse of production/consumption. By ultimately dismantling both, and by implication the very conventions of visuality inherent in them, they firmly established an emergent aesthetic of administration.

The diversity of these proto-Conceptual objects would at first suggest that their actual aesthetic operations differ so profoundly that a comparative reading, operating merely on the grounds of their apparent analogous formal and morphological organization—the visual topos of the square—would be illegitimate. Art history has accordingly excluded Haacke's *Condensation Cube*, for example, from any affiliation with Minimal Art. Yet all of these artists define artistic production and reception by the mid-1960s as reaching beyond the traditional thresholds of visuality (both in terms of the materials and production procedures of the studio and those of industrial production) and it is on the basis of this parallel that their work can be understood to be linked beyond a mere structural or morphological analogy. The proto-Conceptual works of the mid-1960s redefine aesthetic experience, indeed, as a multiplicity of *non-specialized* modes of object—and language-experience. According to the reading that these objects generate, aesthetic experience—as an individual and social investment of objects with meaning—is constituted by *linguistic* as well as by *specular* conventions, by the institutional determination of the object's status as much as by the reading competence of the spectator.

Within this shared conception, what goes on to distinguish these objects from each other is the emphasis each one places on different aspects of that deconstruction of the traditional concepts of visuality. Morris's *Mirrored Cubes*, for example (once again an almost literal execution of a proposal found in Duchamp's *Green Box*), situate the spectator in the suture of the mirror reflection: that interface between sculptural object and architectural container where neither element can acquire a position of priority or dominance in the triad between spectator, sculptural object, and architectural space. And in so far as the work acts simultaneously to inscribe a phenomenological model of experience into a traditional model of purely visual specularity and to displace it, its primary focus remains the sculptural object and its visual apperception.

By contrast, Haacke's *Condensation Cube*—while clearly suffering from a now even more rigorously enforced scientistic reductivism and the legacy of Modernism's empirical positivism—moves away from a specular relationship to the object altogether, establishing instead a biological/physical system as a link between viewer, sculptural object, and architectural container. If Morris shifts the viewer from a mode of contemplative specularity into a phenomenological loop of bodily movement and perceptual reflection, Haacke replaces the once revolutionary concept of an activating "tactility" in the viewing experience by a move to bracket the phenomenological within the determinacy of a "system." For his work now suspends Morris's tactile "viewing" within a science-based syntagm (in this particular case that of the process of condensation and evaporation inside the cube brought about by temperature changes due to the frequency of spectators in the gallery).

And finally, we should consider what is possibly the last credible transformation of the square, at the height of Conceptual Art in 1968,

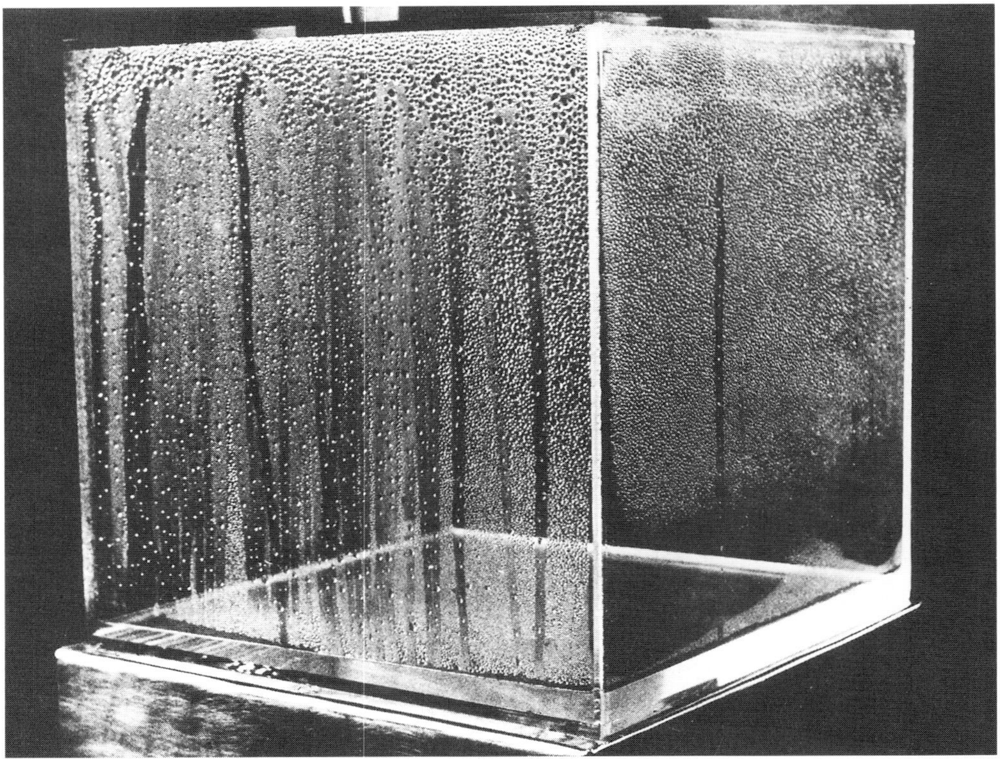

Hans Haacke, *Condensation Cube*, 1963–65. Acrylic, plastic, water, and climate in area of display, 12 × 12 × 12 in. (30 × 30 × 30 cm). © 2015 Hans Haacke/Artists Rights Society (ARS), New York/VG Bild-Kunst, Bonn.

in two works by Lawrence Weiner, respectively entitled *A Square Removal from a Rug in Use* and *A 36″ × 36″ Removal to the Lathing or Support Wall of Plaster or Wallboard from a Wall* (both published or "reproduced" in *Statements*, 1968[31]), in which the specific paradigmatic changes Conceptual Art initiates with regard to the legacy of reductivist formalism are clearly evident. Both interventions—while maintaining their structural and morphological links with formal traditions by respecting classical geometry as their definition at the level of shape—inscribe themselves in the support surfaces of the institution and/or the home which that tradition had always disavowed. The carpet (presumably for sculpture) and the wall (for painting), which Modernist idealist aesthetics had always declared as mere "supplements," are now foregrounded not only as parts of their material basis but as the inevitable future location of the work. Thus the structure, location, and materials of the intervention, at the very moment of their conception, are completely determined by their future site and destination. While neither the surface of the rug nor that of the wall are explicitly specified in terms of their institutional context, this ambiguity of dislocation generates two oppositional, yet mutually complementary readings.

On the one hand, it dissipates the traditional expectation of encountering the work of art only in a "specialized" or "qualified" location (both "wall" and "carpet" could be either those of the home or the museum, or, for that matter, could just as well be found in any other location such as an office, for example). On the other, neither one of these surfaces could ever be considered to be independent from its institutional location, since the physical inscription into each particular surface inevitably generates contextual readings dependent upon the institutional conventions and the particular use of those surfaces in place.

Transcending the literalist or perceptual precision with which Barry and Ryman had previously connected their painterly objects to the traditional walls of display, in order to make their physical and perceptual interdependence manifest, Weiner's two squares are now

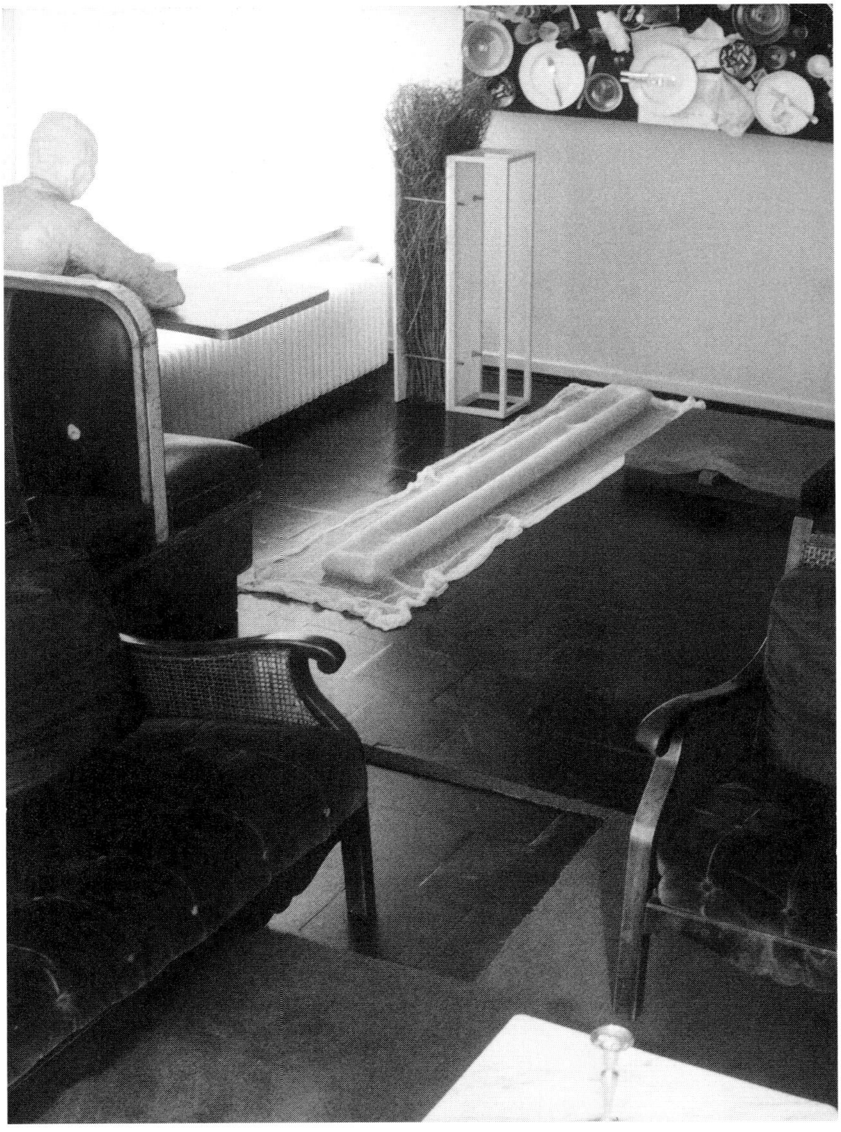

Lawrence Weiner, *A Removal of the Corner of a Rug in Use,* 1969. Wolfgang Hahn Residence, Cologne, Germany. Collection of Wolfgang Hahn, Museum Ludwig, Vienna. © 2015 Lawrence Weiner/Artists Rights Society (ARS), New York. Photo: Courtesy of Moved Pictures Archive, New York.

physically integrated with both these support surfaces and their institutional definition. Further, since the work's inscription paradoxically implies the displacement of the support surface, it engenders not only an experience of perceptual withdrawal but one of a critical intervention as well. Just as the work negates the specularity of the traditional artistic object by literally withdrawing rather than adding visual data in the construct, so this act of *perceptual* withdrawal operates as a physical (and symbolic) intervention in the institutional power and property relations underlying the supposed neutrality of "merely" artistic devices of presentation. The installation and/or acquisition of either of these works requires that the future owner accept an instance of physical removal/withdrawal/interruption on both the level of institutional order and on that of private ownership.

It was thus only logical that, on the occasion of Seth Siegelaub's first major exhibition of Conceptual Art, the show entitled *January 5–31, 1969*, Lawrence Weiner would have presented a formula that then functioned as the matrix underlying all of his subsequent propositions. Specifically addressing the relations within which the work of art is constituted as an open, structural, syntagmatic formula, this matrix statement defines the parameters of a work of art as those of the conditions of authorship and production, and their interdependence with those of ownership and use (and not least of all, at its own propositional level, as a linguistic definition contingent upon and determined by all of these parameters in their continuously varying and changing constellations):

With relation to the various manners of use.

1. The artist may construct the work

2. The work may be fabricated

3. The work need not be built

Each being equal and consistent with the intent of the artist the decision as to condition rests with the receiver upon the occasion of receivership.

Entering the arsenal of Conceptual strategies here, then, is a critique that operates at the level of the aesthetic "institution." It is a recognition that materials and procedures, surfaces and textures, locations and placement are not only sculptural or painterly matter to be dealt with in terms of a phenomenology of visual and cognitive experience or in terms of a structural analysis of the sign (as most of the Minimalist and Post-Minimalist artists had still believed), but that they are always already inscribed within the conventions of language and thereby within institutional power and ideological and economic investment. However, if, in Weiner's and Barry's work of the late 1960s, this recognition still seems merely latent, it was to become manifest very rapidly in the work of European artists of the same generation, in particular, that of Marcel Broodthaers, Daniel Buren, and Hans Haacke after 1966. In fact an institutional critique became the central focus of all three artists' assaults on the false neutrality of vision which provides the underlying rationale for those institutions.

In 1965, Buren—like his American peers in Conceptual Art—initiated his own work from a critical investigation of Minimalism. His early awareness and critical understanding of the work of Flavin, Ryman, and Stella rapidly enabled him to develop positions from within a strictly painterly analysis that soon led to a reversal of the traditional painterly and sculptural concepts of visuality altogether. On the one hand Buren was engaged in a critical review of the legacy of advanced modernist (and postwar American) painting and on the other, in an analysis of Duchamp's legacy, which he viewed critically as the utterly unacceptable negation of painting. This particular version of reading Duchamp and the readymade as acts of petit-bourgeois anarchist radicality—while not necessarily complete and accurate—allowed Buren to construct a successful critique of both: Modernist painting and Duchamp's readymade as its radical historical Other. In his writings and his interventions from 1967 onwards, through his critique of the specular order of painting and of the institutional framework determining it, Buren succeeded single-handedly

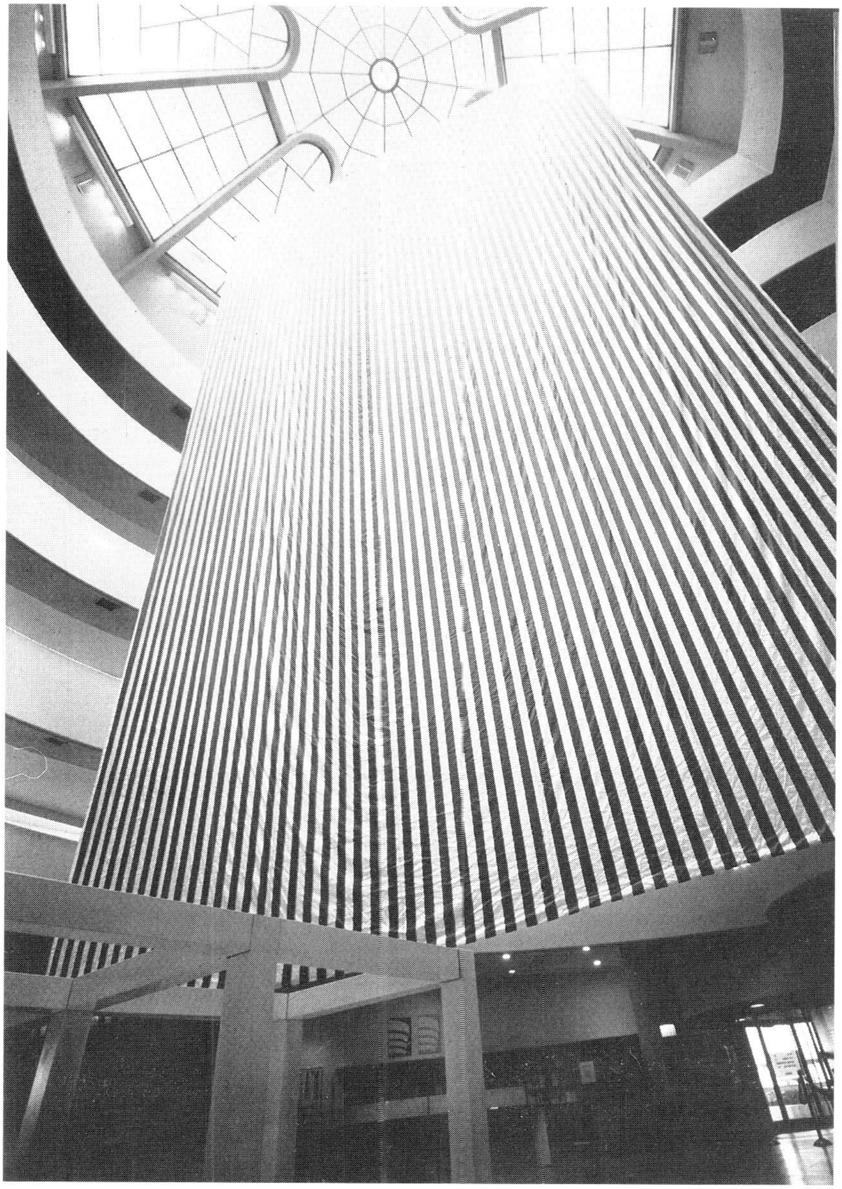

Daniel Buren, photo-souvenir: *Peinture-Sculpture (Painting-Sculpture)*, 1971. Work in situ. Solomon R. Guggenheim Museum, New York. © DB-ADAGP, Paris/Artists Rights Society (ARS), New York 2015.

in displacing both the paradigms of painting and that of the readymade (even twenty years later this critique makes the naive continuation of object production in the Duchampian vein of the readymade model appear as utterly irrelevant as the uncritical delivery of painterly products, regardless of whether they are abstract or representational).

From the perspective of the present, it seems easier to see that Buren's assault on Duchamp, especially in his crucial 1969 essay "Limites Critiques," was primarily directed at the conventions of Duchamp reception operative and predominant throughout the late 1950s and early 1960s, rather than at the actual implications of Duchamp's model itself. Buren's central thesis was that the fallacy of Duchamp's readymade was to obscure the very institutional and discursive framing conditions that allowed the readymade to generate its shifts in the assigment of meaning and the experience of the object in the first place. Yet, one could just as well argue, as Marcel Broodthaers would in fact suggest in his catalog of the exhibition *The Eagle from the Oligocene to Today* in Düsseldorf in 1972, that the contextual definition and syntagmatic construction of the work of art had obviously been initiated by Duchamp's readymade model first of all.

In his systematic analysis of the constituting elements of the discourse of painting, Buren came to investigate all the parameters of artistic production and reception (an analysis that, incidentally, was similar to the one performed by Lawrence Weiner in arriving at his own "matrix" formula). Departing from Minimalism's (especially Ryman's and Flavin's) literalist dismemberment of painting, Buren at first transformed the pictorial object into yet another model of opacity and objecthood. (This was accomplished by physically weaving figure and ground together in the "found" awning material, by making the "grid" of vertical parallel stripes his eternally repeated "tool," and by mechanically—almost superstitiously or ritualistically one could say with hindsight—applying a coat of white paint to the outer bands of the grid in order to distinguish the pictorial object from a readymade.) At the same time that the canvas had been removed from its traditional stretcher/support to become a physical cloth-object (reminiscent of Greenberg's notorious "tacked up canvas which already exists as a picture"), this strategy in Buren's arsenal found its logical counterpart in the placement of the stretched canvas leaning as an object against the support wall and floor.

This shifting of support surfaces and procedures of production led to a wide range of forms of distribution within Buren's work: from unstretched canvas to anonymously mailed sheets of printed striped paper; from pages in books to billboards. In the same way, his displacement of the traditional sites of reading and artistic intervention resulted in a multiplicity of locations and forms of display that continuously played on the dialectic of interior and exterior, thereby oscillating within the contradictions of sculpture and painting and foregrounding all those hidden and manifest framing devices that structure both traditions within the discourse of the museum and the studio.

Furthermore, enacting the principles of the Situationist critique of the bourgeois division of creativity according to the rules of the division of labor, Buren, Olivier Mosset, Michel Parmentier, and Niele Toroni publicly performed (on various occasions between 1966 and 1968) a demolition of the traditional separation between artists and audience with each performing their respective roles. Not only did they claim that each of their artistic idioms should be considered as absolutely equivalent and interchangeable, but also that any anonymous audience production of these pictorial signs would be equivalent to those produced by the artists themselves.

With its stark reproductions of mug shots of the four artists taken in photomats, the poster for their fourth manifestation at the 1967 Biennale de Paris inadvertently points to another major source of contemporary challenges to the notion of artistic authorship linked with a provocation to the "audience" to participate: the aesthetic of anonymity as practiced in Andy Warhol's "Factory" and its mechanical (photographic) procedures of production.[32] The critical interventions of the four artists within

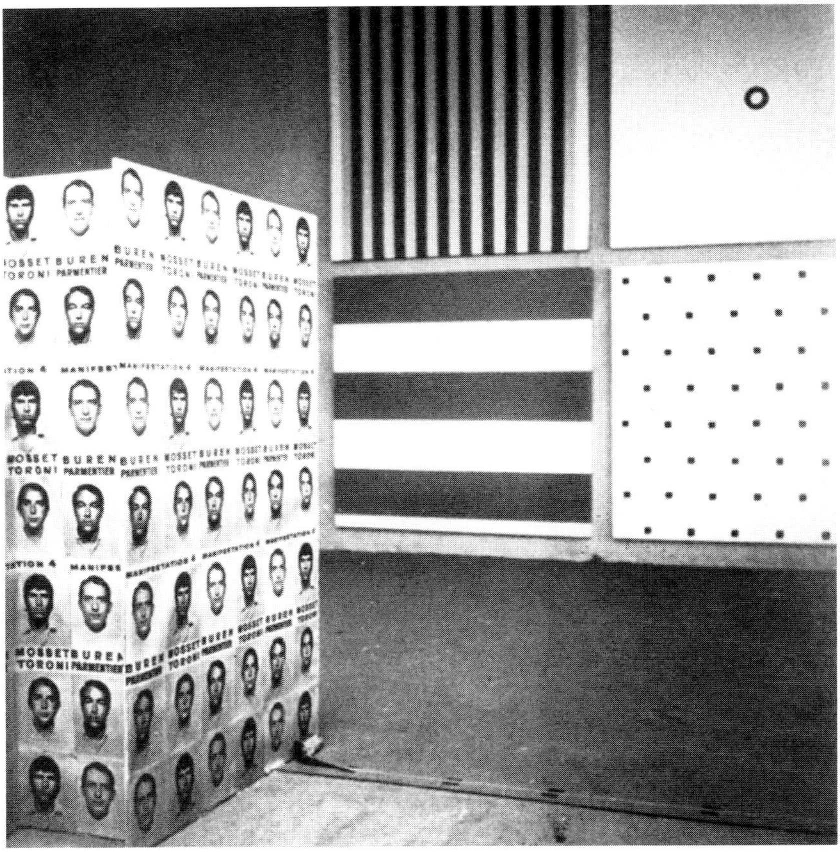

Daniel Buren, Olivier Mosset, Michel Parmentier, and Niele Toroni, *Manifestation No. 4, Photo-souvenirs No. 20 and No. 21*, September 1967. Fifth Biennale de Paris, Musée d'Art Moderne de la Ville de Paris.

an established but outmoded cultural apparatus (represented by such venerable and important institutions as the Salon de la Jeune Peinture or the Biennale de Paris) immediately brought out in the open at least one major paradox of all conceptual practices (a paradox incidentally which had made up the single most original contribution of Yves Klein's work ten years before). This was the recognition that the critical annihilation of cultural conventions itself immediately acquires the conditions of spectacle culture, and that the insistence on artistic anonymity and the demolition of authorship paradoxically produces all the more attractive instant brand names and identifiable products, and that the campaign to critique conventions of visuality with textual interventions, billboard signs, anonymous handouts, and pamphlets inevitably ends by mimetically following the pre-established mechanisms of advertising and marketing campaigns themselves.

All of the works mentioned coincide, however, in their rigorous definition of relationships between audience, object, and author. And all are concerted in the attempt to replace a traditional, hierarchical model of privileged experience based on authorial skills and acquired competence of reception by a structural relationship of absolute equivalents that would dismantle both sides of the equation: the hieratic position of the unified artistic object just as much as the privileged position of the author. In an early essay (published incidentally in the same 1967 issue of *Aspen Magazine*—dedicated by its editor Brian O'Doherty to Stéphane Mallarmé—in which the first English translation of Roland Barthes's "The Death of the Author" appeared), Sol LeWitt had laid out these concerns for a programmatic redistribution of author/artist functions with astonishing clarity, presenting them by means of the rather surprising metaphor of a performance of daily bureaucratic tasks:

> The aim of the artist would be to give viewers information. … He would follow his predetermined premise to its conclusion avoiding subjectivity. Chance, taste or unconsciously

> remembered forms would play no part in the outcome. The serial artist does not attempt to produce a beautiful or mysterious object but functions *merely as a clerk cataloguing the results of his premise.*[33]

Inevitably the question arises how such restrictive definitions of the artist as a cataloging clerk can be reconciled with the subversive and radical implications of Conceptual Art. And this question must simultaneously be posed within the specific historical context in which the legacy of an historical avant-garde—Constructivism and Productivism—had only recently been reclaimed. How, we might ask, can these practices be aligned with that historical production that artists like Henry Flynt, Sol LeWitt, and George Maciunas had rediscovered, in the early '60s, primarily through the publication of Camilla Gray's *The Great Experiment: Russian Art 1863–1922.*

This question is of particular importance since many of the formal strategies of early Conceptual Art appear at first glance to be as close to the practices and procedures of the Soviet Productivist avant-garde as Minimal sculpture had appeared to be dependent upon the materials and morphologies of the Russian Constructivist avant-garde.

Not unlike Constructivist practices, Conceptual Art emphasized a self-reflexivity transcending the boundaries of modernist self-referentiality, and it equally foregrounded the transparency of production processes as much as the work's internal and contextual operations. And not unlike the artists who developed Productivist positions, Conceptual artists were concerned with a radical alteration of the work's object status and its distribution form. And—most importantly perhaps—Conceptual Art, in its shift to the linguistic definition of artistic practice and its critique of conventional notions of visuality, was engaged with the project of broader audiences and establishing different audience relations, attempting to develop a more general reading competence of artistic structures and altering the conditions of artistic reception altogether (without of course specifying these new audiences in terms of social class or geo-political location).

The profoundly utopian (and now unimaginably naive) nature of the claims associated with Conceptual Art at the end of the 1960s was articulated by Lucy Lippard (along with Seth Siegelaub, certainly the crucial exhibition organizer and critic of that movement) in late 1969:

> Art intended as pure experience doesn't exist until someone experiences it, defying ownership, reproduction, sameness. Intangible art could break down the artificial imposition of "culture" and provide a broader audience for a tangible, object art. When automatism frees millions of hours for leisure, art should gain rather than diminish in importance, for while art is not just play, it is the counterpoint to work. The time may come when art is everyone's daily occupation, though there is no reason to think this activity will be called art.[34]

While it seems obvious that artists cannot be held responsible for the culturally and politically naive visions projected onto their work even by their most competent, loyal, and enthusiastic critics, it now seems equally obvious that it was precisely the leftist utopianism of earlier avant-garde movements (the type that Lippard desperately attempts to resuscitate for the occasion) that was manifestly absent from Conceptual Art throughout its history (despite Robert Barry's one-time invocation of Herbert Marcuse, declaring the commercial gallery as "Some places to which we can come, and for a while 'be free to think about what we are going to do'"). It seems obvious, at least from the vantage point of the early 1990s, that from its inception Conceptual Art was distinguished by its acute sense of discursive and institutional limitations, its self-imposed restrictions, its lack of a totalizing vision, its critical devotion to the factual conditions of artistic production and reception without aspiring to overcome the mere facticity of these conditions. This became evident as works such as Hans Haacke's series of *Visitors' Profiles* (1969–70), in its bureaucratic rigor and deadpan devotion to the statistic collection of factual information, came to refuse any transcendental dimension whatsoever.

Furthermore, it now seems that it was precisely a profound disenchantment with those political master-narratives that had empowered most of the 1920s avant-garde art that, acting in a peculiar fusion with the most advanced and radical forms of critical artistic reflection, accounts for the peculiar contradictions operating within Conceptual Art of the mid-to-late 1960s. It would explain why this generation of the early '60s—in its growing emphasis on empiricism and its skepticism with regard to all utopian vision—would be attracted, for example, to the logical positivism of Wittgenstein and would confound the affirmative petit-bourgeois positivism of Robbe-Grillet with the radical atopism of Samuel Beckett, claiming all of them as their sources. And it would make clear how this generation could be equally attracted to the conservative concept of Daniel Bell's "end of ideology" and Herbert Marcuse's Freudo-Marxist philosophy of liberation.

What Conceptual Art achieved at least temporarily, however, was to subject the last residues of artistic aspiration toward transcendence (by means of traditional studio skills and privileged modes of experience) to the rigorous and relentless order of the vernacular language of administration. Furthermore, it managed to purge artistic production of the aspiration toward an affirmative collaboration with the forces of industrial production and consumption (the last of the totalizing experiences into which artistic production had mimetically inscribed itself with credibility in the context of Pop Art and Minimalism for one last time).

Paradoxically, then, it would appear that Conceptual Art truly became the most significant paradigmatic change of postwar artistic production at the very moment that it mimed the operating logic of late capitalism and its positivist instrumentality in an effort place its autocritical investigations at the service of liquidating even the last remnants

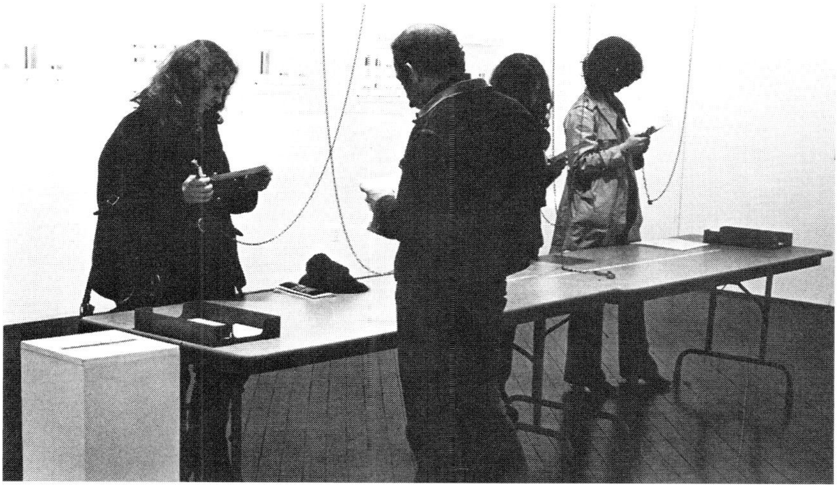

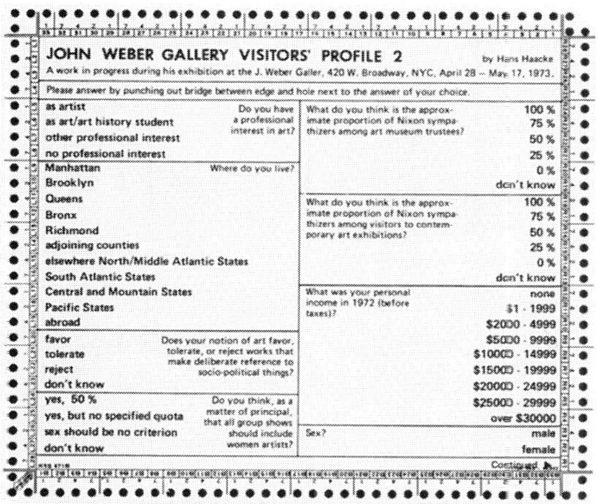

JOHN WEBER GALLERY VISITORS' PROFILE 2 by Hans Haacke
A work in progress during his exhibition at the J. Weber Galler, 420 W. Broadway, NYC, April 28 – May 17, 1973.
Please answer by punching out bridge between edge and hole next to the answer of your choice.

Do you have a professional interest in art?
as artist
as art/art history student
other professional interest
no professional interest

Where do you live?
Manhattan
Brooklyn
Queens
Bronx
Richmond
adjoining counties
elsewhere North/Middle Atlantic States
South Atlantic States
Central and Mountain States
Pacific States
abroad

Does your notion of art favor, tolerate, or reject works that make deliberate reference to socio-political things?
favor
tolerate
reject
don't know

Do you think, as a matter of principal, that all group shows should include women artists?
yes, 50 %
yes, but no specified quota
sex should be no criterion
don't know

What do you think is the approximate proportion of Nixon sympathizers among art museum trustees?
100 %
75 %
50 %
25 %
0 %
don't know

What do you think is the approximate proportion of Nixon sympathizers among visitors to contemporary art exhibitions?
100 %
75 %
50 %
25 %
0 %
don't know

What was your personal income in 1972 (before taxes)?
none
$1 - 1999
$2000 - 4999
$5000 - 9999
$10000 - 14999
$15000 - 19999
$20000 - 24999
$25000 - 29999
over $30000

Sex?
male
female

Continued

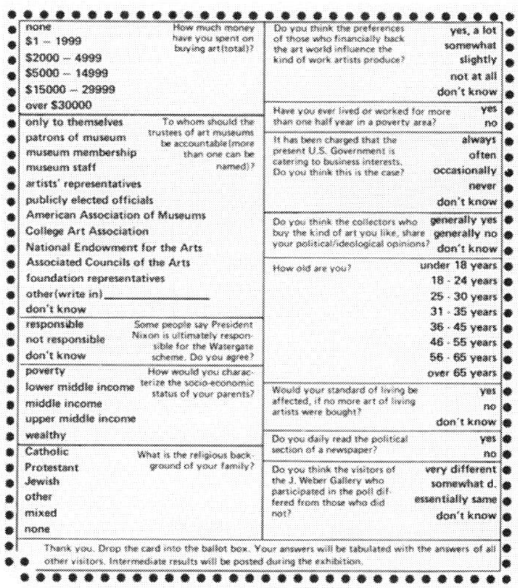

How much money have you spent on buying art (total)?
none
$1 – 1999
$2000 – 4999
$5000 – 14999
$15000 – 29999
over $30000

To whom should the trustees of art museums be accountable (more than one can be named)?
only to themselves
patrons of museum
museum membership
museum staff
artists' representatives
publicly elected officials
American Association of Museums
College Art Association
National Endowment for the Arts
Associated Councils of the Arts
foundation representatives
other (write in) ________________
don't know

Some people say President Nixon is ultimately responsible for the Watergate scheme. Do you agree?
responsible
not responsible
don't know

How would you characterize the socio-economic status of your parents?
poverty
lower middle income
middle income
upper middle income
wealthy

What is the religious background of your family?
Catholic
Protestant
Jewish
other
mixed
none

Do you think the preferences of those who financially back the art world influence the kind of work artists produce?
yes, a lot
somewhat
slightly
not at all
don't know

Have you ever lived or worked for more than one half year in a poverty area?
yes
no

It has been charged that the present U.S. Government is catering to business interests. Do you think this is the case?
always
often
occasionally
never
don't know

Do you think the collectors who buy the kind of art you like, share your political/ideological opinions?
generally yes
generally no
don't know

How old are you?
under 18 years
18 - 24 years
25 - 30 years
31 - 35 years
36 - 45 years
46 - 55 years
56 - 65 years
over 65 years

Would your standard of living be affected, if no more art of living artists were bought?
yes
no
don't know

Do you daily read the political section of a newspaper?
yes
no

Do you think the visitors of the J. Weber Gallery who participated in the poll differed from those who did not?
very different
somewhat d.
essentially same
don't know

Thank you. Drop the card into the ballot box. Your answers will be tabulated with the answers of all other visitors. Intermediate results will be posted during the exhibition.

Hans Haacke, *John Weber Gallery Visitors' Profile 2*, April–May 1973. Results: 29 sheets drawing paper, 11 × 8½ in. (28 × 21.5 cm). Private collection. © 2015 Hans Haacke/Artists Rights Society (ARS), New York/VG Bild-Kunst, Bonn.

of traditional aesthetic experience. In that process it succeeded in purging itself entirely of imaginary and bodily experience, of physical substance and the space of memory, to the same extent that it effaced all residues of representation and style, of individuality and skill. That was the moment when Buren's and Haacke's work from the late 1960s onwards turned the violence of that mimetic process back onto the ideological apparatus itself, using it to analyze and expose those very social institutions from which the laws of positivist instrumentality and the logic of administration emanate in the first place. These institutions, which determine the conditions of cultural consumption, are the very ones in which artistic production is transformed into a tool of ideological control and cultural legitimation.

It was left to Marcel Broodthaers to construct objects in which the radical achievements of Conceptual Art would be turned into immediate travesty and in which the seriousness with which Conceptual artists had adopted the rigorous mimetic subjection of aesthetic experience to the principles of what Adorno had called the "totally administered world" were transformed into absolute farce. And it was one of the effects of Broodthaers's dialectics that the achievement of Conceptual Art was revealed as being intricately tied to a profound and irreversible loss: a loss not caused by artistic practice, of course, but one to which that practice responded in the full optimism of its aspirations, failing to recognize that the purging of image and skill, of memory and vision, within visual aesthetic representation was not just another heroic step in the inevitable progress of Enlightenment to liberate the world from mythical forms of perception and hierarchical modes of specialized experience. But that it was also yet another, perhaps the last of the erosions (and perhaps the most effective and devastating one) to which the traditionally separate sphere of artistic production had been subjected in its perpetual efforts to emulate the regnant episteme within the paradigmatic frame proper to art itself.

Or worse yet, that the Enlightenment triumph of Conceptual Art—its transformation of audiences and distribution, its abolition of object status and commodity form—would most of all only be short lived, almost immediately giving way to the return of the ghostlike apparitions of perhaps prematurely displaced painterly and sculptural paradigms of the past. So that the specular regime, which Conceptual Art claimed to have dismantled, would soon be reinstated with renewed vigor. Which is of course what happened.

Notes

First published in *L'art conceptuel: Une perspective* (Paris: Musée d'art moderne de la Ville de Paris, 1989). First English version in *October* 55, (winter 1990): 105–143. Minor corrections have been made for consistency.

1. La Monte Young's *An Anthology* was in fact published by Heiner Friedrich in 1963. A second contestant for the invention of the term was Edward Kienholz with his series of *Concept Tableaux* in 1963 (in fact, he is occasionally still credited with the discovery of the term. See for example Roberta Smith's essay "Conceptual Art," in *Concepts of Modern Art*, ed. Nikos Stangos (New York: Harper & Row, 1981), pp. 256–270.

Joseph Kosuth claims in his *Sixth Investigation 1969 Proposition 14* (Cologne: Gerd de Vries/Paul Maenz, 1971, n.p.) that he used the term "conceptual" for the first time: "in a series of notes dated 1966 and published a year later in a catalogue for an exhibition titled Non-anthropomorphic Art at the now defunct Lannis Gallery in New York."

And then there are of course (most officially accepted by all participants) Sol LeWitt's two famous texts from 1967 and 1969, the "Paragraphs on Conceptual Art," first published in *Artforum* 5, no. 10 (June 1967): 56–57; and "Sentences on Conceptual Art," first published in *Art & Language* 1, no. 1 (May 1969): 11–13.

2. For a typical attempt to write the history of Conceptual Art by blindly adopting and repeating uncritically the claims and convictions of one of that history's figures, see Gudrun Inboden, "Joseph Kosuth—Artist and Critic of Modernism," in *Joseph Kosuth: The Making of Meaning*, ed. Gudrun Inboden (Stuttgart: Staatsgalerie, 1981), pp. 11–27.

3. Joseph Kosuth, *The Sixth Investigation 1969 Proposition 14* (Cologne: Gerd De Vries/ Paul Maenz, 1971), n.p.

4. Dan Graham, *End Moments* (New York, 1969), n.p. The other Minimalists with whose work Graham seems to have been particularly involved were Dan Flavin

(Graham wrote the catalog essay for Flavin's exhibition at the Museum of Contemporary Art in Chicago in 1967) and Robert Morris (whose work he discussed later extensively in his essay "Income Piece" in 1973).

5. Mel Bochner, "Less Is Less (for Dan Flavin)," *Art and Artists* (summer 1966).

6. Joseph Kosuth, "Art after Philosophy (Part II)," in *The Making of Meaning*, p. 175. The list would seem complete, if it were not for the absence of Bochner's and On Kawara's names, and its explicit negation of the importance of LeWitt. According to Bochner, who had become an instructor at the School of Visual Arts in 1965, Kosuth worked with him as a student in 1965 and 1966. Dan Graham mentioned in an interview with the author that during that time Kosuth was also a frequent visitor to On Kawara's and LeWitt's studios. Kosuth's explicit negation makes one wonder whether it was not precisely Sol LeWitt's series of the so-called "Structures" (such as *Red Square, White Letters*, for example, produced in 1962 and exhibited in 1965) that would become one of the crucial points of departure for the formulation of Kosuth's *Proto-Investigations*.

7. Roland Barthes, *Mythologies*, trans. Annette Lavers (New York: Hill & Wang, 1972), p. 158.

8. The first of the two quotations is to be found in Ad Reinhardt's Skowhegan lecture, delivered in 1967, quoted by Lucy Lippard in *Ad Reinhardt* (New York: Abrams, 1981), p. 195. The second statement appears in an interview with Mary Fuller, published as "An Ad Reinhardt Monologue," *Artforum* 10 (November 1971): 36–41.

9. John Cage, statement in reaction to the controversy engendered by the exhibition of Rauschenberg's all white paintings at Eleanor Ward's Stable Gallery, New York,, September 15–October 3, 1953. Printed in Emily Genauer's column in the *New York Herald Tribune*, December 27, 1953, p. 6 (section 4).

10. Ad Reinhardt, "Art as Art," *Art International* (December 1962). Reprinted in *Art as Art: The Selected Writings of Ad Reinhardt*, ed. Barbara Rose (New York: Viking, 1975), p. 56.

11. Duchamp voiced this critique repeatedly, for example in the famous quip: "All my work in the period before the *Nude* was visual painting. Then I came to the idea. ..." See Marcel Duchamp, interviewed by Francis Roberts (1963), *Art News* (December 1968): 46.

12. Stella's famous statement was made in Bruce Glaser's "Questions to Stella and Judd," in February 1964, published in *Art News* (September 1966): 55–61.

13. Robert Morris, unpublished interview with Jack Burnham, November 21, 1975, Robert Morris Archive. Quoted in Maurice Berger, *Labyrinths: Robert Morris, Minimalism, and the 1960s* (New York: Harper & Row, 1989), p. 25 (emphasis added).

14. Sol LeWitt, "Sentences on Conceptual Art," first published in the journal edited by Vito Acconci, *0 to 9* (1969): n.p., and *Art & Language* (Coventry, May 1969): 11.

15. Robert Morris, as quoted in Maurice Berger, *Labyrinths: Robert Morris, Minimalism, and the 1960s*, p. 22.

16. Robert Morris, "Some Notes on the Phenomenology of Making: The Search for the Motivated," *Artforum* 9 (April 1970): 63.

17. It would be worthwhile to explore the fact that an artist like Arshile Gorky under the impact of the WPA program would still have been concerned with the aesthetics of mural painting when he was commissioned to decorate the Newark Airport building, and that even Jackson Pollock tinkered with the idea of an architectural dimension for his paintings, wondering whether they could be transformed into architectural panels. As is well known, Mark Rothko's involvement with the Seagram Corporation to produce a set of decorative panels for their corporate headquarters ended in disaster and Barnett Newman's synagogue project was abandoned as well. All of these exceptions would confirm the rule that the postwar aesthetic had undergone the most rigorous privatization and a reversal of the reflection on the inextricable link between artistic production and public social experience as they had marked the 1920s. The most notable exception would of course be the development of urbanist and architectural concerns in the context of the activities of the Independent Group in England in the mid-1950s.

18. This work claims to document photographically the existence of everyone alive in order to produce the most authentic and inclusive representation of the human species that may be assembled in that manner. Editions of this work will be periodically issued in a variety of topical modes: "100,000 people," "1,000,000 people," "10,000,000 people," ... etc.

19. Victor Burgin, "The Absence of Presence," in Burgin, *The End of Art Theory* (Atlantic Highlands, N.J.: Humanities Press International, 1986), p. 34.

20. In the preparation of this essay I have not been able to find a single source or document that would confirm with definite credibility Kosuth's claim that these works entitled *Proto-Investigations* were actually produced and existed physically in 1965 or 1966 when he (at that time twenty years old) was still a student at the School of Visual Arts in New York. Nor was Kosuth able to provide any documents to make the claims verifiable. By contrast these claims were explicitly contested during my interviews with all the artists who knew Kosuth at that time, none of them remembering seeing any of the *Proto-Investigations* before February 1967, in the exhibition *Non-Anthropomorphic Art by Four Young Artists*, organized by Joseph Kosuth at the Lannis Gallery (or Lannis Museum as it is often referred to by Kosuth who directed this gallery, financed by one of his relatives). The artists with whom I conducted interviews in the preparation of this essay

were Robert Barry, Mel Bochner, Dan Graham, Sol LeWitt, and Lawrence Weiner. I am not necessarily suggesting that the *Proto-Investigations* could not have been done by Kosuth at the age of twenty (after all, Frank Stella had painted his *Black Paintings* at age twenty-three), nor that the logical steps fusing Duchamp and Reinhardt with Minimalism and Pop Art leading up to the *Proto-Investigations* could not have been taken by an artist of Kosuth's historical awareness and strategic intelligence. But I am saying that none of the work dated by Kosuth to 1965 or 1966 can—until further evidence is produced—actually be documented as 1965 or 1966, or dated with any credibility. By contrast the word paintings of On Kawara (whose studio Kosuth visited frequently at that time), such as his important early work *Something* which anticipates the *Proto-Investigations* in every respect, are reproduced and documented in 1965.

21. Seth Siegelaub, "On Exhibitions and the World at Large: An Interview with Charles Harrison," in *Studio International* (December 1969).

22. This differentiation is developed in Hal Foster's excellent discussion of these paradigmatic differences as they emerge first in Minimalism. See his essay "The Crux of Minimalism," in *Individuals* (Los Angeles: Museum of Contemporary Art, 1986), pp. 162–183.

23. Rosalind Krauss, "Sense and Sensibility," *Artforum* 12 (November 1973): 43–52, n. 4.

24. Introduction, *Art & Language* 1, no.1 (May 1969): 5.

25. Joseph Kosuth, "Art after Philosophy," *Studio International*, nos. 915–917 (October–December 1969). Quoted here from Joseph Kosuth, *The Making of Meaning*, p. 155.

26. Joseph Kosuth, *The Sixth Investigation 1969, Proposition 14.*

27. Hans G. Helms, *Die Ideologie der anonymen Gesellschaft* (Cologne: Dumont Buchverlag, 1968), p. 3.

28. Roland Barthes, *Mythologies*, pp. 152–153.

29. Guy Debord, *The Society of the Spectacle* (1967), trans. Donald Nicholson Smith (New York: Zone Books, 1994), p. 15.

30. Donald Judd, in Lucy Lippard, "Homage to the Square," *Art in America*, (July–August 1967): 50–57.

31. Lawrence Weiner, *Statements* (New York: The Louis Kellner Foundation/Seth Siegelaub, 1968), n.p.

32. Michel Claura, at the time the critic actively promoting awareness of the affiliated artists Buren, Mosset, Parmentier, and Toroni, has confirmed in a recent conversation with the author that the reference to Warhol, in particular to his series *The Thirteen Most Wanted Men*, which had been exhibited at the Ileana Sonnabend Gallery in 1967, was quite a conscious decision.

33. Sol LeWitt, "Serial Project #1, 1966," *Aspen Magazine*, nos. 5–6 (1967), n.p. Emphasis added.

34. Lucy Lippard, "Introduction," *955.000* (Vancouver: Vancouver Art Gallery, 1970), n.p.

11

Residual Resemblance: Three Notes on the Ends of Portraiture

For example, it is accepted as a certainty that Foucault, adhering in this to a certain conception of literary production, got rid of, purely and simply, the notion of the subject: no more oeuvre, no more author, no more creative unity. But things are not that simple. The subject does not disappear; rather, its excessively determined unity is put in question, what arouses interest and inquiry is its disappearance (that is, the new manner of being which disappearance is), or rather its dispersal, which does not annihilate it but offers us, out of it, no more than a plurality of positions and a discontinuity of functions (and here we reencounter the system of discontinuities, which, rightly or wrongly, seemed at one time to be a characteristic of serial music).

—*Maurice Blanchot, "Michel Foucault as I Imagine Him"*[1]

I

A recent surge in photographic portraiture (from Thomas Struth and Thomas Ruff on one end of the spectrum to Nan Goldin on the other) confronts spectators and collectors with questions that could be phrased from both the perspective of social history and that of art history. These questions would address the historical necessity, if not the legitimacy, of the desire to confide oneself (or one's self) again and again to the genre of portraiture, both as an author and as a subject.

We should remember that photography's initial promise to provide each subject with an iconic likeness—as much as the quest had been legitimate—had been proven to be fraudulent already by the mid-nineteenth century. Just at that moment when the representation of all subjects had become technically possible, it became also apparent that iconic representation alone would not suffice to recognize the collective participation in the processes of production. Quite to the contrary: to the very degree that photographic representation had been disseminated (for example in the discovery and industrial exploitation of Adolphe Disdéri's *carte de visite* portraits), the democratic potential of portrait photography unleashed its dialectical counterpart; it now provided a new and singular image: the substitution of the subject by the mere image.

Early theoreticians of photography like Walter Benjamin failed to recognize this dialectic: they failed to see that the seemingly emancipatory practice of the photographic dissemination of the image of subjectivity, and the concomitant loss of the auratic uniqueness of the subject's individual features, would bring about its opposite: a hypertrophic representation of a lost subjectivity that could now be sold back as a substitute, as commodity and cult imagery, to those who had never been given access to the subject's physiognomic—let alone its actual—political realization. We therefore already confront the first of the many contradictions innate to the genre of portraiture: the photographic portrait ultimately substituted the subject's photographic representation in the place of his or her political representation.

The second dialectic dimension of the portrait, both in painting and in photography, originates from the genre's historically determined bond with class specificity. Any historical claim for a self-determined subject, and certainly any cultural practice claiming to represent it, loses its credibility when that model of free subjectivity is neither universally accessible, nor derives exclusively from the boundaries and privileges of class. If subject formations depend on residual class privileges and conventions of self-representation, as for example, the painted portrait once depended upon the aristocratic or high bourgeois conception of the self, such formations will inevitably appear as obsolete or grotesque. This is all the more so if such formations claim to redeem an already precarious model of subjectivity and resuscitate the obsolete genre. This dialectic demarcates the obstinate survival of portraiture in the twentieth century in both its painterly and photographic epiphanies; the latter's claim on technical veracity and neutrality provides only a semblance of protection from these contradictions.

II

Among the many traditional pictorial (and sculptural) categories to be dismantled in the cubist campaigns between 1907 and 1912, the portrait appears to have been the most formidable opponent. While at least temporarily sharing the fate of disappearance alongside the genres of the *nude*, the *still life* and the *landscape*, the *portrait* as a pictorial category seems to renew itself and rear its heads (like those of the Hydra) almost instantly after their inevitable decapitation. The conclusion of cubism in Picasso's work was announced first of all by the return to the mimetic portrait in the neo-classical renderings of Max Jacob and Ambroise Vollard, executed in 1915. Physiognomy functions here not just as the reaffirmation of a biological foundation of subjective identity, but also as the foundational guarantee of a mimetic model of artistic representation. Inevitably, a crucial question arises in retrospect: was the literal disappearance of the sitter from painting in 1910 primarily determined by a pictorial necessity, or more importantly by an epistemic change in the conception of subjectivity? Any answer to that question will have to precede all attempts to clarify why claims for the validity of the portrait as a genre of painting and photography, and as a model of pictorial mimesis, were continuously re-staged on the ruins of representation after 1915.

If cubism initiated representation's transition from a model of mimesis to one of structural difference, it argued for the end of a "motivated" visual sign.[2] Therefore, inasmuch as portraiture instantiates the subject within a "naturally given" iconic resemblance, it would have to be the genre discredited first and foremost. In portraiture, a seemingly guaranteed nexus between object and representation appears evident; in fact, mimetic resemblance was one of the category's founding conditions. The desire for the lasting depiction of subjects reinforced physiognomic truth as a naturally given fact. If such depictions were at all a departure from that perceived fact, then they were so only by virtue of the painter's hand and competence; more frequently, however, such exceptional mimetic skills would *enhance* the naturalized relation between object and representation.[3]

It does not surprise us that, unlike the landscape, the still life, and the nude—pictorial genres that have all but vanished since the moment of their cubist deconstruction—the portrait has been resurrected again and again. In fact, it became the site where the myth of a natural motivation of the sign—that is, the mimetic model of representation, as much as the myth of a foundational concept of subjectivity—could be avidly reaffirmed by every generation of twentieth-century modernists. Thus we can propose that actual correspondences exist between the pictorial and the epistemic, correspondences that attest to a causal nexus between rapidly changing conceptions of the subject, and the equally

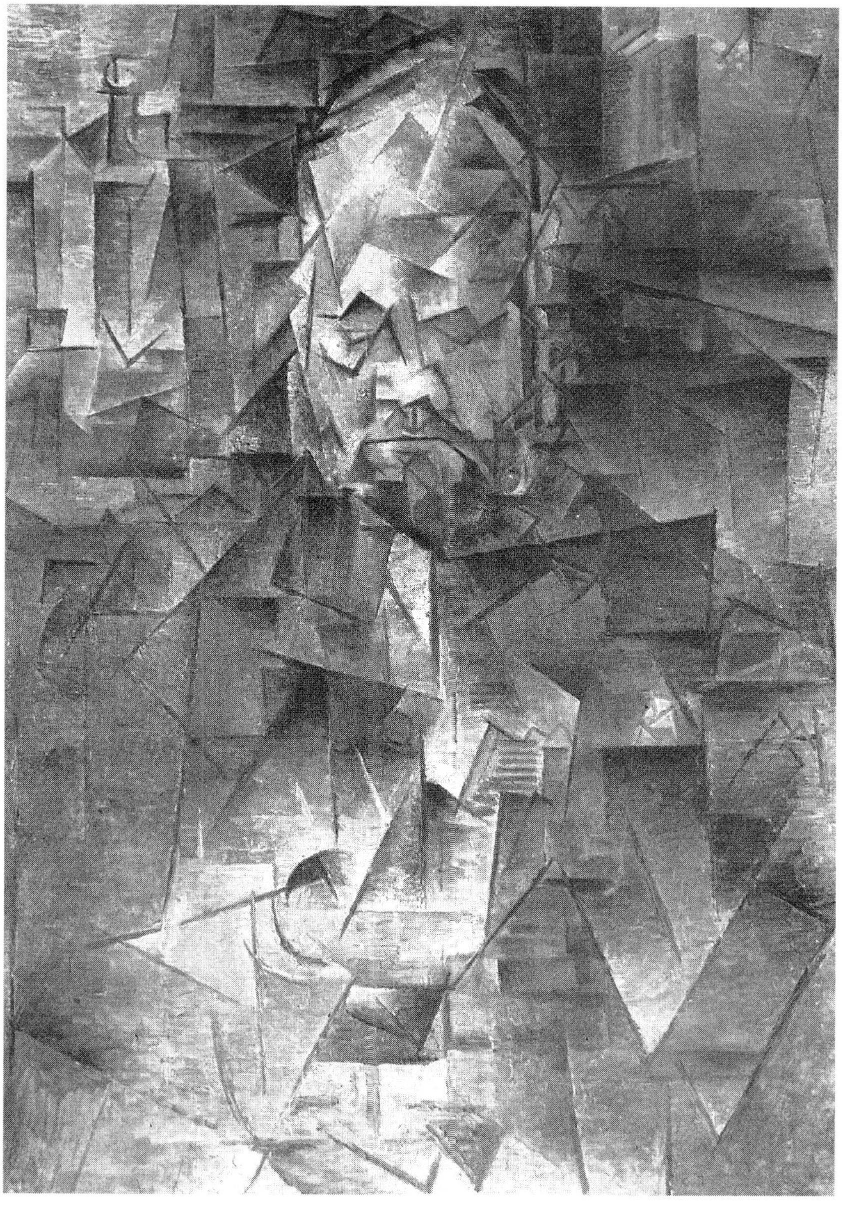

Pablo Picasso, *Portrait of Vollard*, 1910. Oil on canvas, 36¼ × 25⅝ in. (92 × 65 cm). Pushkin Museum, Moscow.

rapid disintegration and desperate resurrection of the traditional genre of portraiture. The photographic portrait as a genre seems to be outlasting even the impact of psychoanalytic and structuralist theories of the subject.

However, before one embraces a theory of radically de-centered subjectivity as a politically emancipatory project, one should equally consider whose interests are served by the incessant dismantling of the traditional conception of the subject. After all, an uncannily complex historical interrelationship operates between the emerging structuralist and socialist models that had initially aimed at dismantling bourgeois subjectivity as an ideological construct, and the late-capitalist agenda that aims to systematically foil the formation of politically conscious and self-determining subjects in the service of an emerging and increasingly enforced culture of consumption and control.

III

> So the Russian feature film was the first opportunity in decades to put people before the camera who had no use for their photographs. And immediately the human face appeared on film with new and immeasurable significance. But it was no longer a portrait. What was it?
>
> —*Walter Benjamin, "A Short History of Photography"*

The reflection on portraiture turns inevitably to photography, which was certainly as foundational for the genre of portraiture in the nineteenth and twentieth centuries as were the emerging concepts of class identity. When Walter Benjamin in 1931 speaks in his essay of the new, politically educated way of seeing that overcomes the cult of interiority of the centered subject, he argues that it will dissolve the subject's privacy and intimacy in favor of a public illumination of social relations and material details. Yet he emphasizes at the same time that the genre of the photographic portrait would resist this transformation longer than any other, stating that "to do without people is for photography the most impossible of renunciations."[4]

Yet among the many roles that photography has played throughout the twentieth century, it has fulfilled one with particular persistence: to compensate for the losses that the agents of the avant-garde inflicted on traditional forms of visual experience. As to be expected, at every such moment, photography would deploy its arsenal of a seemingly unshakeable, guaranteed iconicity. But the project of restoring physiognomic likeness in 1915 via traditional single-frame painted or photographic imagery, however, amounted to more than just redeeming mimetic representation. It reassured the spectator of the continuing validity of essentialist and biologistic concepts of identity formation. This foundational—if not outright ideological—promise is a latent argument found in every traditional photographic portrait of the twentieth century.

In an astonishing—and hardly examined—comparison between the work of August Sander, the eminent portrait photographer of German *Neue Sachlichkeit*, and the works of the Soviet filmmakers Sergei Eisenstein and Vsevelod Pudovkin, Benjamin describes the historical predicaments of the photographic portrait and the conditions necessary for a resurrection in the present of legitimate portraiture.[5] One such condition is a new systematicity of physiognomic investigation. According to Benjamin it was precisely Sander's quasi-scientific approach to the interrelation between the subject's physiognomic nature and its social constructedness that made *Menschen des 20. Jahrhunderts* (*People of the 20th Century*) an exemplary project

To conceive of the subject as constituted by and through its social functions seems to have been in fact one of the principles of Sander's undertaking. The conception was made in the mid-1920s and a first selection published in 1929 under the title *Antlitz der Zeit* (Face of Our Time). Sander's project in fact did construct an historical archive of a

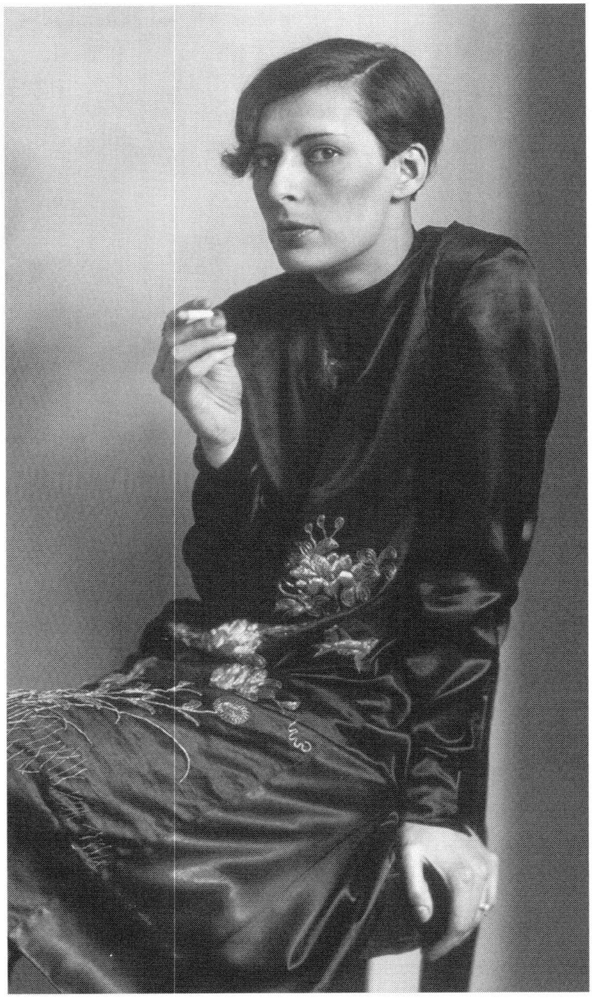

August Sander, *Secretary at West German Radio in Cologne*, 1931, from *People of the 20th Century*. © 2015 Die Photographische Sammlung/SK Stiftung Kultur—August Sander Archiv, Cologne/Artists Rights Society (ARS), New York.

highly differentiated subjectivity that he perceived as being still embedded in social relations and professional identities.[6] His liberal, social-democratic political convictions attempted to rescue the remaining spaces of subjective self-determination that soon would be foreclosed altogether by the rise of German Nazi fascism.

With hindsight it is easier now to recognize to what extent such a model of subjectivity, based primarily on the definition of professional identity, already had become obsolete at that time. This is especially so given that such a model of subjectivity was, in Sander's case, at least partially founded on a nostalgic longing for the seemingly naturally given social order of the medieval guilds. The contradictions and shortcomings of this obsolete model of social identity became glaringly evident in the portraits of those marginal figures whom Sander incorporated in what Benjamin would soon call his *Übungsatlas* (an "instruction manual"). After all, these social outcasts—beggars, the unemployed, circus people, the blind and the debilitated—exemplify, unwillingly perhaps, the relativity (if not the failure) of a concept that defines identity primarily by a subject's professional formation. This crisis of the traditional portrait reaches its climax in Sander's photographs of Nazi soldiers, which he incorporates into his project as demanded by both his era and by the comprehensive aspirations of his survey. Such photographs pose the urgent question (among others) of how to name the historically founded and professionally anchored identity of the fascist.

Furthermore, we must assume that it was Sander's serial approach to the traditionally unique, single-frame portrait that engendered Benjamin's enthusiastic response to the first publication of a small selection from Sander's vastly ambitious work. Undoubtedly it was also this feature that would have contributed to Benjamin's surprising comparison of Sander's work with the film of the Soviets. Abandoning the individual sitter, depicted in the unfathomable artificiality of the photographer's studio, Sander presented his subjects as both constituted within social relations and as determined by their professional functions within society at large.

Given that *Menschen des 20. Jahrhunderts* was planned as a project of forty-five portfolios, each containing twelve photographic portraits, the formal organization of Sander's project equally emphasized seriality and contextuality. Although this clearly constituted a departure from both the traditional portrait aesthetic as much as the aesthetic principles of German *Neue Sachlichkeit* photography (an aesthetic that Benjamin had vehemently criticized in the same essay in his remarks on Albert Renger-Patzsch's book *Die Welt ist Schön*), the equally evident conservative dimensions of Sander's project are ignored altogether in Benjamin's discussion.

While serial in its organization, Sander's model of portraiture nevertheless argues the case of social determinism, and supports the notion of a social "ontology" where each individual finds his or her natural place and position in a hierarchically and cyclically structured pre-established order. In Sander's portraits, the statuary singularization of the sitter retains aspects of the traditional forms of representation, now transferred onto different social identities that have become eligible for hieratic depiction. Despite its serial organization, Sander's hierarchical and cyclical archive affirms foundational concepts of subjectivity as grounded in nature and religion, and in the solid determinations of class, if not ethnicity. But the balance set up by Sander is fragile and tenuous. It shifts between a reactionary impulse to restore the credibility of essentialist notions of subject formation, along with a revision of the traditional hierarchical and mimetic models of representation, and a tenuous affirmation of the radical, immediate, and universal applicability of an open model of subject formation—both in photographic and in socio-political terms. Sander's project in fact seems to question whether any model of a radically non-hierarchical and anti-essentialist meaning in photography can be enacted in the face of unchanging politics and economics of class relations and ideological subject formation, and whether traditional forms of portraiture can be abolished with any greater credibility under these circumstances.

Like other counter-modernist gestures emerging at the very moment of modernism's most radical articulation (such as de Chirico's and Picasso's, in 1915), Sander's project inscribes the mnemonic evidence of the loss of an earlier concept of subjectivity. It mediates this loss at the very instant when the structural and the psychoanalytic models of subjectivity were first articulated within the larger cultural theories of the subject and systems of representation, if not necessarily within the political realities of that moment. In the face of dramatically increasing evidence of the destruction of any form of autonomous and self-determining subjectivity with the imminent rise of Fascism in Sander's country, that mediation would inevitably become ever more tenuous. The same would be true for each attempt to rescue the vanishing categories and conventions of subject depiction by photographic and painterly means.

Benjamin's comparison between what he calls Eisenstein's and Pudovkin's "tremendous physiognomic gallery" and Sander's project to document all the professions and trades of the Weimar Republic astonishes a contemporary reader. First of all, given Benjamin's overall acuity and precision in the observation of the specific characteristics and functions of different media, the apparently unproblematic correspondence, if not outright equation of film and photography, suggested by the author, is all the more surprising. Second, only a few years before the publication of Benjamin's essay, a debate concerning the functions of photography in modern industrial (socialist) societies had emerged in the pages of *Novyi lef* among the artist Alexander Rodchenko and the critics Ossip Brik, Boris Kushner and Sergei Tretyakov.[7] This by now notorious "photography debate" of 1928 had precisely taken the genre of the photographic portrait as its point of departure, and it had posed the question of whether it would be at all possible to continue portraiture in the twentieth century, and if so, in what forms and material organization it could be sustained.

The photographic avant-garde of the Soviet Union situated portraiture now in explicit opposition to the traditional principles of pictorial isolation and singularity. By contrast, the photographic image was defined as dynamic, contextual, and contingent, and serial structuring of visual information emphasized open form and a potential infinity. Yet this did not only apply to the question of who would be eligible to become the new photographic subject in the social collective. It equally acknowledged that an infinity of contingent, photographically recordable details would indicate to what extent each individual subject was actually constituted within perpetually changing activities, social relations, and object relationships. Thus, Ossip Brik argued, for example, that

> differentiating individual objects so as to make a pictorial record of them is not only a technical but also an ideological phenomenon. In the pre-Revolutionary (feudal and bourgeois) period, both painting and literature set themselves the aim of differentiating individual people and events from their general context and concentrating attention on them. … To the contemporary consciousness, an individual person can be understood and assessed only in connection with all the other people—with those who used to be regarded by the pre-Revolutionary consciousness as background.[8]

The argument implied a radical redefinition of the photographic object itself; it was to be no longer conceived as a single-image print, carefully crafted by the artist-photographer in the studio, framed and presented as a pictorial substitute. Rather, at least in Rodchenko's definition, a photograph would now become precisely the cheaply and rapidly produced snapshot that would displace the traditional synthetic portrait. Consequentially, the newly defined genre of the *photo-file* would become the organizational and distributional form. A loosely organized archive, a more or less coherent accumulation of snapshots, would now document any given protagonist. Lenin serves as the primary example in Rodchenko's argument:

> Here is an example of the first big collision between art and photography, a battle between eternity and the moment. Moreover, in this instance, photographs were taken casually, but painting attacked photography with all its heavy and light artillery … and failed miserably. … I mean Lenin … it should be stated firmly that with the appearance of photographs, there can be no question of a single immutable portrait. Moreover, a man is not just one sum total; he is many, and sometimes they are quite opposed.[9]

Rodchenko could not have made a more provocative choice to illustrate his ideas about the new photographic portrait than selecting the recently deceased Lenin as his example, since cult and hero worship of Lenin had assumed already quasi-religious dimensions. Whether the new socialist culture would succeed at all would depend precisely on this issue, the memorialization of Lenin. What was at stake was not only the defeat of bourgeois forms of commemoration (such as the bronze statue, the plaster bust, and the oil portrait) but, more importantly, the triumph of new forms of public representation that were non-hierarchical and anti-monumental; mechanisms that would allow viewers to disinvest themselves from the experience of power and domination that the category of the portrait had traditionally mediated.

Yet another discursive change in the portrait genre merits discussion here, if only in the form of an outline. In 1917 the American photographer Paul Strand developed technical methods that allowed him to record anonymous figures in the street with hidden cameras in order not to draw their attention. This strategy of hidden cameras would be deployed later by Walker Evans in his *Subway Portraits* of the 1940s and in Helen Levitt's street photography at a slightly later point. Thus, a new chapter is added to the history of portrait photography, one that formulates the genre's problematic in manifest opposition to Sander's approach.

This clandestine recording of anonymous figures acquires the qualities of an authentic depiction because it articulates the actual condition of fragmentation and transience of the subject's status and experience within the collectivity. Typically, the temporal structure of the portrait is now reversed: rather than attempting to familiarize himself/herself in numerous sessions with the sitter, presumably in order to reconcile the sitter's physiognomic appearance with the artist's epiphany of psychological complexity, the rapid and vicariously executed "snapshot" forfeits such claims from the start. By contrast, Strand's and Walker Evans' clandestine "portrait sessions" now become an assault whereby the photographer robs the subject of his or her momentarily distracted physiognomic appearance in an attempt to attain a higher degree of authenticity. Now the subject can only become a sitter by subjecting himself or herself to intense fragmentation; only under these circumstances can the genre of the "portrait" be redeemed.

Yet it is not merely the temporality of the portrait's production that allows us to recognize the structural changes occurring within the genre. Changes in its spatial parameters appear with equal, if not more devastating evidence. If in Strand's work (and later in Walker Evans') the subject still appears as embedded in the public urban spaces of sociality, that spatial and social dimension disappears altogether in postwar portraiture; from then on, the conditions of portraiture are as much structured by spatial isolation as by social fragmentation, anonymity as much as assault. Best embodied in the work of Diane Arbus, for example, the postwar portrait will depend increasingly on its intrusion into the privacy of alienated existence, the secret spaces of society's hidden victims.

Both Sander's and Strand's radical transformations of portrait photography in the first decade of the twentieth century point toward the ever increasing evidence of that genre's precarious survival. This

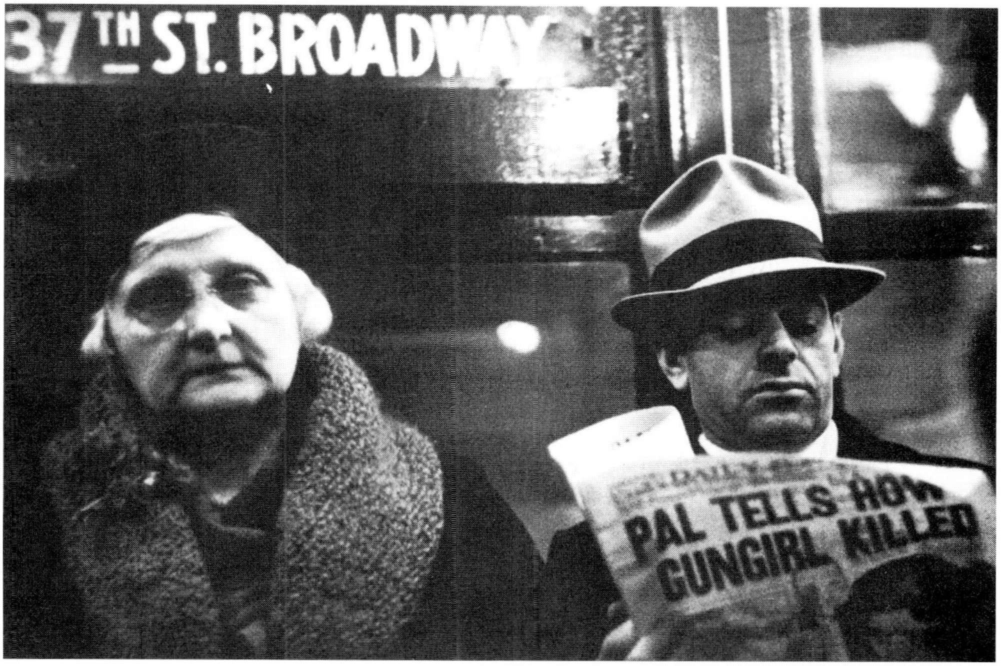

Walker Evans, [Subway Passengers, New York], 1938. Gelatin silver print, 4 13/16 × 5 15/16 in. (12.2 × 15 cm). Gift of Arnold H. Crane, 1971 (1971.646.18), The Metropolitan Museum of Art. © Walker Evans Archive, The Metropolitan Museum of Art, New York. Image Source: Art Resource, NY.

becomes all the more evident if one compares their projects with those of the postwar portrait photographers who seem to have operated under the assumption that they were to continue along the lines of Sander's and Strand's trajectory.

But in the new portrait photography of the New York School in the 1950s, the subject will increasingly be presented as a grotesque figure, as the merely farcical residue of a lost opportunity for subjecthood (e.g., Diane Arbus). Or it will appear as the industrially produced hypertrophic image of the mythical subject, as the spectacle of the ostentatiously displayed substitute of subjectivity, the *star* (e.g., Richard Avedon). If the socially marginalized figures of the cripple, the destitute, and the demented appeared in Sander's work as integral elements of a social texture that—while strained—was nonetheless somewhat cohesive, such isolated figures now take center stage in the representation of the social subject.

It is, however, not evident if this new condition of the sitter as victim or as star, the subject's spectacularized substitute, is the result of a genre's despair concocting such subjects in order to ascertain its own vicarious and precarious survival; or, if such subject positions—the victim and the star—are the only remaining formations of subjecthood available to the portrait genre.

These processes of subject formation are of course first implemented through the universally (and now globally) operative terms of image production and consumption. This fact alone should suffice to discredit any claim to represent subjectivity as a physiognomic phenomenon with photographic means. Under the regime of total reification, where subjectivity is increasingly constituted in the production of sign exchange value, the public (i.e., artistic) display of such a model of physiognomic subjectivity, as the unique and particular essence of a being, can at best provide a compensation for the losses of subjective experience, at worst constitute an ideological legitimation of such mythical conceptions of subjectivity. The portrait genre thus legitimizes itself only by testifying to the historically grotesque claims to provide an adequate representation of the subject. Or, as fashion and advertisement photography make all too evident, the genre functions not only as a mere ideologeme of a failed and obsolete model of subjectivity; it actually glosses over its own complicity in the subject's current destruction.

IV

> This fine word—the commonplace—has several meanings; it refers without doubt to the most hackneyed of thoughts, but the fact is that these thoughts have become a meeting place for the community. Everyone recognizes both themselves and others in them. The commonplace is everyone's and mine; it is the presence of everyone in me. It is, in essence, the generality; to appropriate it for myself, I must perform an act, an act by which I divest myself of my particularity in order to attach myself to what is general, to become the generality. Not simply to resemble everyone, but to be precisely the incarnation of everyone. By this eminently social act of association, I identify myself with all other beings in the indistinctness of the universal.
>
> *—Jean-Paul Sartre, preface to Portrait d'un inconnu by Nathalie Sarraute, Paris, 1948*

To the very extent that subjectivity is now universally manufactured in the processes of collective image production and their social organization, the portrait's defense of its own survival by virtue of its capacity to depict "the individual subject" borders on the obsolescent if not on the obscene. To the very extent that subjectivity under conditions of reification is now universally transferred onto the object itself, thus systematically destroying subjectivity through the daily practices of consumption, the portrait—in its residual forms—will either have to become grotesque, or it will have to become spectacular.

In the rarest of critical aesthetic articulation and dialectical inversion, the portrait succeeded in representing the subject in the metonymy of objecthood. The first instance in which such a radical displacement of traditional portraiture by the complete reduction to the metonymical object occurred was in Francis Picabia's famous mechanomorphic portraits from 1915, such as the portrait of Alfred Stieglitz and that of Paul Haviland, in which a diagrammatic object of consumption and advertisement stands in as a substitute for the subject.

Thus a drastic inversion of depicted figures occurs in the historical and mental distance that separates the photographic work of Sander from that of such postwar portrait photographers as Diane Arbus, Richard Avedon, and Irving Penn. Their emphasis on the persistence of the photographic and pictorial category of the portrait is as desperate as that of the depicted "subjects" themselves. Such photographers retrieve the "subject" in its last forms of eccentricity and—in their attempt to shore up traditional bourgeois conceptions of originality—they spectacularize the subject either as victim and freak, or as the grand artistic and aristocratic exception from the rule of the collective sabotage and prohibition of subjectivity.

Yet, what would drive such an enterprise is not immediately evident: Is the motivation a reactionary impulse to salvage the obsolete genre of the photographic portrait, or is it fueled by a conception of photography as an ideological handmaiden that attempts to sustain and prolong the mythical concepts of subjectivity? One is not even certain any longer if photography can be situated in such a parasitical relationship to ideology, or whether—in its habitualizing effects—photography actually *operates* as an ideological force itself. This is especially true in early cases such as Avedon's, where there was never a threshold between an "artistic" avant-garde practice and a visual enforcement of ideology; here, all operations—fashion and advertisement photography as well as the "artistic" ambitions of the master—partake of the same logic of an enforced mythification of the lost subject.

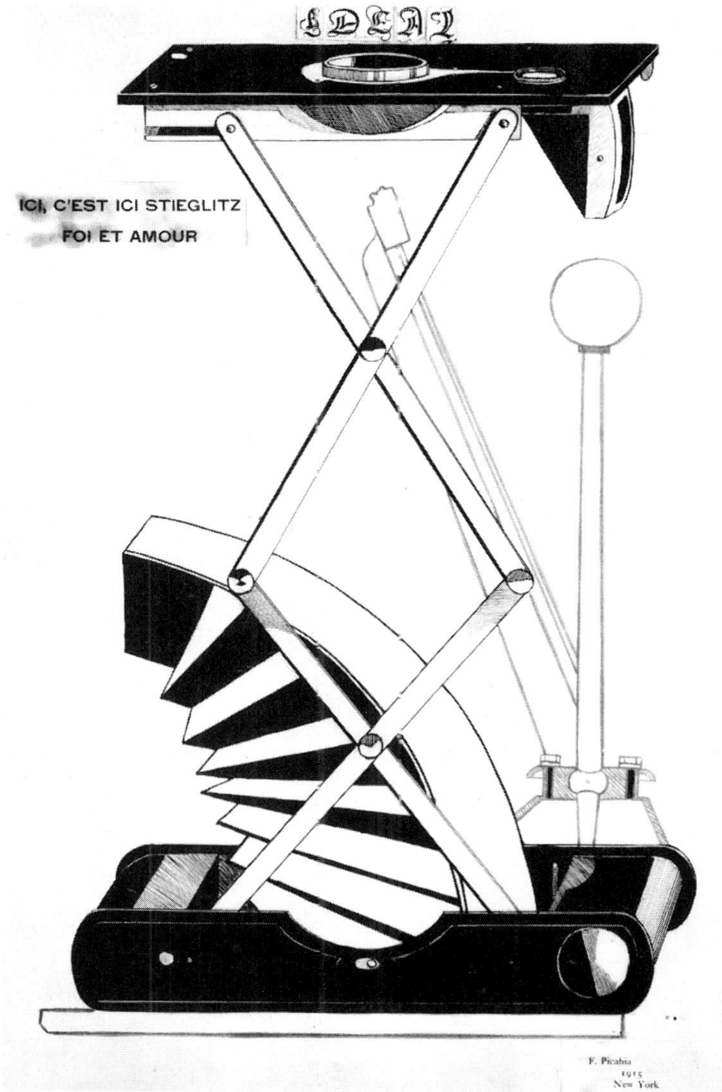

Francis Picabia, *Ici, c'est ici Stieglitz*, 1915. Pen, brush and ink, and cut and pasted printed papers on paperboard, 29⅞ × 20 in. (75.9 × 50.8 cm). Alfred Stieglitz Collection, 1949 (49.70.14), The Metropolitan Museum of Art. © 2015 Artists Rights Society (ARS), New York/ADAGP, Paris.

A comparison between these highly commercial and visible photographic practices and the artistic practices of the early 1960s reveals an astonishing discrepancy of attitudes toward the category of the portrait. Commercial photographers such as Avedon struggle to resurrect the historically inaccessible genre at all costs, risking even the image's total loss of truth value, while artists of this generation such as Andy Warhol actually struggle to undo the category as definitively as possible. In 1961, Robert Rauschenberg had already executed the signal (and single most important) gesture in this historical process when he mailed a telegram with the following statement to his Paris dealer: "This is a Portrait of Iris Clert if I say so. Robert Rauschenberg."[10]

Barring even the last trace of photographic iconicity from his definition of the portrait, Rauschenberg now fully shifts the representation of subjectivity onto the register of the performative declaration, re-enacting and re-radicalizing the Duchampian principle operative in the readymade. In the process of doing so, Rauschenberg not only articulates one of the first instances of postwar conceptual art, but he also asserts that the introduction into language and its iteration is one of the fundamental principles of the construction of subjectivity. Rather than theorizing subjecthood as a definite status, or as a representable given, Rauschenberg's work conceives of the subject as a continuous performative *process*.

This complication of the concepts of subjectivity and its representation culminated in the late 1960s and early 1970s in the work of conceptual artists such as Douglas Huebler and On Kawara. One of Huebler's proposals expressly addresses these questions and (perhaps unknowingly?) seems to fulfill Rodchenko's quests for an open photo-file as the archive of a truly non-hierarchical collective subjectivity:

> Throughout the remainder of the artist's life, he will photographically document, to the extent of his capacity, the existence of everyone alive in order to produce the most

> authentic and inclusive representation of the human species that may be assembled in that manner.[11]

The historical conflict between a photographic practice that resurrects reactionary conceits of subjectivity under the auspices of fashion and consumption, and an avant-garde photography that opposes these fraudulent claims, further unfolded in the early 1960s when Pop Art paid renewed attention to found, rather than fine-art photography. And once again, it was precisely on the site of the portrait genre that this conflict was played out in Pop Art's critique of the myths of mass cultural representation. While exceptions occur, especially in Warhol's later and largely irrelevant portrait production, and in almost all of the works by Rauschenberg, Warhol, Lichtenstein, Richter and Ruscha which re-identify an inextricable relationship between the pictorial with the photographic and which present iconic figures, the traditional individual portrait—pictorial or photographic—is all but absent from their work. Thus, Ruscha for example explains the "absence of people" from his photographic books:

> I have always tried to keep people out of my books ... just to eliminate the unnecessary human aspect. The first thing Andy Warhol said when he saw my book—I gave him *Twenty-six Gasoline Stations*—was, "How do you get all these pictures without people in them?" and I hadn't even thought about it before, but there aren't any people in them. Every once in a while you will spot one. I seem to unconsciously eliminate people from them ... I don't like imagery of people. Instead of using people, I'll use something else.[12]

Ruscha's statement confirms our assumption that the conscientious *exclusion* of figures and faces from representation has now become as significant a strategy as their traditional, seemingly "natural" *inclusion* had been up to the moment of Cubism. This decision to eliminate the representable subject altogether renders a reading of the resulting iconography of the human physiognomy, and its paradoxical persistence in Pop Art, all the more complex, since what is at stake in the exclusion of the figure seems to be precisely a fundamental and irresolvable dialectic: at this point, a subject can only be recognized—in fact, will be at its most visible—if it is mediated by forms of object production, consumption and exchange.

In their approach to the category of the portrait, the artists of that generation, in particular, Lichtenstein and Warhol, now share the ability to articulate that absence of subjectivity, which is as visibly missing in the technical execution of their works as it is in their iconography. In their hands, the genre now appears emptied both of individual painterly performance and of any remnants of the sitters' interiority and privacy. The subjects depicted are either, as in the case of Warhol, already the public substitutes of subjectivity, the mere myths of the subject in the spectacular appearance of the "star," or, in the case of Lichtenstein, the pathetic residue of subjectivity living on in the comic book and the cheap romance novel.

Warhol's intervention in the genre of the portrait has been discussed extensively, yet it is astonishing that Lichtenstein's equally subversive and persistent deconstructions have been all but ignored in this context. One could argue that the category of the portrait, with its traditional promises of resemblance and identity, of the centrality of an integrated subjectivity, is played out almost continuously in Lichtenstein's farcical interventions within the genre. Lichtenstein announced this position in a statement almost as programmatic as Rauschenberg's telegram, when, in 1961, he painted a double portrait (rarely reproduced) in which the same sparkling young man (who seems to have stepped out of a dry-cleaning advertisement) is painted twice; the first painting is entitled *Portrait of Allan Kaprow*, and the second, identical painting, *Portrait of Ivan Karp*.[13]

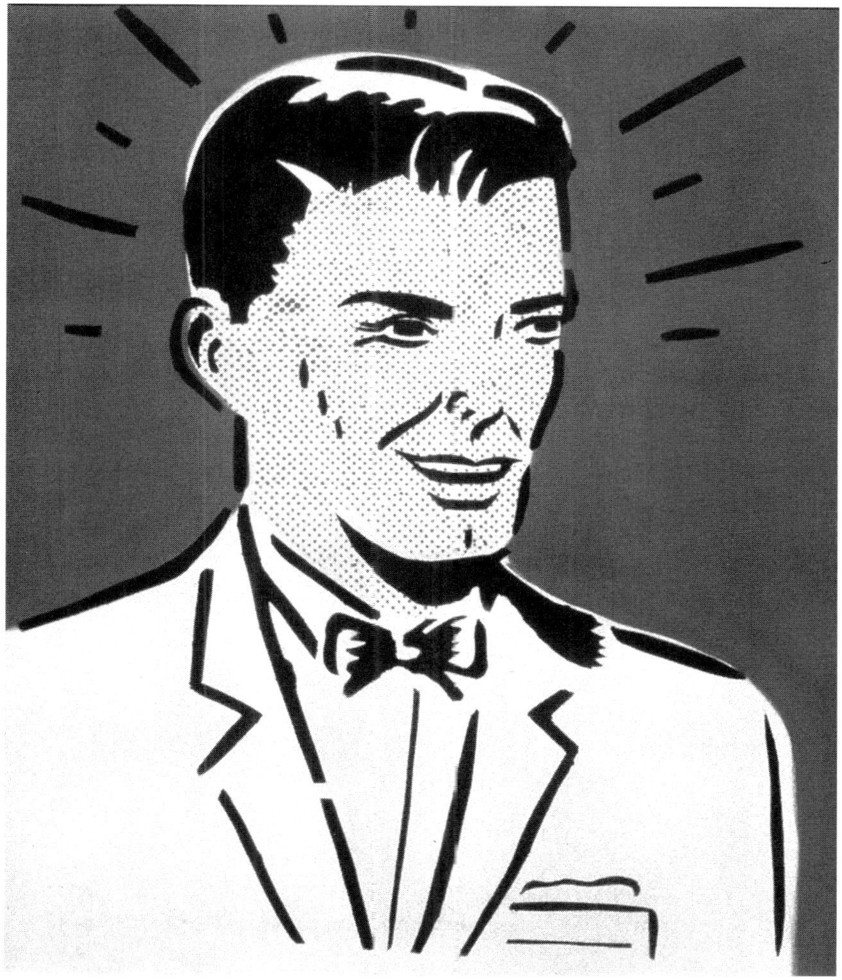

Roy Lichtenstein, *Portrait of Allan Kaprow*, 1961. Oil on canvas, 24 × 20 in. (70 × 50.8 cm). © Estate of Roy Lichtenstein.

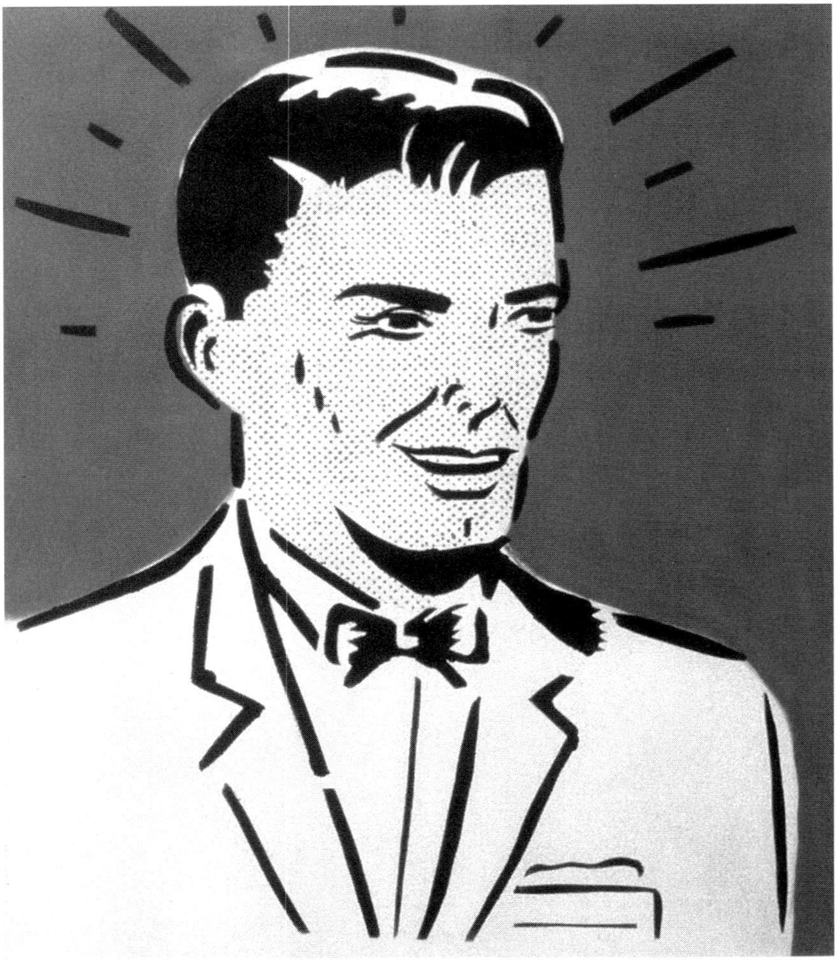

Roy Lichtenstein, *Portrait of Ivan Karp*, 1961. Oil on canvas, 24 × 20 in. (70 × 50.8 cm). © Estate of Roy Lichtenstein.

Too numerous to mention are the subsequent examples of Lichtenstein's paintings from 1962 onward, in which all the conventional figures and topoi of portraiture appear, yet they are always mediated through the mirror of mass culture, already estranged within the imagery of the comic strip or the advertisement. We encounter portraits of the artist (for example *Masterpiece*, 1962), the soldier/war hero (*Torpedo Los*, 1963), the tragic muse (*Drowning Girl*, 1963), the exotic beauty (*Aloha*, 1962), or even the historical figure (*George Washington*, 1962). The continuous reflection on this problem persists far into Lichtenstein's later work, and is approached with a similarly precise dissection. In 1977, a "physiognomic figure," consisting of a rectangular mirror fragment, placed above the graphic shorthand for a substitute person (tie-shirt-suit), surfaces for the first time in a painting called *Reclining Nude*. It will reappear a year later, as an empty T-shirt, again carrying a small rectangular mirror in place of the head, entitled *Self-Portrait*, only to become a fixture in the subsequent iconographic program of the artist, which will undergo even more hilarious variations when the mirror is substituted by a piece of graphically textured plywood, as in *Razzmatazz* (1978), or by perforated Swiss cheese in drawings such as *Study for Portrait* (1977).

In this regard the radical anonymity of Lichtentein's comic-book characters complements the immediate and universal recognizability of Warhol's star imagery, since the traces of the personal and the private, the subjective and the psychological are encoded in the grotesque exaggeration of the cartoon imagery that had persistently voided the validity of mimetic resemblance.[14]

V

Whenever a generation of artists has developed strategies within which structural transformations of social relations are anticipated or retroactively articulated, a younger generation will respond by developing counter-strategies. Rather than being merely reactionary, these will most often deny the radical implications of the work of their predecessors, perhaps in favor of a more conciliatory approach to the continuing viability of the genres, and they might opt for more moderate claims concerning the social consequences of artistic strategies at large. Such a reversal, with regard to the radical implications of Pop Art and Conceptual art, occurred in the early 1980s in the work of numerous photographic artists, among them Thomas Ruff and Thomas Struth. They positioned themselves not only within the trajectory of their teachers, Bernd and Hilla Becher, but also within the broader legacies of *Neue Sachlichkeit* photography, in particular that of August Sander.

The Bechers bequeathed to their disciples an anti-modernist project of re-skilling photography, which brought about an even more manifest resistance to the conceptual radicality of the Pop artists and the Conceptualists (i.e., the Warhol-Ruscha-Graham positions). Alongside this reconstitution of photographic skill emerges the recuperation of the photographic genres, and once again we witness the rise of portraiture and the re-figuration of individual subjectivity, be it isolated or within the group, as in the individual or the family portraits of Ruff and Struth in the mid-1980s. The selection of the sitters is determined, at least initially, by already existing relationships between photographer and sitter, or by an increasing communicative familiarity resulting from the preparatory sessions for the portrait. Thus in Struth's work, for example, the procedure of taking a portrait photograph depends upon a complex process of repetitions and revisions, a process that may well incorporate commentaries and criticisms by the sitter or that might not lead to a result at all.[15]

In constituting the portrait out of residual communicative relations, or by making the photograph the occasion to establish such relations, Struth's work opposes the presumed conditions of a universally governing social anomie and a fully deconstructed subjectivity that had been articulated by the work of the preceding conceptualist generation. In

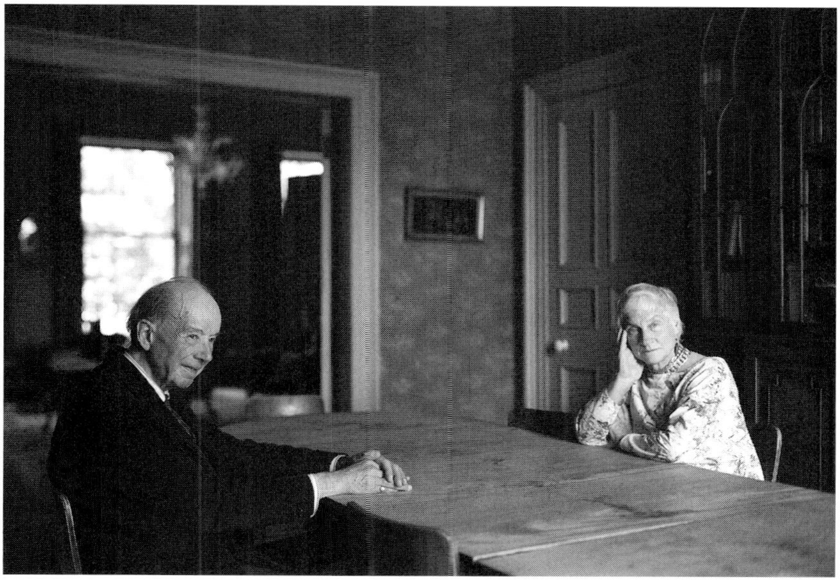

Thomas Struth, *Eleanor and Giles Robertson, Edinburgh*, 1987. C-print, 26½ × 33¾ in. (67.3 × 85.7 cm). © Thomas Struth. Courtesy the artist and Marian Goodman Gallery, New York/Paris.

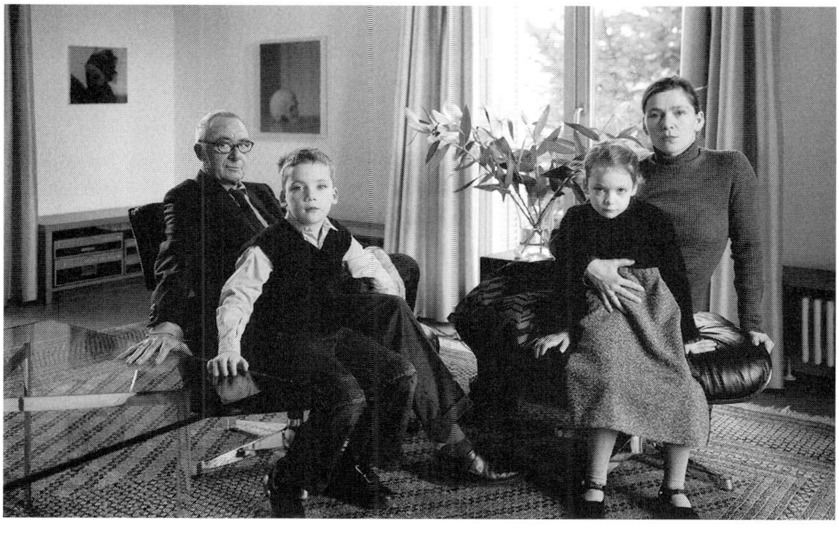

Thomas Struth, *The Richter Family 1, Cologne*, 2002. C-print, 53⅛ × 76⅛ in. (134.9 × 193.4 cm). © Thomas Struth. Courtesy the artist and Marian Goodman Gallery, New York/Paris.

Struth's symbolic construction of protected social spaces the subject reappears at least as a reminder of its presumably long-lost plenitude, and communicative relations appear as accessible reality. It is certainly not accidental that the most successful portraits in Struth's oeuvre are those that present their subjects as either distinguished by their dignity and age (as for example in the portraits of *Eleanor and Giles Robertson, Edinburgh, 1987* or in *Anci and Harry Guy, Groby, Leicestershire, 1989)*, or by the exceptional indication of their practices and profession (as for example in the outstanding images *The Restorers, San Lorenzo Maggiore, Naples, 1988*), or by the unusual geopolitical location determining their identity (as for example in the *Shimada Family, Yamaguchi, 1986)*: all of these images situate identity in a relative distance from the pre-established set of common characteristics presently determining the subject's appearance.[16] If this is occasionally not the case, and the physiognomy and the attributes of the sitters are in every respect defined by their utter commonality and by their adaptation to the ruling standards of dress and physiognomy (as for example in the portrait of the *Schäfer Family, Düsseldorf*), the photograph itself becomes questionable and with it the enterprise of portraiture at large.

A project that attempts to construct a protective, if not a celebratory, reservation of residual forms of bourgeois subjectivity might at first appear as both artistically and politically precarious, if not as outright culturally conservative. It is precisely the protectionism of this operation that makes the portraits appear as images of a privileged subjectivity and of exempted forms of social solidarity, since these constructions claim that residual forms of sociability and subjectivity can still be detected within and against a universal regime of anomy. Inevitably, the question arises then whether it is only the melancholic image of a lost subjectivity that appears here in the obsolete genre of the portrait because the subject is *de facto* deprived of any access to the structures of its economic and political self-determination, or whether the actually existing residual forms of subjectivity necessitate the deployment of obsolete genres and representational conventions in order to claim credibility against intensifying anomic relations and the loss of traditional forms of subjectivity.

Inevitably the resurrection of the subject with artistic means has a historical price to pay: as opposed to the exact focus on the professional and socio-political aspects of the constitution of identity in Sander's project, we learn hardly anything from Struth's portraits about the attributes of enforced daily economic reproduction and its enormous importance for the interdiction or the enactment of the formation of subjectivity in the present. While Sander's work showed occasional *family* images, Struth's portraits refuse to recognize professional sociability as integral to the processes of subject formation. If the photographs of the Bechers eliminate all human presence from the public spaces of industrial production, Struth's portraits, in a strange inversion of that principle, bracket the sites and the attributes of production from the enforced privacy of protected subjectivity.

Perhaps more importantly, one should recall that the social transparency in Struth's topographical archive of the vanishing public spaces of architectural urbanity could only be constructed (with few exceptions) by eliminating the actual inhabitants of these spaces. By contrast, the social and architectural space within which his portrayed subjects are now presented is always the private space of the "family" and the "home." It is at times hard to decide whether this social unit is central to Struth's portrait project because it is sustaining the communicative bonds in its smallest context or whether Struth is recording the conditions of this social unit in the last phases of its own disintegration.

One result of this rigorous separation between the "private" and the "public" is the implicit recognition that public space in the present can either no longer tolerate the presence of traditional forms of subjectivity and sociality, or that the latter—if they exist at all—can only survive and be represented in those spaces and forms that are confined to privacy. Subject formation and identity construction appear in Struth's oeuvre therefore as being constituted outside of the parameters of social production and are shifted to the private sphere of family relations and the home. Inevitably then, the genre of portraiture as historically formed is *dehistoricized* in exact correspondence to the extent that the category of subjectivity is *naturalized*.

Yet another problematic aspect of this artificial redemption of the subject becomes immediately apparent. Instead of learning—as we did in Sander's work—about class differences, social practices, profession, and politically determined relations, Struth's archive constructs a compendium of globalized middle class identities, contained in nuclear family units. Thus we confront an incipient naturalization of subjectivity, newly presented as an ontological, if not a biological, category, and the condition of subjecthood appears here as restricted to those who are fortunate enough to have access to the proper economic framework, the ideological apparatus of subject formation, and the proper conventions of representing subjectivity, i.e., to the Western European genre of portraiture offered by the producers of subjectivity's mythical image.

What is perhaps even more problematic than Struth's limited class matrix is the fact that this matrix inevitably brings with it an equal, if not greater, limitation of sexual and ethnic parameters. Those ethnic groups who would differ dramatically from the gestural, physiognomic, and dress code appearances of the globalized middle class that circumscribes the eligible group of available subjects in Struth's oeuvre, or those whose family structure would differ considerably from the Westernized standards of assimilation, seem to have fallen completely outside of Struth's purview. In a similar manner, there does not seem to be any room in Struth's middle-class compendium for those who have chosen to construct their identities outside of the parameters of a compulsory heterosexuality and its attendant nuclear family formation.

But we would read Struth's construction of a social compendium in a reductivist manner if we did not understand a totally different set of implications at the same time: as a photographer in the tradition of New Objectivity, Struth records these frameworks of middle-class identity precisely at the very moment when the nuclear family confronts its most fundamental crisis, its threat of actual disintegration and disappearance. Processes of globalization erase the credibility of any and all Eurocentric hegemonic claims to privileged access and forms of subjecthood. Undoubtedly, the fundamental duality of photography's mnemonic structure, namely its simultaneous impulse both to rescue images from and to simultaneously deliver them to oblivion, also operates in Struth's project, inasmuch as his photographs attempt to preserve precisely those formations that are currently vanishing at an astonishing rate.

It is perhaps even more important to recognize the critical distance that his work establishes with regard to those practices where disintegrated subjectivity appears merely as a spectacularized "Other," or as outright victim photography. Nothing clarifies this distance better than a comparison of Struth's portraits with those of his American contemporary, Nan Goldin. As if the dialectic of a redemption of bourgeois subjectivity on the one hand, and one of an outright declaration of the death of that subject on the other, could no longer be sustained in a single artistic or photographic proposition, both practices appear now as diametrically opposed and as totally irreconcilable. Thus one could describe Goldin's seemingly radical work as a typical example of recent victim photography, even though it claims to build an archive of the "Other," to give voice and representation to those who had been traditionally marginalized from the field of the image. In spite of the work's ostentatiously declared solidarity, and in spite of all tokens of a private bond between photographer and sitters, the work ultimately merely delivers these images of the "Other" to the panoptic impulses of social taxonomy and control and to the voyeuristic desires of its clientele, the collectors, and the institutions.

By contrast one could recognize in the conservative dimension of Struth's project a counter-impulse, one that is directed precisely against a practice that victimizes its sitters. In fact, it could be read as a critical position that counters the exploitative complicity in Goldin's work,

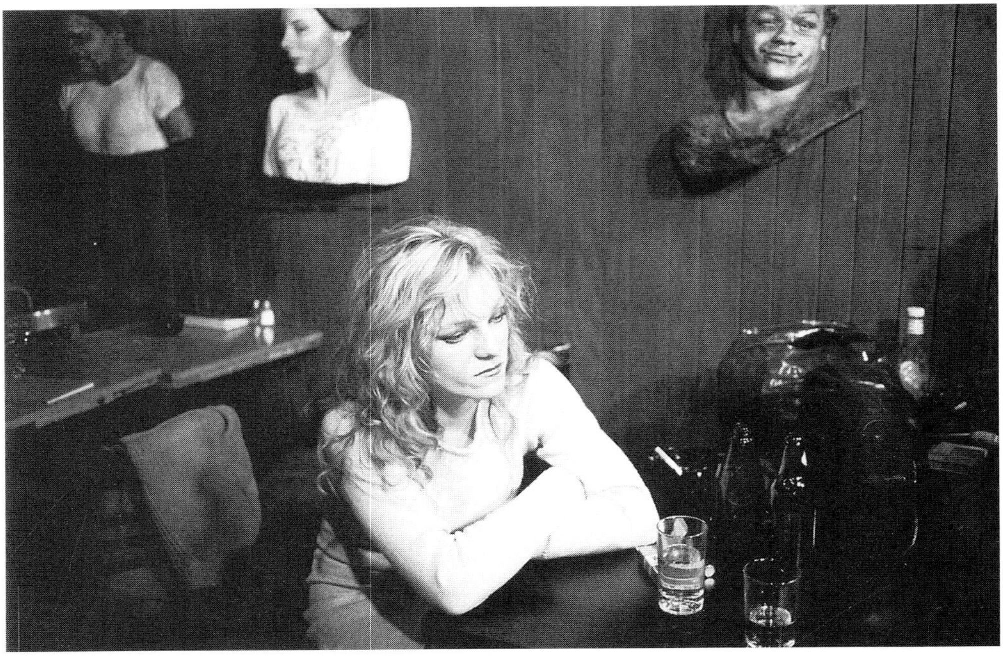

Nan Goldin, *Cookie at Tin Pan Alley, NYC*, 1983. Cibachrome, 20 × 24 in. (51 × 61 cm).

which offers only a spectacularization of the exceptional "Other" in order to confirm and consolidate the existing social and sexual order. Thus, Struth's portraits would grant us another insight: these "radical" examples of post-bourgeois portrait photography only accelerate the subject's demise without recognizing the continued existence of residual practices of interaction that oppose the socially enforced destruction of subjectivity.

Concerning the conjunction of group portraiture and color photography, which seems to be relevant both for Struth's portraits in particular and for a discussion of the genre in general, a last observation might still be useful. With few exceptions, Struth's portraits are color photographs, produced with the same consistency with which his topographical work had mobilized black-and-white photographs (with approximately the same number of exceptions in both categories).

It is equally noteworthy that the black-and-white portraits which make up the exceptions are for the most part single-figure images. In their apparent interchangeability with all other generic portrait photographs, these photographs make the precarious condition of a resuscitation of traditional portraiture all the more evident. How then could one possibly explain the peculiar correspondence that governs these images, the fact that the portraits seem to succeed when presented in color and that the topographical images retain their highest credibility in the traditional format of black-and-white photography?

Admittedly, the argument is highly speculative, but it could provide a first step into the rather enigmatic connection between color and the genre of the portrait in Struth's work. The model of subjectivity reasserted by the artist depends, as we have argued, to a considerable degree on a rather narrow definition of sociality that is provided by a network of family and friends.

To reassert this model by representing subjects in the portrait genre and in black-and-white photography would evidently risk revealing the obsolescence of such a project. To deploy color, with its inherent emphasis on the simultaneity and equivalence of all depicted objects and figures in a more or less non-hierarchical manner, generates precisely the dialectic of dissolution and reification of subjectivity that imbues these photographs with a more contemporaneous, rather than merely conservative, dimension. Perhaps one could even suggest that it is precisely this nexus between the clandestine equivalence of subjects and objects and the precarious conditions of subjectivity that Struth's color portraits make all the more evident. What is at stake then in his work would not be the disappearance of the traditional models of subjectivity as such, nor, even less so, the attempt to recuperate that loss through photographic means; rather his photographs frame that subjective dissolution as a constitutative condition of subject experience itself. Thus, we are returned to the beginning of this essay, forced to grapple with the full weight of Blanchot's pronouncement that it is not the dispersal of the subject as such that primarily interests us, but the possibility of discontinuity that follows "this new manner of being."

Notes

First published in *Face-Off: The Portrait in Recent Art*, ed. Melissa E. Feldman (Philadelphia: Institute of Contemporary Art, 1994), pp. 53–69. Minor corrections have been made for consistency.

1. Maurice Blanchot, "Michael Foucault as I Imagine Him," in *Foucault/Blanchot*, trans. Jeffrey Mehlman and Brian Massumi (New York: Zone Books, 1987), p. 76.

2. The crucial essay on these questions remains Yve-Alain Bois, "Kahnweiler's Lesson," in Bois, *Painting as Model* (Cambridge, Mass.: MIT Press, 1990), pp. 65–100. My brief rehearsal of the argument here is obviously indebted to his.

3. It is well known that only when Picasso decided in the fall of 1906 to substitute the rigid structures of an Iberian mask for the mimetic drawing of Gertrude Stein's features, did he consider her portrait to be completed. A few months earlier, he had literally effaced the portrait, after having spent some eighty sessions with Stein to bring about a physiognomic resemblance. But even in the subsequent, programmatic instances when Picasso disassembled portraiture, by depicting his dealers, Kahnweiler, Vollard and Uhde, in the three magisterial portraits of 1910 that pronounce the death of the genre

in an uncontradictable manifesto, the mimetic residue of physiognomic traces works as counter-evidence throughout the paintings. These anti-portraits fuse the sitter's subjectivity in a continuous network of phenomenological interdependences between pictorial surface and virtual space, between bodily volume and painterly texture, as all physiognomic features merge instantly with their persistent negation in a pictorial erasure of mimetic resemblance. Yet, remnants of characteristic subjectivity still appear in Wilhelm Uhde's squinting face and Ambroise Vollard's patriarchal demeanor—even if only in a passing gesture that seems to acknowledge that the disappearing conventions of mimetic depiction of the physiognomic are now, at best, embodied in the features of the caricature. It is worthwhile, then, to ponder what the caricature and the mask share, in order to understand why they served, around 1910, as tools in the dismantling of a mimetic, physiognomic depiction-based portraiture.

First, both the caricature and the mask reduce physiognomy to a fixed structure, rather than conceive it as a fluid field; in singling out particular traits, they reduce the infinity of differentiated facial expressions to a metonymic set. Thus, the fixity of the mask and the caricature outright deny the premise of the fullness of the subject's features, and outright negate all traditional aspirations toward an organic mediation of the essential characteristics of the differentiated subject in portraiture. Moreover, in singling out particular traits, the caricature reveals a certain mechanicity of those features of the subject whose rigidity displays the individual as grotesque. In cubism then, the caricature and the mask attest to the character of identity as always already constructed, and serve to denaturalize the model of physiognomic evidence and mimesis in the construction of representation.

4. See Walter Benjamin, "A Small History of Photography," in *One Way Street and Other Writings*, trans. Edmund Jephcott and Kingsley Shorter (London: Verso, 1979), p. 251. The title of this essay is variously translated as "A Short History" (Patton) or as "A Small History" (Jephcott). Although the latter corresponds more literally to the original adjective *kleine*, it is, for once, Phil Patton's otherwise totally flawed translation that is closer to the original.

5. The association of *Neue Sachlichkeit* photography and Soviet film is all the more astonishing since the general tendencies of the German movement aimed for a "return to order" in the arts, emphasized the separation of genres and categories, and resuscitated the transhistorical validity of skillful painterly execution and mimetic representation.

6. August Sander, *Antlitz der Zeit* (Munich: Transmare Verlag/Kurt Wolff, 1929).

7. Obviously, the texts in the photography debate could not have been known to Benjamin, since his extended visit to Moscow began in December 1926 and lasted until January 1927. But given his awareness of the Soviet avant-garde, especially its filmic, theatrical, and literary protagonists, it still seems surprising that he did not know, or feel

the necessity to research, any of the photographic work, or any of the writings on photography by Brik and Tretyakov when writing his essay in 1931.

8. Ossip Brik, "From Painting to Photography," in *Photography in the Modern Era*, ed. Christopher Phillips and trans. John Bowlt (New York: Metropolitan Museum of Art/ Aperture, 1989), pp. 231–232. Later in the same essay, Brik explains very specifically how the conflict between traditional forms of representation and new social and political realities has to be addressed with the means that photography provides:

> Whenever a people's commissar is isolated from his environment, the result is iconography: he is being regarded as a heroic figure, just like Napoleon, who might seem to be the central figure in the Napoleonic campaigns. … To take a snapshot, a photographer does not have to differentiate the individual. Photography can capture him together with the total environment, and in such a manner that his dependence on the environment is clear and obvious. The photographer, then, can resolve this problem, something that the painter cannot do.

Alexander Rodchenko argues in almost identical terms for the formal transformation of perceptual experience in accordance with political changes:

> There is no revolution if, instead of making a general's portrait, photographers have started to photograph proletarian leaders—but are still using the same photographic approach that was employed under the old regime or under the influence of Western art.

See Alexander Rodchenko, "A Caution," *Novyi lef*, no.11 (1928), 36–37; repr. in *Photography in the Modern Era*, pp. 264–265.

9. Alexander Rodchenko, "Against the Synthetic Portrait, for the Snapshot," in Phillips, *Photography in the Modern Era*, pp. 238–242.

10. The title of the exhibition *Les 41 présentent Iris Clert* announced that forty-one artists had been commissioned by Iris Clert to submit a portrait of the dealer for this exhibition. The argument made recently by some scholars that Rauschenberg sent the telegram only because he had forgotten to submit his contribution to the exhibition seems all the less plausible if one recognizes the degree of radical conceptualization in the works that Rauschenberg had produced prior to the telegram, such as his notorious *Erased de Kooning Drawing* (1953), or his *Automobile Tire Print*, done in collaboration with John Cage in 1953.

11. Douglas Huebler, text accompanying an ongoing series of works. See *Variable Piece*, No. 70 (in process), *Global 598* (1975): 31. To what extent the depiction of subjectivity slides into the linguistic performative in the context of Conceptual art is evident in the numerous examples one can quote from the work of On Kawara. As if taking a clue

from Rauschenberg's telegraphed portrait, Kawara begins in the late 1960s to mail telegrams and postcards to a select number of artworld figures and friends stating the following: "I am still alive," "I got up," and "I went."

12. Edward Ruscha, interviewed by Willoughby Sharp, in *Avalanche* (winter–spring 1973): 30–39. Ruscha all but states in this interview that he never admitted people into the iconography of his books, when he suddenly pauses. At least in one work, close in form to the serial object arrangements of the books, Ruscha used a series of found portrait photographs, taken by various anonymous professional photographers. The work is called *Five 1955 Girlfriends, Oklahoma City, Oklahoma*, and it was submitted by Ruscha for the 1969 exhibition and catalog entitled *Konzeption/Conception*, curated by Konrad Fischer and Rolf Wedewer, in Leverkusen.

Certainly, one would have to take into account that Ruscha's decision, however infrequent, to include human figures in his serial arrangements of photographs was partially motivated by the desire to intervene in what must have appeared to Ruscha by this time as the rather orthodox and academic definition of Conceptual art. The submission of the photographs of five (fictitious or authentic) girlfriends from the 1950s, provincial beauties from Oklahoma in their campy hairdos and dress, must have appeared as both a provocative statement on the rapidly changing habits of identity formation in fashion and art, and an uncharacteristic turn to the private and the erotic, the past and the personal, in an exhibition that programmatically pronounced the end of all that.

13. The radical exchangeability between the two characters is all the more hilarious in this case since both were, at the time, of crucial importance to the development of Lichtenstein's career: Ivan Karp, then the director of the Leo Castelli Gallery, had offered him his first exhibition; Allan Kaprow, then a crucial friend and colleague at Douglas College of Rutgers University, had brought Lichtenstein's work to Karp's attention, and was the artist who was generally perceived as seminal in the formulation of anti-pictorial Happening and Pop aesthetics.

14. By enforcing and exaggerating the subject, the cartoon imagery also insists on the normalization and naturalization of its characters, the reduction to the most standard and stereotypical figures imaginable (for example, the "Blonde" in Lichtenstein could be the result of a computer printout of all the advertisement, television, and film blondes of the fifties and sixties put together). Similarly, the fragments of speech inserted in the paintings often record moments of great intensity of experience that are, at the same time, the most vacuous clichés (e.g., "That's the way it should have begun! But it is hopeless."), only to be recognized immediately as pre-processed forms, lacking any reality within the available spaces and patterns of behavior.

15. Since both Ruff and Struth portray mostly friends and personal acquaintances of the artists, their photographs convey an uncanny intimacy and familiarity, thereby already negating one of the Bechers' fundamental positions on historical subjectivity: their

insistence on the anonymity of the architectural authors, and on the absence of the producers from the sites of production. This artistic gesture had clearly allied itself with a concept of collective subjectivity rather than bourgeois individuality. This principle of excluding the social subject, embodied in photographic figuration, was also precisely what had distinguished the Bechers' work most notably from the spectacular and grotesque distortions of subjectivity in New York School photography. "Anonymity" had of course also been the selection principle of Gerhard Richter's photographic iconography, and Richter had been—along with the Bechers—the other important teacher for Struth's artistic development.

Already in 1942, in his introductory essay to the catalog of the exhibition *Twentieth Century Portraits*, the curator, Monroe Wheeler, noticed this condition, without, however, attempting to understand it, when he writes the following:

> Even the specialists seem to have often done their best work when there happened to be some intimacy between them and the sitter, or at least some mutual enthusiasm. And many artists refuse to undertake any pre-arranged painting of strangers at all.

See Monroe Wheeler, *Twentieth-Century Portraits* (New York: Museum of Modern Art, 1942), p. 9.

16. Isabelle Graw has pointed out in her interview with Thomas Struth that the artist had sought out locations in his topographical work that were distinguished by both a considerable historical density and a relative marginality with regard to the most common denominators or currencies of architecture and urban spaces. See Isabelle Graw, "Ortskunde: An Interview with Thomas Struth," *Artis* (December 1989): 36–40.

12

Sculpture: Publicity and the Poverty of Experience

> As is true of any other convention, sculpture has its own internal logic, its own set of rules, which, though they can be applied to a variety of situations, are not themselves very much open to change. The logic of sculpture, it would seem, is inseparable from the logic of the monument. By virtue of this logic a sculpture is a commemorative representation. It sits in a particular place and speaks in a symbolic tongue about the meaning or use of that place.
>
> —*Rosalind Krauss, "Sculpture in the Expanded Field"*[1]

The manifest obsolescence of this definition, formulated almost twenty years ago, is in and of itself an indication of the rapidly changing approach to the theorization/historicization of sculpture. Already at the end of the 1970s it could have been obvious to what extent the definition itself was limited by the futile attempt to rehearse the functions of the sculptural one more time according to the traditional definition of the monument. Already at this moment one could have envisaged a range of contrary definitions, as for example the following one:

> The logic of sculpture, it would seem, is inseparable from the logic of the commodity fetish. By virtue of this logic a sculpture is always already a fetishized object whose function is disavowal. It lacks any particular location and it is universally accessible. It speaks in a symbolic tongue about the meaning or use of the fetish.

Or, another version could have been equally plausible:

> The logic of sculpture, it would seem, is inseparable from the logic of spectacle. By virtue of this logic a sculpture is always already part of spectacle culture. It lacks any particular location and it is universally accessible, and its function is the destruction of historical thought. It speaks in a symbolic tongue about the meaning or use of spectacle.

Thinking about sculpture in the present moment then confronts first of all two questions and tasks: the first one has to clarify the concealed, yet actually existing status of subject/object relationships and its impact on the production and reception of sculpture. The other one results from an increasing evidence about the disappearance of the last vestiges of social interaction in the residually existing forms of public space. Both questions have of course been undercurrents within the sculptural production of the twentieth century, as they are present for example in the historical dialectic between Brancusi and Duchamp and they point the way toward the developments of the future. Art historians and aesthetic theoreticians, however, have failed to develop even the beginnings of an adequate theorization of these phenomena.

All sculptural production since the last fifty years finds itself knowingly or naively suspended between two realms of object definition and their registers of articulation. On the one hand it is positioned within the mythical domain of the public sphere where sculpture receives the traditional placement and function of the monument (especially under the auspices of a newly flourishing memory industry of public and officious assignments of commemoration). On the other hand, it is positioned within the equally mythical but more powerfully "real" dimension of the world of industrially produced "signs."[2] This tradition, obviously initiated by Marcel Duchamp's readymades, had recognized first of all the inescapable analogy between sculptural production and the industrialized object/commodity fetish. This analogy would eventually lead up to the dematerialization of sculpture altogether, making the congruence between sculptural object and sign structure increasingly evident. Sculpture is thus constituted in an uneasily balanced double reference, operating simultaneously in a discursive/semiotic space and in a socio-political space. Yet one should be careful to imagine that the foundational reality of sculpture, its presumed transhistorical "essence" so to speak, would be found first of all in mass, volume, matter, and its location in mythical public space. Neither is it self-evident that the artistic recognition of the elementary character of sculpture as "fetish" and as "sign" would bar it essentially from access to the "real." After all, even the most contradictory conceptions of "publicity" and "public sphere" as elaborated upon by Jürgen Habermas and Alexander Kluge/Oskar Negt have in the meantime faced considerable critical responses with regard to their continuing credibility and feasibility, if not desirability, even.

Public democratic institutions (such as the museum) and public conventions of communication (such as the practice of sculpture) are increasingly subjected to the pressures of the formations of what Negt/Kluge have identified as the "production public sphere," i.e., the system of forces and enforcements operative in the culture industry and the world of corporate administration at large. It should be obvious that the language conventions within which public consciousness originally articulated itself would also become the first to vanish under the pressure of such changes within the traditional conception of the public sphere.

Only the epistemic rigidity of art historical discourse can explain that "sculpture" is still associated with the fiction of a more or less immediately accessible public space and the promise to provide instant acts of commemoration. At the same time—when it comes to a theory of the object in sculptural production and the irreversible conditions of fetishization of sign exchange value—a similarly naive situation prevails: in spite of the legacies of Duchamp and Surrealism, art history still theorizes the object of sculpture outside of a psychoanalytic or a socioeconomic/semiologic model of the object.

The paucity of object experience and the destruction of concepts of use value associated with the traditional definition of material objects were of course at the center of Duchamp's critique of the newly emerging conditions of fetishization. The readymade object internalized the violence of everyday life, and its constructed objects no longer criticized the existing modes of object experience but embraced them as inescapable conditions within which the aesthetic gesture henceforth would have to constitute itself.

Autonomy, resistance, transcendence, and affirmation could be considered four types of articulation within the sphere of sculptural production. While these are by no means the sole articulations, they seem to be primarily structuring the relation of sculpture to the generally existing conditions of object experience. Rarely—if ever—would a sculptural work follow one of these models alone. Rather one would surmise that the most important sculpture of the twentieth century has been defined by a hybrid synthesis of all of these models within a single structure.

I SCULPTURE FROM SPITTLE: GIACOMETTI AND NEWMAN

It is difficult to identify the exact moment in the history of twentieth-century sculpture and the exact circumstances when the loss of public space and the increasing poverty of public experience became manifestly determining factors in the production of sculpture. It is less difficult, however, to describe the symptoms within the history of twentieth-century sculpture when the actual crisis between the bourgeois public sphere and the production public sphere manifested itself for the first time with full intensity.

The first example we could point to in the post–World War II period in Europe would obviously be the work of Alberto Giacometti (obvious in the break that his work from the 1940s and '50s constitutes with regard to his earlier work as much as from the rupture that his work inserts into the history of twentieth-century sculpture at large). Giacometti's work gains its historical tension from the articulation of a tripartite structure of loss and disappearance.

First of all from the articulation of a loss of the self-evidence of figuration: in Giacometti's work from the 1940s it becomes apparent that the fact of figuration can no longer be read as a proof of a continuing credibility of traditional concepts of subjectivity. Neither can it be taken for granted any longer that figurative sculpture still operates in the spaces of the public sphere where it could stand for the actually existing forms of social interaction. To the very degree that Giacometti's walking figures reiterate the question of the possibility of representing the anonymous subject in public space (and thereby implicitly reflect upon the potential continuity of sculpture functioning as a monument), to the very degree the walking figures seem to radically deny the possibilities of such a continuity. Furthermore, to the degree that the figures insist on their fragile verticality, that they retain the uprightness of the traditional sculptural idiom, they convince us of the inescapable disintegration of verticality—the withering away of one of the unquestionable paradigms of anthropomorphic sculpture.

The extreme fragmentation of the body in Brancusi's work or the definitive shift toward abstraction had of course pronounced the loss of anthropomorphic sculptural figuration in various instances in the first half of the twentieth century, but it is in Giacometti's work of the postwar period that this disappearance is formulated with renewed vehemence. First of all in the process of an extreme reduction of "scale," in the proportional reduction of the human body to the size of a miniature figurine. Secondly—developed only after the first strategy had proven to be untenable—Giacometti's decision for an extreme reduction of "volume" and "mass" to the paradoxical threshold of the modeling of the body as a "linear" structure.[3]

The second loss to be concretized in Giacometti's work is the definitive disappearance of artisanal production from both the modeling process and the procedure of the sculptural cast. Giacometti is in fact one of the last traditionalists in sculpture who understood the dialectic between artistic and artisanal self-determination and the externality of technological determination. While the phenomenological interpretation of Giacometti's work is generally precise in its argument that it is the process of perception itself that is physically incorporated into the modeling procedure, it fails to recognize other determining factors that led to the disintegration and disappearance of the most hallowed traditions of sculptural production at that time. Even the phenomenological theory of the 1940s did not exclude socio-political, let alone psychoanalytic dimensions, from its argument, and it seems therefore all the more adequate to theorize an artist's contribution to the phenomenology of perception inside the full range of that theory's parameters.

The paucity of representation as much as the poverty of means in the precarious modeling process indicates the traditionalist's awareness of just how tenuous the most fundamental production principles of sculpture had in fact become. This condition resulted from both the radical transformations in collective object experience as well as from an awareness of the reduction of the public and social dimensions of spatial experience. It was not accidental therefore that Barnett Newman suggested upon his first encounter with Giacometti's sculptures in Pierre Matisse's gallery in 1949 that they appeared to have been made from spit.[4]

The third loss concretized in Giacometti's sculpture after the catastrophe of bourgeois humanism is the disappearance of the guaranteed institutions of public space (both spatial and discursive). Already in Giacometti's Surrealist sculptures this reflection on the publicity of urban space had been a peculiar preoccupation, but it would return with greater urgency in the postwar period. Public space—in Giacometti's work represented by the urban plaza—appears now, just like the figurines, in a miniaturized form as though these were already the mnemonic models of a conception of publicity long past. This conception had been one in which subjectivity and publicity had been mutually interdependent, had defined the subject as public, both through the social institutions, discursive conventions as well as through urban/architectural spaces, and early modernist sculpture (e.g., Rodin and Rosso) had still succeeded to make this strenuous relationship between the private and the public remain one of its integral dimensions.

Giacometti's work entitled *Figurine dans une boîte entre deux maisons* (1950) acquires almost prognostic qualities in this perspective. The figurine appears here for the last time in striding motion (all subsequent ones would be depicted as stationary). The most striking quality of the sculpture, however, is its combination of various public and private spatial structures with various incompatible object types, constructing an unlikely synthesis between an exhibition showcase, vernacular architecture, and modernist domestic furniture. This hybrid structure positions the figurine in an unidentifiable spatial container (its design seems to come close to television sets of the fifties, but television technology was only about to emerge at that moment in France).

The total reduction of subjectivity to the private sphere and the emerging depoliticization of individual existence resulting from the enforcement of consumer culture are uncannily anticipated in Giacometti's hybrid sculptural construction. The figurine, enclosed between three sheets of Plexiglas,[5] appears like a scientific specimen from a prehistoric period, a subject no longer accessible. At the same time, it offers

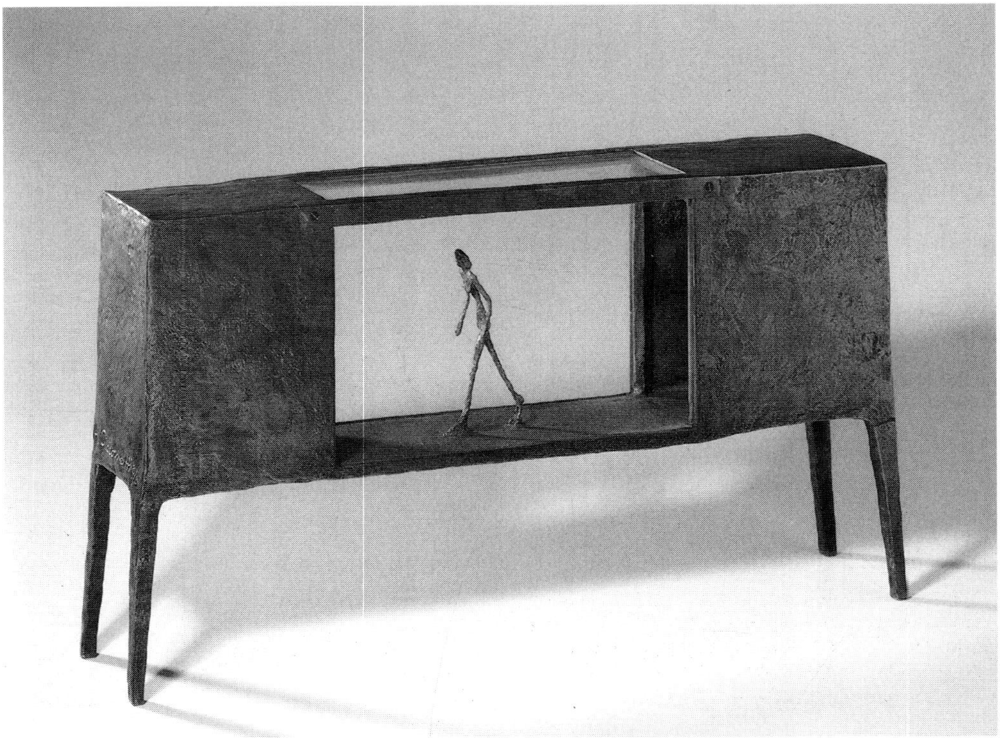

Alberto Giacometti, *Figure in a Box between Two Houses* (*Figurine dans une boîte entre deux maisons*), 1950. Bronze, glass, figure painted white, 11 13⁄16 × 21½ × 3¾ in. (30 × 54 × 9.5 cm). Musée National d'Art Moderne, Centre National d'Art et de Culture Georges Pompidou, Paris. © 2015 Alberto Giacometti Estate/Licensed by VAGA and ARS, New York.

a radically new paradigm for sculpture's forms of presentation and its inherent structure of publicity: the display case.

This paradigm surfaces then for the first time in the postwar period in the work of the traditionalist Giacometti concretizing the privatization of subjectivity and the fetishization of object experience. What might have appeared in 1950 still as a bizarre prognosis and a strange aberration on Giacometti's side, becomes now recognizable—with the hindsight of almost half a century—as an uncanny work predicting the governing conditions of social space and object relations on every account.

Barnett Newman would produce one of his first rare sculptural works in direct dialogical response to his encounter with Giacometti's exhibition in 1949, entitled *Here I* (1950). Giacometti's extremely attenuated figures return in Newman's sculpture already as mere wooden lattices, bereft of even the last residual resemblance to the anthropomorphic figure. And in response to Giacometti's extremely subtle modeling where the remnants of the privileged artisanal forms are redeemed in the phenomenological and purely procedural aspects, Newman's emphasis on process now abandons even those dimensions in favor of a pure indexicality of the casting procedure.

Instead, the ensemble of found objects, wooden sculptures (such as a milk crate that the artist found in front of his doorstep or the simple lattices used for construction) insist on the banality of their objecthood as much as the production process insists on the transparency of "its" procedural and material conditions. This sudden and seemingly finite disqualification of manually produced plasticity is as integral to the reading of Newman's sculpture as is the sudden exemption of sculpture from all representational anthropomorphic functions.

Newman's observation that Giacometti's work appeared to be made from spit has now been taken literally and has been radicalized in his own modeling procedure. All conventions now seem to have to be liquidated: the traditional assumption of sculpture as mass and volume as

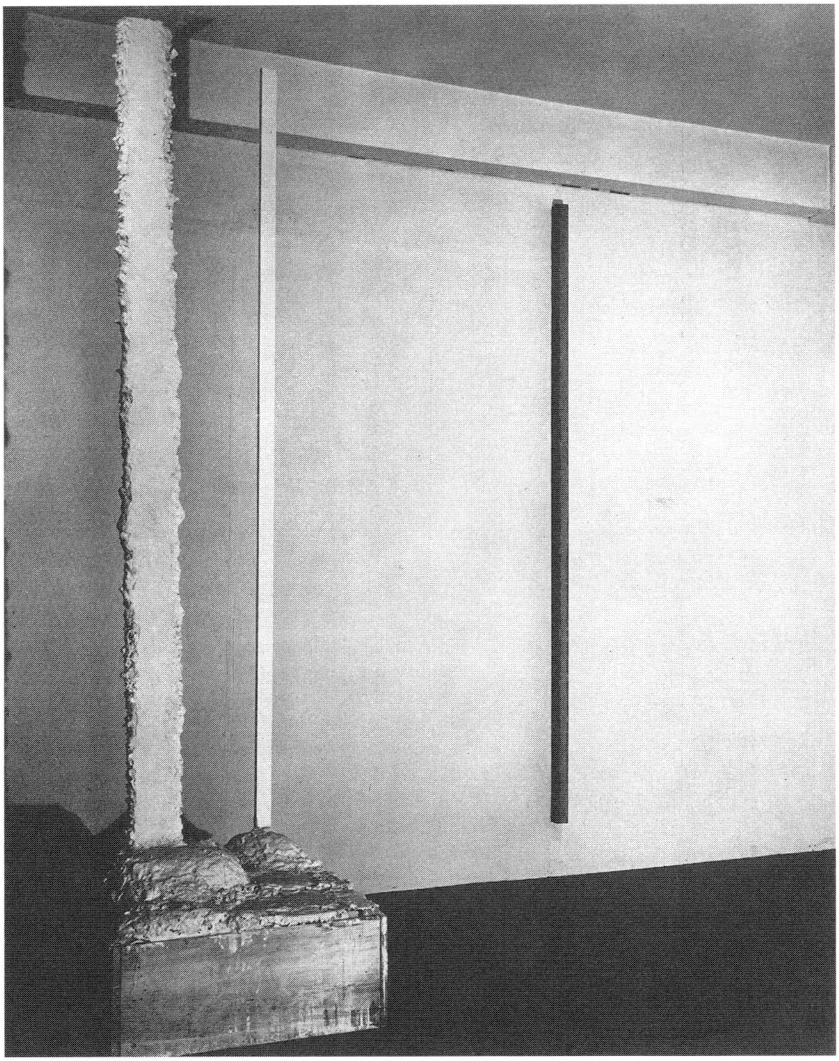

Installation view of Barnett Newman, *Here I* (plaster) and *The Wild* (oil on canvas) at the Betty Parsons Gallery, New York, during Newman's second one-man show, April 23–May 12, 1950. Photograph by Hans Namuth. © Hans Namuth.

much as the process of modeling itself. The relative liquidity or the relative density of the plastic mass alone seems to determine the structuration of the sculptural form. The transparency of this indexical formation finds its correlative in the cheap rigidity and ostentatious verticality of the lattices planted into the plaster mold heaped onto the wooden crate. The vertical elements are precisely not—as overly eager interpreters have frequently argued—a reiteration of the motif of the funeral "stele" but first and most of all a baring of the device of the basic principle of the armature that had traditionally kept vertical anthropomorphic sculpture in its upright position.

Yet in their almost pathetic poverty of means and in the paucity of procedure in the execution of the sculpture these vertical lattices seem to signal yet another loss. Reminiscent of an Odradek character or appearing like the masts of a childishly constructed barge, these objects recognize the victory of objecthood over the traditional concepts of subjectivity by purging from their structure both the competence of manual execution and the representative function of earlier sculpture. Exemplary sculpture thus emerges from a process of extreme elimination in which—as in the language of Samuel Beckett—the negation of the traditional concepts of subjectivity not only negates the conventions of its representation, but redeems them mnemonically at the same time.

2 SCULPTURE FROM DEBRIS: ARMAN AND OLDENBURG

At the beginning of the 1960s the conception of sculpture responds more systematically to the radical transformation of the object- and publicity-conditions in a society of advanced and enforced consumption, and it is not surprising that the display case of the fetish object becomes the presentational paradigm of the most advanced work of that moment: as for example in the work of Arman (his *Poubelles* and his *Accumulations*) or in the work of Oldenburg and his *Ray Gun Wing* and his *Mouse Museum*. An understanding seems to have asserted itself now more vigorously than that which had already emerged at the time of Surrealism—namely that sculpture in actuality could make no other credible claim any longer than to structure itself as an accumulation of serialized industrially produced objects.

As was the case for Giacometti's *Figurine dans une boîte entre deux maisons*, it is not incidental at all that this paradigm shift has remained equally ignored in the writing of the history of postwar sculpture, since the reflection on conditions of framing and presentation were perceived at best as supplementary to the actual conditions concerning the production and the reception of sculpture. By contrast to the conditions of the object in the context of Surrealist assemblage, however, where the rediscovery of obsolete spaces of experience and of outdated fashion objects could set free sudden insights of mnemonic experience, the accumulation of found objects of Nouveau Réalisme recognizes that this potential evaporates from the object under the circumstances of an artificially enforced and accelerated obsolescence. The consumer culture of advanced capitalist production cannot even tolerate the aging of objects through use any longer. Now, even the actually existing spaces of the outdated and the residual objects of use value have to be instantly spectacularized in order to generate on the level of sign exchange value and spectacle, a compensation for those lost forms of experience that had once been tied to the experience of time and of use value in the aging of the object. It is precisely this transition that is clearly articulated in the transformation of object-structures and the presentational devices from Surrealism to Nouveau Réalisme and that leads to a dramatic change in the aesthetic of assemblage in the late 1950s.

In the context of Surrealism the container had still functioned as a framing device of a presumed spatial and psychological interiority of experience, deriving partially from the cultic spaces of the shrine and the votive painting and the private images of commemoration, leading up to the obsessive secrecy of the private image/object of the fetish: after all, this is the triad of experimental forms that had for example

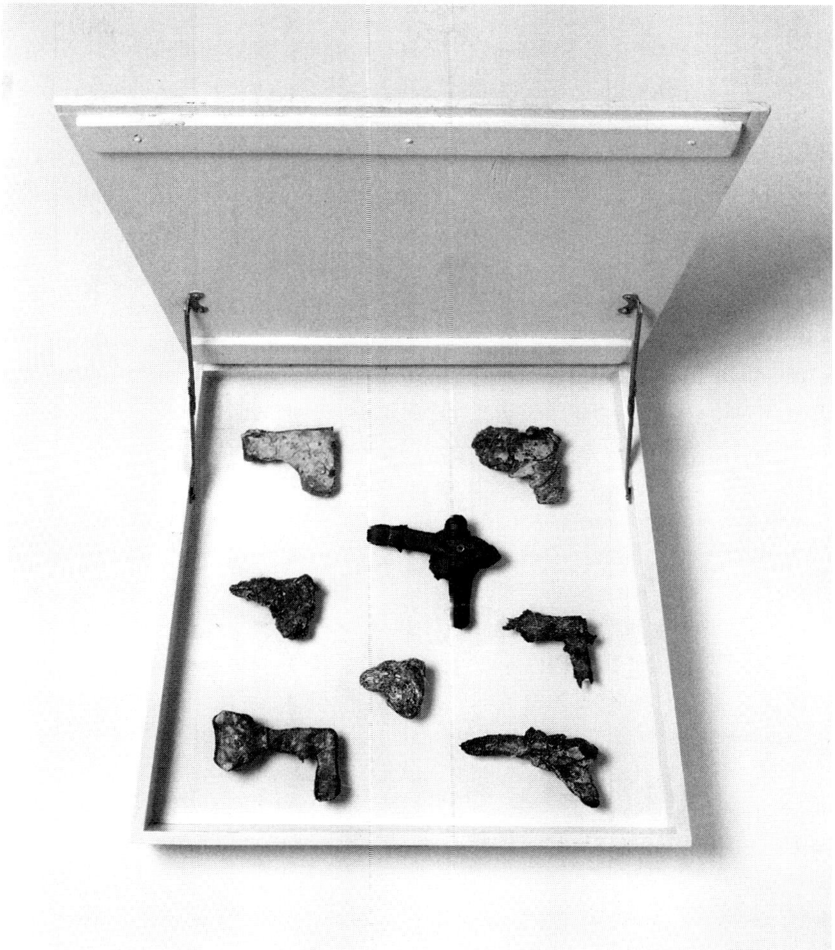

Claes Oldenburg, *Street Ray Guns*, 1959. Eight objects painted with enamel and casein, mounted in a painted wood box, 16½ × 13¼ × 4 in. (41.9 × 34.9 × 10.2 cm). Private collection. © Claes Oldenburg. Courtesy the artist and Paula Cooper Gallery, New York.

constituted the mystery of the work of Joseph Cornell, where the amassing and combination of objects ultimately still appeared as the work of a "collector." It is precisely this shift from the collection to the mere "accumulation" of more or less identical objects in the work of Arman and Oldenburg at the beginning of the 1960s that makes the universalized conditions of fetishization apparent and with them the rapid disappearance of those forms of experience that had been tied to the knowledge of use value and the temporality and intimacy of the object. In this transition from collection to mere accumulation the object is handed over to exhibition value/sign exchange value alone. This becomes all the more evident in Arman's structures where the seriality and the similarity/identity of the accumulated objects within the exhibition container prohibit even the slightest aspects of a mnemonic dimension.

If the Surrealists could still claim to have uncovered history in obsolescence and to have generated—in sudden juxtapositions—the experience of shock that could be converted into the energy of defetishization, the Nouveau Réalist's object no longer makes any such claims or promises and it presents itself as voided of all magical, mnemonic and therapeutic powers. Yet this aesthetic of the showcase reveals more than merely a growing sense for the increasing congruence between sculptural object and commodity fetish. Sculpture appears here once again—as was already the case in the work by Giacometti discussed above—as a preserved specimen.

Preservation does, however, not necessarily signal a reactionary or melancholic attempt to rescue cult value and the intimacy of contemplative object experience from disappearance, nor the attempt to liberate the object from its functions by withholding it from its standard transactions in consumer culture. Rather we would argue that a new type of publicity is constructed in the new sculptural paradigm of the display case and the principles of the presentational devices of commodity culture.[6] Namely the insight that even the constructions of historical

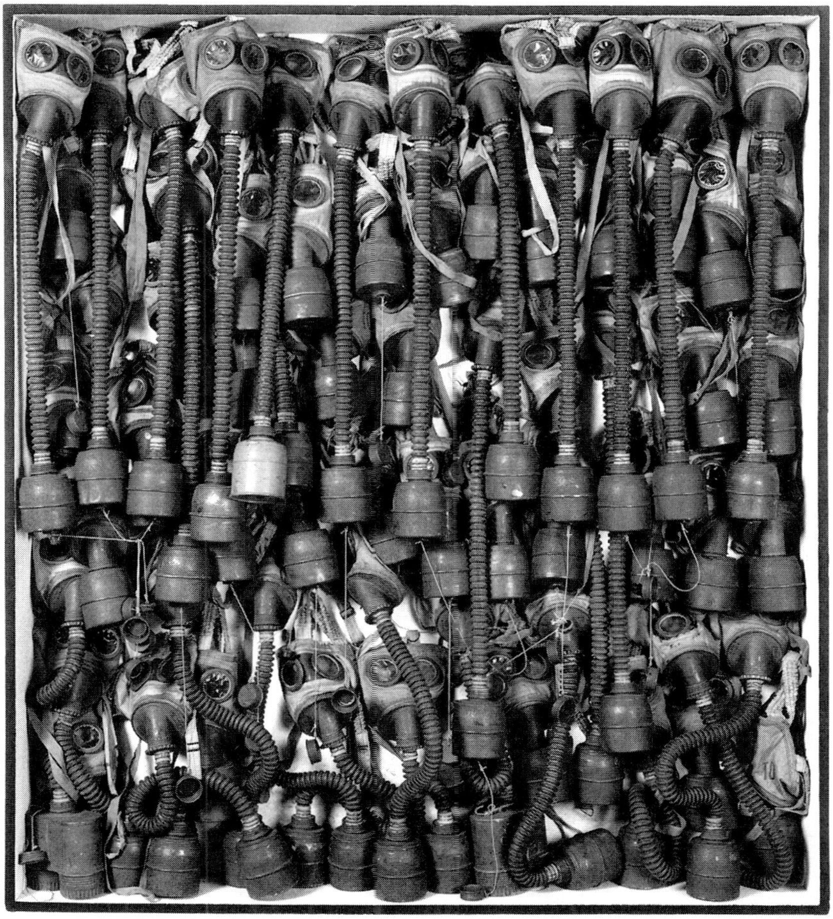

Arman, *Home Sweet Home* (1960). Accumulation of gas masks in box, 63 × 55 × 7⅞ in. (160 × 140 × 20 cm). Musée National d'Art Moderne, Centre National d'Art et de Culture Georges Pompidou, Paris. © 2015 Artists Rights Society (ARS), New York/ADAGP, Paris.

experience in the spaces and the displays of the museum institution are not exempt from the radical transformation occurring inside those institutions themselves: to be gradually altered from spaces of public historical experience and self-definition to becoming a branch of a newly emerging memory industry. In fact it makes evident to what degree the organization of history and the accumulation of commodity objects in the department store were evolving toward each other from the start that once an object had been isolated from its function and contexts and had been given over to exhibition value it would inevitably fuse with the condition of the isolated and fetishized commodity object as the central category of the definition of object experience.[7]

It is crucial to understand at the same time, however, that this resignative gesture, which seemingly accepts sculpture's extreme limitations of publicity in the commodity object and its display systems, simultaneously creates a fair recognition of the actually existing possibilities of public experience in the construction of sculpture. Or perhaps one should invert this observation instantly and phrase it in less optimistic terms: that the sculpture which voluntarily assumes the morphology and the display of the commodity fetish articulates the actually existing lack of public experience and the poverty of social experience still to be generated by sculptural constructs and thereby delimiting the threshold where sculpture can—if at all—mediate between publicity and the object.

Finally, a few more theoretical and fundamental questions could be asked, deriving from the historical sketch outlined above: first of all the problem of which modes of object experience could still be considered adequate for the production and available to the perception of sculpture if the modes of the commodity fetish and of sign exchange value are in fact the universally governing conditions of object experience. Second, if these conditions would in fact apply, could any alternative registers of perception and experience remain at all accessible to the construction of sculpture's insistent claim for its inherently integral constitution in publicity? Sculpture would either have to withdraw (as it does in most cases) into a seemingly protected realm of specific discursive traditions and the specificity and autonomy of the sculptural object (i.e., it would have to invent an "essence" of sculpture outside of any of the really prevailing conditions of object production and perception) or it would become desiccated and irrelevant.

If we begin with the assumption that in fact it is ideological interpellation that establishes communication between subjects and objects through the medium of sign exchange value, we would have to rethink sculptural production in terms of interpellation. What types and forms of critical opposition could be articulated under those circumstances with the traditional means sculpture had available to voice transcendence, transgression, opposition, and dissent? More difficult yet, which would be the forms of a construction of memory that sculpture could supply under these conditions without relapsing simply into the conventions of a false monumentality? Or, put differently, in Althusser's concept of interpellation: what type of critical interpellation—if any—is accessible to sculptural production outside of the totality of the regime of sign exchange value?

We have attempted to sketch out a historical trajectory in which it became evident that radical and relevant sculpture of the last fifty years results precisely out of the recognition to what extent collective publicity has become "inaccessible" and to what degree all objects increasingly follow the law of fetishization and sign exchange value. Paradoxically it is the sculpture which articulates the loss of simultaneous collective experience and which refuses to pretend that commemoration and monumentality could still be accomplished with sculptural means that has produced the meaningful work of the past fifty years. Publicity and experience were constructed precisely by those works whose extreme differentiation of subjective spectatorial response demythified even the last remnants of the monumental and of the contemplative object experience that sculpture had once provided.

Yet to the extent that phenomenologically oriented sculpture such as Richard Serra's or Dan Graham's fails to confront itself with the very circumstances that have transformed public space into either a space of absolute fetishization or a space of absolute spectacle, the radical work of the 1960s and 1970s now faces a fate similar to that of the most radical positions developed at the moment of abstraction in the context of the historical avant-garde in the 1910s and 1920s: to have failed to recognize that the abstraction of perceptual models neither guarantees their universality nor provides a space of protection or exemption from the power of opposite models (e.g., those of ideology and advertisement).

Critics and historians should admittedly be careful to act as prognostics, yet I would like to conclude by pointing toward the continuation of these questions in a subsequent text. Precisely the question, which—if any—would be the strategies that artistic (and in particular, sculptural) practices could engage with to go beyond the limitations of abstraction and phenomenology and to confront the spaces of ideological interpellation and of sign exchange value without simply enacting their laws (as is of course most manifestly the case with the all-time travesty of sculpture as a public structure performed by the Christo Couple in Berlin and elsewhere).

Without pointing toward any particular example in current artistic practice (even though some do certainly exist) I would argue that the work which will perform the most detailed and the most accurate analysis of the difficulties of constructing the representation of the real and of the social under the conditions of spectacle culture and sign exchange value will most likely also be the practice that would resist the totalization of these conditions most successfully.

Notes

First published in English and German in *White Cube/Black Box*, exh. cat. (Vienna: Generali Foundation, 1996), pp. 151–173. Minor corrections have been made for consistency.

1. Rosalind Krauss, "Sculpture in the Expanded Field," *October* 8 (spring 1979): 31–44.

2. If we use the term "mythical" in the discussion of the terms "public sphere" and "public space" we understand it more in the traditional conception of myth, hinting at the condition of a rapidly disappearing form of experience, such as models of thought, perception and social interaction which are on the brink of extinction if not already extinct. If we use the term "mythical" in the discussion of the sign, it refers to the more precise definition provided by Barthes forty years ago: namely the profoundly ideological dimension of powerful images and structures of publicly imposed and held beliefs as well as in Jean Baudrillard's economic/ideological definition of the concept of "sign exchange value."

If we use the term "public" in the first instance we refer to the tradition of thought exemplified by Jürgen Habermas. Alexander Kluge and Oskar Negt focus on the assumption that within democratic societies, emerging institutions and discursive practices or residual forms of communication could take place within which individuals constituted and determined themselves. Evidently, artistic practices—if only hesitatingly admitted by Habermas within the public sphere—would be affected first of all by radical transformations occurring within the political definitions of the public sphere; more specifically even the practices of sculpture, since they were tied in most cultures (certainly those in Western Europe) to forms of public display and instruction since the Middle Ages and to forms of public commemoration (if often, at first, only the commemoration of rulers or of ideals of antiquity) at least since the Renaissance.

3. The development of Giacometti's postwar work is discussed in an essay by Franz Meyer. See "Giacometti et Newman," in *Alberto Giacometti: Sculptures, Peintures, Dessins*, ed. Suzanne Pagé (Paris: Musée d'art moderne de la ville de Paris, 1991), pp. 59–66. While Meyer's essay already traces the comparison between Giacometti and Newman, his phenomenological approach yields rather different results from my own comparison argued in the following part of this essay.

4. It is of course not accidental that Newman would point to spittle, the least likely material for the modeling of sculpture. Already in 1929, in the notorious definition of the "Informe" in the "Dictionnaire critique" of his journal *Documents*, Georges Bataille had identified the "Crachat" as the essence of formlessness. Simultaneously two other articles were to appear in *Documents* dealing with the subject of oral secretion as well: the first one by the ethnographer/anthropologist Marcel Griaule entitled "Crachat/Ame" (Spittle/Soul) and the second one by Michel Leiris entitled "L'eau à la bouche" (Mouthwater). I owe this information to Y.-A. Bois's excellent essay on the subject, "La valeur d'usage de l'informe," in the exhibition catalog *L'Informe: mode d'emploi* (Paris: Musée national d'art moderne/Centre Georges Pompidou, 1996), pp. 9–37.

By no means do we want to suggest that Newman was in any way aware of the discussions of spittle and the *informe*. However, the precision with which he detects this aspect in the work of Giacometti seems quite unusual, and it indicates at least to what extent Newman was capable of perceiving and personally close to the key aesthetic conceptions developed in post-Surrealist French aesthetics.

5. Even though it seems unlikely in the context of the material choices made by the artist in general and the availability of materials at that particular moment, the description of the work in the Paris catalog lists in fact Plexiglas as the material enclosing the figure. See Pagé, *Albert Giacometti*, p. 236.

6. Beyond the two examples mentioned one should point to other artists whose work develops slightly later yet deploys—in many objects if not generally—the same strategy of presenting itself primarily as a commercial vitrine or showcase design from the late 1950s. In the work of Beuys, Boltanski and Broodthaers, the display case as a sculptural framing device appears as one residual form of the bourgeois public sphere that is now being dismantled and overwhelmed by the emerging principles of the production public sphere.

7. For a more extensive discussion of this problem and its evidence provided by the work of Claes Oldenburg in the early 1960s in particular see my essay "The Museum Fictions of Marcel Broodthaers," in *Museums by Artists*, ed. A. A. Bronson and Peggy Gale (Toronto: Art Gallery of Ontario/Art Metropole, 1983), pp. 45–57, reprinted in this volume.

Index

Note: Page numbers in italic type indicate illustrations.